FOREIGN POLICY IN WORLD POLITICS

FOREIGN POLICY

PRENTICE-HALL, INC., *Englewood Cliffs, New Jersey*

IN WORLD POLITICS

fourth edition

ROY C. MACRIDIS, Editor

Contributing Authors

VERNON V. ASPATURIAN

KARL W. DEUTSCH

LEWIS J. EDINGER

LEON D. EPSTEIN

ROY C. MACRIDIS

HANS J. MORGENTHAU

RICHARD L. PARK

ROBERT A. SCALAPINO

GEBHARD L. SCHWEIGLER

KENNETH W. THOMPSON

ALLEN S. WHITING

FOREIGN POLICY IN WORLD POLITICS
fourth edition

Roy C. Macridis, *Editor*

© 1972, 1967, 1962, 1958 by Prentice-Hall, Inc.
Englewood Cliffs, New Jersey

ISBN: 0-13-326470-X

Library of Congress Catalog Card No.: 77-172678

10 9 8 7 6 5 4 3 2

Printed in the United States of America

Prentice-Hall International, Inc., London
Prentice-Hall of Australia, Pty. Ltd., Sydney
Prentice-Hall of Canada, Ltd., Toronto
Prentice-Hall of India Private Limited, New Delhi
Prentice-Hall of Japan, Inc., Tokyo

CONTENTS

FOREIGN POLICY OF THE GERMAN FEDERAL REPUBLIC, 119

KARL W. DEUTSCH, GEBHARD L. SCHWEIGLER,
AND LEWIS J. EDINGER

SOVIET FOREIGN POLICY, 174

VERNON V. ASPATURIAN

Chapter Six

THE SOVIET UNION AND INTERNATIONAL COMMUNISM, 238

Vernon V. Aspaturian

FOREIGN POLICY OF COMMUNIST CHINA, 289

ALLEN S. WHITING

THE FOREIGN POLICY OF MODERN JAPAN, 321

ROBERT A. SCALAPINO

PREFACE

When the first edition of this volume appeared in the spring of 1958, the contributors had no way of knowing that it would be received as well as it was. We knew that we were involved in subject matter that was new, and all that we could hope for was to give to the student and the teacher supplementary material for courses in comparative government and international relations. This fourth, revised, edition is now being presented with the full knowledge that comparative foreign policy has become a recognized field of study.

Our new edition maintains essentially the format of the previous ones. We have updated our material and rewritten rather extensively many of the individual essays—particularly those dealing with Great Britain, France, the Federal Republic of Germany, Japan, and of course China. We have also added a note on the evaluation of foreign policy to our introductory chapter only in order to raise one of the most difficult questions in foreign policy analysis. We have updated our bibliographical references without, I am sure, doing full justice to the wealth of publications that have come out in the last few years.

It is our hope that this volume will continue to serve as an introduction to courses in comparative foreign policy and international relations. My deepest thanks for cooperation and patience go again to all the contributors and to Roger Emblen and Stanley Evans of Prentice-Hall.

RCM

FOREIGN POLICY IN WORLD POLITICS

Chapter One

THE COMPARATIVE STUDY OF FOREIGN POLICY

KENNETH W. THOMPSON

ROY C. MACRIDIS

TWO BASIC APPROACHES TO FOREIGN POLICY

Two approaches to foreign policy have vied with one another in Western thought at least since the days of the French Revolution. One is the *ideological* approach, according to which the policies of states vis-à-vis the rest of the world are merely expressions of prevailing political, social, and religious beliefs. In this approach, foreign policies are classified as democratic or totalitarian, libertarian or socialist, and peace-loving or aggressive. The second approach to foreign policy is *analytical*. At the heart of this viewpoint is the proposition that policy rests on multiple determinants, including the state's historic tradition, geographical location, national interest, and purposes and security needs. To understand foreign policy, the observer must take into account and analyze a host of factors.

The Ideological Approach

In the twentieth century, it has been commonplace for critics to proclaim that the United States, or Britain, or France has no foreign policy or has been unfaithful to liberal or socialist or conservative principles, as the case may be. This is one way to think about foreign policy; to the present day it is perhaps the prevailing approach. Periodically, the domestic political arena rings with angry charges that a set of political leaders, a political party, or an administration is opportunistic in foreign affairs and

1

faithless to its political creed or ideology. Governments are condemned for not supporting democracy, or free enterprise, or a particular social class everywhere around the world. This dominant approach views foreign relations primarily in psychological terms; it looks to the motives or ideologies of leaders or governments as the essential, if not the sole, determinant of policy. It maintains that a democratic regime pursues one type of foreign policy, an autocratic government another, a communist government a third, and a democratic-socialist administration still another. There is a fairylandlike simplicity about this that makes it widely acceptable and easily understood. Foreign policy is considered a function of a political system in action or of the preferences or convictions of political leaders who carry out its programs.

The Analytical Approach

There is a second approach to foreign policy, however, which has at least as respectable a heritage. It was a ruling point of view throughout much of the eighteenth and nineteenth centuries, whether in doctrines of raison d'état or in broader historical interpretations, and it is being revived in our day by a handful of analysts and scholars.

Its renaissance is partly an outcome of the apparent shortcomings of the psychological or ideological approach, especially in accounting for present-day international developments. That approach has been shaken and discredited by inner contradictions, and it has faltered and failed in describing the continuities of objective and purpose in the policies of states. Regardless of the party in power or the leaders and their private or public philosophies, British, American, French, and Russian foreign policies display unities that transcend individual beliefs or ideologies. In the early postwar period, the Labour government in England, despite longstanding protests against Tory imperialism and power politics, turned inevitably to the protection—in Western Europe, in the countries of the British Commonwealth, in the Iberian Peninsula, and in the Near and Middle East—of substantially the selfsame interests that Tories and Whigs had considered vital for several centuries. In the United States, the Kennedy, Johnson, and Nixon foreign policies have looked to the central goals with which the administrations of Roosevelt and Truman were concerned. The means, methods, or techniques may have changed, but the interests and objectives have been relatively constant.

Therefore, in a period of a little more than two decades there has been a reaction against the ideological approach to the study of international relations. It should perhaps have been obvious that a conception in which foreign policy is nothing more than a by-product of domestic politics could hardly do justice to the elements of continuity in national policy. At some point, it became necessary to recognize that objective requirements of the national interest place certain irremovable limits upon any statesman seeking to formulate foreign policy. Regardless of the intentions, social philosophy, or religious outlook of individuals, there are broad strategic interests intimately bound up with a nation's geographic position and international role that must be safeguarded if its independence is to be preserved. Not only are these interests permanent for Bolsheviks as well as tsars, but continuity also appears in the approach of a nation's statesmen, who stand guard over their country's security and whose conception of that security has been formed and molded by the same institutions and traditions. However intangible, the "national mind," which interprets the national interest, is itself a factor in the permanence of foreign policy. Out of the interplay of a durable international position with permanent traditions and institutions, the larger nation-states have fashioned foreign policies that, in broadest outline, have been consistently maintained over long periods, even in the face of drastic changes on the domestic political scene.

According to this second approach, foreign policy demands, of policy makers, choices and discriminations of a basic order. Not only are the interests of a nation permanent in character, but they range themselves in a hierarchy of greater and lesser interests. In a classic statement intended as a guide in the formulation of Belgium's foreign policy but with relevance for all foreign policy, M. Paul-Henri Spaak observed:

There must be a hierarchy in international obligations. The nations of a continent cannot reasonably be asked to consider with the same realism and sincerity of judgment affairs which directly concern them and events which are taking place thousands of kilometers away in regions where they have neither interests nor influence.

Certain interests must be defended at all costs; others should be safeguarded under particular circumstances; and certain others, although desirable, can almost never be defended. It is the task of foreign policy, in the first instance, to determine its own hierarchy of interests and, next, to examine the scale of interests revealed in the principles or practice of other nations' foreign policies. Even when national leaders forswear the formulation of hierarchies of interests,

the hard tests of practice often evoke underlying conceptions of vital interests. The United States' decision, in World War II, to bring the fighting to a successful conclusion in Europe and the North Atlantic before turning to destroy the enemy in the Pacific, or Britain's waiting, at the turn of the nineteenth century, until Poland was attacked and other nations were invaded before forming coalitions against Napoleon—these are examples of action in terms of a basic perception of interests.

The interests of states, and their power to pursue their claims, are of course immutable for any given historical period only in the sense that they set broad limits within which choices in foreign policy are made. They set the framework within which the domestic political contest over external policies must be waged. In the same way that no German political party today can afford to ignore the sometimes latent but ever-present demands for German reunification, no American government can take steps that would compromise the security of the Western Hemisphere. It is obvious that both power and interests can be made responsive to the forces of change. For example, a so-called peace-loving nation, faced by threats to its security, can translate its resources into military power, its influence into foreign bases and real estate, and its industrial and military potential into forces in being. This has, in effect, been the trend of postwar American foreign policy. Or a state may suffer a loss of power, as Britain did in World War II, with the consequent need for revising its estimates of national interest. Technology can require continuing reappraisals of national security and of the means of preserving it, and may lead to changes in the ranking of the great powers. Britain may have fallen in the hierarchy of powers as other nations belatedly experienced the industrial revolution, but it may recapture at least some of its vaunted supremacy in an era of atomic energy and hydrogen bombs. The existence of continuities in the foreign policies of states is admittedly more subject to debate in an era when one of the few certainties is the continual unrelenting pace of technological change.

Yet most students of international politics are persuaded that those recurrent patterns of the foreign policies of nations that most diplomats appear to take for granted are amenable to study and analysis by the modern scholar. These patterns have been approached along several distinct if parallel lines. Scholars have engaged in more general studies of the geographical, industrial, and physical position of nations, of the peculiar historical circumstances in which these conditions have operated, of the actual adjustment of nations on the basis of their objective position to successive historical circumstances, and of the claims and declarations made by statesmen engaged in pursuing a certain historic foreign policy. Obviously, the intent of the studies in this volume is not to do basic research in any or all of these areas, but significantly, and almost without exception, each separate inquiry starts with an examination of some aspect of the objective patterns and conditions of foreign policy in the respective countries. At the same time, in successive chapters, the writers go on to consider the role of ideology, of those changing institutions and domestic political factors which give to the policies of states that endless subtlety and richness that throws into question every simple generalization about the conduct of states. In effect, the theme of the book is one of continuity and change, of unities and coherences alongside the unique and particular in foreign relations.

The authors, although wary of what Burckhardt described as "grand simplilcations," are nevertheless compelled by their interests as political scientists to examine what can be said in general about foreign policy. This provides a unifying theme or central core of intellectual interests, not everywhere made explicit but unquestionably at hand for those who seek understanding in this complex and fascinating realm.

THE ELEMENTS OF FOREIGN POLICY

The study of foreign policy, despite the two major approaches described above, provides no ready-made categories that can be applied to every nation. Perhaps even in the physical sciences, the effort to uncover total systems, at least in these terms, is less fruitful than is sometimes imagined. In any event, there is marked diversity in the categories of analysis by which foreign policy has been studied in the present volume. To a considerable extent, this results from differences in national context. For example, social stratification has implications for the making of foreign policy in Britain that it seems not to have in the Soviet Union, and the policy-making process in Britain has greater continuity and tradition even than the American system. A fortiori, the newer states cannot point to the same political experience and diplomatic tradition in which the older nations can take pardonable pride. Despite these individual variations in the species, the nation-states whose policies are described have much in common. Their foreign policies are susceptible of analysis in terms of a checklist of elements that exist, that can be identified, and that merge and compromise the bases of foreign policy.

The elements of foreign policy may

be thought of in terms of concentric circles. At the center are certain elements that are more or less material in character. Some of these are relatively permanent, such as geography and natural resources. Others, like the economic, industrial, and military establishments, are more responsive to change and human manipulation. Then there are human factors, largely quantitative in the case of population, and qualitative as regards national character, social structure, national morale, political institutions and experience, and an effective tradition of diplomacy. From these elements and the instrumentalities of the policy-making process, the substance of foreign policy derives, and major historic policies and the vital interests of countries emerge.

It may be worth at least passing mention that students of international politics have for the most part concentrated their attention on the elements of foreign policy. By contrast, writers on comparative politics have dealt more particularly with the policy-making process, including the influence of political parties, interest groups, effective political ideologies, and the peculiar executive-legislative relations in a country. The attempt has been made in the present volume to marry these two approaches, and to combine the study of objective factors in foreign policy with the study of processes by which decisions are reached and policies implemented.

Significant Factors in the Study of Foreign Policy

The Elements of Foreign Policy
A. The relatively permanent material elements
  1. Geography
  2. Natural resources
    a. Minerals
    b. Food production
    c. Energy and power

B. Less permanent material elements
  1. Industrial establishment
  2. Military establishment
  3. Changes in industrial and military capacity
C. The human elements: quantitative and qualitative
  1. Quantitative—population
  2. Qualitative
    a. Policy makers and leaders
    b. The role of ideology
    c. The role of information

The Foreign Policy-making Process
A. The governmental agencies
  1. Executive (e.g., prime minister, relevant ministries, and interministerial or interdepartmental organizations)
  2. Legislature (including relevant committees)
B. The nongovernmental agencies
  1. Political parties
  2. Interest groups
  3. Media of communication
  4. Characteristics of public opinion

Trends and Issues
A. National purposes
  1. Peace as national purpose
  2. Security as national purpose
  3. Power as national purpose
  4. Prosperity and economic development as national purpose
B. Diplomacy
  1. Diplomatic practices
  2. The transformation of diplomatic practices
  3. The rediscovery of diplomacy
C. Democratic and totalitarian systems
D. The impact of the Cold War

The Relatively Permanent Material Elements

Geography. The more or less permanent elements of foreign policy obviously include geography, perhaps the most stable factor undergirding a nation's policies. It is not without significance that "except for Japan . . . Britain has been the only major power of modern times to be based on an island rather than a large continental area."[1] Its separation from the European continent by a narrow but strategic body of water, the English Channel, proved as decisive in frustrating the designs of Hitler and Napoleon as it had those of Julius Caesar or Philip II. No less an authority than Sir Eyre Crowe observed: "The general character of England's foreign policy is determined by the immutable conditions of her geographical situation on the ocean flank of Europe as an island State with vast oversea colonies and dependencies, whose existence and survival as an independent community are inseparably bound up with the possession of preponderant sea power."[2] This passage gives a clue to an important source of one of the most successful foreign policies in history. Going back to the fifteenth and sixteenth centuries, England, with but two exceptions, has neither been invaded nor defeated; and the exceptions—the American Revolution and the Afghan Wars—are hardly impressive evidence to challenge the importance of its geographic position. Until quite recently, England remained an island with what Winston Churchill described as threefold commitments to Europe, the British Commonwealth, and the "New World." Historically and down to the present, it has striven to retain for itself sufficient freedom of action to harmonize its commitments in each of these orbits, and only at points where they overlapped have new undertakings been possible. It is true that technology, through inventions like the airplane and submarine, has transformed the character of

Britain's location, and that its interests today are drawing it ever closer to Europe. In part, political factors have prompted this trend, including the British failure to pursue a successful independent foreign policy when its interests were in conflict with those of the superpowers, as in the Suez crisis in the autumn of 1956. But in Arnold Toynbee's apt words, "in this postwar age, the English Channel is no broader—in the subjective human terms of measurement which have to be applied in this context— than a Dutch dyke in the age of Alva and William the Silent; and the Atlantic itself is no broader than the Channel at the time when Napoleon's army of invasion was encamped at Boulogne."[3] Nonetheless, there are reasons for treating with some reserve claims about the annihilation of distance, for this statement dates back to 1934—only a few short years before the backbone of Nazi strategy was broken by an island state whose geography continued to make a difference.

No one would doubt that communications and modern warfare have shifted the emphasis that can properly be laid on geographic location, but its influence continues in various ways, not least in the case of the great powers. The territorial expanse of the Soviet Union, whose land mass extends over one-seventh of the land area of the earth, or the vast reaches of the Chinese empire—both make military conquest and control problematical even with absolute weapons. The policies that the United Nations was able to pursue in Korea were circumscribed by the magnitude of the military effort of fighting a successful war on the seemingly endless terrain of the mainland of China. At the same time, the difficulties of maintaining

---

[1] See chap. 2.

[2] Eyre Crowe, "Memorandum on the Present State of British Relations with France and Germany, January 1, 1907," in *British Documents on the Origins of the War: 1898–1914*, ed, G. P. Gooch and H. Temperley (London: Her Maiesty's Stationery Office, 1938), 3:402–3.

[3] Arnold J. Toynbee, *A Study of History* (London: Oxford University Press, 1934), 3: 353.

communication networks within these vast areas can be a source of weakness in defense. For Russia, the lack of natural frontiers in the west or of natural obstacles to invasion across the plains of Poland and eastern Germany has been a source of conflict and weakness from the fourteenth century up to the present day. This condition must be considered at least partly responsible for Soviet policies toward the satellites and for the insistence of the late Premier Stalin that "Poland is a matter of life and death."

Consequently, experienced diplomats like Ambassadors Charles E. Bohlen and Llewelyn Thompson warn that the most probable *casus belli* for the Russians could be a sudden change in the status of Eastern Europe. Short of a general settlement, they would fight to preserve their position in this area, as was evident in Hungary in 1956 and in Czechoslovakia in 1969.

Natural Resources. The crisis in the Middle East provides a reminder that natural resources continue to be a vital element in foreign policy. The decisive importance of the countries in the Arabian peninsula rests primarily in the control they exert over oil. In practice, modern technology has made Middle Eastern oil production an increasingly vital necessity, especially for regions like Western Europe. Instruments of production, transportation, and war require oil as a source of energy—Clemenceau once observed that "one drop of oil is worth one drop of blood of our soldiers"— and its importance has led to a shift in the relative power of major regions of the world (as in the rise to importance of the Middle East) and of some of the major nations. Self-sufficiency in this natural resource has enhanced the power of Russia and the United States while Britain and other European nations have been made weaker

by their want of oil. The Middle East still furnishes a large proportion of Western Europe's oil supplies and, barring major conflicts, this fact will continue to influence policy. Other estimates suggest that with the expansion of industrial production and national income and the flagging output of Europe's coal industry, Western European oil consumption may be trebled in twenty years. Hence control of oil becomes a crucial stake in world politics, and "oil diplomacy" has emerged as a term of art among policy makers.

Other natural resources influence foreign policy; the most basic has tended to be food production. Germany's military and political strategy in two world wars was influenced by the need to gain a comparatively early victory before its limited food reserves were exhausted. For much the same reason, Britain, which before World War II produced only 30 percent of its food, ran the risk of destruction when its external lines of communication were threatened by submarines and air power. Britain, by economic enterprise, had extended its influence until, by the 1930s, there was no part of the world not economically linked in some way with London; but its security became more precarious in proportion to its dependence on tenuous and extended lines of communication. Liberals, prompted by their zeal for international trade, frequently decry a nation's quest for autonomy and self-sufficiency, yet in wartime self-sufficiency becomes a decisive source of strength. Food and energy are the lifeblood of a nation; its leaders must find ways, whether domestically or internationally, to satisfy these needs.

Less Permanent Material Elements

Industrial Establishment. The twin forces of the Industrial Revolution and the contemporary political revolution, symbolized by the fact that approximately seventy new nations have gained recognition since World War II, underscore the vital importance of another element of foreign policy. In the nineteenth and twentieth centuries, the industrial establishment of a country has been the most basic index of world power. So long as Britain had no equal as an industrial power, its weight in the balance of power was bound to be decisive. With the increase in industrial strength of Germany and the Soviet Union or of Italy and Japan, to say nothing of the United States, Britain's capacity to influence the course of world politics was substantially reduced. Britain, having lost its industrial supremacy, also lost its capacity to serve as a balancer. France's industrial decline in relation to Germany meant that it was no longer able to resist German expansionism. Industrial capacity in both world wars, even more than peacetime military preparedness, proved to be the *ultima ratio*. It was the latent power of the United States, reflected in its industrial resources, that tipped the scales and gave the victory to the allied powers:

In any comparison of the potential resources of the Great Powers the United States, even before Hitler's war, far outstripped every other nation in the world in material strength, in scale of industrialization, in weight of resources, in standards of living, by every index of output and consumption. And the war, which all but doubled the American national income while it either ruined or severely weakened every other Great Power, has enormously increased the scale upon which the United States now towers above its fellows.[4]

[4] *The Economist* (London), May 24, 1947, p. 785.

The realities of industrial capacity, can therefore be ascertained and measured, at least in approximate terms. India, for example, seems to have been lacking in the industrial resources essential to a great power. Although it has substantial deposits of coal and iron and ranks high in manganese production, it has in the past lagged far behind the first-rate powers in the level of its industrial establishment. Only a tiny percentage of its total population has been engaged in industry, and its industrial plants have been severely limited. India is but one of a number of new nations whose rising political expectations are echoed in their demands for expanded industrial capacity. Its five-year plans are in part the expression of the drive for economic development and industrialization. Most of the nations that have only recently attained independence seek economic growth as the indispensable prerequisite of status in the international society. For some, the quest for rapid industrialization cannot be other than abortive. The observer can suggest that they might play a more significant role if they held to a more modest view of their destiny and cast their lot with neighboring states in a regional development program. In so doing, however, they would accept a permanently inferior position in which their freedom of action would be hedged about, and this they are unwilling to do.

Military Establishment. The military establishments of nations comprise another, and possibly the most explicit, element of foreign policy. Diplomacy and military strength go hand in hand. In an earlier day, the great powers sent gunboats up the rivers of states they were seeking to influence; today a show of strength involves air forces, fleets, and satellites. The postwar distribution of power was an outcome of the position of the Red Army at strategic points in the heart of Europe. Germany's demoniacally successful diplomacy in the period between the two world wars was clearly the direct outgrowth of superior military preparedness. The explosion and testing of atomic weapons by the Soviet Union has been joined with strategic moves in the Cold War. The frontiers separating the spheres of influence of warring states often demarcate the limits of their effective military forces, as, for example, in both Korea and Indochina. As long as force remains the final arbiter of rivalries among nations, the comparative strengths of military establishments will set boundaries to actions in foreign affairs.

Military strength quite obviously lacks the permanence of the elements of geography or natural resources. Throughout history it has been subject to the compulsions of technological changes that have brought far-reaching shifts in power. The phalanx was the key to Sparta's victory over Athens in the Peloponnesian War of 431–404 B.C. Its effectiveness lay in the use of heavy infantry in close-order formation and in reliance upon shock techniques. The Athenians recovered from their defeat and, thirty-three years later, employed swarms of light infantry to conquer the Spartans. Somewhat later, the Thebans improved the phalanx by distributing its power in depth, thus introducing an element of surprise that had been missing. The Macedonians revamped the Spartan phalanx, made use of Greek mercenaries, and put their stress on a war of movement. But Macedonia was succeeded by the military genius and mobile legions of Rome. Hardened in civil and border wars, the Roman army proved versatile enough to fight as skirmishers or heavily

armed infantrymen in open country and in villages and towns. However, the battle of Adrianople against heavily armed cavalrymen from the east brought the challenge Roman military leaders had foreseen but for which they were unprepared. In modern times, technology has given dramatic opportunities to those military leaders who proved capable of adaptation and innovation. By contrast, failure to respond to change has usually meant failure even for those whose traditional military resources appeared to be adequate. The Germans were defeated in World War I because they used the strategy of 1870 against their opponents' order of battle of trench warfare and economic blockade. The French, expecting another costly and brutal war of attrition, built the Maginot Line in the 1930s to fight the kind of struggle that military technology had already rendered obsolete. Short of warfare itself, the failure of military establishments to keep pace with fast-moving technological changes can also reduce nations' influence in the chancelleries of the world. This was the tragedy of France before World War II.

The difficulties inherent in maintaining military establishments that will not suffer defeat are more complex than mere responses to technological change. A nation may recognize the need for military organs capable of supporting the foreign policies it pursues but be limited in the margin of its economic resources that can be turned to military use. Some countries exhaust their resources in attaining a viable economy; others, like the United States, have a surplus with which to meet foreign military and political commitments. Belgium cannot afford to devote the same part of its gross national product to military ends as can the Soviet Union or the United States. Thus, both in absolute and relative terms, the military establishment of smaller powers must lag behind.

However, it should be remembered that technology is not the only important element in military strength. A technically weaker nation can, if it is sufficiently determined, tie down if not defeat outright a stronger nation in a guerilla combat. Most recently, the effectiveness of this method has been shown in Algeria and in Indochina.

Three errors are commonly made in appraising the military component of foreign policy. First, military power is often confused with national power, and a nation's capacity to impose its will is equated with its military establishment. Military power is like the first whose force depends on the health and vitality of the body politic and the whole society. Troops are an important determinant of a successful foreign policy, but without other foundations they will not suffice. Second, the military element is often viewed in more static terms than is appropriate. The democracies, although the last to arm in two world wars, rallied their forces to gain the victory in the end. Third, it is difficult to analyze and foresee, in advance of a particular war, the most effective distribution of the components of military force. For example, what comprises a strong military force today? Is it large ground forces, hydrogen bombs, or intensive research? Is a small, highly specialized army more desirable than a large number of ground forces, or are both essential for a nation that seeks to be strong? The answers to these questions will probably be decisive in determining a state's future influence in the world, yet it is sobering that estimates must be made on the basis of contingencies that cannot now be foreseen. We know in a general way that an effective foreign policy must be supported by a military program that can safeguard national security. But this leaves those who make decisions with the painful task of distributing resources among alternative means of defense without any certainty of the kind of war they may have to fight.

Changes in Industrial and Military Capacity. Beyond the factors discussed above, the weapons of today may not be used in future wars because technology has rendered them obsolete. It is said that conventional weapons are fast being supplanted by new and more deadly weapons, and that, therefore, traditional armaments fail to provide an adequate basis for foreign policy. On the other hand, there are military experts who question whether atomic and hydrogen weapons will ever be used, given the prospect of mutual annihilation. Is it not fair then to ask whether the stockpiling of an unlimited supply of weapons that no nation would dare to use furnishes a state with the requisite military support? A military establishment grounded in conventional weapons may fall short of providing a defensible military posture, but so may a military program aimed at superior atomic capacities. These are the horns of the dilemma on which defense strategists could be impaled.

The Human Elements: Quantitative and Qualitative

Quantitative—Population. Students of foreign policy have stressed another set of elements that make up a third concentric circle of factors of policy. They constitute the human forces—both quantitative and qualitative. Population is a quantitative factor that obviously must be considered in every calculation of the capacity of states. The importance of China and India rests partly in the size of their populations, which exceed 400 million people; both the Soviet Union and the United States, numbering less than half the populations of these countries, have shown respect for their potential. Conversely, nations with falling birth rates have lost influence among the society of nations, as France did after World War I. In the past, the wide diversity in technological skills, for instance between an Englishman and a Chinese, meant that population was not a factor. In recent years, this situation has been changing. The 50 million people now living in the United Kingdom enjoy a high degree of scientific skill, but there is no longer any certainty that the peoples of underdeveloped areas may not eventually approach them, or even that the combined skills of so large a population may not compensate for a persistent technological lag.

The use of population statistics and forecasts suggests that the science of estimating and predicting the relative populations of states is simple and precise. Yet demography is subject to many of the vicissitudes to which other research in the social sciences is exposed. For example, World War I virtually wiped out a whole generation of Frenchmen. France's casualties from 1914 to 1918 numbered 1,400,000 young men. By 1938, the French birth rate no longer compensated for the death rate, and in World War II, France lost 625,000 men—almost three times America's losses in a country one-fourth America's size. Yet, since World War II, the French birth rate has reversed direction, and, since 1946, the surplus of births over deaths has been about 225,000 a year—a surplus greater than that of Italy or West Germany. France, which had been static and immobile between the world wars, has witnessed a renewal of its rate of growth. In more general terms, then, population is an element of for-

eign policy that is not absolutely predictable and that depends on other related elements. It may enable or prevent a state from achieving its national purposes, but, in either role, it is also subject to change and fluctuation.

Qualitative—Policy Makers and Leaders. Another crucial element of policy is the role of policy makers within a political system. The study of the methods, style, and quality of the process by which policies are implemented is the concern of students of both international and comparative politics. Moreover, the capacity for rational and responsible foreign policy varies greatly from state to state.

From a formal point of view, a policy maker is the official empowered with making the relevant decisions in foreign policy. In some political systems, the officials are the effective decision makers, as is the case in stable democratic systems and well-established authoritarian systems. In other cases, the officials are not the effective decision makers. The matter is one for empirical observation, knowledge of existing domestic systems, and study of historical patterns of foreign policy action. In most cases, observation will disclose the effective wielders of power and the real centers of decision making, but there will always be some doubt, especially when competing groups and elites have different views or when there is conflict on goals or on the means of achieving them. In societies where the officials are not the true wielders of power, the search for the centers of power may lead us to the political party, the military, the trade unions, the tribal chiefs, or the intellectuals. No prediction about foreign policy trends can be made, for many countries, without a careful assessment of the relative strength of the students, the trade unions, the military, the church, and the business groups.

Formal or informal decision makers reflect the existing balance of forces in any given political society, from the most consensual to the most divided and fragmented. There are some long-range trends, however, that are very relevant to the study of foreign policy. These include the growing managerial control of advanced industrialized societies, the growing influence of the natural scientists, both as policy makers and as an important group, and the relative independence of the military. Industrialization and technological improvement, together with rising material expectations and their satisfaction, create similar societies in which ideologies progressively give place to pragmatic and technical considerations. Ideological conflicts become secondary. Such a trend inevitably leads to emphasis upon peace, since material satisfaction and the utilization of technology for this purpose are possible only if there is peace. Although there are qualifications to be made, one might well hypothesize that present industrial and technical developments put primacy upon fulfillment of material goals and satisfaction of material expectations, rather than upon international conflict. However, the growing importance of the military in all contemporary societies is prima-facie evidence of the reverse trend.

Political leadership, in most societies, acts in order to maintain the security of the national state. An indispensable ingredient of security is power. The "realists" in international relations claim that power is a primary consideration in the behavior of the ruling groups of any nation-state, and that ideology and all other considerations are subordinate. This is undoubtedly true, and the quest for power often comes into conflict with national welfare or even internal status; thus, groups in power, in order to increase the power of the nation-state, may sometimes undermine their own position. The extent to which considerations of power will come into conflict with considerations of internal status, wealth, and leadership is a matter for empirical and historical study. In order to study comparative foreign policy, we ought to know how well entrenched are the effective wielders of power, and how likely is it that their decisions will be obeyed. International conflict will strengthen or weaken leadership, depending on the existing constellation of the various groups in a society. It is important to discover the circumstances under which an external threat leads to the consolidation of the power of an existing leadership group and when it leads to an undermining of that leadership.

It is also important to define the relations between the various decision makers or wielders of power. The question applies with equal relevance to the "Soviet world" and the "free world."

The Role of Ideology. What is the role of ideology within the international system? The term *ideology* applies not only to the manner in which objectives are shaped, but also to how the given objectives will be pursued. There is a range of means, extending from outright violence to attachment to the established procedures. As long as international rules for the adjustment and accommodation of conflict have a very low degree of legitimacy, conflict will always involve a threat of violence. At what point is conflict likely to lead to war? It is difficult to make an accurate prediction, but certain obvious alternatives can be envisaged.

Some nation-states and their political leadership are likely to resort to violence more readily than others.

The available instruments of violence are an important consideration in assessing the likelihood of war. The more destructive the weapons available, the less likely their use; hence, the effort will be to accommodate conflict. "Total" destructive power in the hands of only two powers may lead to a number of alternatives: progressive disarmament of all other political systems; progressive polarization, in the form of alliances under the leadership of the two states, or an effort to redress the balance by the manufacturing of weapons by a third power or bloc, as was true with de Gaulle's France. Polarization may be stable if it brings about either complete disarmament of the rest of the world, with the express or tacit agreement of the two states involved, or the physical division of the world into two clearly demarcated and integrated spheres. All other situations are bound to be highly unstable.

This appears to be the case more than twenty-five years after the end of World War II. The two superpowers, unable to reach an agreement, have permitted a slow drift towards multicentrism. France and China have developed their atomic weapons while the Atlantic alliance and the Russian-controlled bloc are going through a process of disintegration. Thus, we have again entered a period of instability mitigated only by the continuing predominance of the United States and the Soviet Union. The Sino-Soviet conflict; the United States involvement in Southeast Asia; far-reaching social and political changes in South America, as in Chile; the *Ostpolitik* of Chancellor Willy Brandt in West Germany; and growing resentment of U.S. and Soviet influence—all are indications of the fluidity of the present situation in which the only discernible pattern is the reassertion of nationalist aspirations by independent sovereign states.

Possibilities of surprise attack and retaliation obey essentially simple rules if there are only two nuclear powers. The moment ultimate weapons are available and held by many states—a threat implicit in the so-called nth-country problem—there can be no stabilizing force such as the one implicit in the balance-of-power theory. The situation is one in which there is no possible balancer; each nation-state, once it possesses a given number of ultimate weapons, is relatively as powerful as the other. At this point, instability is so great that it is safe to predict that conflict inevitably will lead to violence on an unprecedented scale. Our world will approximate Hobbes's model of the state of nature.

The Role of Information. What importance does information have in shaping policy? The problem of available information, which forms the basis of the policy maker's decision, is very complex. Game theory postulates its free flow, much as the liberal economics assumed perfect mobility and price competition. The "liberal model" is useful because, on its basis, we can make inferences about events and developments even when empirical reality does not fit the model. Game theory does not have this advantage, because it assumes a game without telling us what the game is about —i.e., whether it is war, peace, accommodation, maintenance of the status quo, surprise attack, or annihilation. Despite the theory's emphasis upon the "rules," we cannot understand what they are unless we assume that the participants have similar objectives, norms, and leadership characteristics, a situation that obviously never obtains. If the participants all play different games with different rules, we have no game amenable to rational observation. Therefore, where and how reality differs from the model cannot be shown in any terms. Game theory, useful in military analysis when we consider the use of weapons and force, is not relevant to the study of foreign policy.

To undertake a discussion of the relationship between information and policy making or formulation of objectives, we would have to consider: (*a*) information available to decision-making and governing elites; (*b*) information as a source of conflict among elites; (*c*) possession of information as a source of power and influence among certain of the political elites or decision makers; (*d*) the manner in which information is perceived; and (*e*) the serious problem of the disparity between the information available to the public and that available to various public policy-making and leadership groups. A subsidiary problem is that of the manufacturing of "information" in different degrees in all political systems.

It is hard to relate the above meaningfully and arrive at certain hypothetical generalizations. The Wilsonian theory, that the free flow of information would keep opinion alert and pave the way to the resolutions of all conflicts without resort to war, was based on the notion that decision makers and governing elites are more prone to conflict and war than are the people. It was further based on the assumptions that the public, when given all the facts, would make rational judgments, and that rational judgment excludes war. There are reasonable doubts, however, that public opinion is the more rational or that it is more easily modified in the light of information received. There is also less evidence than had been assumed that the withholding of information

by the decision makers, or the limiting of access to it to only a small group of persons with leadership positions, is more likely to lead to war.

Diplomacy: National Purposes

Another element of foreign policy is the quality of a nation's diplomacy. At one level, this involves a clear conception of national purposes; at another, it involves prudence and skill in the use of the tools of statecraft. For purposes of analysis, both can be examined in the context of American foreign policy.

It is well to remind ourselves that issues confronting the makers of American foreign policy compete for attention, crowding out and succeeding one another in headlines of the daily press. Brazil, Nigeria, East Africa, Cambodia, Israel, Laos, and Cuba—to say nothing of the overriding attention to Vietnam—flash kaleidoscopically across each of our horizons as we seek to understand international affairs. Sensing this process, it is tempting to second-guess the future. When one is asked what will be the most compelling and troublesome problems of the next six months or a year, he can prophesy the continued threat of war in the Middle East, the continuing conflict in Indochina, or agreement on arms controls. But behind these issues and affecting their resolution are deep-seated, underlying questions relating to this country's basic goals and national purposes. What do Americans seek in the world? Is it peace? Power? Prosperity? Each of these goals is often set forth as a national fundamental aim. Sometimes peace, especially in this atomic age, is made an absolute purpose; prosperity sometimes seems to emerge as the one end Americans seek above all others in the conduct of their affairs in the world. We shall look in turn at each of these goals, seeking to ascertain its relevance to the real issues in America's foreign affairs.

Peace as National Purpose. It is sometimes considered a mark of bad judgment to recite a succession of "great generalities" at the outset of any discussion. However, the present crisis imposes upon us responsibilities of perceiving more clearly the ebb and flow of certitude and truth with respect to the root principles of world affairs. Recent events have shaped and molded the dimensions of the international problem in a manner that few anticipated. Take, as an example, the issue of peace. For the first time in centuries, rational men have been claiming—apparently with some accord—that war has become obsolete as an instrument of national policy. President Eisenhower reiterated this view, and he maintained again at the First Geneva Conference that victor and vanquished alike would be casualties in any thermonuclear war. His successor, President Kennedy, continued negotiations until the Limited Nuclear Test Ban Treaty was signed and ratified by the Senate in 1963. President Nixon has committed us to protracted negotiations in the SALT talks. But does this mean that peace is inevitable and atomic warfare impossible? Apparently not, if we consider recent policy statements, the informed opinions of experienced leaders, or events in the Middle East and above all, in Southeast Asia—without mentioning, of course, the Sino-Soviet conflict.

Power as National Purpose. The most celebrated and controversial policy statements in the mid-fifties were those attributed by *Life* writer James Shepley to Secretary of State John Foster Dulles. In discussing the policy of "massive retaliation," Mr. Dulles observed: "The ability to get to the verge without getting into the war is the necessary art. If you cannot master it, you inevitably get into war. If you try to run away from it, if you are scared to go to the brink, you are lost." Earlier he had said that a potential aggressor must know that his acts would be met by such retaliation and that he would lose more than he could gain. Specific targets for retaliation had to be selected and agreed upon in advance: "The way to deter aggression is for the free community to be willing and able to respond vigorously at places and with means of its own choosing." Its response should be massive and overwhelming.

If we separate the chaff from the grain, the political from the inescapable truth in this contested statement, it seems clear that the possibility of resort to military measures has not been cast out from the armory of American foreign policy. Since the Eisenhower administration stressed, wherever possible, the replacement of manpower with decisive weapons, the risk of warfare with ultimate weapons can hardly be said to have passed. Nor is this possibility made any less ominous by the boasts of Soviet leaders that they too have developed a strategy of retaliation. The Soviet resistance to a neutral administrator of a disarmament agreement and their refusal to accept other suggested procedures are further evidence. In this situation an accident, a miscalculation, or an act of desperation could easily set off the conflict that Geneva was said to have made impossible. The "Nixon Doctrine," which preserves American commitments to come to the aid of allies who suffer aggression while reducing conventional American military resources for supporting these commitments, further increases the risk of using ultimate weapons in conflicts.

Prosperity and Economic Development as National Purpose. Turning to the issue of prosperity, we enter the presence of the most appealing of the current trends of informed thinking on our foreign policy. This trend of thought maintains, with varying reservations, that most of the tensions between the West and the uncommitted countries of the world are the result of mutual suspicions, and that these can be composed through economic cooperation and aid. Put in the proper perspective, a policy of contributing modestly and consistently to prosperity and the raising of standards of living in the world is a viable, if not an utterly essential, goal of American foreign policy. Its emphasis is all the more crucial because of the neglect of this facet of American thinking in the past. However, prosperity, like peace, is at best a proximate guide to action. It offers no panacea to the ills that engulf the world. Tensions may be eased when the fruits of economic development and growth are more widely shared at home and abroad, yet American experiences of intense strife and national division during the past decade should caution us against excessive optimism.

On a world scale, the limits of a form of inverted Marxism that looks to economic development as a miraculous device for purging tensions and strife are even more graphic. India and the United States have not been deterred from misunderstandings by India's phenomenal economic growth. The fact that India has literally raised herself by her own bootstraps, that she increased real income 28 percent in the period from 1949 to 1965, and attained, in 1953/54, the highest rate of economic growth in the world has, if anything, prompted her to press claims more vigorously, even when they conflicted with those of the West.

Furthermore, those who would lay the disparities in standards of living throughout the world on the conscience of the West sometimes seek to exact a heavier tribute than any nation or civilization can fulfill. These developments in other countries are intimately bound up with cultural traditions, with political order and stability, with resources, attitudes, population pressures, and a thousand local conditions that Western powers can only slightly shape or affect. If Western efforts can assist others to inch their way to a happier and more promising state of economic well-being and political justice, this will be enough, and it may even stem the advance of hostile forces. However, it can lead at best to public disillusionment and perhaps a deep and festering embitterment with the West's role in the world if public justification of these programs claims more than is warranted.

That the West should be left to find its way gropingly, painfully, and with uncertainty can come as a shock only to those who forever seek simple absolutes and an easy pathway. Peace, more than ever before in America's history, is a paramount goal of American foreign policy. However, it is a goal that knows its limits. Power throws a spotlight on those dark corners of American action that were but dimly lighted throughout the era of intellectual pacifism and political neutralism. Prosperity—especially in Asia, Africa, and the Middle East— must be as much America's aim as military security, particularly since the foe becomes ever more cunning and resourceful in his pursuit of this enterprise. Yet prosperity is a means and not an end. The interests of progressive, no less than oppressed, states clash and must be accommodated. Diplomats and not the experts in technical assistance must be called to this task.

We will be on surer ground if we recognize that peace, power, and prosperity are rough guidelines to action. They show us the perimeters within which to work, but in no way remove the demands placed on leaders for political judgment and practical wisdom.

Diplomacy and Democracy

Democratic theory rests on the supposition that, while the very broad goals of foreign policy must be decided by the people, the concrete decisions and implementation within these goals is the function of the political leadership, primarily the executive branch of the government. Bryce argued, in the heyday of the Wilsonian "populism" in matters of foreign policy, that the broad ends of foreign policy should be decided by the people, and he produced evidence to show why democracies had displayed more "wisdom" than despotisms in the formulation of such broad objectives. Most democratic theorists tempered their remarks with a realization that popular awareness and popular infallibility were more restricted in matters of foreign policy than in domestic matters. Bryce himself put this in the following terms: "One of the strongest arguments for democratic government is that the masses of the people, whatever else they may not know, do know where the shoe pinches, and are best entitled to specify the reforms they need. In foreign policy this does not apply. . . ."[5]

These basic presuppositions about the role of public opinion and the relationship between leadership and public opinion require comparative analysis and study. To begin with, the rationalist assumptions about public opinion have been subjected to careful criticism and reconsideration ever

since the publication of Walter Lippmann's *Public Opinion* and *The Phantom Public*. Secondly, the apathy of public opinion in matters of foreign policy in contemporary systems calls for the reconsideration of those presuppositions. When the European Defense Community sharply divided the French Parliament and stalemated any legislative action in the second legislature of the Fourth Republic, "four-fifths of the public [in France] had heard about the project but [were] uncertain as to whether the plan had been voted or not. . . ."[6] The surveys carried on by the Institute of Public Opinion in France reveal the colossal ignorance of foreign policy matters among an electorate that has been traditionally considered alert and sophisticated. In the United States, 75 percent of the electorate have been considered as unaware of, or uninformed on, foreign policy questions.[7] Strangely enough, if public opinion polls have any relevance, the postwar German public opinion has been consistently more alert and informed than that of the traditionally democratic and enlightened nations. A recent study indicates the same general division between an informed active minority and a large mass of uninformed and passive public. It may be warranted, therefore, to raise this fundamental question as an invitation to comparative study of foreign policy. Are the democratic presuppositions

[6] Pierre Gerbet, "*L'influence de l'opinion publique et des partis sur la politique étrangère en France*," in *La politique étrangère et ses fondements*, ed. Jean-Baptiste Duroselle, (Paris: Librairie Armand Colin, 1954).

[7] Lester Markel, ed., *Public Opinion and Foreign Policy*, Martin Kriesberg, *Dark Areas of Ignorance*. When Secretary of State Dean Acheson was under severe attack for the Truman-Acheson foreign policies, only 23 percent of those polled could identify the secretary of state.

[5] James Bryce, *Modern Democracies* (New York: Macmillan Co. 1921), 2:370.

valid? If not, why? If so, under what conditions do they obtain?

Diplomatic Practices and Diplomacy. In diplomacy, the choice of methods and techniques is no less vital than clarity about objectives. Democracies sometimes assume that the demands of coherence and consistency in diplomacy fall less heavily upon them than upon other states. In part, this stems from the prevailing outlook about democracy and foreign policy.

The first two decades of the twentieth century witnessed the flowering of a philosophy of international politics that was unambiguously simple, straightforward, and capable of engendering widespread popular appeal. Those who held this view looked, in a spirit of buoyant optimism, to democracy and national self-determination as the twin sources of international peace and order. The creation of popular regimes on the Anglo-American model everywhere throughout the world was heralded as a sure corrective to the harsh conflicts that for centuries had wracked international life. New nations, brought into existence at the will of a self-conscious community of peoples, would dissolve the rivalries and frictions that had always led to conflict among contiguous social groups. The faith of modern Western Homo sapiens in man's potentialities for unending progress found its expression on the international scene in the assurance that a brave new world merely awaited the fulfillment of these goals.

It is ironic that this illusion, based on an excess of faith in what is essentially the divine right of the *vox populi* has, in the recent past, been rudely shaken on numerous fronts. The phenomenon of totalitarian democracy, unknown in the nineteenth century, has not only left political rivalries and conflict intact but has heightened and made virtually irreconcilable the disputes among the new collectivities. Inflamed public passions, playing on statesmen, have made moderation and compromise more difficult of attainment. National leaders, by pandering to popular passions, have often reduced the alternatives open to responsible makers of foreign policy. Nationalism has not led to more peaceful relations among peoples who rested content with their political status, but instead has bred the most embittered antagonisms between new nations and their former colonial masters or between non-Western states and their erstwhile exemplars in the West. National self-determination and democracy can hardly be said to have ushered in a new era of hope; our more serious observers find deep anguish in the steep and sudden decline of influence and self-confidence of the Western democracies. The West succeeds in engendering resentment and suspicion more often than it earns respect. Yet many students and statesmen insist on talking in bated breath about the causes and conditions of our decline. The bulk of those who assume leadership in intellectual and political life are singularly inhibited when it comes to diagnosing the source of our ills. It is commonplace to respond to a critical evaluation of the conduct of foreign policy in a democracy by pointing the finger of scorn at nondemocratic societies that are still more obviously the authors of our most recent historic catastrophes. The key to this difficult problem is surely not loss of faith in democracy. It is rather a deeper awareness of the methods of diplomacy.

Democratic diplomacy, like all diplomacy, must adhere to certain sound principles and rules. It must prove its consistency with the diplomatic tradition and the imperatives of effective negotiation. Majority votes in multilateral conference, dialectics, invective, or propaganda may hold a certain fascination for the spectators of world affairs. But more often than not, their effect is to sow international distrust and to increase, rather than alleviate, world conflicts. The first principle worth noting is that, historically, diplomacy and foreign policy have not been considered identical. Foreign policy has been viewed as the legislative aspect, and diplomacy as the executive aspect, of managing foreign relations. Diplomacy has called for experts with freedom of action; policy is a matter for the most responsible branches of government, including at some point the legislature. Diplomacy is not the framing of policy, but rather its execution. It is no more a point of focus for public attention than is the execution of the national budget, as distinct from its authorization.

The *Oxford English Dictionary* defines *diplomacy* as "the management of international relations by negotiation; the method by which these relations are adjusted and managed by ambassadors and envoys; the business or art of the diplomatist." This definition suggests a second principle: the test of diplomacy is not the vindication of some abstract moral principle or the rewarding or punishment of virtuous or evil forces; it is rather the most effective accommodation of state relations that are sometimes in harmony, but other times in conflict.

Third, diplomacy calls for an intimate knowledge of the mechanics of negotiation, for endless patience in the use of numberless expedients in working out agreements, and for consummate skill in adjusting national proposals and making them acceptable at home and abroad without sacrificing vital objectives.

In recent years, many serious writers have questioned whether or not diplomacy has measured up to the standards inherent in these principles. Hugh Gibson, who has few peers among twentieth-century American diplomatists, has written:

What we have come to call diplomacy . . . has failed to achieve results and has led into all sorts of disasters. But it wasn't really diplomacy. It was the usurpation of diplomatic functions by politicians and inept amateurs; it was the new method of having the negotiation of infinitely complicated world problems handled by politicians, amateurs, and adventurers; the forcing on the world in critical times of new and untried methods; publicity stunts and hurried personal discussions between the political leaders, who should stay at home and be the heavy artillery in reserve rather than trying to direct operations on hurried visits to the front-line trenches.[8]

These words have even greater relevance today than they had a little less than three decades ago.

The Transformation of Diplomatic Practices. For nearly four centuries, the statecraft of Europe had certain salient features. It sought, in theory at least, to mitigate and reduce conflicts by means of persuasion, compromise, and adjustment. It was rooted in the community of interests of a small group of leaders who spoke the same language, catered to one another as often as to their own people, and played to one another's strengths and weaknesses. When warfare broke out, they drew a ring around the combatants and sought to neutralize the struggle. The old diplomats carried on their tasks in a world made up of states that were small, separated, limited in power, and blessed, ironically enough, by halfhearted political loyalties. Patience was a watchword; nego-

[8] Hugh Gibson, *The Road to Foreign Policy* (Garden City, N.Y.: Doubleday & Co., 1944), p. 63.

tiations were often as protracted during war as in peace. It was taken for granted that talks would be initiated, broken off, resumed, discontinued temporarily, and reopened again by professionals in whose lexicon there was no substitute for "diplomacy."

Today not one of these conditions any longer prevails, and the search for new formulas in diplomacy has gone on apace. The first and most novel pattern to crystallize after World War II found expression in the United Nations and in what is called "popular diplomacy." International forums and majority votes in the General Assembly were to substitute for the tortuous paths of traditional diplomacy. It must be said that this choice was expressed more rigorously in practice than in the United Nations Charter, which emphasized talks among the parties to a dispute before placing an issue on the agenda. Popular diplomacy reflects the faith in parliamentary procedures, in the rule of the people, and in straightforward, rational, and open discussion. It is the joint product of an age of rationalism and an age of popular government. It translates into global terms supreme political attainments of free people within the democratic state. Popular diplomacy, despite the role of the Great Powers in the Security Council, marks a swing of the pendulum to diplomacy by all the peoples of most of the nations. It is the antithesis of secret diplomacy by a concert of leaders of the preeminent countries.

Because popular diplomacy has been the basis of much of our postwar diplomacy, we are able to make a modest estimate of its success. To use former Canadian Prime Minister Lester Pearson's phrase, we find that the problems of "diplomacy in a goldfish bowl" are more intractable than we had supposed. Publicity has been both a virtue and a vice. It has kept the spotlight of public opinion on world affairs, but it has encouraged the actor in world politics to take inflexible positions from which it is difficult to retreat. Majority votes on Korea have demonstrated who has controlled greater support; they have left conflicts of interest unaffected or have actually contributed to their increase. When this new pattern of diplomacy has worked, it has been flavored with more ancient techniques, as with the private diplomacy of Mr. Ralph Bunche in Palestine and of Mr. Jessup on Berlin, the "quiet diplomacy" of late Secretary-General Dag Hammarskjöld of the United Nations on Suez and the Congo, and the efforts of U.S. envoy Cyrus Vance in Cyprus.

These successes, however noteworthy, failed to arrest the sharp swing of the pendulum to another type of international diplomacy. The Eisenhower administration espoused personal diplomacy as a means of correcting the excesses of public negotiations. The first Geneva Conference, the United States-Canadian-Mexican conference at White Sulphur Springs, and the meeting with India's late Prime Minister Nehru and with former Prime Minister Macmillan of England illustrated a new and emerging pattern. It was a pattern based upon the President's partiality "for talking things out rather than negotiating things out" in an atmosphere of genial informality. It reflected the view that some of the roots of conflict would dissolve when leaders from other nations, sitting across a table from Mr. Eisenhower, became persuaded of his good intentions. The personal touch of a famous personality had been placed on the scales of world diplomacy. It is perhaps too early to assess the style, and the successes or failures, of the late President Kennedy and of former President

THE COMPARATIVE STUDY OF FOREIGN POLICY

Johnson. The first successfully combined personal diplomacy and negotiations with what we have called "popular diplomacy." The manner in which he handled the Soviet thrust in the Cuban missile crisis was an excellent display of a combination of diplomacy and power. His successor showed a greater penchant for popular diplomacy. With both Presidents Johnson and Nixon there has also appeared a shift away from a realistic approach in favor of ideological commitments —so common in American foreign policy.

The Rediscovery of Diplomacy. The two novel approaches—personal and parliamentary diplomacy—are at opposite ends of the spectrum. One emphasizes public speeches, mass assemblies, and resolutions emerging from open forums; the other stresses informality and man-to-man conferences free of protocol, agendas, and advance preparation. (At White Sulphur Springs, on the eve of the so-called Little Summit Conference, the Canadians were unaware of the topics to be discussed.) Yet these new patterns, so divergent in conception and design, share one thing in common: they constitute a revolt against traditional diplomacy.

For diplomats, the first rule has always been that negotiations are essential when national interests are in conflict. Since such conflicts arise from causes more basic than personal hostility, personal amiability can hardly resolve them. Sir Harold Nicolson has argued:

Diplomacy is the art of negotiating documents in a ratifiable and dependable form. It is by no means the art of conversation. The affability inseparable from any conversation . . . produces illusiveness, compromises, and high intentions. Diplomacy, if it is ever to be effective, should be a disagreeable business, and one recorded in hard print.

The trouble with approaches that set aside the lessons of the past is that history has a way of returning to haunt us. Both popular and personal diplomacy have their place, especially if we safeguard them against their excesses. The best way of doing this is to remember that foreign policy has a memorable tradition, not all of which is folly.

REFLECTIONS ON THE STUDY OF FOREIGN POLICY IN THE CONTEXT OF THE COLD WAR

Theories of social science run the risk of departing too sharply from social reality. By contrast, advances in the medical sciences are often accounted for by the phrase "the scientist is never too far from the patient in the sickbed." The scientist is close to nature so long as he poses relevant and researchable questions. The focus of his interest must be "operationally relevant." Economics, particularly since Walras and more notably since Keynes, has become at once more scientific and more useful. Practitioners of foreign policy are often critical of the unfortunate irrelevance of much theorizing in such approaches as the theory of decision making and behaviorism. They charge that theories remain on the drawing board without being tested or applied against reality.

At the same time, policy makers are the first to signal the need for principles of wider application or for a manageable body of doctrine on foreign policy. Public leaders need help, not merely from efficiency experts, but also from political and constitutional theorists, on problems involved in the organization of the government for the conduct of foreign policy. How should foreign policy be carried on in a democracy? Who takes responsibility and who should be the coordinator of policies and programs? What aspects of foreign policy are the appropriate concern of appointed or elected officials? What part is the responsibility of the whole of the body politic? What are the objectives of foreign policy, how should they be ranged, and in what hierarchical order? For example, how should statesmen order and relate the goals of most Western countries, which include national security, avoidance of thermonuclear war, the preservation of Western values, and support for the rising expectations of newly independent peoples?

These issues are clearly amenable to study, to the ordering of facts and data, to trial and error in testing alternative hypotheses, and to building a body of more generalized theory with relevance for practice. Propositions put forward by one observer will invariably be challenged by others. This is the story of evolving knowledge. If scholars and writers with commitments to rigorous and systematic analysis leave this rich field to others, understanding will suffer. Yet it is disheartening to note how many serious scholars prefer the simpler if tidier tasks of abstracting from reality those problems on which great masses of data are at hand, regardless of their significance.

Policy and Public Opinion. The first obstacle is inherent in the problem of marshalling domestic support for American policies while at the same time putting America's best foot forward in the eyes of the rest of the world. To mobilize support for policies, Americans say things to themselves that, from the standpoint of other peoples, might better be left unsaid. (In this the United States is, of course, not unique.) America is a vast sprawling continent of great diversity of political and religious beliefs; in its constitutional system,

power and responsibility are broadly diffused, although less so in foreign affairs than in the conduct of domestic affairs. Thus Americans speak in many voices, some raucous and strident, as they seek to persuade one another of the right course to follow. The language of domestic politics is not the language of political theory. It aims to unite as many as will join to support policies or programs. It looks to a common denominator that can more often be found in broad principles and moral generalities than in specific directives of strategy that, like military policies, must be cast in practical alternatives to meet circumstances. It prefers militant slogans to qualified truths, a crusade to public conversations about a problem.

Above all, it is a permanent part of the landscape of international relations that American foreign policy must draw its support from a union of the experts, the public, and friends and allies abroad. History demonstrates that no American statesman can ignore any point on the triangle without courting disaster. Before World War II, the public ostensibly lagged behind the thinking on foreign affairs of experts and allies. Following World War II and up to 1950, American policy—especially with respect to Europe—was acceptable alike to the authoritative views of the experts, to the public, and to the members of the postwar Grand Alliance. This day has passed, and the demands of the three groups have tended increasingly to go their separate ways.

Colonialism. Another obstacle to effective policy making stems from the colonial dilemma, which reaches beyond America's national life and touches conflicting interests at work throughout the rest of the world. We know that the colonial problem stands at the top of every agenda for discussion of American foreign policy. Responsible officials are encouraged to issue proclamations and to throw America's weight behind independence movements. In this setting, it is tempting to take general and sweeping positions and to express an American doctrine on the rights of peoples everywhere to independence and self-government. This is particularly true because Americans' own experience is so rich in its lessons and apparently pregnant with meaning. The fruits of attempts thus far made to propound a dogma should serve, however, to give us pause, for the record of America's efforts to align itself squarely with either colonial or anticolonial powers is sprinkled with as many failures as successes.

Nevertheless, Americans face new situations today and demands crowd in upon them for new and more vigorous policies. Nationalism is on the march in Asia, the Middle East, and Africa, and Americans implore one another to identify their country with these movements rather than appearing to stand in their pathway. Unhappily, the colonial problem is less tractable than those exhortations suggest. For at the same time as the fight is waged to end old imperialisms, a new and more demoniac expansionism threatens. To meet it, some feel that America must cleave to its trusted friends and allies with whom it has interests and military bases in common, striving to preserve a more stable world balance of power. Yet, in itself, this is not likely to be enough. The present equilibrium of power will be upset unless America can join with new forces in the so-called underdeveloped areas. We may say, therefore, that the United States faces the triple challenge of stemming the tide of Russian imperialism and Chinese communism, uniting the other Western states, and drawing closer to non-Western

peoples only recently emerging as independent states. In a manner of speaking, policy makers must keep three balls in the air. This is the unenviable task of American statesmanship.

The pathos of our present position may be illustrated briefly from events in the last two decades. First there was the U.S. statement on Goa, recognizing Portugal's authority in the tiny enclave in India, prompted doubtless by the zeal of European officers in the State Department to display a sense of community with Portugal. This provoked deep resentment in India and, perhaps, throughout much of Asia. Next came the expression of "sympathy" for Greek feelings in the Cyprus dispute, which loosed a torrent of British protest. Then the Dutch voiced dismay at Dulles' warm and friendly comments during a visit to the Indonesian Republic. The United States aroused its European friends when it appeared to take sides with Egypt and Middle Eastern friends by reassuring Turkey against Syria and Russia, and more and more in the past few years by supporting Israel in its conflict with the Arabs. More recently the changing objectives of Soviet foreign policy, the emergence of a new and independent but powerful Communist China in Asia, and the specter of communism of the Castro variety in Latin America have underscored the predicament of American foreign policy. The Soviet image is rapidly changing among our Western allies, and the need for accommodation with the Soviet Union is a view that is beginning to be shared by many American experts. Yet we remain somehow still committed to an "anticommunist posture" that paralyzes our reflexes and makes negotiations on common interest between the two countries more difficult. Similarly, there is a tendency to view the war in

Vietnam in global and absolute terms —as the extension of communist aspirations for domination and expansion instead of considering it as a manifestation of a limited and negotiable area of conflict. Events in Latin America have provoked an increasing nervousness with popular revolutions—which we often championed in the past—and a tendency to equate them with anti-American subversive moves directed and inspired by "worldwide communism." Such attitudes have accounted for the progressive decline of our influence and position in Western Europe.

Perceiving these problems, can we say anything about this perplexing picture that will offer some guidance to the juggler or policy maker of whom we have spoken? Perhaps there are guidelines or principles we can enunciate to spotlight a few of the darker corners of this colonial problem. First, we must start with the presumption that the colonial problem is fraught with dilemmas with which America must learn to live. Dogmas for or against colonialism will not waft them away: solutions must be worked out case by case. Second, timing is of the essence. The statement supporting Indonesia stirred up a hornets' nest because Dutch-Indonesian tensions at that time were great. Third, if any general solution can be found, it rests in the coordinating of mutual interests, not in the wholesale sacrifice of one set of interests to another. In North Africa, the French, American, and African interests appeared to coincide, in that all wanted "liberal solutions." Likewise, in other regions, the goal should be the harmonizing of interests. This calls for a judicious balancing of claims. Fourth, it is one of the ironies of history that force may be necessary to preserve colonial arrangements, not in order to perpetuate them, but so that their orderly liquidation may be achieved.

Finally, conflicts of interest—as past conflicts between Britain and India or between the Dutch and the Indonesians—may be swept along by powerful historical movements until one side emerges supreme. It may be necessary for American policy makers to choose sides, and so inevitably give offense. These facts need not preclude prudence and restraint, but the end of the colonial era has changed the form, if not the substance, of choices Western leaders must make.

The Moral Problem. A final obstacle has roots in the moral problem. The question of right and wrong is continuously raised in international relations, as in all the other social orders. Nations, as individuals, either seek to do, or claim to have done, what is right. The nature of Western values, as embodied in American culture, assures that America persistently aspires to justice and to the goal of international order. We are pained when some aspect of national conduct cannot be justified in broader international terms, yet we can take comfort from the fact that, historically, this has been among the most baffling philosophical problems. The question is whether an action shall be called "good" if it serves the group of primary loyalty, or whether it must serve a more inclusive purpose. Political morality, as distinct from pure law or justice, dictates the answer in terms that give it a unique flavor. We must look for the point of concurrence between the particular and the general value or interest, rather than calling for the sacrifice of the part to the whole. Politically, there always remains a residual egotism or self-interest that represents the creative potential of individuals and groups. The nascent international community must guard against extreme forms of parochial loyalty, which end in nations claiming too much and reserving to themselves the right to suppress and overwhelm weaker neighbors. Short of this, however, the larger community is able to harness, beguile, and deflect the more limited national purposes even though it cannot easily transcend them. In Reinhold Niebuhr's words, "the individual or the group may feel called upon to sacrifice an immediate value for the sake of the more ultimate or general interest. But the community cannot demand this sacrifice as its right." Nor, one might add, can another sovereign state.

America's policy makers look for shortcuts to the moral problem. They talk a great deal more about promoting the impact of morality than about determining its content. They seize on the most available expressions congenial to their tastes and interests, like "majority rule" and "the will of the United Nations." The workings of political machinery are invested with all the trappings of a religious exercise, and political pronouncements are equated with the glorification of God. Repelled by all the talk of "missions" and "crusades," one of our most sensitive critics has said, "I would rather *be* moral than claim to be it; and to the extent we succeed in lending moral destruction to the conduct of our affairs, I would rather let others discover it for themselves." The deep pathos of the moral problem calls more for Christian humility than for a moralistic self-righteousness, which can win few friends abroad and serves only to lower the currency of moral principles.

EVALUTION OF FOREIGN POLICY

When it comes to studying foreign policy in its various manifestations, and most particularly international conflict—including war—the social scientist is in a difficult position. He is asked to explain and predict attitudes whose complexity makes a mockery of the few "scientific" tools we have. The layman presses us to predict American or Chinese foreign policy; to unwrap the famous riddle of the Soviet foreign policy; or to explain the nature and conditions of conflict in our contemporary world.

The more stubborn and complex the material, the greater the temptation to move into the realm of abstraction. The canons of science call for simplicity and economy in the formulation of hypotheses that are to be tested. It is only when simple hypotheses are tested that the scientist moves into the more complex, slowly relating and checking his findings with the outside world. We, in contrast, find that we cannot test. As a result, many of us today find it easier *not* to relate our speculations to the outside world at all, and to create propositions, conceptual schemes, and models that have logical coherence, but fail to pass the test of empirical relevance. There is much futility in this.

The way out, in our opinion, is to assume from the start that the range of indeterminacy in our social and political world is great. This is even more applicable to the behavior of states that goes under the name of "foreign policy." To attempt to construct generalizations and models that will give us a rigorous scientific understanding and prediction of foreign policy is a hopeless task.

As we move more into the realm of abstraction in the name of "science," we become more likely to evade—and perhaps evasion is the basic reason for the "scientific" trend toward a high degree of abstraction and conceptualization—our responsibilities in advancing an understanding of politics, notably in international relations and conflict. Therefore, we would, for instance, suggest a better understanding and study of the existing laboratory, i.e., history. (We cannot understand why simulated war games are more important to devise and study than actual or historical conflict from which all degree of simulation is eliminated by the stark and brutal necessity of real choice and decisions.) Second, we believe that case studies of the individual foreign policy-making process, including conflict of various states in terms of the descriptive categories suggested, would give us considerable food for thought and might lead us to more fruitful hypotheses.

One of our aims should be to find regularities in the behavior of nations and to develop general propositions by setting forth carefully the conditioning factors that account for types of behavior. Thus we may hope to reduce the range and degree of indeterminancy. But ours is also a world where exercise of will and choice calls for more than a scientific knowledge of man and nations.

The analytical approach to foreign policy, as distinct from the ideological approach, is no miracle-working device for understanding the complex problems of international affairs. It gives no clue to the specific decisions that must be reached daily. It is not a cookbook with recipes for action to fit every contingency. It does, however, provide a way of thinking about the foreign policy of any country and ordering the factors that contribute to the conduct of foreign relations. If prediction is still beyond the reach of scholars, analysis in the face of varying contingencies may be attainable. In some form or another, this method is useful in studying the acts of great and small powers. Amid all the variations of individual scholars writing about unique national policies, the present book serves to demonstrate the role and the limits of the systematic analysis of foreign policy.

EVALUATION OF INDIVIDUAL POLICY DECISIONS

As the reader goes through the analysis of the foreign policy making of individual countries, he unavoidably is concerned with evaluating them. Have the policy makers made a "good" or a "bad" decision? Has the foreign policy pursued by a given country been "successful" or "unsuccessful"? In terms of what criteria and what canons shall we judge and render a verdict? The intense debate that has been going on over U.S. policy in Vietnam, just as was the case in France over Indochina and Algeria, clearly demonstrates that clearcut and objective tools for analysis and judgment are not always available.

To begin with, there is the perennial problem of "good" and "bad"—i.e., of *normative* criteria and goals. Such goals generally indicate the overall commitment of a society to a way of life and naturally influence policy making and foreign policy as well. The aversion of the average citizen in the United States to the Nazis or to the invasion of China by Japan in the 1930s was real and reflected a normative posture on the part of the American people and its policy makers. There is no doubt that some of the same values and normative criteria play an exceedingly important role in the minds of those who have criticized our involvement in Vietnam and its military manifestations. For a long time American isolationism was based squarely on normative considerations —primarily the belief that the American way of life was distinct and superior to those of the European countries, and that any involvement in their affairs and any involvement on their part in the affairs of the American continent would "contaminate" and perhaps corrupt the American democracy. By the same token, many French political leaders and intellectuals believed that the French colonies were a major challenge for the dissemination of the French culture and the French language through which the "natives" would be assimilated to a higher and better way of life.

The student generally is inclined to be very sympathetic to foreign policy analysis in terms of basic ethical criteria. It is not, however, an easy job—nor is it analytically satisfactory. The first difficulty is that of agreeing on ethics. For those who consider an ethical principle more important than human life, outright destruction in its name is preferable to peace; for those who consider communism a danger far outweighing the well-being of any given generation, war and sacrifice is above that of welfare and well-being; for those who consider democracy and an open society more valuable than one man's life, again, war and destruction may be inevitable to preserve what is so highly valued. In other words, it is not always easy to find people agreeing on the highest normative goal. Even if we did, a second difficulty emerges: how to implement it. As we noted, isolationism was for a long period of time a policy related to the preservation of American democracy. The Cold War and our intervention in Vietnam are related exactly to the preservation of the same ideals. So is NATO. The same normative goal can, in other words, be pursued by foreign and military policies that appear to be on their face antithetical. There is a second difficulty—that of the choice of the means to the pursuance of an accepted goal. Means can be proximate; they can be intermediate. To illustrate what we have in mind: Is it possible in the name of a given ethically accepted goal to pursue means that appear to be incompatible with it? The argument is a very old

one—and in foreign policy the illustrations are abundant. Richelieu had no scruples in allying himself with Protestant powers against Catholic Spain. And Churchill in the war against Nazi Germany solemnly proclaimed that he would ally himself not only with Stalin but with the Devil himself, if he could find him! In the pursuit of freedom and democracy, American foreign policy makers seemed to have gone just as far in forming alliances or giving support to some of the most repressive regimes in the world. At what point—and again, in terms of what criteria—can we convincingly argue that certain means distort the end? That certain policy or policies are incompatible with the posited ethical values? If human life is the highest end, is slavery to be preferred to loss of life? If freedom is the highest end, is it higher than life itself?

The truth is that as in domestic politics there are many values, many ethical norms, and many ways of life that claim primacy in our international community. We live in a pluralistic universe, and nothing can destroy our world more easily than the unqualified assertion of one ethic or one way of life over all others. Unabashedly speaking, there is a relativist ethic. In the words of Pascal, "what is 'good' [acceptable] on one side of the Pyrenees Mountains may well be 'bad' [unacceptable] on the other." This may be so without there being a compelling necessity for either country to extirpate by force what each considers bad and therefore to fight with each other to the ultimate destruction of one or perhaps both. Many nation-states today seem to hold values that are antithetical to each other. Many can live side by side without attempting to impose their will upon the other. That which many hold to be the epitome of morality and their demands that policy must be harnessed to it may well lead directly to conflict and war.

In a pluralistic universe, then, judgment and evaluation in terms of ethical considerations is hazardous and highly unpredictable. We prefer and we suggest here a more instrumental approach to the evaluation of foreign policy. It is based on the assumption that, at least for the time being, nation-states are here to stay and that their foreign policy must be evaluated in terms of the success and failure to implement the goals they pursue. In the international community each and every state is allotted some power, which alone or in combination with others allows it to keep its autonomy and way of life—or, conversely, prevents its destruction by others. The international community has been in this sense a world of power relations differing in degree rather than in kind from domestic politics.

Power relations, it must be noted, express themselves in a number of ways, of which war is the extreme form. Alliances, international law, cooperative schemes, and even integrative schemes express and regularize power relations just as a constitution, a judiciary, and a police system do at the domestic level. A world based upon power relations is not a jungle. Systems providing for balance or limitations or deterrence often are more stable and less likely to lead to the use of force than situations where power relations are unrecognized and ignored. For power, while occasionally erupting in the outright use of force, more often seeks to find, in the world of nations, affinities, compatibilities, and safeguards that will prevent it from becoming destructive. The problem is not to negate power or to ignore it, but to build restraints and to prevent its potentially destructive manifestation by the use of force. The recognition and legitimation of one nation-state's power means, in the last analysis, its preservation in order to exclude the use of force.

Finally, an analysis based upon power must also take into consideration that it is not an end in itself. It is an instrument for preserving a national community and its way of life. Its use, therefore, must always be subjected to this test: Does it preserve the national community? Does it enhance its security and well-being? Is its use consistent with the basic interests of the national community? Was dropping the atomic bomb on Hiroshima, for instance, necessary for the United States' *preservation,* in the broadest sense of term? By presumably shortening the war in the Far East, did its use safeguard basic American interests? Was its use indispensable for the preservation of such interests? Undoubtedly, the student will now raise objections to the trend of this argument. He will point out that we have reintroduced normative considerations just after arguing in favor of their exclusion. *Who* can decide, and *how,* whether the use of the bomb was necessary or indispensable? Some will say that it was if one American life was saved at the cost of hundreds of thousands of Japanese civilians. Others will argue precisely the opposite. However, the normative argument need not enter into the picture (despite our abhorrence of the sacrifice of human life that the use of the bomb entailed); indeed, it cannot be answered even if it is allowed to enter into the picture. The question can be answered by a careful analysis of means and ends. Our purpose was to bring the Japanese to terms—to force them to unconditionally surrender. If the use of the bomb had been the only way to do it, then and only then can we differ about its ethical connotations. The analysis we suggest, however, involves a number of steps *before* we confront the thorny ethical question. Were there other means available to make the Japanese come to terms? Were they used? If not, why not? If so, with what results? Did the policy makers balance carefully the damage to the image of the United States by the use of a new weapon that destroyed and maimed many, many thousands against the benefit that was to be derived from its use? Did other considerations enter into the picture—our desire, for instance, to finish the war there before the Russians were able to join our forces in full force and create serious dissensions and problems—as the case proved to be in Europe? Whatever the answers, the questions raised suggest the approach we follow in evaluating a foreign policy: we link the policy to a goal and discuss it in terms of the implementation of the posited goal.

We propose simply to suggest a set of instrumental criteria in terms of which "success" or "failure," or at least a discriminating bill of particulars, can be determined. Foreign policy decisions are generally made in order to alleviate a country's predicaments or to create favorable conditions for it—specifically, in terms of the United States, to increase our security, power, or influence in the world. In this sense, a decision may be simply defensive in nature (i.e., to remove a perceived predicament, as in Santo Domingo) or promotive (i.e., to create conditions conducive to the exercise of American influence and power). Very often a defensive policy cannot be easily distinguished from a promotive one.

To assess the success or failure of a decision—or a set of decisions that constitutes a policy—the outside observer must have a series of unambiguous facts and figures before him. This is not always an easy situation to come by. First, we must have a fairly explicit statement of the goals desired by the decision maker. Secondly, we must try to establish a connection between a series of acts and decisions that are made to implement the major goals posited. Thirdly, in assessing the nature and effectiveness of such a series of intermediate decisions, we must be constantly aware that the goal posited remains the same, or that, if it has changed in response to changes in the international environment, there is a clear awareness of such a change. Fourthly, we must undertake a cost-factor analysis—that is to say, we must try to assess the nature of the means used and their effectiveness in terms of the costs they entail. Given a scarcity of resources, a high-cost policy, even if successful, may be a failure if it is shown that it has deprived a given system of the means required to meet other and perhaps more pressing predicaments. By the same token, a low-cost policy that has succeeded may be considered to be a failure if it has created conditions that render its future use ineffective or has created unanticipated difficulties that entail high costs. Last but not least, irrespective of whether a given policy has succeeded or failed, it is incumbent upon the analyst to show that success could not be obtained by any other means or, alternatively, that failure could have been averted by the choice of different means. Otherwise, no conclusive and coherent explanation can be given regarding the relationship between means and ends.

The difficulties in evaluating foreign policy, it should now be clear, may well be insurmountable. They are only compounded by the following requirements, which alone can provide the proper context in which we may dare evaluate:

1. We must first provide a clear description of the predicament; for instance, what was exactly the predicament for

the United States in the rebellion in the Congo? But this is not always relevant. It is more important to identify how the predicament was perceived—in other words, to determine why a certain situation was or is considered by policy makers to be a predicament.

2. The next step, related to the first, is to make an effort to assess the flow of information and intelligence that goes into the formation of the perception of the policy makers: Is there only one source? Which one? Are there many sources? Do they provide the same facts and figures, or do they differ? If they differ, how are differences resolved in accepting one set of information flows and rejecting another?

3. This leads us to our third required piece of information: Which governmental units are most responsible for coping with the predicament? And if it falls (at least technically) within the jurisdiction of more than one, what types of intergovernmental and interunit arrangements exist to allow for a concerted action?

4. At this stage, assuming that the information sources, the nature of the predicament, the perception of the predicament, and the particular governmental units and procedures used in order to make a decision are known, we need to have a clear statement and description of the action resulting from the decision actually made—e.g., an ambassador was recalled; economic aid was offered; an official was bribed; the Marines were dispatched.

5. A knowledge of the action taken (or contemplated) must be coupled, at least when analyzing democratic foreign policy making, with the possession of an unambiguous declaration of the anticipated consequences of the action or decision. The simpler and the smaller the number or numbers of consequences anticipated, the easier the evaluation. The greater the number and the more complex the goal, the more difficult the assessment—unless one is able to peel off the rhetoric that often accompanies a decision from its substance, or unless we can establish a set of priorities of goals ranging from the imperative ones through the desirable ones down to the least-expected but simply hoped-for. Such priority assessments are not always easy to make, for the time dimension within which policies are implemented constantly forces reconsideration and reshuffling of priorities.

Only after the above steps have been carefully followed can the analyst, hopefully, survey the actual consequences that flowed from the policies made and arrive at a very quiet, and always highly qualified, verdict. Our frame of analysis, in other words, is *instrumental*, relating means to ends and linking the two by study of decision-making procedures and intermediate steps. It evades normative questions; it is based on a power theory of international politics in which the ultimate analysis of "success" and "failure" can be measured in terms of the plusses and minusses in the increments of power and influence for a given nation.

To summarize, foreign policy evaluation involves: assessment of the goals of a given country; analysis of the various predicaments that seem to endanger these goals; an examination of the instrumentalities (policies) pursued to alleviate the predicaments; a careful examination of the manner in which such policies were formulated, with regard to both the predicament involved and the manner in which the policy was to be implemented; an account of the major governmental organs responsible for the implementation of the policy; a careful examination of the availability of alternate means and instrumentalities (were they considered? were they rejected after being considered, and if so why?); and finally, an assessment— i.e., did the policy as formulated and implemented bring about the desired goals? If so, then our verdict is positive—as may be the case with the Marshall Plan for aiding the European nations. If not, we must then ask: Why not?

Even a negative verdict to a given foreign policy, however, calls for a reevaluation, which should take at least two major forms. First, we must determine whether failure was due, not to implementation or to the means used, but rather to the goals posited. Generally, we must assume that, if the goals were completely or considerably beyond the available means at the disposal of a country, the policy was doomed to failure, no matter how well it was implemented. By the same token, even if the policy is successful at a very high cost, it must be considered a failure because it makes the country involved vulnerable to other potential predicaments. But even if the goals posited are compatible with the power resources of a given nation, failure may be due to a number of factors and reasons already mentioned: the given predicament may have been alleviated, but the policy responsible may have caused a series of unanticipated predicaments; or the policy pursued may have alleviated the predicament temporarily, only to allow it to appear in a more virulent form later on; or, finally, the policy used may be so far at odds with the posited goals as to insidiously distort the goals themselves. As an illustration, we might cite the case of U.S. foreign policy respecting Greece formulated in 1947 by President Truman, who promised aid to Greece (and Turkey) in order to safeguard their security from communist aggression and infiltration and in order to promote free, democratic institutions. Twenty-five years later, Greece is a military dictatorship and Turkey seems to be in the process of becoming one. American presence and help has, all along, so emphasized the military

importance of these countries at the expense of all the other goals explicitly stated by President Truman in 1947 that one of the overt goals of American foreign policy makers—the preservation of free institutions in the "free world"—has been preverted and distorted.

SELECTED BIBLIOGRAPHY

ALMOND, GABRIEL A. *The American People and Foreign Policy*. New York: Praeger, 1960.

ARON, RAYMOND. *A Century of Total War*. Garden City, N. Y.: Doubleday, 1954.

———. *Peace and War: A Theory of International Relations*. Garden City, N.Y.: Doubleday, 1966.

BELOFF, MAX. *Foreign Policy and the Democratic Process*. Baltimore: Johns Hopkins, 1955.

BOULDING, KENNETH. *Conflict and Defense*. New York: Harper & Row, 1961.

BUCHANAN, WILLIAM. *How Nations See Each Other: A Study in Public Opinion*. Urbana: University of Illinois Press, 1953.

CLAUDE, INIS. *Power and International Relations*. New York: Random House, 1962.

DE JOUVENEL, BERTRAND. *The Art of Conjecture*. New York: Basic Books, 1967.

DEUTSCH, KARL W. *The Analysis of International Relations*. Englewood Cliffs, N.J.: Prentice-Hall, 1968.

DE VISSCHER, CHARLES. *Theory and Reality in Public International Law*. Princeton: Princeton University Press, 1956.

DUROSELLE, JEAN-BAPTISTE. *La Politique etrangere et ses fondements*. Paris: Librairie Armond Colin, 1954.

FALK, RICHARD A., and MENDLOVITZ, SAUL H., eds. *Toward a Theory of War Prevention*. New York: World Law Fund, 1966.

FARRELL, R. BARRY, ed. *Approaches to Comparative and International Politics*. Evanston, Ill.: Northwestern University Press, 1966.

FEHRENBACH, T. R. *This Kind of Peace.* New York: McKay, 1966.

GROSS, FELIKS. *Foreign Policy Analysis.* New York: Philosophical Library, 1954.

HAAS, ERNST. "The Balance of Power: Prescription, Concept, or Propaganda?" *World Politics* 5 (1950): 459–479.

HAAS, ERNEST B., and WHITING, ALLEN S. *Dynamics of International Relations.* New York: McGraw-Hill, 1956.

HALLE, LOUIS J. *Civilization and Foreign Policy.* New York: Harper & Row, 1955.

HINSLEY, F. H. *Power and the Pursuit of Peace.* New York: Cambridge University Press, 1963.

HOFFMAN, STANLEY, ed. *Contemporary Theory in International Relations.* Englewood Cliffs, N.J.: Prentice-Hall, 1960.

KAHN, HERMAN, and WEINER, ANTHONY J. *The Year 2000—A Framework for Speculation.* New York: Macmillan Co., 1967.

KAPLAN, MORTON A., ed. *New Approaches to International Relations.* New York: St. Martin's, 1968.

KENNAN, GEORGE F. *American Diplomacy: 1900–1950.* Chicago: University of Chicago Press, 1951.

————. *Realities of American Foreign Policy.* Princeton: Princeton University Press, 1954.

KISSINGER, HENRY. "The Policymaker and the Intellectual." *Reporter,* March 5, 1959, pp. 30–35.

KISSINGER, HENRY, ed. *Problems of National Strategy.* New York: Praeger, 1965.

LALL, ARTHUR. *Modern International Negotiation.* New York: Columbia University Press, 1966.

LEVINE, ROBERT. *The Arms Debate.* Cambridge: Harvard University Press, 1963.

LISKA, GEORGE. "Continuity and Change in International Systems." *World Politics* 16 (1963): 118–36. [Review of Richard Rosecrance, *Action and Reaction in World Politics.*]

MARSHALL, C. B. *The Limits of Foreign Policy.* New York: Holt, Rinehart & Winston, 1955.

MEEHAN, EUGENE. *Explanation in Social Science: A System Paradigm.* Homewood, Ill.: Dorsey, 1968.

————. *The Theory and Method of Political Analysis.* Homewood, Ill.: Dorsey, 1965.

MORGENTHAU, HANS J. *Politics Among Nations.* New York: Knopf, 1954.

————. *The Purpose of America.* New York: Knopf, 1960.

————, and THOMPSON, KENNETH W. *Principles and Problems of International Politics.* New York: Knopf, 1951.

NICOLSON, HAROLD. *Diplomacy.* New York: Harcourt, Brace & World, 1933.

————. *The Evolution of Diplomatic Methods.* New York: Harper & Row, 1955.

ORGANSKI, A. F. K. *World Politics.* 2d ed. New York: Knopf, 1968.

ROSECRANCE, RICHARD. *Action and Reaction in World Politics.* Boston: Little, Brown, 1963.

ROSENBAUM, NAOMI. *Readings in the Western Political Systems.* Englewood Cliffs, N.J.: Prentice-Hall, 1970.

RUSSETT, BRUCE M.; ALKER, HAYWARD R., JR.; DEUTSCH, KARL W.; and LASSWELL, HAROLD D. *World Handbook of Political and Social Indicators.* New Haven: Yale University Press, 1964.

SCHELLING, THOMAS C. *Arms and Influence.* New Haven: Yale University Press, 1966.

————. *The Strategy of Conflict.* New York: Oxford University Press, Galaxy Edition, 1963.

THAYER, CHARLES W. *Diplomat.* New York: Harper & Row, 1959.

THOMPSON, KENNETH W. *American Diplomacy and Emergent Patterns.* New York: New York University Press, 1962.

————. *Christian Ethics and the Dilemmas of Foreign Policy.* Durham, N.C.: Duke University Press, 1959.

————. *The Moral Issue in Statecraft.* Baton Rouge: Louisiana State University Press, 1966.

————. *Political Realism and the Crisis of World Politics.* Princeton: Princeton University Press, 1960.

WADSWORTH, JAMES. *The Glass House.* New York: Praeger, 1966.

WALTZ, KENNETH N. *Foreign Policy and Democratic Politics.* Boston: Little, Brown, 1967.

WOLFERS, ARNOLD. *Discord and Collaboration.* Baltimore: Johns Hopkins Press, 1962.

Chapter Two

BRITISH FOREIGN POLICY

LEON D. EPSTEIN

Americans especially have often admired British foreign policy making for its method if not its substance, believing that diplomatic wisdom and shrewdness prevailed over political emotions and parochial concerns. Prestige of this kind was understandable during the centuries when so small an island kingdom stood as a major world power and even, at times, as the leading world power. Long and evidently successful experience, as measured by imperial territory, international trade, and general influence, enhanced the reputation of the process by which British foreign policy was made, supported, and executed. There had to be, it seemed, special political attributes to explain how the limited British population could exert power over vast overseas populations, notably in the late nineteenth and early twentieth centuries, while maintaining a leading influence among European nations.

Sustaining this reputation was less likely during Britain's decline in status among the great powers of the mid-twentieth century. Apparent failures in foreign policy, such as the collapse of the attempt to appease Hitler in the 1930s or the frustrated effort to reoccupy the Suez Canal zone in 1956, were charged against the political process and not simply regarded as the product of diminished relative power. So too was the expensive perpetuation into the 1950s and 1960s of the increasingly unsubstantial if symbolically useful policies of independent nuclear deterrence, Commonwealth leadership, and responsibility flowing from a "special relationship" with the United States. A sympathetic observer, it is true, could have discerned even during the decades of decline that Britain adjusted successfully to second place in a military alliance and accomplished its massive imperial withdrawal with relative graciousness. No other nation ever surrendered so much in so short a time as did Britain in the fifteen or twenty years after 1945, but this accommodation was hardly awesome, as had been the old accumulation and maintenance of power. In particular, it was not awesome to Americans who, during the very years of British decline and withdrawal, were concerned with the enormous expansion of the American nation's role in the world. A policy-making process associated with decline, then, attracted little admiration. Its past glories seemed to belong to another world. The 1970s, however, may put the matter in a new perspective. Now that Americans are becoming disenchanted, often bitterly so, with the nation's role as world power, there is a likely tendency to see virtue in Britain's postimperial accommodation and so to devote attention to the process by which the accommodation is achieved. Moreover, as Americans become conscious of failure in recent foreign policies, the failure is associated with defects in the American policy-making process. One begins to wonder whether the process of another democratic nation might not be superior or at least have desirable features worthy of emulation. Americans could thus again expect too much rather than too little from the study of another nation. Transferability of political experience cannot generally be assumed, and Britain's situation is plainly different from the United States' if only because of the existence of allied American power. Just as Britain's ascendancy was achieved in a world then dominated by several European powers, so its recent retreat has been accomplished in another environment that differs from anything that the United States itself can hope for.

THE NATIONAL BACKGROUND

Economic Geography

Except for Japan, whose days of imperial glory were few, Britain has been the only major power of modern times to be based on an island rather than a large continental area. It is easy to forget how small the British island home is. The whole of the United Kingdom, including the six counties of Northern Ireland plus England, Wales, and Scotland, comes to just over 94,000 square miles—an area smaller than Oregon and only slightly larger than Minnesota. Over 57 million people now live in the United Kingdom, and nearly 50 million of this total are in England and Wales, which together have one of the highest population densities of any white community of comparable size. Over 10 million persons live in London and its immediate environs, and almost every Englishman is within a day's rail journey of London.[1] This densely populated island is separated from the northwest coast of Europe by only 21 miles of open water, but even this distance has been sufficient for British life to develop its own distinctive pattern. Although isolation from European power struggles (in the nineteenth-century American manner) has never been feasible, the British long avoided identification as a purely European power.

Britain's island location and the absence of a nearby frontier, either in Britain or on the Continent, made it

[1] Demographic and economic data are published by the Central Statistical Office, *Annual Abstract of Statistics* (London: Her Majesty's Stationery Office).

natural for Englishmen to seek their fortunes in faraway places. This meant sea trade as well as colonial settlement, and both ventures were highly developed before the Industrial Revolution. Almost from the start, British factories supplied an established overseas trade in addition to a domestic market. By the mid-nineteenth century, the large-scale exchange of domestic manufactures for overseas raw materials and foodstuffs had become the cardinal feature of the British economy. Abundant coal, originally inexpensive to mine, provided an important base for the early British industrial supremacy. Not until 1870 did this supremacy begin to fade in relation to the more rapid industrial growth of Germany and the United States.[2]

Nineteenth-century industrialization made the British almost entirely an urban people, and reduced agriculture to a decidedly secondary status. Workers engaged in agriculture have long constituted a lower proportion of the gainfully employed than in any other country in the world.[3] Despite recent successful efforts to increase agricultural production, the British must remain predominantly a manufacturing people and also a people largely dependent on outside sources of food and raw materials. Well over half of the nation's food is now imported, and in order to pay for the food Britain must export a very high percentage of its manufactured products. Although British real income, per capita, stands fairly high in the world, it rests heavily and uneasily on the vicissitudes of international economic relations.

Social Structure

Class differentiation, on various bases, is treated more openly as a fact of life in Britain than in the United States, and this may lead to an exaggeration of the relative importance of class in British politics. It is true, however, that working-class consciousness has, at least until very recently, been definite and substantial. Despite the occupational rise of many Englishmen in each generation,[4] a rise resembling American patterns of mobility, the working class long retained a distinctive status resting on the assumption that most children of workers would themselves become workers. The sense of status, especially in the past, was linked to a deferential attitude toward a traditional ruling class, but it has also been significantly associated with the solidarity of manual laborers, both in industrial unions and in political movements. Class consciousness of this kind is stronger in Britain than in the United States because of the residue of a feudal past and because of the sharply unequal distribution of the benefits of early industrialization. An important sense of differentiation remains despite the material advantages afforded the working class by the egalitarian governmental policies of the 1940s and the general prosperity of the 1950s and 1960s. Status may now be more fully identified with occupation than with income, and also with intangibles such as style of life or manner of speech. These cultural marks have only begun to lose their significance.

The British educational system has played an important part in preserving class distinctions. Best known in this respect are the "public schools,"

[2] W. Stanford Reid, *Economic History of Great Britain* (New York: Ronald Press Co., 1954), pp. 337, 377.

[3] P. Sargent Florence, *The Logic of British and American Industry* (London: Routledge & Kegan Paul, 1953), p. 5.

[4] D. V. Glass, ed., *Social Mobility in Britain* (London: Routledge & Kegan Paul, 1954), p. 20.

which are really private secondary schools operating on a boarding or day basis for children whose parents can afford the fees. These schools include the limited number of famous and prestigious institutions such as Eton, Harrow, Winchester, and Rugby, but altogether the fee-paying private sector has enrolled no more than about 5 percent of all secondary school-age students. Government-supported grammar schools, also designed to provide academically superior secondary education, have enrolled a much larger minority—over three times as large in the mid-1960s. This minority, selected by competitive examination of children at about age eleven, has been characterized by its intellectual promise rather than by the fee-paying capacity of parents, but it has been drawn much more heavily from middle-class backgrounds than has the majority of secondary students assigned, also as a result of examination, to less academically distinguished government schools. Thus the system, at least until very recently, has separated students, at an early age, in paths that seemed related to demonstrated abilities partly associated with family backgrounds. Whatever the social and educational disadvantages, especially for the majority consigned to schools of lesser status and quality, there is no doubt that the government grammar schools have provided at least some lower-income students with a first-class education enabling them to compete, with the products of the fee-paying schools, for the limited number of places in British universities and for the financial support to attend these universities. The pattern seemed designed to produce an able and trained intellectual elite, selected largely on the basis of merit.[5] But it is

challenged by the growing movement for comprehensive secondary schools in which, as in American high schools, courses are conducted under one roof for students of different abilities. Developed in many communities particularly after World War II, these comprehensive schools remained the less conventional and less frequent path before the late 1960s, when the Labour government sought to establish them as the norm for planning secondary education. Although the new Conservative government of 1970 is not similarly dedicated, a continued trend toward comprehensive schools in most areas appears likely. What is more uncertain is whether this trend will in itself modify the essentially differentiated character of British academic training. The differentiation rests not only on a strong elitist private sector, but also on the perpetuation of the public sector's grammar-school tradition as a quality stream within a comprehensive school.

Still more definitely a bulwark of education only for the talented minority are British universities. Following a decade of what was, by past British standards, an enormous expansion, these universities enrolled only about 200,000 students at the end of the 1960s. Even if all other postsecondary students, particularly those in teacher training, are added so as to be as inclusive as we are in defining enrollment in American colleges and universities, there are fewer than 400,000 British postsecondary students compared with about 7 million American—or about one-twentieth as many students in a total population over one-fourth that of the United States. Only somewhat less dramatically unfavorable numerical comparisons exist between Britain and most other developed nations. The fact is that Britain seems committed to university-level education for only a modestly growing minority.

[5] Michael Young, *The Rise of the Meritocracy* (London: Thames and Hudson, 1958).

Partly this relates to the expensiveness of British-style universities; quality rather than quantity is stressed, and the students fortunate enough to be admitted receive not only considerable faculty attention but also in most instances government grants enabling them to attend residential institutions without part-time employment. So, regardless of background (often middle class), British university students are treated as an elite even before graduating to the professional and managerial careers for which their education prepares them.

Apart from social class and the related differentiation of an educational elite, the British people appear relatively homogeneous. The population, despite substantial immigration in the 1950s and early 1960s from the West Indies, India, and Pakistan, remains about 98 percent white, and the near-elimination, by recent restrictive legislation, of further immigration of Asian and African peoples will not allow this proportion to change greatly from the present level. The white population is overwhelmingly of a "British stock," formed by successive invasions of long ago. The Scots and the Welsh preserve distinctions, but their national background is assuredly British. Irish immigrants must be noted separately, but they, along with smaller numbers of continental refugees, are decidedly exceptional minorities. The great bulk of Britain's inhabitants, unlike Americans, have no national background save their present one. The British also have a considerable religious homogeneity. The nation is largely Protestant, with about 5 million Roman Catholics and a half-million Jews.

Political Experience

Not only are the British old as a people, but they are also old as a nation. The unity of England and Wales goes back to the Middle Ages, and the union with Scotland dates from the beginning of the eighteenth century. The island was small enough to be dominated early by a single political authority, mainly representing the numerically superior English population. National political institutions are of such long standing that loyalty to them can be taken for granted in a way that would be difficult in a more recently created nation.

The supremacy of Parliament, in relation to the monarch, has been constitutionally established since 1688. Traditionally, the parliamentary regime was liberal and aristocratic—liberal in the sense of standing for the liberty of individuals and of property, and aristocratic in that relatively few were eligible to choose parliamentary representatives. Like British society in general, the political system remained nonegalitarian until the late nineteenth century, when the vote was extended to the mass of the population. That the political institutions, managed over centuries by a special ruling class, should thus have been democratized without revolution distinguishes British history from much of the European continent's. That history is also distinguished from America's in that Britain had a long predemocratic political experience and adapted universal suffrage to an old institutional pattern.

The liberalism of the British tradition has been associated particularly with the toleration of dissenting and unpopular opinions. Although there have been lapses, respect for individual liberty of expression has been characteristic of modern British history. To some degree, this is the heritage of Protestant religious differences which, since the seventeenth century, have been tolerated for the sake of internal peace. Whatever the source, there is no doubt about the vitality of the tradition in political as well as in religious matters. It means toleration of eccentrics and even of those regarded at times as subversive elsewhere in the democratic world.

Persistent External Concerns

Historically, Britain has had two major international concerns. The first has been to maintain oceanic access to the rest of the world, and the second to prevent any potentially hostile power from dominating the continent of Europe. Both concerns have been vital to the national interest. Without overseas connections, Britain would have been cut off, not just from imperial possessions or Commonwealth partners, but also from the world trade which sustains British life. Even more directly would Britain have been adversely affected if any single nation controlled Europe and threatened to dominate Britain as well.

In the days when the British Empire was at its zenith and when most of the currently equal partners in the Commonwealth were imperial colonies, the simplest way for Britain to maintain overseas access was to command the seas. This is just what Britain did on its own until about the time of World War I. As long as "Britannia ruled the waves," the nation's trade routes were secure, as were its military communications with the empire. The growth of American naval power ended exclusive British control of the seas, but the advantages of that control remained because the United States became an ally and not an enemy. The most direct threat first came from the German navy, and especially from German submarines in both world wars. For the first time in modern history, an enemy was equipped with a force that could just

possibly cut the British lifeline to the outside world. And this was not yet all. The airplane and the rocket bomb threatened the island even more dramatically during World War II. Ruling the waves, although still within the power of Britain joined by the United States, was no longer enough to provide security for the island and its people. It is surely not enough now.

The classic British concern with the European balance of power has sometimes been explained as a corollary of the nation's general position in the world. In his famous Foreign Office memorandum of 1907, Eyre Crowe assumed that Britain's capacity to command the seas, which he regarded as essential, would inspire fear and jealousy among other countries.[6] To avert an anti-British combination based on such fear and jealousy, Crowe thought, Britain needed to make special efforts to develop a policy that harmonized with the interests of other nations. First among these interests, he wrote, was independence, and therefore Britain had rightly championed (and should continue to champion) the independence of nations against any single powerful and ambitious state. In practice, this meant a grouping of forces against first one strong European power and then another, "but ever on the side opposed to the political dictatorship of the strongest single State or group at a given time."[7] So explained, Britain's policy in Europe was a striking instance of high-mindedness coinciding with national self-interest.

[6] Memorandum by Eyre Crowe, in *British Documents on the Origins of the War, 1898–1914,* ed. G. P. Gooch and Harold Temperley (London: Her Majesty's Stationery Office, 1928), vol. 3.
[7] Ibid., p. 403. On the balance of power, see also Harold Nicolson, *Diplomacy* (London: Oxford University Press, 1950), p. 135.

Neither of Britain's major concerns has diminished in the nuclear age. Access overseas, even without large imperial possessions, remains vital for economic reasons, and the avoidance of hostile domination of continental Europe is politically as well as economically important. It is the means for dealing with these concerns that have changed. With limited resources in a new world of superpowers, Britain's old command of the seas is impossible. Even when allied to the much greater American naval strength, Britain is now unable to achieve its earlier kind of security. Similarly, the problem of preventing hostile domination of the European continent has greatly changed. Britain itself cannot supply the crucial element in a coalition against the single strongest Continental power. This is even clearer when that power is the Soviet Union, as after World War II, than when it was Germany. In both instances, the United States became the decisive force.

Another and still newer circumstance renders obsolete Britain's balance-of-power method in Europe. The integration of the Western nations of continental Europe, economically and to some extent politically, required that Britain choose either to become more completely and unreservedly European by joining the European Economic Community (the "Common Market"), or to become more sharply and definitely an outsider enjoying less influence as well as suffering economic disadvantages.

THE POLICY-MAKING PROCESS

Traditionally, in considering the conduct of British foreign affairs, American observers tended to admire what appeared to be the capacity of a well-informed executive to act without frustrating pressures from legislative authority or other domestic political forces. This capacity might in part have been attributed to British aristocratic customs, more characteristic of the nineteenth than of the twentieth century, as well as to the greater experience of an old European power. But it has also been associated, in American minds, with the parliamentary-cabinet form of government as opposed to the separation of executive and legislative powers, and with the special British development of a non-populist yet responsible democratic government. Perhaps British politics were thus idealized by the once-prevailing Anglophiles in the American intellectual community. There might always have been significant political pressures at least indirectly influencing British foreign policy, and these pressures could well have come from a fairly large section of the public whose support, in recent times, would have been essential in fulfilling any major national commitment. But the picture of strong, effective, and coherent British policy making remained dominant until the 1950s and 1960s, when the decline of Britain's national fortunes caused even the effectiveness of its political process to be challenged. It was then that an American political scientist could argue that British government had performed less well in foreign policy making, during the twenty years following World War II, than had the American system, and that the inferior performance resulted in large part from weakness rather than strength in executive leadership.[8] The supposed "weakness," however, may not seem so undesirable to Americans who now react against the consequences in Vietnam of strong presi-

[8] Kenneth N. Waltz, *Foreign Policy and Democratic Politics* (Boston: Little, Brown, 1967).

dential leadership. Once again, as already observed, we Americans turn to the British model, but this time in the hope of finding effective restraints on executive commitments rather than a formula for bold and positive action.

Governmental Agencies

The Executive Authority. No legal restraints are to be discovered. Rather the political executive, representing the crown, is formally supreme in foreign policy making. Foreign policy, while ordinarily presented to Parliament at some stage, does not formally require legislative action (as does domestic policy). There are no constitutional provisions resembling the American requirements for congressional—particularly Senate—approval of certain significant international commitments. Legally, the present-day political leadership of prime minister and cabinet is heir to the traditional prerogative of the crown in making Britain's foreign policy.

The search for restraints must, therefore, enter the political instead of the legal sphere. Here it is common to assert that prime minister and cabinet, conventionally holding office only while supported by a parliamentary majority, are clearly limited by the threat of ouster from office as the result of unpopular or unsuccessful policies, foreign as well as domestic. Stated so baldly, however, the assertion is of doubtful relevance for twentieth-century British politics. Apart from a brief transitional period in the 1920s, there has been not only a sufficiently stable two-party pattern producing a majority party in the House of Commons, but also a sufficiently cohesive majority party precluding the kind and the number of parliamentary defections that would vote its own political leadership out of office. Only the electorate, every five years—or sooner at the prime minister's option—is expected to decide whether to have a new executive, by returning a majority of M.P.'s who belong to what had been the opposition party. Between general elections, it must be stressed, a parliamentary majority party now serves effectively to protect its leadership from ouster by formal votes of censure or no confidence in the House of Commons. But this is still to speak of the most readily observable formalities, although no longer merely of the legalities, of the governmental process. The political sphere also involves the possibility of less blunt and more subtle restraints. To start with, we know that prime ministers—four of the last eight—have left office without losing general elections and without losing majority support in parliamentary voting. Although age and illness account at least in part for three of the four resignations, even these instances suggest a flexibility of tenure that the American presidency lacks. More pointedly, in the fourth instance, Neville Chamberlain's departure in 1940 was the known political consequence of a revolt in which members of the prime minister's own party refused their support in such numbers as effectively to threaten, without actually destroying, Chamberlain's majority. Smaller and less dramatic revolts, only partly surfaced in parliamentary voting, are reasonably assumed to have been factors in the resignations of Eden in 1957 and Macmillan in 1963, if not in the departure of the aging Churchill in 1955. Even without the evidence of open revolts through parliamentary speeches or voting abstentions, many of which may only pressure without threatening a government, there are known to be other intraparty limits on the policy-making power of a leadership that hopes to retain its position. Continued parliamentary-party support must often be sought by persuasion, compromise, and concession.

A prime minister, it should be well understood, seeks and obtains that support within the context of the collegial leadership represented by the cabinet. The word is the same as the American term for the president's chief administrative appointees, but the political significance of the British cabinet is almost entirely different. The difference, it is true, has been obscured in recent years by the growth of the prime minister's authority, especially as party leader and dominating public figure; and for a time in the 1960s, observers began to describe Britain as having "prime ministerial" rather than cabinet government. Granting that the prime minister is now a great deal more than merely "the first among equals," which he was supposed to have been in the original conception of cabinet government, nevertheless it is almost certainly an exaggeration to consider the prime minister so dominantly responsible for executive policy making as is the American president. Politically he cannot be nearly so independent of his cabinet as the American president can be of his. The prime minister shares executive authority with his cabinet colleagues even though, like the president, he appoints these colleagues. What is crucial is that British cabinet members, by custom amounting to political necessity, are chosen so as to include almost all of a parliamentary party's important leaders. It is their support, or that of nearly all of them, that is essential for a prime minister. With it he maintains his parliamentary majority; without it he can be isolated and driven to resign or to change his policy to accord with that of his colleagues. Nothing about this description denies the likely predominance of a prime minister in cabinet policy making. As the party leader

elected by his parliamentary-party colleagues in the first place, he has both the political status and the personal respect to be able ordinarily to persuade colleagues to accept his policies; but he has so to persuade or, as may happen, to accept policies emerging from cabinet discussions in which he was no more than a leading participant. The cabinet, and especially its most important members, is thus itself a kind of restraint in relation to the policy-making authority of a chief executive. Another and more usual way to put the matter is to say that Britain has collective rather than strictly individual responsibility for the executive decision making that is so characteristic of foreign affairs. Or, to be more careful, since the prime minister's special importance should not be disregarded, Britain has greater collective responsibility in these matters than has the United States.

A closer look at the cabinet should help explain its complexities. There are about twenty members, varying by two or three in either direction as recent prime ministers have found politically convenient. Always included are the heads of the most important ministries (*departments* in American terminology), some of which, such as the Foreign Office, Defense, Home Affairs, and the Treasury, are consistently so defined while others might be important enough only in certain periods. There are, in other words, some ministers (like the minister for overseas development) as well as junior ministers (undersecretaries, for example), outside the cabinet but in the larger "government" of about seventy executive appointees from parliamentary ranks. Because the most important political figures in the majority party are naturally chosen to head the most important ministries, they thus are cabinet members. So often are a few other similarly important politicians assigned traditional cabinet-status titles without specific departmental responsibility, but perhaps with special negotiating assignments (such as for the Rhodesian problem or for Common Market entry). In this way, the prime minister can include in his cabinet the members of his parliamentary party who are the ablest, most experienced politicians, and simultaneously the chief officers of the major departments of state. The basic political character of the appointments is not substantially qualified by the inclusion of a few members of the House of Lords, named either because of their political consequence in that body or because of special skills justifying a new peerage to accompany ministerial appointment. The latter suggests freedom to name a cabinet member who lacks prior parliamentary experience, but this is a freedom sparingly exercised. Certainly parliamentary experience, ordinarily meaning lengthy membership in the House of Commons, is a virtual prerequisite for cabinet appointment. On the other hand, such experience, however long, does not itself guarantee either cabinet or junior ministerial appointment. Seniority alone is not enough. Nor is political prominence a sufficient additional quality leading to appointment for an experienced M.P. if he seems, perhaps by holding extreme views, to be politically embarrassing for the prime minister and his government. The facts of political life require that *almost* all, but not every single one, of the prime minister's important political party colleagues be included in the cabinet. He can—and occasionally almost has to—omit a major rival, although in so doing the prime minister risks open disaffection that successful cabinet cooptation might avoid.

Most directly concerned with foreign affairs in the cabinet are the prime minister himself and the foreign secretary (whose full title is now secretary of state for foreign and commonwealth affairs, following the merger in 1968 of the Foreign Office with the previously separate Commonwealth ministry, which had earlier absorbed the old Colonial Office). The relationships between prime minister and foreign secretary vary considerably from government to government. One man can even hold both positions, but the last time that the prime minister was also foreign secretary was in 1924. On the other hand, a prime minister can effectively be his own foreign secretary without holding the title if, as a strong-minded leader experienced in foreign affairs, he chooses as his foreign secretary an especially close and loyal confidante to act virtually as a deputy. At the other extreme, a prime minister more fully absorbed in domestic affairs, or one perceiving his role as less positive generally, can appoint a foreign secretary possessing considerable independent authority in Parliament. That authority need not flow from specialized expertise; for example, it was primarily political in the case of Ernest Bevin, the powerful trade unionist who was the Labour government's foreign secretary under Prime Minister Clement Attlee. Bevin seems exceptional in the degree of his political power, but a considerable standing within the parliamentary majority party (and probably a measure of respect from the Opposition) is useful for any foreign secretary—at least as much as it is for any other cabinet member. The standing may well combine specialized experience with personal popularity in the parliamentary party. So it did for Sir Alec Douglas-Home when he returned to the foreign secretaryship in Heath's Conservative government of 1970. Still, the prime minister must share in the parliamentary defense of foreign policy as well as in the making of it. He is always the leading member of the collegial group responsible for policy. He cannot avoid that responsibility.

Other cabinet members are regularly involved in foreign policy. The defense secretary is plainly important, especially as he heads, since 1964, a unified military establishment without the formerly coexisting Admiralty, War Office, and Air Ministry. Under the defense secretary are now two ministers of defense, one for equipment and the other for supply, and three parliamentary undersecretaries, one for each service. But only the defense secretary has cabinet status. In this, he resembles the foreign secretary, whose several subordinate ministers of state and undersecretaries are also outside the cabinet. Included, however, as a cabinet member in both Wilson's Labour government of the late 1960s and Heath's Conservative government of 1970 was another minister definitely concerned with foreign affairs, specifically one charged with Common Market negotiations and given the honorific title of chancellor of the Duchy of Lancaster to signify cabinet status. Still one other member of the cabinet, the chancellor of the exchequer, has to be mentioned as concerned with foreign affairs because he is necessarily involved in all policies that require government funds. International commitments have been known to be expensive, even prohibitively so for a nation whose economy is as strained as Britain's. Responsible for the political direction of the Treasury, which in Britain combines budget making and many other tasks of administrative supervision along with the more limited functions of the U.S. Treasury Department, the chancellor of the exchequer is often in a position to be the crucial decision maker. He is always a leading figure

in the majority party; certainly he would become so by virtue of being made chancellor if he were not so already.

It is reasonable to assume that the chancellor of the exchequer would be included—along with prime minister, foreign secretary, defense secretary, and perhaps a few others—in any "partial cabinet" organized to consider major foreign policy decisions. There is a good description of such a "partial cabinet" by a former participant, Patrick Gordon Walker, who also provides a careful analytical exposition of its relation to other cabinet groupings.[9] It differs, he explains, from what has been called an "inner cabinet" of the prime minister's friends who meet only informally. The partial cabinet is an organized committee, of a kind often used to expedite business by having only the relevant ministers meet on a given interdepartmental problem before bringing a policy proposal to the full cabinet. In significant foreign affairs, the committee seems more impressive because of its likely membership, and so the aptness of the term *partial cabinet* in such instances, although probably also in the case of a somewhat differently constituted committee contemplating a major domestic decision. Regardless of the term, some such collegial group, smaller than the whole cabinet, is an important part of the British decision-making process: it represents cabinet authority without usurping it. As Gordon Walker, himself a former foreign secretary, rightly observes, this constitutes the "very opposite of Prime Ministerial government; it presupposes that the Prime Minister carries influential Cabinet colleagues with him, and that these

[9] Patrick Gordon Walker, *The Cabinet* (New York: Basic Books, 1970), pp. 39–40, 88–90.

will, with the Prime Minister, convince the Cabinet if policy is questioned when the Cabinet is informed."[10] The same British collegial principle is illustrated most persuasively by the testimony that Labour's prime minister and foreign secretary, in the 1960s, were once overruled by the cabinet on a matter of great importance.[11]

The Foreign Service. So far only the political leadership of the government has been discussed. Under its executive authority is a sharply differentiated career service that does not change with political turnovers. As in other nations, foreign-service officers are international subject-matter specialists in a way that politicians need not be (although they occasionally are). The career members of the British Foreign Office appear to have a greater prestige and influence than their American counterparts. The prestige is partly traditional, and it is closely associated with continued heavy recruitment, by competitive examination, from the upper layers of the educational elite produced by the fee-paying public schools and by Oxford and Cambridge universities.[12] The foreign service is separated from the domestic civil service both in its recruitment and in its managerial direction.[13] Its relative influence, however, depends on more than traditional educational elitism and the presumably associated professional competence. There is also the structural fact that the most experienced and successful foreign-service officers occupy crucial positions in relation to

the foreign secretary and to other ministerial policy makers. Compared to the United States—where an administration appoints a substantial layer of its own politically chosen specialists, in the relevant departments as well as in the White House—a British government makes little more than the limited number of ministerial and junior ministerial appointments already noted. And most of these are chosen for their parliamentary political talents rather than for their specialized knowledge of a given field. They are more directly dependent on career service advisers than are American presidents and cabinet members.[14] Understandably, this works to increase the influence of the foreign service (much as the similar situation works in the same direction for Britain's domestic civil service). Yet it is well to remember that the role remains that of influence; however weighty the advice from career officials, policy making is the responsibility of the political executive—prime minister, foreign secretary, and others functioning within the cabinet. The political leadership must defend foreign as well as domestic policy in the House of Commons and before the country. Attacks on policy are not directed to the career officers. Even the permanent undersecretary for foreign affairs, the very top career official, does not participate in the political debate, although it may well have been his influential advice that a government chose to follow. Disregarding that advice, it is recognized, is possible. Political leaders have occasionally done so, and the foreign service, accordingly, executes the very policy with which it disagrees. But this is not the expected relationship.

Parliament. British legislative authority, embodied now overwhelmingly in

10 Ibid., p. 91.

11 Ibid., p. 92.

12 Anthony Sampson, *Anatomy of Britain Today* (New York: Harper & Row, 1965), p. 322.

13 On recruitment, see Lord Strang, *The Foreign Office* (New York: Oxford University Press, 1955), chaps. 4 and 5.

14 Waltz, *Foreign Policy*, p. 137.

the popularly elected House of Commons, provides the most significant arena for debate and controversy concerning foreign as well as domestic policy. It does so even though, as previously observed, it does not itself make the policy or even exercise power to reject either a government policy or the government that makes a policy. Whatever the influence of the Commons, it is exerted within the context of parliamentary voting that through a majority party formally supports the government. The context is limiting, but not so completely as it might appear from parliamentary voting itself. Government policy, made in the cabinet, is originally formulated with some concern for the preferences, explicit and implicit, of the more than three hundred M.P.'s who compose the majority parliamentary party. Intraparty discussion and pressures are common, and regular opportunities exist for communication between backbenchers and their leaders. All of a party's M.P.'s meet from time to time, while some meet regularly in their own party committees, including one devoted to foreign affairs. These same M.P.'s, of the majority party, will, it is true, eventually vote in sufficient numbers even in support of a policy that they may have argued against in intraparty councils and continued to dislike. A few will abstain or, more rarely, vote against their government without causing it to lose its parliamentary majority; these are danger signals for the leadership, which is thereby being told of the extent of disaffection with its policy. Admittedly, such parliamentary behavior is far different from the independent exercise of power by American congressmen either on the floor or in their decision-making committees.[15] British M.P.'s of

15 Max Beloff, *Foreign Policy and the Democratic Process* (Baltimore: Johns Hopkins Press, 1955), pp. 25–26.

the majority party are so likely to observe the political exigencies requiring public support for their executive leadership that their influence must be exerted more subtly, usually behind the scenes when policy is formulated or by a critical speech or abstention designed to affect the next policy formulation.

Members of Parliament of the opposition party, both individually and collectively through their leadership, have a different and perhaps immediately even less consequential role to play. In parliamentary voting, of course, they regularly lose and are meant to lose to a cohesive majority party backing its government when policies are under attack. Individual M.P.'s belonging to the opposition party are not potential participants—as are many American congressmen of the nonpresidential party—in a bipartisan majority supporting foreign policy. For support of its policy, in foreign or in domestic affairs, the government rests on its usual partisan majority. Thus, much more plainly than in the United States, legislative debates are not conducted in order to persuade members of the chamber which way to vote on a given issue. Yet British parliamentary debates are treated seriously, and, as would be expected, more often in the popularly elected House of Commons—although occasionally in the Lords—the government must defend its policies. Here, although each parliamentary party contains a variety of individual views which find expression in debate if not in voting, major attention is ordinarily focused on the give-and-take between party leaders. On an important occasion, the government's policy will usually be presented and defended by the foreign secretary, one or two of his political aides, and the prime minister; the Opposition will then be represented by appropriate members of its "shadow cabinet"—that is, particularly by its prospective foreign secretary and its prospective prime minister (the opposition leader). Thus a Commons debate is mainly between those responsible for policy and those who would like to be, and might well become, responsible. It is a discussion between a government and its alternative.[16]

How much does a debate really matter, in the face of the fact that a poor governmental showing does not modify majority approval in the immediate circumstances? It can weaken the position of the cabinet leaders within their own party, and so possibly lead to changes in personnel or policy. And it can strengthen the opposition party in the country, thus influencing future elections. Similarly, a weak opposition case can damage the leadership of the minority party. There is not much doubt that British politicians take careful note of performance in debate, and no minister is likely to survive if his own supporters find him a poor spokesman for the government and the party.

Foreign policy debates in the Commons occur, in one form or another, with considerable frequency. Usually they are scheduled in order to discuss a currently controversial policy or subject, so that the interval between debates varies with the number of

international crises. However, there is a foreign affairs debate about every three or four weeks. The politically conscious members of the community may follow the full reports in the nation's best newspapers and read the columns of critical comment in the serious intellectual weeklies. Although little parliamentary news is carried in the large popular dailies, the serious press keeps the sizable educated minority informed of the course of parliamentary discussion.

In addition to full-fledged debates on foreign affairs, the government is subject to attack during the regularly scheduled Commons question period —the first hour of each of the first four meeting days of the week. During this period, questions are addressed to ministers concerning their various policies. Foreign affairs receives its share of questions, both from opposition members and from members of the majority party. Sometimes the questions are directed to the prime minister instead of to the foreign secretary or his political aides. More often than is possible for other subjects, foreign affairs questions can be turned away on the ground that to answer would violate national security. However, there are many questions, sometimes difficult and embarrassing, that government spokesmen attempt to handle, for it is politically unwise for ministers to dodge too many questions. The question period, as well as the general debate, serves to exemplify the usefulness of Parliament's role with respect to policy making: to question and criticize, but not to defeat the government.

The same can be said for the parliamentary performances reflecting individual and intraparty dissent concerning world affairs; M.P.'s, simply because they are M.P.'s, command a certain amount of public attention for their views, whether presented in or

---

[16] The most dramatic example was the prolonged debate between the Labour opposition and the Conservative government over Britain's Suez intervention, reported in 558–560 *House of Commons Debates*, passim (October 30–November 8, 1956). See also Leon D. Epstein, *British Politics in the Suez Crisis* (Urbana: University of Illinois Press, 1964), chap. 5. For a strong argument concerning the efficacy of the parliamentary role in general, see Alexander J. Groth, "Britain and America: Some Requisites of Executive Leadership Compared," *Political Science Quarterly* 85 (June, 1970): 217–39.

out of the House of Commons. There is a fairly good chance that what is said in the House will be reported outside. The most famous twentieth-century example is Winston Churchill's use of the Commons, as well as of other public arenas, to expound his critical view of the governing Conservative party's policy toward Hitler's Germany in the 1930s. Churchill was then a dissident nonministerial member of that governing party. More recently, there have also been dissenting M.P.'s within each major party. Left-wing and pacifist-minded Labour M.P.'s have disputed their party's military commitments—particularly those involving the American alliance—throughout the decades of the Cold War, and they have done so both when Labour has been in office and—perhaps more vigorously and on a larger scale—when their party has been in opposition. On the other side, imperialist Conservative M.P.'s have attacked their party's policies during Britain's nearly steady postwar retreat from its former power and glory, and this often meant criticism of their own government when it, instead of Labour, happened to be managing the retreat (from Suez, for example). Always, as with the Labour left M.P.'s, the imperialist Conservative M.P.'s used the Commons as the place to let their leaders and the country know that there were nonconsensual views that had to be taken into account, if not followed, in making foreign policy.

Nongovernmental Agencies

Political Parties. As their parliamentary behavior indicates, British parties, despite internal disagreements, function as collective adversaries with respect to foreign as well as domestic policy. The considerable interparty consensus about the general lines of policy does not, except during wartime coalitions, keep the opposition party from criticizing, conventionally and legitimately, either the substance or the execution of the government's policy. Related to this function, as well as to a majority party's defense of government policy, are the large membership organizations that each major party (and also the Liberal party during its periods of revival) maintains outside of Parliament in loosely defined connection with the strictly parliamentary groups. The extraparliamentary organizations are not simply cadres of officeholders and prospective officeholders[17]; nor are they skeletonized structures to be filled out only during election campaigns. Rather, they contain large numbers of regular dues-paying members.

On this score, the Conservative structure is simpler than Labour's. Conservative membership is entirely individual and direct. The member joins a Conservative constituency association, which is affiliated to the National Union of Conservative and Unionist Associations. Total membership in recent years has been about 1.5 to 2 million. Labour's more complicated structure allows both direct and indirect memberships. In addition to about one-half million who belong to Labour constituency associations, over 5 million are counted as members because they belong to trade unions that are affiliated to the Labour party and that pay dues to the party.

From the viewpoint of each party's parliamentary leadership, the principal purpose of the mass membership is undoubtedly to help win elections. Advice, let alone direction, on policy

[17] The fullest account of the relationship of mass membership to parliamentary parties is R. T. McKenzie, *British Political Parties* (London: William Heinemann, 1963).

questions is hardly desired, but this does not prevent the organized membership from offering and even urging such advice. Regular dues-paying members have often become active in the first place in order to have a role affecting policy. There are two levels at which rank-and-file members can try to influence decisions. The first is through the constituency organization, which in either case—Conservative or Labour—selects its parliamentary candidate, and would therefore appear to have the means of influencing decisively the position of an M.P. How much and how often this channel of influence is used cannot readily be discovered. Certainly there are very few instances in which sitting M.P.'s have been locally rejected for subsequent candidacy because of policy disagreements, and in such cases (as those occurring after the Suez crisis of 1956), the M.P.'s were rejected because they violated national party positions.[18] Indeed, the constituency associations seem to reinforce national party leadership by using their candidate-selection power to make it unlikely that any M.P.'s would move toward the parliamentary opposition. This is understandable, since members of a constituency association are recruited on the basis of loyalty to the national party cause. They may tolerate M.P.'s who occasionally deviate toward a position more extreme than that of party leaders—that is, a position farther removed from that of the other party—but they do not want M.P.'s whose deviation tends to help the Opposition. This means, among other things, that a constituency association is unlikely to press an M.P. to adopt a policy at variance with that of the national party leaders. That an association would have such a policy is

[18] Epstein, *Suez Crisis,* chap. 6.

itself unlikely in the highly centralized system of British politics.

The second level for rank-and-file influence is the national conference held annually by each major party. The conference seems designed for this purpose, and avowedly so in Labour's case. Delegates to each conference, chosen by the various units of the national party, have the opportunity to present, discuss, and vote on policy resolutions. On foreign affairs as on other matters, the mass membership of each party has had distinctive views which it has sought, via conference resolutions, to persuade or pressure party leaders to adopt. The Conservative conference has done so without claiming the power to fix the parliamentary leadership's policy, but the Labour conference has often acted as though it and the executive committee elected by the conference did have such power. The Labour party constitution does give the external mass organization the power to decide general policy, but this is at odds with the usual British conception that policy is made by parliamentary representatives who are individually and collectively responsible to the electorate. It is also at odds with much of Labour's own practice, especially in the really significant periods of 1945–51 and 1964–70, when the party formed the government. Labour government leaders usually succeeded in getting the party conference to support foreign policy positions already adopted by the government. And the parliamentary leaders were able, during most of Labour's opposition years of 1951–64, to keep the initiative and to persuade the conference delegates to accept official policy, occasionally in compromised form. Only in 1960 did the Labour conference adopt foreign policy resolutions advocating unilateral nuclear disarmament, which were flatly opposed by the parliamentary leadership—the leadership, under Hugh Gaitskell, refused to accept these resolutions as binding on the parliamentary party. Whether Gaitskell would eventually have been forced either to adopt the conference's policy or to resign was never answered, because he succeeded in a campaign to have the next annual conference, in 1961, reverse its position. The fact, however, that he and the bulk of the Labour M.P.'s persisted in a year's defiance of conference resolutions is pretty strong evidence of the primacy of the elected M.P.'s and their leadership. That primacy, especially of the leadership, was even more striking during the Wilson governments of 1964–70.

Regardless of their disputed role in determining policy, organized parties do serve, much more regularly than in the United States, as media for the expression of public opinion, and thus as agencies of popular pressure if not of popular control. This is plainer and more significant in the Labour party, largely because of the already-noted claims of the annual conference. The left-wing critics within the Labour party have been numerous and persistent—whether defeated, as on a variety of resolutions in the 1950s, or temporarily successful, as on unilateral nuclear disarmament in 1960. They represent a strong tendency among many Labour party activists and trade union leaders, and their persistent left-wing advocacy in foreign affairs is rooted in both socialism and pacifism. Opposition to "power politics" and "imperialism" has been traditional Labour party ideology; so has a commitment to a distinctively "socialist foreign policy." Thus the left wing opposed German rearmament following World War II, suspected the Anglo-American alliance (most of the time and especially during the Vietnam war), and rejected

nuclear weapons.[19] It is true that such left-wing views did not become official Labour policy, and that they seemed to exert less influence than ever during Prime Minister Wilson's governments of the late 1960s. Yet they remained to be faced by Labour leaders at most party conferences, and perhaps in revised and more formidable shape in the early 1970s with Labour again in opposition.

Lessening except in residual form at an earlier date was the comparable, if ideologically opposite, campaign to move the Conservative party leadership from its usually moderate position of accepting Britain's diminishing status in world affairs .More accurately called "imperialist" than "right-wing," it represented a substantial force at party conferences as well as among Conservative M.P.'s until the late 1950s.[20] "Empire" long remained the emotive word for Conservatives, as "socialist" has been for Labour, but efforts to save the empire or to halt its "scuttling" ceased to be relevant in the 1960s, when virtually all of the large British dependencies of the past had become self-governing nations. The new multiracial Commonwealth, to which these nations belonged along with Britain and the old white dominions, did not have the same imperialist appeal. More significant for many rank-and-file Conservatives were the remaining ties to British settlers in Africa—notably in Southern Rhodesia, where the effort of the white minority to maintain its dominance was met with less hostility among Conservative activists than it was among Labour activists. Somewhat similar sentiments could be associated with Conservative

[19] Labour conference debates are reported verbatim in *Annual Reports* published by the party.
[20] Conservative conference debates are reported verbatim in *Annual Reports* published by the party.

party support for the sale of arms to the Union of South Africa. Another kind of residual imperialist sentiment was displayed in Conservative willingness to support or even encourage the use of British military force when the nation's overseas interests appeared to be challenged; thus there was strong rank-and-file party sympathy for the abortive campaign of Eden's government in 1956 to reverse the Egyptian seizure of the Suez Canal. Much less dramatically, this same kind of sympathy could be counted on by Conservative leaders who presently want to postpone Britain's military departure from positions east of Suez, which had been scheduled for abandonment by the Labour government of the late 1960s. In neither the later Conservative decision nor in the Labour leadership's original decision to withdraw military forces can rank-and-file pressure be considered crucial in government policy making, or even a significant influence. All that is evident or likely is that the party leaders would be comforted in their respective decisions by party popularity.

Party membership, in or out of annual conferences, has played an even less definite part in the development of policy concerning British entry into the European Economic Community (EEC). During the period in which this has been a live issue in British politics (often in the 1960s and again in the early 1970s), the decision to seek British entry has first been taken by the government, Conservative or Labour, and then subject to debate within each party. At certain times, as in the early 1960s, when the Conservative government was negotiating entry (eventually vetoed by de Gaulle), there was an apparent interparty divergence. Then Conservatives (if sometimes reluctantly and with reservations) supported their leadership's efforts, and Labour conferences backed their leadership's evident opposition—at least to the supposed terms of entry. Subsequently, when Wilson's Labour government sought to join the EEC, the party was carried along while Conservatives did not oppose what they had so recently tried themselves. Yet even when both parties formally approved of entry, there can be no doubt that at almost all times, including 1969–70, there was large-scale dissent within each major party. It was expressed at party conferences where each party's leadership, in order to obtain at least majority support on this issue, had to present its policy so as to stress negotiations without firm commitment in the absence of favorable terms. Each party contains both nationalist and practical economic critics—often reflecting widespread opposition outside party channels as well—in addition to ideological objections—socialist dislike for the big-business orientation of the Common Market, and residual imperialist dislike for the European (as opposed to an overseas) involvement. Neither of these latter tendencies was strong enough on its own, after the early 1960s, to cause a major party to adopt a doctrinal line against joining the EEC regardless of the terms of entry that might be negotiated. Thus, while socialist and nationalist principles contributed in 1971 to Labour's opposition to the Conservative government's negotiated entry, the Labour party conference as well as the parliamentary Labour party officially opposed only the specific terms of entry. In practice, of course, this meant opposing *the* terms evidently obtainable for Britain to enter the EEC during the early 1970s. Yet, by confining official opposition to the specific economic terms, Labour avoided a commitment to try subsequently to withdraw Britain from the EEC. At the same time, the party probably satisfied some of its more ideological anti-EEC activists whose rank-and-file pressure seemed indirectly influential.

Rank-and-file pressures in constituencies and in party conferences are often closely related to differences of opinion between the party's M.P.'s. It is really the M.P.'s who are the direct objects of whatever influence the external organizations can bring to bear. Despite the advantages, already described, of the party's leaders in maintaining parliamentary cohesion—especially when they hold government office—the fact remains that the few hundred M.P.'s who compose a majority party have a final authority: their backing for a policy has to be secured by a government. And when a party is out of power, its M.P.'s even have room for some initiative. Labour formally gives control of its opposition policy to its M.P.'s; the Conservative party maintains an equivalent, though less clearcut, means for backbenchers to express their opinions, which may also be the opinions of their constituency followers.

In discussing the role of parties it should be pointed out that, despite extremists within each party, the moderate Conservative and moderate Labour leaders have occupied a good deal of common ground with respect to Britain's postwar foreign policy. The really important matters of maintaining a substantial if now limited defense establishment, preserving the American alliance, and surrendering imperial possessions have not been basically at issue between the two major parties (or between them and the Liberal party). Insofar as the parties have disagreed on these matters, it has ordinarily been at the margins of policy. For example, while the Labour party officially disputed, from 1960 to 1964, the Conservative government's policy favoring an independent nuclear arsenal for Britain,

Labour's alternative was to place Britain's nuclear force in a joint Atlantic force with the United States and to rely openly on American military capacity. Much more unusual was the sharp and nearly total Labour opposition to the Conservative government's Suez campaign of 1956. Even in 1971, when Labour opposed the terms of EEC entry, its party solidarity was much less substantial.

There is a danger of overstating the importance of British parties in foreign policy, which may be averted simply by calling attention to their greater organization and cohesion around policy positions in comparison with American parties.[21] The fact remains that British parties do not regularly present competing foreign policies to the electorate. Even when they seem to present marginally different policies, as on the independent nuclear force in the 1964 general election, the issue may not be especially relevant to the voters. Party appeals have usually focused on domestic issues, and there is convincing evidence from opinion surveys in 1964 that the British electorate regarded these issues as much more important than any defense or foreign policy question.[22] The 1964 electorate is probably not exceptional in this respect. Without a notable crisis in world affairs, it now seems that most British voters are unlikely to regard their electoral decisions as primarily concerning international questions. Perhaps they never did have any such view, but it would have been less unrealistic to have expected it several

[21] This view of British parties is advanced most vigorously by Samuel H. Beer, *British Politics in the Collectivist Age* (New York: Knopf, 1965).

[22] National Opinion Polls, Ltd., *Political Bulletin* (London), October, 1964, Appendix A. See also David E. Butler and Donald Stokes, *Political Change in Britain* (New York: St. Martin's Press, 1969), pp. 343–44.

decades ago, when Britain was a more consequential force in world affairs.
Interest Groups. The old view of the unimportance of interest groups in the British political process has been abandoned. The study of such groups has disclosed that they play a large role, at least in domestic matters; and no one now doubts that, on such questions as tariffs, British manufacturers, unions, and farmers have means of effectively conveying their preferences to the government. However, it is evident that British interest groups, although as multifarious as those anywhere else, operate differently from their American counterparts. The very fact that the political parties are national in character and cohesive in parliamentary organization makes it of limited value to pressure legislators, directly or through constituents, for individual votes. To affect the main lines of government policy, certainly in foreign affairs, a British interest group would have to influence a party's leadership—or, more remotely, the bulk of its M.P.'s. Neither of these avenues seems feasible except for the biggest interest groups; although on lesser matters, particularly those involving administrative decisions, it may be assumed that smaller groups exert influence. Certainly it is established government practice to consult representatives of interest groups likely to be affected by contemplated policies, but this practice is highly institutionalized.

Major British interest groups tend to have direct connections with a political party. The outstanding example is that of the trade unions, most of which are affiliated with the Labour party and thus share directly, often dominantly, in that party's policy making. The unions also have a general organization, the Trades Union Congress, which is not part of the Labour party and which confers with the governments, regardless of which party is in power, in behalf of union interests. Somewhat similarly, the cooperative movement works both within and outside the Labour party. The Conservatives have no precise organizational counterparts, but industrial leaders maintain close connections with the party. This they do personally, as important Conservatives themselves, and through the usual business organizations established in particular trades and in general categories such as manufacturing. Trade associations, like individual trade unions, may maintain communication with party leaders on policy matters of direct concern. A distinctive feature of this political communication, from the American point of view, is that individual M.P.'s often openly serve as agents for interest groups—business, union, farm, and others; M.P.'s are even subsidized for this purpose by the groups they represent. There is ready access and, therefore, influence—but not overwhelming influence. For example, the British farm organization, working closely with the Conservative party, might have contributed to the delay in the Macmillan government's decision to negotiate for entry to the Common Market, but it did not prevent the decision or set all the terms for entry.

Generally, the most substantial interest groups concerned with foreign policy decisions are not organized primarily to influence such decisions. This holds for the important domestic economic groups noted above, and also for other types of organizations. Churches are plainly in this category; through their official representatives, they express opinions bearing on British foreign policy, although the expression of such opinions is only incidental to their main role. Veterans' groups are another case in point, although their efforts to influence general policy are less prominent in Britain than the efforts of comparable groups in the United States. The same can be said, for a different reason, of the activities of ethnic groups. Such groups are simply less significant in Britain because of the absence of large ethnic minorities of the sort that compose so much of the American population. Although there are, and almost always have been, Continental refugees in Britain, their numbers have not been sufficient to constitute serious pressure on British foreign policy making. Even the Jewish population of a half-million cannot be said to be an electoral factor in determining British policy toward Israel, despite a vigorous Zionist movement—represented particularly in the Labour party. Neither is the Irish minority, largely centered in a few seaports and manufacturing centers, a major influence, although it does, like the Zionists, have parliamentary spokesmen.

In addition to the groups whose varying influence on foreign affairs is incidental to their main purpose, there are also many British groups organized entirely around foreign policy issues. These may be less substantial, but they are often most active propagandistically. Some organizations are devoted to particular causes, such as justice or freedom for certain people in a certain place, and they wax and wane with the excitement of the issue. Others are broader in scope and more durable. One example is the United Nations Association; another, operating at a scholarly and almost official level in order to influence opinion makers, is the Royal Institute of International Affairs; a third, also of limited membership, is the newer Institute of Strategic Studies, which combines key government personnel with other selected persons who are professionally concerned with the analysis of foreign and defense poli-

cies. At an altogether different level of activity is the mass-membership organization, the Campaign for Nuclear Disarmament. Developed in the late 1950s to oppose Britain's retention of nuclear weapons, the CND undoubtedly mobilized the residual pacifism and neutralism of socialists, students, intellectuals, and miscellaneous middle-class citizens. Their most spectacular tactic was a well-publicized protest march each spring from a nuclear weapons center to a Trafalgar Square rally. The Nuclear Disarmers became active not only in this way and through a flood of speeches and literature, but also in the Labour party, where their position was accepted by important trade union leaders as well as by many constituency party workers. To a large degree, the Labour party conference's decision in 1960 to support unilateral nuclear disarmament was a victory for the campaign of the previous few years; after that, the campaign lost momentum.

Media of Mass Communication. The most basic point to note about British mass media is their national character. Strictly local and regional newspapers are of minor importance in relation to the media centered in London. The British magazine, radio, and television audience is essentially national. Opinion concerning foreign policy, like that concerning most domestic policy, is formed nationally and not regionally.

British communication has also taken on a special character by virtue of the continued monopoly (perhaps to be broken at the local level in the 1970s) of radio broadcasting by the government-owned British Broadcasting Corporation (BBC), and by a similar monopoly of telecasting, which lasted until 1955, when supervised commercial television began to compete with the BBC The government-owned service has avoided the editorialized commentary on the news typical of American radio and television. The news is reported straight and without dramatization, and a similar standard is expected of commercial television. Radio and television facilities are used by government spokesmen, particularly the prime minister and the foreign secretary, for official expositions of foreign policy, the importance of this means of communication with the nation having been firmly established by the successful wartime speeches of Winston Churchill. Some radio and television time is divided, according to an agreed-upon formula, between political parties for a presentation of their views on international as well as other issues. Occasionally, too, there are programs devoted to discussion of foreign policy. Television, as in the United States, is the most important means of reaching a mass audience; but in no case is there any purchase of time for the presentation of opinions.

The neutrality of British radio and television stands in contrast to the sharply partisan attachments of the press. A majority of newspapers lean toward the Conservatives, but the largest London paper, the *Daily Mirror*, is often pro-Labour. Although none of the mass-circulation dailies (such as the *Daily Mirror* and its several pro-Conservative counterparts) give much serious attention to international affairs, it is through their headlines, often slanted by partisan considerations, that a large share of the British population forms its perspective on international policies. Nevertheless, the quality press, even with its small circulation, deserves more attention as a molder of opinion, for it reaches most Englishmen who have opinion-making roles. Except in Scotland, where there are equivalent newspapers, almost every person seriously concerned with national or international affairs reads the *Times* of London, the liberal Manchester *Guardian*, or the Conservative London *Daily Telegraph*. Moreover, at least one of three London Sunday papers—the *Observer*, the *Sunday Times*, and the *Sunday Telegraph*—is read by virtually the whole of the serious English public. In addition, the special importance of the weekly *Economist* should be noted; more so than other intellectually oriented weeklies (such as the *Spectator* and the left-wing *New Statesman*), the *Economist* reaches the influential. Although these various papers and periodicals often present divergent views, there is an intimacy about the English circle of discussion that is absent in larger and less centralized political communities.

Other media of communication also play an important role in Britain. Pamphlets, for instance, are still widely used by party and party-affiliated groups to reach the public. Furthermore, Britain is a book-reading nation, and it is worth mentioning that both scholarly and popular volumes on foreign policy reach the attentive public. Speeches at public meetings, even though they are declining in popularity as a result of television, are still a means of influencing political audiences. A speech by a major public figure remains an important occasion, at least for the membership of a political party.

The Role of Public Opinion

Many of the "nongovernmental agencies" discussed in the preceding section are often conceived as representing public opinion, in contrast to the official agencies of governmental policy making. For analytical purposes it has been useful to adhere to this distinction, although there is a considerable overlapping of persons and functions. The term *establishment*, now widely used pejoratively in the United States, seems to have been invented in Britain to refer to an inner circle of important ministers, top civil servants, editors of quality newspapers, and a miscellany of academic and other public figures all capable of informal consultation with each other. Possessing common social and educational backgrounds, the members of this "establishment," it is thought, both make policy and expound it. The small, homogeneous nature of the British community lends credibility to this notion, especially when we are considering the somewhat detached area of foreign policy.

No doubt there is more divergence among the influential British than the concept of an "establishment" conveys. But with or without the term, the British community frankly recognizes the leadership groups that, in Gabriel Almond's phrase, "carry on the specific work of policy formulation and policy advocacy."[23] As Almond has also pointed out (although in reference to the United States), an elite of this sort does not operate independently of "certain policy criteria in the form of widely held values and expectations."[24] The British public, like the public elsewhere, sets such criteria, and the policy makers are limited thereby—as, for instance, by the public's manifest desire for peace. The subtlety of these relations has been well described by Kenneth Younger, a former minister of state for foreign affairs. Control of foreign policy, he says, is more oligarchic than control of domestic policy, and on first reflection he could think of no occasion when he or his superiors "had been greatly affected by public opin-

ion in reaching important decisions."[25] But this first impression, he realized, was misleading, because public opinion did affect ministers in a general way. "The Government," he writes, "tends to identify itself almost unconsciously with a vaguely sensed general will, and no clear formulation of the pressure of public opinion upon Government policy ever occurs."[26] Younger believes that a government identifies itself especially with its own supporters.

THE SUBSTANCE OF FOREIGN POLICY

Ordinarily, it is assumed that major tendencies in British foreign policy are not subject to drastic change as a result of general elections or other internal political events. No such change can be observed in any of the shifts in party government during the last twenty-five years—from Conservative to Labour in 1945, to Conservative in 1951, back to Labour in 1964, and again back to Conservative in 1970. Each of these successive governments faced a world situation in which Britain had limited choices, often confined to methods, timing of a military withdrawal, or marginal issues such as whether to sell arms to the Union of South Africa or how hard a line to take against Southern Rhodesia's white government. Maintaining close relations with the United States, remaining militarily within the North Atlantic Treaty Organization, and continuing the gradual withdrawal from imperial responsibilities were not regarded as reversible by the dominant forces in either major party. Nor, once negotiations were begun to enter the European Economic Community, was

---

23 Gabriel Almond, *The American People and Foreign Policy* (New York: Harcourt Brace & World, 1950), p. 5.

24 Ibid., p. 6.

25 Kenneth Younger, "Public Opinion and Foreign Policy," *British Journal of Sociology* 6 (June, 1955): 169.

26 Ibid., 171.

it thought likely that a subsequent government would abandon negotiations altogether or seek to reverse a negotiated entry if actually accomplished. Admittedly, however, the decision to seek entry at all, since it had been rejected by both British parties until the early 1960s, represents a genuine choice of policy whose adoption was less than an inevitable consequence of Britain's situation.

Commonwealth Relations

Especially in the past, Britain's relations with the other member nations of the Commonwealth and with its strictly imperial dependencies, might not have seemed properly to belong within the sphere of foreign affairs. Now, however, that the British government itself blurs the distinction by having only one merged ministry to deal with foreign and Commonwealth relations as well as with what remains of colonial affairs, it is clearly reasonable to consider policy toward the Commonwealth as an aspect—albeit a special aspect—of British foreign policy. The term *Commonwealth of Nations* is of recent coinage, succeeding *British Commonwealth of Nations* as well as the still older *British Empire*. For a time during the years between the two world wars and just afterward, Englishmen often spoke of *Commonwealth and Empire*, meaning by the first part of the phrase the already self-governing member nations (or "dominions," as they were also called), and by the second part the still vast areas and populations that were British dependencies governed in some degree from London. Gradually, however, *Commonwealth* has come to be used almost exclusively as most of the formerly imperial dependencies have become self-governing member nations; the word *British* was simultaneously dropped as the prefatory adjective for a group of nations now so largely Asian and African.

Commonwealth, it can be seen, is the single general name for an entity consisting of and developed from two very different elements of modern British overseas expansion. The first element is largely British in the literal sense of those nations—Canada, Australia, and New Zealand—which were settled and dominated numerically and politically by peoples from the British Isles, and augmented by other European immigrants. The Union of South Africa, which along with Canada, Australia, and New Zealand joined Britain in the original Commonwealth and remained a member until the early 1960s, was always a special case, since its British-derived population was not dominant over time in relation to the white settlers of Dutch descent—and certainly not in relation to the black African population. But even taking into account the Union of South Africa and the large French minority in Canada, the Commonwealth before 1945 was principally British in many significant ways. It is true that the spacious, remote, and growing nations of Canada and Australia, however British in origin, were bound to develop and pursue interests of their own, for which reason they had become self-governing even in the nineteenth century; but they also shared many interests with Britain and consequently displayed considerable support for British policy, as in their almost immediate move to participation in both world wars. Whether this kind of cohesion would have continued after World War II, even in an old Commonwealth, is doubtful; it was surely too much to expect in the newly enlarged and extremely diverse Commonwealth. The new member nations were overwhelmingly Asian and African by population, not just by geographical location. Neither India (by far the largest) nor any of the other new Commonwealth states had ever been so heavily populated by British settlers as to make for a British nation. Mainly, these nations had simply been governed by Britain following military conquest and accompanied by economic involvement by way of trade and industry. Only in certain parts of eastern and southern Africa were there substantial settlements of Britishers, and even in these exceptional instances the colonial settlers were no more than a large privileged minority whose capacity to dominate, in Southern Rhodesia as in the Union of South Africa, depended on sternly enforced racial discrimination. Much more characteristic in Africa were Ghana and Nigeria, which, like India and Pakistan and almost all of the other former African and Asian dependencies of any size, had no large minority of British or other white settlers. The thin line of British civil servants, military officers, and businessmen did not realistically constitute a colonial settlement. Therefore, self-government could only mean non-British government without any claims to the contrary. The most the former British governors could hope for was that the new, indigenous government would be in the British style, which they had usually sought to implant through the establishment of elected parliaments and native civil services before the achievement of complete self-government. This hope was (perhaps surprisingly) fulfilled during the first decades of Indian government in particular, and also of certain other (but by no means all) the new governments; but its achievement is by no means a substitute for common interest flowing from a common national origin. In short, the Commonwealth ceased to be British in much more than name when it became multiracial in the decades after World War II.

Some exposition is required in order to understand the maintenance of this Commonwealth and its apparent significance in recent British experience. It is a residual symbol of two age-old British ambitions. One ambition was to lead a "Greater Britain" that combined, in a kind of union—economic as well as political—Britain itself and the British-populated overseas dominions (and perhaps the United States). The other ambition, really meaningful only for a few decades of the late nineteenth and early twentieth centuries, was to possess an imperial power through domination of huge Asian and African portions of the globe. There did not appear to be any other way for Britain to achieve great-power status once it became clear, as it did even before 1900, that it had to compete with the larger Continental states of Germany and Russia, and with the United States. But neither ambition, it also became clear, could be fulfilled after World War II. The possibility of a reintegration of English-speaking dominions was obviously remote, given the increasingly national identities of Canada and Australia, not to mention the Union of South Africa; in any event, Britain could hardly expect to lead these nations when it was economically weak and militarily dependent—as so indeed was Australia—on the United States. And, of course, Britain had neither the will nor the capacity to hold, for a prolonged period, the large imperial territories against their now-rebellious Asian and African populations. It did not follow, however, that Britain was obligated to encourage Commonwealth membership for these territories when they became self-governing. It would have been possible, while extending self-government in Asia and Africa, perhaps even more rapidly than was actually done, to have eliminated even the residual special ties to Britain, and so to have kept the Commonwealth exclusively, or almost exclusively, a grouping of "British" nations. This would have meant an effort to achieve a somewhat closer community even if well short of a union of "Greater Britain." Appreciating the British rejection of this option is to comprehend how postwar Britain still sought greatness in the world through a liberalized mid-twentieth century version of "empire." A Commonwealth large enough to include India and most of the other formerly Asian and African dependencies was necessary in order to magnify Britain's role commensurate with the old ambitions. Moreover, the very multiracial character of the new Commonwealth seemed itself an accomplishment in a world otherwise divided so sharply along racial lines. With pride, then, a British ambassador to the United States could say, in 1956: "Britain lies at the heart of the Commonwealth, and the Commonwealth contains over six hundred million people, more than a third of the population of the free world."[27]

Unquestionably there does remain, even now, a genuine if limited association of nations called the "Commonwealth." Twenty-nine nations, including Britain, are members (as of 1970), and thirty other, mostly very small, territories are dependencies, although six of these are so thoroughly self-governing as to be called "associated states." The total Commonwealth population has risen to 800 million, and is now even more overwhelmingly Asian and African than it was twenty years ago. Each member nation acknowledges the queen of England as

27 Roger Makins, "The Commonwealth in World Affairs," *Labour and Industry in Britain* 14 (September, 1956): 116.

the symbolic head of the Commonwealth, but the new Asian and African nations do not accept the queen as their own crowned head of state. There is no central authority, in any practical political sense, above that of the respective governments themselves, although there are essentially administrative arrangements of intergovernmental committees and staffs in a multitude of cooperative ventures. There are also regular meetings of prime ministers and other political leaders at Commonwealth conferences, at which efforts are made to adopt common policies at least on matters of intra-Commonwealth concern. It has not been possible, however, for the Commonwealth to present a united front on many of the most important international issues of concern to Britain. Not only have the African and Asian member nations been at odds with any seeming reassertion by Britain of an imperialist role, as at Suez in 1956, but the established Afro-Asian position in the Cold War has been neutralist under Indian leadership and so most distinct from Britain's alignment with the United States. Broadly speaking, the new Commonwealth nations have defined their global interests differently from Britain's—no doubt because those interests are in fact different in many basic respects.

Yet Britain has exerted considerable effort, often at considerable expense, to maintain the multiracial Commonwealth. It loosened what was already a loose intergovernmental structure in order to accommodate first India and then other Asian and African nations when they insisted on republican regimes without the British queen as their crowned chief of state. Britain also accepted the Commonwealth's numerically predominant antagonism to the Union of South Africa, and joined in policies leading to the

Union's exit from the Commonwealth. It is true, of course, that by the 1960s many Englishmen shared the African and Asian hostility toward the Union's racist domestic policies, but there remained (and still remains) many closer British ties with the Union and the people in it than with the newer Commonwealth nations. These ties are economic as well as ethnic and personal—at least with respect to the large English-speaking white minority. Yet such ties have been overridden with respect to Southern Rhodesia, whose white minority is almost completely British in origin. Britain rejected the claim of a regime based on that minority to become self-governing and, as such, presumably a member nation of the Commonwealth. In fact, after rejecting the asserted independence of that regime in 1965, Britain attempted to give effect to the rejection by economic sanctions along with withdrawal of legal recognition. Again, it must be said that the British policy coincided not just with Afro-Asian attitudes, but also with widespread antiracist sentiments in Britain itself. But it is by no means clear that Britain would have taken quite so hard a line without the desire to maintain its Commonwealth ties with Asian and African nations. There were limits, of course, to the policies Britain would or could adopt because of Afro-Asian pressure; thus Britain refused to use its military force to attempt to overthrow the white minority government of Southern Rhodesia, even though legally and morally, and in the eyes of world opinion, the action could have been justified. Apart, however, from the expense of launching a military expedition in Africa, there was another reason why Britain could not seriously contemplate such an action to please most of the Commonwealth: sending British soldiers to fight British settlers in behalf of a black major-

ity was hardly attractive politically in Britain itself.

An even clearer indication of the inherent limits on an Afro-Asian orientation for Britain's Commonwealth policy is to be found in the postwar history of Britain's immigration legislation. Adhering at first to an idealistic conception of Commonwealth citizenship, Britain was open throughout the 1950s to immigrants from the African, Asian, and West Indian member nations and dependencies, just as it was to immigrants from the old British dominions. And this was at a time when Britain was by no means open on the same basis to immigrants from southern and eastern Europe. Commonwealth citizens were treated as British citizens rather than as foreigners. Consequently, during the years of full employment in Britain and of unemployment or underemployment in other parts of the Commonwealth—in the overpopulated Asian and West Indian nations particularly—there was a fairly large-scale movement of nonwhite people to British cities, bringing their total numbers near the 2-percent figure, as noted earlier, and producing, in certain cities considerable popular agitation against the immigration. Responding to this pressure in the 1960s, successive British governments, Conservative and then Labour, acted first to curtail the immigration and then to try to eliminate it almost altogether. Governmental leaders, it is likely, acted reluctantly insofar as they were committed to Commonwealth ideals, but politically they appreciated that they had little choice, even though they might well have been able to cite strictly economic benefits for Britain in securing additional workers.

In other instances, Britain has pursued a Commonwealth policy that could be questioned on purely economic grounds and that, on such grounds, has recently been curtailed. Overseas economic aid to the less-developed nations of the Commonwealth is an obvious case in point, although it might be argued that Britain continued to be relatively generous in this respect. Military commitments have seemed more burdensome partly because they may have derived from an older imperial role rather than from a strictly contemporary Commonwealth purpose, even though serving it as well. Britain has sought to defend territories not only while they were still dependencies—as in providing a military force in Malaya during the earlier postwar years—but also afterward, as when, in the middle 1960s, Britain helped the self-governing Commonwealth nation of Malaysia fight Indonesian attacks. More generally, Britain has regularly maintained expensive overseas bases— the so-called East-of-Suez policy—for such purposes, and has only scheduled their abandonment, or near-abandonment, for the early 1970s. Perhaps Britain would have wanted in any case to retain these tangible signs of influence in the postwar world, but the Commonwealth tie surely encouraged and legitimized the expenditure for at least two extra decades. The virtual withdrawal that is now occurring may thus be understood as reflecting a diminishing Commonwealth emphasis as well as Britain's generally diminishing influence in world affairs.

From an American and perhaps also from a broader Western viewpoint, Britain's postwar involvement in the new Commonwealth appears useful if only because it means that Britain has assumed some of the military burden, east of Suez and elsewhere, that would otherwise have become the sole responsibility of the United States— unless Western influence were surrendered altogether in large areas of the world. Much of this could also have been justified from a strictly British viewpoint on the widely held assumption that Britain, as a Western power, has a considerable stake in the American-led effort to contain hostile forces and to preserve Western communication with less-developed nations. But it is not clear that quite as much of the actual British overseas undertaking could thus have been justified during the quarter-century after World War II. It was one thing for an economically weakened but still substantial power like Britain to contribute, as it did on a large scale, to the military defense of Europe, where British interests were most directly involved. Large-scale military expenditures elsewhere seemed less obviously necessary, and they were not forthcoming on a similar scale for so long a time from other Western European nations of similar size. It is hard to escape the conclusion that Britain retained a disproportionate overseas commitment, and that it did so partly because of its residual imperial attachment to Commonwealth responsibilities. That attachment may now be diminishing, at least in its capacity to influence material commitments. After all, the generation of Englishmen growing up since World War II has not really lived in the era of imperial glory or even of great-power status. On the other hand, preceding generations, including those in policy-making positions until now, must have found the symbolism of Commonwealth a useful mid-twentieth-century substitute for imperialism. Especially during the decades of Britain's withdrawal from territories it had once governed, the existence of the Commonwealth could assuage what was aptly called a "sense of personal loss—almost of amputation,"[28] which Englishmen felt when a

[28] John Strachey, *The End of Empire* (New York: Praeger, 1964), p. 204.

colony became independent. Substitution of the Commonwealth association for the empire could thus help account for the relatively slight resistance to the withdrawal process and so to the absence of persistent attempts to hold territory that had become unmanageable for Britain.

As against the usefulness of the Commonwealth in this internally relevant symbolic respect and in various more tangible respects as well, it is sometimes argued that Britain suffered more than just the financial costs of maintaining its overseas military and economic commitments when it decided to maintain the Commonwealth. It is contended that Britain was thereby distracted from prompt recognition of its European status, holding back as it did from Continental economic union in 1950 when the Schuman plan for a six-nation coal and steel community was proposed, in the late 1950s when the Common Market was developed by the same six nations, and even in the 1960s when Britain was unwilling to pay a high enough price to join the Common Market despite negotiations to that end. Certainly in each instance British spokesmen did cite Commonwealth relations, among other reasons, for holding back. The relevant relations were both symbolic —in the sense that the Commonwealth suggested a larger overseas identification that was an alternative to a strongly European identification—and economic, in that Britain had established arrangements with Commonwealth nations for tariff preferences incompatible with membership in the Common Market. By the 1960s, however, Britain appeared ready to sacrifice these preferential arrangements, negotiating only for a transitional period, and also to risk losing the overseas identification in order to obtain the supposed benefits of membership in the thriving European Economic Community. At most, the Commonwealth attachment might have delayed this decision or influenced the terms that Britain preferred to obtain on entering the EEC. And there were always other factors, (to be discussed subsequently) that also seemed responsible for the delay or for influencing the negotiating terms. At any rate, Commonwealth policy has not longer looms so large as to stand in the way of Britain's entry into the EEC, now that entrance is otherwise being arranged. Nor with respect to overseas military commitments, as observed, will Commonwealth considerations in and of themselves lead to future expenditures. This hardly means the disappearance, suddenly or gradually, of the Commonwealth, but it does signify a decreasing relative significance in British policy making.

English-Speaking Ties

Britain's links with other English-speaking nations are based on a political heritage along with a common language and an ethnic background associated with the language. These links are not everywhere identical with those of the Commonwealth. Most of the present multiracial Commonwealth is no more English-speaking than it is British; on the other hand, the largest and most powerful English-speaking nation, the United States, is not a Commonwealth nation. Neither is Ireland, and yet its association with Britain, despite centuries of religious and political animosity now readily revived by Northern Ireland's internal difficulties, is a fact dictated by geographical propinquity and economic dependence as well as by the common use of the English language. Ireland, no less than Canada, Australia, and New Zealand, has parliamentary institutions clearly derived from British tradition. So, in certain respects, do the Union of South Africa and Southern Rhodesia, but they must now largely be set aside since their English-speaking populations (plus a larger non-English-speaking white population in the Union of South Africa) are minorities capable of governing only by a racial supremacy ideologically unacceptable in Britain. Here the ties derived from language and associated background factors appear to be greatly weakened if not actually severed along with Commonwealth membership itself. Perhaps Ireland, too, should be treated as a separate case, since its ties of language and democratic ideology would probably be insufficient for a special relationship if there were not also geographical and economic facts to override the ancient enmity. This leaves, among English-speaking nations, Canada, Australia, and New Zealand, along with the United States.

Surely the ties with these nations make Britain unique among European countries, and indeed less exclusively European than any Continental country. So much can be said without ignoring the fact that France, Spain, and Portugal each have language links with non-European nations, and that these links derive, as do Britain's, from an older imperial expansion. Yet the French, Spanish, and Portuguese ties are of a lesser order of political significance. With respect to France, only in Canada, chiefly in the province of Quebec, is there a large overseas population of French descent that can be said to resemble a nation, and it is a population within a larger nation dominated by an English-speaking majority; moreover, the French-speaking population of Canada has been estranged from its mother country culturally and ideologically as well as politically for almost two-and-a-half centuries. Elsewhere there have been no large overseas French settlements,

except in Algeria where the settlement always represented a minority of the total population and was eventually displaced in power by representatives of the non-European native majority. French influence remains in Algeria as it does in other former French dependencies in North Africa and south of the Sahara, but the influence resembles that of Britain in its former Asian and African dependencies rather than resembling British ties with other English-speaking nations. Both Spain and Portugal have important linguistic, and to some extent ethnic, links with other countries—particularly with Latin American nations—but, with few exceptions, the Spanish and Portuguese settlements were limited relative to native populations. The maintenance in Latin America of mother-country influences, especially political influences, was not at all like the British-related experiences of the nineteenth and early twentieth centuries. Neither Spain nor Portugal was a likely model, in the British manner, for successful modern nationhood.

Granting the unique nature of Britain's overseas linguistic ties, as demonstrated by the European comparisons, how significant are these ties in terms of contemporary British foreign policy? They are not the ties of a political union or even of an economic union. The five English-speaking nations of the world—Britain, the United States, Australia, New Zealand, and Canada (only two-thirds of which is English-speaking)—do not coincide with the Commonwealth, since much of the latter is excluded while the United States is added. Yet there can be little doubt that many Englishmen can more readily identify their own nation with the other English-speaking nations than with the multiracial Commonwealth. Americans are less likely to be considered foreigners than are Indians and Pakistanis, or even Europeans whose language if not race seems more foreign than that of the more geographically distant English-speaking American. Sir Winston Churchill was not alone among his countrymen in cherishing Britain's status among the "English-speaking peoples."[29] The very phrase, perhaps partly because it is a twentieth-century euphemism for "Anglo-Saxon world," conveys, especially in Britain, much of the feeling associated with a racial or ethnic bond. As such, the ties may readily be exaggerated. Neither in Canada nor in the United States, and probably no longer in Australia, is the national background of the population so completely British. In addition to Canada's French (and French-speaking) population, there are large numbers of people of various continental European backgrounds in all of the English-speaking overseas nations except New Zealand. The United States in particular is surely not British except in its origins.

Dealing with the United States represents a very special problem in Britain's relations with the English-speaking world if only because the United States has over twice as many people and over twice the power of all the rest of that English-speaking world. Thus British identification as part of this world means that Britain, even if joined by Canada, Australia, and New Zealand, is distinctly a junior partner in an American-led or American-dominated combination. Earlier in the twentieth century this was by no means so evident; during World War I and even during World War II, Britain primarily regarded American power in terms of helping further British policy—or at least the

policy of the English-speaking nations. After World War II and especially since the first few postwar years, Britain had to face the fact that the United States was now so greatly predominant in the Western alliance that Britain was being asked to assist in pursuing policies that often seemed primarily American in conception even if designed to serve general Western purposes. Understandably, Britain has been uneasy in this new and unaccustomed relationship. Generally, Americans seemed, to the British, brash and inexperienced in international affairs—especially so in the Middle East, where the United States was perceived as a usurper of Britain's old leading role and as unwilling to back what Britain believed to be its own interests (as in Iran or the Suez Canal). Moreover, the American involvement in Asia, whether with regard to nationalist China, Korea, or Vietnam, was not one that many Englishmen wanted to share. Always the preference was for the maintenance of American power and interest in Europe in order to hold the line where it had been drawn, in 1945, between Eastern and Western Europe. Here Britain feared, at different times, either that the United States would be too belligerently anti-Soviet, or that the United States would weary of the Cold War task of containment and simply withdraw into isolationism or into deeper Asian involvements. But neither uneasiness nor irritation with American ways kept Britain from maintaining its place in the alliance. The broad central sector of British opinion, including almost all of the leaders of both major parties, accepted the alliance as essential and American leadership as inevitable although hopefully subject to British influence. At least this was certainly true of the first quarter-century after World War II, during which period only fairly

---

[29] As, for instance, in Winston Churchill's famous Fulton, Missouri, speech. See the *New York Times*, March 6, 1946, p. 4.

extreme ideological critics seriously urged alternatives to the American alliance. These critics, both on the imperialist fringe of the Conservative party and, more significantly, on the socialist Left of the Labour party, found their position increasingly weakened as their supposed alternatives—reasserted imperialism, going it alone, Commonwealth leadership, or socialist Third Force membership—became plainly less viable in the postwar world. This did not mean that they or many less extreme critics ceased to question the terms of the alliance or the particular policies of American leadership. There is no doubt, for example, that broad sections of British opinion have been troubled about the involvement of the United States in Vietnam, and that the official governmental unwillingness over several years openly to criticize American policy has concealed misgivings beyond those vigorously asserted by the left wing of the Labour party.

Perhaps what is suggested by Britain's willingness in such a circumstance to go along with, or to acquiesce officially in, American policy is that the dependence on American power militarily and economically has become so great that there is virtually no other national choice. If so, what has this to do with "English-speaking ties" as such? Surely it is not the simple fact that Americans and Englishmen speak the same language that then accounts for maintenance of the alliance. Nor is it likely to be the association of ideology, culture, and institutions with the language. Such common grounds were not always sufficient in the nineteenth century for Anglo-American agreement on international matters. On the other hand, given the contemporary facts of British and American power, it can be argued that the ties of language and

associated factors facilitate the alliance just as they probably made it seem natural in the first place. It has been possible for Englishmen, especially those in government leadership positions, to believe that their country had a "special relationship" with the United States, different from that of the continental European nations that appeared similarly joined in the North Atlantic Treaty Organization. Within this special relationship, which from time to time seemed to be recognized by American officials, the British government sought throughout the postwar era to exert its influence on American policy—often privately and informally—and to maintain a distinctive place for Britain in the highest councils of the Western world. Good personal communication between a prime minister and the American president has been an important part of the special relationship. To maintain such communication and its effectiveness as a means of exerting influence appeared to require that British officials avoid public dispute with American policy.

As with the British attachment to the Commonwealth, so the English-speaking ties and notably the special American relationship have often seemed to be juxtaposed against Britain's integration in Western Europe. This has not been a matter of American policy suggesting that Britain should choose between the United States and Western Europe; on the contrary, postwar American policy has been to urge Britain to join Western European integration, specifically that of the Common Market, while at the same time maintaining ties with the United States. It often seemed as though the American government wanted to deal with Britain as one of several Western European allies rather than as a special kind of partner. Britain, rather than the United States, has emphasized the special relationship, and in such a way as to stress an extra-European role for itself. This role, as a member of an Atlantic community of primarily English-speaking nations, is in many cultural and ideological respects a more congenial one for many Englishmen than is a more fully integrated European role. Apart from an intellectual minority who occupy cultural as well as linguistic common ground with continental Europeans, there are, for Englishmen, fewer barriers of "foreignness" in working with English-speaking nationals, even with Americans. Perhaps this will change as more Englishmen visit Continental countries and as the image of unstable political institutions in France, Germany, and Italy recedes with prolonged Continental democratic experience. Or, put the other way, perhaps the English-speaking ties will diminish in relative significance as American democratic institutions, never entirely equated by Englishmen, in terms of efficacy, with their own, come to be perceived as increasingly unstable. By the 1970s the capacity of American government was already being questioned in a way that it had not been since World War II.

Foreign Economic Policy and the EEC

Britain's dependence on overseas trade means that economic matters are always in the forefront among foreign policy issues. Since World War II, the most consistent national concern has been the maintenance of a sufficient volume of manufactured exports, along with so-called invisible earnings from various services, to pay for needed imports of food and raw materials, as well as to compensate for Britain's overseas expenditures for military and economic-aid purposes. This represents the well-known balance-of-payments problem with which

Britain has struggled from crisis to crisis during the last twenty-five years. At first, in the decade of general European recovery after World War II, Britain received loans and assistance under the American Marshall Plan primarily to help bridge a dollar gap —meaning that Britain needed more dollars than could then be earned in order to purchase goods principally from the United States and Canada, while rebuilding and modernizing manufacturing industry from its war-damaged state. But Britain's balance-of-payments problem has persisted long after the postwar recovery period and despite a considerable degree of success, in that period, in the effort to increase manufacturing output and its sale abroad. The success in this respect has often been offset by increased domestic demand both for Britain's own products and for imported goods, and so the government has restrained this demand by various fiscal measures. In the early postwar years there was a stringent austerity program which, through the use of high purchase taxes and other means, prevented Englishmen from buying their own exportable products (cars, for example) and which virtually prohibited the importation of many foreign products. Even after this program was relaxed, there remained restrictions on foreign-travel expenditures, made more or less stringent from time to time, and various other controls designed to limit domestic consumption, especially when exports lagged behind imports. Moreover, recurrent crises, signified by the declining value of the British pound sterling in international exchange, pushed the British government on two occasions to devalue its official currency rate and at various times to arrange international loans, economies in government expenditures (particularly overseas), and even a slowdown in domestic economic growth in order to curb the inflation that raised the price of British products sold abroad. All of these measures, including devaluation, had to be undertaken even during the late 1960s; and although a surplus in the balance of payments had been achieved by early 1970, there was no assurance that this was any more permanent an accomplishment than that produced by earlier, similar efforts. Britain's international economic difficulties appeared to be nearly chronic.

To a certain extent, these difficulties should be understood as they relate to Britain's leading role as a banker for what is called the "sterling bloc" of nations—the Commonwealth (except Canada) plus a few other small nations closely tied economically to British trade. Within this bloc, free exchange is encouraged, and earnings of gold and dollars are pooled for dealing with other countries. Thus the bloc as a whole, as well as Britain itself, seeks a balance of trade with the rest of the world. London is the banker for the sterling bloc, and its financial service helps to facilitate the residually imperial exchange of British manufactures for the Commonwealth's food and raw materials. Also, much of the modest amount of British capital recently available for export has been directed to nations of the sterling bloc; but the practical limits of this effort contrast sharply with the old British pattern of massive overseas investment that was ended by enforced wartime liquidation. Whether Britain in recent years has really benefitted economically from its maintenance of the sterling bloc is open to question. In and of itself, the bloc appears to carry advantages. Not only is there some British profit in retaining London as a world financial service center, but there is probably an advantage, at least at times, in having certain dollar-earning raw materials, notably Malay-

sian rubber, to use in adjusting balance-of-payments accounts. On the other side, however, there are British expenses, already noted, involved in maintaining the Commonwealth ties with which the sterling bloc is associated. And, more significant if less readily measured, there is the possibility that leadership of the sterling bloc, like leadership of the Commonwealth itself, has served to keep Britain from accommodating itself to a new reality in which there is no place for British leadership of any overseas grouping and no hope, realistically, that the old economic supremacy of the nineteenth century can be reestablished on a residual imperial base.

An important portion of Britain's twentieth-century economic policy did appear to rest on that hope. Empire and then Commonwealth trade was supposed to act as a substitute for the vanished capacity of Britain to compete successfully in free-world markets as it had against the less-developed competing nations of the mid-nineteenth century. What Britain faced, even before 1900 but certainly after that, was the competition of newer and more efficient industrial powers, and at a time when Britain already had to export manufactured goods in order to obtain necessary food and raw materials. After World War II, the problem was only more acute but not new. Britain had been seeking a solution for several decades. Its situation dictated the continued encouragement of food imports because, even with the considerable revival of domestic agriculture in the twentieth century, foreign food in large quantities was going to remain essential for the large and still growing urban population. Thus the old policy of no tariff—or at least a very low tariff—on food imports remained desirable. But it could be so applied as to discriminate in favor of Commonwealth nations;

that is, their foodstuffs could be allowed to enter Britain at a tariff level much lower, if a tariff were in existence at all, than that used for the foodstuffs coming from non-Commonwealth nations. In return, the Commonwealth nations could discriminate in favor of British manufactured exports. Some such system was part of a grandiose scheme at the turn of the century, when Joseph Chamberlain urged an imperial economic customs union. But it was not until the decades between the world wars that Britain developed the tariffs and accompanied them with what was called "imperial preference" ("Commonwealth preference" after World War II) to implement the objectives of intra-Commonwealth trade. It is true that these arrangements, chiefly made in the 1930s, constitute the British variant of the economic nationalism of the interwar era; other nations, led by the United States, were raising their tariffs to protect home markets against foreign competition. Britain was trying to enlarge its home market, in effect, so as to coincide with the imperial boundaries. However well imperial preference seemed to work in the 1930s, associated as it was with British economic recovery from the interwar depression, its further development after World War II could not be realized either materially or in the broader political sense desired by its staunchest champions. Other Commonwealth nations—particularly Canada and Australia, with whom the preferences of the 1930s had been important—did not find it in their postwar interest to extend the preferences on a broad scale, and Britain's own need for more American trade and aid was not compatible with any increased discrimination in favor of Commonwealth producers. The alternative presented by the new American encouragement of general free trade was more attrac-

tive and more feasible. Consequently, imperial preference, although not abandoned, declined greatly in relative importance after 1945. Not only were no new preferences negotiated, but the existing ones ceased to be as significant, in terms of competitive advantage, as they had been in the 1930s.[30]

The remaining special Commonwealth trade relationships, however, have already been observed to be significant enough to influence, without precluding, British negotiations in the 1960s and 1970s for entry into the European Economic Community. On economic grounds, it is easy to understand why Commonwealth trade would not now determine the rest of British policy: there is simply not enough of it, currently or prospectively. British trade with Europe has been greater and it has grown much more rapidly even without EEC membership. The lesser-developed and largely impoverished Afro-Asian nations of the Commonwealth do not have and are unlikely soon to possess the capacity to purchase British manufactured goods as can the prosperous nations of Western Europe. The English-speaking nations of the Commonwealth, while indeed prosperous, are limited as markets for British goods because of their still fairly small populations, their closer proximity to other developed nations (Canada to the United States and Australia to Japan), and their desire, with an ability, to expand their own manufacturing industries. Britain's economic future, in other words, cannot rest primarily or even heavily on Commonwealth trade. Nevertheless, disengaging from it involves more than the abandonment of sentimental

[30] Political and Economic Planning, *Commonwealth Preference in the United Kingdom* (London: George Allen & Unwin, 1960), p. 5.

hopes. There are also serious economic adjustments. Striking among these, at least during the EEC negotiations of the 1960s, has been the problem of New Zealand's large food exports—large especially from New Zealand's standpoint—that enter the British market under more favorable terms than will be retained when Britain is required, as an EEC member, to discriminate in favor of continental European products rather than Commonwealth products. Adjustment here is more difficult than it seems to be for Commonwealth trade in tropical foodstuffs or in other products not available in large quantities from continental Europe. Not only might Britain, by abandoning preferential arrangements with New Zealand, be forced to pay more for Continental substitutes, but a blow dealt the New Zealand economy, through the loss of its major British market, would in turn seriously curtail the capacity of New Zealand to purchase British manufactured goods. Thus there have been compelling reasons for Britain to argue that the EEC allow special transitional arrangements for reducing Commonwealth preferences, especially in relation to New Zealand. But even in this instance it has been evident, from 1961 on, that the preferences themselves would be surrendered, gradually if not suddenly, as part of the price of EEC entry. More strictly domestic economic circumstances, along with political considerations, soon became larger obstacles to entry than the once-cherished Commonwealth trade.

These other factors can best be explained through a review of Britain's developing relations with the EEC. The relations cannot be overemphasized now that Britain has negotiated, in 1970–71, apparently acceptable terms for joining the EEC. The significant point is that the decision, as

presented, involves genuinely crucial policy making with respect to Britain's future place in the world. This means that the decision, while evidently economic in its primary impact, has much broader political consequences as well. But it is not only for convenience that the subject is discussed mainly under an economic heading. Economic factors are evidently responsible for all the British efforts to try to join the EEC, although arguments about joining now, as always, mix political with economic considerations. Some of these considerations have already been noted in discussing British ties with the Commonwealth and with the United States. Awareness of these ties makes it easy to appreciate why Britain stood apart from the earliest continental European integration, the Schuman plan of 1950, which placed the coal and steel industries of France, Italy, West Germany, and the Benelux countries under a supranational European authority; for at that time Britain was still able to conceive of itself as a world power only recently victorious in a war that had vanquished, in one way or another, each of the Continental powers. Merging the British national identity, or the national sovereignty, with the then still economically unrecovered and politically unstabilized Continental powers was hardly attractive for a nation whose Commonwealth, if not empire, remained promising. As the center of this Commonwealth, Britain seemed still to have the opportunity, once itself economically revived, of playing the World War II role as the third great world power (with the Soviet Union and the United States). The unlikelihood of this prospect was not as plain in 1950 as in 1970; and although the most perceptive observers, even among Englishmen, probably realized that the days of overseas glory had ended, it was still hard to act accordingly. Surely there was no overwhelmingly strong economic argument for Britain joining the Schuman plan.

Nor did there seem to be so strong an argument for Britain to join the EEC when this was first proposed in the mid-1950s as a means of extending, among the same six Continental nations, the coal and steel integration to a common market for all agricultural and industrial products, again with a supranational authority administering the integrated economic structure. But by the late 1950s the economic situation dictated a much greater British concern with European trade. Continental growth was now plainly more rapid and impressive—especially in Germany, and becoming so in France—and the integrated coal and steel community was already a functional success. Commonwealth trade had not developed on any massively enlarged scale. Moreover, Britain's confidence in its future as a Commonwealth leader and overseas power was shakier than in 1950, notably after the display of weakness during the Suez crisis of 1956. Consequently, Britain was ready for some intra-European preferential trade arrangement, but not yet for the supranationalism or the common external tariff being developed by the six Continental nations after 1955. As the EEC, or Common Market, began to succeed, the first British response was to try in 1957–58 to persuade the six nations to join Britain and several other European nations in a looser free-trade organization that would afford only mutual tariff preferences for those countries unwilling to accept the other features of the EEC. The advantage for Britain was plain: it would be able to sell its products within any EEC country, as it had done before, without being discriminated against, but it would not have to abandon any of its other trad-

ing advantages by virtue of adopting the EEC's common external tariff. After this suggestion was rejected by the six Continental nations, Britain led in the separate development of the European Free Trade Association, which in the early 1960s reduced tariffs among its seven members (Sweden, Denmark, Norway, Portugal, Austria, Switzerland, and of course Britain). Although this association worked effectively to increase trade among the nations involved, it was hardly much of a rival to the EEC. The total population was much smaller than that of the six Continental nations, and so the economic growth potential was much more limited. The political potential was meant to be limited, and the noncontiguous character of the association's membership worked in the same direction.

From its inception (or at least separate development), the EFTA was plainly not an economic alternative to the EEC. It was not so for Britain or for the other EFTA member nations, several of which, like Britain, sought membership or association with the EEC as that organization shortly proved itself as the dynamic market of Europe. Britain's own effort to reverse its initial decision against joining the EEC came in 1961, when Prime Minister Harold Macmillan led his Conservative government to begin negotiations for entry.[31] These negotiations lasted until early 1963, when President de Gaulle made it painfully clear that France was vetoing British admission. This veto, abrupt and contemptuous of Britain's continued conflicting desire to be a non-European Anglo-Saxon power, came only after persistent British efforts to obtain eco-

[31] Miriam Camps, *Britain and the European Community, 1955–1963* (Princeton: Princeton University Press, 1964), chaps. 9 and 10.

nomic concessions.[32] These concessions involved a transitional period for reducing the Commonwealth preferences (previously noted), as well as arrangements for adjusting domestic British agriculture to the EEC's price-support structure. This latter point has not been a trivial matter either in British politics or in the negotiations. Britain's method of subsidizing agriculture has been to keep prices for domestic farm products at low levels, as are the imported tariff-free products, and to pay British farmers, from the government treasury, the difference between their costs plus profits, on the one hand, and the lower prices of the marketplace. British consumers were thus accustomed to apparently inexpensive food. The EEC method is radically different in that there is a common external tariff (and other restrictive measures) against food imports, while consumers pay more nearly the actual cost of the relatively expensive farm products from the continental European countries (especially France) and as taxpayers contribute in other ways as well, through their governments, to the subsidy of farming. Although it is not clear that the net cost of one method is really greater than that of the other, there is no doubt that the EEC method, when enforced in Britain, would seem much more expensive to British consumers: food prices might rise sharply. Yet some British farmers could suffer at the same time since—while still subsidized, only in a form different from the old British scheme—they might be less successful in selling certain products in the face of freely admitted Continental competition. Altogether there has been no politically painless way for a British government to accept the EEC's agricultural arrangements; but since these arrangements must be

accepted as entry is obtained, the best that has been done is to negotiate for a period of transition so as to ease the pain.

So it was that first Macmillan, from 1961 to 1963, and then Prime Minister Harold Wilson for a Labour government in 1967, sought to gain British admission to the EEC. Perhaps Wilson was able to negotiate with less concern for adversely affected domestic economic interests. Once he committed his own government and party, he had a measure of bipartisan support that Macmillan lacked in the early 1960s when the Labour party, in opposition, seemed hostile to entry. But special transitional arrangements of some kind, both for Commonwealth and for domestic agriculture, remained necessities for British negotiators, as they seemed to be again in 1970 for Prime Minister Heath's government in beginning Britain's third effort to join. What was changed, however, was that de Gaulle, who vetoed Wilson's 1967 bid as well as Macmillan's earlier attempt, no longer commanded French policy. Conceivably his successors, not sharing all of de Gaulle's feeling that Britain was too non-European for the EEC, were much more willing to grant the transitional economic arrangements that Britain still desired. Much depended on Britain's own posture. Was the nation in fact ready to assume a more definitely European role? Economically it would seem so. Although there are special British economic interests that would suffer, especially in the short run, there is a widespread realization in industry and government that Britain needs to belong to a larger internal market in order to share in the growth of modern technology and that, in this respect, there is no alternative to the EEC. Politically also, the time appeared right, since the Commonwealth mirage had

[32] Waltz, *Foreign Policy*, chap. 9.

more definitely receded and, for a time at any rate, the American alliance had lost some of its counterattraction as the United States had become increasingly troubled by its own internal difficulties. Britain may finally become more fully European because it has nowhere else to turn. But as EEC entry is thus apparently obtained, it is not in a surge of popular enthusiasm. British public opinion seemed less attracted by the EEC in 1970–71 than it had been several years earlier. Hence, when Heath's Conservative government presented its negotiated entry terms of 1971, it faced political problems that were soon magnified by the Labour leader, Harold Wilson, who asserted, controversially, that the terms were not those that he would have accepted. Enough Labour M.P.'s, it is true, broke with their leader and their official party position to provide a comfortable parliamentary majority for Heath's entry terms in 1971—more than compensating for a smaller number of Conservative defections. But Labour promised to continue its parliamentary battle into 1972.

Security Policy

The reasons for Britain's assumption that it cannot protect itself against aggression without help are obvious. The island's location, vulnerability, and limited resources require that protection come from collective arrangements with other nations. Strictly speaking, modern Britain has never relied solely on its own military capacities. Its tradition of trying to maintain a European balance of power has necessarily involved joining alliances with some nations against others. And before World War I, this policy, combined with command of the seas, allowed Britain considerable freedom of action and certainly a sense of having the national destiny in its

own hands. The change in Britain's relative position may not have been fully appreciated until World War II, but in 1940 even the magnificent stand against Hitler could not conceal Britain's inability to protect its far-flung interests without the aid of a stronger power.

After World War II, and partly as its consequence, Britain appeared distinctly less imposing than either of the superpowers, the Soviet Union and the United States. Security against Soviet domination of the Continent required American help. Accordingly, the cornerstone of Britain's postwar European policy was to obtain an American commitment, of a sort denied before World War II, to defend Western Europe and by this means to deter aggression. Thus the act of securing American involvement in the North Atlantic Treaty Organization (NATO) was considered a prime diplomatic success. As a leading British diplomatic historian wrote of the treaty, "It is indeed in one sense the culmination of British policy during the last half century."[33] Britain had at last, through an outside ally, succeeded in righting the European balance of power. From this viewpoint, British participation in the military arrangements of the Western European Union, though a sharp departure from British policy, became decidedly subordinate to membership with America in NATO.

The North Atlantic Treaty Organization has continued to be Britain's principal instrument of military security. There has been no tendency to follow France's more nationalistic policy, developed by de Gaulle, of withdrawing from NATO commitments and specifically rejecting Ameri-

[33] Charles Webster, in *United Kingdom Policy*, ed. Charles Webster (London: Royal Institute of International Affairs, 1950), p. 26.

can predominance within the alliance. Even outside Europe, and so apart from NATO itself, British security policy has ordinarily been pursued in conjunction with American power rather than independently. The abortive Suez expedition of 1956 was a striking exception, since it was actually at odds with the announced policy of the United States. Otherwise, even distinctively British actions, as in Malaysia, have been consonant with American policy, and so, for the most part, have been the campaigns to preserve order in remaining British dependencies. Yet there have been general strains in Britain's security relations with the United States. Some derive from the relative novelty of Britain's junior-partner status in an alliance. The inherent difficulty of such status has been exacerbated by a persisting economic dependence on the United States. Needing American aid for general as well as for military purposes has at times caused Britain to seem, or perhaps just to feel, more a satellite than a partner of any kind. Certainly Britain has sought to avoid such an appearance; the best-known instance of this was Britain's long-standing policy of recognizing Communist China despite the United States' refusal to do so. Less plain but probably more significant has been the fairly steady British effort to stand apart, privately if not officially, from any large-scale involvement in apparently aggressive American military policies in Asia. Britain's objective has always been to concentrate military efforts in Europe and closely related areas. Britain has not wanted either itself or the United States to be distracted from the task of European defense, which remained primary even when in the late 1950s and 1960s it began to appear less urgent as the Soviet military threat became less ominous.

Heavy dependence on American power has not made for an inexpensive British security policy. Partly this is a matter of Britain wanting some independent force of its own, so as to avoid complete dependence; partly it is a matter of doing enough within the alliance to encourage the continued American commitment and to try, on these terms, to influence American policy. In other words, maintaining the "special relationship" with the United States as well as remaining a distinctively British power has meant substantial military expenditures. As late as the mid-1960s, Britain was calculated to be spending more proportionately on defense than any other nation of comparable size.[34] Expenditures included overseas military bases east of Suez as well as in the Mediterranean, large contributions of armed forces to NATO in Western Europe, and nuclear weapon development on a partially independent basis. There is no question that these expenditures have strained British resources. In fact, the strain has been so great that the bases east of Suez have been scheduled for early abandonment, or at most token maintenance. Also, the nuclear development has had to be pooled, in effect, with American deterrent capacity after it became apparent that Britain could not afford its own delivery system even though it had its own nuclear bombs. American missiles had to be obtained if Britain was to have a deliverable nuclear weapon capacity. In other ways as well, British military efforts, while still large in relation to limited national resources, continue to be gradually reduced. The navy has ceased to be a really large force in any comparative sense, and the air force, it was finally decided in the late 1960s, would not be modernized through the purchase of the latest American aircraft. Conventional

[34] Waltz, *Foreign Policy,* p. 179.

ground troops have been cut back to the point where there is no substantial home reserve ready for military action. Conscription, ended in 1960, has not been necessary given the decisions to limit total military force levels in accord with financial necessities. As of 1970, Britain's only continuing major commitment was its contribution to NATO, especially in the form of troops stationed in West Germany; and there is even increasing British concern about the expensiveness of this contribution. Reducing it, or persuading Germany to pay for more of it, must be considered at least a possibility in the near future; but it is significant that it remained substantial after Britain decided drastically to reduce, almost to eliminate, its capacity for major overseas military action. Thus the current emphasis of security policy is plainly on home or close-to-home defense, so far as conventional British forces are concerned, and on American capacity, nuclear or otherwise, in the larger world arena. This latter reliance, it is well to add, has involved Britain as a base for American bombers, as a launching site for intermediate-range ballistic missiles, and as a supplier of harbors for missile-carrying submarines. Admittedly, these involvements lessen in importance with the development of intercontinental missiles, but some remain as visible signs of the significance of the alliance.

A point that remains to be discussed is British membership in the United Nations. As one of the founding Big Five, Britain is a permanent member of the Security Council and a prominent participant in U.N. affairs generally. Except in the Suez altercation and on certain other less dramatic residual imperial issues, Britain has tended to join in majority decisions of the organization. However, it has never been official British policy to rely primarily on the United Nations as the agency for securing Britain against aggression. Although many Englishmen, particularly liberals and Labour party members, display a considerable emotional attachment to U.N. ideals, British policy makers have understandably found alliances such as NATO sturdier shields than the U.N. Charter. Britain has been anxious primarily to maintain the United Nations as a gathering place for all nations, including communist nations, so that opportunities for discussion, negotiation, and compromise are readily available.

SUMMARY

British foreign policy during most of the past quarter-century can be summarized as an attempt to meet immense responsibilities with limited resources; it can also be summarized as a fairly steady reduction of those responsibilities in accord with a national realization of a reduced capacity for exercising world power or leadership. Perhaps future historians will be able to add that this process coincided with the eventual if reluctant British acceptance of a more completely European identification marked by admission to the EEC on European terms. Now, however, the evidently forthcoming admission to EEC has an uncertain meaning. Its consequence might be less that of europeanizing Britain, in anything but an economic sense, and more that of turning the EEC as a whole into an outward-looking world force. There are Englishmen who thus perceive the EEC as providing a means for Britain once more to play a major international role, substituting leadership of an integrated Europe for the now-unpromising leadership of the Commonwealth. Blocking the realization of this vision are not only the strength and determination of the Continental nations,

France and West Germany in particular, but also the unwillingness of Britain, in present circumstances, to reduce significantly its ties to the United States. These ties, while manifested in terms of economic assistance and military security, rest heavily on the evidently durable foundations of common language, culture, political institutions, and ideology. So significant have the foundations seemed that they helped to disqualify Britain, in de Gaulle's eyes, for membership in a European community that was to be developed apart from American influence. In this perspective, even without de Gaulle himself, continental Europeans might still regard British leadership as potentially that of an American agent within the EEC.

No matter how Britain functions as a member of EEC, there is the drastic alternative course of discontinuing altogether the exercise of international power. Militarily, this would probably mean neutralism after the model of Switzerland or Sweden, and no responsibility for helping to defend any overseas territory or even the rest of Western Europe against Soviet, Chinese, or any other nation's aggression. The American alliance, in or out of NATO, would thus be put aside, as would any exclusively Western European military organization and the remaining Commonwealth defense arrangements. For a major world trading nation long accustomed to international political involvements, this alternative appears to be so drastic as to be virtually out of the question in the foreseeable future. The American alliance may not be immutable, given the difficulties facing the United States; but Britain nevertheless seems likely to cling to it, even though it may contribute somewhat less than before, as long as the world contains other major powers believed to threaten British interests. Neutralism appears to carry greater

risks at least as long as "British interests" are broadly defined so as to include the protection of those European and overseas areas with which the security of the island home has traditionally been identified. Only a really new and very different generation of Englishmen is at all likely to think just of "little England."

SELECTED BIBLIOGRAPHY

CAMPS, MIRIAM. *Britain and the European Community, 1955–1963.* Princeton: Princeton University Press, 1964.

LIEBER, ROBERT J. *British Politics and European Unity.* Berkeley: University of California Press, 1970.

MANSERGH, NICHOLAS. *The Commonwealth Experience.* New York: Praeger, 1969.

MILLER, J. D. B. *The Commonwealth in the World.* Cambridge: Harvard University Press, 1965.

MULLEY, F. W. *The Politics of Western Defence.* London: Thames and Hudson, 1962.

NEUSTADT, RICHARD. *Alliance Politics.* New York: Columbia University Press, 1970.

NORTHEDGE, F. S. *British Foreign Policy.* New York: Praeger, 1962.

SNYDER, WILLIAM P. *The Politics of British Defense Policy.* Columbus: Ohio State University Press, 1964.

STRANG, LORD. *The Foreign Office.* New York: Oxford University Press, 1955.

THORNTON, A. P. *The Imperial Idea and Its Enemies.* London: Macmillan & Co., 1959.

VITAL, DAVID. *The Making of British Foreign Policy.* New York: Praeger, 1968.

WALTZ, KENNETH. *Foreign Policy and Democratic Politics.* Boston: Little, Brown, 1967.

WARD, A. W., and GOOCH, G. P., eds. *The Cambridge History of British Foreign Policy, 1783–1919.* London: Cambridge University Press, 1922–23.

YOUNGER, KENNETH. *Changing Perspectives in British Foreign Policy.* London: Oxford University Press, 1964.

Chapter Three

FRENCH FOREIGN POLICY

ROY C. MACRIDIS

The dilemma facing France at the end of World War II may be stated in rather simple terms: France, one of the great powers in the world, found her position drastically weakened. But the aspirations of greatness and rank have persisted. These aspirations were expressed succinctly by the architect of France's post-World War II policy, General de Gaulle. "I intended," he wrote in his *Memoirs,* referring to the period immediately after the defeat of Germany,

to assure France primacy in Western Europe by preventing the rise of a new Reich that might again threaten its safety; to cooperate with the East and West and, if need be, contract the necessary alliances on one side or another without ever accepting any kind of dependency; to transform the French Union into a free association in order to avoid the as yet unspecified dangers of upheaval; to persuade the states along the Rhine, the Alps and the Pyrenees to form a political, economic and strategic bloc; to establish this organization as one of the three world powers and, should it become necessary, as the arbiter between the Soviet and the Anglo-Saxon camps.[1]

This was an ambitious scheme, and, as he admitted, the means available to his country "were poor indeed." But it was a goal widely shared by the majority of the French elites.

In 1944, after the liberation of Paris, with the return of General de Gaulle and the establishment of his provisional government on the French territory, France and her overseas possessions were in a state of dependency. Drained of

[1] *War Memoirs,* vol. 3, *Salvation* (New York: Simon & Schuster, 1960), p. 204.

manpower, with her economy seriously undermined after four years of occupation, facing urgent problems of social and economic reconstruction at home and powerful centrifugal forces in the empire, the power and even the political will to fashion the instruments that would lead to an independent course of action were lacking. France was dependent upon Britain and, primarily of course, upon the United States. In terms of Walter Lippmann's axiom that commitments in foreign policy must be commensurate with strength, it was very clear that there were few commitments that France could undertake and carry out successfully without Anglo-American support. France's liberty of action, therefore, was limited. Her aspiration to remain a top-rank power seemed to be at variance with her capabilities.

Thus the dilemma confronting France's post-World War II governments and her political elites was either to accept the situation as it developed after World War II or to continue to seek "greatness" and "rank" without the physical, military, and economic resources to implement it. It called for difficult political decisions and choices; it demanded the rapid reconsideration of some of the traditional French foreign policy patterns; and, above all, it required a meaningful debate among political leaders and elites about alternatives and choices. Neither the political system under the Fourth Republic nor the political parties and the press managed to provide for such a debate. There was no "great debate" to redefine the French position and status in the world. Strangely enough, it was only after the return of General de Gaulle to power in 1958 and the establishment of the Fifth Republic that foreign policy themes began to be stated with enough clarity to invite debate, to elicit support or to provoke criticism. The Fifth Republic under de Gaulle was a decade during which options were examined, choices made, and instruments for their realization fashioned. It was the decade during which many of the goals felt and shared by many of the French elites were given shape, form, and direction. Curiously enough, the leadership of the Fifth Republic (from 1958 to the present) does not differ fundamentally in its foreign policy aspirations from that of the Fourth Republic (1946–58). The difference lies primarily in its clearcut and authoritative—if not authoritarian—formulation of goals and in the stability of its political leadership to implement them.

In this chapter we shall examine the background factors that have shaped France's foreign policy—her geographic position, her economic and social development, her ideology and culture, the persistent national interests pursued in the past, and the foreign policy objectives, as they were reformulated in the years of the Fourth Republic and, more particularly, as they have been in the years of the Fifth Republic under de Gaulle and (since June, 1969) under the new president, Georges Pompidou.

BACKGROUND FACTORS

A number of interacting factors constitute the setting in which foreign policy operates. Some of these factors are objective ones; they can be easily measured and compared. Others are subjective, and constitute a community's image of itself in the world. Among the objective factors, the most important are the nation's economic strength, its geographic position, its military potential, its technological skill, its culture, and the diffusion of its culture in other parts of the world. The subjective factors are primarily ideological; they can be studied with reference to the various elites of the system and to the particular conception the elites have of their country's role in the world. Important among those elites is, of course, the political leadership.

Subjective and objective factors constantly interact to give to foreign policy a dynamic and ever-changing pattern; however, such interaction may be impeded for various reasons, so that reality—i.e., the objective factor—may be at variance with ideology—i.e., the subjective factor. As we have pointed out, this might be a tenable hypothesis for the study of French foreign policy in the twentieth century.

The Economic Foundations

The most significant feature of the French economy was, until the last two decades, its relative decline. While industrialization went forward rapidly throughout the nineteenth century in England, Germany, Japan, and the United States, and also in the Soviet Union in the twentieth century, France's economy advanced at a snail's pace.

Yet France began with a marked head start over *all* other countries. During the Napoleonic era and until the middle of the nineteenth century, France was one of the best economically developed nations of the world. From then on, despite a wealth of resources and skilled labor, her economy declined in comparison with almost all the other countries of Western Europe. Her total national income, between 1870 to 1940, rose by about 80 percent; that of Germany increased five times; that of Great Britain, three-and-a-half times. In the years between the two world wars (1918–1940), investment declined to a point below zero—that is, France was living on her capital, using her factories and equipment without replac-

ing them in full. She was going through a period of disinvestment. The destruction wrought by World War II, estimated at approximately $50 billion, was an additional setback. With her industrial equipment destroyed or dilapidated and her transportation network paralyzed, France's economy was in a state of collapse.

There were many long-range factors associated with this stagnation—notably, the very slow growth of population, a backward agriculture, the protectionist policies of the state and, finally, the attitudes of the business groups.

Population. In 1800 France had the largest population of any country in Europe and the Americas, excepting only that of Russia. The Napoleonic armies were recruited from, and supported by, 26 million French men and women, when England had only 11 million inhabitants, the United States 5.5 million, and the German states, including Austria, about 23 million. France maintained this advantage until about 1860, when she had about 38 million. From then on, her population remained virtually static. In 1940, for instance, it was almost exactly 40 million, while that of the United States was close to 150 million, that of Great Britain was 50 million, and that of Germany (West and East, but without Austria) was 65 million. In the years between 1930 and 1940, the French population actually declined—that is, there was an excess of deaths over births. Two wars had taken a heavy toll, also, of the young and active part of the population. The percentage of the aged (over sixty-five) became disproportionately heavy, thereby contributing to economic stagnation.

Agriculture. France's agricultural problem developed in the period between 1870 and 1940. The proportion of farmers—about 35 to 40 percent of the active population—was the largest in Western Europe excepting Italy and Spain, but their productivity was one of the lowest in Europe. There were a great number of small, marginal farms, divided and subdivided into parcels to which new techniques and mechanization could not be applied. Until 1940 France used less fertilizer than any other Western European country, and the use of tractors remained insignificant.

Protectionism. That much of the population remained on relatively unproductive farms was due partly to the tariff policies of the state. Agricultural interests formed powerful lobbies which demanded and got a high protectionist tariff, sheltering French business and agriculture from foreign competition. They also received special subsidies and guaranteed price supports. Those profiting from these measures were not only wheat producers and growers of beets (from which large quantities of alcohol are distilled), but wine growers, fruit growers, and dairy interests as well. High tariffs also sheltered manufacturing concerns. The state was perpetuating and supporting a situation that consecrated the weakness of the economic system.

Business Attitudes. Industrialists and business groups did not show, in France, the initiative and willingness to take risks that we generally associate with capitalism. Many business enterprises were family affairs. Production remained geared to a limited demand instead of seeking new markets. Profits were often saved instead of being reinvested.

A particularly vulnerable part of the economy was in the distribution sector. Large chain stores were the exception, and small merchants and shopkeepers eked out a living through a limited volume of trade. As a result, efficient techniques to reduce costs and bring prices down were not developed. Retail prices kept far ahead of wholesale prices, with the many middlemen who handled the product making small profits. This unduly inflated the price the consumer paid. The middlemen in France, like the agricultural population, formed an oversized and relatively unproductive sector of the economy. They, too, organized in strong pressure groups and demanded subsidies and protection.

The end of World War II brought to light the weaknesses of the country and accentuated a number of them. The greater part of the foreign assets and investments of France had been wiped out, millions had lost their lives or health as a result of the war and the enemy occupation, and the industrial equipment of the country had reached obsolescence. The tasks ahead were to stop inflation and put the currency back on a healthy basis; to rebuild the communication systems as well as the schools, factories, and homes; to improve the productive resources in order to bring production up to the prewar level and surpass it; to rationalize and reorganize the agriculture; and, above all, to catch up with the "world outside" and to build strength without which survival as a nation might well be impossible.

Geographic Position

France's geographic position had created contradictory interests and commitments. On the one hand, she has been a Continental power with frontiers that include, to the east, Belgium, Germany, Switzerland, and Italy, and, to the southwest, Spain; on the other hand, she has had a colonial empire with possessions throughout Asia and Africa and in the Pacific, Indian, and Atlantic oceans.

The French Empire had been developed and consolidated by the end of the nineteenth century. On the Continent, the Spanish frontier, and that facing Belgium and Switzerland, presented no problems. The threat came from Germany—a Germany that after 1870 had been unified and that after 1930, despite its defeat in 1918, confronted France once more with a population of some 65 million and an economic and industrial system more productive than her own. At the same time, the empire required everlasting vigilance against potential marauders, particularly England, and against nationalist independence movements. This required the maintenance of a strong army at home as well as a strong navy. The position of France, therefore, involved heavy economic sacrifices.

This situation accounted for the existence of two distinct groups within the French political leadership. One tended to favor a rapprochement with Germany. It was anti-British, since the traditional obstacle to French imperial ambitions and naval power had been Great Britain. The other tended to emphasize the Continental position of France, to plead for a strong army, and to underplay her imperial commitments. It tended to be pro-British and anti-German. Neither point of view could or did prevail. Germany was naturally in favor of encouraging France's imperial commitments, in exchange for a free hand in Europe—particularly in eastern Europe and in the Middle East, which ultimately would endanger France's position in Europe. England, on the other hand, was anxious to encourage France in her Continental policy, with the full realization that a strong French army would be a deterrent against Germany and hence would allow England to concentrate on its naval strength and the development of its own empire, ultimately at the expense of the inter-

ests of France in the world at large.

From whichever point of view one looks at the situation as it developed in the latter part of the nineteenth century, one cannot help but realize that the French predicament was a serious one. France, more than any other country of the world, had to assume the heavy burdens both of a Continental power and of an empire. The end of World War II and the subsequent developments indicate, as we shall see, that France stubbornly attempted to preserve both positions.

Cultural Diffusion

It would hardly be an exaggeration to say that France was, in the nineteenth century, the cultural center of the world. In politics, art, literature, and education, French thought radiated everywhere. The French Revolution had given to the cause of freedom a clearcut formulation which was carried to all parts of Europe by Napoleon's armies. The French Napoleonic Code was plagiarized by almost every Latin American and other European nation. The French language was the medium of communication in international conferences and the second language of the educated classes of the rest of the world. France's philosophers, intellectuals, and scientists pioneered the cause of human and scientific knowledge.

Innumerable cultural ties linked France with most other countries. Such links constituted, without any doubt, a capital that, like the *Marseillaise*, was just as important as ships and soldiers, just as important as the investment of the British merchants and storekeepers in the British Empire. But it was the kind of capital whose logic calls for continuous reinvestment. It was also the kind of capital that tends to pervert the lender. With the relative decline of the French economy in the twentieth century, other nations began to attract scientists and intellectuals. The use of the French language in diplomacy and in other aspects of international relations began to be challenged. The French political system itself showed signs of strain, as her colonial policy revealed obvious incompatibilities with the universal ethical postulates that the French Revolution promulgated. The colonial elite, who had studied in France and for whom French was a second language, chose to engage her in a dialogue in which the lessons they had learned became increasingly embarrassing for the teacher. But at the very moment the dialogue was engaged—particularly between the colonies and the metropolis —French cultural preeminence had become permanent and incontrovertible in the minds of the French; it became a myth, an *idée fixe*. French cultural supremacy was taken for granted. This produced innumerable reflexes which account for some of France's more recent actions: her prolonged reluctance to change her policy with regard to the empire; her extreme sensitivity to criticisms from abroad; a blind pride, considering her own system as superior to that of any other nation in the world; and finally a strong belief in the unique mission of France —to educate, to cultivate, and to humanize.

Persistent Patterns

A number of patterns underlie the French conception of foreign policy. In the nineteenth century they reflected France's strength, but they slowly crystallized into dogmas and myths that were ultimately separated from twentieth-century reality. It is, nonetheless, in terms of such myths that France's foreign policy was shaped—immediately after World War II—rather than in terms of the new factors that developed partly as a result of the war and partly as the result of a number of social, economic, and ideological forces that stirred the world.

The basic objectives of foreign policy remained (a) the continuation of France's imperial position, and (b) Continental strength. The first meant, as we have seen, the maintenance of the far-flung empire with all the financial difficulties and obligations it entailed. Not for a moment was the notion of federalism and self-government for its members seriously entertained. Maintenance of the empire was conceived as a part of France's mission and as a continuous challenge to French culture and influence. The resurrection of France as a Continental power was also an automatic reflex; no political leader doubted it. The end of World War II by the defeat of Germany was, in a sense, their revenge for the German occupation of France. Victory, it was thought, simply reestablished the prewar balance. To implement France's Continental position, the same alliances with the West and with the East were contemplated—all of them directed against a Germany that lay prostrate and divided. The fact that the Soviet Union had gained a foothold in the heart of Europe did not alter the traditional French reflexes; Germany was the enemy of France. A weak Germany and a Franco-Russian alliance remained the conditions for French security. When General de Gaulle visited Moscow and signed the Franco-Russian treaty in December, 1944, he was preserving French security according to the best traditions of the nineteenth century. Underlying his actions was the belief that France, with her empire, and secure from the resurrection of German might and German attack, was once more a great power ready to fill the power vacuum that lay in the heart of Europe; moreover she was poised to throw her weight on one or the other side of the scale of the conflict for power that emerged between the Soviet Union and the United States.

THE SUBSTANCE OF FOREIGN POLICY: TRENDS AND PROBLEMS

France has followed two basic foreign policy objectives ever since the eighteenth century. The first is the policy of *natural frontiers* and the second is the policy of what might be called *European status quo*, or *balance of power* in Europe.

The natural frontiers of France have been considered to be on the Rhine and on the Alps. They include Belgium, Holland, Luxembourg, and the German territories that lie west of the Rhine. This was interpreted to mean that France's strategic and military interests extended to those areas, and that no other power could set foot there without jeopardizing her interests. The continuity of this policy is remarkable. Danton stated in 1793, "The frontiers [of the Republic] are marked *by nature*. . . . They are the Rhine, the Alps and the Pyrenean mountains." Clemenceau affirmed in 1919, "The move towards the Rhine was the tradition of our ancestors. . . . It was the tradition to create a frontier, a *true* frontier marking the French territory." General de Gaulle, in 1944, stated, in the name of a weak and defeated country, "The Rhine *is* French security and I think the security of the whole world. But France is the principal interested party. . . . She wishes to be solidly established from one end to the other of her *natural frontier*."[2]

[2] See the excellent article by J. Raoul Girardet, "L'influence de la tradition sur la politique étrangère de la France," in *La Politique étrangère et ses Fondements*, ed. Jean-Baptiste Duroselle (Paris: Librairie Armand Colin, 1954), pp. 143–63.

The policy of status quo, on the other hand, was based upon three assumptions that became in turn three basic objectives of policy:

1. France was not interested in any European conquest.
2. No single power should gain preponderant strength in Europe. The status quo—consisting of a number of competing political units, small if possible—should be maintained so as to give France the role of an arbitrator.
3. France became the protector of small states throughout Europe, since it was owing to the existence of many of them that she could effectively play the role of arbitrator and maintain her position of supremacy in Europe. As Vergennes wrote, in 1777, "France, placed in the center of Europe, has the right to influence all the great developments. Her King, like a supreme judge, can consider his throne as a tribunal established by Providence to guarantee the respect for the rights and properties of the sovereigns."[3]

This providential role of France has been restated many times.

In 1919 the two policies converged. The theory of natural frontiers led to the demilitarization of the Rhine area, to the control of the Saar, and to the military hegemony of France over the Low Countries. The policy of the status quo, as redefined, led to an effort to divide Germany, to the breakup of the Austro-Hungarian Empire, and to the establishment of a number of new nations all over eastern and south-eastern Europe, with which France established close political, economic, and military ties. Of course, a number of other factors entered into the picture. The Wilsonian idea of self-determination encouraged the establishment of small states which France was only too pleased to take

[3] Quoted in J. Raoul Girardet, Ibid.

under her protection, while the creation of a number of small states east of Germany formed a *cordon sanitaire* against the Soviet Union and, at the same time, prevented Germany from moving east.

By 1919, then, the two traditional French foreign policies had found a happy reconciliation. Despite a number of difficulties (the dismemberment of Germany did not take place, for instance), the general settlement gave France both a position of preponderance in Europe and a great degree of security and safety. If only the world had stood still, France might have maintained that position.

The policy of a European balance of power, plus security, also became France's worldwide policy. The empire had been consolidated by the end of the nineteenth century and World War I. The imperial vocation, and with it the world vocation of France, continued side by side with its Continental vocation in the years after World War II—years that we intend to discuss now. We shall divide our discussion into three parts: France and Europe; France and the empire; and France and the world.

France and Europe:
The Insoluble Dilemma

The immediate reaction of France after liberation in December, 1944, was to attempt to reestablish her traditional position of security in Europe and of independence as a world power. From 1944 until mid-1947, a policy was followed that for all practical purposes was identical to that of 1919. France proposed the following:

1. The dismemberment of Germany and prolonged occupation of the country
2. Heavy reparations and tight control of German industrial output
3. The reestablishment of French control

in the area west of the Rhine by the detachment of these territories from Germany
4. A prolonged occupation, if not annexation, of the Saar
5. The independence of the small nations of Europe
6. An alliance with the Soviet Union directed against a threat to French security from Germany
7. An alliance with Great Britain

Under the government of General de Gaulle, this policy was pursued with great tenacity. After the liberation, a Treaty of Mutual Assistance was signed with the Soviet Union. The two countries agreed to take "all the necessary measures in order to eliminate any new menace coming from Germany and to take the initiative to make any new effort of aggression on her part impossible" (Article 3). Immediately after the signing of the pact, General de Gaulle declared, "Because two of the principal powers of the world—free from any conflict of interest in any part of the world—decide to unite under specific conditions, it does not mean that either the one or the other envisages to organize the world and even its security without the help of other nations."[4]

But one might ask whether the haste with which General de Gaulle went to Moscow to sign the treaty was not motivated by considerations other than the security of France from an attack by Germany, which lay literally prostrate before the Anglo-American and Soviet armies. By the treaty with Moscow, France was indeed serving notice to her former British and American allies that she intended to pursue an independent policy.

Throughout 1946, every effort was made by France to gain the support of *either* the Soviet Union *or* the

[4] Quoted in *Année politique, 1944–45*, p. 89.

United States (along with Great Britain) in the implementation of her German policy. Neither of her two allies, however, responded favorably, since they both hoped to see, ultimately, an economically and politically unified Germany *on their side,* something that would have meant the end of French aspirations for European security and leadership. When Soviet Foreign Minister Molotov declared himself, in July, 1946, in favor of a politically unified Germany, *Année politique* commented, "There was reason for France, which could count on the support of her ally in the East *against* the Anglo-Americans, to be disappointed."[5]

There were more disappointments to come. The Soviet Union feared that France would ultimately become part of the Anglo-American camp, and refused to support her aspirations to see the Ruhr and the Rhine provinces detached from Germany. The Soviet-American conflict in Europe revolved around the control of the whole of Germany, and the prize seemed far more important than France. By the time that it became quite clear that the conflict could not be resolved except by a partition of Germany, France discovered that her policy had failed; she had failed to gain the support of either the Soviet Union or the United States. She was faced with the dilemma of either accepting the division of Germany into two zones, a division that could confront France with a highly industrialized and powerful West Germany, or of following an independent policy by maintaining her occupation of a small part of West Germany and the Saar.

The Cold War and the Development of Western Alliances. The Cold War, whose origin can be traced to Yalta

and Potsdam, erupted in the middle of 1947. Conferences in Moscow and London had failed to produce any kind of agreement on the problem of Germany. The lines were being drawn, and the division of Germany into two zones—Soviet and British-American—became a certainty. The conflict implied the strengthening of both zones, and hence the development of a strong West German Republic supported by the United States and England.

France managed to maintain control over the Saar, but failed in all her other claims. After June, 1947, the whole of Western Europe and Great Britain received massive American aid to develop their economy. In 1948 the Brussels Pact brought together the Benelux countries, France, and Great Britain. It provided for a permanent consultative council and negotiations to promote economic development of the countries concerned, and included a military clause calling for immediate consultations to take common action against a German attack or aggression and to cope with a situation that constituted a menace to peace, no matter where it occurred or from where it came. In 1949 the creation of a large military umbrella was logically called for. Not only the Brussels signatories, but also all the Western countries, including ultimately Greece and Turkey, participated. The United States became a permanent part of this alliance that still continues as the North Atlantic Treaty Organization (NATO). Article 5 stipulates that an attack against any one of the signatories, either in Europe or in North America, would be considered an attack against all. It further provides (in Article 9) for a permanent deliberative organization and the establishment of a common military command. West Germany was originally excluded from NATO.

These developments determined

5 *Année politique, 1946,* p. 400.

France's position. She became a member of NATO and of the various Western alliances, under the overall leadership and military direction of the United States. Such an alliance underwrote her security and, in general terms, the integrity of her empire. The exclusion of Germany continued to give her a strategic position in Western Europe, as well as the semblance, if not the reality, of national power and independence. But the question of Germany's future had been only postponed. A military Western alliance without Germany hardly represented a solution of the problems of military defense. Furthermore, as the struggle between the East and the West not only continued but was intensified with the Korean War, the prize of Germany became more important for the two major opponents. For the United States, the rearmament of West Germany seemed, rightly or wrongly, the logical step for the construction of a strong defensive wall in the West against a potential Soviet attack.

For France, however, such a rearmament was a threat. German economic development and the revival of German strength across the Rhine evoked the traditional reflexes. Yet by 1950 or 1951, there could be no imminent danger to France's security. The military alliance with Great Britain, the Brussels Pact, NATO, and the presence of American and British forces on the continent constituted adequate guarantees. Only France's notions of independence and European supremacy were really at stake. A Western alliance in which an armed West Germany participated might, to the French mind, come under the domination of the strongest country—West Germany.

The European Defense Community and Its Alternatives. The defensive arrangements of the Western world and the Atlantic powers did not include West Germany. Yet West German resources were considered indispensable by the United States. The problem, therefore, was to integrate West Germany's power within the frame of a Western alliance, without alienating France and the signatories of the Brussels Pact.

It was, strangely enough, the French who came forth with the answer: the creation of a West European army, the European Defense Community (EDC), involving a genuine integration of national forces and a unified —and, if possible, a supranational— command. The United States became convinced that such a policy was preferable to the rearming of West Germany within NATO. There were many tangible indications of a widespread movement in favor of European cooperation. The Council of Europe, representing the Western European nations, had been established in 1949; the Organization of European Economic Cooperation was a European body studying the resources and needs of Western Europe and attempting to liberalize trade relations. The Western European Payments Union was functioning in order to control and regulate the deficits in the balance of payments of various European countries. Above all, the European Coal and Steel Community, initiated by France, had become a reality that involved a supranational authority with power to make decisions on matters of investment, production, and transportation of coal and steel among the six signatory powers—West Germany, France, the Benelux countries, and Italy. The establishment of a European army, ambitious though it appeared to be, was welcome in the context of these moves toward European cooperation and integration.

No sooner had the European Defense Community been announced and formulated, however, than it provoked a storm of protest in France. The political parties were actively either for or against it. Extreme right-wing and extreme left-wing parties joined hands against the treaty, which was defended by a sharply divided center. To French public opinion, the most controversial part of the treaty was the envisaged German rearmament. A majority of the members of the National Assembly considered German rearmament, even within the EDC, a direct challenge to French sovereignty, clearly spelling the end of France's aspirations to remain a leading European nation. The memory of Nazi Germany was too fresh in the minds of many; the possibility that West Germany, once rearmed, might attempt to provoke a war with the Soviet Union in order to achieve its unification, and thus drag the whole of Europe into a war, was pointed out; the assumption by Germany of a predominant role in Europe, at a time when France was heavily engaged in protecting her empire, was also mentioned. Each party and each parliamentary group saw specific reasons for refusing to accept the treaty, while its proponents defended it also for different reasons. Since there was no genuine majority for or against the treaty,[6] it was on a procedural motion that, in August, 1954, the EDC was rejected by the French National Assembly. In the meantime, all the other prospective members had honored the signature of their governments. Only the French assembly used its constitutional prerogatives and refused to ratify the treaty. The rejection climaxed four years of equivocation. It was only in December, 1954, that the National Assembly, six months after defeating the EDC for fear of German rearmament, allowed Germany to become a member of NATO and to rearm herself within the context of the NATO alliance.

A Third Force? While the EDC was being debated and criticisms against it multiplied, the movement in favor of neutralism assumed great importance. It is hard to define or describe it briefly without doing injustice to its manifold aspects and characteristics. Essentially, it was a movement that answered the profound hopes of the French people that, in case of war, France would be allowed to remain out of it. Some 70 percent of the French people answering a poll conducted by the French Institute of Public Opinion expressed this hope in 1951, when Cold War tensions were at their highest. At the same time, neutralism was a movement that tended to reassert the traditional French claims to independence and a balance of power. Since the world was divided into two camps, France alone, or France at the head of Western Europe, could afford to say, "A plague on both your houses!" and, if need be, to arbitrate between them.

The neutralist position was advanced by the Communist party and by some left-wing intellectuals for other motives. Essentially, they wanted to weaken American dominance over Western Europe. Many of the left-wing intellectuals were motivated by subtler considerations: the independence of the French nation to continue to develop her own way of life;

---

[6] The division of the political system in the French Parliament and in the various coalition cabinets reflected very closely the division of public opinion: in July, 1954, 36 percent of those asked were "for" or "rather for" the EDC, 31 percent were "against" or "rather against," and 33 percent did not answer.

the rejection of the realities of a polarized world; an emphasis upon France's cultural and intellectual vocation. For some it was mere anti-Americanism and a declaration of France's independence from American tutelage; for others it was the belief that France had more to gain than to lose from a pro-Soviet orientation; for many others it was a constructive step toward the building of a solid Western alliance with Great Britain as a partner, which would develop enough strength to play the role of "third force" that France could not play alone. Neutralism and nationalism were often linked.

But the German problem was again an obstacle. A third force in Europe, without West Germany and without wholehearted British commitment, could not be strong enough. A third force with Germany, however, was one in which Germany, rather than France, might assume a preponderant role. The real tragedy was that France, weak alone, found that any form of European integration and alliance underscored her weakness and subordination—to the United States, to the Soviet Union, or possibly to England or West Germany. By 1954, therefore, France found herself, after interminable zigzags, equivocations, and soul-searching, in the Atlantic camp to which a fifteenth member had been added—West Germany.

France and the Empire

France emerged from World War I as one of the three big powers. Russia lay in the throes of revolution; the United States still was unwilling to assume international responsibilities that involved continuous commitments abroad; and elsewhere in the world, the stirrings of nationalist awakening were making themselves

heard, but not sufficiently to cause concern to the colonial powers, of which England and France were the most important.

The French Empire extended over every continent of the world. Its administration was a vestige of the Napoleonic conceptions of a highly centralized bureaucratic system—an administration in which Paris, through the colonial officials, made the ultimate decisions and legislated for the whole empire. Its cementing ideology was that of "assimilation"— the notion that ultimately every inhabitant would become a French citizen and be represented in the French Parliament—a notion at marked variance with the Anglo-Saxon conception, according to which political and cultural evolution of the colonial peoples would ultimately bring about political autonomy and self-government.

In 1944 the basic charter of colonial policy had been drafted at the Brazzaville Conference. There it was decided that "the purpose of the civilizing work accomplished by France in the colonies excludes any idea of autonomy, any possibility of an evolution outside of the French Empire. The establishment, even in the remote future, of 'self-government' in the colonies must not be considered."[7] In 1945, when a trusteeship committee was appointed within the United Nations, the French made it quite clear that they would not accept its jurisdiction. The empire was French, and hence a matter of domestic policy.

In almost every case, the French insisted upon assimilation and maintenance of French sovereignty. In 1945 France refused to withdraw her army from Syria and Lebanon. Within a year she had to give in. In 1947 she

[7] *Année politique, 1944–45.*

refused to enter into negotiations with Ho Chi-minh, and engaged in a war that lasted until 1954. The war in Indochina cost France more than a billion dollars a year, retarded her internal investment policy, and paralyzed her alternate plans for an economic and social reconstruction of the North African territories. It was in part responsible for France's inability to keep pace with German economic reconstruction in Western Europe.

But the Indochinese war brought other problems to a head. In Algeria, Tunis, and Morocco, the independence movements were gaining strength. These movements, however, envisaged continued cooperation with France. In every case, the French political leaders and representatives and the various military leaders in command of the French troops reiterated the philosophy of the French vocation. Time after time, the legitimate interests of France were evoked. Time after time, the representatives of the French government and army intervened. By 1956, both Morocco and Tunisia became independent. The refusal to grant self-government left only one alternative: secession.

This situation was most evident in Algeria, where there was a very strong movement in favor of self-government after the liberation of France in 1944. It gained strength after the independence of Morocco and Tunisia. Yet there were many opportunities to cope with the Algerian situation, and progress was made in 1947, when special legislation granting considerable political autonomy to Algeria was passed, although never implemented. Claims of French sovereignty in Algeria and assertions that France "intends to stay there," made in the last years of the Fourth Republic, sounded very similar to the assertions made about Syria, Lebanon, Indochina, Tunis, and Morocco.

France and the World: The Vocation of Greatness

The explanation of the predicament of the French Empire lies in the postwar vocation of France to maintain her top-rank power status in the world. The French Empire, as a French commentator wrote in an excellent but highly optimistic analysis of the prospects of the French Union, "corresponds without any doubt to the profound interest of France. . . . France cannot aspire to play an important international role except in terms of her ability to represent a powerful association of peoples."[8]

The fate of France was invariably presented in terms of the destiny of the nation in the world. The answer was given in terms of traditional historical reflexes—France's military power, her cultural superiority, her civilizing mission, and her empire.

Over and above these misconceptions, the assessment of national strength was also couched in terms of nineteenth-century imperial perspectives. The equation, however, was no longer valid in view of the development of colonial nationalism. The British saw in it something the French refused to realize: that to maintain an empire by force is far more expensive and far more debilitating to a nation's strength than to abandon it.

THE LEGACY OF THE FOURTH REPUBLIC (1946–1958)

ELEMENTS OF STABILITY

Speaking on October 28, 1966, in his fourteenth press conference, General de Gaulle stated with remarkable suc-

8 "L'union française: Bilan politique de l'année 1947," in *Année politique, 1947*, p. 275.

cinctness the objectives of French foreign policy in terms that apply to the Fourth Republic as well:

In the world as it is people sometimes feign surprise over the so-called changes and detours of France's action. And there are even those who have spoken of contradictions or Machiavellism. Well, I believe that while the circumstances are changing around us, in truth there is nothing more constant than France's policy. For this policy, throughout the extremely varied vicissitudes of our times and our world—this policy's essential goal is that France be and remain an independent nation.

Despite the divisions of the political system under the Fourth Republic and the fact that they often spilled over into the area of foreign policy, there was continuity in the pursuit of basic objectives of foreign policy. The political elite, the political parties (with the exception of the Communists), and the public remained steadfast in their attachment to the traditional interests of France, in spite of rapidly changing world conditions. Discontinuities were occasionally introduced, but only in the form of decisive choices. This was the case in 1954–55, with the termination of the Indochinese war, the granting of autonomy and later independence to Morocco and Tunisia, and the Paris agreements that consecrated West German sovereignty and allowed for German participation in NATO. The political system remained, by and large, committed to the following objectives: (a) the maintenance of an Atlantic and world position that implied a weak Germany and a militarily independent France; (b) a European rapprochement in terms of which France could gain strength at the head of Western Europe; and (c) the maintenance of a top-rank world position.

What has been called *la politique du grandeur* ("the policy of great-

ness"), according to which France's vocation is that of a world power and therefore a partner in the development of world strategy or—under propitious conditions—an independent force, was ever present. General de Gaulle's policy, after he returned to power on June 1, 1958, was a faithful expression of the broad objectives pursued by the political leadership of the Fourth Republic.

The Empire: The Foundation of a New Policy. It was only in the last two years of the republic, between 1956 and 1958, that France's leadership decided to move ahead of the irresistible trend of colonial emancipation rather than attempt to oppose it. In 1956, the French Parliament began consideration of new legislation to put an end to the theory and practice of assimilation. A *loi-cadre* ("framework law") empowered the government to enact executive orders in order to give considerable autonomy to the African republics and Madagascar. They became semi-independent republics, with their own parliaments and responsible executives. France retained jurisdiction over important areas of policy making such as defense, foreign policy, trade, and education. But the first path toward gradual political emancipation had been made, and it proved to be irreversible.

Economic and Military Policy. The Fourth Republic also laid the groundwork of France's economic and military recovery. The Atomic Energy Commissariat, founded in 1945, continued in operation throughout the years when the cabinet was unstable, and it was endowed with adequate credits. The possession of an atom bomb in a world in which only three powers had developed nuclear weapons became associated, in the eyes of the French political leaders and public alike, with France's national independence and security. Throughout the latter years of the republic, all French governments favored the suspension of the fabrication of the bomb *and* the gradual destruction of nuclear weapons. Only if the latter condition were accepted would France have been willing to abandon her manufacture and testing of the bomb.

Although favoring the Atlantic alliance, the political leaders of the Fourth Republic never agreed to play a secondary role and acquiesce to American or British and American supremacy. They did not accept any genuine integration of military command within NATO and, alleging their colonial obligations, insisted on maintaining autonomy over their military forces. They remained reluctant to permit the United States to establish stockpiles of nuclear weapons or to construct launching sites on French soil. The same fear of integration of the military forces applied to a purely European army, as we have seen.

Thus, while accepting participation in an Atlantic and European military alliance, the French governments made sure that these alliances never took a form that undermined France's independence and freedom to use her own military forces at her own discretion. By the same token, they were unwilling to participate in any defense system with the British and the Americans unless France were given full and equal power on all global decisions and strategy.

Public Opinion[9]

Studies of opinion throughout the Fourth Republic indicate that there was a striking coincidence of the

9 I am indebted to the summary of public opinion trends, "La politique étrangère de la France et l'opinion publique, 1954–1957," *Sondages: Revue Française de l'opinion publique*, nos. 1 and 2 (1958).

action of the political leaders and public opinion. French attitudes toward the Cold War, the Soviet Union or the United States, the problem of French military independence and West Germany, and European cooperation show stability and continuity.

The Cold War. Generally, the attitude of the French with regard to the Cold War can be summed up as one of neutrality and considerable hostility toward both protagonists. One out of every ten Frenchmen polled believed that the United States was to be blamed, two out of ten put the blame on the Soviet Union, and four out of every ten on both. At the same time, the French public thought that neither the United States nor the Soviet Union was doing all it could to avert the Cold War. Fifty-two and 57 percent of those interrogated in 1957 believed that the United States and the Soviet Union, respectively, were not doing as much as possible. From 1952 until 1957, the public expressed itself as follows:

To which camp should France belong?

		The West	The East	Neither
Sept.,	1952	42%	4%	43%
Nov.,	1954	36	2	39
June,	1955	18	3	57
Aug.,	1955	23	4	51
Dec.,	1955	35	5	45
May,	1957	28	4	39
Dec.,	1957	21	3	51

If there were a war between the United States and the Soviet Union, to which camp should France belong?

		U.S.	USSR	Not take part
Sept.,	1952	36%	4%	45%
Nov.,	1954	22	2	45
June,	1955	19	3	58
Aug.,	1955	25	5	51
Sept.,	1957	15	3	62

Europe. While the French continued to fear West Germany and to be reluctant to see her rearm, there was a general resignation to Germany's participation in European cooperation schemes. From 1947 until December, 1957, French public opinion favored a European union. Fifty-five to 70 per cent were in favor, and those opposed never exceeded 21 percent. In only two polls, taken in 1955, did less than 50 percent favor a European union. Support for the European Common Market, for the Schuman Plan, and for the European atomic cooperation program was equally strong. The rearmament of West Germany, however, was considered, until 1954, to be a danger, and the consensus of opinion favored a demilitarized Germany. In 1955, 53 percent were against the participation of West Germany in the defense of Western Europe.

Atomic Weapons, NATO, and the United States. Although they still chose neutrality and condemned the manufacture and potential use of atomic weapons, the French, in December, 1957, favored "giving more attention to atomic weapons" for the defense of their country. Forty percent were in favor and 20 percent were opposed; 40 percent declined to answer.

In December, 1957, the French were also asked, "Under the present circumstances, how can France best assure her security?" Sixteen percent favored the maintenance of the existing alliances in Western Europe, within NATO and with the United States; 5 percent favored a military alliance limited to Western Europe only; 21 percent favored a general security system including the United States, Western Europe, and the Soviet Union; and 34 percent favored withdrawal *from all alliances* and the assumption of an independent and neutral posture.

In the same context, the general reaction of the French public with regard to NATO was one of relative indifference. Not more than 50 or 60 percent were prepared to answer on the basis of any knowledge of the organization. Of those answering, only a small percentage favored the organization and considered it important for the security of France. Such a reaction stemmed primarily from the realization that the United States was exerting too much influence on French foreign policy. Forty to 42 percent of the French interrogated between 1952 and December, 1956, thought that the United States had too much influence. In the same manner, more than 60 percent believed, in 1956 and 1957, that France was not treated by the United States as an equal in matters concerning the two countries. Some 27 to 40 percent believed that Americans and French had common interests, while some 25 percent believed that the interests of the two countries were different. More than 33 percent of those asked in December, 1956, believed that a European union would diminish American influence, and 35 percent of them believed that such a diminution of American influence would be "a good thing."

Thus, throughout the period of the Fourth Republic, the public, even if badly informed, reacted with a remarkable degree of unity in favor of neutrality and European cooperation, feared Germany, suspected NATO, and in general agreed that independence and security could be based only on national strength and freedom of action. Despite an underlying realization of France's reduced world status, the public continued to cling to the image of a strong and independent France. They deplored the reduction of French strength and accepted European unity as an instrument for the realization of national security vis-à-vis both the United States and the Soviet Union.

Foreign Service

An important factor in the continuity of the French foreign policy was the existence of a small but competent body of civil servants attached to the Ministry of Foreign Affairs. A hard core of some four thousand foreign-service officers constitute the administrative network of the foreign service; about a thousand are in Paris, and roughly three thousand are scattered over the various embassies, legations, consulates, and other foreign service posts. They are admitted into the foreign service on the basis of competitive examinations and, since 1945, all candidates complete two or three years of study in the National School of Administration. Thus a greater percentage of candidates of modest fortune may enter the foreign service. Less than 5 percent of the applicants pass the examination, which requires a high level of intellectual competence.

The structure and the personnel of the Ministry of Foreign Affairs have not undergone serious modification in the last century. The consular and the diplomatic corps have been combined, and a number of foreign-service personnel were purged after the liberation. The organization of the ministry continues to be based on functional rather than geographic divisions: it includes the General Office of Political and Economic Affairs, the General Office of Personnel and General Administration, the General Office of Cultural and Technical Affairs, the Office of Administrative and Social Affairs, the Office of Protocol, the Archives, and the Legal Service section. However, there are certain broad geographic subdivisions: (a) Europe and European organizations, (b) Asia and Oceania, (c) Africa and the Middle East, and (d) America.

The hard core of the foreign service has been a stable and efficient body, but it has shared and, in a way, contributed to the perpetuation of many of the myths on which French diplomacy has been based, such as the supremacy of French culture and the top rank of France. What is more, it has long remained, because of the education of many of its officers, tradition-bound and legalistic. Problems have not been considered in terms of the dynamics of the ever-changing relations of power in our world.[10]

A New Economic Policy. There was a clear perception among most of the political leaders of the Fourth Republic that France could not recover its prewar position without drastic economic effort. A rapid modernization of the French economy and a gradual movement toward increasing European cooperation were required. A strong France in a well-integrated western European economy could be far stronger than if she acted alone. Therefore, the Fourth Republic, after many equivocations, moved after 1956 in the direction of the European Economic Community (EEC) providing for liberalization of trade, lowering and ultimately elimination of all tariffs, and free movement of capital and labor among West Germany, Italy, France, and the Benelux countries. The treaty formalizing the EEC ("Common Market") was signed in Rome in 1957 and put into effect on January 1, 1959.

The Beginning of Economic Modernization. The task facing the country immediately after World War II was twofold: reconstruction and produc-

10 As Prof. J.-B. Duroselle points out, "The service remains a caste ever prone to believe in its omniscience" (Quoted in Kertesz and Fitzsimons, eds., *Diplomacy in a Changing World* [South Bend, Ind.: University of Notre Dame Press, 1959], p. 227).

tive investment, to renew the industrial equipment of the nation and to expand its weak sectors. This was the objective of the first Monnet Plan (1947–1950).

Production and modernization programs for six basic industries—coal mining, electric power, steel, cement, farm machinery, and internal transportation—were adopted for 1947, 1948, 1949, and 1950. A second and a third plan were developed. These began to build upon healthier foundations. Whatever the weaknesses of the Fourth Republic, whatever the vacillations of the various governments, massive public investment was followed scrupulously and expansion and growth became the commonly accepted policy. By 1956–57 the impact of the economic plans was clearly discernible. France was modernizing fast, at a tempo that began to compare favorably with that of Germany in 1952–56. By 1958 the gross national product had almost doubled. The population also began to grow, registering a rise for the first time since 1870. It grew by about 15 percent since the end of the war, and has now exceeded the 50 million mark.

ELEMENTS OF INSTABILITY

The governmental institutions of the Fourth Republic adversely affected the implementation of the long-range objectives, but only to a degree. Despite the instability of the cabinet—there were twenty cabinets under the Fourth Republic—foreign policy was directed by only a very small number of foreign ministers. Under the Fourth Republic there were, in all, five ministers of foreign affairs: Robert Schuman and Georges Bidault, Edgar Faure and Pierre Mendès-France (from the Radical Socialists), and Christian Pineau (of the Socialist party). Divi-

sions, however, in domestic and colonial issues and growing parliamentary interference provided serious internal difficulties and a marked immobility in policy making. This was the cause, for instance, of the equivocation on the European Defense Community. The instability of the cabinet undermined consistency in execution of policies.

The formulation of foreign policy, like the formulation of any other policy at the governmental level, involved the cooperation of the prime minister and his cabinet with the Parliament. As a result, its formulation suffered because of certain inherent weaknesses of the governmental process in France. These weaknesses were (a) the coalition character of the cabinet, and (b) the instability of the cabinet.

Coalition Cabinet. In France the cabinet was, and to a great extent continues to be, composed of the leaders of a number of political parties. Ever since the establishment of the Third Republic, hardly a party or a combination of two parties managed to provide a majority in the legislature. The cabinet was a coalition of the leaders of many parties and groups. As a result, the desired homogeneity of views on policy in general and on foreign policy in particular was lacking. Very often, the members of one and the same cabinet held opposing views on matters of foreign policy. That happened, for instance, between 1952 and 1954, when members of the same cabinet were in favor of and against the European Defense Community.

Instability of the Cabinet. Under the Third and Fourth Republics, the average life of a coalition cabinet was short. In the last two decades of the Third Republic, the average life of a cabinet hardly exceeded eight months. From the establishment of the Fourth

Republic to the middle of 1958, there were twenty cabinets. The succession of cabinets at this rate was responsible for the following consequences:

1. Lack of continuity in the implementation of foreign policy
2. Lack of planning for goals

Both these evils were to some degree alleviated, as we have noted, by the relative independence of the minister of foreign affairs and by his continuity in office. However, this continuity in office of the minister of foreign affairs could not compensate for the instability of the cabinet, since issues of foreign policy could not be dissociated from other issues of policy. They were part of a whole that engages the cabinet and, as a result, called for common policy and planning in the cabinet.

The only two semipermanent coordinating cabinet committees were (a) the general secretariat attached to the Organization of European Economic Cooperation (OEEC), composed primarily of civil servants of the various economic ministries; and (b) the permanent Secretariat of the National Defense, operating under the Ministry of the National Defense—a staff organization with rather limited functions and a turbulent history of continuous reorganizations. All the other existing coordinating organizations operated either at the administrative level and were composed of civil servants or were ad hoc organizations formed to deal with a particular problem. As Professor Duroselle pointed out, "There were no coordinating agencies between the different bureaus of the *Quai d'Orsay* [the Ministry of Foreign Affairs] and the other Ministries."[11] There were some min-

isterial committees but, because of the instability of the cabinet, they were just as short-lived as the cabinet itself. Furthermore, there was no permanent planning agency. To quote again Professor Duroselle, "The most striking fact is the complete absence of planning organisms. French policy was organized exactly as if decisions were to be taken on a day-to-day basis."[12]

The only planning agencies that existed, it may be argued, were the Ministry of Foreign Affairs and the cabinet as a whole. But the first, as we have pointed out, was unable to cope with the volume and the complexity of the work involved, while the instability of the latter made planning in foreign policy impossible. It was generally admitted that, since the liberation, and despite the continuity of her objectives, France had no foreign policy on many grave matters that concerned her. There were many Algerian policies, a number of European policies, and a great number of North African policies succeeding each other, but never forming a whole and never followed in terms of a coherent plan.

Such a situation could not but invite growing parliamentary interference, which aggravated the situation. Disagreements on foreign policy inevitably reached the Parliament and became, in turn, matters over which political parties and parliamentary groups took sides, thus intensifying party warfare in the National Assembly, causing frequent dislocations of the existing majorities, and accentuating the instability of the cabinet.

Conclusion

Tenacity and continuity in the perception of common goals; inability to implement these goals because of great disparity between aspiration and

---

[11] Jean-Baptiste Duroselle, "L'élaboration de la politique étrangère française," *Revue Française de la science politique* 6, no. 3 (July–September 1956): 418.

[12] Ibid., 516.

means, a disparity brought about by the influence of stronger powers, notably the United States; and a deadlock created by the sharp internal divisions that produced discontinuities and vacillations in the overall carrying out of foreign policy—this is perhaps the best way to summarize the foreign policy of France in the twelve-odd years of the Fourth Republic.

It was only at the very end that, after numerous setbacks, a new note of realism was injected into the relations between France and her Western neighbors. The domestic economic efforts were beginning to pay off, and the French business elite became increasingly reconciled to the notions of decolonization and of European unity. The Schuman plan had functioned moderately well, and the prospect of an enlarged European market began to appeal to many French manufacturers, undermining the traditional protectionist mentality of business groups. By 1957 most political parties were willing to go along with the establishment of the Common Market. For many, however, close economic and political European cooperation implied something else—the creation of a strong European bloc, possibly under the leadership of France, that would give her an opportunity to play a genuinely independent role in world affairs.

Colonial disengagement, economic modernization, the abandonment of a protectionist economic policy, the rapid development of resources—including the discovery of rich deposits of oil and gas both on the soil of France and in Sahara—were beginning to provide a sense of strength and recovery where in the past there had been only a feeling of weakness and frustration. The dismal way in which the Fourth Republic came to an end, and the difficulty of finding a solution to the Algerian problem, did not hide

from the vast majority of French men and women the promise that lay ahead.

THE FIFTH REPUBLIC AND GENERAL DE GAULLE (1958–1969)

The failure of the Fourth Republic rapidly and effectively to translate into action the commonly shared foreign policy objectives was one of the major reasons for its ultimate downfall. France's diminished status in the world, the successive defeats or withdrawals in the many and elusive colonial wars, the failure of France and Great Britain in Suez, the growing strength of West Germany in NATO and in Western Europe under a stable political leadership were all factors in the growth of a spirit of nationalism in the country, contrasting sharply with governmental instability. Parliament and coalition cabinets continued to mirror the perennial and multiple divisions of the body politic at the very time when the public demanded unity and the realization of national objectives.

Whatever the factors and the immediate causes associated with the uprising of May 13, 1958, in Algeria, it was to General de Gaulle that most of the political groups and leaders turned. Army officers, veterans, the political parties from the Socialists to the Independents, and a great number of intellectuals—some with considerable misgivings—turned to de Gaulle as the symbol and the person around whom this new spirit of French nationalism could find expression.

The Basic Assumptions

De Gaulle's basic assumptions—what we may call his overall philosophy— begin and end with the notion that there is one social force—the "reality of the nation" (*le fait national*)—that overshadows all others. No other force or forces—ideological, social, or economic—have succeeded in undermining the nation-state as the focal point of the ultimate loyalty of man.

From the postulate of national reality a number of inferences flow. They do not always have the logical consistency that an academician would desire; but consistency is not a necessary ingredient of statecraft. Situations change so fast in our world that the only consistency lies in the ability to adjust.[13] Consistency means, in the last analysis, realism. Yet the inferences that follow from the postulate on national reality constitute guides to action and must be spelled out.

The Reality of the Nation and the Means of Achieving Independence. The reality of the nation requires power in order fully to manifest itself. Surveying the world situation before the Allied victory in Europe, de Gaulle could not restrain his bitterness: "How dull is the sword of France at the time when the Allies are about to launch the assault of Europe."[14] Although not the only one, the basic ingredient of power is the military. In the ruins of France after the liberation, de Gaulle set himself to recreate the French army. He was haunted with the certainty that the Allies were blocking his efforts because they were unwilling to allow France to develop the military strength that would enable her to become an equal. When the matter of Germany's occupation seemed in doubt, he ordered his divisions onto German soil, suspecting, perhaps rightly, that the Allies might prevent France from participating in settling the future of Germany and remembering, also, that in war possession is nine-tenths of the law. His vision remained the same throughout the months following the liberation— to recreate the French armed forces. When there was not enough gas to heat French stoves, he established a Commission for Atomic Energy.

But there are other important factors in the equation of power. De Gaulle recognized many and used them all: alliances; diplomacy and skill in negotiations; cultural relations; spiritual influence; economic resources; and population.

A strong ingredient of power—indeed, the only valid expression of a nation—is the state and its political organization. Gaullist revisionism, both before and throughout the Fourth Republic, was predicated upon de Gaulle's ideas about world relations and the role of the French nation. To play the proper role, France needed a strong state. In this state, one man, the president of the republic, should make foreign policy on behalf of the nation—the "real France"—incarnating the national interests over and above the welter of particular interests and ideological factions.

A third ingredient of power that de Gaulle evoked very frequently led him to follow policies to which he had seemed firmly opposed. This is what he called the imperative of the *grands ensembles* ("great wholes"). Nations must establish cooperative "wholes" that provide the structural bases and the resources for the economic development and defense of each one and all. This is not contrary to his emphasis upon national uniqueness, nor did it lead him to the espousal of projects of military integration. The building of large wholes creates more than an

---

[13] Almost always, for instance, de Gaulle, speaking on international issues, inserted the phrase "given the present conditions in the world," or "in the actual state of developments," or "things being as they are."

[14] *War Memoirs*, vol. 2, *Unity* (New York: Simon & Schuster, 1959), p. 245.

alliance and less than a federation. It is a close association and cooperation between nation-states which, by pooling some of their resources, find the strength to sustain a common purpose. Whether it stemmed from a profound realization on de Gaulle's part of contemporary economic trends or was simply a tactical answer to the "two great empires" (the Soviet Union and the United States), whether it applied to Western Europe or to the French community, he was one of its most forceful advocates, reminding the African republics time after time that independence nowadays is a fiction unless sustained by strength, and that strength can never be attained by geographically small political fragments that go under the name of "sovereign states."

The Idea of Balance. De Gaulle's emphasis upon the reality of the national phenomenon and its concomitant accessories—power, both military and political—led him to a theory of international relations that is often referred to as "realist." International relations comprise an arena of conflict in which every participant nation-state attempts to increase its strength at the expense of the other. Every political leadership, no matter what ideology inspires it, acts in terms of national consideration. *If so, it is only power that can check power—and the only possible international world is one in which an equilibrium of powers is reached.* This led de Gaulle to follow conclusions that directly shaped his actions and are likely to influence his successor.

The present balance is unnatural, precarious, and unwise—unnatural, because it involves a polarization of the world and the creation of political satellites, which are inconsistent with the secular realities and interests of nations; precarious, because both the

big and small nations are continuously on the brink of war; unwise, because it gives to the two of the less qualified nation-states (the United States and the Soviet Union) full liberty to act, the independence to decide their fate and with it the fate of the world.

Both the American and the Soviet efforts are expressions of national power, in one form or another, and de Gaulle had no illusions about either. If they are allowed free sway, they might enter upon armed conflict. If they find a temporary accommodation, it will be in order to establish a joint hegemony over the world. *Either eventuality will be to the detriment of the other nation-states* including, of course, of France and Europe as a whole. This can be avoided only by creating a balance of power consistent with the growing realities of the world, in which the economic and political development of Europe is bound to play a growing role.

General de Gaulle's conception of a balance was a permanent trait of his thinking and action. It took a number of forms. In the third volume of his *Memoirs,* de Gaulle pointed out that the only way to keep the Soviet Union out of the heart of Europe was to dismember Germany. Thus the threat of a new Germany would be eliminated, and the fears of the Soviet Union and the Eastern European nations alleviated. Moreover, a treaty with the Soviet Union, directed against the revival of German power, would free France to pursue her other world obligations. It was the failure of Yalta to revive the pre-World War II arrangement in Europe that also accounted for the bitter denunciations against the settlement. Although France received a number of compensations, perhaps far beyond what the French leadership had a right to expect in terms of her real power at the time, Yalta became slowly identified with a betrayal of Europe and France by the Anglo-Saxons.

As late as August of 1968 the response of de Gaulle to the Soviet invasion of Czechoslovakia was a condemnation of Yalta! He then stated that

the armed intervention by the Soviet Union in Czechoslovakia shows that the Moscow Government has not freed itself from the policy of blocs that was imposed on Europe by the effect of the Yalta Agreements, which is incompatible with the right of peoples to self-determination and which could and can only lead to international tension. . . . France, who did not take part in these Agreements and who does not adopt that policy, notes and deplores the fact that the events in Prague —besides constituting an attack on the rights and the destiny of a friendly nation—are of the kind to impede European détente, such as France herself practices and in which she urges others to engage, and which, alone, can ensure peace.[15]

De Gaulle made an open offer to Churchill in November, 1944, to combine forces so that the two countries with their far-flung empires would be able to act independently of the Soviet and the Americans. It is worth quoting his remarks to Churchill:

You can see, France is beginning to recover. But whatever my faith in her is, I know that she will not recover soon her former strength. You, English, will finish this war on the other hand with glory. But nonetheless your relative position may well be weakened in view of your losses and sacrifices, the centrifugal forces that undermine the Commonwealth and above all the ascendancy of America and Russia, and later on of China. Well then, our two ancient countries are both weakened at the time when they are to confront a new world. . . . But if England and France agree and act together in the

15 Ambassade de France, Service de Press et d'Information, no. 1121, August 21, 1968.

future negotiations, they will have enough weight to prevent any decision that will not be acceptable to them. . . . It is this common will that must be the basis of the alliance that you are proposing to us. . . . The equilibrium of Europe, . . . the guarantee of peace on the Rhine, the independence of the states on the Vistula, the Danube and the Balkans, the keeping on our side of the peoples to whom we opened up civilization in all parts of the world, the organization of the nations in a manner that will provide something else than a battlefield for the quarrels of the Russians and the Americans, finally the primacy in our policy of a certain conception of man, despite the progressive mechanization of the societies, . . . is it not true that these are the great interests of the Universe? These interests, let us put them together and safeguard them together.[16]

A third scheme involved an alliance with the Soviet Union, directed against German recovery and guaranteeing the status quo of Europe. Speculating before his trip to the Soviet Union in December, 1944, only a few weeks after he had made his offer to Churchill, de Gaulle wrote wistfully, "Perhaps it might be possible to renew in some manner the Franco-Russian solidarity, which even if misunderstood and betrayed in the past, was nonetheless compatible with the nature of things *both with regard to the German danger and the Anglo-Saxon efforts to assert their hegemony.*"[17]

A fourth and perhaps more persistent effort to recreate a balance is the revival of Europe as a "third force." What "Europe" meant to de Gaulle, exactly, is a difficult matter. In his *Memoirs* he spoke of an organization

16 Quoted in *War Memoirs*, vol. 3, *Salvation* (New York: Simon & Schuster, 1960), p. 52. Author's translation.
17 Quoted in ibid. p. 54. Author's translation; italics supplied.

of the peoples of Europe from "Iceland to Istanbul and from Gibraltar to the Urals." Sometimes Russia is part and sometimes it is not, although emphasis is often put on the European destiny of Russia. Sometimes it is Western Europe and sometimes the whole of Europe. Sometimes "Europe" implies a dismembered Germany, sometimes a divided Germany, and sometimes a Franco-German rapprochement without qualifications. Two things are certain: "Europe," whatever it is, is distinct from the "Anglo-Saxon powers." It is also separate from Soviet Russia, without, however, always denying the European position of Russia and hence its participation.

With the economic recovery of West Germany and the continuing division of this country into two blocs, de Gaulle's conception of Europe became clearer. A strong France in Western Europe could assume the leadership of the Western bloc and speak for it. But to be strong in Western Europe, France must maintain good relations with a West Germany that is, all the same, never to be allowed to match France's leadership. So, underlying the new conception of balance in which Western Europe is perhaps to become for the first time a genuine third force, there is always an emphasis on France's interest, which means France's strength. A leader of Western Europe, France, can put all her weight, in the name of the new force, into world strategy and world leadership.

In the name of balance, de Gaulle envisaged in the course of less than twenty years the following alliances: (a) with the British, in order to create an independent bloc vis-à-vis the Soviets and the Americans; (b) with the Soviet Union, in order to maintain French supremacy in Europe vis-à-vis Germany; (c) with all against the revival of a unified, militarized, and strong Germany; and (d) with West Germany and the other Western European states, in order to create an independent bloc—a third force in Europe that might lead to drastic changes in the balance of power.

A New Style

Harold Nicolson, in his *Evolution of Diplomacy*, distinguishes between the "old diplomacy" and the "new diplomacy." The distinction has both procedural and substantive traits. Substantively, the old diplomacy assumed the primacy of Europe, the objective gradation of nations in terms of power, and the responsibility of the big powers for the course of international events and, more particularly, for matters of peace and war. Procedurally, the old diplomacy used diplomacy and negotiations and shied away from appeals to world opinion, large conferences, and ideologic confrontations. The new diplomacy is the work of secular forces that changed the balance of forces. Europe was progressively overshadowed. It was also the work of Woodrow Wilson, who introduced diplomacy by conference, utilized ideological slogans, and stressed the equality of all nations.

All of de Gaulle's sympathies remained with the old diplomacy. While conceding basic alterations in the balance of forces that ought to be considered, he had no patience with the new procedures. The old Concert of Europe, he was willing to concede, ought to become the new "Concert of the World," in which the United States has a permanent place—perhaps, also, China and even India. But Europe was to remain a dominant force—perhaps, under the proper conditions, *the* dominant force. The powers that have global interests and global responsiblities are few; they must continue to play a leading role in all matters of international relations, and particularly in matters of war and peace.

Negotiations and carefully prepared treaties must be once more the rule. Such negotiations must be conducted by experts, as in the past, in secret, and communicated at the appropriate time to parliaments and publics. Neither the United Nations, as organized today, nor the various summit meetings, past, present, or future, appealed to de Gaulle. In his press conference of November 10, 1959, he specifically criticized assemblies whose only purpose seemed to be the airing of grievances and the agitation of public opinion. Again, when France decided no longer to provide funds for the United Nations operations in the Congo, de Gaulle explained in his press conference of April 11, 1961, why support had been withdrawn. The Security Council, where decisions were to be made by five big powers, had lost virtually all power, he said. The General Assembly, he pointed out acidly, "has assumed all powers. It can deliberate on everything." This assembly, furthermore, would soon consist of some 130 states, "many of which are improvised states and believe it their duty to stress grievances or demands with regard to the older nations." The meetings of the United Nations "are no more than riotous sessions. . . . As the United Nations," he concluded, "becomes a scene of disturbance, confusion, and division, it acquires the ambition to intervene in all kinds of matters." France, he hinted, would maintain its aloofness toward "these United, or Disunited, Nations."[18] At the end of July, 1961, France refused to acknowledge the

competence of the United Nations in dealing with the French-Tunisian conflict in Bizerte.

De Gaulle's actions while president exhibited all the traits associated with the "old diplomacy": his firm commitment to European revival under the leadership of France; his emphasis upon the global responsibilities and global strategy of the Great Powers; his underplaying of the United Nations and NATO (to the extent to which it consecrates the hegemony of the Anglo-Saxons and allows only them, especially the United States, freedom of action); and, above all, the exclusive jurisdiction he assumed, as president of the republic, for foreign affairs.

The new style continues to be reflected in the constitutional arrangement and institutional development of the Fifth Republic.

The Constitution. The Constitution of the Fifth Republic provides that the cabinet "shall determine and direct the policy of the nation" and that "it will be responsible to Parliament."; in addition, "the Prime Minister is responsible for national defense" (Articles 20 and 21). The president of the republic, on the other hand, "shall be the guarantor of the national independence, of the integrity of the territory, and of the respect . . . of treaties" (Article 5). He "shall negotiate and ratify treaties" and "he shall be informed of all negotiations leading to the conclusion of an international agreement" (Article 52). All major treaties, however, must be "ratified by law" (Article 53).

The contrasts with the constitutional arrangement of the Fourth Republic lie primarily in the conception of the role of the president. He was given both implicitly and explicitly broader powers. The president is the guarantor of the national integrity;

18 News conference, April 11, 1961, in *Speeches and Press Conferences,* trans. Press and Information Service, French Embassy (New York), no. 162, pp. 7–8.

the commander-in-chief, presiding over the meetings of the various defense councils; and the possessor of large emergency powers. He is the "moderator" (*arbitre*), making presumably final decisions whenever there appears to be division and conflict in the country or his cabinet. He has the power to dissolve the legislature and to ask the public, in a referendum, to endorse or reject his policy.

Under de Gaulle, the presidency became the coordinating office for the major decisions: military policy, foreign policy, and colonial policy. His successor has fully endorsed this position. Cabinet meetings are simply for the execution and implementation of the decisions made by the president and his immediate advisers. The president is not simply informed of foreign policy negotiations. He negotiates directly with foreign representatives, prime ministers, and heads of state; he outlines the goals of the government—at times taking even the cabinet and the prime minister by surprise. Matters pertaining to NATO, to the ties among the members of the Common Market, to negotiations concerning suspension of atomic tests, to the advisability of a summit meeting—all are decided by the president.

The role of Parliament is greatly diminished. Negotiations and formulations of policy are kept secret in the best tradition of the old diplomacy. Only general developments and over-all policy have been discussed. Since the establishment of the Fifth Republic, there have been a number of major foreign policy debates, lasting two or three days each. Debate, however, is limited to the exposition of the prime minister's or the minister's views and to foreign policy pronouncements by various party leaders.

The parliamentary Committee on Foreign Affairs of the National Assembly has heard the minister of for-eign affairs frequently, and many questions on foreign policy have been addressed to the prime minister and the minister. They have been perfunctory, however. Since the possibility of engaging the responsibility of the president of the republic and the cabinet is lacking, in the first place, and highly restricted in the second, debate is little more than academic.

Occasions for the expression of dissatisfaction have not been lacking, however. For instance, when the debate on the government's program on atomic weapons and the development of a retaliatory atomic force for France took place (in connection with the voting of military credits), the Senate twice defeated the measure that had been passed in the National Assembly. The opposition in the National Assembly had the opportunity to introduce a motion of censure which was endorsed on the last two occasions by 215 and 217 votes, respectively—some 60 votes short of the majority required to bring the cabinet down. Again, in the spring of 1966, de Gaulle's decision to withdraw from NATO led to a full-dress debate triggered by a censure motion against the government. Not more than 140 deputies out of 482 voted for the motion.

THE GAULLIST YEARS: THE SUBSTANCE OF FOREIGN POLICY

The Gaullist years will no doubt be considered by future historians to have set the guidelines for French foreign policy. Both de Gaulle's philosophy (which we discussed briefly earlier) and his actions set a pattern that can be described in one simple phrase—the reassertion of independence. In a highly fluid and ever-changing world it was the vocation of a nation-state to establish its freedom to act—to seek its allies and pursue its interests. The objective of independence and of independent action became almost an obsession often obscured by the changing tactics in order to preserve and maximize all possible options and never to create a situation or to allow an arrangement to develop that took ultimate choices and decisions away from the hands of France. The obsession often led the country, under de Gaulle, perilously close to isolationism, to a Maurassian *France seule* posture, in a world where the solitary state—even for the superpowers—is an anachronism. At times in an effort to keep all choices open, France, unable to both please its allies and placate possible enemies, found herself ignored by both. In Europe unwilling to commit herself to a genuine political union but always anxious to speak on behalf of Europe and the European interest, de Gaulle antagonized his partners without being able to provide them with leadership and strength. If one were to single out one connecting thread in de Gaulle's actions, it would be his desire and his efforts to see both American and Soviet forces withdraw, in one form or another, from Eastern and Western Europe.

In his last press conference, on September 9, 1968, de Gaulle summed it up thus:

Since 1958, we French never ceased to work in order to put an end to the regime of the two blocs. Thus, while building close relations with the countries of Western Europe, even to the extent of transforming our former estrangement with Germany into cordial cooperation, we have slowly detached ourselves from the military organization of NATO which subordinates the Europeans to the Americans. Thus, while participating in the Common Market we have never consented to the establishment of a supranational system which will drown France in a . . . whole which will have no other

policy but the one of the protector from across the seas. . . . By the same token, . . . we have restored our relations with the countries of Eastern Europe and above all with Russia. . . . We have given to the great Russian people to understand . . . that the whole of Europe expects from them something much better than to shut and chain their satellites within the barriers of a crushing totalitarianism.[19]

We shall discuss the Gaullist decade with regard to (*a*) colonial and economic policy, (*b*) NATO, (*c*) Europe and the Common Market, (*d*) the atom bomb, (*e*) relations with the Soviet Union, and (*f*) tactics.

End of Empire; Economic Growth

In 1958, General de Gaulle pledged to all overseas territories a new political arrangement—the French Community—and, if they wished it, their independence. All of the territories, with the exception of Guinea, entered the French Community. They became republics federated with France. They were governed by the president of the French republic, who was also president of the community, with the assistance of an Executive Council which consisted of the president of the republic, a number of French ministers charged with community affairs, and the prime ministers, or their delegates, of the African republics and Madagascar. A Community Senate, with primarily consultative powers, was also established, as well as a community arbitration court, to hear and pass on controversies among the member states.

In the course of 1959–60, the community was abandoned. It still exists in name, but its institutions have been set aside. Speaking in Dakar, Senegal, in December, 1959, de Gaulle promised to grant "international sover-

19 Quoted in *Année politique, 1968*, p. 392.

eigny"—that is, complete independence—to all of France's African territories. Special accords between France and the member states were passed and ratified by the French Parliament, providing for diverse modes of cooperation between France and the individual republics in economic, social, cultural, and military affairs. All provisions can be renegotiated and possibly cancelled by new accords in the future. All the African republics have become independent, and all of them have become members of the United Nations as independent, individual states with the freedom to vote as they please in the United Nations General Assembly and to participate in its organs and specialized commissions.

Thus France, under de Gaulle, put an end to colonialism. In doing so, she improved her position in Africa, where she is assured of a reservoir of good will. Large subsidies to the African republics and Madagascar guarantee a good rate of modernization and industralization there, which is bound to favor French trade and investments in Africa and improve the living standards of the Africans themselves. Thus, politically and economically, the road was paved for better relations.

Algeria. It was not until July 3, 1962, after a series of zigzags and equivocations into which we need not enter here, that Algeria was finally granted her full independence. The leaders of the rebellion were released from jail, and the French settlers began their return to France. Between 1962 and 1965, almost 1 million European French citizens and a sizeable number of Algerians who had fought in the French army or in territorial units were resettled in the metropolis with substantial financial aid from the state. Thus the war in Algeria (1954–1962) that, like the war in Vietnam,

had sapped the energy of the country, that had provoked sharp and, at times, irreconcilable conflicts, that had seriously qualified France's freedom of action, that had gravely undermined her prestige among her former colonies, particularly in Africa, came to an end. France retained a temporary foothold—the naval base of Mers-el-Kebir and her atomic and space testing grounds in Sahara. As for her rapidly growing oil installations in Algeria, the French companies were allowed to continue their exploitation subject to negotiated agreements with an independent Algerian government. The last military adventure had come to an end, and in 1962, for the first time since World War II, French soldiers were no longer fighting anybody, anywhere. Relations with Algeria itself rapidly improved, and France continued to extend considerable economic and cultural aid to the newly created state.

The National Economy. Under de Gaulle, the economic development of the country continued to improve. The improvement was partly due to measures, originally suggested by a "special" committee of experts, designed to eliminate inflationary tendencies and restore monetary stability. This plan aimed "to restore to France its international status" in the economic field and "to establish the nation on a foundation of truth and severity, which alone can enable it to build its prosperity."

In order to achieve a sounder monetary position and a better competitive position for French goods in foreign markets, the franc was devalued by 17.5 percent in December, 1958. France restored the convertibility of the franc, thus giving foreign companies the guarantees necessary to enable them freely to invest and remit profits. Foreign capital began to flow into the country, contributing appreciably to the improvement in the balance of payments. The new price of the franc made it again possible to liberalize trade, and enabled France to fulfill its commitments toward its Common Market partners. On January 1, 1959, France implemented, in full, the European Common Market treaty provisions for the reduction of customs duties and the liberalization of trade. Moreover, because devaluation had lowered the prices of French goods, the country's foreign trade improved rapidly. In May, 1959, for the first time in a very long period, France's foreign trade balance showed a surplus. Her gold and foreign exchange reserves steadily mounted, rising to over $5 billion by 1966. Exports rose at a rapid rate. Industrial production, after a slight decline in 1963–64, resumed its upward trend and was followed by a steady rate of increase that has averaged 4.5 percent until 1968, when, as a result of the May-June uprisings and strikes, production fell off sharply and the balance of payments was seriously affected. In August, 1969 (after de Gaulle had retired), France had to adopt restrictive policies and devalue the franc by some 13 percent; exports then began to rise again, causing a rapid improvement in the balance of payments.

NATO: Participation; Reform; Withdrawal

Immediately after his return to power, de Gaulle asserted that it was not the purpose of France to limit her foreign policy "within the confines of NATO." On September 23, 1958, he addressed a memorandum, still technically secret, to Belgian Prime Minister Paul-Henri Spaak, Prime Minister Macmillan, and President Eisenhower. It is, however, common knowledge that the memorandum contained a diagnosis of the problems facing NATO and a statement of French policy. De Gaulle indicated the common responsibilities imposed upon the alliance in case of war, but pointed to the inequality in armaments and, what is more, to the disparity in the freedom of the member states to make decisions. Events in Egypt and Algeria contrasted sharply with those in the Near East, Formosa and, later, Vietnam. He proposed, therefore, the establishment within NATO of a "directorate" of three—England, France, and the United States—with responsibility for elaborating a common military and political strategy for the whole of the planet, for the creation of allied commands for all theaters of operation, for joint deliberations about strategy, and for joint decision on the use of atomic weapons. "The European states of the continent," he stated on April 11, 1961, ". . . must know exactly with which weapons and under what conditions their overseas allies would join them in battle."[20] He reminded President Kennedy, who was to visit him within a matter of weeks, that "the threats of war are no longer limited to Europe" and that NATO should accordingly revise its organization to meet joint non-European problems. There was also a threat in the memorandum: France would reconsider its NATO policy in the light of the response of England and the United States.

Although ostensibly addressing problems related to NATO, de Gaulle was actually attempting to place France on a level to which no other continental European power in NATO could aspire. NATO was to remain a broad organization, according to his proposal, but with three of its members—France, England and the

[20] News conference, April 11, 1961, in *Speeches and Press Conferences,* no. 162, pp. 7–8.

United States—jointly in charge of global strategy. The three great powers were, in the best tradition of the old diplomacy, to be in charge, at the NATO level, of the Atlantic problems, and jointly in charge of planetary strategy. De Gaulle remained adamant. When his suggestions were rejected, France withdrew its Mediterranean fleet from NATO command; she refused to integrate her air defense with NATO; she prevented the building of launching sites and the stockpiling of atomic warheads over which she could have no control. But this stand against military integration was to bring France in conflict with West Germany. This became painfully evident during Chancellor Adenauer's visit in December, 1959, and throughout 1960, when de Gaulle and his advisers talked freely about an "independent" Western European strategy and apparently foresaw even the possibility of the withdrawal of American forces.

After the memorandum of September 23, 1958, de Gaulle continued to simultaneously emphasize France's Atlantic commitment and her European and world vocation. His emphasis on France's European vocation inevitably raised the question of the status of NATO. As a treaty signed at the time of the peak of the Soviet peril in 1949, when Western Europe was still suffering from the economic, social, and—to some extent—political aftereffects of World War II, NATO consecrated American hegemony and placed Western Europe under American military tutelage. The United States could deploy its strength and assert its interests in other parts of the world, but the European nations, especially France, found themselves tied to a regional alliance that deprived them of freedom of action in Europe and elsewhere. According to General de Gaulle, the situation was unaccept-

able on both counts. As the European nations developed in strength, as France began to withdraw from the heavy imperial commitments she had assumed in Asia and in North Africa, as her economy began first to recover and then to move rapidly ahead, and as, finally, she began to develop atomic weapons, the contradiction between the conditions of 1949 and those of the 1960s became increasingly apparent.

With the end of the Algerian war, there was no doubt at all as to where de Gaulle stood and what he wanted. First, European problems had better be left to the European nations. This involved even the problem of German reunification. Second, European nations, notably France, had worldwide commitments that transcended the regional limits of NATO, just as did the United States. Hence the future of the national armed forces and their deployment and posture was a national matter belonging to France. Third, without ever stating it, de Gaulle seemed to infer that the presence of American troops in Europe was becoming, at least politically, a liability. Fourth, NATO and its integrative aspects were to be thrust aside and replaced, at most and on the basis of expedience and contingency, by a classic alliance among individual and separate states—an alliance that was to be negotiated and renegotiated as the circumstances demanded. De Gaulle never rejected the desirability of such a classic alliance, but while insisting on its form—a pact between individual sovereign states—he never specified its content. It has seemed clear, however, that such an alliance was to be construed narrowly. The partners would be free to differ on everything that did not involve their defense against a specified foreign attack under the stipulated conditions. France would be free to move in her own way in China, in Southeast Asia, and in Latin

America, as well as reconsider her relations with the Eastern European countries or the Soviet Union. De Gaulle's revisionist policy with regard to NATO was, in other words, an explicit reformulation of France's full-fledged independence to act as a world power. If and when the interests of the United States and France converged, so much the better; if they diverged, each would be free to act independently of the other. This, in effect, would put an end to NATO. To quote one of de Gaulle's pronouncements on the subject at some length:

Nothing can make a treaty wholly valid when its object has changed. Nothing can make an alliance remain as such when the conditions in which it was concluded have changed. It is therefore necessary to adapt the law, the treaty and the alliance to the new factors, failing which the texts, emptied of their substance, will, if circumstances so require, be nothing more than useless papers in the archives, unless there is a harsh break between these obsolete forms and the living realities.

Well! If France considers, today still, that it is useful to her security and to that of the West that she be allied with a certain number of States, particularly with America, for their defense and for hers in the event of agression against one of them; . . . at the same time she recognizes that the measures for implementation taken subsequently no longer correspond to what she deems satisfactory, with respect to herself, in the new conditions.

I say, the new conditions. For it is quite clear that, owing to the internal and external evolution of the countries of the East, the Western world is no longer threatened today as it was at the time when the American protectorate was set up in Europe under the cover of NATO. But, at the same time as the alarms were dying down, there was also a reduction in the guarantee of security—one might say absolute—that the possession of the nuclear weapon by America alone gave to the Old Continent, and in the certainty that

America would employ it, without reservation, in the event of aggression. For Soviet Russia has since that time equipped itself with a nuclear power capable of striking the United States directly, which has made the decisions of the Americans as to the eventual use of their bombs at least indeterminate, and which has, by the same token, stripped of justification—I speak for France—not the Alliance, of course, but indeed integration.

On the other hand, while the prospects of a world war breaking out on account of Europe are dissipating, conflicts in which America engages in other parts of the world—as the day before yesterday in Korea, yesterday in Cuba, today in Vietnam—risk, by virture of that famous escalation, being extended so that the result could be a general conflagration. In that case Europe—whose strategy is, within NATO, that of America—would be automatically involved in the struggle, even when it would not have so desired. It would be so for France, if the intermeshing of her territory, of her communications, of certain of her forces, of several of her air bases, of some of her ports with the military system under American command were to continue much longer. . . . Lastly, France's determination to dispose of herself, a determination without which she would soon cease to believe in her own role and be able to be useful to others, is incompatible with a defense organization in which she finds herself subordinate.

Consequently, without going back on her adherence to the Atlantic Alliance, France is going, between now and the final date set for her obligations, which is April 4, 1969, to continue to modify successively the measures currently practiced, insofar as they concern her. What she did yesterday in this respect in several domains, she will do tomorrow in others, while taking, of course, the necessary measures so that these changes take place gradually and so that her allies cannot be suddenly, and because of her, inconvenienced. In addition, she will hold herself ready to arrange with one or another of them, and in the same manner in which she has already proceeded on certain points, the practical relations for cooperation that will appear useful on both sides, either in the immediate present or in the eventuality of a conflict. This naturally holds for allied cooperation in Germany. In sum, it means re-establishing a normal situation of sovereignty, in which that which is French as regards soil, sky, sea and forces, and any foreign element that would be in France, will in the future be under French command alone. This is to say that it in no way means a rupture, but a necessary adaptation.[21]

Subsequently, in three separate memorandums—on March 11, March 29, and April 22, 1966—the French government communicated its decision to withdraw its forces from NATO on July 1, 1966, and demanded the withdrawal, by April 1, 1967, of all United States armed forces and military personnel and of all NATO instrumentalities from the French soil. The only remaining possibility was that American forces could be stationed in France, and French forces in Germany, on the basis of bilateral arrangements. The alternative left to the United States was to persist in the continuation of NATO without France, but with the support of England and West Germany, which has been the official position of the three governments concerned.

The Common Market and England

De Gaulle's acceptance of the Common Market was motivated in part by economic reasons and in part by considerations favoring the development of a European "whole." The crucial reason, however, was political. It gave him a bargaining position with the British with respect to the demands of his memorandum of September 23, 1958, and on a number of other issues,

[21] News conference, February 21, 1966, in *Speeches and Press Conferences.*

notably Berlin, atomic weapons, and the agenda of the ill-fated summit conference of June, 1960. In repayment for Adenauer's participation in the Common Market, and as a compromise of their disagreements about the extent and nature of military integration in NATO, de Gaulle became a staunch supporter of the Berlin status quo. However, he also accepted Germany's existing frontier arrangements with Poland. Many still think, on the basis of his *Memoirs*, that he continued to consider the future of Germany the crucial problem of our times, and that under no circumstances was he prepared to make any concession to Germany other than on Berlin, which has only a symbolic value and does not alter the balance of forces.

After 1960, the political and military reasons that accounted for de Gaulle's acceptance of the economic provisions of the Common Market became increasingly apparent. The Common Market suggested the possibility that a larger European whole could be placed under the leadership of France, armed with atomic weapons that were denied to Germany by virtue of the 1955 Paris accords. Britain's participation was highly desirable, provided Britain was willing to abandon the intimate Atlantic connections that underwrote the dominance of the United States, and also provided that Britain brought into a European pool —under some form of Franco-British control—her atomic and hydrogen weapons and knowhow. Britain's nuclear power was to be its dowry in the contemplated marriage with the Common Market. When it became clear that England was unwilling to cut her intimate ties with the United States, de Gaulle decided to refuse entry to England. His decision became a foregone conclusion when, after meeting with President Kennedy, Macmillan virtually placed British nuclear weapons under the control of the United States. In his now famous press conference of January 14, 1963, de Gaulle, alleging economic and cultural reasons, rejected England's entry. The heart of the matter, however, was political and strategic; England, de Gaulle feared, would remain under the domination of the United States, and her entry into the Common Market would thus reinforce America's influence.

With England at least temporarily out of the picture, de Gaulle turned to Germany. A Franco-German alliance providing for frequent consultations and possibly for the elaboration of common policy on military, foreign, cultural, and economic questions, would provide the hard core for consolidating Western Europe and, given France's military superiority, safeguard French leadership at the same time. In January, 1963, a Franco-German treaty, embodying the principle of consultations on matters of defense, foreign policy, and cultural affairs, was signed. However, the very logic of the treaty raised serious questions. It was again based on the assumption that West Germany would accept French, rather than American, leadership and protection. But in the light of its military and economic ties with the United States, and especially in the light of the overwhelming superiority of the United States in these areas, it was unlikely that any German political leader would acquiesce to this. Gradually, the treaty was bypassed and the policies of the two countries on military and foreign policy questions began to diverge, with Germany supporting the United States. Thus, what accounted for de Gaulle's rebuff of Britain seemed to be also called into play by Germany. It was only de Gaulle, and only France, that seemed to believe that

Western Europe could do without the United States, and it was only France that pressed for a European solution of the European problems at the very time when the heart of the European defense establishment continued to lie across the Atlantic.

But the Common Market remained a successful economic arrangement. It had, by 1965, reached the stage when increasing commitments to supranationality were to be made, and when some decision could be made by a qualified majority of the participants. In other words, the Common Market had moved to the critical stage when it was about to assume, even to a limited degree, genuine supranationality. However, such a supranationality is, as we have seen, contrary to de Gaulle's basic assumptions about the nature of international relations. Alleging the unwillingness of the other five members to accept common agricultural policies (policies, incidentally, quite advantageous to French agriculture), de Gaulle instructed his ministers, in the middle of 1965, to withdraw from the Council of Ministers of the Common Market. He also attacked the supranational character of the Rome treaty establishing the EEC and claimed that the assumption of power by a body of "stateless" functionaries was prejudicial to the independence of the sovereign member states. The Rome treaty, he concluded, had to be revised in order to do away with all supranational clauses. In effect, he urged that the Common Market remain a purely economic arrangement, held together by the will of sovereign and independent states, and subject to the veto power of each and all.

Nothing illustrates better the tactical flexibility and the effort to preserve all options better than de Gaulle's European policy: he argued for "the Europe of Six," for "the

Europe of Seven," for "a Europe from the Atlantic to the Urals," and for "a European Europe." He remained willing to accept the economic integration of the Common Market without allowing for its political unification—indeed, while opposing it. He favored the "Market" but not the "Community." Occasionally he threatened to weaken even the economic ties by creating an open free-trade community including a number of other European states. For instance, in his remarks to the British ambassador early in 1969, he apparently suggested that the Common Market could become a free-exchange area among a number of countries provided the Atlantic organization was phased out and a political directorate for Europe —consisting of France, West Germany, Italy, and England—established. Yet when the British attempted to use the defunct Western European Union—consisting of the six countries of the Common Market and England—to discuss a number of political questions, the French refused to participate. At one and the same time, the Gaullists exalted the uniqueness of "the Six"—especially when England was interested in entering—and threatened to dismantle the Common Market when England showed interest in entering.

Nuclear Strategy

Since the Allies seemed unwilling to subordinate overall strategy and the use of atomic weapons to a "directorate," France proceeded with the explosion of her own atom bomb. A number of additional reasons were given: the uncertainty about the use of the bomb by the United States, except in self-defense; the need of a French deterrent to war; the injection of a new pride and a higher morale in an army that had experienced one frustration after another; and, finally,

the worldwide commitments of France. As long as other powers have nuclear weapons, the only policy consistent with French interests, according to de Gaulle, was to develop nuclear weapons. At the Geneva disarmament conference, the French continued to favor the liquidation of stockpiles of weapons and delivery missiles before the suspension of manufacturing and testing of nuclear weapons.

On February 13, 1960, in accord with the timetable set before de Gaulle returned to office, France exploded her first atomic device in the Sahara. Since then, there have been seven additional atomic tests in the atmosphere and a number of underground ones. Nuclear devices were tested in the Polynesian possessions of France in the Pacific in the summer of 1970.

By 1967, France had a minimum of a hundred atomic bombs, averaging in strength at least three times that of the first bomb which fell on Hiroshima. With nuclear capabilities to be added soon, it was estimated that France's force would exceed 100,000 kilotons by 1970. The army has been trimmed down, and increasing emphasis has been placed on atomic weapons and the production of delivery vehicles, some of which are now operational.

The reality of French nuclear capability, even if limited, was bound to cause a reconsideration of strategic thinking. General de Gaulle himself was particularly anxious not to allow France to meet a crisis with antiquated ideas and weapons. Atomic weapons are considered today to be the best deterrent against war, by giving to the nation possessing them the possibility of retaliating against the centers of an aggressive enemy's power. However, given the nuclear capabilities of the United States and the Soviet Union, the confrontation of American and Soviet forces in the heart of Europe and, finally, the particular interests of France in Europe, the French hope to perform a number of interrelated and often contradictory strategic tasks. France wishes to maintain a special and privileged position in Western Europe, including West Germany, without, however, allowing herself to be overshadowed by Germany; to keep the substance of the Atlantic alliance, without conceding to the United States a free hand in Western Europe; and to promote a détente with Eastern Europe.

The French atomic weapons are of course not calculated to provide a solution to the above problems. The atomic weapon itself is only a means to *one* goal—independent French action—rather than part of a comprehensive strategy. The acquisition of military independence, or at least of a semblance of independence, can and will provide freedom for France to move in one or another direction as the world situation changes. This is the heart of Gaullist doctrine, and it is, of course, at odds with American efforts to reduce to a minimum anything and everything that might upset the United States' control and initiative.

A French *force de frappe* ("striking force"), wielded by France under the control of the French government, provides for a certain degree of independence. It gives France a degree of freedom, especially within a decade or so, to do away with American protection, which virtually all now consider necessary; it maintains France's superior position in Western Europe vis-à-vis West Germany; it has given the French impressive reasons for reconsidering NATO. These points, taken one by one, appear to be only mildly persuasive, but if we were to accept the central argument of French government circles and of de Gaulle—i.e.,

if we were to accept the uniqueness of the nation-state and the exclusively national character of defense and military preparedness—then the *force de frappe* indeed gives the French nation-state a weight and a position that it did not and could not have before. This is especially so in the light of the contingent and fluid nature of international politics and the narrow margin of resources and power that often spells the difference between national survival and national disaster.

Thus, the French *force de frappe*, when viewed in the abstract, can, or at least *may*, play a number of roles. Which role it will play, in political or military terms, cannot be assessed à priori, however. The important thing, for France, is to have the bomb and be ready to play *any* given role that the situation demands. It strengthens France's position in NATO, if NATO is still desired, or it can give France the freedom to move completely out of NATO; it gives France the possibility of assuming the military leadership of Western Europe, but at the same time the possibility of breaking away from the confines of a European context and coming to terms with the Soviet Union at least on matters concerning Europe. It may be the strongest argument against MLF, controlled exclusively by the United States, but it is also one of the strongest trumps in France's hands if it suits her interests to reshape MLF; it is both an argument with which to silence Germany's desires to get nuclear weapons and to undermine American efforts to provide Germany with such weapons, and it also gives Germany a strong incentive (how strong depends upon a number of factors) to enter a European military arrangement and share in the control of a European strategy. Thus the French bomb can destroy European unity or become the basis for European common military arrangements. It can cause proliferation, or it can help put an end to it, if the powers that have the bomb now—including France and China—were to be given the proper voice in the deliberations against proliferation. The bomb might conceivably hasten American withdrawal from Europe, but it can well have the opposite effect. It may incite the Soviet Union to greater belligerence in Europe, but it may also provide the basis for a Franco-Soviet understanding with regard to a new settlement of European problems, particularly the German problem.

In sum, it is highly unrealistic to condemn the French effort because of the contradictions it involves. These contradictions do not impede choice; on the contrary, they allow, depending on the circumstances, a certain freedom of choice. And this is the basic postulate of a sound strategy! The bomb is only a condition for the development of strategy. It would, therefore, be a mistake and perhaps irrelevant to speculate at length on the exact character of French strategy. There is little of it, and what does exist is rather primitive. It is only in the last few years that French military, political, and intellectual leaders, as well as the various "clubs," have entered into the debate about atomic weapons; in this connection, the interested reader is referred to *Le grand débat*, Raymond Aron's succinct exposition and criticism of the French position.[22] Since Aron's publication,

one authoritative study has produced a particularly strong argument in favor of the possession of the nuclear deterrent by a country the size of France. The bomb provides, it is argued, a deterrent against a potential aggressor—even a superpower—but only where the stakes are not high for the aggressor but are deemed to be a matter of survival by France. In such a particular case, the aggressor—even a superpower—will be discouraged by the French deterrent.[23]

The Soviets: The "Opening to the East"

As we have seen, de Gaulle never accepted the arrangements made at Yalta. Yet it was quite obvious that, as long as the Soviet threat continued and Soviet power was countered by American power, the division of Europe along the lines laid down at Yalta was inevitable. With the emergence of the Sino-Soviet split, with the relative weakening of the Soviet Union's expansionist trends, with the growing preoccupation of the Soviets with many internal problems, and last, with the emerging aspirations of many Eastern European nations for independence, the time appeared propitious to reopen the Yalta settlement. This necessitated, first, a reconsideration of the problem of German reunifi-

[22] Publications on French nuclear strategy are rapidly increasing in number. The most important are the following: General Gallois, *Stratégie de l'âge nucléaire* (Paris: Calman-Levy, 1960); General Beaufre, *Introduction à la stratégie* (Paris: Librairie Armand Colin, 1963); Alexander Sanguinetti, *La France et l'armée atomique* (Paris: Julliard, 1964); Jules Moch, *Non à la force de frappe* (Paris: Robert Lafont, 1963); Club Jean Moulin, *La force de frappe et le citoyen*

(Paris: Editions du Seuil, 1963); Club de Grenelle, *Siècle de Damocles: Du nouveau sur la force de frappe* (Paris: Les éditions Pierre Coudere, 1964); Raymond Aron, *Le grand débat: Initiation à la stratégie atomique*, 1964.

The reader will find a review of some of the most important recent publications in "Le grand débat nucléaire," *Bulletin sedeis*, February 10, 1965, no. 910, supplement. Significant articles have also appeared in *La politique étrangère*, and *Revue de la defense nationale*.

[23] *Notes et études documentaires, 6 Decembre 1966*, "La defense: La politique militaire de la France."

cation and, second, the assumption by Western Europe of a relative degree of independence vis-à-vis the United States. For as long as NATO remained what it was, and as long as there was direct Soviet-American confrontation in the heart of Europe, there would be no relaxation of Soviet controls in Eastern Europe.

De Gaulle's emphasis upon a "European Europe," his often-repeated statements about a Europe stretching from the Urals to the shores of the Atlantic, were designed to suggest such a relaxation. Its implementation proved to be a much harder problem. One way was to achieve a genuine Franco-German entente within the context of the Common Market, and then to begin a dialogue with the Soviet Union on matters of German reunification. This proved difficult because of the unwillingness of the Germans to substitute French protection for American, and because of the legitimate doubts of American policy makers about the advisability of such a course of action. De Gaulle then made repeated overtures in the direction of the Eastern European satellites. Cultural and economic ties were stressed; visits were exchanged, a number of leaders of Eastern European countries visiting Paris; and France refused to consider any arrangement that would give the Germans a say about nuclear arms. Thus, under de Gaulle, France was returning increasingly to the pre-World War II arrangements—in which an understanding with the Soviet Union is indispensable to the maintenance of peace in Europe, and in which Germany must reenter the concert of European powers, but without the ultimate weapons. This might well have been the objective of General de Gaulle's visit to the Soviet Union in the summer of 1966 and of Premier Kosygin's return visit to France six months later.

Tactics

A shrewd use of all the trumps that France held characterized, as we have seen, the Gaullist diplomacy. France has appeared to be both European and Atlantic. De Gaulle blocked England's entry to the Common Market, but never for a moment claimed that this was a final decision. He attempted to build the foundations of European power on the basis of a Franco-German alliance but, at the same time, held out the prospect of a new Franco-Soviet agreement, first with the visit of his foreign minister to Moscow in the winter of 1965 and later, in the summer of 1966, visiting Moscow himself. While urging the drastic reform of NATO, he never came out openly in favor of the abandonment of his close contacts or, indeed, the alliance with the United States. While ridiculing and deriding the United Nations, he did not refrain from using it to advance the cause of the admission of China. Disclaiming all colonial ambitions, he reasserted France's interests in the peace and security of Vietnam, and in the neutralization of that area in which France fought a long and unsuccessful war. Finally, neither the rapprochement with the Soviet Union nor the profession of strong Atlantic ties stopped him from recognizing China and establishing trade relations with it. The goal is one and only one —the assertion and the realization of French independence. To achieve this, he picked and chose allies, promoted French interests as the situation shifted and changed, and exploited any opportunity in order that France might climb once more to the level of both a Continental and world power.

As André Fontaine wrote, with justice, in the influential *Le Monde*:

Everything is aimed to accomplish an objective, however remote. A Europe to its full geographic limits, with African, Near Eastern and—who knows—South American extensions. . . . A Europe that will no longer be divided between American and Soviet zones of influence, a Europe which might even receive Russia the day it becomes "Russian" as it is predestined by history, a Europe that will once more become the nerve center of the world and which might if it were necessary arbitrate between the great empires.[24]

De Gaulle's objectives appeared to be the following: the liquidation of the European status quo as created by Yalta and its substitution by something more closely resembling the situation that existed in Europe before 1939—but without the resurrection of German strength; a free hand for France to exert political, cultural, and economic influence in all parts of the world; and, ultimately, the freedom to reconsider all alliances with and commitments to the West or, as the case may be, the East.

AFTER DE GAULLE

Only after we understand fully that de Gaulle was a national spokesman and that his foreign policy was widely accepted not only by the public but also by very significant elements of the French elite, and that he not only expressed but effectively implemented many of the general orientations that the unstable governmental institutions of the Fourth Republic could not manage to translate into policy, can we evaluate the changes since his official departure on April 28, 1969, and, of course, since his death on November 10, 1970. Even in the midst of the most serious upheaval his regime faced—the student-worker rebellion in May and June, 1968—de Gaulle was serenely preaching his "opening to the East" policy with a visit to

24 *Le Monde* (Paris), March 10, 1960.

Rumania. He urged the Rumanians to free themselves of Soviet tutelage without eschewing Soviet friendship, as France had done with NATO without abandoning the Atlantic alliance. Dissatisfied with relations with West Germany and extremely restive with the efforts of many Europeans to endow the Common Market with genuine supranational capabilities in accord with the Rome treaty, he outlined to the British ambassador his plan for a "larger Europe" to include not only England but others at the expense of the integrative institutions and ultimate supranational orientations of "the Six." In fact, both he and his foreign minister insisted upon the "economic" arrangements of the Common Market while evading—indeed, opposing—the political arrangements through which a modicum of political integration could be attained.

In his last formal pronouncement on international politics, his New Year's address of December 31, 1968, de Gaulle cast France in the role of a world power. He did not mention the Common Market or Germany or England's entry; he did not refer to the ruthless Soviet military intervention in Czechoslovakia—a regrettable incident that he attributed, as we have seen, to Yalta and to the division of the world into two blocs; he said nothing about the American-Soviet confrontation in the eastern Mediterranean. He lectured of East-West détente, and urged: an end to the war in Vietnam; the withdrawal of Israeli forces from all occupied territories under the proper frontier guarantees; the entry of China in the United Nations; self-determination for Biafra; a free expression of national life for the French in Canada; aid to the underdeveloped areas of the world and a new international monetary system that would do away with the primacy of the United States currency. In this grandiloquent peroration, the only item missing was France's nuclear strength—conveniently forgotten because economic difficulties had brought about the postponement of French tests. The hard realities of the situation, as we shall see had called for some reconsideration of French atomic strategy.

It is wrong to assume that, with de Gaulle's death, a docile France will return again to the Atlantic fold, or that the Fifth Republic will collapse without leaving any trace on domestic institutions and foreign policy. France is more powerful, has a better sense of its role in the world, has tasted the fruits of independence and the poison of the atomic era, and has regained the posture she had temporarily lost after the shattering defeat of 1940. But it will be also difficult to believe that, in the years to come, France will be in a position to maintain her present intransigent attitude of independence. There will be no return to a position of tutelage and dependence upon the United States, as happened after 1947; but it is unlikely that there will be a full-fledged separation and independence from the Atlantic commitment. It is also unlikely that the development of closer European ties can be thwarted. It is very unlikely, in other words, that there will be a serious crisis of succession—at least with regard to basic foreign policy goals. On the other hand, the new president and the Gaullist leaders may not be able to pursue with the same adroitness all the various and often incompatible options that de Gaulle pursued at high risks, and may have to settle for some clearcut commitments and choices. Lip service will continue to be paid to many of the Gaullist themes, including the general's solicitude for the fate of the French in Canada. Gradually, however, the Gaullist vocabulary is likely to give way to more realistic and pragmatic pronouncements; ambiguity will be replaced with clearcut commitments, and a European rank in terms of a firmly entrenched European base of power will replace worldwide ambitions. But for the foreseeable future, continuity is likely to be the theme.

There are many reasons for this. First, President Georges Pompidou had been as close to de Gaulle as anybody could have ever been and served as prime minister for over six years; secondly, the new president enjoys a solid majority in the National Assembly; thirdly, the combination of the institutions of the Fifth Republic—and more particularly of the office of the presidency—with the massive Gaullist majority in the National Assembly (indeed the two may have to remain linked) gives Pompidou wide latitude for action and effective means of implementing it. French foreign policy is very likely to follow the blueprint traced by General de Gaulle.

Yet differences are likely to develop. Some may be due to a greater degree of realism shared by the younger Gaullists; others, to a genuine feeling in favor of a European commitment; still others, to the realization that nuclear strategy is an expensive proposition and that the Atlantic umbrella should remain intact if France is to maintain both her independence and her security. Finally, there is the problem of the Franco-German relations. The increasing independence of West German foreign policy under Chancellor Willy Brandt to pursue an opening to the East, with treaties with the Soviet Union and Poland and more accommodating relations with East Germany, may spring West Germany loose from the Western European entanglement that Adenauer had fashioned and that de Gaulle wanted to exploit to his own ends. France is not prepared to allow this.

These considerations indicate one of the major directions toward which French foreign policy is likely to move. It will become more and more concerned with European rather than worldwide problems. It will become regionalized and retrenched and by so doing perhaps far more effective than under General de Gaulle. Realism calls for a more careful assessment of resources and a better evaluation of means and goals. The uprisings of May and June of 1968 revealed France's economic weaknesses when compared to West Germany. Military expenditures had to be deferred or scaled down; as a result, nuclear capabilities—in particular, delivery capabilities—cause continued doubts about France's deterrent. Moreover, the rate of technological development in this field is so great among the superpowers that middle-rank nuclear powers such as France are left with the clear realization that obsolescence may well be the payoff for their efforts! The alternatives are either to scale down the nuclear effort—which simply means to reduce the deterrent effect of the French weapon and underline her vulnerability—or to acquiesce to the Atlantic protection and even to reinforce it through individual agreements with the United States, or to seek a European nuclear military arrangement. It is quite likely that France in the coming decade will seek either or both of the last two alternatives.

The European urge shared by many Gaullists is closely linked with the question of Franco-German relations. The new foreign minister, Maurice Schumann, had been a member of a pro-European party. Both at the summit meeting of Hague in December of 1969 and in a number of subsequent addresses, Schumann outlined his famous European "triptych" in this order of priority: the completion of the Common Market, its internal strengthening, and its enlargement. By *completion* he meant the full development of an agricultural market and the ushering in of the final and definitive stages in all economic arrangements, which is an irreversible step. Furthermore, he supported fully the proposal to endow the Common Market with its own resources, to be used under the control of a European parliament. While paying lip service to the Gaullist anti-supranationalist and anti-integrationist themes, Schumann time after time stated that economic union and political union are "two sides of the same coin." By *strengthening* he meant the development, by member nations, of new cooperative and integrative arrangements in technology, fiscal policy, monetary policy, and investment policy. All differential traits in the economies of "the Six" should be eliminated until a genuine whole had been established—one that would assimilate each of the six countries to the American states. Finally, *enlargement* means the addition of new members, notably England. In what appeared a policy shift, treaties between England, Denmark, Ireland, and Norway were signed (January 22, 1972) admitting them to the Common Market. The pro-European commitment, either out of a realistic appreciation of the situation or out of ideological inclination or out of necessity—or because of all three—is obvious, and is likely to continue.

The entry of England into the Common Market is not as surprising as it may appear; it was even supported by some die-hard Gaullists. It is in line with one of the basic patterns of French foreign policy—security from Germany. To dilute the institutions of the European Economic Community at this stage, to return to a Europe with loose ties, may simply give West Germany its head. The direction to which it will be pointed is not important—whether it remains, as it is likely to, in the American orbit, or develops growing economic and diplomatic ties with the East, it will be a threat to and a source of insecurity for the French. At the Hague summit meeting and afterward, the French made concessions not only for the sake of maintaining the EEC, but also in order to show that their intentions were no longer the same as de Gaulle's. These concessions were based upon the realization that cooperation now—even in the political field—among "the Six," was the only way to avoid the disintegration that the Gaullists had threatened so often. Such cooperation among the powers could be achieved and the Community enlarged only when it became clear that a franco-british rapprochment was necessary to offset German power. For the alternatives to the present setup are either a Europe of separate states—with Germany in a far more powerful position to go its way— or a genuine political community in which the French will participate on a basis of equality with its five partners. Closer cooperation—even the prospect of political union—appears now to the French leaders far preferable to the isolation to which the Gaullist policy may have led them or to bilateral Franco-German contacts that were not acceptable to the other European states.

It is, therefore, because of the convergence of a number of factors—a growing realism among the political leaders of the Gaullist majority, the mounting expenses of a nuclear strategy, and the increased strength and independence of West Germany— that France opts for an enlarged Europe and for continuing European commitment. This, it is claimed—how realistically remains to be seen—in no way impedes the so-often stated claims in favor of strengthening the Community ties. As the communiqué issued

late in 1969 states, "What has been done must be jealously preserved and the completion [of the Community] must become a definite reality."[25]

Such an emphasis inevitably calls for a reconsideration of the role of the United States in the context of the Atlantic alliance. French strategy, based until recently upon massive retaliation against the "aggressor," is neither possible nor credible. Further, the notion that France should be prepared to defend herself against any aggressor coming "from any side," in the words of the former chief of staff, the late General Ailleret, could not be reconciled either with international realities or with France's capabilities. Even before de Gaulle had left office, the French military thinking began to change. The enemy was likely to come "from the East," and the French deterrent has no meaning, except in extreme cases, except in the context of the Atlantic alliance and the realities of the United States' overall nuclear strategy and military presence in Europe.

But closer and even integrative political ties among "the Six"—possibly in close military cooperation with England—cannot be excluded. Indeed, France may now demand such ties in order to offset German power. If they were to develop, then France in Western Europe, in cooperation with England and West Germany, will be a powerful entity within an extremely powerful regional bloc. With de Gaulle's departure, France's vocation for rank may become in fact enhanced —but only through regional and European entrenchment. The coming decade may indeed be once more the decade of Western Europe, with the prospect of its becoming truly a third

25 "France at the European Summit Conference," Ambassade de France (The Hague), December 1–2, 1969.

force capable of mediating between the two empires!

This prospect was clearly evoked by de Gaulle's successors. The new president has stated that the tasks ahead appear to be *"entente, détente* and *cooperation."* France continues to insist on the disappearance of the two blocs that divide Europe and supported respectively by the United States and the Soviet Union. The Western European Community will be "open." The new president has visited both the United States and the Soviet Union, and no doubt will be visited in the normal course of time by the heads of both states. Special Franco-Soviet committees have been working out trade relations and technological exchange, and both countries have agreed to consult with each other on all serious foreign policy questions. But France continues also to participate in the meetings of the states that comprise NATO, and the new French leaders have been far more receptive to U.S. investments than was de Gaulle. West Germany's opening to the East has been fully endorsed by the French, and the effort initiated by de Gaulle to befriend the Arab states continues. So has been the demand for peace in Vietnam. Interest in wide-ranging world problems, in other words, continues.

The future role of France is suggested by the analysis, by the minister of foreign affairs, of the changing nature of world relations in the last twenty-five years. The American territory is now vulnerable, he pointed out, the monolithic structure of the Communist world has come to an end, and the "third world" has become a political dimension to be reckoned with. The bipolar world has broken down, and a new flexibility has been introduced. It is a flexibility full of opportunities and risks that France intends to exploit as a European power in concert with the other nations of "the Six" from a position of strength that few would have anticipated a generation ago. The goal still remains to undo Yalta, but only through the creation of a strong Western European entity open both to the West and the East. Both its strength and openness will facilitate the erosion of the two blocs and the respective gradual withdrawal of Soviet and American forces—and with it of their confrontation in Europe.

SELECTED BIBLIOGRAPHY

AILLERET, CHARLES. *L'Aventure atomique française.* Paris: Grasset, 1968.

Année politique. Annual volumes published since 1944. It constitutes one of the best sources of material on French foreign policy.

ARON, RAYMOND, and LERNER, DANIEL. *France Defeats the EDC?* New York: Praeger, 1957.

———. *France, Steadfast and Changing: The Fourth to the Fifth Republic.* Cambridge: Harvard University Press, 1960.

BEAUFRE, ANDRE. *NATO and Europe.* New York: Knopf, 1967.

BELOFF, NORA. *The General Says "No."* Baltimore: Penguin Books, Inc., 1964.

BROGAN, D. W. *France Under the Republic, 1870–1939.* New York: Harper & Row, 1940.

BUCHAN, ALASTAR. *Europe's Futures, Europe's Choices.* New York: Columbia University Press, 1969.

DE CARMOY, GUY. *Les politiques Étrangères de la France, 1944–66.* Paris: La Table Ronde, 1967.

DE GAULLE, CHARLES. *Discours et Messages.* 5 vols. Paris: Plon, 1969–70. This is the most authoritative and detailed collection of all of de Gaulle's utterances from June 18, 1940, to April 28, 1969, when he withdrew from the presidency.

———. *War Memoirs.* vol. 1, *The Call to Honour.* New York: Viking Press, 1955. Vol. 2, *Unity.* New York: Simon & Schuster, 1959. Vol. 3, *Salvation.* New York: Simon & Schuster, 1960.

————. *Le renuveau.* 1971.

————. *L'effort.* 1971. This and the above volume cover de Gaulle's presidency.

DEUTSCH, KARL W., et al. *Elite Attitudes and Western Europe.* New York: Charles Scribner's Sons, 1966.

DUROSELLE, J. B. *La politique étrangère et ses fondements.* Paris: Librairie Armand Colin, 1954.

FURNISS, EDGAR, JR. *France: Troubled Ally.* New York: Harper & Row, 1960.

DE LA GORSE, ANDRE-MARI. *La France Contre les Empires.*

GROSSER, ALFRED. *La politique extérieure de la 4iéme République.* Paris: Librairie Armand Colin, 1963.

————. *La politique extérieure de la 5iéme République.* Paris: Éditions Sevil, 1963.

HOFFMANN, STANLEY. "De Gaulle's Memoirs: The Hero in History." *World Politics*, October, 1960, no. 1, 140–56.

HOFFMANN, STANLEY, et al. *In Search of France.* Cambridge: Harvard University Press, 1964.

HOWARD, J. E. *Parliament and Foreign Policy in France.* London: Cresset Press, 1948.

JOUVE, EDMOND. *Le General de Gaulle et la construction de l'Europe, 1940–66.* 2 vols. Paris, 1967.

KERTESZ, STEPHEN D., and FITZSIMONS, M. A. *Diplomacy in a Changing World.* South Bend, Ind.: University of Notre Dame, 1959. See the section by Prof. J.-B. Duroselle, "French Diplomacy in Post-World War," pp. 204–50.

KISSINGER, HENRY. *The Troubled Alliance.* New York: McGraw-Hill Book Co., 1965.

KULSKI, W. W. *De Gaulle and the World System.* Syracuse, N.Y.: Syracuse University Press, 1967.

LUETHY, HERBERT. *France Against Herself.* New York: Praeger, 1955.

MCKAY, DONALD D. *United States and France.* Cambridge: Harvard University Press, 1951.

MACRIDIS, ROY C. *De Gaulle—Implacable Ally.* New York: Harper & Row, 1966.

————. "De Gaulle's Foreign Policy and the Fifth Republic." *Yale Review*, Winter, 1961.

MACRIDIS, ROY C., and BROWN, BERNARD E. *The De Gaulle Republic: Quest for Unity.* Homewood, Ill.: Dorsey Press, 1960.

NORTHEDGE, F. S., ed. *The Foreign Policies of the Powers.* New York: Praeger, 1968. See especially pp. 187–220.

STEEL, RONALD. *The End of Alliance: America and the Future of Europe.* New York: Viking Press, 1964.

Sondages: Revue française de l'opinion publique, "La politique étrangère de la France et l'opinion publique: 1954–1957," nos. 1 and 2, 1958. Also subsequent issues between 1960 and 1970.

WILLIAMS, PHILIP. *Politics in Post-war France.* New York: Longmans, Green & Co., 1954.

WILLIS, ROY. *France, Germany and the New Europe, 1945–1967.* New York: Oxford University Press, 1968.

Pompidou's major pronouncements have been translated and disseminated by the French Press and Information Service, 972 Fifth Ave., New York, N.Y. 10021. The reader will find them also in the *Année politique*, 1969, 1970, 1971.

Chapter Four

FOREIGN POLICY OF THE GERMAN FEDERAL REPUBLIC

KARL W. DEUTSCH

GEBHARD L. SCHWEIGLER

LEWIS J. EDINGER

THE HISTORICAL SETTING AND BASIC ATTITUDES

In all countries, the making of foreign policy is influenced by the legacy of the past. Among the small groups of influential persons, as well as among the broad masses of the voters, memories of the past help to shape the images of what foreign policy is and what it could be. Such memories guide men's imagination as to what tasks any present or future foreign policy could accomplish, what persons and institutions should accomplish them, and by what methods. People turn to memories for answers to their basic questions: "Who are we?" "What do others expect of us?" and "What should we expect of ourselves?" In all countries, memories thus fashion expectations; everywhere they influence the interplay between foreign policy and the ongoing process of national self-perception and self-definition. In Germany, however, these historical memories are, in some respects, more self-contradictory than in any other large country.

The Heritage of Memories

From the tenth to the thirteenth century, the medieval German empire was the leading power of Europe, claiming the symbolic and, at times, the actual leadership of Western Christendom. For another three centuries, from the thirteenth to the sixteenth century, German princes and cities, German knights and German merchants were predominant in central and eastern Europe without finding serious rivals. Generations of German schoolchildren have had impressed upon them those three centuries of universal greatness and six centuries of unchallenged German predominance in central Europe; but they have been given a far less clear picture of the processes that were at work in the centuries of decline and catastrophe that followed.

By the sixteenth century, although Germany had had no effective central government for almost three hundred years, it had not suffered any serious risk of foreign military invasions. With the rise of more effectively organized states in western Europe, this situation changed. France, at times allied with Sweden, fought the Spanish and Austrian empires on German soil for almost two centuries, leaving the country divided into innumerable independent states. The political fragmentation of Germany was made far more serious by the religious cleavages of the Reformation of the early sixteenth century, which left the German people approximately two-thirds Protestant and one-third Catholic. In the same period, the routes of world trade shifted away from central Europe to the Atlantic coast, and to the ocean lanes to countries overseas. These economic processes were subtle and anonymous, but their results were disastrous and conspicuous, like the decline of a patient who is weakened by a serious disease of which he remains ignorant. In any case, it seemed as if the world were turning cold and hostile toward Germany. Many of the prosperous German cities declined, while French and English trade centers increased in size and influence. These unfavorable economic developments left the German middle class economically and culturally backward, as well as politically weak and lacking in self-reliance, during the period

when the middle classes to the west became more prosperous and more self-reliant.

Throughout the sixteenth and seventeenth centuries, German states, German cities, and German politics remained, on the whole, petty; no effective economic or political centers for the entire area developed. Both in spite and because of this situation, a new concept—Germany (*Deutschland*) —came into use, and a vague notion spread that the Germans were a single people with some sort of common identity, some common destiny, and some common need for safety and prestige.

Early in the seventeenth century, when economic decline and political frustration had become well established on the German scene, the full force of political catastrophe struck. From 1618 to 1648, about one-third of the German people perished in the Thirty Years' War, waged essentially by foreign countries for reasons of European power politics, with no significant result for the German people other than suffering and devastation. During the rest of the seventeenth and eighteenth centuries, Germany remained a battlefield of foreign powers; in the course of these two centuries, Germans acquired an image of Germany as the "land of the middle," helplessly exposed to attacks, surrounded by hostile powers, and condemned to be the perpetual victim of foreign aggressors because of her own lack of unity, organization, and concentrated military power.

By the end of the eighteenth century, two major patterns of response to this situation had become widespread. One consisted in accepting the political and religious division of the country and the almost total absence of significant military power on the part of most of the petty states into which the country was divided. Resigned to viewing politics as hostile and evil—as Martin Luther had already pictured it—some Germans felt free to concentrate their energies on diligent productive work in trades and crafts, in economic activity, and, perhaps most important of all, in the arts and sciences.

A contrasting but related pattern of response developed in the state of Brandenburg-Prussia: if politics was evil, force and cunning were its only realistic methods. This view stressed the strengthening of the state as the only organization that could safeguard the individual in a world of enemies. To make this state ever larger, stronger, more efficient, and more disciplined was believed the only way of ensuring a minimum of security and dignity for its population. The subjects of the king of Prussia might at least live in a state of law, with an orderly administration and some security against the arbitrary whim of foreign powers. Thus military assertiveness and political passivity—symbolized by Potsdam, the town of the Prussian soldier-kings, and Weimar, the town of the German poets—became the two equal and opposite responses of the Germans to their predicament.

In the course of the nineteenth century, these two German traditions were partly fused under the impact of the German industrial revolution and of the German political unification movement, which culminated, in 1871, in the establishment of a united German Empire under Prussian leadership. The new political and social system linked much of the German intellectual and literary heritage to the Prussian tradition of widespread public education and instruction. The German intellectuals of the generation that reached maturity after 1809, and that experienced the closing phases of the Napoleonic wars, were receptive to nationalism and impressed with the need for national political power. It was not only the memories of the humiliating French occupation in the days of Napoleon that made national military power seem ever more important; the growth of German industry and commerce created a whole series of conflicts with the neighbors of Germany. There were disputes—with the Netherlands about the shipping tolls on the lower Rhine, with Denmark about the duchies of Schleswig and Holstein and, hence, about the territory of the proposed German Kiel Canal between the Baltic and North seas, for example. Only military power seemed likely to prevent endless frustrations in these conflicts and to resolve them in accordance with what were considered German needs.

In the course of the nineteenth century, and particularly after 1848, the German middle class and the German liberal parties turned increasingly to an alliance with their own princes, with the aristocracy and the military castes of Germany and, in particular, to an alliance with the Prussian state. Bismarck's policy of "blood and iron," which accomplished the reunification of Germany in three wars between 1864 and 1871, found in the end the overwhelming support of the German intellectuals and the German middle class, as well as of most of the German people. The coming of the railroads and the triumph of industrialization and urbanization took place in the same decades as these triumphs of power politics, and Bismarck's empire was credited with all.

The popularity of Bismarck and the empire which he founded remained remarkably high during the early years of the German Federal Republic; in 1952, 36 percent of a cross-section of West German adults said that, among great men, Bismarck had done most for Germany. However, as Chancellor Konrad Adenauer succeeded in consolidating West Germany's position in the world and bringing about a widely noted *Wirtschaftswunder* ("economic miracle") at home, his popularity began to increase rapidly. In 1952 only 3 percent of all respondents had indicated that they felt Adenauer, of all great Germans, had done most for Germany; in May, 1967, shortly after Adenauer's death, 60 percent of all West Germans considered him to have done most for Germany. Nevertheless, the fact that, in 1967, 17 percent of the respondents still named Bismarck as Germany's greatest benefactor provides some indication of his lingering popularity as one of Germany's major historical figures.[1] However, the empire over which Bismarck had ruled no longer looms as a golden age in the memories of West Germans. When they were asked, in 1951, when in this century they felt that Germany had fared best, 45 percent of a representative sample of West German adults answered, "before 1914," while only 2 percent said, "today." When the same question was asked in May, 1970, only 5 percent claimed, "before 1914," while an overwhelming majority (81 percent) voted for "today" as the period in which they felt Germany had been best off.[2]

But the memories of the period of Bismarck's empire are by no means all idyllic. They include memories of international rivalries in the age of imperialism, and images of the envy and resentment of foreign countries at German commercial and political suc-

cesses. They include the beginning of the themes of a German bid for "living space," for a "place in the sun," and the double image of empire-building and colonialization by other Western powers, such as France and England. These countries were seen as models and reference groups whom the Germans should imitate and from whom they had to learn how to get on in the world; at the same time, they were viewed as envious enemies ready to encircle and destroy Germany.

By 1914, a very large number of Germans saw themselves engaged, at one and the same time, in a bitterly competitive struggle for world power and a desperate defensive effort for national survival. They welcomed the seemingly clearcut state of open war as a long-awaited release from the tensions and frustrations of the prewar years. World War I was thus at first accepted with enthusiasm; about 3 million published poems celebrated the event within the first nine months after its outbreak in August, 1914. At the beginning, volunteers for combat duty were numerous, and the fighting morale of front-line troops remained high until close to the end. Even after 1918, many Germans refused to accept the fact of defeat; about one-quarter of the German voters continued to support parties that insisted that with better home-front morale the war would have been won.

Some of these memories of an inevitable power struggle against foreign envy and hostility were revived and reinforced by the impact of the great economic depression that hit Germany in 1929, and which, by early 1933, had produced 6 million unemployed—almost one-third of the industrial labor force. The image of a hostile international environment; the image of a German empire, similar to the British Empire, as a solution to Germany's difficulties; the image of a

[1] Elisabeth Nölle and Erich Peter Neumann, *Jahrbuch der öffentlichen Meinung, 1965–1967* [Yearbook of public opinion] (Allensbach: Verlag für Demoskopie, 1967), p. 144. All data in this yearbook are for samples of the adult population—i.e., above sixteen years—unless otherwise indicated.

[2] Institut für Demoskopie Allensbach (IfD), *Allensbacher Berichte,* "Geliebte Gegenwart" (Allensbach, May, 1970).

desperate bid for living space and a place among the leading imperial nations of the world—all played their part among the appeals by which Hitler rose to power. At the beginning of the Nazi terror, in the elections of March, 1933, as many as 43 percent of the German voters supported Hitler's National-Socialist party; another 8 percent supported Hitler's close allies in matters of foreign policy at that time, the German Nationalist party. Fifteen years later, in October, 1948, 41 percent of a cross-section of West German voters recalled that they themselves had approved of the Nazi seizure of power in 1933. In the same month, 57 percent agreed that National Socialism was a good idea that had been badly carried out.

After World War II

At the end of World War II, Germany was utterly defeated, thoroughly destroyed, completely occupied, and forcibly divided. Defeat, destruction, occupation, and division thus marked the beginnings of a new period in German history; it is to their consequences one must turn in the effort to explain and understand postwar German politics, both domestic and foreign. Defeat brought feelings of guilt and shame and efforts to overcome these feelings either through repression or through *Wiedergutmachung* ("restitution," literally "making-good-again"); destruction necessitated the concentration of all remaining strength in the domestic sphere, leaving little for any foreign policy endeavors; occupation meant government by Allied commanders, and only a gradual return of governmental powers to appointed and elected German officials; and division, finally, led to the expulsion of millions of Germans from their homes in Eastern Europe, the severing of most ties between the Soviet occupation zone and the Western occupation zones, and ultimately to the creation of two new—and in many ways hostile —German states on German soil which might eventually become nation-states in their own right. How the West Germans atttempted to cope with these problems through their foreign policy, how public attitudes on these questions developed, and what the prospects for the future are will be discussed in this and the following sections.

The utter defeat of Germany in 1945 faced most West Germans with the psychologically difficult task of coming to terms with their country's and their own immediate past; *die Vergangenheit bewältigen* ("mastering the past") became one of the key

TABLE 4.1

"It is, of course, difficult to say, but what would you think— whose fault was it that war broke out in 1939?"

	Oct., 1951	May, 1955	Apr., 1956	May, 1959	Aug., 1962	May, 1964	Apr., 1967
Germany	32%	43%	47%	50%	53%	51%	62%
Other states	24	14	12	11	9	9	8
Both sides	18	15	11	10	10	7	8
International capitalism	6	5	5	6	3	2	2
Circumstances	4	3	3	3	5	2	2
Other	1	1	2	2	1	2	2
Don't know	15	19	20	19	20	28	16

Source: *Jahrbuch 1967*, p. 146.

TABLE 4.2

"Do you believe that we are more capable and more
gifted than other peoples?"

	May, 1955	June, 1956	May, 1959	Jan., 1960	July, 1960	Feb., 1965
No	38%	42%	50%	55%	55%	50%
Yes, basically	39	33	30	29	27	28
Yes, certainly	21	23	18	13	15	17
Don't know	2	2	2	3	3	5

Source: *Jahrbuch 1967*, p. 154.

TABLE 4.3

"Do you believe that Germany will one day rank again as one
of the most powerful states in the world?"

	June, 1954	Sept., 1955	June, 1962	Feb., 1965
No, I don't believe	41%	48%	53%	52%
Yes, I do believe	38	25	19	17
Impossible to say	21	27	28	31

Source: *Jahrbuch 1967*, p. 155.

phrases in postwar German politics. The dangers inherent in "stab-in-the-back" theories of defeat, advanced after 1918 by nationalist parties, were all too vividly remembered. A massive education—indeed, "re-education"—effort was launched by the occupation powers in order to forestall a rebirth of militant nationalism. Judging from the results presented in table 4.1, such efforts met with a slow, but steadily increasing, measure of success.

While a constantly growing number of West Germans faced up to their country's responsibility for World War II, a similarly increasing number of them, as table 4.2 indicates, began to feel less certain about the Germans' superiority over other people.

During the same period of time an increasingly large number of West Germans had given up all dreams of ever living in a powerful state again, as table 4.3 clearly shows. A poll taken in November, 1968, shows that only 6 percent of a representative sample of

West Germans believed the German Federal Republic to be a "great power" today, while 53 percent ranked her a "middle power," and 35 percent a "small power."[3] When the Institut für Demoskopie Allensbach (IfD) asked two thousand carefully selected West Germans in July, 1969, whether they thought that the political position of the Federal Republic in the world had improved or deteriorated during the past ten years, a large majority of 68 percent said, "improved," only 11 percent claimed, "deteriorated," and 21 percent were "undecided."[4] Together with the pre-

[3] INFAS, "Report," May 5, 1969.
[4] IfD, "Die Stimmung im Bundesgebiet," Aug. 26, 1969. This is one in a series of such reports prepared by the IfD for the Press and Information Office of the Federal Government. The authors gratefully acknowledge the help of Conrad Ahlers, chief of the Press and Information Office, and Prof. Elisabeth Nölle-Neumann, director of the IfD, in obtaining these data.

viously reported results on polls concerning when Germany was best off and which historical figure had done most for Germany,[5] these results clearly show that an overwhelming majority of West Germans has come to accept the Federal Republic's limited role in world politics, partly because of a heightened awareness of past mistakes and partly because of a sharpened sense of what is possible within the present international system.

During the twelve years of the Third Reich, the Germans had inflicted the most terrible of sufferings upon the Jews, upon their western neighbors, and upon the eastern European countries. German attacks on Poland, Russia, France, Belgium, the Netherlands, Norway, Yugoslavia and Greece had caused many millions of deaths and huge devastation; German annihilation camps and execution squads had slaughtered six million Jews, men, women, and children. When the war had come to an end, the Germans faced the difficult task—difficult psychologically as well as materially—of making restitution. A large number of West Germans initially were not prepared to do so. After Adenauer had single-handedly negotiated a restitution agreement with Nahum Goldmann, president of the World Jewish Congress, in 1952, 44 percent of those West Germans asked in a public

opinion poll felt it "unnecessary" that "Germany should make restitution to Israel in the form of 3,000 million marks' worth of goods"; 24 percent agreed with the idea of this restitution, but thought the amount was too high; 11 percent expressed unqualified agreement; 21 percent were undecided.[6] However, after Adenauer's death in 1967, 38 percent of a representative sample of West Germans agreed that restitution to the Jews and reconciliation with Israel had been one of his greatest achievements, ranking in their estimation before West Germany's joining NATO, the founding of the EEC (the Common Market), and the recovery of the Saar.[7] Finally, during the Middle East war of June, 1967, 59 percent of those West Germans polled said they were on the side of the Israelis, while 6 percent were for the Egyptians; 27 percent expressed a sense of neutrality.[8] These figures indicate how West Germans have tried to come to terms with that terrible aspect of their past.

As noted in footnote 5, 70 percent of all West Germans polled in 1967 considered the reconciliation and establishment of friendship with France one of Adenauer's greatest achievements. Many fears and prejudices—on both sides of the Rhine—had to be overcome before this effort at mutual reconciliation culminated in the Franco-German treaty of friendship in 1963. However, as table 4.4 indicates, this policy of reconciliation met, from the very beginning, with a relatively large degree of public approval. In May, 1955, 83 percent of those West Germans asked said they personally

---

[5] It is an interesting reflection of the West Germans' sense of priorities in foreign affairs that they gave the following answers, when they were asked in May, 1967, after Adenauer's death, what they considered to be his greatest achievements:

Arranging for the return of German
  prisoners of war from Russia . . . 75%
Reconciliation and friendship with
  France 70
Having helped Germany to regain
  stature and importance in the
  world 65

Source: *Jahrbuch 1967*, p. 187.

[6] IfD, *The Germans: Public Opinion Polls, 1947–1966* (Allensbach: Verlag für Demoskopie, 1967), p. 188.

[7] Nevertheless, of course, this achievement was ranked below those mentioned in footnote 5.

[8] *Jahrbuch 1967*, p. 473.

TABLE 4.4

"Do you feel it is right, or wrong, of Adenauer to seek to establish
a good relationship with France?"

	Feb., 1952	Nov., 1953	Sept., 1954
Right	48%	65%	59%
Right, with reservations	17	10	13
Wrong	13	5	9
Undecided	22	20	19

Source: Institut für Demoskopie Allensbach (IfD), *The Germans*, p. 535.

TABLE 4.5

"Do you feel it is possible, by and large, for us to establish lasting friendship
with France, or do you think there are too many differences between us?"

	May, 1955	July, 1962	Sept., 1962
Lasting friendship possible	40%	52%	59%
Too many differences	32	16	15
Undecided	28	32	26

Source: IfD, *The Germans*, p. 535.

wanted to see the achievement of a permanent reconciliation with the French. But when they were questioned whether they felt that this was possible, a considerable number of them indicated that they saw too many differences between the Germans and the French. Such answers reflected a general feeling of distrust which decreased only slowly during the years to come, as table 4.5 shows. After the treaty of friendship between France and West Germany had been concluded, 51 percent of West Germans, as polled in July, 1963, said the treaty was a good thing; only 17 percent indicated that they thought the treaty bad because it might prejudice relations with other Western allies; and 32 percent were undecided or had not heard about the treaty.[9] Today, despite some ups and downs in Franco-German relations, close cooperation with France is one of the cornerstones of West German foreign policy, sup-

ported by an overwhelming majority of the West German people.

However, as much as the Germans seem to value their newly found friendship with France, most West Germans, when asked directly, put close cooperation and friendship with the United States above their friendship with France. Americans are in general more admired than the French (22 percent vs. 4 percent in a January, 1967, poll[10]); their importance for most West Germans is unquestioned: maintaining good relations with the United States has been and continues to be *the* overriding issue in West German foreign policy. In part, this may reflect a certain amount of distrust between the Germans and the French, as has been argued elsewhere.[11] In the

[10] *Jahrbuch 1967*, p. 429. The number of those claiming that they liked Americans increased from 37 percent in 1957 to 58 percent in 1965. See also IfD, *The Germans*, p. 543.

[11] See, e.g., Karl W. Deutsch et al., *France, Germany, and the Western Alliance* (New York: Charles Scribner's Sons, 1967).

[9] IfD, *The Germans*, p. 536.

TABLE 4.6

"With which of the following countries should we cooperate
particularly closely?"

	Mar., 1953	Aug., 1954	Dec., 1956	Sept., 1959	June, 1962	Aug., 1963	Jan., 1967	Apr., 1970	Nov., 1970
U.S.	83%	78%	84%	81%	82%	90%	72%	80%	86%
France	55	46	42	48	60	70	76	58	75
England	62	58	39	49	54	65	52	50	62
Russia	18	22	18	31	22	27	41	32	52
Japan	42	35	31	32	31	31	22	28	43
Italy	44	34	30	31	36	30	22	22	36
Poland	11	11	17	25	22	27	27	19	35
Israel	15	13	9	19	18	17	16	14	24

Source: IfD, "Die Deutschen als Kosmopoliten," *Allensbacher Berichte,* Jan. 16, 1971.

main, however, this admiration for and reliance on the United States simply reflect postwar political developments, as well as the position of the United States in the world today. The American occupation regime, for one, was considered by many the most lenient and beneficent; and in the context of European security requirements, the West Germans are very clearly aware that only close military cooperation with the United States can provide some measure of security for the Federal Republic. The results presented in table 4.6 are, therefore, by no means surprising. In a series of polls taken by the Institut für Demoskopie in May, 1965, a consistent majority of around 60 percent expressed their belief that it was more important for Germany to cooperate closely with the United States than with France, particularly with regard to the economy (58 percent for U.S. vs. 20 percent for France), and even more so in military matters (63 percent vs. 11 percent); but in cultural relations the West Germans seem more willing to seek closer relations with France (37 percent) than with the United States (26 percent).[12]

There can be no doubt but that an overwhelming majority of West Ger-

mans "side with the West in the present world conflict" (72 percent in April, 1966).[13] This fact is evident in their insistence on closer relationships with the United States as well as in their complete acceptance of West German membership in a North Atlantic Treaty Organization dominated by the United States. (In January, 1969, the Institut für Demoskopie asked a West German sample whether the Federal Republic should remain in NATO: 79 percent agreed and only 4 percent disagreed; at the same time, 81 percent said that the United States had the most influence in NATO. Presumably, then, the prevailing influence of the United States over NATO is completely acceptable to most West Germans, since they have no desire to cancel West German membership in NATO.)[14] But yet, throughout the short history of the Federal Republic, a consistently large number of West Germans, when polled, have indicated a certain preference for neutrality. In September, 1965, the IfD asked its respondents, "Should we continue with our close military alliance with the United States or should we try to take up a neutral position, like Switzerland,

[12] *Jahrbuch 1967,* p. 446.

[13] Ibid., p. 435.
[14] IfD, "Die Stimmung im Bundesgebiet," March 6, 1969.

for instance?"; 46 percent wanted to remain allied with the United States, 37 percent wanted to become neutral, 17 percent were undecided.[15] What these and other polls reflect appears to be a certain reluctance on the part of many West Germans to become involved in political disputes of the big powers (in early 1967, over 80 percent of those asked repeatedly agreed with the proposition that "we should keep out of the quarrels of the Big Powers").[16] Even more so, such polls point toward a deep fear of a war between two superpowers in which Germany would be caught in the middle, a war which undoubtedly would leave Germany utterly destroyed once more, whether actually defeated or not. It seems, therefore, not too surprising that, despite a general support for the West and the United States, most West Germans—throughout the 1950s, at least—wanted to stay out rather than take sides "if it should come to a war between Russia and the U.S."[17] Similarly, it can only be called logical if an overwhelming majority of West Germans consistently have expressed their disapproval of the Federal Republic's acquiring access to nuclear weapons, despite promises of increased security and raised status linked to such a move.[18] Most West Germans, in short, appear today to

have resigned themselves to their country's role as a small or middle power, content with the amount of military security guaranteed by military cooperation with the United States, but unwilling to pursue the goal of military security beyond the maintenance of close ties with the United States.

Europe

In general, most West Germans today appear to share relatively little interest in foreign affairs. In fact, to most West Germans, foreign policy means primarily the pursuit of economic advantages which eventually would benefit each person. Foreign policy goals pursued for idealistic reasons—such as European unity—or because of national concerns—such as the reunification of Germany or regaining the so-called lost territories beyond the Oder-Neisse line—are meeting increasingly with benign neglect, although the level of purely verbal support for such goals remains fairly high. Thus, on the question of the unification of Europe, a consistently large majority of between 70 percent and 80 percent of all respondents asked between 1955 and 1967 have indicated that, if it ever came to a vote, they would vote for the creation of a "United States of Europe," while only around 5 percent said they would vote against it.[19] On the other hand, between 1953 and 1967, a surprisingly consistent one-third of all West Germans polled said that they did not expect to see the creation of a United States of Europe; another third was optimistic, while the remaining third was undecided.[20] Such expectations, of course, in many ways reflect at once an assessment of the willingness of others to work for that

---

15 IfD, *The Germans*, p. 523.

16 EMNID Institut, "Monatliche Berichte" (Bielefeld, February–April, 1967). The authors gratefully acknowledge the help of Viggo Graf Blücher in obtaining these reports prepared for the Press and Information Office of the Federal Government.

17 See Richard L. Merritt and Donald J. Puchala, *Western European Attitudes on Arms Control, Defense, and European Unity, 1952–1963* (New Haven: Yale University Political Science Research Library, January, 1966), p. 37.

18 See IfD, *The Germans*, p. 441, as well as many polls on "the most important questions today" throughout the *Jahrbücher*.

19 *Jahrbuch 1967*, p. 454.
20 Ibid., p. 453.

goal as well as one's own willingness.

By the 1970s a large majority of West Germans appeared to support various European institutions as well as the inclusion of other countries, such as Great Britain and some Scandinavian countries, in the European Common Market. However, their degree of interest in these institutions and issues seems to be quite small. In one series of polls, for example, EMNID Institut in 1967 asked a number of West Germans whether they were for a direct election of representatives to the European Parliament in Strasbourg; 34 percent said they were for it, 15 percent were against, 10 percent gave no answer, and 41 percent said they thought the question was "uninteresting." Similarly, when asked what common tasks European institutions in Strasbourg and Paris should concern themselves with, 34 percent said this question did not interest them, while 40 percent mentioned a common foreign policy and 31 percent a common defense.[21] In general, it could be said that most West Germans support in some idealistic sense the goal of European unification, but that they are bewildered by the complexities of emerging political and economic institutions with which they find it difficult to identify. They seem to be willing, as in March, 1970, to have one European currency instead of national currencies (52 percent in favor, 26 percent against); they admit that the Common Market has had beneficial effects on their personal standard of living (49 percent); but a slight majority of 51 percent is not prepared to make personal sacrifices of a financial nature to bring about European unification (42 percent would do so). And when respondents were asked whether they favored having one team to represent Europe at the Olympics, only 25 percent agreed, while 51 percent were against the idea. Finally, only 35 percent of those West Germans polled indicated that they were in favor of having a European flag flown at important functions, while 41 percent said they preferred the national flag.[22] In short, national symbols and institutions appear to maintain their strong hold over the imagination of a large number of West Germans today.

However, despite the persistence of national symbols and institutions, most West Germans are not prepared to pursue the goal of becoming once again a completely independent nation-state. In a series of polls taken between 1950 and 1966, a consistent majority of West Germans preferred a Germany as a member of a united Europe with equal rights to a Germany completely independent and with its own customs borders; in fact, by 1966, 62 percent preferred membership in a united Europe, while only 23 percent expressed more nationalistic sentiments.[23] In part, of course, these results reflect the postwar German desire for a restoration of equality with other European powers, a goal which was to be achieved through active participation in European unification policies. Even so, the results of these polls portray the slow increase of a pro-European unification sentiment (at nearly one percentage point per year, from 48 percent in 1950) that allowed successive administrations to pursue European policies.

The priority of national goals becomes evident in another context: the

21 EMNID Institut, "Meinungsbild zur aktuellen Europapolitik in der deutschen Bevölkerung" (Bielefeld, August, 1967).

22 Europäische Gemeinschaft, "Dokumentation," September, 1970, pp. 30–31.

23 EMNID Institut, "Einstellung der Deutschen über den gemeinsamen Markt und den Europagedanken" (Bielefeld, July, 1967), p. A6.

TABLE 4.7

"Which, in your opinion, is the most important question we in West Germany
should at present occupy ourselves with?"

	1951	1955	1959	1962	1965	1967	1969	1970
Reunification	18%	34%	45%	30%	45%	18%	22%	12%
Economy	45	28	15	20	27	62	24	40
Peace	20	16	16	26	9	4	15	11

Sources: IfD, *The Germans*, p. 214, and "Die Stimmung im Bundesgebiet," March 25, 1970.

choice between European unification and the reunification of Germany. When these alternatives were presented to a sample of West Germans between 1951 and 1965, a consistent minority of around 25 percent voted in favor of European unification, while an equally consistent majority of around 70 percent (with the exception of 1951 and 1953, when 57 percent expressed that opinion) wanted to see German reunification achieved first.[24] These data point once more to the conclusion that a really effective political demand for the unification of Europe was lacking in West Germany, while a generally high level of support for some measures of unification gave the federal governments considerable leeway in their policies, as long as such policies did not commit major resources or give up important West German goals.

Ostpolitik

Just how low the goal of a united Europe has always ranked as a political issue among the West German population becomes evident in a series of polls taken by the Institut für Demoskopie every year since 1951; these polls disclose also some of the real priorities of West German politics. The respondents were asked: "Which do you consider the most important question we in West Germany should at present occupy ourselves

[24] Ibid., p. A5.

with?"; the question was open-ended and allowed more than one answer. Three areas of main concern have remained over the years, but with some very interesting shifts of attitudes at critical points in the history of the Federal Republic. In short, whenever the economy was going well, the goal of reunification received most support; during times of economic difficulties, such as in the early fifties and the late sixties, the improvement of economic conditions was considered to be the most important political task; and finally, at times of foreign policy crises, such as in 1961 after the building of the Berlin Wall, as many as 26 percent believed maintaining peace in Europe to be the most important goal for West German politics. (Table 4.7 summarizes some of the most relevant data.) The goal of European integration was mentioned by as many as 12 percent in January, 1963, at the time the Franco-German friendship treaty was concluded; however, before and after that date, European integration was included as a "most important task" by only 2–3 percent of all respondents.

The data in table 4.7 reveal, of course, the great emphasis a large number of West Germans place on their economic well-being to the exclusion of most other political goals when times appear relatively bad. This seems understandable, since the Germans after the war were faced with the task of rebuilding their destroyed country, a task which came to preoccupy their minds for a long time to come. In the process they resigned themselves to small-power status and showed very little interest in foreign policy, imposing on successive federal governments few restraints, with one exception—that regarding *Ostpolitik* ("Eastern policy").

To be sure, available public opinion polls seem to indicate a high degree of willingness on the part of most West Germans to pursue an active foreign policy toward the Eastern bloc countries throughout most of the history of the Federal Republic. When the prime minister of the German Democratic Republic, Grotewohl, invited Adenauer in 1950 to meet with him in order to discuss measures for the reunification of Germany, 49 percent of those asked thought Adenauer should accept the invitation (only 27 percent disagreed).[25] When another such proposal was made (and declined by Adenauer) in 1951, 64 percent of all respondents said the federal government should meet with representatives of the East German regime (15 percent disagreed).[26] Even after the Berlin Wall, dividing both parts of the city, had been built on August 13, 1961, only 32 percent of a sample of West Germans agreed with a statement to the effect that "only when the wall is gone should negotiations with the East begin, but in no case sooner"; 54 percent said "I am of a different opinion. . . . Now there is nothing else to do but to negotiate so that the situation won't become worse."[27] When the Institut für Demoskopie polled West Germans regarding the suggestion that a proposed exchange of speakers between the SPD (Social Democratic party) and the SED (*Sozialistische Einheitspartei Deutsch-*

lands—the Communist party of East Germany) in the summer of 1966 should not take place as long as refugees were shot and killed at the Berlin Wall, 65 percent insisted on having the talks anyway; only 16 percent agreed with the suggestion.[28] And finally, even after the invasion of Czechoslovakia in August, 1968, 58 percent of those West Germans polled said that the federal government should "continue to insist on talks between ministers from Bonn and East Berlin," while only 22 percent said "no talks" should be held.[29] In short, the federal government appears always to have had ample room for official contacts with representatives from East Berlin as well as from other Eastern European countries, in particular the Soviet Union,[30] despite official West German claims that such contacts would undermine the West German right of sole representation of all of Germany.[31]

The fact that consecutive administrations, particularly under chancellors Adenauer and Erhard, both members of the Christian Democratic Union (CDU), did not make use of such public latitude may in part reflect their reluctance to engage in an effort to seek reunification at the expense of West German integration

---

[25] *Jahrbuch 1955*, p. 318.
[26] Ibid.
[27] *Jahrbuch 1964*, p. 524.
[28] *Jahrbuch 1967*, p. 397.
[29] IfD, "Allensbacher Berichte," September, 1968, p. 5.
[30] In June, 1955, after the Soviet government had invited Adenauer to come to Moscow, 82 percent of those West Germans polled said that he should accept the invitation; only 3 percent were against it (IfD, *The Germans*, p. 246).
[31] Most West Germans never seem to have accepted such claims; in May, 1966, 54 percent of a representative sample indicated that this view was not correct, while only 14 percent felt that contacts would undermine this right; 32 percent were undecided. (Poll taken by INFAS, Bad Godesberg, and published in *Polls* 2, no. 2, 34).

into Western Europe, as has often been argued.[32] On the other hand, of course, public opinion did limit considerably the amount of freedom any West German government would have had in serious negotiations with Eastern bloc countries. Primarily, the overwhelming majority of West Germans were simply unwilling formally to recognize the existence of the German Democratic Republic (often referred to in public statements as either the "Eastern zone," a "phenomenon," or simply "over there") and the permanency of the western border of Poland—the Oder-Neisse line, separating Poland and the G.D.R. shown below. As will be seen shortly, it was only after public opposition to such measures had eroded over a long period of time that a more active Eastern policy could be pursued by a federal government not connected with the policies of the past.

Such policies of the past included the strong Western orientation of German foreign policy under the Adenauer administration, a policy which in many ways seemed unavoidable considering the heavy influence of the Allied powers over the foreign policy of the Federal Republic. In particular, the so-called Germany treaty of 1954 had specified the rights of the Allied powers pertaining to Germany as a whole; subsequently this right was interpreted in West Germany as a responsibility on the part of the Western powers to seek the reunification of Germany, while the role of the Federal Republic was considered to be limited at best. While there existed a great deal of awareness that a solution to the "German problem" had to be sought in Moscow, the policy makers in Bonn were reluctant to deal di-

rectly with Moscow, partly because to do so seemed outside their responsibilities, partly because such a policy might have raised fears of another "Rapallo"-type agreement with the Russians at the expense of the Western powers; and finally—and perhaps most important—because Adenauer's "policy of strength" vis-à-vis the Soviet Union rested on a strong sense of anti-communism widely shared by the West German public. This hatred and fear of the Russians, partly understandable in the light of wartime and postwar experiences with Soviet troops, not only prevented a more open foreign policy toward the East, it also precluded a realization on the part of the Germans of their responsibility for much of Russia's sufferings during the war and thus interfered with any attempt to come to terms with that aspect of their past. It was only after some of these attitudes had gradually changed that the new *Ostpolitik* did, in fact, become a political reality.

The "Soviet Threat"

The dramatic decline in the number of West Germans feeling threatened by the Russians becomes evident in table 4.8. This table also shows that the Soviet interventions in Hungary in 1956 and in Czechoslovakia in August, 1968, caused only short-lived fears and anxiety, influencing the overall trend only slightly. It also seems important to note that the younger age groups included in these polls (sixteen to twenty-nine years) felt, in 1969, less threatened by almost 10 percent; similarly, supporters of the SPD perceived considerably less of a threat than those identifying with the CDU.

The apparent fact that today a majority of West Germans no longer appear to feel threatened by the Soviet Union does not necessarily mean that

---

[32] See, for instance, the excellent study by Arnulf Baring, *Aussenpolitik in Adenauers Kanzlerdemokratie* (Munich: Oldenbourg, 1969).

TABLE 4.8

"Do you have the feeling that we are threatened by
Russia or that we are not threatened?"

	July, 1952	Oct., 1954	Apr., 1956	Mar., 1958	Nov., 1964	Apr., 1965	Apr., 1966	Nov., 1968	Sept., 1969
Threatened	66%	64%	45%	51%	39%	50%	37%	54%	32%
Not threatened	15	21	27	27	37	27	37	32	55
Undecided	19	15	28	22	24	23	26	14	13

Source: IfD, "Die Stimmung im Bundesgebiet," November 7, 1969.

they consider the Russians to be their friends, or consider them even willing to negotiate in good faith with the West. In a series of polls conducted by the IfD between April, 1959, and April, 1970, the number of those who believed that the Russians "today basically have the good will to come to an agreement with the West" increased only from 17 percent to 33 percent; the number of those who did not believe in Russia's good will decreased only from 57 percent to 46 percent.[33] In other words, most West Germans still do not seem overly optimistic about arriving at meaningful agreements with the Soviet Union. The important fact, however, has become their willingness to try. This willingness has already become evident in table 4.6, where the number of respondents identifying the Soviet Union as the "country with which we should cooperate particularly closely" increased from an 18 percent low in December, 1956, to a 52 percent high in November, 1970.

Some of the reasons underlying this increasing West German emphasis on cooperation with the Soviet Union and other Eastern bloc countries become apparent in a poll taken by the INFRATEST Institut in 1969. Their interviewers presented respondents with a list of possible consequences of the new Ostpolitik and asked which

of these consequences might be expected. The results were that 56 percent of all respondents expected that "we could make a contribution to the relaxation of tension in world politics"; also, 56 percent expected that "great new markets will open up for us"; and 53 percent thought that "the citizens of the G.D.R. will have some benefit."[34] Furthermore, 48 percent felt it might bring closer a united Europe and 41 percent thought it would increase Germany's standing in the world; only around 15 percent expected any negative consequences, such as coming under communist influence, losing the support of the United States, or putting up with the permanent division of Germany. An earlier poll, taken in the summer of 1967, highlights some of the reasons underlying these responses. Interviewers for INFAS gave their respondents a choice between two statements. One was, "With all the steps which we undertake vis-à-vis the East, a solution to the German question must always stand in the foreground. All other problems must be put behind this goal": only 21 percent agreed. The other choice was, "Our Eastern policy must serve foremost to aid in achieving peace, détente, and reconciliation; the German question must recede into the background for

[33] IfD, "Die Stimmung im Bundesgebiet," April 26, 1970.

[34] INFRATEST, "Das Publikum der Sendereihe 'Kontraste,' " (Munich, May, 1970), p. 16.

the time being"; 61 percent voted for this alternative. (Another 18 percent were undecided or did not answer).[35] Again, in October, 1968, a question was asked about the priorities of foreign policy for the Federal Republic: "Should we continue without change our policy of relaxation of tension vis-à-vis the East, or should we instead make much stronger efforts to achieve the political unification of Europe?" Of this representative sample of West Germans, 48 percent said they were for relaxation of tension; only 39 percent expressed their sympathy for the goal of a united Europe.[36] In short, then, the themes standing behind the Eastern policy of the Federal Republic today appear to be the following: (1) the continuing effort to come to terms with the past through a reconciliation with *all* former enemies; (2) the pursuit of ever-larger markets for German industry in order to increase the personal well-being of the average West German; and (3) the quest for some means to overcome the political division of Germany and, even more important, the often painful separation of the German people.

Reunification

The decreasing importance West Germans are likely to attach to all questions pertaining to the reunification of Germany can be documented from a variety of different polls; but the results of one poll taken by the Institut für Demoskopie in May, 1969, emphasize this likelihood particularly strikingly. Respondents were con-

fronted with the following statement: "It would be nice if East and West Germany could be reunified, but nowadays one finally has to admit that there are many much more important problems for us than reunification"; 37 percent shared this attitude, 44 percent "would not put it that way," and 19 percent were undecided. However, a breakdown of all respondents into age groups reveals that the younger generations (those sixteen to forty-four years old) believed to a much higher degree—namely, 44 percent of them—that "there are more important problems today" (39 percent named reunification); while of those over forty-five years of age, only 28 percent saw more important problems for the Federal Republic than reunification (51 percent named the latter).[37] This generational difference in attitudes toward the national problems of reunification is evident in almost all public opinion polls on this question as well as carefully documented in more specific studies among young West Germans today. In short, generational effects appear to be largely responsible for a general decline in the importance attached to the so-called German question.

Next to generational differences in attitudes toward the problems of Germany, a generally growing sense of disillusionment—or perhaps better, realism—has had the effect of changing attitudes in this regard. Considering first the case of the so-called lost territories beyond the Oder-Neisse line, public opinion polls taken between August, 1953, and November, 1969, reveal that the number of those who believed that "Pomerania, Silesia, and East Prussia will one day belong to Germany again" decreased from 66 percent in 1953 to 16 percent in 1969,

35 INFAS, "Die Bundesrepublik und Osteuropa," report prepared for the Press and Information Office of the Federal Government (Bad Godesberg, Summer, 1967).
36 EMNID, "Monatliche Berichte," report prepared for the Press and Information Office of the Federal Government (Bielefeld, October, 1968).

37 IfD, "Wiedervereinigung" (Allensbach, May, 1969).

TABLE 4.9

*"Do you think we should acquiesce in the present German-Polish
border—the Oder-Neisse line—or not?"*

| | Natives | | | Refugees | | |
	Yes	No	N.A.	Yes	No	N.A.
Mar., 1951	8%	77%	15%	7%	89%	4%
Dec., 1956	10	69	21	5	85	10
Mar., 1962	27	47	26	21	65	14
Feb., 1966	27	51	22	25	62	13
Apr., 1970	58	23	19	57	33	10

Source: IfD, "Die Stimmung im Bundesgebiet," June 7, 1970.

while the number of those who did not share this belief increased from 11 percent to 68 percent.[38] In the course of those years, ever more West Germans became willing to accept the Oder-Neisse line as a final border, as table 4.9 clearly shows. The results presented here also indicate that on the whole refugees seem to be almost as willing as native West Germans to recognize the Oder-Neisse line. Considering also the fact that between September, 1957, and November, 1969, the number of those refugees who said it was "out of the question" that they would return to their "homeland" if it belonged to Germany again, increased from 26 percent to 59 percent,[39] it seems safe to assume that the political role of refugee organizations —very great indeed during the first twenty years of the Federal Republic —will greatly diminish during the years to come, giving the Federal Government even more leeway in its Eastern policy.

The national goal of reunification of the two parts of Germany similarly appears to have lost most of its importance in the minds of West Germans today. In part, of course, this decreas-

ing emphasis on national reunification stems from the fact that more and more West Germans simply are getting used to the political division of Germany, as table 4.10 indicates. On the other hand, a significant shift in public attitudes toward the issue of reunification has taken place since 1960, after the German philosopher Karl Jaspers first suggested that humanitarian considerations ought to be more important than national ones; in a widely discussed book[40] he suggested that the improvement of living conditions for East Germans should be the primary goal of West German foreign policy, not the political reunification of the two parts of Germany. The Institut für Demoskopie sought to determine public attitudes on this issue in August, 1960, when it asked a number of West Germans whether they agreed with the following proposition: "Some people say the important issue is that the Germans in the Eastern Zone regain their liberty, that is, become liberated from Communism and be able to live just like us in the Federal Republic. Suppose the Russians would free the Eastern Zone only if East and West Germany enter into a binding and final agreement to foresake any reunification: should we Germans then foresake reunification, if

[38] *Jahrbuch 1955*, p. 313; IfD, *The Germans*, p. 482; IfD, "Die Stimmung im Bundesgebiet," February 21, 1970.

[39] IfD, *The Germans*, p. 483, and "Die Stimmung im Bundesgebiet," June 7, 1970.

[40] *Freiheit und Wiedervereinigung* (Munich: R. Piper, 1960).

TABLE 4.10

"Do you find the division of Germany to be an untolerable condition or
would you say that people have gradually become used to it?"

	Sept., 1956	June, 1962	July, 1963	Dec., 1967
Untolerable	52%	61%	53%	31%
Become used	33	28	32	54
Undecided	15	11	15	15

Source: IfD, "Die Stimmung im Bundesgebiet," January 8, 1970.

that would free the Eastern Zone?"
Only 18 percent said yes, 48 percent
were against the idea, and 34 percent
were undecided.[41] In March, 1962, 28
percent felt that "we should renounce
reunification" to achieve decent living
conditions and liberty for Germans in
the Eastern zone; 51 percent thought
that "reunification is the most important thing" and that the problem
would take care of itself once reunification had been achieved.[42] By March,
1967, a strong minority of 36 percent
supported the priority of humanitarian goals, expressing agreement
with a suggestion made by Herbert
Wehner (then minister of all-German
affairs) of the SPD that West Germany
might recognize the G.D.R. if conditions there were to become freer for
the population; 38 percent still disapproved, while 26 percent were undecided.[43] In September, 1970, finally,
57 percent of a carefully selected sample of West Germans said they felt the
Federal Republic should recognize
the G.D.R., but only if the G.D.R.
made some concessions (presumably,
in the area of better living conditions
for its population); 15 percent thought
the G.D.R. should be recognized even
if it did not make any concessions; 20
percent were strictly opposed to recognition under any circumstances; and

8 percent were undecided.[44] In short,
the number of those insisting on the
priority of national reunification appears to have dropped to the relatively
small minority of 20 percent.

As living conditions in the German
Democratic Republic improved substantially after the political and economic consolidation brought about
after the building of the Berlin Wall,
the goal of seeking better living conditions for those living in the G.D.R.
became somewhat less urgent for most
West Germans, particularly since on
the whole they seemed to be well
aware of some of the advances in education, health care, and social security
made by the East German regime.[45]
This development left a large number
of West Germans with the more
modest goal of trying to improve relations between the Federal Republic
and the G.D.R. to the point where
easier contacts across the border might
become possible. This goal has, in fact,
become the one pursued in Willy
Brandt's new Ostpolitik, which culminated, for the time being, in the meetings between Brandt and G.D.R.
Prime Minister Willy Stoph in Erfurt
and Kassel in the spring of 1970.
These meetings did not produce any
immediate results as far as improvement of relations between the two

[41] Jahrbuch 1964, p. 486.
[42] Ibid., p. 487.
[43] Jahrbuch 1967, p. 390.

[44] IfD, "Allensbacher Berichte," October,
1970.
[45] See, for instance, "Was soll Bonn tun?"
Der Spiegel, November 16, 1970, p. 102.

TABLE 4.11

*"If you had to make the decision—should the Federal Republic recognize
the G.D.R as a state or should she not?"*

	Mar., 1967	May, 1969	Apr., 1970	May, 1970
Recognize	34%	29%	47%	52%
Not	57	52	38	37
Depends	7	18	12	9
Undecided	2	1	3	2

Source: IfD, "Die Stimmung im Bundesgebiet," May 28, 1970,

parts of Germany are concerned. However, as table 4.11 clearly demonstrates, the meetings did have the result of dramatically increasing the willingness of West Germans to recognize the G.D.R. as a state. These results suggest that the federal government can count on little public opposition to a recognition of the G.D.R. when it considers the time ripe for such a move and when it can expect some small improvements as a result of such recognition. In any case, as time goes on and as most West Germans resign themselves to the division of Germany; as living conditions in East Germany improve to the point where the East Germans themselves do not want West German help any more (there are some indications that this point has already been reached); as the estrangement between the peoples on opposite sides of the border deepens; as East Germans and West Germans each begin to develop a national consciousness of their own—while all these deveopments are taking place, the issue of the reunification of Germany is likely to fade into the background of West German politics, kept alive only by possible crises over the situation of Berlin.

Domestic Issues

All of the trends of public attitudes in West Germany developed here seem to add up to one impression:

West Germany is on the way to becoming a nation-state in its own right. National issues concerning all of Germany appear to be slowly losing their importance, while concerns touching on the well-being of West Germans are becoming ever more salient. West Germany appears to have found itself as its citizens seem to have accepted their country's new role in world politics. In short, then, these public opinion trends suggest a gradual development toward normalcy among the West German public—a receding preoccupation with issues arising from the past and an increasing emphasis on solving the problems of the present and the future.

Such a return to normalcy in the sphere of attitudes in the Federal Republic is paralleled by a return to normalcy in West Germany's socioeconomic realm. Like other highly developed countries, West Germany is becoming increasingly urbanized, more middle class, and better educated. The effects of increasing urbanization, growth of the middle class, and higher educational levels on the foreign policy of the Federal Republic can hardly be overestimated, as the following discussion of the 1969 Federal election will show.

In the September, 1969, election of deputies to the Bundestag (who in turn elect the federal chancellor), the Social Democratic party (SPD) for the first time succeeded in gaining enough votes—and electing enough deputies—to form a federal government together with the Free Democratic party (FDP), thus ending twenty years of uninterrupted rule by the Christian Democratic Union (CDU). The election of Willy Brandt as federal chancellor symbolized in yet another way the West Germans' coming to terms with their own past, having elected as chancellor the illegitimate son of a workingwoman, a man who had emigrated to Norway and Sweden during the Nazi regime and who had returned to Germany in the uniform of a Norwegian officer. Brandt resumed his German citizenship and helped build the SPD in West Berlin into a strong political base for his move from mayor of West Berlin to chancellor of the Federal Republic.

To be sure, foreign policy issues played a minor role in the electoral success of the SPD, although Brandt had gained considerable personal stature among the electorate as foreign minister during the three years that the CDU and the SPD had formed a "Grand Coalition" government. That government, considered by many observers as contrary to democratic values because it left the Federal Republic without a functioning opposition, had come into being in response to an economic crisis in 1966. Economic issues were to dominate the 1969 election campaign as well, as Minister of Economics Karl Schiller, the star performer of the SPD, became the man most West Germans thought could deal best with the Federal Republic's economic problems. In this sense, the SPD had earned its success at the polls through a creditable performance of its cabinet members in the areas of economics and foreign affairs.

However, detailed analyses of the underlying factors affecting the SPD's win in 1969 reveal that the gradual changes in the socioeconomic structure of West Germany's population correlated highly with SPD electoral successes. In short, the SPD made significant gains in urban areas with their high concentration of blue-collar workers, white-collar workers, and intellectuals (since the SPD had always been the workers' party, most of the SPD's gains in the 1969 election were due to increased support by white-collar workers and intellectuals), and generally improved its position in Protestant areas of the Federal Republic. The CDU, on the other hand, found its bastions of strength reduced to primarily rural areas and to the more predominantly Catholic parts of West Germany; its gains in votes were primarily among the self-employed—a group which had formerly been the mainstay of the FDP, which, as a consequence, lost almost half of its former voters to the CDU.[46] Election statistics also show that, in general, men were more inclined to vote SPD than women; and that older people were more likely to vote CDU than SPD.

Some of the surveys and analyses undertaken in an effort to understand and explain the 1969 election results clearly show that the predominant ideological cleavage in West Germany today is no longer one between friends and enemies of the Federal Republic, between supporters of democracy and adherents of dictatorship. It rather appears to have become the cleavage between liberals and conservatives observable in most other Western countries today: between those who want to change the domestic and international status quo and those who cling

[46] These conclusions are based on studies by Max Kaase, "Determinanten des Wahlverhaltens bei der Bundestagswahl, 1969," and by Hans D. Klingemann and Franz U. Pappi, "Die Wählerbewegungen bei der Bundestagswahl 1969," both in *Politische Vierteljahresschrift*, March, 1970.

to the values, traditions, and policies of the past. It is, in West Germany as elsewhere, also largely a cleavage between young and old. Politically, the SPD and the CDU represent this ideological cleavage between liberals and conservatives, respectively.

The combined historical experience of democracy and economic progress in the Federal Republic served to convince most West Germans fairly quickly of the value of democracy. In a series of polls taken between 1953 and 1965, the number of those who identified "democracy" as the "best form of government for us Germans" increased from 57 percent to 79 percent, while the combined number of those preferring monarchy or an authoritarian regime declined from 19 percent to 6 percent.[47] Similar response patterns were obtained in polls seeking to determine whether West Germans preferred several parties offering free expressions of opinion to one party representing national unity: between 1951 and 1958, the number of those preferring several parties increased from 61 percent to 77 percent.[48] A more detailed analysis of the values West Germans associate with democracy or with dictatorship shows that by fall, 1965, they appeared to have learned the lessons of history well. For instance, more than 70 percent in each case associated with democracy: the public good, security, safety, well-being, justice, order, and freedom; associated with the Nazi regime were, by more than 70 percent: regime of violence, deception of the people, suppression, and threats.[49]

However, even though there may be some doubt as to the firmness of democratic convictions, most analyses show that such convictions are held more firmly by a significantly larger number of West German youth than West German adults, and in particular by large numbers of West German students.[50] Thus when the Institut für Demoskopie, in a poll taken a few weeks before the 1969 election, asked respondents whether they preferred several persons to make political decisions—even though that might lead to occasional confusion—to one person exercising all governmental power in the interest of greater efficiency, 75 percent of all young voters preferred more than one political decision maker, while only 20 percent expressed their sympathy for efficiency through one man's rule. Of those respondents who were potential CDU voters, only 62 percent wanted several decision makers, the former alternative, while 30 percent favored one-man rule; among SPD identifiers, the distribution of opinion was 69 percent vs. 25 percent.[51]

Throughout this particular preelection study of public opinion, one finds CDU supporters expressing more conservative opinions and SPD supporters sharing the more liberal convictions, with the younger voters usually ahead of SPD identifiers in their liberal attitudes. Asked, for instance, whether they thought it was good that many students wanted to change conditions radically in the Federal Republic, only 9 percent of all CDU voters agreed, while 18 percent of the SPD supporters agreed, and 28 percent of the young voters shared that opinion.[52] When asked whether they thought it

[47] Klaus D. Eberlein, *Was die Deutschen möchten* (Hamburg: Wegner, 1968), p. 99.

[48] Ibid., p. 103.

[49] Ibid., p. 100.

[50] See, for instance, Rudolf Wildenmann and Max Kaase, "Die unruhige Generation" (University of Mannheim, 1968), for a large number of public opinion polls comparing attitudes of students, youth, and the general public.

[51] IfD, *Wählermeinung—nicht geheim* (Allensbach: Verlag für Demoskopie, 1969), p. 128.

[52] Ibid., p. 131.

was "time to travel new roads in politics and elect new leaders to do so" or
whether security was more important
and, therefore, it was better to retain
the well-known leaders, an almost
equal number of young voters and
SPD supporters opted for new roads
and new leaders (53 percent and 56
percent, respectively), while—by no
means surprising—72 percent of the
CDU sympathizers preferred security
and (their own) old leaders.[53]

In the field of foreign policy, the
liberal attitudes of young voters in
particular and of SPD supporters in
general are also evident. Indeed,
responses to the statement, "The German youth must be educated to love
its fatherland," verify that CDU voters
could be considered most nationalistic, since 47 percent of them agreed;
of SPD voters, only 31 percent expressed their agreement; while young
voters flatly rejected the proposition
aimed at them: only 15 percent
showed their sympathy with this demand.[54] Again, regarding the question
of recognition of the Oder-Neisse line
and of the G.D.R., CDU voters appeared to be much more reluctant (19
percent for recognition of the G.D.R.)
than SPD supporters (31 percent) and
young voters (40 percent).[55] In looking at what supporters of each party
considered to be their party's major
goals, the difference in attitudes toward problems of domestic and foreign policy becomes strikingly evident.
Supporters of the CDU ranked the
following goals according to their
importance:[56]

1. Job security (72%)
2. Law and order (66%)
3. Military security (62%)
4. Maintaining Germany's good position
   in Europe and the world (62%)

53 Ibid., p. 80.
54 Ibid., p. 85.
55 Ibid., p. 68.
56 Ibid., pp. 133–34.

5. Progress in European cooperation
   (60%)

SPD supporters thought the following
to be their party's major goals:

1. Job security (81%)
2. Social justice for workers (80%)
3. Price stability (70%)
4. Relaxation of tension toward East
   (68%)
5. Solution of problems in education
   (67%)

In short, while these polls reflect
the basically domestic context in
which the 1969 election campaign was
held, they also show the differences in
foreign policy outlook—the CDU more
concerned with military security and
Germany's position in the world, the
SPD striving to improve relations with
the East and to bring about a relaxation of tension. It is clear from these
polls that the foreign policy of the
Federal Republic is likely to undergo
significant changes in emphasis, if not
direction, every time the chancellorship should change from one party to
the other.

How likely are such changes? At the
moment, the SPD clearly appears to be
holding the edge over the CDU. All
the trends, socioeconomic as well as
attitudinal, depicted so far would
seem to work in the SPD's long-run
favor. Increasing urbanization will
open up new converts to the SPD's
kind of liberalism; rising educational
levels will favor the SPD; and certainly the inclusion of ever more
younger voters in the electorate can
hardly hurt the SPD. Before the 1969
election, young voters ranked the two
parties according to what they thought
were their special areas of competence, as indicated in table 4.12. Only
in the field of military security was
the CDU judged to be more competent than the SPD; but then other

TABLE 4.12

Young Voters' Perception of Parties' Special Competence

	SPD	CDU
Foreign policy	52%	26%
Price stability	44	20
Education and science	40	26
Closer contacts between F.R.G. and G.D.R.	37	17
Military security	18	43

Source: IfD, *Wählermeinug—nicht geheim* (Allensbach: Verlag für Demoskopie, 1969), p. 48.

polls quickly reveal that among young voters today, the question of military security for the Federal Republic is considered to be relatively unimportant. When asked whether they thought that security from a military attack from the East was important, only 47 percent of the young voters interviewed agreed, whereas 70 percent of the CDU supporters shared that conviction; 57 percent of all SPD identifiers said that they considered military security important.[57] Taking these results into consideration, it seems by no means surprising that the younger voters were overwhelmingly in favor of the SPD during the 1969 election campaign.

In the context of West German politics, the Brandt administration is likely to stand and fall on the domestic issues of price stability, job security, and constant economic growth. Secondary considerations will be the social reforms promised in the field of health services, education, and workers' codetermination. Foreign policy issues are likely to be of tertiary importance, a fact the chancellor learned soon after his initial foreign policy successes in The Hague, Erfurt, Moscow, and Warsaw. Thus the future course of the Federal Republic's foreign policy is likely to be determined by the federal government's perfor-

[57] Ibid., pp. 55–62.

mance at the domestic front. However, the long-term trends outlined above would seem to indicate that the SPD can tolerate even a certain amount of domestic failure; and certainly, no CDU government could long maintain a leading position if it did not in some ways change its attitude toward the question of more open and liberal foreign and domestic policies. While the future is hard to predict, it seems safe to assume that the policies initiated by Chancellor Willy Brandt since 1969 will be continued for some time to come. While the ideological cleavage between left and right, liberals and conservatives, will undoubtedly continue to contribute a good deal of heated argument over the merits of each policy, the secular shifts of West German opinion clearly appear to favor the forces of liberalism.

But even though the administration elected in 1969 came into office with a mandate—however small—for new policies at home and abroad, it is still bound to the constitutional, legal, and administrative policy-making framework of the Federal Republic. This policy-making framework exerts an important influence not only on the decision-making process itself, but also on the kind of decisions eventually reached. It is for this reason that we must now direct our attention to the role of governmental and nongovernmental institutions in the making of foreign policy.

THE ROLE OF GOVERNMENTAL AND NONGOVERNMENTAL INSTITUTIONS IN THE MAKING OF FOREIGN POLICY

Under the constitution of the German Federal Republic, foreign policy is the responsibility of the federal government. The ten constituent states of the Federal Republic and their governments are bound by federal actions in the realm of foreign policy; if required, they are expected to pass enabling legislation to incorporate into state law commitments undertaken by the federal government toward foreign governments. To a limited extent, the states participate in the formation of foreign policy through the upper house of the federal legislature (*Bundesrat*); this house is composed of representatives of the ten state governments, and each state has from three to five votes, according to the size of its population. This chamber has an absolute veto over all constitutional changes, but only a suspensive veto over ordinary legislation. Prior to the conclusion of treaties affecting the particular interest of one or more states, the state governments have the right to make their views known, but these opinions are not binding on the federal government and may formally be ignored by it, although political considerations may induce the federal government to take them into account in deciding a course of action. As under the constitution of the Soviet Union (and unlike the American system), the states have the right to conclude treaties of their own with foreign nations—subject to the approval of the federal chancellor —when these deal with matters not specifically reserved for federal jurisdiction or with subjects of concurrent jurisdiction not yet preempted by the federal government. These, however, are minor matters; in the main, foreign policy is federal in theory and practice.

The Key Role of the Chancellor

Within the federal government, the federal chancellor (*Bundeskanzler*) is constitutionally the principal decision maker in the realm of foreign policy. His cabinet, the federal president, the two chambers of the federal legislature, and the federal constitutional court may, under certain circumstances, share in the decision-making process but, constitutionally, the final source of authority is the chancellor, who alone has the power and responsibility for determining public policy.

The framers of the Basic Law of 1948—the constitution of the Federal Republic—deliberately endowed the chancellor with considerable power in the hope of avoiding the sort of governmental instability that is common in many countries where an all-powerful legislature is divided into many bitterly antagonistic factions. At the same time, they wanted to prevent a recurrence of the sort of irresponsible executive absolutism that had prevailed in Germany before 1918 and in the early 1930s. Designed for the traditional German multiparty system, the Basic Law strives for executive responsibility by providing for a chief of government elected by and responsible to a majority of the popularly elected lower house of the federal legislature. It strives for governmental stability by providing that a chancellor remain in office until either (*a*) a majority, or at least a plurality, of the lower house agrees on a replacement; (*b*) a new lower house is elected; or (*c*) the incumbent chancellor dies, resigns, or is convicted of certain criminal acts. The chancellor cannot be impeached. Thus, it was hoped by the fathers of the constitution, neither the disintegration of a coalition nor the opposition of a parliamentary majority unable to agree on a replacement should force the fall of a government. Such "chancellor government" (*Kanzlerregierung*) is intended to make the head of the government less dependent upon the legislature than under a pure parliamentary system, yet more so than under the United States' presidential form of executive leadership.

In accordance with these principles, the chancellor alone—and not the entire government—is supposed to determine government policy, see to its execution, and account for it to the legislature. There is no collective responsibility of the entire government. Accordingly, the chancellor, in effect, appoints and dismisses the members of his cabinet; his recommendations are binding on the federal president, who has the formal power of appointment and dismissal. In turn, the ministers of the chancellor's government are solely responsible to him as his advisors and subordinate administrators, and their tenure ends automatically with his.

Constitutionally, neither the president nor the legislature can compel the chancellor to include anyone in his government or to dismiss any minister. Chancellor Adenauer successfully maintained this point in 1955, when one of the parties in his coalition broke with him and sought to withdraw its representatives from the government. The ministers, Adenauer insisted, were his agents once they joined the government, and not those of their party. Subsequently, he dropped some cabinet members on his own because their presence in the government apparently no longer seemed politically advisable to him. Adenauer's actions underlined the fact that a strong chancellor, one who commands a majority in the lower house of the legislature, can afford to defy suggestions concerning the composition and size of his government. On the other hand, a weak chancellor —that is, one who did not command such a majority, or even a plurality— presumably would have to be far more considerate toward the leaders of parties whose support he sought in connection with the makeup of his cabinet. In order to gain such support, he might be forced to accommodate them, to give ministerial portfolios to representatives of parties whose support he wanted, and perhaps to create new portfolios or appoint ministers without portfolios. He might have to offer important ministries to powerful political leaders who were not necessarily qualified for these posts, but who would bring him the parliamentary support he needed.

Other Offices and Officials

Individually, the members of the chancellor's government are supposed to administer the affairs of their ministries in accordance with the general policy determined by their chief. As in the case of the chancellor himself, the personality, experience, and qualifications of the incumbent play an important part in determining the actual role he plays in the decision-making process and the extent to which he relies on subordinate officials.

Chief among the ministries concerned with foreign policy is, of course, the Foreign Office (*Auswärtiges Amt*). It is officially charged with "attending to foreign affairs," and unless the chancellor makes special exceptions (as in the case of the minister for economic cooperation, in the second Adenauer government), other ministries may deal with foreign governments and international organizations only with its approval. Jurisdictional conflicts are resolved either by the entire cabinet or by the chancellor alone. Other ministries directly or indirectly concerned with foreign policy decisions are those of Defense (*Bundesministerium für Verteidigung*); Finance (*Finanzen*); Economics (*Wirtschaft*); and the Ministry for Inner-German Relations (*Innerdeutsche Beziehungen*), which has special responsibility for matters pertaining to the reunification of divided Germany. Since 1961, the Ministry for Economic Cooperation (*Bundesminis-*

terium für Wirtschaftliche Zusammenarbeit), previously responsible for questions pertaining to European economic cooperation, deals exclusively with economic aspects of West German foreign policy toward the developing countries. (European matters are now dealt with by the competent ministries in cooperation with the European agencies at Brussels.)

Collectively, the ministers form the chancellor's cabinet and, as such, are supposed to advise him on matters of general policy and to decide on government proposals to be submitted to the legislature. The actual role of the cabinet and its individual members in decision making would also appear to depend very largely upon the personalities and relative political power of the chancellor and his ministers. A strong chancellor, such as Adenauer, could largely dictate policy; a less determined incumbent, like Erhard, depended more upon the approval and support of at least the most powerful of his ministers, and of the parties or factions which they represent.

A relatively recent creation is the Federal Defense Council (*Bundesverteidigungsrat*), a sort of inner cabinet (somewhat similar to the U.S. National Security Council), whose members are selected and appointed by the chancellor. The membership varies; normally, only select members of the cabinet are included, but other ministers and important officials may be invited to attend meetings at the chancellor's discretion.

Two other agencies of the executive branch of the federal government have, in recent years, played a considerable role in the making of West German foreign policy, largely owing to the intimate relationships existing between their respective chiefs and the incumbent chancellor. The first of these, the Chancellor's Office (*Bundes-kanzleramt*), is formally charged with assisting the chancellor in his relations with other branches of the government and important nongovernmental agencies, with keeping him informed on political developments at home and abroad, and with preparing for the decisions that the chancellor may decide to take on the basis of this information. The second, the Press and Information Office of the Federal Government (*Presse und Informationsamt der Bundesregierung*), is supposed to assure close relations between the executive branch and the media of mass communication (both foreign and domestic), to gather and evaluate data on public opinion, and, generally, to interpret the policies, decisions, and actions of the government to the public at home and abroad. In terms of actual as well as potential influence over the foreign policy-making process, leading officials in both these offices are important members of the decision-making elite within the executive branch, the extent of their influence varying with the prevailing relationship between their incumbents and the chancellor.

The Powers of the President

The role of the federal president in the foreign policy-making process is normally insignificant. Although he has the right to submit a candidate for the chancellorship to the lower house of the legislature, he must appoint the choice of the majority of the deputies, whether he approves or not. The incumbent chancellor is supposed to keep the president informed, and consult with him on the policies of his government; but the president, for his part, is constitutionally bound to cooperate loyally with a man who has the support of a majority of the deputies. He must sign such treaties, bills, and decrees as are submitted to him by the chancellor or his ministers, appoint or dismiss officials on the chancellor's advice and, in general, exercise his formal powers at the discretion of the chief of government, who bears ultimate responsibility for the actions of the executive branch. Some constitutional commentators would concede the president's limited influence over diplomatic negotiations, but even here a strong chancellor would appear to have the final word, as principal decision maker.

A few constitutional commentators have claimed that the powers of the president, particularly in foreign policy making, might be used more decisively in the hands of a powerful incumbent. Such an interpretation may have led Chancellor Konrad Adenauer to consider exchanging the chancellorship for the presidency in 1959. His decision not to become a candidate for the presidency, and his subsequent efforts to maneuver the popular minister of economics, Ludwig Erhard, into running for the office so that he could not succeed Adenauer as chancellor, seemed to indicate that the president has little or no influence on policy making under present circumstances.

The president's role might become more important if the parliament should be so deeply divided that its members would neither support the incumbent chancellor nor agree upon a successor. Given the present division of parliament into two major parties, more-or-less tightly organized and united, such a development is not likely. Should a multiparty system re-emerge at some future date, as seems unlikely today, and should a deadlock then develop between the incumbent chancellor and a majority of the deputies, the role of the president might temporarily become more significant.

The Powers of the Parliament

Of the two chambers of the federal legislature, the lower house (*Bundestag*) has by far the greater power in most matters, including foreign policy. Treaties that regulate the political relations of the federation, or that relate to matters of federal legislation, can become the law of the land only with its consent. Similarly, the transfer of sovereign rights of the state to international institutions, such as the EEC (Common Market), require legislative action. Finally, all treaties and other legislation that conflict with the Basic Law require constitutional amendments, which must be approved by two-thirds of the membership of the lower house.

Apart from its legislative functions, the lower house is granted certain other powers designed to give the members a voice in the foreign policy-making process. A majority elects a chancellor and can dismiss him by choosing a successor. The deputies of the lower house provide half the votes in the Federal Assembly (*Bundesversammlung*) which, every five years, chooses a federal president, and which can initiate impeachment proceedings against him before the federal constitutional court.

In the lower house, the deputies have the right to investigate and criticize the actions of the executive in plenary sessions or in committees. They may summon and question members of the government when they choose; the latter, for their part, have the right to demand to be heard by the deputies at any time, providing themselves with potential opportunities to influence important deliberations of the house at decisive moments.

Most of the important contacts between the executive branch and the deputies occur in the sessions of the standing and select committees of the lower house, rather than in plenary sessions. It is here that experts from the various parties examine the actions and requests of the government and question its members thoroughly. The vote in the committee is usually decisive, and committee recommendations are usually approved in subsequent plenary sessions. With respect to foreign policy issues, the key committees are Foreign Affairs (*Auswärtige Angelegenheiten*), Defense (*Verteidigung*), Budget (*Haushalt*), Inner-German Relations (*Innerdeutsche Beziehungen*), Economics (*Wirtschaft*), and Economic Cooperation (*Wirtschaftliche Zusammenarbeit*).

The role that the deputies of the lower house may play in West German foreign policy appears to depend primarily on the authority that the chancellor exercises in the chamber. If he comands a stable majority—or better, two-thirds of the votes—his powers are fairly absolute and his position firm. However, if he lacks such strength, his freedom of action would seem to be more limited; he may be forced to rely on the cooperation of uncertain and demanding allies in order to see his program through the legislature and to prevent the election of a successor.

In the event of constitutional disputes arising out of foreign policy issues, the federal constitutional court may enter the picture. It may be called upon to adjudicate jurisdictional disputes between the federal government and the states or between the executive and the legislative branches of the national government. The court may also be asked to render advisory opinions on the constitutionality of certain pending actions, either upon the joint request of the executive and the legislature, or upon that of the federal president alone. The president has the right to refuse to place his signature on treaties, acts of the legislature, or government decrees pending an advisory opinion from the court. Thus, in 1952, President Theodore Heuss tried to withhold his signature from the treaty providing for the arming of the Federal Republic until the constitutional court had advised him that it did not conflict with the Basic Law, but he finally signed the treaty on Chancellor Adenauer's advice.

To summarize what has been said about the formal role of various governmental institutions in the making of foreign policy: foreign affairs are a federal matter; and, within the federal government, the principal decision maker is the chancellor, while lesser roles are assigned to the ministers, president, legislature, and constitutional court of the Federal Republic. How this formal arrangement actually functions depends primarily on the prevailing relationship between a chancellor and the lower house of the legislature. A strong chancellor, who commands a comfortable majority in the lower house, will have a great deal of freedom in the conduct of foreign affairs; a chancellor who lacks such support is likely to be far more dependent on the cooperation of the legislature and the president.

Experience during the first twenty years of the Federal Republic's existence indicates that the chancellor's position vis-à-vis both president and legislature rests largely on his relationship to his party and on that party's strength and cohesion. A future chancellor might not necessarily be a party man at all—not even a member of the legislature; nonetheless, his power to make decisions would still depend primarily on his ability to gain the support of the majority party or coalition in the legislature. The formal organization of the foreign policy-making process thus becomes a functioning party system, although it does provide the chancellor with some limited means of governing temporarily without parliamentary support, should the parties fail to produce a stable majority behind him.

The Role of the Political Parties

The Basic Law of the Federal Republic is unique in its specific recognition of the decisive role of political parties in the formulation of national policy. Through their representatives in the executive and legislative branches of the national government, the parties are supposed to act as the responsible agents of the electorate in the conduct of government. The existing electoral law compels all aspirants for seats in the popularly elected lower house to belong to a party and thus to identify themselves with, and bear responsibility for, its policies and actions. Referendums, plebiscites, and other devices for "direct democracy," which bypasses parties and legislature, have been deliberately omitted from the constitution; its framers were all too aware of the antidemocratic uses to which such devices had been put in the past by demagogues who appealed to the "popular will" against the "selfish" interests of parties.

Anyone may organize a political party in the republic, as long as its objectives and organization accord with the democratic principles of the constitution and do not aim at the overthrow of the present state. In fact, however, the electoral laws have made it almost impossible for any party receiving less than 5 percent of the electoral votes to gain representation in the national legislature.

Contrary to the apparent expectations of the framers of the constitution, the traditional German multiparty system has been gradually eliminated, and the two major parties have become the principal representatives of the electorate. These are the Christian Democratic Union (CDU) and the Social Democratic party (SPD). Between them, these parties received 60 percent of the votes and 67 percent of the seats in the 1949 election; 74 percent of the votes and 83 percent of the seats in 1953; 82 percent of the votes and 88 percent of the seats in 1957; 82 percent of the votes, and 87 percent of the seats in 1961; 87 percent of the votes and 90 percent of the seats in 1965; and nearly 89 percent of the votes and 94 percent of the seats in 1969.

The Christian Democratic Union (*Christlich Demokratische Union*), operating in Bavaria as the Christian Social Union (*Christlich Soziale Union*, or CSU), is a departure from the traditional German parties. Instead of following the traditional pattern of parties in Germany and becoming closely identified with some particular ideology, religious group, or economic interest, this party has managed to attract the support of rather heterogeneous elements among the voters in the name of its "Christian principles." It is moderately conservative in its domestic economic and social program, and has faithfully followed the lead of its first and long-time chairman, Konrad Adenauer, in the realm of foreign policy. Its professed aims have been the reunification of Germany "in peace and freedom"; the peaceful recovery of the German lands presently "administered" by Poland and the Soviet Union; permanent and intimate collaboration with the Western powers; and the economic, military, and—ultimately—political integration of the states of Western Europe.

The Social Democratic party (*Sozialdemokratische Partei Deutschlands*) is more strongly rooted in the past than the CDU (or CSU)—in terms of both its objectives and its supporters. The SPD was for long primarily a workers' party, as it was before the advent of Hitler and its prohibition in 1933, and many of its supporters have been adherents for many decades. Heretofore far more homogeneous in both membership and electorate than the CDU (or CSU), the SPD since the late 1950s has made strenuous efforts to broaden its support among the voters. Most West Germans appear unwilling to cast their ballots for a "workers' party," and even many manual workers no longer want to be considered proletarians. Seeking to become a progressive "peoples' party" similar to the Scandinavian labor parties, the SPD has thrown overboard most of its traditional Marxist principles. In its domestic program, the party has gone far toward accepting the social and economic tenets of the Christian Democrats, while in foreign affairs it has abandoned its former neutralist inclinations and has embraced rearmament and NATO membership. These efforts have produced the desired effect of changing the image of the SPD among the electorate. In every election since 1953, the SPD has gained an average of 3.7 percent of the votes; by 1969 it received 42.7 percent of all votes cast—enough to allow it to take over the government together with the FDP.

None of the minor parties represented in the national legislature has played a very significant role in matters of foreign policy, with the exception of the one remaining small party, the Free Democratic party (*Freie Demokratische Partei*). Aspiring to hold the balance of power between the two major parties, the FDP was long under the influence of the CDU, with which it formed a coalition government until December, 1966. But while its appeal to the voters declined steadily (from a 13 percent high in

1961 to a bare 5.4 percent in 1969), it gained considerably in power in 1969, when its *Fraktion* in the *Bundestag* found itself in a position to decide which major party would form the government in coalition with the FDP. Largely because of its views on foreign policy, the FDP leadership decided on a coalition with the SPD, thus making Willy Brandt chancellor of the Federal Republic, while its own party chairman, Walter Scheel, took over the Foreign Office.

Until 1967, extremist parties had been conspicuous by their absence. The insignificant Communist party had no representation in the national legislature even before it was outlawed in 1956; when the formation of a new Communist party was permitted in 1969, it polled less than 1 percent of the votes. However, a newly formed combination of formerly insignificant neo-Nazi parties, the National Democratic party (*Nationaldemokratische Partei*, or NPD), won up to eight percent of the vote in various *Landtag* (state legislature) elections between 1967 and 1969, mostly in rural areas where dissatisfaction with Bonn's farm policies ran high. However, the NPD's influence over dissatisfied voters and old Nazis declined to the point where, in the 1969 *Bundestag* election, it polled only 4.3 percent of all votes—not enough to gain entry into the *Bundestag*. Since then the NPD has lost heavily in various *Landtag* elections and appears headed for political oblivion.

The formulation of West German foreign policy, therefore, has been primarily in the hands of the two major parties. As the governing party since the establishment of the Federal Republic in 1949 until 1969, the CDU bore prime responsibility for initiating and executing foreign policy decisions. The SPD was compelled to play the role of a permanent opposition, endeavoring, with mixed success, to influence foreign policy through criticism of the government, through attempts to amend government bills in the national legislature, and through efforts to mobilize public opinion to compel the government to modify its position. During much of the 1950s, both parties sought, between elections, to establish a clear distinction in the public mind between their respective policies, in order to present the electorate with a decisive choice at election time. In the early 1960s, however, these distinctions became increasingly blurred. By 1966, the CDU and the SPD shared policy outlooks similar enough to allow them to form a "Grand Coalition" government. During the three years that this government lasted, however, policy differences became increasingly apparent once again, particularly in the area of foreign policy toward the East. Now that the CDU finds itself in the unusual and uncomfortable role of opposition, it is attempting to offer its old policies as developed by Konrad Adenauer as foreign policy alternatives to the electorate. As we have already seen, it seems doubtful at best whether a majority of the West German people will embrace these alternatives advanced by the CDU.

The Role of the Interest Groups

The constitution grants all West Germans the right to form organizations to represent their particular political, economic, or religious interests, as long as such groups are not directed against "the principle of international understanding." As in the United States, there exist in the German Federal Republic numerous associations that, in one way or another, seek to influence the conduct of foreign affairs in accordance with their perceived interests. However,

West German interest groups are more inclusive, more tightly organized, and occupy a more privileged position in public life than do their American counterparts. On the other hand, the West German public tends to be more critical and suspicious of the influence of such interest groups than do Americans.

Economic and political interests are organized into large national organizations (*Spitzenverbände*), all of which are ostensibly nonpartisan, but by no means nonpolitical. Religious interests are primarily represented by the two major churches, the Roman Catholic and the Protestant, and their affiliated lay organizations.

In general, the influence of interest groups on the conduct of foreign affairs has increased in direct proportion to the gradual restoration of West German sovereignty and the recovery of independence of action by the government of the Federal Republic. Most of them have endeavored to exercise their influence over national policy through the political parties and, particularly, through party leaders in the executive and legislative branches of the federal government.

Economic interest groups in the Federal Republic fall roughly into two major categories: (*a*) employers' organizations; and (*b*) organizations representing employees, independent farmers, independent craftsmen, and the professions. The employers' groups have the greater financial resources, but the others have a greater voting strength to offer to political leaders and parties. Individually or collectively, these organizations endeavor to influence the foreign policy-making process whenever they consider their special interests to be involved. In the past this has meant, for example, that representatives of the employers' organizations sought a more open policy toward the East in order to open up new markets. Industrial interests in the Federal Republic have also been influential in the field of national security policy, where they have attempted to commit the federal government to policies beneficial to the West German armaments industry—that is, to policies designed to increase West German armaments spending and exports of armaments to other countries. In this respect, West Germany's industrial organizations have exercised a great deal of influence over the Federal Republic's foreign policy. The role of employee groups, by comparison, has been less influential, although various trade union representatives have at times attempted to influence foreign policy decision making in regard to countries where trade union movements are repressed (such as Spain). In general, however, the influence of such organizations appears to be limited to matters where their immediate interests are at stake.

One particularly successful organization in this regard has been the League of German Farmers (*Deutscher Bauernverband*), which represents more than three-quarters of the country's 1.6 million independent farmers. Despite the shrinking of the agricultural sector since 1950, West German farm organizations still have considerable political influence. This influence has been effectively directed toward specific demands, such as agricultural subsidies, prices of produce, and, especially, the accommodation of West German agricultural prices within the framework of the European Economic Community. By 1970, the federal government was subsidizing West German farmers at the rate of almost 6.8 billion DM—that is, roughly $1.9 billion (or about as much as the federal government spent for institutions of higher learning in 1970). More than two-thirds of these

subsidies went to support West German farmers vis-à-vis the EEC. The net effect that such subsidies have had on the agriculture of the EEC as a whole has been the accumulation of tremendous surpluses of wheat, corn, butter, and milk. The EEC estimated that in 1969 it spent approximately 8 billion DM (more than $2.2 billion) to finance this surplus of agricultural goods, most of which were eventually sold substantially below value to countries outside the EEC. This large amount of governmental subsidy to West German agriculture, paid in order to maintain a common EEC agricultural policy—as well as the seemingly constant haggling over the implementation of Common Market standards in all EEC countries, from wheat to wine to beer—has contributed substantially to a common feeling among West Germans of dissatisfaction with European institutions. In this sense, then, West Germany's agricultural interests have exercised—and continue to exercise—a heavy influence on West German foreign policy.

Only a few of the special-interest groups play any significant role in the Federal Republic. The most important of these are the organizations of expellees—German citizens and ethnic Germans who fled or were expelled from German lands that are east of the Oder-Neisse line (which are presently administered, under the Potsdam agreement of 1945, by Poland and the Soviet Union) and from other parts of Eastern and southeastern Europe. About 9 million of these expellees live in the Federal Republic today, constituting about 15 percent of the total population; approximately half of them are former residents of Silesia and the Sudetenland. However, almost 45 percent of all officially recognized refugees in 1970 were forty years and younger; in other words, they were either children at the end of World War II or were born after 1945. Only a fraction of the expellees are organized into the various groups that claim to defend their common interests. The most important of these are the League of Expelled Germans (*Zentralverband Vertriebener Deutscher*) and the League of Regional Groups (*Verband der Landsmannschaften*), with its major affiliates of Silesians (*Landsmannschaft Schlesien*) and Sudeten Germans (*Sudetendeutsche Landsmannschaft*). There are also more than 4 million refugees from the Soviet zone of Germany in the Federal Republic (about 7 percent of the population) but, although there are numerous organizations that would like to represent their interests, few of the refugees belong to them. Together, expellees and refugees number more than 13 million persons, almost one-quarter of the population, but most of them appear to have found adequate representation of their interests within the major political parties.

THE SYSTEM IN OPERATION: THE SUBSTANCE OF FOREIGN POLICY

The actual operation of West German foreign policy making is heavily influenced by three factors: the aims of West German policy makers; the pressure of various interest groups; and, to a lesser extent, the involvement of the West German economy with the United States, first through various forms of U.S. aid, during the late 1940s and early 1950s, and, later, through private business relations. The intra-German factors will be discussed shortly, but the West German stake in its political and economic relations with the United States is so substantial that we must say something about its magnitude at the outset.

The Economic Influence of the United States

To indicate even the order of magnitude of the American dollar flow into the Federal Republic and West Berlin during the immediate postwar decade is not an easy task. The aid has always been given in a large variety of ways, under a bewildering succession of alphabetical agencies: GARIOA, ECA, MSA, FOA, and others. Although these accounted publicly for their operations, data for other channels of dollars into the West German economy have not been so readily available. In West Germany, as in some other countries, many of these extraordinary dollar receipts, as a report of the U.N. Economic Commission for Europe points out, "belong to the twilight zone of quasi-strategic information: at best, only general orders of magnitude are known."[58]

What is this general order of magnitude? The German Federal Ministry for Economic Cooperation acknowledged, in 1956, that West Germany had received almost $10 billion up to June 30, 1956, presumably for a period since early 1948.[59] Of the exact total, which was $9,935 million, $6,355 million was listed as aid to the Federal Republic in general, and $3,580 million as aid to West Berlin.[60] Even if one assumes that this total includes all dollar aid since 1946, one would arrive at an average of $1 billion per year, approximately $20 per

[58] United Nations, Department of Economic Affairs, Economic Commission for Europe, *Economic Survey of Europe in 1953* (Geneva, 1954), pp. 19–20.

[59] Bundesministerium für wirtschaftliche Zusammenarbeit, *Der europäische Wirtschaftsrat—OEEC: Handbuch, 1956* (Godesberg: Verlag für Publizistik), p. 70.

[60] Ibid. The latter sum may have included orders placed in West Berlin for work done elsewhere in the Federal Republic.

year for every German man, woman, and child.

The value of these dollars to the West German economy was greatly increased by the manner in which they were employed and by the efficient response of West German management and labor. Through counterpart funds and other devices, a considerable part was used to increase capital investment—and thus the technological equipment of West German industry—without any of the sacrifices that consumers would otherwise have had to make for an investment program of this magnitude. The result was an increase in both capital equipment and consumer goods. An official West German publication sums it up thus:

> To use a medical term, it was "dollar therapy" and the tonic effect of an American blood transfusion. . . . Every Marshall Plan dollar spent in Germany has resulted in $10 to $20 worth of goods produced and services rendered.[61]

The Federal Republic's economy remains fundamentally dependent on the United States. Although the increasing consolidation and growth of the German economy has translated this dependence from one-sided aid to a mutual interplay, West Germany's need for warm relations with the United States has remained greater than the United States' need for even minimal good relations with West Germany. West Germany exports, as well as domestic goods, have continued to depend in good part on American defense installations and on American tax and tariff policies, as well as on the continuing confidence of American investors. A decline of the American stock market, such as that of "Blue Monday," May 28, 1962, or the American ten percent surcharge on import

61 *Germany Reports,* 1953, pp. 239–43.

duties in 1971, has an immediate effect on the economy of the Federal Republic. American taxes on the investments of its nationals abroad, or fears among American and European investors of military or political instability in West Germany, could alter the country's prosperity and balance of payments very rapidly, indeed.[62]

The economic influence of the United States is heavily reinforced by psychological, social, and military considerations that make American friendship appear to be the most important basis of whatever security the makers of West German foreign policy can hope for in this uncertain world. The results of this relationship have been conspicuous. In almost every major West German foreign policy decision, the government of the United States has been an invisible—and sometimes not so invisible—partner.

Nevertheless, there has been a growing autonomous component in West German foreign policy. The interplay of West German aims and United States influence with the various West German domestic interests can be seen best by glancing briefly at a few actual cases. The questions of West German membership in the European Coal and Steel Community, of West German rearmament, and of negotiations with the Soviet Union about German reunification are the cases in which we shall try to watch the making of West German foreign policy.

Toward the Recovery of German Influence

A primary objective of West Germany's foreign policy, since the creation of the Federal Republic in 1949,

62 See Karl W. Deutsch, "The German Federal Republic," in *Modern Political Systems: Europe,* ed. Roy Macridis and Robert E. Ward (Englewood Cliffs, N.J.: Prentice-Hall, 1963), pp. 301–2.

has been the recovery of West German influence in international affairs. There have been differences among the elite and among the public at large over the means to be employed, but there is solid unanimity about the general objective. The man primarily responsible for the conduct of West German foreign policy from 1949 to 1963, Chancellor Konrad Adenauer, was singularly successful in his efforts to regain independence of action in the conduct of foreign policy without losing the political, military, and economic support of the West, particularly the United States. Adenauer's policy was to establish West Germany as the leading power and the senior partner of the United States on the European continent, by means of adroit and subtle moves that gained for the Federal Republic full sovereignty and a leading position within the Western alliance in the course of a few years. In the face of frequently bitter opposition at home, particularly from the Social Democratic leadership, and often without the specific support of public opinion, he gained his ends through close collaboration with the Western powers, particularly the United States. Adenauer gambled, successfully, that temporary concessions would eventually lead to major gains for West German foreign policy, and that the voters would sustain him at election time. He owed his success to a combination of factors: his unrivaled position as the leader of the governing political group; his remarkable prestige, both inside and outside West Germany; his ability to enlist the support of crucial West German leaders for specific foreign policy moves, in the face of public opposition or indifference; his influence among leading policy makers in Western countries; and last, but not least, the exigencies of the international situation. In general, Adenauer ex-

ploited, to the fullest, his great formal and informal powers as chancellor and as leader of the largest West German party—if necessary, in the face of widespread public opposition at home and abroad—in order to gain his ends in foreign affairs.

The European Coal and Steel Community Treaty. The first step toward the recovery of West German sovereignty and liberation from allied controls, after the creation of the Federal Republic, was taken with the creation of the European Coal and Steel Community (ECSC), popularly known as the Schuman Plan. Under the Occupation Statute of 1949, the new West German state gained only limited independence from control over its affairs by the three Western occupation powers—the United States, Great Britain, and France. A tripartite Allied High Commission was established, endowed with broad powers designed to assure that the Federal Republic would conform to Western plans for a democratic and demilitarized Germany and that it would honor the political and economic obligations it had undertaken in return for allied agreement to the establishment of the new state. The Allied High Commission controlled the organization and operation of German business, endeavoring to prevent its reconcentration in cartels and trusts, and diverting a considerable share of the production of the Ruhr's coal to those foreign countries which had been victims of German aggression. The commission regulated political and economic relations between the new state and foreign countries, and, for all practical purposes, represented the interests of the Federal Republic and its citizens abroad.

The new West German government, a coalition led by Adenauer, immediately sought ways and means of gaining freedom from allied supervision. These efforts were helped immeasurably by the rapid economic recovery of the new German state and by the intensification of the conflict between the Western allies and the Soviet Union. The failure to achieve agreement with the Soviet Union on the reunification of Germany, and the belief that the USSR might attack Western Europe through the territory of the Federal Republic, led the Western occupation powers to yield to Adenauer's demands for complete sovereignty. Even before the outbreak of the Korean conflict in July, 1950, Western policy toward West Germany had begun to change. Instead of continuing to treat the Federal Republic as a defeated enemy, the West began to seek its inclusion in the Western alliance as a major bulwark against Soviet aggression. These developments played directly into the hands of the leaders of the Federal Republic, who offered intimate collaboration to the Western powers in return for independence and West German equality in the councils of the Western alliance. Their first opportunity to move toward their objective came almost as soon as the new state had come into being, in May, 1950, when French Foreign Minister Robert Schuman called for the pooling of French and German coal and steel production in an economic union, which he invited other interested European states also to join.

Chancellor Adenauer immediately hailed Schuman's proposal as "epochmaking" and called for its speedy implementation in the form of a treaty. However, the spokesmen of the Federal Republic let it be known that their country would join the proposed community only if all existing restrictions on the republic's sovereignty, imposed by the occupation powers, were removed. The Occupation Statute of 1949, therefore, was gradu-

ally revised in the course of the negotiations leading to the signing of the ECSC treaty in April, 1951. The Federal Republic was given partial control over its foreign relations, and some of the most severe allied controls over its domestic affairs were gradually dropped. In January, 1952, the *Bundestag* approved the ECSC treaty by a vote of 232 to 143.

Bundestag approval of the ECSC treaty was not due to overwhelming public support. The "attentive public" in favor of the proposed coal and steel community declined steadily during negotiations, and the opposition to it increased. The largest number of West Germans appeared to have become increasingly indifferent toward the issue, however, leaving the final decision to the makers of foreign policy.

West German Armament as an Instrument of Foreign Policy. On May 9, 1955, the black, red, and gold flag of the German Federal Republic rose at the Supreme Headquarters, Allied Powers Europe (SHAPE), while the band played the old German national anthem, *Deutschland, Deutschland über alles, über alles in der Welt.* It signified the admission of a free and sovereign West German state to NATO—almost ten years to the day since its new allies had dictated armistice terms to a vanquished state. After almost six years of determined efforts to throw off Western allied controls over German affairs, Chancellor Adenauer and his associates appeared at last to have obtained their goal. In exchange for the promise of a German military contribution to the defense of Western Europe, they had gained for the Federal Republic "the full authority of a sovereign state over its internal and external affairs," a national military establishment, a major voice in the councils of the Western powers, assurances of Western military and political support against the Soviet Union, and, finally, Western recognition of the Bonn government as "the only German Government . . . entitled to speak . . . as the representative of the entire German people in international affairs."[63]

As in the case of ECSC, the negotiations leading to the abolition of Western controls and the recognition of the Federal Republic as a sovereign and equal member of NATO demonstrated the far-reaching and generally uncontested independence of West German foreign policy decision makers from the influence of domestic public opinion. The price that the Adenauer government agreed to pay for sovereignty and NATO membership was the setting up of a national military establishment—a decision repeatedly opposed, during the period of negotiations, by more Germans than supported it.

Adenauer and his closest associates sought to achieve their objective—as in the case of the ECSC—in the name of European integration. In December, 1949, Adenauer launched a trial balloon by suggesting that the West Germans should contribute to the defense of Europe in a European army. Apparently anticipating that the West would soon demand a West German contribution to European defense, and basing this prediction on formal and informal suggestions from Western political and military leaders, he maintained his position in the following months despite intense opposition both in the Federal Republic and

abroad. Adenauer sought to impress Western leaders with the value of the Federal Republic as an ally and to prove to them that it might play a crucial role in a future conflict between the Soviet Union and the NATO powers. He claimed that the industrial and demographic resources of the Federal Republic might prove decisive in a future war; and he stressed the danger of large-scale Soviet troop concentrations in central Germany and of the growing power of the Peoples' Police of the communist-dominated German Democratic Republic, suggesting that, short of a military contribution from the Federal Republic, the Western powers lacked the forces to repel an attack from the East. For political as well as military reasons, Adenauer maintained, the Western powers needed the loyal support of the people of the German Federal Republic; he offered it in exchange for an end to allied controls and the termination of existing limitations on the sovereignty of the Federal Republic.

To gain his objective, Adenauer was willing to risk Soviet threats against the Federal Republic and the possibility that the reunification of Germany might be deferred indefinitely; as in the case of ECSC, he was prepared to sacrifice *potential* sovereign rights in return for the surrender of *actual* sovereign powers by other nations participating in the creation of a European defense community. The same ideological motives that influenced the CDU, under Adenauer's leadership, to support the Schuman Plan of May, 1950, also led it to support concurrent proposals for the creation of a European army, even though ten opinion polls between 1950 and 1954 each showed more opponents than supporters for this policy.

However, political considerations were every bit as important. Member-

[63] United States Congress, Senate, *Protocol on the Termination of the Occupation Regime in the Federal Republic of Germany and Protocol to the North Atlantic Treaty on the Accession of the Federal Republic of Germany*, 83d Cong., 2d sess., Executives L and M, 1954.

ship in a European integration scheme held out, for a West German state both wealthier and more populous than any other Continental state, the prospect not only of equality but of potential leadership of the democratic nations of continental Europe. Instead of remaining merely a rump German state, facing the prospect of indefinite occupation and control by foreign powers, the Federal Republic might become "first among equals," playing a leading role in international affairs as the leader of the Continental nations, particularly in relation to the United States and the Soviet Union, the two superpowers of the world. Finally, such a role for Germany in a European military union promised to make it less dependent on foreign powers and to give its leaders a greater voice in matters affecting the defense of the Federal Republic against attack from the East. To gain these ends, Adenauer was prepared to defy popular opposition to German rearmament. Sovereignty and equality for the Federal Republic, through European integration, were to him worth the price of a West German military contribution, as Adenauer's official biographer was to note.[64]

Adenauer's arguments for a German military contribution to the defense of Western Europe against communist attack seemed substantiated by the North Korean attack on South Korea in July, 1950. Particularly in the United States, government, military, and political leaders—some of whom had favored a German military contribution, at least since 1949—reportedly interpreted the unexpected invasion as a clear warning that

either the Soviet Union or its East German satellite might invade the Federal Republic, too. Western allied forces in Germany, never very strong, and further weakened by the diversion of military resources to Korea, appeared inadequate to meet the threat. Simultaneously, the French government informed the United States that it was not interested in an allied strategy that depended primarily on American atomic weapons, but wanted Western Europe to be defended by ground forces, as far east as possible.

While the United States sought desperately to stem the North Korean sweep down the peninsula, Chancellor Adenauer pointed with increasing emphasis to the exposed situation of his country, and of Western Europe in general. In August, 1950, he suggested to the Western Allies the formation of a "special force of German volunteers" of the same size and strength as the Peoples' Police in the Soviet zone of Germany—estimated at 50,000 to 80,000 trained soldiers. He coupled this appeal with the renewed suggestion that the Federal Republic might make a sizeable contribution to a European army in return for an end to allied controls and complete equality within a defense arrangement. Simultaneously, Adenauer appointed a former general to head a new office in the federal government that was to lay plans for such a West German military contribution.

The United States government, responding to the urgings of its own military leaders, replied to Adenauer's proposals by openly calling for the use of West German productive resources and military manpower for the defense of Western Europe. Secretary of State Dean Acheson asked the British and French to agree to the inclusion of about ten German divisions in the NATO forces in Europe. But, in the

---

[64] Paul Weymar, *Konrad Adenauer: Die autorisierte Biographie* (Munich: Kindler, 1955), pp. 500, 557. See also Fritz René Allemann, *Bonn ist nicht Weimar* (Cologne-Berlin: Kiepenheuer and Witsch, 1956), pp. 187–212.

face of French opposition to the creation of an independent German army, the three Western governments agreed that the West Germany military contribution demanded "by democratic leaders in Germany" should become part of an integrated European army.

Urged on by the United States, the governments of the Federal Republic of Germany, France, Italy, Belgium, the Netherlands, and Luxembourg hammered out a scheme for a European Defense Community (EDC) that would more or less parallel the pattern agreed upon for the European Coal and Steel Community. French negotiators, led by Adenauer's friend, Foreign Minister Robert Schuman, sought to limit West German influence in the proposed military arrangement, but the representatives of the Federal Republic demanded complete equality and the termination of allied controls over West German affairs. The West Germans were aided not only by strong United States support but, paradoxically, by popular opposition to rearmament in West Germany itself. Pointing to gains for the opposition Social Democrats—strongly opposed to the scheme—in various local elections, Adenauer extracted major allied political concessions for the more "cooperative" West German leaders.

When the EDC treaty was finally signed, in May, 1952, it provided for the creation of twelve German divisions, an air force, and a small navy, which were to become major components of a European military establishment. True, the German Federal Republic was not yet admitted to NATO, but Chancellor Adenauer had no doubts that membership would follow as soon as the German defense contribution had begun to take concrete form. Simultaneously with the signing of the EDC treaty, the Federal Republic concluded a contractual

agreement with the three Western occupation powers which was to replace the Occupation Statute of 1949. In effect, this agreement terminated the occupation and put an end to practically all allied controls. However, Western forces, remaining in Germany as "allies," retained the right to intervene in case the democratic order in the Federal Republic should be threatened either from within or without. In May, 1953, the *Bundestag* approved the two agreements by a majority of 59 votes, a considerably smaller margin of victory than Adenauer's policies had achieved for the ECSC, only a few months earlier.

Despite widespread popular opposition to rearmament, the promised restoration of German sovereignty and the gains in Germany's international position impressed many voters. Adenauer won a resounding personal victory in the election of 1953. His prestige and reputation as an effective representative of German interests gave the Christian Democrats an absolute majority in the *Bundestag* for the first time; the ruling coalition now commanded the two-thirds majority required for the constitutional changes which rearmament might necessitate. Adenauer's policy of German political recovery in international affairs through European integration was dealt a setback in August, 1954, however, when the French Chamber of Deputies rejected the EDC treaty and thus defeated the scheme. Following this defeat, interestingly enough, only 37 percent of the respondents in a West German poll expressed regret for the failure of the project.

The German chancellor immediately demanded complete sovereignty for the Federal Republic, maintaining that it had fulfilled its part of the bargain and was not to blame for the failure of the armament scheme. However, the British and American governments insisted that a West German military contribution, agreed to by the French, remained the *sine qua non* of political sovereignty. On British initiative, representatives of the United States, Britain, Canada, and the six Continental countries that had signed the EDC treaty formulated a hasty substitute. It provided for the creation of a national West German military establishment, and the admission of the Federal Republic to NATO as a sovereign and equal partner, subject only to certain limitations on its future military power, and a ban on any production of "ABC" weapons, (i.e. atomic, biological, or chemical) weapons, and the retention of a few formal rights by the former occupation powers pertaining to West Berlin and German reunification. By May, 1955, all the governments concerned had ratified these "Paris Agreements," a major goal of Adenauer's foreign policy. The immediate political gains for the Federal Republic were even greater than under the proposed EDC arrangement; however, many West German proponents of European integration paid the price only reluctantly. The gains of sovereignty, NATO membership, and a national military establishment did not appear to them to be worth the sacrifice of the European army scheme and its apparent promise of German leadership in Europe.

Originally, NATO was promised 500,000 troops by 1957, but the projected pace was subsequently slowed, so that only about 400,000 West German troops were under arms by 1970. The percentage of West German national income spent for defense purposes, however, climbed from about 4 percent during most of the 1950s to about 7 percent in the early 1960s, close to that of France and Britain but less than the roughly 11 to 12 percent

spent by the United States in 1965–66 and the perhaps still higher level of the Soviet Union. By 1970, however, this percentage had again dropped to only 4.7 percent, reflecting the decreased importance the *Bundeswehr* ("federal defense" force) played in West German politics.

OSTPOLITIK

Between 1945 and 1956, West German foreign policy makers were highly successful in obtaining their objectives in negotiations with the Western occupation powers, primarily because the West was willing and able to pay the price demanded. To obtain the political, military, and economic participation of the Federal Republic in the Western alliance against the Soviet Union, they agreed to Adenauer's demands for sovereignty and equality. Reunification, however, was another matter. Here, West German foreign policy makers were faced with a double deadlock on the formula for German unity: the stalemate between the Soviet Union and the United States on the one hand, and the lack of clear agreement among Western leaders— not only between West Germany and France, but perhaps even between West Germany and the United States —on the other. In respect to the Soviet-American deadlock, both sides conceived the potential status of a united Germany as a matter so vital to their respective interests that they found it impossible to make the concessions that a compromise solution would require. Western leaders saw the terms for reunification proposed by Soviet leaders as designed to give control over this strategic area to the USSR, while the latter insisted that a Germany united according to Western plans would constitute a menace to the Soviet Union and its allies in Eastern Europe. The resulting deadlock, while leaving little room for maneuver, has left West German policy makers with difficult decisions over the past twenty-five years.

The Basic Law of the Federal Republic of Germany made it a constitutional requirement of the federal government "to complete the unity and the liberty of Germany in free self-determination" of the whole German people. However, the writers of the Basic Law wisely left open the question of the means by which the goal of reunification was to be achieved; subsequently, the federal constitutional court, West Germany's highest court, has repeatedly refused to accept the argument that a particular administration had acted against the Basic Law in pursuing a certain policy apparently in contradiction with the constitutional demand for reunification. West Germany's foreign policy makers have thus been relatively free in designing policies geared to the goal of reunification.

Under Konrad Adenauer's leadership as chancellor, the goal of reunification was pursued through a "policy of strength." Adenauer claimed that this "policy of strength" formed the link between what many West Germans felt were two contradictory goals: the Federal Republic's integration into the Western alliance with rearmament the major domestic consequence and the reunification of Germany as well as the regaining of the formerly German territories beyond the Oder-Neisse line. The debate over the priorities of West Germany's foreign policy raged even within Adenauer's own party, the CDU. Thus Gustav Heinemann, at the time minister of the interior in Adenauer's cabinet, resigned in 1951 in protest over Adenauer's rearmament policy, claiming it was immoral, impractical, and detrimental to real West German interests. (Subsequently Heinemann

joined the SPD, whose representatives, aided by those of the FDP, voted him president in 1969 of the Federal Republic in yet another demonstration of *Vergangenheitsbewältigung* ["mastering the past"]). Adenauer, however, remained firm, refusing even to consider seriously a Soviet offer transmitted in 1952 which promised the reunification of Germany in exchange for neutrality. From Adenauer's point of view, the Federal Republic simply could not afford to engage in such an uncertain political adventure. Western support would have been lacking; he was afraid of a rekindling of German nationalism; and neutrality did not appear to be a feasible alternative to his policy of firm integration into the West. As long as international tensions remained acute, a united Germany would have seemed too dangerous to either side in the East-West contest.

In 1955, when the Federal Republic gained full sovereignty and joined NATO, Adenauer's "policy of strength" appeared to bring its first results: the leaders of the Soviet Union invited Adenauer to come to Moscow in September, 1955. Adenauer accepted, possibly sharing the widespread West German view that his bargaining position was strong enough to extract favorable terms from the Soviet government. If he did so, it turned out, however, that he had overestimated his own position and underestimated that of the Soviet leaders. The latter refused to discuss reunification, but suggested that he negotiate directly with the leaders of the German Democratic Republic, a move which no political leader in the Federal Republic was then willing to make. Adenauer refused, but he agreed to the establishment of diplomatic relations between the Federal Republic and the Soviet Union in return for the release of several thousand German prisoners of war still in captivity. To many leading West Germans, it seemed that Adenauer had walked into a Soviet trap. By agreeing to the establishment of diplomatic relations, he seemed to have accepted the Soviet claim that there were two German states, both represented in Moscow, and that unification could only come about by negotiations between their respective governments. However, Adenauer quickly sought to dispel the impression that he had abandoned the claim of the federal government to be the only German government and that he was moving toward recognition of East Germany. He did so by announcing a policy of breaking off all diplomatic relations with countries recognizing the East German regime. This policy came to be known as the Hallstein doctrine and remained virtually in effect until 1971, albeit with diminishing vigor since the mid-1960s. The presence of a Soviet ambassador in Bonn, and of a West German ambassador in Moscow, represented a relative increase in German independence and bargaining power vis-à-vis the West; and Adenauer had gained these points without injuring in any way his reputation for rock-solid reliability as an ally of the West. However, it was evident that the Federal Republic could ill afford to go much further in the way of independent negotiations with the Soviet Union, and that it still depended upon the Western powers—particularly the United States—to achieve the professed major foreign policy objective of its leaders: German unity.

Throughout Adenauer's tenure as federal chancellor, *Ostpolitik* was pursued—or perhaps better, neglected —under the assumption that reunification was a precondition for a relaxation of tensions in Europe. Indeed, this policy represented the West German corollary to John Foster Dulles's

"roll back" policy: through an increase of Western power, the Soviet Union was to be forced into a position where it had to relinquish its hold over most of Eastern Europe. It was thus natural that Adenauer and Dulles, who shared essentially similar views on issues of Cold War politics, should maintain the closest of relations until Dulles's death in 1959.

The year 1961, however, brought two significant developments which were to put a severe strain on the Federal Republic's domestic and foreign policies: in January, John F. Kennedy became president of the United States, and on August 13 the East German regime began construction of the wall that was to divide East and West Berlin.

The Kennedy administration came to power with the declared intention of trying to seek a détente between the East and the West. While it also put great emphasis on the idea of an Atlantic partnership between the United States and a united Europe (to which end it considered various schemes of Atlantic integration, such as a Multilateral Nuclear Force), the more open-minded policy toward the East which Kennedy initiated conflicted heavily with Adenauer's ideas. The problem was confounded by Adenauer's personal dislike for Kennedy, a man almost twice as young (and presumably twice as inexperienced) as Adenauer. But even though Adenauer tried to resist the foreign policy changes originating from Washington, his position was by no means strong enough to do so. As he became more at odds with the prevailing Western foreign policy images, his international as well as his domestic stature declined rapidly, until he was finally forced by his own party (and its coalition partner, the FDP) to resign in favor of Ludwig Erhard, then minister of economics, in 1965.

The erection of the Berlin Wall underlined dramatically the failure of Adenauer's "policy of strength." Instead of having forced the Soviet Union to abolish its hold over East Germany, this move served to stabilize the Ulbricht regime to the point where it could actually claim the support of a large sector of the East German population. In the years prior to 1961, a large stream of refugees had left the G.D.R. in search of the "Golden West." Of the roughly 3 million East Germans who took this step, taking along only their bare necessities, almost half were young people up to the age of 25. This meant a serious depletion of qualified workers for the East German economy, which until 1961 had struggled hard to achieve an economic recovery comparable to the Federal Republic's. On the other hand, the refugee movement had the beneficial effect for the East German regime of eliminating almost all serious and organized opposition to the Ulbricht regime. Therefore, when, in the summer of 1961, the refugee stream temporarily rose to unprecedented proportions (due in large part to the forced collectivization of East German agriculture then taking place at the time), the East German regime found the time ripe to close off the border.

The repercussions in West Germany were widespread, although, as our discussion of public opinion polls has shown, not of very long duration. Certainly the most serious direct consequence of the closing of the border was the fact that East and West Germans could no longer communicate with each other. While movement across the border had by no means been easy even before 1961, the level of contacts between East and West had remained fairly high. Particularly in Berlin, due to its special status as a city under Four Power Administration, it had always been possible to cross the border in both directions. This had enabled East Germans to stay in contact with West German developments and vice versa. This avenue of communication, as well as others, was now cut off. This complete cutoff of almost all cross-border contacts except for mail (and even here public opinion polls showed a decline in the number of people claiming to write and receive mail across the border) raised previously expressed fears of a process of estrangement between the two parts of Germany to new heights. In the years since 1961, therefore, attempts to overcome this separation of Germans in East and West replaced in priority the goal of reunification.

Following the lead of the Kennedy administration, West German foreign policy makers, in particular Foreign Minister Gerhard Schröder, soon initiated a policy of détente without reunification as a precondition. Where previously the Cold Warriors of the Federal Republic had insisted that a relaxation of tension was impossible without prior reunification, the more realistic foreign policy makers of the 1960s conceded that, if reunification were to be achieved at all, it could come only after a long process of relaxation of tension. The new policy toward the East called for the cautious establishment of semidiplomatic relations with Eastern bloc countries, primarily through the establishment of so-called trade missions (so as not to give up the Hallstein doctrine); in the process of this *Ostpolitik*, the German Democratic Republic was to be isolated from the rest of the Eastern bloc countries, which would then presumably be more in favor of a reunification of the two parts of Germany. However, as the G.D.R. made dramatic gains in its economic development after the building of the Berlin Wall, it not only became indispensable to the economy of the Eastern bloc as a whole, its leaders also gained enough political power in Moscow and elsewhere to withstand Bonn's efforts to isolate them. This policy, while leading to increased trade relations with Eastern bloc countries, was thus no more successful in bringing reunification closer to reality than the previous "policy of strength." Even the goal of humanitarian improvements, so important after 1961, met with only limited success in Berlin, where SPD Mayor Brandt had managed to negotiate an agreement with the East German government allowing West Berliners to visit their relatives in East Berlin during Christmas and Easter holidays. Even this agreement, endorsed most reluctantly by Bonn's foreign policy makers (who did not like the fact that the mayor of West Berlin, a prominent member of the SPD at that, had negotiated directly with East German governmental authorities and not with the mayor of East Berlin, thus implying international recognition of the German Democratic Republic), did not last very long; since 1966, most West Berliners have not been able to visit East Berlin. And, with the exception of persons over sixty-five years of age, who are allowed a yearly visit to relatives in West Germany—since 1964, more than 1 million a year have come and returned!—almost no East German citizens are allowed to visit West Germany.

By late 1966, the foreign policy makers of Erhard's CDU government had come to a dead end. Even the highly touted "peace note" sent to Eastern bloc countries in March, 1966, offering negotiations on a renunciation of force, had brought almost no response, primarily because the note contained an attack against the Soviet Union reminiscent of earlier Cold War politics. When the economy took

a turn for the worse, Erhard was forced to resign, again under pressure from the CDU's coalition partner, the Free Democrats. At this point, the SPD saw its long-awaited chance. After having pursued throughout the 1950s a policy of vigorous opposition to Adenauer's foreign policy, the SPD in 1959 had adopted a new party program at Bad Godesberg in which it threw overboard most of its old, partly Marxist political doctrines. This realignment with the prevailing political forces in West Germany had become complete in 1960, when the party's chief parliamentary spokesman, Herbert Wehner, announced in a widely noted speech in the *Bundestag* that henceforth the SPD would support the basic foreign policy programs of the government. This political change of face did not result in a victory at the polls in either 1961 or 1965, as the architects of the change, Wehner and Brandt, had hoped. But it did increase the SPD's public stature until, in December, 1966, it could enter into a "Grand Coalition" government with the CDU, thus for the first time since the Weimar Republic sharing in the responsibility of policy making at the national level. The announced purpose of this "Grand Coalition" was to form a government of national unity, capable of tackling the pressing problems of a sagging economy and worsening relations with the East. Significantly enough, the ministers responsible for overseeing the policies in these areas, Karl Schiller in economics and Willy Brandt in foreign affairs, were both members of the SPD, while the chancellor Kurt Georg Kiesinger, was a member of the CDU.

Under the guidance of Willy Brandt, West Germany's *Ostpolitik* took a new turn. Already in 1963, Egon Bahr—a close friend of Willy Brandt, who was later to conduct the negotiations leading to the Moscow treaty of 1970—had formulated a new policy designed to overcome the division of Germany: *Wandel durch Annäherung* ("change through rapprochement") was its catchword. This policy called for the establishment of close contacts between East and West Germany at all levels so as to induce a gradual change in East German political behavior; a change eventually leading, if not to reunification, at least to a *reguliertes Nebeneinander* ("regulated living side-by-side"), allowing the human contacts most Germans were by now so very much interested in. In other words, Schröder's policy of isolating East Germany was to be replaced by a policy of friendly relations with all Eastern bloc countries, including the German Democratic Republic. The SPD had attempted to implement this foreign policy program even while it was out of power, when in early 1966 it accepted a challenge by the SED, the governing party of the G.D.R., calling for an exchange of speakers. But excitement in both parts of Germany ran so high that eventually the SED felt threatened and called off the project.

After the SPD had joined the government in the making of foreign policy, Brandt pushed vigorously his policy of furthering relations with Eastern bloc countries. Claiming that these countries did not have much choice in the matter, the new government began to dismantle the Hallstein doctrine, which had called for no diplomatic relations with countries recognizing the German Democratic Republic. The new policy proved successful inasmuch as the Federal Republic succeeded in establishing diplomatic relations with Rumania and Yugoslavia. However, the high hopes thus raised were dashed when negotiations with Poland and Czechoslo-

vakia proved unsuccessful. It was clearly evident that the East German regime under Walter Ulbricht had managed to undercut West Germany's diplomatic drive in the East. When the combined armies of the Warsaw Pact, including East German troops, invaded Czechoslovakia in August, 1968, the Grand Coalition's new *Ostpolitik* ground to a halt. Fears of further Soviet moves and a general anger and frustration prevented further efforts. Besides, it was now evident that the G.D.R. had become one of the major powers of the Eastern bloc, capable of sabotaging almost any policy it disapproved of. Despite a first exchange of letters between East German Party Chairman Walter Ulbricht and Chancellor Kiesinger, no further contacts were made. The federal government was not yet prepared to enter into direct negotiations with the East German regime.

As already indicated, the 1969 election campaign was fought primarily over domestic issues of economics and social reform. Nevertheless, foreign policy issues were raised, and as a consequence the differences between the major parties' outlooks sharpened. The role of the FDP in bringing foreign policy issues to public attention should not be underestimated. Running a cleverly designed campaign of "Let's get rid of old hats," the FDP stood on a platform of better relations with the East, recognition of the Oder-Neisse line, and official contacts with the G.D.R. It was in large measure because of this foreign policy stand that the FDP, which had previously formed coalitions with the CDU, for the first time found it possible to form a coalition with the SPD, thus giving the coalition the slight majority of twelve seats in the *Bundestag* and the chance to put its foreign policy program into action under the leadership of FDP Chairman Walter Scheel, now foreign minister of the Federal Republic.

The change of leadership in Bonn had a large effect on the chances of successfully initiating yet another new *Ostpolitik*. Ideologically, the Eastern bloc countries felt much more comfortable about a Social Democratic regime in Bonn than they did about the governments under Adenauer, Erhard, and ex-Nazi Kiesinger, who used to espouse the right-wing, refugee-organization-inspired claims to former German territories, the right to a homeland, and the indivisibility of the German fatherland. Under Brandt, the federal government lowered its voice as well as its sights.

The Brandt administration, having come to power in October, 1969, wasted little time in preparing the groundwork for its *Ostpolitik*. First it cleared the international political atmosphere by signing the Nuclear Non-proliferation Treaty. The West German signature to this treaty had been opposed—vehemently by some, such as Franz Josef Strauss, chairman of the Bavarian sister party of the CDU, the CSU—on the grounds that the inspection procedures specified in the treaty would harm West German industrial interests in the sphere of the civilian use of nuclear power, where West German scientists had made considerable advances. The more outspoken opposition, like Strauss, also argued that for the Federal Republic to sign the treaty would mean a "Versailles of cosmic proportions," since it would lead to a "demotion of the Federal Republic in the international rank order." Brandt and Scheel, however, relatively unconcerned over the Federal Republic's alleged ranking in international politics, and reassured by the United States and the Soviet Union that the treaty would not be injurious to West German industrial

interests, made signature of the treaty their first order of business.

Next came the effort to initiate an inter-German dialogue. In January, 1970, Brandt wrote a letter to Willy Stoph, prime minister of the G.D.R., suggesting negotiations between the two states on the basis of "equality and nondiscrimination." The East German regime, which had always insisted on such contacts, could ill afford to decline the invitation; after some haggling over the location of the talks (Stoph had suggested East Berlin; Brandt accepted on condition that he would travel there via West Berlin, to which Stoph objected because of East German insistence that West Berlin form a political unity separate from the Federal Republic), the two representatives of two German states met in Erfurt, East Germany, on March 19, 1970. The meeting represented a personal triumph for Brandt when an enthusiastic crowd of East Germans called him to a window of the hotel where the meeting was held, but proved to be singularly unsuccessful in bringing about any changes in the relations between East and West Germany. Stoph insisted on the diplomatic recognition of the German Democratic Republic by the Federal Republic before any negotiations over an easing of restrictions could be held; Brandt refused to do so, claiming that intra-German relations could not be of the same nature as international diplomatic relations, since the two states were still united by the special bond of the German nation. When the two German leaders met again two months later in Kassel, West Germany, their positions remained the same. No progress was made.

However, these two meetings between two German statesmen did bring about significant changes within each German state. The East German leaders, who had refused to recognize the validity of West German claims to a special bond uniting the two states, had to reckon with the outburst of emotion for Brandt in Erfurt. Subsequently, the Ulbricht regime initiated a campaign to educate the East German citizenry about the evils of "Socialdemocratism" in general and of West German Social Democratic ideas in particular. It also proceeded full steam ahead in its effort to eradicate the last vestiges of all-German feelings among the East German population by striking out the word *Germany* wherever it could. Thus East German industrial products no longer bear the phrase, "Made in Germany"; East German coins no longer carry the word *Deutschland*; and East German athletes competing internationally no longer compete for the glory of "Germany," but only for the glory of their "socialist fatherland," the German Democratic Republic.

In West Germany, the primary effect of the meetings was to increase radically the willingness of the population to recognize the German Democratic Republic. This fact has already been noted in the public opinion data presented earlier. The Brandt-Stoph meetings also served to launch an occasionally intense public debate over whether the two German states were indeed united by the bond of the German nation.[65] Behind this claim, which Brandt reiterated in his January, 1971, address on "the State of the Nation," stands the familiar German distinction between *Staatsnation* (nation-state) and *Kulturnation*—the former defined in political and constitutional terms and the latter in terms of cultural unity and a common historial background. This distinction may be valid; but even if it is, the

question remains whether the cultural unity of the Germans still exists today. Some of evidence to the contrary is available which points to the conclusion that the "complementary habits of communication" (which is one definition of culture)[66] between West Germans and East Germans are in a state of gradual dissolution. People in East and West Germany are experiencing ever more difficulties *understanding* each other. The West German federal government, fully aware of this process, is of course attempting, in its policy vis-à-vis the G.D.R., to stem this tide of cultural erosion. To maintain some measure of German unity by increasing inter-German contacts has become the federal government's primary goal in its *Deutschlandpolitik*. The East German government, on the other hand, also very much aware of this development, is seeking to speed it up. Thus the two German states appear today locked in combat over the preservation of cultural unity.

Deutschlandpolitik, of course, represents only one aspect of *Ostpolitik*, although a very important one indeed. The main focus of any West German *Ostpolitik* must, however, remain Moscow. In an attempt to improve relations with the Soviet Union, Brandt soon after taking office offered the Soviet leaders once again a treaty renouncing all use of force between the two powers. The Soviets, who pre-

---

65 See, for instance, Hellmut Diwald, *Die Anerkennung: Bericht zur Klage der Nation* (Munich: Bechtle, 1970).

66 "A common culture, then, is a common set of stable, habitual preferences and priorities in men's attention, and behavior, as well as in their thoughts and feelings. Many of these preferences may involve communication; it is usually easier for men to communicate within the same culture than across its boundaries. In so far as a common culture facilitates communication, it forms a *community*" (Karl Deutsch, *Nationalism and Social Communication* [Cambridge: M.I.T. Press, 1966], p. 88).

viously had shown only lukewarm interest at best in such a proposal, now agreed to enter into negotiations over the precise content of the proposed treaty. The negotiator for the federal government, Egon Bahr, secretary of state in Brandt's chancellery, found himself in a difficult position vis-à-vis his Soviet counterpart. Quite clearly his dilemma was that the powerful Soviet Union would not be content with a *quid pro quo* renunciation of force; after all, the Soviet leaders have little to fear from West Germany's comparatively small army without nuclear weapons. So the Soviets bargained for more: West Germany's recognition of "postwar realities"—the Oder-Neisse line and the border between East and West Germany. Article 3 of the treaty put this West German concession into precise terms:

In accordance with the foregoing purposes and principles the Federal Republic of Germany and the Union of Soviet Socialist Republics share the realization that peace can only be maintained in Europe if nobody disturbs the present frontiers.
—They undertake to respect without restriction the territorial integrity of all States in Europe within their present frontiers;
—they declare that they have no territorial claims against anybody nor will assert such claims in the future;
—they regard today and shall in future regard the frontiers of all States in Europe as inviolable such as they are on the date of signature of the present Treaty, including the Oder-Neisse line which forms the western frontier of the People's Republic of Poland and the frontier between the Federal Republic of Germany and the German Democratic Republic.[67]

[67] *The Treaty of August 12, 1970, between the Federal Republic of Germany and the Union of Soviet Socialist Republics* (Bonn: Press and Information Office of the Federal Government, 1970).

But now that the Federal Republic had made concessions beyond renouncing the use of force—concessions which altered radically most of West Germany's previous foreign policy goals—the West Germans had to seek some concessions in return. Already a strong public campaign had been launched by right-wing newspapers (such as publisher Springer's chain) and politicians, such as Kiesinger and Strauss, denouncing the treaty as a West German sellout. When Walter Scheel traveled to Moscow to conclude the final negotiations, he was under extreme pressure to return with something to show as a concession by the Soviet Union to German wishes. Everything considered, he did as best he could. He succeeded in having the treaty worded in such a way that the Soviet Union implicitly renounced articles 53 and 107 of the United Nations Charter (which had allowed the victorious nations of World War II to take direct actions in order to stop new aggressions on the part of former enemy states), thereby binding the Soviet Union to the nonintervention clause of the U.N. Charter. The treaty, it was further stipulated, "shall not affect any bilateral or multilateral treaties or arrangements previously concluded" by the Soviet Union and the Federal Republic; this clause kept in force the agreement of 1955, when the Soviet Union had accepted a letter by Adenauer noting that the establishment of diplomatic relations with the Soviet Union did not mean that the Federal Republic would cease working toward the reunification of Germany. In order to cement this previous understanding, Scheel wrote a letter to the Soviet foreign minister, in which he stated that "this treaty does not conflict with the political objective of the Federal Republic of Germany to work for a state of peace in Europe in which the German nation will recover its unity in free self-determination"; when this letter was accepted by the Soviet Foreign Ministry, it became part of the treaty. A reference in the text of the treaty to a desire "to improve and extend cooperation between [the signatories], including economic relations as well as scientific, technological and cultural contacts" was designed to appeal to German industrial interests (who support mainly the CDU). Finally, Scheel issued a statement to the effect that the federal government would present the treaty to the *Bundestag* for ratification only when a "satisfactory solution" to the Berlin problem had been agreed upon among the Four Powers. In short, then, what had started out as a treaty of mutual renunciation of force had turned into a subtly worded treaty in which West Germany finally recognized the losses of World War II, while the Soviet Union agreed not to act as a victor any longer, while holding out the promise of increased trade and a solution to the Berlin problem.

This treaty, as well as an almost identical treaty concluded with Poland later that year, had immediate repercussions on the West German domestic scene, as might well be expected in a policy change of such magnitude. Brandt, in a television address to the West German people after he had personally signed the treaty in Moscow, considered some of the arguments advanced by opponents of the treaty—mainly, that it amounted to a sellout of West German interests. To counteract such claims, Brandt pointed to the Soviet Union's partial responsibility for the fate of Berlin and to the lucrative Soviet market for West German industry. Brandt, in his talks with Soviet leaders, apparently had gained the impression that the Soviet Union was prepared to push for an acceptable Berlin settlement which would guarantee Western access

rights, West Berlin's close links with the Federal Republic, and perhaps even the West Berliners' rights to travel to East Berlin. However, in the months following the conclusion of the treaty, little progress was made at the Four Powers' Berlin talks. On the contrary, the East German regime found it expedient to harass Berlin traffic on numerous occasions (usually claiming "unlawful" activities by the West German federal government in Berlin as its reason for interfering with the traffic). Such actions underlined the relative position of strength enjoyed by the G.D.R. It was only after Ulbricht had relinquished his hold over the East German government (under circumstances not yet quite clear) that the new East German leadership under Erich Honecker gave up its opposition and allowed a successful conclusion of the Berlin talks.

The promised increase in trade relations with the Soviet Union has run also into difficulties. Prior to 1969, West Germany had already become one of the major economic partners of the Soviet Union in the West. For instance, the state of Bavaria had concluded an agreement with the Soviet Union providing for a large supply of natural gas through a pipeline from Russia (the pipeline, in turn, to be built with West German steel pipes). At the time the Moscow treaty was concluded, prospects for additional trade were made public. The Soviet invitation to the Daimler-Benz factory, makers of Mercedes cars and trucks, to build a plant in Russia for the construction of Mercedes trucks received wide publicity, especially after the Ford Motor Company was forced by the U.S. Department of Defense to decline a similar offer. However, the conclusion of this deal ran into economic and political difficulties; for a while it appeared as if the Soviet government was holding out until the *Bundestag* ratified the treaty. Again, this failure immediately to conclude lucrative bargains with the Soviet Union put the pressure on the Brandt government, which had hoped that the prospect of better trade relations with the Soviet Union might induce West Germany's industrial interests to exert pressure on the CDU to support Brandt's *Ostpolitik*.

With no immediate success on either the Berlin issue or the matter of trade relations in sight, Brandt and the SPD came under increased attack and suffered a number of setbacks in various state elections. However, since apparently most of the electoral dissatisfaction with the SPD had its roots in a general dissatisfaction with the state of the economy, Brandt's *Ostpolitik* did not seem threatened directly. Indirectly, of course, any further decline of the public's confidence in the SPD's economic policies could lead to a reversal in West German foreign politics, if the voters should turn to the CDU to register their disapproval. In order to forestall future losses, the Brandt government in late 1970 began to concentrate more on domestic politics while waiting for some favorable results of its initial push toward the East.

Even if the SPD should be voted out of office, it seems unlikely that West German foreign policy could be reversed. As we have seen, the effect on public opinion has been dramatic; and although a decline in some of the favorable responses to Brandt's *Ostpolitik* might be expected, the long-term trends undoubtedly will continue, probably at an increased rate. Already, the official recognition of European realities has brought changes at the symbolic level; West German maps, for instance, are now being rewritten. Former German territories, until 1970 labeled "presently under Polish administration" are now simply labeled "Poland." Similarly, the German Democratic Republic will now officially be referred to under this name, instead of as the "Soviet Zone of Occupation." And in what amounts to a painful reevaluation of present conditions, the federal government is considering changing the wording of the oath sworn by West German soldiers upon entering the service: instead of vowing to "defend the liberty of the whole German people," future West German soldiers may simply pledge to defend the Federal Republic. In short, such small symbolic changes will serve to heighten a public awareness of the basic irreversibility of present conditions in Europe. Willy Brandt's new *Ostpolitik* is bound to remain the Federal Republic's official policy toward the East for a long time to come.

Prospects for West German Foreign Policy

This study of the evolution of the foreign policy of the Federal Republic of Germany suggests that, as West Germany has come to find an identity of its own, its foreign policy has begun to focus on easily identifiable patterns. While this fact does not remove all the risks involved in making predictions about the future course of West Germany's foreign policy, it does allow a number of relatively safe predictions.

Quite obviously, the Federal Republic will continue its present policy of European cooperation, focusing on functional integration in the area of economics, but providing also for increasing measures of political integration. However, it might well be expected that in years to come there will be less emphasis on the unification of political institutions in Europe. In the years following the catastrophe of 1945, many West Germans supported the goal of a unified Europe either because such support might offer proof of the Germans' change of attitudes or because only in a unified Europe could present dreams of great-power status become future realities. Today, most West Germans no longer feel a need to achieve some measure of great-power status. Thus they might support in a general way the goal of a "United States of Europe," but they are unlikely to press hard for its realization.

Undoubtedly, the Federal Republic's present policy of close cooperation with the United States will undergo no major changes. However, the nature of this cooperation may well change in emphasis as the expressed need for military cooperation is likely to diminish over the years. Most West Germans are becoming less concerned about matters of military security; as in most other countries of the world today, they will probably make increasing demands for public efforts in the domestic sphere which would limit the amount of funds available for the military. This development is already visible in West Germany today. In the future, this might lead to an acquiescence to American troop withdrawals from Europe as long as the American security guarantee can be maintained with a smaller presence of American troops in the Federal Republic. This guarantee would most likely be sought within the framework of NATO or some such organization, the role of which might however, gradually decline in importance.

As the need for military security against aggression from the East becomes less acute, West German foreign policy makers can pursue more actively the goal of a mutual reduction of forces in Europe. The federal government has already expressed great interest in the idea of a European security conference to be held

some time in the future. While no dramatic results should be expected from this conference, long-range developments in the area of troop reductions appear likely, provided no major crisis upsets the present process of a general relaxation of tension. Certainly a reduction of forces would seem at least a logical consequence of a treaty of renunciation of force.

Much, of course, will depend on the progress made in the issues touched upon by the Moscow treaty, particularly regarding Berlin. In December 1971 an agreement was reached under substantial pressure on the GDR from the Soviet Union (which wanted the agreement because of Western insistence that discussion about a European Security Conference would not begin until the Berlin issue had been settled. The whole process pointed once again to the Federal Republic's dependence in matters of foreign policy on the big powers in both East and West.) The Berlin Agreements guarantee Western access rights to East German border guards controlling, but not interfering with, sealed transportation units. West Berliners regained their right to visit East Berlin. In return for these concessions, the Federal Republic appeared prepared to agree to limit its political presence in West Berlin; that is, West Berlin would become somewhat more independent from West Germany in terms of common political institutions, while retaining its close economic and cultural contacts.

In regard to the goal of bettering relations with the German Democratic Republic, it seems rather likely that only after West German leaders have given up their hopes for inducing any change in East Germany will the possibility for closer human contacts increase significantly. In short, West Germany will have to give up all hopes for some scheme of institutional reunification. As indicated earlier, there seems to be a good chance that most West Germans will, in fact, do so. The two parts of Germany appear headed for an "Austrian solution" to the German problem: peaceful coexistence, some cooperation, but no demands for reunification or *Anschluss* ("annexation").

If the Federal Republic of Germany should succeed in accepting such limited goals and seeing them through to their realization, then, in Willy Brandt's words, "it will serve peace, Europe, and us all." The award of the Nobel Prize for peace to Willy Brandt in 1971, and its widespread favorable echo, suggested that a good part of the world agreed with him.

SELECTED BIBLIOGRAPHY

ADENAUER, KONRAD. *Erinnerungen.* 4 vols.: *1945–1953, 1953–1955, 1955–1959, 1959–1963.* Stuttgart: Deutsche Verlagsanstalt, 1968.

———. *Memoirs, 1945–53.* Chicago: Henry Regnery Co., 1966.

ALLEMANN, FRITZ RENE. *Zwischen Stabilität und Krise: Etappen der deutschen Politik, 1955–1963.* Munich: R. Piper, 1963.

ALMOND, GABRIEL A., ed. *The Struggle for Democracy in Germany.* Chapel Hill: University of North Carolina Press, 1949.

ALMOND, GABRIEL A., and VERBA, SIDNEY. *The Civic Culture.* Princeton: Princeton University Press, 1963.

ALTMANN, RÜDIGER. *Das Deutsche Risiko: Aussenpolitische Perspektiven.* Stuttgart: Seewald, 1962.

BAADE, HANS W. *Das Verhältnis von Parlament und Regierung im Bereich des auswärtigen Gewalt der Bundesrepublik Deutschland.* Hamburg: Hansescher Gildenverlag, 1962.

BACKER, JOHN H. *Priming the German Economy: American Occupational Policies, 1945–1948.* Durham: Duke University Press, 1971.

BALABKINS, NICHOLAS. *Germany Under Direct Controls.* New Brunswick, N.J.: Rutgers University Press, 1964.

BARING, ARNULF. *Aussenpolitik in Adenauers Kanzlerdemokratie.* Munich: Oldenbourg, 1969.

BARZEL, RAINER. *Gesichtspunkte eines Deutschen.* Düsseldorf: Econ, 1968.

BENDER, PETER. *Zehn Gründe für die Anerkennung der DDR.* Frankfurt: Fischer, 1968.

BESSON, WALDEMAR. *Die Aussenpolitik der Bundesrepublik.* Munich: R. Piper, 1970.

BIRNBAUM, IMMANUEL. *Entzweite Nachbarn: Deutsche Politik in Osteuropa.* Frankfurt: Scheffler, 1968.

BIRRENBACH, KURT, et al. *Aussenpolitik nach der Wahl des 6. Bundestages.* Opladen: Leske, 1969.

BLUHM, GEORG. *Die Oder-Neisse-Linie in der deutschen Aussenpolitik.* Freiburg: Rombach, 1963.

BÖLLING, KLAUS. *Republic in Suspense.* New York: Praeger, 1965.

BRACHER, KARL DIETRICH. *Deutschland zwischen Demokratie und Dikatur.* Bern-Munich-Vienna: Scherz, 1964.

———, ed. *Nach 25 Jahren: Eine Deutschlandbilanz.* Munich: Kindler, 1970.

BRANDT, WILLY. *Aussenpolitik, Deutschlandpolitik, Europapolitik: Grundsätzliche Erklärungen während des ersten Jahres im Auswärigen Amt.* Berlin: Berlin-Verlag, 1968.

———. *A Peace Policy for Europe.* New York: Holt, Rinehart & Winston, 1969.

BRAUNTHAL, GERARD. *The Federation of German Industry in Politics.* Ithaca, N.Y.: Cornell University Press, 1965.

BUCHANAN, WILLIAM, and CANTRIL, HADLEY. *How Nations See Each Other: A Study in Public Opinion.* Urbana: University of Illinois Press, 1953.

CHALMERS, DOUGLAS A. *The Social Democratic Party of Germany.* New Haven: Yale University Press, 1964.

CRAIG, GORDON. *From Bismarck to Adenauer.* New York: Harper & Row, 1965.

DAHRENDORF, RALF. *Gesellschaft und Freiheit in Deutschland.* Munich: R. Piper, 1961.

————. *Society and Democracy in Germany.* Garden City, N.Y.: Doubleday & Co., 1969.

DAVISON, W. PHILLIPS. *The Berlin Blockade: A Study in Cold War Politics.* Princeton: Princeton University Press, 1958.

DEHIO, LUDWIG. *Germany and World Politics in the Twentieth Century.* New York: Norton, 1967.

DEUTSCH, KARL W. *Arms Control and the Atlantic Alliance.* New York: Wiley, 1967.

————. "The German Federal Republic." In *Modern Political Systems: Europe,* 2d ed., edited by Roy C. Macridis and Robert E. Ward. Englewood Cliffs, N.J.: Prentice-Hall, 1967.

————. *Nationalism and Social Communication.* 2d ed. Cambridge: M.I.T. Press, 1966.

DEUTSCH, KARL W., and EDINGER, LEWIS J. *Germany Rejoins the Powers: A Study of Mass Opinion, Interest Groups, and Elites in Contemporary German Foreign Policy.* Stanford, Calif.: Stanford University Press, 1959, New Haven: Archon Press, 1971.

DEUTSCH, KARL W., et al. *France, Germany and the Western Alliance.* New York: Charles Scribner's Sons, 1966.

DEUTSCH, KARL W., et al. *Political Community and the North Atlantic Area.* Princeton: Princeton University Press, 1957, 1968 (paper).

DIEHL, GÜNTER. *Denken und Handeln in der Aussenpolitik.* Freudenstadt: Lutzeyer, 1970.

DIWALD, HELLMUT. *Die Anerkennung: Bericht zur Klage der Nation.* Munich: Bechtle, 1970.

EBERLEIN, KLAUS D. *Was die Deutschen möchten.* Hamburg: Wegner, 1968.

EDINGER, LEWIS J. "Continuity and Change: Some Data on the Social Background of German Decision Makers." *Western Political Quarterly* 14. no. 1 (March, 1961): 17–36.

————. *Kurt Schumacher: A Study in Personality and Political Behavior.* Stanford, Calif.: Stanford University Press, 1965.

————. *Politics in Germany.* Boston: Little, Brown, 1967.

ELLWEIN, THOMAS. *Das Regierungssystem der Bundesrepublik Deutschland.* Cologne: Westdeutscher Verlag, 1963.

ERDMENGER, KLAUS. *Das folgenschwere Missverständnis: Bonn und die sowjetische Deutschlandpolitik, 1949–1955.* Freiburg: Rombach, 1967.

ERLER, FRITZ. *Democracy in Germany.* Cambridge: Harvard University Press, 1965.

ESCHENBURG, THEODOR. *Staat und Gesellschaft in Deutschland.* Stuttgart: Schwab, 1962.

FAUL, ERWIN, ed. *Wahlen und Wähler in Westdeutschland.* Villingen: Ring, 1960.

FREUND, GERALD. *Germany between Two Worlds.* New York: Harcourt, Brace, 1961.

FRÖSE, LEONHARD, et al. *30 Thesen für eine neue Deutschlandpolitik.* Hamburg: Wegner, 1969.

GROSSER, ALFRED. *Die Bonner Demokratie.* Düsseldorf: Karl Rauch, 1960.

————. *The Federal Republic of Germany.* New York: Praeger, 1964.

HAAS, ERNST B. *The Uniting of Europe.* Stanford, Calif.: Stanford University Press, 1958.

HALLSTEIN, WALTER. *United Europe: Challenge and Opportunity.* Cambridge: Harvard University Press, 1962.

HANRIEDER, WOLFRAM. *West German Foreign Policy, 1949–1963: International Pressure and Domestic Response.* Stanford, Calif.: Stanford University Press, 1967.

————. *The Stable Crisis: Two Decades of German Foreign Policy.* New York: Harper & Row, 1970.

HARTMANN, FREDERICK H. *Germany between East and West: The Reunification Problem.* Englewood Cliffs, N.J.: Prentice-Hall, Spectrum Books, 1965.

HEIDENHEIMER, ARNOLD J. *The Governments of Germany.* 2d ed. New York: Crowell-Collier & Macmillan, 1966.

HISCOCK, RICHARD. *Democracy in Western Germany.* London: Oxford University Press, 1957.

INSTITUT FÜR DEMOSKOPIE ALLENSBACH. *Wählermeinung—nicht geheim.* Allensbach: Verlag für Demoskopie, 1969.

JACOBSEN, HANS-ADOLF, with VON BREDOW, WILFRIED. *Misstrauische Nachbarn: Deutsche Ostpolitik, 1919–1970.* Düsseldorf: Droste, 1970.

JANOWITZ, M. "Social Stratification and Mobility in West Germany." *American Journal of Sociology* 64: (1955), 6–24.

KAISER, KARL. *German Foreign Policy in Transition: Bonn between East and West.* London: Oxford University Press, 1968.

KAISER, KARL, and MORGAN, ROGER. *Strukturwandlungen der Aussenpolitik in Grossbritannien und der Bundesrepublik.* Munich: Oldenbourg, 1970.

KIRCHHEIMER, OTTO. "Germany: The Vanishing Opposition." In *Political Opposition in Western Democracies,* edited by Robert A. Dahl. New Haven: Yale University Press, 1966.

KITZINGER, U. W. *German Electoral Politics.* Oxford: Clarendon Press, 1960.

LOEWENBERG, GERHARD. *Parliament in the German Political System.* Ithaca, N.Y.: Cornell University Press, 1966.

MEISSNER, BORIS, ed. *Die deutsche Ostpolitik, 1961–1970: Kontinuität und Wandel—Dokumentation.* Cologne: Wissenschaft und Politik, 1970.

MERKL, PETER H. *Germany: Yesterday and Tomorrow.* New York: Oxford University Press, 1965.

———. *The Origin of the West German Republic.* New York: Oxford University Press, 1963.

MERRITT, ANNA J., and MERRITT, RICHARD L. *Public Opinion in Occupied Germany: The OMGUS Surveys, 1945–1949.* Urbana: University of Illinois Press, 1970.

MERRITT, RICHARD L. "West Berlin: Center or Periphery?" In *Comparing Nations,* edited by Richard L. Merritt and Stein Rokkan. New Haven: Yale University Press, 1966.

MERRITT, RICHARD L., and PUCHALA, DONALD J. *Western European Attitudes on Arms Control, Defense, and European Unity.* New Haven: Yale University

sity Political Science Research Library, January, 1966.

MÜLLER-HERMANN, ERNST. *Bonn zwischen den Weltmächten: Perspektiven der deutschen Aussenpolitik.* Düsseldorf: Econ, 1969.

NÖLLE-NEUMANN, ELISABETH. "Der Staatsbürger und sein Staat." In *Zwanzig Jahre danach—eine deutsche Bilanz 1945–1965,* ed. Helmut Hammerschmidt. Munich: K. Desch, 1965, pp. 79–104.

NÖLLE, ELISABETH, and NEUMANN, ERICH PETER. *The Germans: Public Opinion Polls, 1947–1966.* Allensbach: Verlag für Demoskopie, 1967.

PARSONS, TALCOTT. "Democracy and Social Structure in Pre-Nazi Germany." In *Essays in Sociological Theory,* rev. ed., pp. 104–23. New York: Free Press, 1954.

PLISCHKE, ELMER. *Contemporary Governments of Germany.* Boston: Houghton Mifflin Company, 1969.

RICHARDSON, JAMES L. *Germany and the Atlantic Alliance.* Cambridge: Harvard University Press, 1966.

RUPP, HANS KARL. *Ausserparlamentarische Opposition in der Aera Adenauer: Der Kampf gegen die Atombewaffnung in den 50iger Jahren.* Cologne: Pahl-Rugenstein, 1970.

SCHATZ, HERIBERT. *Der parlamentarische Entscheidungsprozess: Bedingungen der verteidigungspolitischen Willensbildung im deutschen Bundestag.* Meisenheim: Hain, 1970.

SCHEUCH, ERWIN K., and WILDENMANN, RUDOLF, eds., "Zur Soziologie der Wahl." In *Kölner Zeitschrift für Soziologie und Sozialpsychologie,* Sonderheft 9, 1965.

SCHMIDT, HELMUT. *Defense or Retaliation: A German Contribution to the Consideration of NATO's Strategic Problem.* Edinburgh: Oliver & Boyd, 1962.

———. *Strategie des Gleichgewichts: Deutsche Friedenspolitik und die Weltmächte.* Stuttgart: Seewald, 1969.

SCHMIDTCHEN, GERHARD. *Die befragte Nation: Ueber den Einfluss der Meinungsforschung auf die Politik.* Frankfurt: Fischer, 1965.

SCHROEDER, GERHARD. "Germany Looks at Eastern Europe." *Foreign Affairs* 44, no. 1 (October, 1965): 15–25.

SCHWARZ, HANS-PETER. *Vom Reich zur Bundesrepublik: Deutschland im Widerstreit der aussenpolitischen Konzeptionen in den Jahren der Besatzungsherrschaft, 1945–1959.* Neuwied: Luchterhand, 1966.

SCHWARZKOPF, DIETRICH, and VON WRANGEL, OLAF. *Chancen für Deutschland: Politik ohne Illusionen.* Hamburg: Hoffmann & Campe, 1965.

SHELL, KURT L. *Bedrohung und Bewährung: Führung und Bevölkerung in der Berlin-Krise.* Cologne: Westdeutscher Verlag, 1965.

SIEGLER, HEINRICH FREIHERR VON. *Wiedesvereinigung und Sicherheit Deutschland,* 2 vols. Bonn: Verlag für Zeitarchive, 1968.

———. *Dokumentation der Europäischen Integration.* 2 vols. Bonn: Siegler, 1961–64.

SMITH, JEAN EDUARD. *The Defense of Berlin.* Baltimore: Johns Hopkins Press, 1965.

———. *Germany Beyond the Wall: People, Politics, and Prosperity.* Boston: Little, Brown, 1969.

SPEIER, HANS. *German Rearmament and Atomic War: The Views of German Military and Political Leaders.* New York: Harper & Row, 1957.

SPEIER, HANS, and DAVISON, W. P., eds. *West German Leadership and Foreign Policy.* New York: Harper & Row, 1957.

STAHL, WALTER. *The Politics of Postwar Germany.* New York: Praeger, 1963.

———, ed. *Education for Democracy in West Germany.* New York: Praeger, 1961.

STRAUSS, FRANZ-JOSEF. *Challenge and Response: A Program for Europe.* New York: Atheneum, 1970.

———. *The Grand Design: A European Solution to German Reunification.* New York: Praeger, 1966.

VALI, FERENC. *The Quest for a United Germany.* Baltimore: Johns Hopkins Press, 1967.

WILDENMANN, RUDOLF. *Macht und Konsens als Problem der Innen- und Aussenpolitik.* Bonn-Frankfurt: Athenaeum, 1963.

WILLIS, ROY. *France, Germany, and the New Europe, 1945–1967.* Rev. ed. London: Oxford University Press, 1968.

WINDSOR, PHILIP. *German Reunification.* London: Elek Books, 1969.

ZAPF, WOLFGANG, ed. *Beiträge zur Analyse der deutschen Oberschicht.* Munich: R. Piper, 1965.

———. *Wandlungen der deutschen Elite.* Munich: R. Piper, 1965.

ZIEBURA, GILBERT. *Die deutsch-französischen Beziehungen seit 1945: Mythen und Realitäten.* Pfullingen: Neske, 1970.

Chapter Five

SOVIET FOREIGN POLICY

VERNON V. ASPATURIAN

CONTINUITY AND CHANGE
IN RUSSIAN FOREIGN POLICY

One of the most baffling aspects of Soviet foreign policy is its remarkable capacity for evoking the most variegated and contradictory responses to its diplomacy. "In its distant objectives," writes Edward Crankshaw, "the foreign policy of the Soviet Union is less obscure and more coherent than that of any other country," yet its immediate intentions and the motivations behind its day-to-day diplomacy often appear incoherent, capricious, and almost always enigmatic.[1]

The foreign policy of any country, the Soviet Union included, is not, however, simply the sum total of its avowed intentions, no matter how sincerely and devotedly they are adhered to, but must depend upon the capacity, in the present or in the future, to carry out its intentions. "In order to transform the world," Stalin told H. G. Wells in 1934, "it is necessary to have political power . . . as a lever of change."[2] Marxist ideology, reinforced by the early experiences of the Soviet regime, thus has persuaded the Kremlin that the capacity to transform intentions into reality is indistinguishable from power, a power which is objectively determined by the economic and social foundations of society, but which, in turn, can dictate the evolution of society toward particular ethical and political goals.

[1] *New York Times Book Review*, July 3, 1949, p. 4.
[2] V. Stalin and H. G. Wells, *Marxism vs. Liberalism* (New York, 1934), p. 14.

In order to draw a proper appraisal of Soviet diplomacy at any given time, the voluntaristic aspects of Soviet foreign policy must always be measured against its power to overcome the deterministic impediments of international reality. Thus, although the Soviet Union can plan the calculated growth of the economic and military foundations of its power, it cannot "plan" foreign policy. This fact was eloquently stated by Maxim Litvinov to the Central Executive Committee in 1929:

Unlike other Commissariats, the Commissariat for Foreign Affairs cannot, unfortunately, put forward a five-year plan of work, a plan for the development of foreign policy. . . . In . . . drawing up the plan of economic development, we start from our own aspirations and wishes, from a calculation of our own potentialities, and from the firm principles of our entire policy, but in examining the development of foreign policy we have to deal with a number of factors that are scarcely subject to calculation, with a number of elements outside our control and the scope of our action. International affairs are composed not only of our own aspirations and actions, but of those of a large number of countries . . . pursuing other aims than ours, and using other means to achieve those aims than we allow.[3]

The balance between the voluntaristic and deterministic components of Soviet foreign policy is neither fixed nor stable, but is in a state of continual and deliberate flux. In the initial stages of the Bolshevik Republic, its foreign policy was virtually at the mercy of external forces over which it could exercise little control, and Soviet diplomacy assumed the characteristic contours of a weak power struggling

for survival under onerous conditions. As its economic and military position improved, it gradually assumed the characteristics of a great power and, given its geographical and cultural context, it took on the distinctive features of its tsarist predecessors and the impulse to subjugate its immediate neighbors.

The Geographic and Historical Inheritance

"Marxism," wrote a more recent Soviet specialist on diplomacy, "teaches that economic factors determine the foreign policy and diplomacy of a state only in the long run, and that politics and diplomacy are, in a certain sense, conditioned by the concrete historical period and by many other elements (not excluding even, for instance, the geographical situation of a given country)."[4] Although Soviet writers may still tend to agree with the observation of the hapless Karl Radek that "it is silly to say that geography plays the part of fate, that it determines the foreign policy of a state,"[5] geography is nonetheless the most permanent conditioning factor in a country's foreign policy; for location, topography, and natural resources are significant— and often decisive—determinants of a country's economic and military power. Geography's effects, however, are relative, rarely absolute, always dependent upon the more variable factors in a country's character, such as its cultural traditions, political institutions, the size and diversity of its population, the exploitation of its natural resources, and the skill of its

---

[3] *Protokoly Zasedani Tsentralnovo Ispolnitelnovo Komiteta Sovetov,* Bulletin 14 (Moscow, 1930), p. 1.

[4] F. I. Kozhevnikov, "Engels on Nineteenth Century Russian Diplomacy," *Sovetskoye Gosudarstvo i Pravo,* December, 1950, no. 12, pp. 18–34.

[5] "The Bases of Soviet Foreign Policy," in *The Foreign Affairs Reader,* ed. M. F. Armstrong (New York: Harper & Row, 1947), p. 173.

statesmen. A country's geography, with rare exceptions, cannot be remade; it can only be utilized more effectively. Thus, although Radek's contention—that "the questions raised by geography are dealt with by each social formation in its own way . . . determined by its peculiar economic and political aims"—remains incontestable, it was the blessing of providence that this vast empire secreted all the basic ingredients for the erection of a powerful industrial and military state, given the necessary will and determination of its leadership. Had Russia been a wasteland with limited raw materials, she would have been doomed to be permanently a preindustrial society. The character of her foreign policy—her very existence—would have been vastly different, and her vaunted ideology would have long been relegated to the ash cans of history.

The Soviet Union, like tsarist Russia before it, is the largest single continuous intercontinental empire in the world. Embracing fully half of two continents, the Soviet Union has the world's longest and most exposed frontier, which is at once both its greatest potential hazard and one of its prime assets in international politics. As a part of both Europe and Asia, and embracing more than 150 ethnic and linguistic groups ranging from the most sophisticated nations to the most primitive, the USSR achieves a unique microcosmic character denied any other country, including the United States with its ethnically variegated but linguistically assimilated population. Russia's serpentine frontier is both a consequence of the indefensibility of the central Russian plain and, at the same time, an important conditioning factor in the further evolution and execution of its foreign policy. For a weak Russia, such a frontier affords maximum exposure to at-tack, but for a powerful Russian state, this extended frontier, bordering on nearly a dozen states, offers an enviable and limitless choice for the exertion of diplomatic pressure. Since 1939, the Soviet Union has annexed four of its former neighbors, seized territory from seven more, and has made territorial demands upon two others; most of this territory was previously lost by a weakened Russia. Of all her bordering states, only Afghanistan has not been imposed on to cede territory to the Soviet Union.

In the past, Russia's geographical position has exposed her to continuous depredations and subjugation from all directions—an inevitable consequence of political disunity in a geographically indefensible community. But if geography simplified the conquest of a divided Russia, it also facilitated the expansion of a united and powerful Russian state, which pushed out in all directions until it was arrested by superior force.

In the absence of more obvious geographical obstacles to her enemies, Russia's physical security became irrevocably attached to land space, while her psychological security became inseparable from political centralization. This conviction was confirmed by Stalin, himself, on the occasion of Moscow's 800th anniversary in 1947:

Moscow's service consists first and foremost in the fact that it became the foundation for the unification of a disunited Russia into a single state with a single government, a single leadership. No country in the world that has not been able to free itself of feudal disunity and wrangling among princes can hope to preserve its independence or score substantial economic and cultural progress. Only a country united in a single centralized state can count on being able to make substantial cultural-economic progress and assert its independence.[6]

6 *Pravda*, September 11, 1947.

It is a persisting fact of Russian history that this dual quest for physical and psychological security has produced, in Russian foreign policy, a unique pattern. A divided Russia invites attack, but a united Russia stimulates expansion in all directions. The revolutions in 1917, and the terrible purges of the thirties which Stalin undertook to enforce unity at home, exposed Russia's internal schisms to the world and stimulated foreign intervention. In each crisis, after surviving the initial assault from without, she embarked on a campaign designed to carry her beyond her self-declared national frontiers. The campaign failed in 1921, but she succeeded, after World War II, in bringing all of Eastern Europe under her hegemony.

The Bolsheviks fell heir not only to Russia's geography and natural resources, but also to the bulk of her population, her language, and the Russian historical and cultural legacy. Marxism gave Russia new goals and aspirations, but once the decision was taken to survive as a national state, even on a temporary and instrumental basis, the Soviet Union could not evade assuming the contours of a Russian state and falling heir to the assets and liabilities of its predecessors. Although Lenin thought that he had irrevocably severed the umbilical cord with Russia's past, it was not entirely within his power to unburden the new Soviet Republic of the disadvantages of tsarist diplomacy. Foreign attitudes remained remarkably constant; fears and suspicions, sympathies and attachments, were reinforced more than erased. Designs on Soviet territory still came from the same quarter, exposure to attack remained in the same places, and the economic and commercial lifelines of the tsars became no less indispensable to the new regime. In short, even if the Soviet Union refused to remain Russia, Japan remained Japan,

Poland remained Poland, and the Straits remained the Straits.

Moreover, the Russian language, permanently encrusted in its Cyrillic shell, became the official speech of Soviet diplomacy, and, as the vehicle of the Marxist dogma, it was pompously proclaimed the "language of the future." Russian cultural and scientific achievement became the basis for Soviet claims to cultural supremacy, of which Soviet science and culture were pronounced a continuation; the symbolism of Holy Russia was revived. Moscow eagerly laid claim to all the advantages of historic Russia, and the outside world just as assiduously refused to permit her to evade the liabilities and vulnerabilities of the Russian past. Thus, partly by choice and partly by necessity, the foreign policy of the Soviet Union could not but assume some of the contours of its predecessors.

The impact of a voluntaristic doctrine like Marxism on the geographical facts of Russia and her messianic traditions not only reinforced the psychological obsession for security, but provided an ideological rationale for assuming the implacable hostility of the outside world and sanctified Russian expansion with the ethical mission of liberating the downtrodden masses of the world from their oppressors. The hostile West of the Slavophils became the hostility of capitalism and imperialism; instead of the parochial messianism of the pan-Slav enthusiasts, Marxism provided Russia with a mission of universal transcendence—transforming the outside world into her own image, in fulfillment of her historic destiny and as the only permanent guarantee of absolute security. Up until the Twentieth Party Congress in 1956, the Leninist-Stalinist thesis that "the destruction of capitalist encirclement and the destruction of the danger of capitalist intervention are possible only as a result of the victory of the proletarian revolution, at least in several large countries,"[7] continued to be in force. Although "capitalist encirclement" was declared ended by Stalin's successors, the recent events in Poland and Hungary may have convinced the Kremlin that this proclamation was premature.

To assume, however, that Soviet foreign policy is merely Russian imperialism in new garb would be a catastrophic mistake on both sides. Soviet foreign policy was bound to assume "Russian" characteristics during one phase of its metamorphosis, but now that the maximum, but still limited, aims of tsarist imperialism have been virtually consummated, the aggressive (no longer necessarily expansionist) aspects of its foreign policy will assume a purely Marxist character, while only the defensive aspects (i.e., the preservation of its present power position) of its diplomacy will retain distinctively "Russian" features. That these two aspects of current Soviet foreign policy are in flagrant contradiction is self-evident, even to the Kremlin and other communist leaders. Chinese accusations of "great-power chauvinism," the de-Stalinization campaign, and the uprisings in Poland and Hungary are all manifestations of this fundamental schism in Soviet foreign policy. Whereas in the past, when the Soviet Union was weak, indiscriminate emphasis on the revolutionary aspects of its foreign policy tended to undermine its basic instinct to survive, now, its defensive reflexes tend to subvert not only its continuing leadership of world communism, but the eventual success of the movement itself.

World Revolution and National Interest in Soviet Diplomacy

Deciphering Soviet motives is an

7 *Kommunist*, January, 1953, no. 2, p. 15.

elusive and hazardous undertaking, yet it must be done systematically and with calculation, otherwise ad hoc and unconscious assumptions acquire priority by default. Miscalculation of motives can often be catastrophic, since foreign policy expectations are built upon assumptions concerning the motives and capabilities of other powers, and diplomatic success or failure often depends on the degree of accuracy with which these assumptions approach actuality. Much of the agony of postwar Western diplomacy can be traced directly to illusory expectations resulting from false calculations of Soviet motives by Western leaders. Diplomacy, however, is not an intellectual exercise, and motives are not always susceptible to rational and logical analysis. Assessment of motives, in any event, is rarely certain and in most cases calls not only for acute analytical intelligence, but also for espionage and, above all, for the intuitive wisdom of long experience in statecraft.

Information concerning Soviet motives is derived from three principal sources: (1) word, (2) conduct, and (3) personal contact with the Soviet leadership. In general, whenever there exists a discrepancy between publicly stated intention and conduct, the latter is a more reliable indicator of motives on a short-run basis. Actually, there are three possible relations between speech and practice in Soviet diplomacy: (1) *identity*; (2) *approximation*, usually implying a temporary accommodation or modification of a preconceived intention, unless the latter itself receives explicit reformation; and (3) *divergence*. Cleavages between word and conduct may, in turn, result from faulty execution, misinformation, miscalculation, or deliberate confusion.

Analyzing Soviet diplomacy purely from documents, speeches, and ideological statements gives undue weight to "rational" factors, since the irrational and accidental aspects of diplomacy can hardly be culled from documentary sources; and, although such a study may give a fairly lucid picture of the long-range outlines of Soviet policy, it is of limited validity as an investigation of Soviet diplomacy. On the other hand, calculating Soviet motives purely on the basis of day-to-day conduct and responses to particular situations can easily produce a distorted conception of Soviet foreign policy and lead to the erroneous conclusion that it is only slightly distinguishable from traditional great-power diplomacy.

Diplomacy is neither impersonal nor automatic in its execution—although its working executors may often be both—but is a human enterprise. Soviet motives cannot be separated from the character and personality traits of the principal decision makers in the Kremlin. Any evaluation of the foreign policy of the Soviet Union, whose principal decision makers are a well-defined oligarchy, without a prudent and careful examination and consideration of the various estimates and observations of the "human equations" in Soviet diplomacy is bound to be defective. The personal factor, particularly in the last fifteen years of Stalin's life and during Khrushchev's incumbency, was of crucial significance in any evaluation of Soviet foreign policy. Personal observations of the Soviet leadership, however, are essentially subjective; they originate with observers who are free from neither ignorance nor prejudice nor gullibility, and the observations are apt to vary accordingly. Any attempt to distill the essence of Soviet diplomacy solely from personality considerations is in fact doomed to hopeless confusion and sterility. A sound analysis of Soviet motives must take into

consideration ideology, conduct, and personalities, not as separate and independent entities, but as basic variables whose relative and relational significance is in a constant state of flux.

One question that inevitably arises is whether Soviet policy is actually motivated by ideological ends, such as world revolution, or by some other more mundane consideration, such as "power" or "national interest." Soviet ideology itself defines *national interest, power,* and *world revolution* in such a way as to make them virtually as indistinguishable and inseparable as the three sides of an equilateral triangle. The transcendental goal of Soviet foreign policy, world revolution, was defined by Lenin even before the existence of the Soviet state, when he declared in 1915 that "the victorious proletariat of [one] country . . . would stand up against . . . the capitalist world, . . . raising revolts in those countries against the capitalists, and in the event of necessity coming out even with armed force against the exploiting classes and their states."[8] "The fundamental question of revolution is the question of power," wrote Stalin, quoting Lenin, and he went on to say that, as the effectiveness of the Soviet Union as an instrument of world revolution is measured in terms of power, "the whole point is to retain power to consolidate it, to make it invincible."[9] As a contrived and temporary nation-state, the Soviet Union assumed particular interests, but "the U.S.S.R. has no interests at variance with the interests of the world revolution, and the international proletariat naturally has no interests that are at variance with the Soviet Union."[10]

8 V. I. Lenin, *Selected Works* (New York: International Publishers Co., n.d.), 5:141.
9 J. V. Stalin, *Problems of Leninism* (Moscow: Universal Distributors, 1947), p. 39.
10 W. K. Knorin, *Fascism, Social-Democracy and the Communists* (Moscow, 1933).

Stalin's final fusion was to identify the consolidation and extension of his own power with the interests of the world revolution.

The abstraction of a Soviet national interest outside the context of Soviet ideology, no matter how superficially attractive it may appear to be as a useful analytical tool, ruptures the image of Soviet reality and results in the calculation of Soviet foreign policy on the basis of false assumptions. Soviet foreign policy is based on the image of reality provided by the Marxist-Leninist ideological prism, and whether this image be faulty or not is totally irrelevant in the calculation of Soviet motives, although such a foreign policy will eventually reap its toll in diplomatic failure. The Soviet conception of "interest" cannot be separated from class categories, and its determination is essentially horizontal rather than vertical. Although the legal expression of class interests is temporarily articulated through the nation-state, and assumes the character of a "national interest," nonetheless in the Soviet view there exist within each state not one but several parallel "national interests," corresponding to its socioeconomic development. The "national interest" reflected by the state in its diplomacy, however, can only represent the interests of the "ruling class," and no other, regardless of its pretensions.

Soviet ideology recognizes the coexistence of three qualitatively distinct national interests in the modern world, owing to the uneven development of society: (1) the national interest of the feudal aristocracy, surviving only in extremely backward societies; (2) the national interest of the bourgeoisie, which allegedly is the dominant expression of most noncommunist states; and (3) the national interest of the proletariat, receiving diplomatic expression only in communist states, which is presumed by the dialectic to be coterminous with that of society as a whole.

Marxism tenaciously holds to the view that the community of interests that binds identical classes of different nations is more fundamental and decisive than that which binds different classes within the same nation-state. Although division and disunity are inherently characteristic of the bourgeois classes of different states, whose conflicts of interest are periodically expressed in war, the interests of all proletarians (together with their peasant and colonial allies) are considered to be in total harmony, their basic identity being temporarily obscured by artificially stimulated national distinctions.

Given the premise of the total identity of interests on a class basis, the Soviet Union, as the only avowed proletarian state in existence and the self-proclaimed embryo of a universal proletarian state, pronounced its interests to be identical with those of the world proletariat:

> The Communist Party of the Soviet Union has always proceeded from the fact that "national" and international problems of the proletariat of the U.S.S.R. amalgamate into one general problem of liberating the proletarians of all countries from capitalism, and the interests . . . in our country wholly and fully amalgamate with the interests of the revolutionary movement of all countries into one general interest of the victory of socialist revolution in all countries.[11]

Although this view is vigorously contested, is far from universally recognized, and does not correspond to actual facts, it is not thereby invalidated as a basis for diplomatic action or analysis.

The presence of one of two factors,

11 *Kommunist*, January, 1953, no. 2, p. 15.

both capable of objective verification, is sufficient to impart to the national interests of a particular state an authentic international quality. These factors are (1) the creation of appropriate forms of political organization designed to articulate the national interests of one state as those of the world at large; and (2) mass recognition in other countries that the national interests of a foreign state are identical with a higher transcendental interest. Not one but both of these desiderata characterize Soviet foreign policy. It was a cardinal aim to replace the nation-state system with a world communist state, by shifting allegiance and loyalty from the nation-state to class. This not only invited the nationals of other countries to recognize a higher, class, loyalty to the Soviet Union, but meant active engagement in fostering the appropriate political institutions, such as the Comintern, foreign communist parties, front organizations, and the like, to implement this fusion.

The Soviet invitation to commit mass disloyalty has elicited wide response, and the formula identifying Soviet interests with the interests of the world proletariat has been accepted by millions of communists throughout the world as a basis for political action. This gives to Soviet national interests an undeniable transcendental quality denied to the national interests of any other state except China. No matter how persistently a state may claim to be motivated by the interests of all mankind, if such a claim is accompanied neither by a serious effort at implementation nor evokes a response in other countries, it remains an empty and pious pretension. Transcendental ethical ends in foreign policy, irrespective of their substantive nature, have relevance only if they function as effective instruments or stimulants for the

limitation, preservation, or further accumulation of power, or as instruments for its focalization. Otherwise, they are meaningless slogans and utopias, devoid of anything but peripheral significance in the calculation of a country's foreign policy.

Expansionism is thus inherent in the Leninist-Stalinist ideology, since the Soviet state was conceived as an ideological state without fixed geographical frontiers. Not only did this idea of the Soviet Union as the nucleus of a universal communist state receive expression in the basic documents of the Comintern,[12] but the Soviet constitution of 1924 proclaimed the new union to be open to all future Soviet republics and a "decisive step towards the union of workers of all countries into one World Socialist Soviet Republic."[13] And at Lenin's bier, Stalin vowed "to consolidate and extend the Union of Republics."[14] Since it was the indispensable instrument and base of the world revolution, the extension of Soviet power and territory, by any means, was equated with the exfoliation of the revolution.

Stalin's attempt to preserve the dominant and privileged status of the Soviet proletariat in the postwar communist fraternity of nations resulted in a specific form of Soviet imperialism that brought about Tito's defection and unleashed corrosive forces within the orbit as a whole. The subsequent failure of Khrushchev and Mao Tse-tung to reconcile their divergent national interests may have produced an irreparable schism in the

[12] See W. H. Chamberlin, ed., *Blueprint for World Conquest* (Chicago: Human Events, 1946).

[13] Full text in M. W. Graham, *New Governments of Eastern Europe* (New York: Holt, Rinehart & Winston, 1927), p. 608.

[14] *History of the Communist Party of the Soviet Union* (New York: International Publishers Co., 1939), p. 269.

movement as a whole. The failure of Stalin and his successors to calculate accurately the persistence and vitality of the community of interests based on national peculiarities is actually a reflection of the inadequacy of Marxist categories to deal with the conflicting interests of national communities, whether they be communist or bourgeois.

Paradoxically, as long as the Soviet Union was the only communist state, its universalistic pretensions were unchallenged by foreign communist parties. But with the eclipse of the Soviet monopoly of the interests of the world proletariat, occasioned by the emergence of a Communist China and national communism in Eastern Europe, the universalistic pretensions of the Leninist doctrine have been blunted, while, at the same time, stimulating a more limited "regional interest" aimed at synthesizing the various national interests of the communist orbit. The transmutation of several national interests into a single supranational interest remains an insuperable difficulty in the communist world, so long as the incompatibility of individual communist national interests, which the Marxist dogma fails to perceive accurately, prevails:

Marxism-Leninism has always strongly advocated that proletarian internationalism be combined with patriotism. . . . The Communist Parties of all countries must . . . become the spokesmen of the legitimate national interests and sentiments of their people [and] . . . effectively educate the masses in the spirit of internationalism and harmonize the national sentiments and interests of these countries.[15]

Less than seven years after this statement, however, it had become quite clear that "the spirit of internationalism" could not prevail over the conflicting and incompatible national interests of the two great communist powers, each with its own national goals, aspirations, and image of the outside world. Since both the Soviet Union and China function within identical ideological matrixes, each has attempted to reshape and subordinate the interests of the communist movement to its own national interests, and each has provided an ideological rationalization for the transmutation of its national interests into the universal interests of all mankind. In 1963, Moscow denounced with eloquence the very vice which she had hitherto practiced with such consummate skill:

The statements of the Chinese leaders reveal a growing tendency to speak on behalf of the peoples of practically the whole world, including the Soviet people, the peoples of other socialist countries, and also the young national states of Asia, Africa, and Latin America. "Yet, who has given the Chinese leaders the right," the Soviet people inquire with indignation, "to decide for us, for the Soviet government, for the communist party, what is in keeping, and what is not in keeping with our interests? We have not given you the right and we do not intend to give it to you."[16]

SOVIET IDEOLOGY AND FOREIGN POLICY

The exact relationship between Soviet ideology and foreign policy has been subject to great controversy, ranging from the view that it is substantially irrelevant to the conviction

[15] Statement by the Chinese Communist Party, "Once More on the Historical Experience of the Dictatorship of the Proletariat." Full text in *Pravda*, December 31, 1956.

[16] Soviet government statement of August 21, 1963, *Pravda*, August 21, 1963.

that foreign policy is rigidly dictated by ideology. Actually, aside from providing the transcendental objectives of Soviet diplomacy, Soviet ideology performs five distinct, additional functions in foreign policy:

1. As a system of knowledge and as an analytical prism, it reflects an image of the existing social order and the distinctive analytical instruments (dialectical laws, and categories like the "class struggle," "historical stages," and so on) for its diagnosis and prognosis.
2. It provides an action strategy with which to accelerate the transformation of the existing social order into the communist millennium.
3. It serves as a system of communication, unifying and coordinating the activities of its adherents.
4. It functions as a system of higher rationalization to justify, obscure, or conceal the chasms that may develop between theory and practice.
5. It stands as a symbol of continuity and legitimacy.

This compartmentalization of Soviet ideology is frankly arbitrary, and actually ruptures its basic unity, which is not necessarily to be found in its logic or reason, but in the intuitive faith and active experience of its partisans—factors which often elude rational analysis. Elements of Soviet ideology that appear logically incompatible, in fact, are, but these rational contradictions can be unified only in the crucibles of revolutionary action, not in the intellectual processes of the mind. The true meaning of the Marxist-Leninist insistence on the "unity of theory and practice" is that contradictions cannot be resolved by logic, but by action, which is the final judge of "truth." Communist "truth" cannot be perceived without intuitive involvement—i.e., revolutionary action and experience—and to the outsider it remains as enigmatic as the mysteries of Zen.

The Soviet Image of the World

The Soviet ideological prism reflects an image of the world that is virtually unrecognizable to a noncommunist, yet it is on this image that Soviet foreign policy is based. It reflects a world of incessant conflict and change, in which institutions, loyalties, and philosophies arise and decay in accordance with the convulsive rhythm of the dialectic, which implacably propels it on a predetermined arc to a foreordained future—world communism. This image is accepted as the real world by Soviet leaders. Their foreign policy rests upon the conviction that Marxism-Leninism is a scientific system that has uncovered and revealed the fundamental and implacable laws of social evolution, and, hence, that affords its adherents the unique advantage of prediction and partial control of events. This conviction has imparted to Soviet diplomacy an air of supreme confidence and dogmatic self-righteousness:

Soviet diplomacy . . . wields a weapon possessed by none of its rivals or opponents. Soviet diplomacy is fortified by a scientific theory of Marxism-Leninism. This doctrine lays down the unshakeable laws of social development. By revealing these norms, it gives the possibility not only of understanding the current tendencies of international life, but also of permitting the desirable collaboration with the march of events. Such are the special advantages held by Soviet diplomacy. They give it a special position in international life and explain its outstanding successes.[17]

The history of Soviet diplomacy, however, is by no means a uniform record of success, although "errors" in foreign policy are ascribed not to the

17 V. P. Potemkin, ed., *Istoriya Diplomatii* (Moscow, 1945), 3:763–64.

doctrine, but to the improper apprehension and application of these infallible laws. Failure to apply these laws properly, according to the Soviet view, divorces foreign policy from international realities, and although it is true that "the record of Soviet diplomacy shows an inability to distinguish between the real and the imaginary, a series of false calculations about the capabilities and intentions of foreign countries, and a record of clumsy coordination between diplomacy and propaganda,"[18] still, it is fatuous to deny that Marxism-Leninism, on the whole, has furnished a system of analysis that gives a sufficiently accurate comprehension of power, its calculation and distribution in the world, and the opportunities and limitations such calculations afford for Soviet foreign policy. The dogmatic reliance on techniques and methods that have proven successful under other conditions, the frequent refusal to jettison concepts that either have outlived their usefulness or consistently produce dismal results in terms of foreign policy aims, and the concentration of all decision-making authority in one man or in a tight oligarchy—these practices at times tend to convert Marxism-Leninism from a unique asset for Soviet diplomacy into a straitjacket.

The Dialectical Image of History. Soviet ideology exposes the forces and tendencies operating in international politics, but it is up to the leadership to calculate these forces properly, seek out the most decisive trends, and coordinate Soviet diplomacy with the inexorable march of history. The suc-

cess of Soviet diplomacy, according to the Soviet view, is maximized as it is attuned to the rhythm of the historical dialectic, and its failures are multiplied as it falls out of harmony. Conversely, the occasional successes of bourgeois diplomacy are due to fortuitous and haphazard coordination with historical development, or to the equally accidental deviation of Soviet foreign policy from the implacable dictates of history. These accidental deviations are attributed to faulty application of historical laws by individual leaders.

Without attempting any extended discussion of Soviet dialectics, it can be said that, in the communist view, history progressively exfoliates as a series of qualitative stages, each with its own peculiar economic organization of society, which gives rise to corresponding social, political, and religious institutions. This inexorable movement from lower to higher forms of economic and social organization is propelled by means of a dialectical duel between perpetually developing economic forces of society and the social and political institutions that attempt to preserve the economic order in the interests of a particular ruling class, whose servants they are. As long as the institution of private property survives, class distinctions between property holders and the propertyless, whose interests are irreconcilable, are perpetuated, and will eventuate in conflict, war, and revolution, only to be replaced by a new economic system that perpetuates class divisions and conflicts in new form. The class struggle, which is the principal motivating force of historical revolution, comes to an end only with the overthrow of the capitalist system by the proletariat, after which class distinctions, conflict, and war are finally eliminated. Once communism achieves victory on a world scale, the state itself

18 Max Beloff, *Foreign Policy and the Democratic Process* (Baltimore: Johns Hopkins Press, 1955), p. 98. See also Vernon V. Aspaturian, "Diplomacy in the Mirror of Soviet Scholarship," in *Contemporary History in the Soviet Mirror,* ed. J. Keep (New York: Praeger, 1964), pp. 243–74.

and its coercive institutions are supposed to "wither away."[19]

The communists recognize five qualitative historical stages—primitive communism, slave-system, feudalism, capitalism, and socialism-communism —all of which, except for the first and last, are characterized by the institution of private property, two main contending classes (owners of the means of production and workers), and a state that represents the interests of the ruling class. Although the movement of history is from lower to higher stages, this movement is neither uniform nor without complications, and it does not pursue a uniform and rigid chronological evolution. This has been particularly true of the twentieth century. At the present time, communists acknowledge the coexistence of all historical stages; and this recognition has had a profound influence on Soviet foreign policy.

Soviet ideology is not self-executing; that is, it does not interpret itself automatically and does not reflect images of reality that can be unambiguously perceived, but rather it is based upon an authoritative interpretation of changing events by the Soviet leaders, who must choose from among a variety of possible interpretations, only one of which can be tested at a time for truth in the crucible of action. As long as Stalin was alive, interpretation of doctrine was a monopoly reserved for him alone and it was his interpretation.

The Two-camp Image. Stalin's image of the world after the Russian Revolution was one of forced "coexistence" between a single socialist state and a hostile capitalist world surrounding it—a coexistence imposed on both antagonists by objective historical conditions. Neither side being sufficiently powerful to end the existence of the other, they were fated to exist together temporarily on the basis of an unstable and constantly shifting balance of power:

> The fundamental and new, the decisive feature, which has affected all the events in the sphere of foreign relations during this period, is the fact that a certain temporary equilibrium of forces has been established between our country . . . and the countries of the capitalist world; an equilibrium which has determined the present period of "peaceful co-existence."[20]

The establishment, in a capitalistic world, of a socialist bridgehead which was inevitably destined to envelop the entire globe was, for Stalin, the supreme and ineluctable contradiction in the international scene. Although the capitalist world was infinitely stronger and could overwhelm the Soviet Republic if it could embark on a common enterprise, it was viewed as torn by internal divisions and conflicts that prevented the organization of an anti-Soviet crusade. Beside the overriding contradiction between the socialist camp and the capitalist camp, the bourgeois world was plagued with four additional inescapable contradictions: (1) the contradiction between the proletariat and the bourgeoisie in each country; (2) the contradiction between the status quo and the revisionist powers (Stalin referred to them as "victor" and "vanquished" capitalist states); (3) the contradiction between the victorious powers over the spoils of war; (4) the contradiction

[19] For a more elaborate statement of the author's views on the nature of Soviet ideology, see Vernon V. Aspaturian, "The Contemporary Doctrine of the Soviet State and Its Philosophical Foundations," *American Political Science Review* 48 (December, 1954).

[20] J. V. Stalin, *Political Report of the Central Committee to the Fourteenth Congress of the Communist Party of the Soviet Union (B)* (Moscow, 1950), p. 8.

between the imperialist states and their colonial subjects.

The contradiction between the socialist and capitalist camps was considered by Stalin the most fundamental and decisive, but it was not to be aggravated so long as the Soviet Union was in a weakened condition. War between the two camps was viewed as inevitable; however, it could be temporarily avoided and delayed by astute maneuvering within the conflicts raging in the capitalist world.

Stalin's postwar policy was predicated on an inevitable conflict with the West, organized by the United States. The organization of the Cominform and the forced unity of the communist orbit, the expulsion of Tito from the communist fraternity, the extraction of public statements of loyalty from communist leaders in all countries, the urgency with which Stalin sought to eliminate all possible power vacuums between the two blocs along the periphery of the communist world, all were preparatory measures based on the false assumption that the American ruling class was betraying anxiety at the growth of Soviet power and was preparing to launch Armageddon. At the founding convention of the Cominform the late Andrei Zhdanov revealed the authoritative Soviet interpretation of the emerging bipolarization of power:

The fundamental changes caused by the war on the international scene and in the position of individual countries have entirely changed the political landscape of the world. A new alignment of political forces has arisen. The more the war recedes into the past, the more distinct become two major trends in postwar international policy, corresponding to the division of the political forces operating on the international arena into two major camps; the imperialist and antidemocratic camp, on the one hand, and the antiimperialist and democratic camp, on the

other. The principal driving force of the imperialist camp is the U.S.A. . . . The cardinal purpose of the imperialist camp is to strengthen imperialism, to hatch a new imperialist war, to combat Socialism.[21]

During the Korean War and just prior to the Nineteenth Party Congress in 1952, a "great debate" had apparently taken place in the Politburo concerning the validity of the expectation of imminent war between the two camps. Two essentially divergent views were discussed by Stalin in his *Economic Problems of Socialism*: (1) that wars between capitalist countries had ceased to be inevitable and hence war between the two camps was imminent, the view that was then current; and (2) that wars between capitalist states remained inevitable, but that war between the two camps was unlikely. Although the first view was the basis of Soviet postwar policy, Stalin ascribed it to "mistaken comrades," and elevated the second to doctrinal significance:

Some comrades hold that the U.S.A. has brought the other capitalist countries sufficiently under its sway to be able to prevent them going to war among themselves. It is said that the contradictions between capitalism and socialism are stronger than the contradictions among the capitalist countries. Theoretically, of course that is true. It is not only true now, today; it was true before the Second World War. . . . Yet the Second World War began not as a war with the U.S.S.R., but as a war between capitalist countries. Why? . . . because war with the U.S.S.R., as a socialist land, is more dangerous to capitalism than war between capitalist countries; for whereas war between capitalist countries puts in question only the supremacy of certain capitalist countries over others, war with the U.S.S.R. must certainly put in question the existence of

21 Full text reprinted in *Strategy and Tactics of World Communism* (Washington, D.C.: Government Printing Office, 1948), pp. 216–17.

capitalism itself. . . . It is said that Lenin's thesis that imperialism inevitably generates war must now be regarded as obsolete. . . . That is not true. . . . To eliminate the inevitability of war, it is necessary to abolish imperialism.[22]

Stalin's only modification of his two-camp image was thus to concede that war between the two blocs was no longer imminent, but would be preceded by a series of wars among the capitalist powers themselves—between the United States and its satellite allies, France and Britain, on the one hand, and its temporary vassals, Germany and Japan, on the other. The resentment of the ruling classes of these vassal countries over American domination would provoke national revolutions and a renewed war over the ever-shrinking capitalist market, occasioned by the emergence of a parallel communist market, which would remain outside the arena of capitalist exploitation. The Soviet Union would remain outside the conflict, which would automatically seal the doom of world capitalism. However, Stalin's policies actually accentuated the very conflict—the one between the two camps—that he wished to temporarily deemphasize, while submerging those —among the capitalist states—which he wished to exacerbate. Soviet policy, by predicting war, was threatening to make inevitable a nuclear holocaust which would destroy both worlds.

The Post-Stalin Image. At the Twentieth Party Congress (February, 1956) Stalin's image of the world was considerably modified, in an attempt to bring it into closer focus with the realities of international politics. These modifications were made to eliminate the threatening schisms in the communist camp, to break up the unity of

22 J. V. Stalin, *Economic Problems of Socialism* (New York: International Publishers Co., 1952), pp. 27–30.

the non-Soviet world and dismantle anti-Soviet instruments like NATO, to head off the impending nuclear war that Stalin's doctrines and policies were unwittingly encouraging, and to enhance the flexibility of Soviet diplomacy in exploiting the contradictions of the capitalist world.

In place of Stalin's fatalistic image of a polarized world, the Twentieth Party Congress drew a more optimistic, and, in many respects, a mellower picture:

1. "Capitalist encirclement" was officially declared terminated, as major speakers like Molotov echoed the Titoist doctrine that "the period when the Soviet Union was . . . encircled by hostile capitalism now belongs to the past." The permanent insecurity of the Soviet Union, pending the worldwide victory of communism, as visualized by Stalin, was replaced with the image of a permanently secured Soviet Union, surrounded by friendly communist states in Europe and Asia, embracing nearly one-third of the world, with imperialism in an irrevocable state of advanced decay.

2. In place of Stalin's fixed vision of coexistence between two irreconcilable camps poised in temporary balance, which was declared obsolete and inapplicable to the postwar world, his successors recognized a third, "anti-imperialist" but nonsocialist, group of powers, carved out of decaying colonial empires, which had separated from the capitalist camp but had not yet joined the communist. Stalin's inflexible two-camp image needlessly alienated these new states and tended to force them into the capitalist orbit. This belt of neutralist states—a concept which Stalin refused to recognize—insulated the entire communist orbit from the capitalist world and, together with the socialist states, was viewed as constituting "an extensive 'zone of peace,' including both socialist and nonsocialist peace-loving states of Europe and Asia inhabited by nearly 1,500,000,000 people,

or the majority of the population of our planet."

3. Stalin's doctrine of the "fatal inevitability" of wars was pronounced antiquated, since its emphasis on coercive and violent instruments of diplomacy tended to render the Soviet peace campaign hypocritical, accelerated the formation of anti-Soviet coalitions, and, in an era of nuclear weapons, appeared to doom both worlds to a war of mutual annihilation.

4. Stalin's five main contradictions were retained as valid and persistent, but the radical shift in the equilibrium of class forces in the world dictated a change of emphasis and the reordering of priorities. Stalin stressed the conflicts among the major capitalist countries as the main object of Soviet diplomacy, relegating other contradictions to minor roles, but his successors saw the main contradiction of the current historical stage to be that between the anticolonial and the imperialist forces. In short, the world has moved out of the stage of the "capitalist encirclement" of the Soviet Union and, during the current phase of coexistence, is moving into the stage of the "socialist encirclement" of the United States, as a prelude to the final victory of communism.[23]

The new image of the world drawn by Khrushchev at the Twentieth Party Congress was by no means the consequence of a unanimous decision. It was opposed by at least four, and possibly five, full members of the eleven-man Presidium. Aside from his vigorous opposition to Khrushchev's adventurist innovations in industry and agriculture, Foreign Minister Molotov and the so-called Stalinist faction bitterly resisted the demolition of the Stalin myth and the entire de-Stalinization program; and they systematically sabotaged the foreign policy

[23] Full text broadcast by Moscow Radio, February 18, 1956. See also *New York Times*, February 19, 1956 (Mikoyan report).

decisions of the Twentieth Party Congress, which they publicly accepted.

Molotov's doctrinal differences had practical consequences in the actual formulation and execution of foreign policy. His constant carping criticism of existing policies, together with the precarious nature of Khrushchev's majority in the Presidium, introduced an uncharacteristic hesitancy into Soviet diplomacy. The vacillations, abrupt reversals, hesitations, discrepancies between policy and administration, and other eccentricities of Soviet diplomacy after Stalin's death were due not only to the incapacitating incompatibilities in the Presidium but also to Molotov's use of the Foreign Ministry and Soviet missions abroad as instruments to subvert the government's policy in favor of his own.

Molotov objected to the decisions to seek a reconciliation with Marshal Tito and to meet President Eisenhower at Geneva. When Khrushchev and Bulganin returned from Geneva, Molotov was waiting with sarcastic and biting comments on their personal diplomacy. As a result of his persistent criticism and obstructionism, he was disciplined by the Central Committee in July, 1955, and his "erroneous stand on the Yugoslav issue was unanimously condemned." This was followed shortly by his forced and pained confession of doctrinal error, which superficially appeared to have no connection with foreign policy but appeared designed to tarnish his ideological orthodoxy and was an unmistakable sign that he was on his way out. His unrelenting sabotage through the Foreign Ministry, in particular his determination to poison relations with Tito, finally led to his ouster as foreign minister in favor of Shepilov on the eve of Tito's visit to Moscow in June, 1956. Apparently, Shepilov also fell out of sympathy with the foreign policy he was supposed to execute and for opportunistic reasons (Khrushchev scathingly characterized him as "the careerist Shepilov who . . . showed himself to be a most shameless double-dealer") cast his lot with the Stalinist faction. The Molotov group suddenly contrived a majority in the December, 1956, plenum of the Central Committee, but when Khrushchev regained control at the February, 1957, plenum, Shepilov was summarily dismissed as foreign minister in favor of Andrei Gromyko, who was a professional diplomat and thus could be counted upon not to pursue a personal foreign policy.

In the bill of particulars against Molotov, the following charges were made:

1. For a long time, Comrade Molotov in his capacity as Foreign Minister, far from taking through the Ministry of Foreign Affairs measures to improve relations between the U.S.S.R. and Yugoslavia, repeatedly came out against the measures that the Presidium . . . was carrying out to improve relations with Yugoslavia.
2. Comrade Molotov raised obstacles to the conclusion of the state Treaty with Austria and the improvement of relations with that country, which lies in the center of Europe. The conclusion of the Austrian Treaty was largely instrumental in lessening international tension in general.
3. He was also against normalization of relations with Japan, while that normalization has played an important part in relaxing international tension in the Far East.
4. Comrade Molotov repeatedly opposed the Soviet Government's indispensable new steps in defence of peace and security of nations. In particular he

24 The last point is probably a reference not only to the Geneva Conference but also to the various junkets of Bulganin and Khrushchev throughout Asia and Europe, none of which included Foreign Minister Molotov.

denied the advisability of establishing personal contacts between the Soviet leaders and the statesmen of other countries, which is essential for the achievement of mutual understanding and better international relations.[24]

"Molotov," Khrushchev bluntly stated in a later speech, "found more convenient a policy of tightening all screws, which contradicts the wise Leninist policy of peaceful co-existence."[25] Thus, it can be assumed that Molotov advocated a continuation of the basic foreign policies of the Stalinist era, as modified during the Malenkov regime, based on a perpetuation of the two-camp image. It was Molotov's contention that Soviet policy could reap its greatest dividends by maintaining international tensions at a high pitch and running the risks of nuclear war, on the assumption that an uncompromising, cold-blooded policy would force Western statesmen, through lack of nerve and under pressure of public opinion, to continually retreat in the face of Soviet provocation, for fear of triggering a war of mutual extinction. It appears that he considered as un-Marxist the idea that the ex-colonial countries could be regarded as having deserted the capitalist camp and as constituting an "extensive zone of peace" together with the Soviet bloc, but rather believed that their behavior in international politics was motivated purely by considerations of opportunism and expediency. The main arena of rivalry for Molotov remained in Western Europe and the Atlantic area—the bastions of capitalism—and not in Asia or Africa, and he continued to view the new countries of Asia and Africa with hostility and suspicion as appendages to the capitalist camp.

Molotov's policy of "tightening all screws" was opposed by the Soviet

25 New York Times, July 7, 1957.

army, and also by Peking, which had its own reasons, although it was later revealed that the Chinese and Molotov seemed to agree on a wide range of issues. Speaking in Peking, Anastas Mikoyan, reputedly the principal Kremlin architect of the new diplomatic strategy, invoked Lenin in support of the current policy. Quoting Lenin's famous formula that "in the last analysis, the outcome of the struggle will be determined by the fact that Russia, India, China, etc. constitute the overwhelming majority of the world's population," he roundly condemned the Stalinist two-camp image to which Moltov still subscribed.

Soviet diplomatic strategy in the underdeveloped countries of Asia, Africa, and Latin America appears to contradict the basic revolutionary strategy of communism. Although Moscow's support of the so-called bourgeois-nationalist (roughly, "neutralist" under existing conditions) independence or revolutionary movements in the underdeveloped regions (colonies and "semicolonies") against Western colonialism, economic dependence upon the West, and internal feudalism is fully compatible with Leninist-Stalinist doctrine on revolution in the underdeveloped world, the Soviet pattern of political and economic assistance to regimes like those in India, Egypt, Iraq, Ghana, and, to a lesser extent, Cuba, does not fully conform to communist doctrine. Red China has stepped into this breach and has challenged Moscow's refusal to encourage and support indigenous communist parties in their efforts to overthrow native "bourgeois-nationalist" governments and establish authentic communist-controlled regimes. Instead, according to Peking, Moscow supports governments which persecute and imprison local communists.

The Soviet position on this point is extraordinarily nondoctrinaire and pragmatic, for whereas China stresses the view that the Communist party is the only reliable instrument of revolution, Khrushchev and his successors appear to be toying with the idea that under favorable circumstances, particularly when the balance of power has shifted decisively in favor of the communist world, native bourgeois-nationalist leaders may be won over to communism and the revolution could be consummated from above rather than below. The transformation of the Castro regime in Cuba, from an anti-imperialist, nationalist regime into a communist regime, was apparently viewed by Khrushchev as a prototype of this process. As a practical diplomatic position, Moscow feels that any move to encourage communist insurrection in these areas would simply stampede them all into the capitalist and anticommunist camp, a development which Peking considers—along with Molotov—as inevitable in any event. Peking's present strategy seems to stem from the conviction that the bourgeois nationalists will betray the Soviet Union (as Chiang Kai-shek did in 1928) and that, by supporting the local Communist parties now, China will have earned their gratitude and support.

THE FORMULATION OF SOVIET FOREIGN POLICY

Any attempt to describe the formulation of Soviet foreign policy in the crucibles of its decision-making organs is bound to be a hazardous and frustrating enterprise. The absence of periodic or systematic publication of documents, the inaccessibility of archives and officials, the virtual non-existence of memoirs or diaries of retiring statesmen, the puzzling duplication of state and party institutions, the perplexing fluctuations in their relationships, the ambiguity of Soviet ideology and the wide discrepancy between theory and practice, the bewildering profusion of constitutional and institutional changes, the arbitrary tendency to ignore or short-circuit elaborately detailed institutional channels, and, finally, the capricious and convulsive turnover of personalities are the more familiar impediments that must be contended with.

The decision-making process itself is a dynamic interaction between institutions and personalities, whose character varies with the effectiveness of institutions to impose limits on the acts of individuals. In constitutional states, characterized by relatively permanent institutions, the restraints on officials are carefully defined, imposing ineluctable limits not only on the range of policy formulation but on the choice of means as well. In a totalitarian system like the Soviet Union, where impermanently rooted institutions have been subordinated to relatively permanent personalities, the institutional aspects of the decision-making process are little more than ceremonial. Decision making is essentially personal, and bound to vary with the evolving ideological convictions, character, and judgment of those in control, the nature of the rivalries between them, and, finally, their reaction to the political and social pressures that bear upon them.

The Soviet political superstructure prior to 1953 was a complicated mosaic of shifting and interlocking institutions resting on an entrenched foundation of one-man dictatorship, in which all powers were delegated from above. The institutions of both party and state, as well as their relationship to one another, were essentially creatures of the late Joseph Stalin and were designed, not to limit his own power, but to limit that of his subordinates and rivals, and to facili-

tate the solidification of his own authority. As the instruments of his creation and manipulation, they could not, and did not, function as restraints on his latitude of decision. Both institutions and subordinates were liquidated with remarkable dispatch when the occasion demanded.

The system of duplicating and overlapping political organs between the party and state allegedly reflects a division of functions between the formulation and execution of policy, with policy formulation a monopoly reserved exclusively for the party, while the function of the government was to be restricted to formalizing and legalizing the decisions of the party into official acts of state. This dichotomy was never either rigid or absolute, but constantly varied in accordance with the degree of interlocking of personnel at the summits of the party and state hierarchies.

The Party Congress

In theory the most exalted, but in practice the most degraded, of the central party institutions in the formulation of policy is the party congress. Traditionally, the most important fundamental pronouncements on foreign policy have been made before the party congress, which is empowered to set the basic line of the party and state, but which in actual fact merely hears and rubber-stamps the decisions made elsewhere. All higher organs of the party, including the Presidium and Secretariat, are responsible and accountable to the party congress, which theoretically can remove and replace their membership.

The actual role of the party congress in foreign policy has varied throughout its existence. Under Lenin, and, in fact, as late as the Sixteenth Party Congress (in 1930), serious debate on foreign policy and international revolutionary strategy frequently ensued, although never with the same intensity or wide range of diversity as on domestic policy. Because of its massive size (nearly 2,000 delegates), the party congress became increasingly unwieldy as an organ of debate and discussion, and it gradually was converted into a forum which heard various sides and finally into a subdued sounding board for Stalin's deadly rhetoric. Discussion and debate first slipped behind the doors of the Central Committee and eventually vanished into the Politburo. All decisions were made in the Politburo, then reported to the Central Committee and, with increasing infrequency, to the party congress. The principal function of the party congress was reduced to hearing the reports of prominent party figures.

The two most important reports to party congresses relating to foreign policy are the Main Political Report of the Central Committee, delivered in the past by Stalin (except at the Nineteenth Party Congress), and a report on the activities of the World Communist Movement. At the Nineteenth Party Congress, Malenkov delivered the Main Political Report. However, Stalin had ordered published his *Economic Problems of Socialism* on the eve of the party congress, and this set the tone and dominated the entire proceedings. At the Twentieth Party Congress, Khrushchev delivered the Main Political Report, incorporating radical doctrinal innovations affecting foreign policy, while Molotov confined himself to praising reluctantly the new policy and resentfully subjecting his own past conduct of foreign policy to self-criticism. The activities of foreign Communist parties were reported by their own representatives.

A close examination of the Main Political Reports betrays an almost

rigid uniformity in organization. The entire first section is devoted to international affairs; an authoritative interpretation of the world situation; an appraisal of the Soviet position; trends, developments, and opportunities to watch for; warnings, threats, boasts, and invitations to bourgeois powers; congratulations and words of praise for friendly countries; and, finally, a summary of the immediate and long-range objectives of Soviet foreign policy. This report, before the emergence of polycentric tendencies in the world communist movement and the onset of the Sino-Soviet dispute, set the line to guide Communists everywhere in their activities, and, thus, the party congress became not a forum for debate, but a unique medium of communication.

Debate and discussion vanished after 1930, and meetings of the party congress became so infrequent that they threatened to vanish altogether. In his secret speech to the Twentieth Party Congress, Khrushchev gave this vivid description of the deterioration of the party congress:

During Lenin's life, party congresses were convened regularly; always when a radical turn in the development of the party and country took place, Lenin considered it absolutely necessary that the party discuss at length all basic matters pertaining to . . . foreign policy. . . . Whereas during the first years after Lenin's death, party congresses . . . took place more or less regularly, later . . . these principles were brutally violated. . . . Was it a normal situation when over 13 years [1939–1952] elapsed between the Eighteenth and Nineteenth Congresses? . . . Of 1,966 delegates [to the Seventeenth Congress in 1934] with either voting or advisory rights, 1,108 persons were arrested on charges of revolutionary crimes.[26]

26 This extract and all subsequent references to Khrushchev's secret report to the

The Central Committee

As the body that "guides the entire work of the Party in the interval between Congresses . . . and . . . directs the work of the Central and Soviet public organizations [i.e., the government],"[27] the Central Committee became the principal arena of debate and discussion of foreign policy during the period preceding 1934. According to the party rules at that time, the Politburo was obliged to report to this body at least three times a year, so that its decisions might be examined, criticized, and judged. The Central Committee elected the members of the Politburo, the Orgburo, and the Secretariat, and theoretically was empowered to appoint, remove, or replace its members. The Central Committee, itself elected by the party congress, was empowered to replace its own members by a two-thirds vote, but Stalin removed and appointed members of the Central Committee virtually at will.

On some occasions, the foreign commissar (who invariably is at least a full member of the Central Committee), as well as high Soviet functionaries of the Comintern, reported to the Central Committee on foreign policy and international communist activities. More often, the secretary general (Stalin) would deliver a report on the nature and scope of the Politburo's work and explain the precise application of the "line" under changing international conditions. A fairly large body, composed of full and alternate members (about equally divided), the

Central Committee was empowered to alter the policies of the Politburo and support the views of the minority. Only full members exercised the right to vote, but candidates had the right to participate in debate. Some of these reports, but not all, were made public, particularly if important modifications of the policies announced at the previous party congress were made. The records of the Central Committee's proceedings during the Stalin era remain generally unpublished and inaccessible for examination.

The Central Committee too, in time, was reduced to little more than a sounding board; its meetings became increasingly infrequent, and there is reason to believe that, after 1934, its decisions were unanimous. In Khrushchev's secret speech, he said:

> Even after the end of the war . . . Central Committee plenums were hardly ever called. It should be sufficient to mention that during the years of the Patriotic War [i.e., World War II] not a single Central Committee plenum took place. . . . Stalin did not even want to meet and talk with Central Committee members. . . . Of the 139 members and candidates of the Party's Central Committee who were elected at the Seventeenth Party Congress [1934], 98 persons, i.e., 70 percent, were arrested and shot.

The Party Politburo

There is no question but that the most important organ of decision making in the Soviet Union has been, and continues to be, the Politburo[28] of the Communist party. In accordance with the principle of "democratic centralism," the ultimate power of the party is entrusted to this organ. Its internal organization and recruiting proce-

---

Twentieth Party Congress are taken from the full text, *New York Times,* June 5, 1956. The speech has been widely reprinted elsewhere.

27 *The Land of Socialism Today and Tomorrow* (Moscow: International Publishers Co., 1939), p. 473.

28 The party's highest organ was called the *Politburo* from 1917 to 1952, and the *Presidium* from 1952 to 1966. In 1966, the name *Politburo* was restored.

dures, the composition and convictions of its factions, and its voting practices remain essentially a mystery. No proceedings of its deliberations have been made public in decades, and, in the absence of any recent defections from this body, information concerning its procedures and activities can be derived only from the following sources: (1) fragmentary records of very early meetings; (2) public exposure of its deliberations by Leon Trotsky and other rivals of Stalin during the period before 1930; (3) accounts by high-ranking diplomats or government and party officials, whose activities brought them to within close range of the Politburo, and who have defected from the Soviet Union; (4) personal accounts and memoirs of foreign statesmen who negotiated with members of the Politburo or with Stalin; (5) accounts of renegade officials of the Comintern and foreign Communist parties; (6) secrets spilled as a result of the Stalin-Tito feud; (7) Khrushchev's secret speech at the Twentieth Party Congress and its aftermath; (8) calculated leaks by the Polish Communist party and government since the rise of Gomulka; (9) examination of the decisions already taken; (10) rare public disputes between leading press organs of the party and government; (11) shifts in party and government officials; and (12) rare Central Committee resolutions, like that of June 29, 1957.

Under Stalin, all decisions of the Politburo on questions of foreign policy were, in one form or another, his own. All rival and dissident views were quashed and their adherents liquidated. The membership of the body was hand-picked by him. In his relations with the Politburo, Stalin could either announce his decisions and expect unanimous approval; submit them for examination and ask for discussion, with or without a vote; simply act without consulting his colleagues; or consult with various members on certain questions, to the exclusion of others. According to a former Soviet diplomat who was an eyewitness to some Politburo meetings in 1933,

a thin appearance of collective work is still kept up at Politburo meetings. Stalin does not "command." He merely "suggests" or "proposes." The fiction of voting is retained. But the vote never fails to uphold his "suggestions." The decision is signed by all ten members of the Politburo, with Stalin's signature among the rest. . . . The other members of the Politburo mumble their approval of Stalin's "proposal." . . . Stalin not only is generally called "the Boss" by the whole bureaucracy, but is the one and only boss.[29]

This general description of Stalin's style of work has been confirmed many times by diplomats and statesmen of many countries who observed that Stalin often made important decisions without consulting anyone, while Molotov and others would request time to consult with their "government." The role of the other members of the Politburo could best be described as consultative, although within the area of their own administrative responsibility they exercised the power of decision. Testimony concerning Stalin's intolerance of dissent is uniformly consistent. "Whoever opposed . . . his viewpoint," complained Khrushchev, "was doomed to be removed."

The relationship between the Foreign Ministry and the Presidium has always been unique. Since relations

29 Alexander Barmine, One Who Survived (New York: G. P. Putnam's Sons, 1946), p. 213. Barmine adds that "thousands of relatively unimportant, as well as all-important, problems, must pass through Stalin's hand for final decision. . . . Weeks are spent in waiting; Commissars wait in Stalin's office."

with other states are viewed in terms of a struggle for power among various "ruling classes," and thus directly involve the security and the very existence of the Soviet state, the party center has always retained a tight supervision over the Foreign Ministry. This supervision assumes different forms, depending upon the party rank of the individuals who hold the posts of foreign minister and of premier. The premier has always been a party figure of the highest rank, while the foreign minister may or may not be a member of the party Presidium.

During the period when Maxim Litvinov was foreign commissar, his work was supervised by Molotov, the premier of the government and his formal superior. Matters of routine interest, not involving questions of policy or fundamental maneuver, were decided by Litvinov himself in consultation with his collegium. More substantial questions were taken to Molotov, who, depending upon the nature of the question, would make a decision or take it to Politburo.[30]

The Politburo itself was broken down into various commissions dealing with different aspects of policy. Questions of foreign policy were first considered by the Politburo Commission on Foreign Affairs, which included the Politburo specialists on the Comintern, foreign trade, and defense. In matters involving exceptional or immediate importance, Molotov would deal directly with Stalin and get a decision.

The procedures of the Politburo were neither systematic nor rigid. Often Stalin would personally consult with the foreign commissar and his chief advisers; and Litvinov, on a few occasions, would be asked to make a

report to the Politburo. The principal function of the Commission on Foreign Affairs was to act as a coordinating agency of all the departments concerned with foreign relations; assemble and evaluate intelligence information flowing from different channels; devise strategy and policy; examine analyses, projects, and reports drawn up by specialists in the Foreign Commissariat; study reports of diplomats abroad; and then make a comprehensive report either to Stalin or to the Politburo as a whole.

Once the decisions were made, they would be transmitted in writing or verbally by Molotov to Litvinov for execution. These bureaucratic channels were often ignored and Stalin would act directly with Molotov, his principal agent, and they would personally give instructions to Litvinov. Deviation or improvisation from instructions by the foreign commissar or his subordinates in the commissariat was neither permitted nor tolerated. According to Khrushchev, the system of Politburo commissions was not primarily for organizational efficiency, but was a sinister device whereby Stalin weakened the authority of the collective body:

> The importance of the . . . Political Bureau was reduced and its work disorganized by the creation within the Political Bureau of various commissions—the so-called "quintets," "sextets," "septets" and "novenaries."

When Molotov replaced Litvinov in May, 1939, this cumbersome procedure was simplified. The Nazi-Soviet Pact was worked out principally by Stalin and Molotov, with Zhdanov and Mikoyan the only other members of the Politburo apparently apprised of the crucial decisions contemplated. The Politburo Commission on Foreign Affairs gradually increased in

30 See Merle Fainsod, *How Russia Is Ruled* (Cambridge: Harvard University Press, 1953), p. 282.

size until, by 1945, it was large enough to be converted by Stalin from a "sextet" into a "septet." As it grew in size, so its importance diminished. During the war, Stalin appeared to consult only Molotov on questions of foreign policy and frequently made decisions on the spot at the Big Three conferences.

Khrushchev's description of how decisions were made by Stalin and the Politburo is probably exaggerated and self-serving, but accurate in its general outline:

After the war, Stalin became even more capricious, irritable, and brutal; in particular his suspicion grew. His persecution mania reached unbelievable dimensions. Everything was decided by him alone without any consideration for anyone or anything. . . . Sessions of the Political Bureau occurred only occasionally, . . . many decisions were taken by one person or in a roundabout way, without collective discussion. . . . The importance of the Political Bureau was reduced and its work disorganized by the creation within the Political Bureau of various commissions. . . . The result of this was that some members of the Political Bureau were in this way kept away from participation in the decisions of the most important state matters.

Decision Making in the Post-Stalin Period: The Agonies of Collective Leadership and Factional Conflict

The death of Stalin stimulated the expression of various opinions, and unleashed a struggle for power among his successors. Six months before his death, at the Nineteenth Party Congress, Stalin radically reorganized the party summit, abolishing the Orgburo and replacing the eleven-man Politburo with a Presidium of twenty-five members and eleven candidate members as the key decision-making organ of the Soviet system. Since many of the new members of the Presidium were burdened with permanent administrative responsibilities far from Moscow, and since it was much too large to function as a decision-making body, there was secretly organized, in violation of the new party charter, a smaller Bureau of the Presidium, whose membership has never been revealed. Whether expansion of the Presidium was designed by Stalin to widen the area of decision making and prevent a struggle for power after his death—thus preparing the conditions for orderly transition from personal to institutional dictatorship—or whether it was a sinister device for liquidating his old associates in favor of a generation ignorant of his crimes remains an intriguing enigma. According to Khrushchev,

Stalin evidently had plans to finish off the old members of the Political Bureau. . . . His proposal after the Nineteenth Congress, concerning the selection of 25 persons to the Central Committee's Presidium, was aimed at the removal of the old Political Bureau members and the bringing in of less experienced persons so that they would extol him. . . . We can assume that this was a design for the future annihilation of the old Political Bureau members, and in this way, a cover for all the shameful acts of Stalin.

Immediately after Stalin's death, the old members of Stalin's entourage reduced the Presidium to its former size. The removal of Beria and the dismantling of his secret police apparatus introduced an uneasy equilibrium among the various factions in the Presidium, none of which was powerful enough to overwhelm the others.

In the post-Stalin Presidium, decisions often were taken only after stormy controversies and agile maneuvering among the various factions. As a consequence, necessity was converted into ideology, and conflicting opinions, within carefully circumscribed limits, were given official sanction. The authoritative theoretical journal *Kommunist*, however, warned that "views that are objectively directed toward dethroning the leadership elected by the Party masses" would not be tolerated.[31] This danger is adumbrated in the party statutes, article 28 of which reads:

A broad discussion, in particular on an all-Union scale concerning the Party policy, should be so organized that it would not result in the attempts of an insignificant minority to impose its will on the majority of the Party or in attempts to organize fractional groupings which would break down Party unity, or in attempts to create a schism that would undermine the strength and the firmness of the socialist regime.[32]

The party statutes, however, were revised in 1961, at the Twenty-second Party Congress, in order to reflect more realistically the more fluid situation which had developed since Stalin's death and, while factionalism was still proscribed, greater emphasis was placed on ensuring the expression of divergent views within the party. Thus, article 27 of the 1961 party statutes stipulates that

wide discussion, especially discussion on a countrywide scale, of questions of Party policy must be held so as to ensure for Party members the free expression of their views and preclude attempts to form fractional groupings destroying Party unity, attempts to split the Party.

The Proliferation of Factional Politics. Diversity and clash of opinion were allowed, initially, to filter down only to the level of the Central Com-

mittee. Eventually however, differences of opinion which reflected various factional views erupted—at first gingerly, and then more boldly, in party congresses, lower-level party bodies, the Supreme Soviet, various professional conferences, newspapers and periodicals, and in professional organizations. The disagreements within the Presidium which were unleashed after Stalin's death threatened to crack the party pyramid down to its very base. It was even possible to envisage the development of a multiparty system, and authoritative voices were openly advocating the nomination of more than one candidate for elective offices.

Decisions in the Politburo are reached by simple majority, with only full members entitled to vote, although alternate members participate in the debate and discussion. Meetings of the Politburo are held at least once a week and, according to both Khrushchev and Mikoyan, most decisions are unanimous. Mikoyan has further elaborated by stating that if a consensus were unobtainable, the Presidium would adjourn, sleep on the matter, and return for further discussion until unanimity was achieved. Since five full members out of eleven were expelled, on June 29, 1957, for persistent opposition to and obstruction of the party line, the unanimity of the Presidium's deliberations appears to have been exaggerated.

In view of Khrushchev's bitter attack on the organization of Politburo commissions under Stalin, the Politburo's internal compartmentalization may not be as rigidly demarcated as before; foreign policy decisions, instead of being merely the concern of the Commission on Foreign Affairs, are discussed and made by the body as a whole. "Never in the past," said Molotov at the Twentieth Party Congress, "has our Party Central Com-

[31] *Kommunist*, August, 1956, no. 10, pp. 3–13.
[32] *Pravda*, October 14, 1952.

mittee and its Presidium been engaged as actively with questions of foreign policy as during the present period."

The sharp and close factional divisions in the Politburo have revived the prominence and activity of the moribund Central Committee. Factional differences have been displayed before plenums of the Central Committee (which are held at least twice a year) where the actions of the Politburo have been appealed. In this relatively large body of 195 full members and 165 alternates, discussion of the various views current in the Politburo is still more ritualized than free, with each faction in the Politburo supported by its own retainers in the Central Committee. Voting is conditioned not only by divisions in the Politburo, but also by considerations of political survival and opportunism, with members being extremely sensitive to the course that the struggle assumes in the higher body. "At Plenums of the Central Committee," according to the revealing statement of one low-ranking member, "Comrade Khrushchev and other members of the Presidium . . . corrected errors in a fatherly way . . . regardless of post occupied or of record."[33]

It was in the Central Committee that Malenkov reputedly indicted Beria and where, in turn, he and Molotov were disciplined and attacked by the Khrushchev faction. Shifts in the balance of factions in the Politburo are almost always immediately registered in the Central Committee, whose proceedings inevitably sway with those of the higher body. The Central Committee, whose decisions are invariably reported as unanimous, is empowered to alter its own membership and that of its higher bodies by a two-thirds vote; and in the June,

1957, plenum it expelled three full members and one alternate from the Presidium and the Central Committee, demoted one to alternate status, and cut off still another at full membership in the Central Committee. Correspondingly, the Presidium was expanded to fifteen full members and nine alternates.

The Central Committee assumed increasing importance during the Khrushchev era, and it is likely that, after the "antiparty group" episode of June, 1957, he considered this body as a counterweight to the opposition which might congeal against him in the Presidium. Khrushchev was almost fastidious in his zeal to enshrine the Central Committee as the ultimate institutional repository of legitimacy in the Soviet system. The body was enlarged and convened regularly by Khrushchev, and all changes in personnel and major pronouncements of policy were either confirmed by or announced at Central Committee plenums. Thus, the Central Committee was convened to expel Marshal Zhukov, former Premier Bulganin, Kirichenko, and Belyayev, as well as others, and met more often than the two annual meetings specified in the party statutes. New appointments to the Presidium and the Secretariat were also announced after Central Committee meetings.

Immediately after the expulsion of the "antiparty group," in mid-1957, and the removal of Marshal Zhukov, the Khrushchev faction appeared to be in full control of both the Presidium and the Central Committee and Khrushchev appeared to be in full command of the ruling faction. Proceedings of the Central Committee were also published more or less regularly under Khrushchev, although selective censorship and suppression persisted. Khrushchev's behavior at Central Committee proceedings was

---

[33] Speech of Z. I. Muratov, first secretary of the Tatar Oblast Committee, Moscow Radio broadcast, February 21, 1956.

often crude, rude, and earthy; commanding, but not domineering. He would deliver a report on the main item on the agenda, which was then discussed in speeches delivered by the other members. These were freely interrupted by the first secretary, who might affirm, criticize, chastise, admonish, correct, and even warn the speakers, and they would respond with varying degrees of deference, familiarity, meekness, fear, or audacity. At the December, 1958, plenum, for example, seventy-five speakers discussed Khrushchev's report, and Bulganin, Pervukhin, and Saburov used the occasion to denounce themselves for complicity in the "antiparty group" conspiracy to oust Khrushchev from power.

Factional Conflict in the Politburo. Differences in the Politburo arise as a result of both personal ambitions for power and fundamental conflict over doctrine and policy. Both factors are so intricately interwoven that attempts to draw fine distinctions between personal and policy conflicts are apt to be an idle exercise. Although Soviet ideology neither recognizes the legitimacy of factional groupings in the party nor tolerates the doctrinal schisms that are their ideological expression, the party, throughout its history, has been constantly threatened with the eruption of both. After Stalin's death, the rival cliques he permitted—and may even have encouraged—to form among his subordinates developed into factions, each with its own aspirations and opinions. Since no single faction was sufficiently powerful to annihilate the others, necessity was converted into virtue and the balance of terror in the Presidium was ideologically sanctified as "collective leadership."

Even before the revelations of the resolution that hurled Molotov and

his associates from their places of eminence, it was unmistakable that serious factional quarrels kept the Presidium in a continual state of turmoil. At least three factions appear to have existed in the Presidium before June, 1957, although the members of each faction were not permanently committed to issues; and personality and tactical shifts, although not frivolous, were also not unusual. The Presidium was divided on four major issues that had important foreign policy repercussions: the Stalinist issue; the relations between the Soviet Union and other communist states and parties; economic policy and reorganization; and relations with the ex-colonial states.

The so-called Stalinist faction had at its core the veteran Politburo members, Molotov and Kaganovich, and was frequently supported by Malenkov. The nucleus of the anti-Stalinist faction was made up of Khrushchev, Mikoyan, Voroshilov, Bulganin, Kirichenko, and the alternate members of the Presidium. This faction was in decisive control of the party apparatus and the Central Committee, and it found crucial support in the army, in Peking, Warsaw, and Belgrade. Pervukhin and Saburov made up the so-called managerial-technical faction, which appeared to have close connections with Malenkov in the past but generally cast its vote with the Khrushchev group on questions of Stalinism. The group deserted Malenkov for Khrushchev when Malenkov appeared to be the apostle for increased emphasis on the production of consumer goods and Khrushchev continued to rely on heavy industry. These factions were bound together by bonds of common ideological and policy considerations, but personal ambitions and opportunism played a considerable role, allowing wide room for maneuver and realignment of positions as the main chance presented itself.

The events in Poland and Hungary, together with the uncompromising attitude of Marshal Tito, encouraged the Stalinists to believe that the Khrushchev group had fumbled, while Khrushchev's sudden interest in decentralizing the economic structure of the state stampeded Pervukhin and Saburov foolishly to join the Stalinist faction in an anti-Khrushchev coalition that made a desperate effort to thwart the proposed dismantling of their economic empires. At the December, 1956, plenum of the Central Committee, this combination was sufficiently powerful to arrest the de-Stalinization program temporarily and to guarantee the preservation of the centralized economic structure by installing Pervukhin as the virtual dictator of the economic system. Relations with Tito were once again inflamed, and satellite policies appeared to harden. During this period, Malenkov—as representative of the new majority—accompanied Khrushchev to the communist gathering held in Budapest, from which both Warsaw and Belgrade were deliberately excluded.

The inconclusive factional strife in the Kremlin, and the ideological ferment in Eastern Europe, provided an opportunity for Peking to intervene, and Chou En-lai embarked upon an emergency trip to Moscow and Eastern Europe to shore up the Khrushchev faction. Because of the unnatural and unstable amalgamation organized against him, Khrushchev's ouster was deferred; but once the crisis had subsided, and it was clear that the armed forces and China preferred Khrushchev's policies to those of his opposition, a realignment of forces in the Presidium enabled Khrushchev once again to reconstitute a majority at the February, 1957, plenum, and Pervukhin was toppled from his brief perch on the economic throne. The economic levers of power were wrenched from his hands, while Shepilov was ousted from the Foreign Ministry in favor of Gromyko.

With the Presidium so sharply and evenly divided, "collective leadership" threatened to abandon Soviet foreign policy to the mercies of an inconclusive see-saw struggle plunging the Kremlin into a condition of perpetual indecision. While key Khrushchev supporters were out of town, Stalinist forces, by engineering a rump meeting of the Presidium—ostensibly to discuss minor matters—regrouped and resolved to unseat Khrushchev through a parliamentary ruse. When the meeting took place on June 17–18, 1957, the first secretary found himself momentarily outmaneuvered and apparently irrevocably outvoted. Saburov and Pervukhin once again voted with the Stalinist faction, as did Khrushchev's erstwhile protégé, Shepilov. But the key figure in the new realignment was Bulganin, who miscalculated the power of the anti-Khrushchev forces and underrated the first secretary's political agility (leading Khrushchev to confide later that some of his colleagues knew more about arithmetic than politics), and in an opportunistic maneuver voted to oust Khrushchev from power in the meeting over which he presided. Refusing to resign, Khrushchev conducted a filibuster while his supporters quickly assembled a special meeting of the Central Committee and its auditing commission (a total of 319 members), which sat June 22–29, 1957.

After a bitter ventilation of all the contentious issues of doctrines and policy, during which 60 members reportedly took part in the debate and 115 filed statements, the Molotov-managerial coalition was overwhelmed by a unanimous vote tarnished only by a single obstinate abstention by Molotov—the first such publicly admitted dissonance in a Central Committee vote in almost thirty years. The Stalinist wing of the coalition was charged in the resolution which expelled them with engaging in illegal factional activity and cabalistic intrigue:

Entering into collusion on an anti-Party basis, they set out to change the policy of the Party, to drag the Party back to the erroneous methods of leadership condemned by the Twentieth Party Congress [i.e., Stalinism]. They resorted to methods of intrigue and formed a collusion against the Central Committee.

The others were not specifically condemned, but Saburov lost his seat on the Presidium and Pervukhin was demoted to alternate status. In their humiliating appearances before the Twenty-first Party Congress, held in February, 1959, both confessed their complicity in the plot against Khrushchev, although they maintained that they later switched to Khrushchev on the vote to actually oust him as first secretary. Saburov was eventually exiled to the obscurity of a factory manager in Syzran, while Pervukhin wound up with the less than exalted post of ambassador to East Germany. Apparently for purposes of concealing the fact that a majority of the Presidium actually voted against him, Bulganin lingered on as premier until March, 1958, and as a member of the Presidium until the following September, although it was clear that his position had been compromised. He was formally charged with being part of the anti-Khrushchev conspiracy on November 14, 1958, and at the December, 1958, plenum, Bulganin made a groveling confession in which he denounced himself as the "nominal leader" of the plot because of his position as chairman of the Council of Ministers. He made an abject plea for forgiveness, unleashed a vicious attack on Molotov and Kaganovich, and was consigned to the demeaning post of chairman of the Stavropol Economic Council.

The victorious group soon betrayed signs of splitting on a wide range of domestic and foreign policies. The leadership tended to polarize into two main factions, a "moderate" group, led by Khrushchev, and a "conservative" group, whose leaders appeared to be M. A. Suslov and F. R. Kozlov, later apparently supported by traditional elements of the professional military and representatives of heavy industry. Generally speaking, the moderate faction sought a relaxation of international tensions and a détente with the United States, even at the expense of alienating China; the conservative faction saw little value in a détente with the United States, especially at the expense of alienating the Soviet Union's most important ally. Domestically, Khrushchev and the "moderates" were willing to tolerate greater relaxation of controls at home and advocated a change in the economic equilibrium in the direction of producing more consumer goods at the expense of heavy industry. The "conservatives" were opposed to further relaxation at home and may have even demanded some retrenchment, and they were virtually dogmatic in their insistence that priority continue to be given to heavy industry over light industry and agriculture. Under these conditions, formalized debate in the Central Committee gave way to a genuine, if largely esoteric, articulation of divergent factional viewpoints, which was also evident from the content of the speeches delivered at the Twenty-first and Twenty-second party congresses, in January, 1959, and October, 1961, respectively.

As long as Khrushchev's policy of seeking a relaxation of international tension and a détente with the United

States seemed to be bearing fruit, he was able to isolate and silence his critics in the leadership, particularly after his meeting with President Eisenhower at Camp David, in mid-1959. Relations with China simultaneously deteriorated catastrophically when Khrushchev unilaterally nullified a secret 1957 Sino-Soviet agreement on nuclear technology, just prior to his meeting with President Eisenhower. Since an improvement in relations with the United States inevitably meant a further deterioration of relations with China, this became an important and crucial issue which agitated the Soviet leadership. The factional opposition to Khrushchev was strengthened in January, 1960, when the Soviet leader alienated the traditional military by calling for a reduction of the ground forces by one-third and shifting the main reliance for Soviet security to its nuclear deterrent capability. This new strategic policy was based upon the expectation of an imminent settlement of all outstanding issues between Washington and Moscow on the basis of the "spirit of Camp David."

After the U-2 incident, Khrushchev's grip on the Central Committee and its Presidium was weakened and came under increasing attack at home, while criticism in Peking mounted simultaneously. Khrushchev's foreign policy was based upon a fundamental restructuring of the image and character of the American "ruling class," which according to the "moderates" had split into a "sober" group, on the one hand, and an intractable group, made up of "belligerent," "aggressive," "irrational," and even "mad" elements, on the other. The sober group—whose leader, according to Khrushchev, was President Eisenhower—was dominant, and it appeared ready to negotiate a settlement with the Soviet Union, on a realistic basis, which to Khrushchev meant a détente based on supposed Soviet strategic superiority. Neither the "conservative" faction, nor the traditional military, nor the Chinese leaders subscribed to this image. The Soviet Union's leader was, in effect, relying upon the self-restraint of the sober forces in the American ruling class, and his opposition viewed his call for troop reductions and cutbacks in heavy industry with considerable alarm. From the Chinese viewpoint, Khrushchev's search for a détente with Eisenhower indicated an erosion in Moscow's commitment to revolutionary goals and a tacit alliance with Peking's principal national enemy.

Although Khrushchev's logic was undermined by the U-2 incident, he managed to remain in power. He pleaded that a new American administration would resume the earlier pacific course of Soviet-American relations, viewed the U-2 crisis as an unfortunate incident, and insisted that the sober American group was still dominant and would be so demonstrated by the forthcoming elections.

Kennedy was unknown to the Russians, but Nixon was a well-known and heartily disliked personality, and so Moscow placed its reliance on a Kennedy victory and a reversal of post-U-2 policy. But the Soviet leader was to be disappointed once again, as the new president embarked on a course of strengthening U.S. military capabilities, supported an attempt to overthrow the Castro regime in Cuba, and refused to be bullied into negotiating a settlement on Soviet terms. The Soviet failure to win a Berlin victory and the steadily growing power of the United States increased the pressures upon Khrushchev both at home and from Peking, and at the Twenty-second Party Congress he adopted a harsher line toward the United States.

From the time of the Twenty-second

Party Congress until Khrushchev's ouster in October, 1964, the Soviet leadership was plagued by constant factional squabbles, and these often found expression in the Central Committee plenums. Khrushchev stayed in power only because the factional balance was extremely delicate, with some leaders supporting him on some issues and opposing him on others. Thus, Soviet factional politics was not only institutionally and functionally oriented but issue oriented as well, and it was the existence of issue-oriented factionalism which provided Khrushchev with the margins necessary to stay in power.

Khrushchev once again narrowly missed being ousted as a consequence of the Cuban missile crisis of October, 1962, when his opposition at home and his critics in Peking seemed perilously close to holding a common point of view. His problems were aggravated, also, by President Kennedy's initial rejection of a Soviet proposal for a limited test-ban treaty based on three annual inspections. The Soviet premier gained a temporary extension of power, however, when the leader of the "conservative" faction, F. R. Kozlov, suffered an incapacitating stroke in April, 1963. Although Khrushchev mused in public about his possible retirement, the incapacitation of Kozlov gave him a new lease on political power, and he quickly took advantage of President Kennedy's offer, made in a speech at American University, to reach an agreement on a limited test-ban treaty, which was signed the following month.

Khrushchev thus appeared to have vindicated himself, for the "sober" forces were indeed in control in Washington; and while the détente was based not upon the assumption of Soviet strategic superiority, but upon the implied assumption of U.S. strategic superiority, it enabled Khru-shchev to turn his attention to pressing economic problems at home and to the dispute with Peking. The Chinese called the limited test-ban treaty an act of Soviet betrayal, and there was strong evidence that the treaty was not enthusiastically accepted by the "conservative" faction or the traditional military.

Khrushchev's inept handling of the dispute with China, his generally crude and unsophisticated behavior as a politician, and his constant boasting in public apparently finally alienated some of his supporters, who saw in his person an impediment to a reconciliation with China and an obstacle to a rational approach to domestic problems. In October, 1964, he was ousted, in a coup engineered largely by his own trusted subordinates, Brezhnev, Kosygin, and Mikoyan. He was indirectly accused of concocting "harebrained schemes," "boasting," and general ineptness. Khrushchev's ouster allegedly took place at a Central Committee plenum, but the proceedings were not made public. The manner and abruptness of his dismissal caused considerable commotion and disturbance in other communist countries and parties, whose leaders demanded and received an explanation in a series of bilateral conferences.

The Chinese, the conservatives, the traditionalistic military, and the moderates all seemed to have a common interest in removing Khrushchev—if for widely differing and even contradictory reasons—and there seems to be little question that the factional situation at home and the criticisms from Peking combined to bring about the Soviet premier's political ouster.

The Central Committee thus began emerging as the most important political organ of power and authority in the Soviet system, although it has not yet eclipsed the Politburo, which, however, must be increasingly responsive to its deliberations. The growing power of the Central Committee reflects the increasingly pluralistic character of the Soviet social order. This body is composed of representatives from the most powerful and influential elite groups in Soviet society. It includes the entire membership of the Politburo and the Secretariat; the most important ministers of the government; the first secretaries of the several republics' party organizations and of important regional party organizations; the most important officials of the Soviet Union's republics; the marshals, generals, and admirals of the armed forces and the police; the important ambassadors; the trade union officials; cultural and scientific celebrities and leaders; the leading party ideologists; and the top Komsomol officials. Increasingly, these representatives perceive attitudes reflecting their institutional or functional roles and status in Soviet society, and this provides the social basis for the political factions which now characterize the Soviet system.

The transition from Stalinist, one-man rule to quasi-pluralistic political behavior is now all but complete. The Khrushchev decade emerges as a sort of transition period between these two types of political behavior. Under Stalin, conflicts were rendered into decisions after a blood purge in which potential opponents were physically destroyed; under Khrushchev, conflicts were resolved into decisions by the clearcut victory of one faction and the expulsion of the others from important positions of power. The blood purge was replaced with public condemnation and disgrace, demotion, or retirement; but since the execution of Beria in 1954, no fallen leader has been executed or even brought to trial. With the element of terror removed from the political process, however, the risks of opposition and dissent were considerably reduced. Victorious factions divided into new factions, and so the factional conflict resumed on a new level, and around new issues. By late 1959, no single group could establish dominance, and control gradually came to be exercised by a kind of consensus, based on compromise, bargaining, and accommodation. This has introduced an element of instability and uncertainty with respect to any given government or administration, but it has simultaneously stabilized and regularized the Soviet political process and has removed much of the uncertainty which hitherto prevailed.

No formal charges of factionalism have been made against any group or individual in the Soviet Union's hierarchy since 1959. Such a charge can only be leveled if a particular faction is soundly defeated and expelled from the leadership, and this was characteristic of the rule by a single faction which flourished between 1953 and 1959. Factionalism is still prohibited by the party rules, but its existence was tacitly admitted by Kozlov at the Twenty-second Party Congress:

Under present circumstances, need the statutes contain any formal guarantee against factionalism and clique activity? Yes, . . . such guarantees as needed. To be sure there is no social base left in Soviet society that could feed opportunistic currents in the Party. But the sources of ideological waverings on the part of particular individuals or groups have not yet been entirely eliminated. Some persons may fall under the influence of bourgeois propaganda from the outside. Others having failed to comprehend the dialectics of society's development and having turned . . . into dying embers, will have nothing to do with anything new and go on clinging to old dogmas that have been toppled by life.[34]

[34] *Pravda*, October 29, 1961.

Interest Groups and Factional Politics. It is at once obvious that factions could neither arise nor flourish unless they received constant sustenance from powerful social forces in Soviet society. Just as party factions do not organize into separate political organizations competing with the party for political power, so interest groups in Soviet society do not constitute separate organizations, but rather seek to make their influence felt as formless clusters of vested interests. Within the context of Marxist ideology, an interest group can only be a social class with economic interests that conflict with the interests of other classes. After the revolution, only the interests of the working class, as distorted by the Marxist prism, were given legitimate recognition—although the concrete political articulation of these interests was usurped by the Communist party—and all other interests and parties were condemned to oblivion. In 1936 Stalin declared the eradication of class conflict in Soviet society, but he continued to recognize the existence of separate social classes, whose interests had merged into a single identity. The Communist party was transformed from a party representing only the interests of the working class into one representing the transcendental interests of all Soviet social classes. Consequently, Soviet ideology neither recognizes the legitimacy of competing interest groups nor tolerates their autonomous existence. In Soviet jargon, an interest group that develops interests that deviate from the party line is a hostile class; the faction that represents it in the party is an attempt to form a party within a party, and its articulated views on policy and doctrine constitute an ideological deviation.

Separate interest groups, however, continue to flourish in Soviet society, but not in conformity with the doctrinaire and contrived premises of nineteenth-century Marxism, nor within the synthetic social divisions given official sanction. The collective-farm peasantry and the working class constitute the numerically preponderant classes in Soviet society, but the major interest groups with sufficient power and influence to apply political pressure do not follow the artificial constructions of Soviet ideology; in accordance with the unique dynamic of Soviet society, the privileged elites find their social differentiation within a single recognized group, the *intelligentsia,* which is not recognized as a social class, but is euphemistically called a *stratum.*

Although the Soviet intelligentsia (roughly identical with what Milovan Djilas labeled the "New Class") is a variegated congeries of differentiated elites, they all have in common a desire to perpetuate the Soviet system from which they have sprung and from which they benefit as privileged groups. But each group is immediately concerned with its own vested stake in Soviet society, and seeks to force doctrine and policy to assume the contours of its own special interests. Since these groups do not enjoy official recognition, they all seek to exert their influence through the Communist party, not outside it, and political rivalry assumes the form of competing for control of the party's decision-making organs and its symbols of legitimacy. Because Soviet ideology rigidly and inaccurately insists on the existence of a single monolithic interest, representing that of society in its collective entity, conflicts between major groups are resolved not by political accommodation, but by mutual elimination and by the attempt of one interest group to establish its supremacy and to impose its views as those of society as a whole. Thus the Communist party, under the pressures of diverse groups seeking political articulation and accommodation, has become a conglomeration of interests whose basic incompatibilities are only partially obscured by a veneer of monolithic unity.

Not all interest groups in the Soviet Union are sufficiently powerful to exact representation for their views by factions in the party hierarchy. There are six principal groups within Soviet society that have accumulated sufficient leverage, either through the acquisition of indispensable skills and talents or through the control of instruments of persuasion, terror, or destruction, to exert pressure upon the party. These are (1) the party apparatus, consisting of those who have made a career in the party bureaucracy; (2) the government bureaucracy; (3) the economic managers and technicians; (4) the cultural, professional, and scientific intelligentsia; (5) the police; (6) the armed forces.

These major groups are by no means organized as cohesively united bodies, speaking with a single authoritative voice, but rather themselves are made up of rival personal and policy cliques, gripped by internal jealousies, and often in constant collision and friction with one another in combination or alliance with similarly oriented cliques in other social groups.

The party apparatus itself has been thus divided into rival cliques, the two main contending groups being those led by Khrushchev and Malenkov. After the denouncement of Malenkov, his supporters in the party apparatus were replaced with followers of Khrushchev. Although the function of the party bureaucracy is essentially administrative rather than policy making, it has a tendency to feel that it "owns" the party, and thus seeks first to subordinate the party to its control and then to force the other major groups to submit to the domination of the party. After Stalin's death, the serious and imminent threat posed to the party by Beria and his secret police caused Khrushchev and Malenkov to temporarily bury their rivalry in the apparatus of the party in order to crush the secret police, which had developed into an independent center of power and threatened to subjugate the party to its will. The secret police was dismembered with the aid of the army.

There appears to be no systematic attempt to select members of the Central Committee and its Politburo from among the major forces in Soviet society; the composition of these bodies appears to depend upon the balance of forces at any given time (see tables 5.1 and 5.2). Ample evidence exists, however, that their composition reflects deliberate recognition of these

TABLE 5.1

Major Groups Represented in the Central Committee

	1952	1956	1961	April, 1966
Party apparatus	103	117	158	155
State and economic officials	79	98	112	136
Military officers	26	18	31	33
Cultural and scientific representatives	. . .	. . .	18	15
Police	9	3	2	2
Others	19	19	9	19
Totals	236	255	330	360

TABLE 5.2

Major Institutions Represented on the Presidium or Politburo

	1952	1953	1956	1957	1961	1963	1966	1970
Party apparatus	13 (5)	2 (2)	4 (3)	10 (6)	7 (3)	8 (4)	6 (6)	6 (7)
State officials:								
Economic sector	5 (3)	4	4	1 (2)	2	2	1	0
Other	4 (2)	3 (1)	3 (1)	3	2 (2)	2 (2)	4 (1)	5 (1)
Military	0	0	0 (1)	1	0	0	0	0
Police	2	1 (1)	0	0	0	0	0	0 (1)
Other	1 (1)	0	0 (1)	0 (1)	0	0	0 (1)	0
Totals	25 (11)	10 (4)	11 (6)	15 (9)	11 (5)	12 (6)	11 (8)	11 (9)

major interest groups. Traditionally, the party apparatus accounts for slightly less than half the total membership of the Central Committee, with the government bureaucracy (including the economic administrators) following close behind. The representation of the other groups is substantially less, although, because virtually all members of the party's two highest bodies who are not career party bureaucrats are employed by the state, it is often difficult to distinguish the main line of work pursued by a particular member of the Central Committee. This is especially true of individuals who move from one group to another. Consequently, all distinctions are provisional and, in some cases, arbitrary. The composition of the Politburo is more accurately differentiated, although even there, because of the interlocking of the top organs of state and party, some ambiguity prevails.

Since the membership of the Central Committee is normally determined by the party congress, which meets every four years, its composition is not normally affected by day-to-day changes in the factional equilibrium. The Politburo, whose membership can be altered by the Central Committee, is particularly sensitive to the fluctuations in the balance of power, and is a fairly accurate barometer of changing political fortunes.

Formerly, it could be said that the composition of the Central Committee was determined from the top, by the Politburo, but the relationship between the two bodies is becoming increasingly reciprocal. Changes in the composition of the Politburo now reflect, to some degree, changes in the factional balance in the Central Committee as groups and individuals maneuver for position and advantage —bargaining, negotiating, and accommodating. The Central Committee's authority becomes crucial, and perhaps even decisive, when the factional balance is delicate. Then, rival groups seek to gain wider support and alter their policies to meet the demands of wider constituencies. Thus, while the Politburo is the more accurate gauge of day-to-day politics, the composition of the Central Committee is apt to reflect more durable, long-range trends. Table 5.2 shows only institutional representation on the Politburo, and it should be noted that interest groups tend, increasingly, to cut across institutional entities.

The party apparatus continues to be the dominant institutional actor in both the Central Committee and its Politburo, but its absolute and relative strength in both bodies, after reaching a post-Stalin high point in 1957, seems now to be diminishing as other groups demand greater representation. As factional cleavages develop within the apparatus, opportunities are created for other groups as they become targets of appeal for support by rival apparatus factions and in turn make demands upon the apparatus. The year 1957, after the expulsion of the "antiparty group," represented the zenith of single-faction rule, which was sustained substantially unimpaired until Khrushchev's assumption of the premiership in the following year. Factionalism, however, infected the victorious Khrushchev group itself, and the overall representation of the apparatus in the Presidium started to decline until, by the time of the Twenty-second Party Congress in October, 1961, two main factions had once again materialized: a "moderate" faction led by Khrushchev and a "conservative" faction, supported by the traditional military, led by F. R. Kozlov, an erstwhile Khrushchev satrap. No less than four full members and four candidate members of the Presidium associated with the "moderate" position were dropped, and the overall size of the Presidium was substantially reduced. In the Secretariat, the "moderate" faction's dominance was eliminated by the appointment of new members associated with the "conservative" group, and the size of this body was raised from five to nine. Thus, the "moderate" faction suffered losses in the Presidium by a trimming of its membership, while in the Secretariat, its presence was diminished through the addition of new members associated with the other faction. Khrushchev managed to hang on as both premier and first secretary, first in order to present a united front to both the United States and China, and second because he adjusted and accommodated his publicly stated views and policies to accord more with the demands of the "conservative" faction, without at the same time abandoning his leadership of the "moderate" faction. From the Twenty-second Party Congress until his ouster in October, 1964, he presided over a regime which was characterized not by single-faction rule but by factional consensus and accommodation.

During the Khrushchev era, the government bureaucracy suffered a drastic decrease in its representation on the Presidium, both in the economic and noneconomic realms. Since 1958, there has been no active representation of either the professional military or heavy industry, while light industry was amply represented by Kosygin and Mikoyan, both of whom were in high favor with Khrushchev. The appointment of D. F. Ustinov as a candidate member of the Politburo and as a member of the Secretariat at the Twenty-third Party Congress (1966) marked the first direct representation of heavy industry in the party's highest body in nearly a decade. A specialist in defense industry, Ustinov represents in his person the symbolic relationship between heavy industry and the traditional military in the Soviet social system. The police were also excluded, although the admission of Shelepin to the Presidium, after he stepped down from his position as chairman of the Committee on State Security, may have given the police some marginal representation. The cultural intelligentsia was represented by professional ideologists like Suslov, who were closely identified with the party apparatus.

The fall of Khrushchev in 1964 did not produce any immediate major dislocations or dismissals in the Soviet hierarchy, except for the demotion of a few individuals who were personally close or related to the Soviet leader. The most conspicuous was his son-in-law, Alexei Adzhubei, who was unceremoniously booted out of the Central Committee and relieved of his job as chief editor of *Izvestia*. Shelepin and Shelest, neither of whom were candidate members, were admitted as full members of the Presidium, and Demichev was appointed a candidate member. Shelepin and Demichev were also members of the Secretariat, and their appointment broadened the overlapping membership in the two bodies. It is possible that their elevation was, in part, a reward for their support in ousting their erstwhile patron. There were other dismissals and appointments at lower levels, but they were accomplished with little fanfare. It was quite clear that Khrushchev's ouster had created a series of minor power vacuums which had to be filled, and this resulted in some maneuvering. Three Khrushchev supporters, Ilyichev, Polyakov, and Titov, were dropped from the Secretariat, reducing its size to eight.

In March, 1965, after a Central Committee plenum, further changes were made. Mazurov was elevated from candidate membership to full membership in the Presidium, and D. F. Ustinov was added as a candidate member. Ustinov's star had appeared to rise, after the Cuban missile crisis, when Khrushchev seemed to be in deep trouble, but it dimmed after Kozlov's stroke and Khrushchev had made a temporary political recovery. Further changes were made in the party summit in December, 1965, when Ustinov, Kapitonov, and Kulakov were appointed to the Secretariat to replace the three members who had been dropped after Khrushchev's political demise, raising its number once again to eleven. Six members of the Secretariat were also full or candidate members of the Presidium, which suggested a resurgence of the party apparatus's representation at the party

summit. Podgorny, at this time, also replaced Mikoyan as chairman of the Presidium of the Supreme Soviet (the Soviet legislature), and subsequently relinquished his membership in the Secretariat.

The definitive post-Khrushchev composition of the party summit was achieved at the Twenty-third Party Congress in April, 1966, when Mikoyan and Shvernik were retired from the Politburo and Pelshe, a Latvian party secretary, was appointed a full member over the heads of all the candidate members. Two new candidate members were appointed—Kunayev, a Kazakh party leader, and Masherov, a Byelorussian party secretary who had become a full member of the Central Committee only in November, 1964, immediately after Khrushchev's ouster, which suggests that he played a key role in the post-Khrushchev factional maneuvering. The composition of the Secretariat remained unchanged, except that Kirilenko, also a full member of the Politburo, replaced Podgorny in the Secretariat, since the latter's new post as chairman of the Presidium of the Supreme Soviet is traditionally disassociated from the Secretariat.

The restructuring of the party summit at the Twenty-third Party Congress strongly suggested that Brezhnev, the general secretary of the party, had strengthened his position and that he enjoyed a factional majority or consensus, but by no means had assumed the power of a Khrushchev or a Stalin, irrespective of the symbolic manipulation of nomenclature at the party congress. Of the eleven full members of the Politburo, four were members of the Secretariat, while of the eight candidate members, two were members of the Secretariat. This meant that six members of the eleven-man Secretariat also sat on the Politburo. The clear dominance of the party

TABLE 5.3

Interlocking of Government and Party Institutions and Personnel in the Soviet Union, 1970

First Secretaries of Republics	Presidium of the Supreme Soviet	Secretariat	Politburo	Presidium of the Council of Ministers	Premiers of Republics	Other
	Brezhnev	Brezhnev (General Secretary)	Brezhnev			
	Podgorny (Chairman)		Kosygin	Kosygin (Chairman)		
		Suslov	Suslov			
		Kirilenko	Podgorny			
			Kirilenko			
			Polyansky	Polyansky (First Deputy)		
			Voronov	Voronov (ex officio)	Voronov (R.S.F.S.R.)	
Shelest (Ukraine)	Shelest		Shelest			
Pelshe (Latvia)			Pelshe			
		Shelepin	Mazurov	Mazurov (First Deputy)		
			Shelepin			Shelepin (Trade Union Chairman)
Mzhvanadze (Georgia)			Mzhvanadze			
Rashidov (Uzbek)			Rashidov			
			Shcherbitsky	Shcherbitsky (ex officio)	Shcherbitsky (Ukraine)	
		Demichev	Demichev			
		Ustinov	Ustinov			
Masherov (Byelorussia)	Masherov		Masherov			
			Grishin			Grishin (Moscow Party Committee)
Kunayev (Kazakh)	Kunayev		Kunayev			
		Ponomarev	Andropov	Andropov (State Security)		
		Kulakov				
		Kapitonov				
		Rudakov				
		Solomentsev				
		Katushev				

apparatus in the Politburo was further indicated by the presence of six party secretaries of republics (Ukrainian, Latvian, Georgian, Uzbek, Byelorussian, and Kazakh) as full or candidate members, thus broadening its ethnic base to include representation from six of the fourteen major non-Russian nationalities, including two central Asian Moslem nationalities, the Uzbek and Kazakh, and giving the apparatus a total of six full members and six candidate members of the Politburo, or twelve votes out of nineteen, a clear majority. In addition to this, career party bureaucrats like Podgorny and Mazurov moved into key state offices. The interlocking of institutions and personnel between the party and the state since the Twenty-third Party Congress is shown in table 5.3.

The rapid and utter defeat of Moscow's Arab client states by Israel in June, 1967, was a traumatic diplomatic debacle for the Soviet leadership and triggered another round of acrimonious debate and controversy in the Politburo and Central Committee. While no major shake-ups resulted in the Politburo or Central Committee, significant reassignments of their personnel were further evidence of factional maneuvering for position. The major consequence of the shifts during this period, which were closely linked to foreign policy issues, was the conspicuous downgrading of the youngest and perhaps most threatening member of the Politburo, Alexander Shelepin, and his coterie of ambitious young *apparatchiki*, who were apparently pressuring the leadership for a more dramatic or militant response to the Egyptian defeat.

Shelepin was dropped from the powerful Secretariat and given the distinctively minor post of chairman of the Central Trade Union Council, although he managed to retain his seat in the Politburo. As a result, V.

V. Grishin, an alternate member of the Politburo, was rotated to become secretary of the Moscow City Party Organization. Shelepin's protégé Semichastny, who earlier replaced Shelepin as chairman of the Committee on State Security (i.e., the KGB, or secret police), was released and reassigned to a minor post in the bureaucracy, thus breaking the grip that the Shelepin group was fastening on the security forces. Under normal circumstances of upward mobility, Semichastny would ultimately have been advanced to alternate membership in the Politburo. His position as head of the security forces was given to a veteran party functionary, Yuri Andropov, whose rising importance was reinforced by his simultaneous promotion to alternate membership in the Politburo, although he was forced to relinquish his position in the Secretariat, since it was incompatible with his membership in the Council of Ministers.

Although the circumstances leading to the occupation of Czechoslovakia in the following year further aggravated the factional alignments in the Kremlin, no perceptible major changes were registered at the apex of the system (see chap. 6 for details). The unexpected postponement of the Twenty-fourth Party Congress meeting from October, 1970, to March, 1971, in patent violation of the party statutes, however, strongly suggested that important changes in the Soviet leadership were impending to correspond more accurately with the shifts in the factional equilibrium. Leonid Brezhnev still appeared to be the single most influential personality in the leadership, but he was clearly far from holding the power of a dictator, or even the power of Khrushchev during his heyday.

It is normal practice to divorce membership in the Secretariat from membership in the Council of Ministers, since the Secretariat is supposed to exercise an independent audit of the government's work and check on the execution and implementation of party directives and resolutions. The only consistent deviation from this practice occurs when the same personality functions as general secretary (first secretary) of the party and as chairman of the Council of Ministers, as was the case during the later years of the Stalin and Khrushchev eras. Similarly, the chairmanship of the Presidium of the Supreme Soviet is considered to be incompatible with membership in the Secretariat. Both Brezhnev and Podgorny relinquished their membership in the Secretariat upon their appointment as chairman of the Presidium of the Supreme Soviet. It is traditional, however, for the general secretary to be an ordinary member of the Presidium of the Supreme Soviet if he holds no other state post, and it is usual for the Presidium to include several other members of the party Secretariat, thus ensuring party audit and control over its activities. It is also customary for membership in the Presidium of the Supreme Soviet to be incompatible with membership in the Council of Ministers, since the latter is jurisdically responsible to the former. Since the death of Stalin, it has been normal practice to include high state and party officials of the R.S.F.S.R. and the Ukraine in the Politburo.

Internal Politics and Soviet Foreign Policy: Interest Groups and Factional Polarization on Foreign Policy Issues

The informal recognition of groups with distinctive special interests of their own and the admission of their representatives to the decision-making bodies of the party cannot but influence the country's foreign policy, although how this influence is exerted,

and in what direction, is difficult to determine.[35] The removal of the managerial bureaucrats from both the Presidium and high government posts was motivated, at least in part, by the fear that their control of the key economic levers of society could be used to frustrate the decisions of the party.

Marshal Zhukov's leadership of the army posed an even grimmer threat to the supremacy of the party apparatus, had he been permitted to remain in the Presidium and the Defense Ministry, where he could seriously question the basic decisions of the party concerning military and foreign policy and frustrate their implementation. His removal, in October, 1957, from both strategic positions was essentially preventive, designed to remove a popular and commanding personality who might at some future date challenge even more crucial decisions of the party and thus produce an internal crisis of incalculable magnitude.

By 1958, the party apparatus, under Khrushchev's direction, had dismembered the police, domesticated the managerial bureaucrats and decentralized their empire, exiled the leaders of factional groupings in the party to Siberia, and subordinated the military to its will. As table 5.2 indicates, neither major instrument of coercion in the Soviet system now has a representative in the party Presidium, which is now overwhelmingly dominated by career party *apparatchiki*.

As the Soviet system matures and becomes inextricably identified with the interests of its various privileged elites, the decision makers must give

---

[35] This section is adapted from the author's "Internal Politics and Foreign Policy in the Soviet System," in *Approaches to Comparative and International Politics*, ed. B. Farrell (Evanston, Ill.: Northwestern University Press, 1966).

greater consideration, in the calculation of foreign policy, to factors affecting the internal stability of the regime; and they will show greater sensitivity to the effects of decisions on the vested interests of the various elites in Soviet society. The rise of powerful social and economic elites in the Soviet Union, and their insistent pressure for participation in the exercise of political power, could only introduce stresses, strains, conflicts, and hence new restraints into Soviet diplomacy.

Within the context of an ideology that imposes a single interest representing society as a whole, each interest group will tend to distort ideology and policy in an endeavor to give them the contours of its own interests; the next step is to elevate these to transcendental significance. Under these conditions, Soviet ideology may be constantly threatened with a series of fundamental convulsions if one interest group displaces another in the struggle for the control of the party machinery. Hence, a rational system of accommodating conflicting interests appears to be evolving. As the vested stake of each major group becomes rooted in the Soviet system, the contours of Soviet diplomacy and national interest will inexorably tend to be shaped more by the rapidly moving equilibrium or accommodation of interests that develop internally than by abstract ideological imperatives, which may conflict with the concrete interests of specific major elites in Soviet society.

Although, ideologically, the basic purpose of external security and state survival is to develop into a power center for the purpose of implementing ideological goals in foreign policy (world communism), increasingly the purpose becomes in fact to protect and preserve the existing social order in the interests of the social groups which dominate and benefit from it. To the extent that the implementation of foreign policy goals, whether ideologically motivated or otherwise, are compatible with the preservation and enhancement of the social order and serve to reward rather than deprive its beneficiaries, no incompatibility between internal and external goals is experienced. If, however, the pursuit of ideological goals in foreign policy undermines or threatens the security of the state and the social groups which dominate it (or even arrests the progress of their material prosperity), the primacy of internal interests is ideologically rationalized and the energies and efforts devoted to external ideological goals are correspondingly diminished.

It must be realized that the relationship between internal interests and external ideological goals is a dynamic one and fluctuates in accordance with opportunities and capabilities, but in the long run the tendency is that ideological goals which threaten internal interests erode and are deprived of their motivating character. The persistence of ideological goals in Soviet foreign policy reflects socio-functional interests which have been traditionally associated with the party apparatus and professional ideologues. The fact that the concrete policies which have resulted from the pursuit of ideological goals in foreign policy have created special vested interests for other socio-political or socio-institutional groups, like the secret police, the armed forces, and the heavy-industrial managers, should not obscure the fact that the definition, identification, and implementation of ideological goals, whether in foreign or domestic policy, has been the special function of the party apparatus and its attendant ideologues. An area of common interest among some members of the party apparatus and the armed forces and heavy-industrial managers in pursuing policies which are tension-producing has thus come into being. Tension-producing policies in an era of increasing technological complexity, however, not only tend to automatically enhance the power of professionalized and technologically oriented groups in the Soviet Union, to the relative detriment of the status and power of the party apparatus, but also tend to alienate from the apparatus other more numerous social groups in society whose interests are more in consonance with tension-lessening policies, such as the consumer goods producers and light-industrial managers; the intellectuals, artists, professionals, and agricultural managers; and finally, the great mass of Soviet citizenry, comprising the lower intelligentsia, workers, peasants, and others, whose priorities are always lower during periods of high international tensions. Since these latter social forces are more numerous than those whose interests are served by tension-producing policies, the party apparatus was in danger of alienating itself further from the great masses of the Soviet citizenry and becoming increasingly dependent upon the traditional military and heavy industry.

The Soviet Union, like the United States, is thus involved in a great debate over foreign policy and national security matters, centering around the issue of whether heightening or lessening international tensions better serves the "national interest."

While only Molotov and the "anti-party group" have been specifically identified by the Soviet leadership with a policy of favoring international tensions, the nature of the factional conflicts in the Soviet Union over budgets, military strategy, the likelihood of war and violence, the nature of imperialism, images of American "ruling class" behavior, and the proper balance between the production of consumer goods and services and heavy industry in the Soviet economy clearly indicate that tension-producing policies tend to favor certain groups within Soviet society while tension-lessening policies tend to favor others. While the residual fervor of a purely ideological commitment to specific goals and policies remains operative in the thought and behavior of Soviet leaders, there has also been an inexorable tendency for individual leaders and functional interest groups to perceive the interests of society as a whole through their own prism and to distort and adjust the national interest to accord with their own. Ideological distortion takes shape in similar fashion in order to impart the necessary symbolic legitimacy to policies and interests which the Soviet system demands as part of its political ritual.

The foreign policy and defense posture of the Soviet state establish a certain configuration of priorities in the allocation of money and scarce resources. Various individuals and groups develop a vested interest in a particular foreign policy or defense posture because of the role and status it confers upon them. Correspondingly, other individuals and groups in Soviet society perceive themselves as deprived in status and rewards because of existing allocation of expenditures and resources and, hence, they might initiate proposals which might alter existing foreign policy and defense postures or support proposals submitted by other groups or individuals.

A particular interest group or social formation may often have a role or function imposed upon it by events, circumstances, policies, and the mechanism of a given social system in response to certain situations that were not of its own making, or, in some instances, which provided the basis for its very creation and existence. While particular interest groups may not have sought such a role, nor have taken the initiative in acquiring it, nor even have existed before the function was demanded, once this role is thrust upon them they adjust to it and develop a vested interest in the role or function imposed upon them, since it constitutes the source of their existence and status. As individual members adjust to their role, develop it, and invest their energies and careers in it, they almost automatically resist the deprivation or diminution of this role or function in their self-interest.

The same is true of groups to which are assigned limited or arrested roles or functions in society, except that these develop a vested interest in expanding their role, dignifying it with greater status and prestige, and demanding greater rewards. Consequently, it is extremely difficult to distill from Soviet factional positions those aspects of thought and behavior which express conflicting perceptions of self-interest on the part of various individuals, factions, and groups as opposed to authentic "objective" considerations of a broader interest, whether national or ideological, since they are so inextricably intertwined and interdependent.

All that we can assert at this point is that certain individuals, factions, and socio-institutional functional groups seem to thrive and flourish and others to be relatively deprived and arrested in their development under conditions of exacerbated international tensions, while the situation is reversed when a relaxation of international tensions takes place. What might be assumed because of these complicated psychological dialogues between perceptions of self-interest and perception of objective reality,

therefore, is that groups that are favored by a particular policy or situation have a greater inclination to perceive objective reality in terms of their self-interest. Thus, groups that are objectively favored by heightened international tension might have a greater propensity to perceive external threats and a corresponding disinclination to recognize that the nature of a threat has been altered, reduced, or eliminated, thus requiring new policies which might adversely affect them. On the other hand, groups that are objectively favored by relaxation of international tensions or a peacetime economy might be more prone to perceive a premature alternation, diminution, or elimination of an external threat and a corresponding tendency to be skeptical about external threats which arise if they would result in a radical rise in defense expenditures and a reallocation of resources and social rewards.

The social and institutional groups in Soviet society which appear to benefit from an aggressive foreign policy and the maintenance of international tensions are (1) the traditional sectors of the armed forces; (2) the heavy-industrial managers, and (3) professional party *apparatchiki* and ideologues. By no means do all individuals or sub-elites and cliques within these groups see eye-to-eye on foreign policy issues. Some individuals and sub-elites, for opportunistic or careerist reasons or functional adaptability, are able to adjust to a relaxation of tensions by preserving or even improving their role and status. The significant point is that the main impetus for an aggressive policy and the chief opposition to a relaxation of tensions find their social and functional foundations within these three socio-functional or socio-institutional groups, whose common perception of interests results in an informal "military - industrial - apparatus complex." Their attitudes stem almost entirely from the function and role they play in Soviet society and the rewards in terms of prestige, status, and power which are derived from these functions in time of high international tensions as opposed to a détente.

The professional military, on the whole, has a natural interest in a large and modern military establishment and a high priority on budget and resources; the heavy-industrial managerial groups have a vested stake in preserving the primacy of their sector of the economy; and the party apparatus traditionally has had a vested interest in ideological conformity and the social controls which they have rationalized, thus ensuring the primacy of the apparatus over all other social forces in the Soviet system. All of these functional roles are served best under conditions of international tension. Consequently, this group, wittingly or unwittingly, has developed a vested interest in either maintaining international tensions or creating the illusion of insecurity and external danger, which would produce the same effect.

To the degree that individuals or sub-elites within these groups are able to socially retool their functions and adapt them to peacetime or purely internal functions, then do they correspondingly lose interest in an aggressive or tension-preserving policy.

For purposes of analytical convenience, those social groups which would seem to benefit from a relaxation of international tensions can be classified into four general categories: (1) the state bureaucracy, in the central governmental institutions as well as in the republics and localities; (2) light-industrial interests, consumer goods and services interests, and agricultural interests; (3) the cultural, professional and scientific groups, whose role

and influence seem to flourish and thrive under conditions of relaxation both at home and abroad; and (4) the Soviet "consumer," the rank-and-file white-collar employees, the working class, and the peasantry, who will ultimately benefit most from a policy which concentrates on raising the standard of living. The technical-scientific branches of the professional military, including the nuclear-missile specialists, also appear to benefit during periods of relaxed international tensions, when the main reliance for national security is on them and the traditional forces are subject to severe budget reductions.

While the contradiction between Soviet security interests and ideological goals in foreign policy has long been recognized by observers of the Soviet scene, a new variable in Soviet policy is the contradiction between enhancing economic prosperity at home and fulfilling international ideological obligations. In Soviet jargon, this emerges as a contradiction between the requirements of "building communism" and the costs and risks of remaining faithful to the principle of "proletarian international-ism."

This new factor has not gone unnoticed by the Chinese, who accused Khrushchev of abandoning Soviet ideological and material obligations to international communism and to the national-liberation movement in favor of avoiding the risks of nuclear war and building an affluent society to satisfy the appetites of the new Soviet "ruling stratum," in the guise of pursuing peaceful coexistence and "building communism." Thus, in a long editorial entitled "On Khrushchev's Phoney Communism and Its Historical Lessons For the World," the authoritative Chinese organ *Jen Min Jih Pao* charged on July 14, 1964:

The revisionist Khrushchev clique has usurped the leadership of the Soviet party and state and . . . a privileged bourgeois stratum has emerged in Soviet society. . . . The privileged stratum in contemporary Soviet society is composed of degenerate elements from among the leading cadres of party and government organizations, enterprises, and farms as well as bourgeois intellectuals. . . . Under the signboard of "peaceful coexistence," Khrushchev has been colluding with U.S. imperialism, wrecking the socialist camp and the international communist movement, opposing the revolutionary struggles of the oppressed peoples and nations, practicing great-power chauvinism and national egoism, and betraying proletarian internationalism. All this is being done for the protection of the vested interest of a handful of people, which he places above the fundamental interests of the peoples of the Soviet Union, the socialist camp and the whole world.

The same charge has also been leveled at Khrushchev's successors, who, Peking maintains, are simply practicing "Khrushchevism without Khrushchev."

The Fragmentation of the Decision-Making Process: The Paralysis of Will

Under Stalin, policy formulation and decision making were tightly centralized in Stalin's person: thought and action were coordinated by a single personality. Under his successors, however, the inconclusive struggle for power has resulted in the fragmentation of the decision-making structure, distributing power among various individuals and factions, each in command of parallel institutional power structures. Ideology has been divorced from policy formulation which in turn has been frequently out of phase with the administration and execution of policy as rival factions have assumed control over policy-making bodies. The fragmentation of

the decision-making structure was initially concealed by the figleaf of "collective leadership," as factional politics replaced one-man decisions in the Soviet leadership. Personalities, factions, and eventually socio-functional and socio-institutional groupings assumed a more variable role in the shaping of Soviet behavior, and a new fluid relationship was established among Soviet capabilities, ideology, personalities, and institutions in the decision-making process. While this made it even more difficult to judge Soviet intentions and predict Soviet behavior, it was compensated for by the corresponding inability of the Soviet Union to pursue the single-minded and precisely calibrated type of foreign policy which was characteristic of the Stalin era, since Soviet leaders are apparently as uncertain as Western Kremlinologists in charting the course and outcome of internal factional conflict.

Factional conflict in the Soviet hierarchy has thus introduced a new and fortuitous element in Soviet behavior, since it is by no means predictable that a given Soviet personality or faction will continue, repudiate, or modify the policies of its predecessors. Even more significantly, Soviet policy may fluctuate not only in accordance with obvious institutional and personality changes, but also with the changing equilibrium of factions within the hierarchy on a more or less continuing basis. As Soviet capabilities expand, these factional conflicts register changing and conflicting perceptions of risks involved in relation to possible returns; they represent shifting configurations of interest, both domestic and external; and finally they represent conflicting and changing sets of priorities as new choices and options proliferate out of expanded capabilities. In the absence of a stable consensus in the policy-making Politburo, the tendency in the post-Stalinist Soviet Union has been for various factions to implement their own views and policies through party or state institutions and organs under their direct administrative control, thus conveying the impression of contradictory, inconsistent, and ambivalent behavior in Soviet policy. While this is the net effect for the Soviet system as a whole, it is not necessarily true of individual groups, factions, or personalities, whose own views may be consistent and firm but who are simply unable to prevail over equally consistent and obdurate views held by other groups and individuals. The possibility of factional vacillation and ambivalence is, of course, not ruled out.

Whereas the United States has always been accustomed to self-restraint in the exercise of its power, the self-restraint introduced into Soviet behavior because of factional politics confronts Soviet leaders with a new and bewildering experience to which they have not completely adjusted. Accustomed to being guided in their behavior by the principle of "pushing to the limit," the Soviet leaders have in the past assumed that the American "ruling class" was guided by the identical principle and have behaved accordingly. It should be emphasized that Soviet behavior in this connection was encrusted in a conceptualized doctrine concerning the behavior of capitalist ruling classes which existed long before the advent of the Cold War and thus could not be explained as a spontaneous response to American behavior, except in concrete cases. Correspondingly, American decision makers have always assumed, on the basis of both Soviet doctrine and past behavior, that the Soviet leaders do not exercise self-restraint and will always "push to the limit," not recognizing that self-restraint is not entirely a subjective phenomenon, but can be imposed upon decision makers objectively as well. Hence, American decision makers have yet to adjust completely to this new departure in Soviet behavior. This element of self-restraint is not necessarily deliberate or calculated in all instances, but has also resulted from institutionalized factors such as internal power rivalries; conflicts of judgment, perception, and interests; and sheer bureaucratic inertia—i.e., the fragmentation of the decision-making process.

The fragmentation of the decision-making process combined with the erosion of Soviet ideology has produced a new element of both instability and uncertainty in Soviet behavior—an institutionalized irrationality, particularly in crisis situations.

Collective leadership, therefore, may not necessarily contribute to more rational or controlled action, but may, under certain conditions, be even more dangerous and difficult to contend with than one-man rule. Under some circumstances, collective leadership may turn out to be collective irresponsibility as decisions are made and unmade by shifting conditions or autonomous action is taken by powerful socio-institutional bodies in the face of factional paralysis or bureaucratic inertia. The deliberations of a divided oligarchy are not only secret, but anonymous as well, and can yield many surprises. In the words of Professor Leo Mates of Yugoslavia in referring to Czechoslovakia:

If it is possible for unprovoked military intervention to follow negotiations and agreement, then the danger to peace is transferred to the domain of the unpredictable, which can but leave deep traces on the general behavior of states in international relations.[36]

This suggests that if the Soviet Union could unleash massive military forces *after* tensions had been presumably dissipated, the Soviet leadership is capable of virtually any kind of rash and irresponsible behavior. More than ever, Soviet decisions in foreign policy may reflect the anxieties, fears, insecurities, and ambitions of individual factions and personalities involved in secret and faceless intrigue and maneuver. This cannot but tarnish the image of rationality, sobriety, and predictability which had emerged during the first years of the Brezhnev-Kosygin regime. We may, of course, be witnessing the disintegration of a hitherto stable equilibrium or consensus sustained by the lowest common denominator of factional interest, i.e., sheer inertia. Whether the assumption of mutual rationality which has formed the foundations of Soviet-American relations has been seriously undermined remains to be seen.

In the absence of crisis situations, whether acute or chronic, the assumption of Soviet rationality will continue to be valid. As personalities and as individual factions, the Soviet leaders appear to be a sober and calculatingly rational group, and in their separate capacities are determined, forceful, and animated by purpose. But in the absence of a stable majority or durable consensus, and with the fluidity of the decision-making process characterized by rapidly dissolving and reconstituted majorities on various issues, the behavior of the Soviet lead-

ership as a collectivity is likely to be fluctuating and inconsistent. The multiplication of divergent rational inputs can thus produce a collective irrational output. It is in this restricted sense that the real possibility of institutionalized irrationality may come to characterize Soviet behavior.

THE ADMINISTRATION AND EXECUTION OF SOVIET FOREIGN POLICY

Party Policy and State Administration: Conflict and Harmony

Responsibility for the actual *execution* of foreign policy, as distinct from its *formulation,* rests with the Council of Ministers and its Presidium, which is nominally accountable to the Supreme Soviet and its Presidium, but in fact is subordinate to the party Politburo, with which it normally shares key personnel. The relationship between the party's highest body and the Council of Ministers and its Presidium in the decision-making process, which is often ambiguous and is currently in a state of transition, depends more upon the degree of interlocking membership between the two organs than upon constitutional forms. Under Stalin, particularly after he became premier in 1941, interlocking membership was virtually complete and was designed to ensure maximum harmony between party policy and state administration. Distinctions between formulation and execution of policy were ambiguous to the point of complete irrelevance under these conditions. Before Stalin held any formal executive position in the government, the institutions of the party were the chief decision-making bodies of the regime, but with Stalin's assumption of the premiership, Stalin, the secre-

[36] Cited by Anatole Shub, "Lessons of Czechoslovakia," *Foreign Affairs* 47, no. 2 (January, 1969):267. See also Vernon V. Aspaturian, "The Aftermath of the Czech Invasion," *Current History* 55, no. 327 (November, 1968):263.

tary-general of the party, made policy, and in his capacity as premier he was also in charge of its execution and administration. As head of both party and government, he did not need to employ all the institutions of decision making, and those of the party virtually withered away. Since all diplomatic relations with the outside world are carried on through state institutions, the organs of the state had to retain sufficient vitality to legalize Stalin's decisions into formal acts of government.

The apparent rise of the state to a position superior to that of the party was undoubtedly a major factor in Malenkov's decision to succeed Stalin as premier rather than as first secretary of the party. Legally, as premier, he had under his control the two principal instruments of violence, the police and the armed forces; and thus he chose the state in preference to the party Secretariat as his instrument with which to subdue his rivals in the Presidium. The police and the army, however, turned out to be virtually separate entities, with their own informal lines of organization and loyalty, which radically departed from constitutional and legal patterns. By relinquishing control of the party Secretariat to Khrushchev in favor of the premiership, Malenkov abdicated the symbols of legitimacy in favor of the shell of power, since within the context of the party rules and institutional controls bequeathed by Stalin, the premier and the government were mere creatures of the party's will. As long as the Secretariat and the premiership are united in a single personality, relationships of control and subordination are irrelevant; but once they are separated, custom and precedent, as well as ideology, favor the Secretariat in any rivalry for supremacy.

With the eruption of factional rivalry in the Presidium and the separation of the party Secretariat from the government, interlocking membership between the Council of Ministers and the party's highest body, instead of ensuring harmony between policy and administration, in fact guaranteed conflict and friction, as the party Presidium came under the control of one faction while key administrative organs of state were in the hands of members of rival factions.

The first overt instance of conflict between party policy and state administration was Beria's attempt to thwart the decisions of the party through his control of the Ministry of Internal Affairs. Since then, both major and minor discrepancies between policy administration have taken place. Thus, while Khrushchev could muster narrow majorities in the Presidium, members of the opposition were in strategic administrative positions where they could subvert the implementation of party decisions. One of the major accusations against Foreign Minister Molotov, and also against Shepilov, was that he was using the Foreign Ministry and Soviet missions abroad to subvert and sabotage, rather than to carry out, the policies formulated by the party. Similarly, Khrushchev's plan for breaking up the concentration of economic power in Moscow was probably opposed by the managerial bureaucrats like Kaganovich, Pervukhin, and Saburov, who controlled key economic levers in the nation's industrial system and could effectively frustrate the dismantling of their own source of power and influence. Thus, before the reorganization of the Presidium in June, 1957, five of the nine members of the Presidium of the Council of Ministers were members of the opposition minority in the party Presidium. If was untenable that the minority faction in the party Presidium should enjoy a majority in the Presidium of the Council of Ministers, whose function it was to implement the very policies rejected, in the party Presidium, by a majority of its members.

The power of the Council of Ministers as a policy-making and executive institution was severely curtailed during the brief period of Bulganin's continued incumbency after the 1957 reorganization. Before June 29, 1957, the nine-man Presidium of the Council of Ministers included seven full members of the party Presidium, but after the reorganization only Bulganin and Mikoyan remained members of both bodies. The displacement of Bulganin by Khrushchev in March, 1958, marked a revival in overlapping membership in the two organs, whereby career party workers moved into top government positions. By 1961, four of the seven-man Presidium of the Council of Ministers were also members of the party Presidium. The situation became highly fluid as Khrushchev's grip on the leadership started to erode after the Twenty-second Party Congress and particularly after the Cuban missile crisis, when only four full members of the party's Presidium of twelve full members were also members of the government Presidium of twelve members.

The Constitutional Basis of Soviet Foreign Relations

Under the Soviet constitution of 1936, as amended, foreign policy is administered and executed at four different institutional levels: (1) the Presidium of the Supreme Soviet, (2) the Supreme Soviet, (3) the Council of Ministers, and (4) the Union Republics, of which there are now fifteen. Although the Soviet constitutional setup is based on the principle of complete fusion of executive, legislative, and administrative power, each institutional level is invested with certain foreign policy functions, which may be permissive, exclusive, or concurrent. These legal relationships, however, do not function in any way as limitations on Soviet diplomacy.

The Presidium of the Supreme Soviet. The Presidium of the Supreme Soviet is vested under the constitution with a wide range of ceremonial, executive, and legislative functions. Juridically a creature of the Supreme Soviet, for which it acts as legal agent, it is, in fact, its institutional superior and surrogate, since it is empowered with virtually the entire spectrum of authority granted to the Supreme Soviet during the long and frequent intervals between sessions of the Soviet legislature. Technically, all of its actions are subject to later confirmation by the Supreme Soviet, but in practice this is an empty ritual.

In the area of foreign affairs, the Presidium, in the person of its chairman, functions as the ceremonial chief of state, much like the British monarch:

In accordance with the universally recognized doctrine of international law, the supreme representation of the modern state is vested in the chief of state, whether he be an actual person (monarch, president of the republic) or a collective body (Presidium of the Supreme Soviet of the U.S.S.R., Federal Council of Switzerland). . . . As a general rule, the competence of the chief of state includes the declaration of war and conclusion of peace, nomination and reception of diplomatic agents, granting powers for the conclusion of international treaties and agreements of special significance, and the ratification and denunciation of these treaties and accords.[37]

[37] Potemkin, *Istoriya Diplomatii*, 3:765.

In its ceremonial capacity, the Presidium confers all diplomatic ranks and titles of a plenipotentiary character, formally appoints and recalls diplomatic representatives of the USSR, and receives the letters of credence and recall from foreign envoys. Although foreign representatives almost always present their credentials to the chairman of the Presidium, they are, in fact, accredited to the Presidium as a collective entity.

The Presidium's substantive powers are considerable. Article 49 of the constitution authorizes it to interpret all Soviet laws, convene and dissolve the Supreme Soviet, annul decisions and orders of the Council of Ministers, appoint and remove the higher commands of the armed forces, and issue decrees in its own right, virtually without limits. Furthermore, the Presidium, during intervals between sessions of the Supreme Soviet, "proclaims a state of war in the event of armed attack ... or whenever necessary to fulfill international treaty obligations concerning mutual defense against agression," can order general or partial mobilization, and can proclaim martial law in individual localities or throughout the country. The exercise of many of these powers is not subject to later confirmation by the Supreme Soviet, although the Presidium remains technically accountable for all its activities to the Soviet legislature, which theoretically can replace its personnel.

Certain important powers vested in the Presidium are provisional and delegated. Thus, the Presidium, during periods when the Supreme Soviet is not in session, can appoint and dismiss ministers upon the recommendation of the chairman of the Council of Ministers, but this is subject to later confirmation. Similarly, if the Presidium promulgates decrees of a fundamental nature, outside its formal constitutional competence, they also are subject to confirmation, although this may be several years later.

Although the constitution appears to give the Presidium a monopoly on the ratification and denunciation of treaties, a law of the Supreme Soviet, "On the Procedure for Ratification and Denunciation of International Treaties," passed on August 19, 1939, defines as treaties requiring its ratification the following: (1) treaties of peace, (2) mutual-defense treaties, (3) treaties of nonaggression, and (4) treaties requiring mutual ratification for their implementation.[38] By implication, and in accordance with past practice, all treaties not specifically enumerated as requiring ratification by the Presidium are left to the discretion of the Council of Ministers. On the other hand, on rare occasions the Supreme Soviet has been asked to ratify or to grant preliminary approval to particularly important treaties, although there exists no constitutional imperative.

The Supreme Soviet. As the "highest organ of state authority in the USSR," the Supreme Soviet has power under the constitution which is coterminous with that of the state.

Composed of two coordinate chambers of approximately equal size—the Council of the Union and the Council of Nationalities—the constitutional competence of the Soviet legislature in foreign affairs surpasses that of any other organ. In practice, it has abdicated most of its powers to the Presidium and has been left only with the empty shell of ceremony, which may sometimes border on consultation. Both chambers are equally potent or impotent, singly or together, and nei-

[38] *Second Session of the Supreme Soviet of the U.S.S.R.* (New York: International Publishers Co. 1938), p. 678.

ther has specific functions or powers denied the other.

The formal authority of the Supreme Soviet in foreign policy falls into seven categories: (1) the enactment of basic legislation and constitutional amendments; (2) the confirmation of the decisions and decrees of the Presidium and the Council of Ministers; (3) ratification of selected treaties; (4) declaration of war and peace; (5) confirmation and authorization of territorial changes and of the creation, admission, promotion, demotion, and abolition of republics; (6) hearing and approving of foreign policy reports delivered by the premier or the foreign minister; and (7) the preliminary examination of treaties prior to ratification by the Presidium. Since Stalin's death, all these activities have been accorded greater publicity.

The sessions of the Supreme Soviet are short. Between 1946 and 1954, the Supreme Soviet sat for a total of only forty-five days, the longest session lasting seven days (June, 1950), the shortest sixty-seven minutes (March, 1953); its performance before and during World War II was even less auspicious. By far the most significant function of the Supreme Soviet is to hear reports on the foreign policy of the government. It is customary, but by no means the invariable rule, that the foreign minister review the government's foreign policy before this body, usually before joint sessions. It listens attentively and enacts the desired legislation. There is "discussion," but a close examination of the official records discloses not a single note of criticism, to say nothing of a negative vote, in all the deliberations of the Supreme Soviet.

In the words of *Kommunist*, "until recently [the Supreme Soviet's] sessions concerned for the most part consideration of budget questions and approval of the decrees of the Presidium"[39]; but after the replacement of Malenkov with Bulganin in 1955, it was given a more conspicuous role in foreign affairs. At that time, the Supreme Soviet issued an appeal to the parliaments of other countries for a program of parliamentary exchanges in the form of visiting delegations addressing each other's legislatures; more than a dozen such exchanges have taken place. In July, 1955, the Supreme Soviet adhered to the Inter-Parliamentary Union (ITU) and sent a delegation to its forty-fourth annual conference in Helsinki.

Although the two Foreign Affairs Commissions of the two chambers of the Supreme Soviet are supposed to make "a preliminary examination of all matters connected with foreign affairs to be considered by the Supreme Soviet (and its Presidium)," this function had all but withered away, and the existence of these bodies was rendered virtually superfluous. They were suddenly brought back to life when the Soviet-Iranian agreement of 1954, the denunciation of the Anglo-Soviet and Anglo-French treaties of alliance, the Warsaw Pact, and the agreement to establish diplomatic relations with West Germany were all submitted to joint sessions of the two commissions (the Supreme Soviet was not in session) for consideration. After hearing reports by Molotov and his deputies, they recommended approval to the Presidium of the Supreme Soviet. At about the same time, the two chairmen of the chambers, together with reputedly prominent members of the two commissions, appeared at diplomatic receptions, received foreign dignitaries, and pompously pontificated on foreign policy in patent, but bogus, imitation of their counterparts in the U.S. Congress.

[39] *Kommunist,* August, 1956, no. 10, pp. 3–15.

It was the Supreme Soviet which proclaimed an end to the state of war with Germany, on January 25, 1955. On August 4, 1955, it was called into special session to hear Bulganin's report on the summit conference at Geneva, a procedure that had not been used since Molotov addressed a special session on the Nazi-Soviet Pact of 1939. On this same occasion, the Supreme Soviet, after "debating" the policy of the government and "interpellating" the foreign minister, issued an appeal to the parliaments and governments of the world to "put an end to the arms race." The regular session of the Supreme Soviet coincided with the return of Bulganin and Khrushchev from their tour of Southeast Asia, and both addressed the Supreme Soviet on the results of their trip.

Although the activities of the Supreme Soviet have been stepped up, there is little reason to believe that there has been a corresponding enhancement of its influence and power. It hears more reports on foreign policy, but it has also retained its absolute unanimity. The invocation of the formal prerogatives of the Supreme Soviet, however, is no idle exercise, since it creates certain advantages for Soviet diplomacy: (1) it serves to infuse the citizenry with the notion that their representatives participate in the formulation of foreign policy decisions; (2) as a propagandistic maneuver, it strives to create the illusion of evolving constitutionalism in the Soviet system; (3) as a purely diplomatic device, it permits the Kremlin to invoke constitutional procedures as a stumbling or delaying mechanism in negotiations, and affords a basis for demanding reciprocal action in the ratification of treaties and other diplomatic instruments.

The possibility, no matter how slight, that ceremony may some day be replaced with substance cannot be ignored, but this expectation must yield to the realization that the flurry of activity we have noted can be arrested as abruptly as it began. Yet it must be stated that periodic suggestions are made in the Soviet press that the Supreme Soviet be given more legislative authority.

The Council of Ministers. As the "highest executive and administrative organ" of the government, the Council of Ministers[40] "exercises general supervision" over the execution and administration of the country's foreign policy, and also directs the state's foreign trade monopoly. Constitutionally, since 1944 the central government no longer exercises a monopoly over foreign affairs, but merely represents the Soviet Union as a whole and establishes the "general procedure in mutual relations between the Union Republics and foreign states," and thus shares the conduct of diplomacy with its fifteen constituent republics. In practice, however, foreign policy in the Soviet Union is the most tightly centralized activity of the Soviet government.

The Council of Ministers has the power to (1) grant or withdraw recognition of new states or governments; (2) sever and restore diplomatic relations; (3) order acts of reprisal against other states; (4) appoint negotiators and supervise the negotiation of international treaties and agreements; (5) declare the adherence of the Soviet Union to international conventions not requiring formal ratification; (6) conclude agreements not requiring ratification with other heads of governments (similar to American executive and administrative agreements); (7) ratify all treaties and agreements not requiring ratifica-

[40] Formerly the Council of People's Commissars, or *Sovnarkom.*

tion of the Presidium; (8) make preliminary examination of all treaties submitted to the Presidium for its ratification; (9) oversee "the current work of the diplomatic organs, effectually direct that work and take the necessary measures in that field"; and (10) appoint and accredit all diplomats below plenipotentiary rank and foreign trade representatives.[41]

Actually, there appears to be a great area of overlapping activity between the Presidium and the Council of Ministers in the conduct of diplomacy, and were it not for the fact that the one-party system makes all basic decisions, rivalries and jealousies would almost certainly develop between these two organs, rendering coordination of diplomatic activity virtually impossible.

(a) The Chairman and his Cabinet. The most influential member of the Council of Ministers is its chairman, referred to in the West as the *premier,* who is always an important figure of the highest rank in the party hierarchy. This office, under the present and previous constitutions, has been filled by only eight men since the establishment of the Soviet state: Lenin (1917–1924); Rykov (1924–1930); Molotov (1930–1941); Stalin (1941–1953); Malenkov (1953–1955); Bulganin (1955–1958); Khrushchev (1958–1964); and Kosygin (1964–   ). Immediately after Lenin's death, when Stalin refused to hold formal office, this post was reduced to a mere shadow of the secretary-general of the party; but after Stalin assumed formal responsibility for the policies of the government in 1941, the post reassumed its former prestige and power. The rivalries that were unleashed

after Stalin's death in 1953 temporarily revived the division of power between the premier and first secretary of the party, and the two positions were again separated, then reunited, and later reseparated. Khrushchev's assumption of the office after Bulganin's resignation reflected the internal and external symbolic significance which it acquired during Stalin's long tenure as well as the fact that it was too risky to permit it to be separately occupied.

The sundering of the two positions, in October, 1964, reflected once again a division of power in the Soviet leadership. The post of premier serves to legitimize and legalize the power of the first secretary, just as the latter imparts to the premiership the necessary ideological sanctity. The position suffered another setback with Khrushchev's ouster and the restoration of the title of secretary general, but the premiership will continue to exert an attraction to any secretary general.

The chairman (premier) has primary responsibility for the conduct of foreign policy and, presumably, the authority to appoint and remove the ministers concerned with its day-to-day execution. Immediately below the chairman are his first deputy chairmen and deputy chairmen, who normally are in charge of specific ministries, or may be without portfolio. The chairman, his first deputies, and his deputies constitute the Presidium (cabinet) of the Council of Ministers.

The Presidium has undergone serious transformations in size and composition in recent years, varying in size by more than a dozen members. Under Stalin the Presidium became so large that a Bureau (inner cabinet) of the Presidium was secretly organized, the composition and membership of which have never been made public. After Stalin's death, the Bureau of the Presidium was technically

---

41 See A. Y. Vyshinsky, *The Law of the Soviet State* (New York: Macmillan Co., 1948), p. 376; Potemkin, *Istoriya Diplomatii,* 3:767–68, 806–7.

abolished, but, in fact, the Presidium was reduced to the smaller size of the Bureau.

The Council of Ministers and its Presidium are actually subordinate to the party Politburo and, in theory, to the Supreme Soviet and its Presidium. If the premier of the government loses a vote of confidence in the Politburo, the decision is reviewed by the Central Committee; if it is upheld there, he submits his resignation to the Presidium of the Supreme Soviet. The Central Committee, through its first secretary, nominates the next premier to the appropriate state organs and a new government is thus formed.

Since the formation of the Bulganin government, the premier and other key members of the Presidium of the Council of Ministers have played an increasingly personal and active role in the country's diplomacy. This pattern was further accelerated after Khrushchev became premier. Not only the premier but also important ministers and the chairman of the Presidium of the Supreme Soviet have made state visits to many countries as a part of the Kremlin's new diplomatic offensive. Kosygin and Brezhnev introduced a division of labor in international affairs, each assuming individual personal roles in Soviet diplomacy. While he was foreign minister, Molotov played an active personal role in the country's diplomacy, but he apparently objected to the interference of the other members of the government in Soviet diplomatic activity. In particular, he objected to the travels of Bulganin and Khrushchev and their meetings with the heads of various governments.

(b) The foreign minister. In forty years of Soviet diplomacy, there have been only seven foreign ministers: Leon Trotsky (November, 1917–April, 1918); Georgi Chicherin (1918–1929);

Maxim Litvinov (1929–1939); Vyacheslav Molotov (1939–1949 and 1953–1956); Andrei Vyshinsky (1949–1953); Dimitri Shepilov (during 1956); and Andrei Gromyko (1957–   ). The typical tenure of a Soviet foreign minister is ten years, and nearly forty-five years of Soviet diplomacy have been directed by only four individuals, thus giving Soviet diplomacy an enviable continuity—except for a few years after Stalin's death, when the changes reflected the bitter conflicts that have raged over foreign policy in the past few years.

The foreign minister's influence depends almost entirely upon his party rank. When the foreign minister is of relatively low rank in the party, he is little more than a caretaker of the department. If he is of top party rank, as Trotsky and Molotov were, he participates in the decisions he is asked to execute and, in at least two cases (Molotov and Shepilov), he has actually flouted the will of the decision makers. Chicherin and Litvinov, like Gromyko, were relatively low-ranking members in the party hierarchy, although this by no means indicates that they were less effective as diplomats. There is ample evidence to suggest that the party leaders would prefer a low-ranking party member as foreign minister to one of first rank (except under critical circumstances), since it enhances the flexibility of Soviet diplomacy while hampering that of other countries, who are forced to accommodate their diplomacy to the bureaucratic channels of the Soviet Foreign Office. Normally, the foreign minister is at least a full member of the Central Committee, although both Chicherin and Litvinov achieved that status some time after they had become foreign commissars. Gromyko was elevated to full membership only at the Twentieth Party Congress. Trotsky and Molotov were the only foreign ministers who were full members of the party's highest body; Vyshinsky and Shepilov were alternate members of the Presidium during their incumbency.

The Ministry of Foreign Affairs

Evolution of the Foreign Ministry. The Ministry of Foreign Affairs,[42] the government department directly charged with the day-to-day administration of Soviet diplomacy, does not materially differ in its structure and organization from its counterparts in the other Great Powers, although its evolution is unique. Since its establishment, it has undergone a triple metamorphosis.

In the beginning, its primary purpose was to trigger a world revolution and thus create the conditions for its own extinction. It was thought that if the world revolution failed, a Soviet diplomacy would be impossible, and, if it succeeded, unnecessary. It was Leon Trotsky's boast: "I will issue a few revolutionary proclamations to the people of the world, and then close up shop."[43] On November 26, 1917, a decree from Trotsky's Foreign Affairs Commissariat virtually disestablished the diplomatic apparatus of the Russian state: all members of the Russian foreign service abroad were summarily dismissed unless they expressed loyalty to the Bolshevik regime. In their places, Bolshevik émigrés abroad were appointed as "unofficial" agents of the new government (Litvinov was such an appointee to Great Britain). Trotsky even neglected to establish a permanent home office; he appeared at his office only once—to dismiss all employees reluctant to pledge loyalty to the new re-

gime and to set up a committee to publish the secret treaties in the archives of the Russian Foreign Office.

The Treaty of Brest-Litovsk imposed upon the new regime diplomatic relations with Germany and its allies, so the Council of People's Commissars was forced to re-create a provisional diplomatic service. With obvious petulance, in a decree of June 4, 1917, it attempted to rewrite unilaterally the principle of diplomatic ranks adopted by the Congress of Vienna in 1815, by abolishing all Soviet diplomatic titles in favor of a single designation, "plenipotentiary representative" (*Polpred*). In a naïve attempt to impose Soviet egalitarian principles upon foreign envoys, the decree peremptorily announced that "all diplomatic agents of foreign states . . . shall be considered equal plenipotentiary representatives regardless of their rank."[44]

Pending the eventual liquidation of the Foreign Affairs Commissariat, the functions of Soviet diplomacy during this initial period fell into three principal categories: (1) the publication of "secret treaties" in order to expose the duplicity and hypocrisy of the Allies and compromise them in the eye of their own people; (2) the conduct of necessary negotiations and diplomatic relations, on a temporary basis, with those capitalist states in a position to impose them; and (3) the utilization of Soviet embassies and legations abroad as centers of revolutionary propaganda, conspiracy, and activity (in clear violation of treaty obligations). In this connection, the Soviet government announced that

the Council of People's Commissars considers it necessary to offer assistance by all possible means . . . to the left interna-

[42] Formerly the People's Commissariat for Foreign Affairs, or *Narkomindel.*

[43] Quoted in E. H. Carr, *The Bolshevik Revolution, 1917–1923* (London: Macmillan & Co., 1953), 3:16.

[44] Full text in T. A. Taracouzio, *The Soviet Union and International Law* (New York: Macmillan Co., 1936), p. 383.

tionalist wing of the labor movement of all countries [and] . . . for this purpose . . . decides to allocate two million rubles for the needs of the revolutionary international movement and to put this sum at the disposal of the foreign representatives of the Commissariat for Foreign Affairs.[45]

The failure of the revolution to spread beyond Russia, the success of the seceding border states in maintaining their independence, and the failure of foreign intervention to subdue the Bolshevik regime forced the expansion of diplomatic contact with the bourgeois world. By 1921 the Soviet foreign office was prepared to pass out of its initial phase into its second, as a quasi-permanent agency for "normalizing" relations with the capitalist powers on the basis of "mutual interests" during the prolonged period of "coexistence" which Lenin now recognized as the inevitable interval between the first and final stages of the world revolution. From an instrument of world revolution, the foreign office was converted into an instrument for furthering the interests of the Soviet state.

Since the revolutionary and conspiratorial activities of Soviet diplomats complicated the establishment of desirable trade and political connections with the bourgeois world, the new commissar of foreign affairs, Georgi Chicherin (who succeeded Trotsky in April, 1918), was instrumental in shifting the function of revolutionary agitation from the foreign office to the party. A new diplomatic service was organized from scratch by Chicherin, and shortly after he assumed office the Foreign Commissariat was organized into more than a dozen departments. The first "Statute on the Commissariat for For-

eign Affairs" was issued by the Council of Ministers on July 6, 1921; it defined the sphere of competence of each of the departments. After the formation of the Union and the centralization of diplomacy in Moscow, the commissariat on November 12, 1923, received its definite statute which still constitutes the juridical basis for the organization and structure of the Foreign Ministry. However, it was not until 1924 that Soviet diplomacy was juridically relieved of its revolutionary mission and entered into its current phase. According to a decree issued November 21, 1924, and still effective:

It goes without saying that diplomatic missions abroad are appointed by each of the parties establishing diplomatic relations for purposes which exclude propaganda in the country to which they are accredited. The Soviet diplomatic missions follow and are to follow this principle with absolute strictness.[46]

Although, technically, the Soviet foreign office is supervised by the Council of Ministers, it has always enjoyed a unique, direct relationship with the party Presidium. Unlike the other departments of government in the new Bolshevik regime, the Foreign Commissariat was unencumbered with holdovers from the old bureaucracy, Chicherin being the only prominent figure who had previous diplomatic experience. Consequently, from the very beginning, it was cherished by Lenin:

The diplomatic apparatus . . . is quite exceptional in the governmental apparatus. We excluded everyone from the old Tsarist apparatus who formerly had even the slightest influence. Here, the whole apparatus, insofar as it possesses the slightest influence, has been made up of Com-

[45] Jane Degras, ed., *Soviet Documents on Foreign Policy* (London: Royal Institute of International Affairs, 1951), 1:22.

[46] Full text in Taracouzio, *The Soviet Union and International* Law, pp. 389–90.

munists. For this reason this apparatus has acquired for itself . . . the reputation of a Communist apparatus which has been tested and cleansed of the old Tsarist bourgeois and petty bourgeois apparatus to a degree incomparably higher than that attained in the apparatus with which we have to be satisfied in the other people's commissariats.[47]

This quality, in the words of a Soviet diplomat, "helped make it a peculiarly well-fitted apparatus for the expression of new policies."[48]

The statute governing the Foreign Affairs Commissariat, decreed on November 12, 1923, which has been frequently amended but never superseded, defined its principal duties as follows:

(a) The defence of the political and economic interests of the U.S.S.R. . . . (b) The conclusion of treaties and agreements with foreign countries in accordance with the decisions of the government. (c) Supervision over the proper execution of treaties and agreements concluded with foreign states, and enabling the corresponding organs of the U.S.S.R. and the Union Republics to exercise rights conferred by these treaties. (d) Supervision over the execution by the competent organs of treaties, agreements, and accords concluded with foreign states.[49]

The Foreign Minister and his Collegium. The administration of the Foreign Commissariat was initially entrusted to a collegium in accordance with the Bolshevik principle of collective responsibility. The foreign commissar was forced to share authority and responsibility with a board of three or four other senior officials of the commissariat.

With the promulgation of the first constitution in March, 1918, the germ of one-man management was implanted, when the commissar was invested with the personal power of decision relating to matters within the competence of his department, with the provision that if a decision conflicted with the views of the collegium, the latter, without the power of stopping execution of the decision, could appeal its differences to the Council of Ministers or to the Presidium. As a consequence, collective responsibility became a convenient evasion of concrete responsibility, and the collegium frequently abused its powers by issuing orders in its own name, thus lowering the prestige and personal responsibility of the foreign commissar.

By 1934, defects of collective responsibility became so serious that Stalin condemned the collective principle as obsolete and subversive of efficient administration; the collegium was abolished and the foreign minister given complete charge of his department; in turn, he assumed full personal responsibility for its work.

Four years later, in March, 1938, the collegium was restored in modified form, but was clearly divested of its former tyrannical power over the commissar. The Council of Ministers, which was too large and unwieldy as a decision-making or even advisory body, was retained as a convenient institution for the diffusion of policy and administrative decisions, and the collegium retained its character as the executive committee of the commissariat. The commissar retained his

[47] *New York Times,* July 1, 1956. Extract is from suppressed Lenin documents distributed at the Twentieth Party Congress and later made public.
[48] Alexi F. Neymann, in *The Soviet Union and World Problems,* ed. S. N. Harper (Chicago: Chicago University Press, 1935), p. 279.
[49] The full text of this statute, with amendments through 1927, is reprinted in *Yezhegodnik Narodnovo Komissariata Po Inostrannym Delam Na 1928 God* (Moscow, 1928), pp. 182–93. All subsequent references and extracts refer to this text. See also Potemkin, *Istoriya Diplomatii,* 3:770–71.

plenary authority and responsibility, but the formal prerogatives of the collegium remained considerable.[50]

The institutional relationship established in 1938 between the foreign minister and his collegium has survived, substantially unaltered, till now. The size and composition of the collegium appear to vary, depending upon the discretion of the foreign minister (except in unusual circumstances), although appointments to the collegium continue to be made by the Council of Ministers. The collegium is presided over by the minister or one of his first deputies. It includes not only the first deputy and deputy ministers, but also about four to six senior officials in the department, one of whom frequently is the chief of the Press and Information Division. The number of first deputies has varied from one to three; their rank roughly corresponds to that of the undersecretary in the American State Department. Immediately below the first deputies are the deputies, whose rank corresponds to that of assistant secretaries in the American hierarchy; there may be up to six deputies (in 1966 there was one first deputy and six deputies). The other members of the collegium are normally department heads. Thus, the size of the collegium may vary by more than a dozen members.

The institutional prerogatives of the collegium fall just short of the power of actual decision, but without weakening in any way the full responsibility of the minister. It cannot overrule the minister's decisions, nor issue orders in its own name, but it is mandatory for the minister to report any disagreement with his collegium to the Council of Ministers for disposition. The collegium retains the

right, individually or collectively, to appeal to the Council of Ministers or to the Central Committee of the party.[51]

The Organization and Structure of the Foreign Ministry. The basic organization and structure of the Soviet Foreign Ministry remain governed by the statute of 1923, which established a flexible system of administration, permitting a wide latitude for internal reorganization at the discretion of the minister. The ministry is organized into "divisions according to the main geographical divisions of the world and the main functions of the department and . . . this apparatus both in its offices in Moscow and its missions in foreign countries does not present any striking differences in structure compared with similar departments in other countries."[52]

At the apex of the ministry stands the minister with his collegium, which is provided with a central secretariat —headed by a secretary general— performing routine secretarial and staff administrative work for the minister, his deputies, and other members of the collegium. The functional divisions, which have become increasingly differentiated with the expansion of Soviet diplomatic activity, have been conventional: Protocol, Political Archives, Courier and Liaison, Passport and Visa, Treaty and Legal, Economic, Consular Affairs, Administration, Personnel, Finance, Supplies, and Press and Information. Several related functional divisions are grouped together and supervised by deputy ministers, and perhaps also by other collegium members. As Soviet power and influence in international affairs has increased, the functional

50 See Vyshinsky, *The Law of the Soviet State,* pp. 387–89.

51 Ibid.
52 Neymann, in Harper, *The Soviet Union and World Problems,* pp. 226–27.

divisions have undergone substantial expansion in recent years. There are now seven functional divisions: Protocol, Press, Treaty and Legal, Consular Administration, Archives Administration, Personnel Administration, and Administration for Servicing the Diplomatic Corps. In addition, attached to the Foreign Ministry are two training institutions, the Institute of International Relations and the Higher Diplomatic School. The old Economic Division has since proliferated into a separate ministry called the State Committee for Foreign Economic Relations, which is in charge of the extensive Soviet foreign aid program. Two other ministries closely related to the Foreign Ministry are the old Ministry of Foreign Trade and the State Committee for Cultural Relations with Foreign Countries.

The political changes of the past twenty years, the massive expansion of Soviet diplomatic relations, and the creation of many new states in Asia and Africa have profoundly affected the internal organization of the foreign office. In the past few years, the number of geographical divisions has been increased, while the number of functional divisions has remained fairly constant. As compiled from press accounts, there are now eight "Western" divisions and eight "Eastern" divisions, plus two separate departments for international organizations and international economic organizations. The present geographical divisions, which closely resemble those of 1925, are as follows:

Western divisions

1. United States of America Division
2. Latin American Countries Division
3. First European Division (France, Benelux, Italy)
4. Second European Division (United Kingdom and white Commonwealth countries)

5. Third European Division (the two Germanies, Austria, Switzerland)
6. Fourth European Division (Poland and Czechoslovakia)
7. Fifth European Division (Balkan countries)
8. Sixth European Division (Scandinavian countries and Finland)

Eastern divisions

1. First African Division (North African states with the exception of Egypt and Sudan)
2. Second African Division (black African states)
3. Third African Division (black African states)
4. Near Eastern Countries Division
5. Middle Eastern Countries Division
6. South Asian Countries Division
7. Southeast Asian Countries Division
8. Far Eastern Countries Division (China, Mongolia, North Korea, and Japan)

Normally, a deputy minister exercises general administrative supervision over the work of several contiguous geographical divisions, and usually he is a former ambassador with diplomatic experience in the geographical area in question.

The appearance of kindred communist states in Eastern Europe and in the Far East has not modified the geographical divisions of the ministry. Relations with communist countries through the Foreign Ministry, however, have been reduced to the bare minimum required by international law and protocol, since substantive and policy questions are handled through corresponding party organizations. Soviet envoys to other important communist countries are considered primarily as functionaries and emissaries from the party, and secondarily as government agents. This has been confirmed and emphasized since Stalin's death, with the adoption of the practice of dispatching high party functionaries as ambassadors to other important communist states.

In view of the deterioration of relations with China, however, party relations between the two countries have virtually ceased, and contact has been limited almost exclusively to formal state relations. Already in 1959, Moscow had replaced a highly placed party official (Yudin) functioning as the Soviet ambassador with Chervonenko, a lower-level party functionary. And in April, 1965, Chervonenko was replaced by a career diplomat, S. G. Lapin, who is not even a candidate member of the Central Committee. Lapin was withdrawn to become head of Tass, the Soviet news agency, in 1967, at the height of China's Great Proletarian Cultural Revolution, when the Soviet embassy was barricaded and its personnel abused and insulted by the rampaging Red Guards. Peking also withdrew its ambassador, and relations were not restored until late 1970, when V. S. Tolstikov, a veteran party functionary and member of the Central Committee since 1961, was appointed to Peking. Tolstikov's party ranking, nearer Chervonenko's level than Yudin's, is nevertheless sufficiently high to suggest that Moscow would prefer to employ him as a conduit to the Chinese party as well as state, in line with its general diplomatic pattern of relations with other communist countries. In sum, there is little question but that the party standing of Soviet ambassadors to other communist countries is indicative of the state of party relations existing between them.

The Soviet Diplomatic Service. The decree of 1918 reducing all diplomatic ranks to the single and equal rank of plenipotentiary representative remained technically in force until 1941, although it was neither possible nor desirable to honor it in practice. The principle of diplomatic equality was based on the discarded theory that "the representatives of . . . the U.S.S.R. do not personify a quasi-mythical Leviathan state, but only . . . the plenipotentiary of the ruling class," and that diplomats from bourgeois countries were likewise emissaries of their ruling classes.[53] This view was condemned as doctrinaire and subversive of Soviet prestige and diplomacy since, in practice, it amounted to unilateral renunciation of all the privileges and prerogatives of seniority and rank under traditional norms of diplomatic intercourse.

Soviet diplomacy gradually accommodated itself to existing international practice through the extralegal exchange of supplementary protocols granting informal recognition of rank, so that Soviet diplomats might avoid forfeiting recognized privileges accorded those of rank and seniority. On May 9, 1941, the Presidium issued a decree establishing three diplomatic categories: (1) ambassador extraordinary and plenipotentiary, (2) minister extraordinary and plenipotentiary, and (3) chargé d'affaires. This decree gave legal sanction to de facto distinctions. Two years later, on May 28, 1943, the Presidium decreed the establishment of eleven grades in the diplomatic service and thus brought Soviet diplomatic ranking into complete focus with general diplomatic practice: (1) ambassador extraordinary and plenipotentiary; (2) minister extraordinary and plenipotentiary of the first class; (3) minister extraordinary and plenipotentiary of the second class; (4) counselor, first class; (5) counselor, second class; (6) first secretary, first class; (7) first secretary, second class; (8) second secretary, first class; (9) second secretary, second class; (10)

[53] E. Korovin, *Mezhdunarodnoye Pravo Perekhodnovo Vremeni* (Moscow, 1924), p. 63.

third secretary; and (11) attaché.[54]

As a rule, Soviet career diplomats do not rank very high in the party hierarchy. The foreign minister is at least a full member of the Central Committee and frequently a member or alternate member of the Presidium. First deputies are normally full members of the Central Committee, while career diplomats rarely achieve higher status than candidate membership in the Central Committee.

Since Stalin's death, the Soviet diplomatic service has been subjected to a unique infusion of new personnel. Alongside members of the career service, who serve as diplomatic technicians, there now exist numerous high-ranking ministry officials and diplomats who are primarily state administrators and party functionaries who appear to correspond to the political appointee in the American diplomatic hierarchy. The transfer of high party officials and state administrators into the diplomatic service has gone through four distinct phases since Stalin's death, corresponding to the principal milestones in the struggle for power after 1953. Each time a major change in the power equilibrium took place in the Presidium, party officials have been shifted to diplomatic work. Consequently, the most obvious trend is that the Foreign Ministry is once again being used as a convenient post of exile from the centers of political power for party bureaucrats wounded in the power struggles. A second trend is the assignment of career party bureaucrats—not all of them in disgrace—to other communist capitals, which has resulted in the formation of a distinct parallel diplomatic pattern which serves to combine both party and state relations in the communist orbit. A third new trend is that a min-

istry long under the control of Molotov and exposed to the temptations of the outside world is being placed under quasi surveillance and provided with party ballast.

Since 1953, not counting Molotov and the late A. Y. Vyshinsky, no less than six full members and five alternate members of the party Presidium elected in 1952 have been shifted to the diplomatic service, most of whom are still there. Many of these new party diplomats enjoy higher party rank than their technical superior, Foreign Minister Gromyko, and they constitute a distinct cluster of party luminaries who outshine any combination of career diplomats. The year 1958 represented the high-water mark of party infusion into the Foreign Ministry, when Gromyko's two first deputy ministers and at least six of his ambassadors appeared to outrank him in the party galaxy, although in most cases their stars were in decline. Five of these new diplomats were admitted to the party Central Committee in 1939, the same year in which Gromyko entered the diplomatic service as a junior official.

Since 1958 some of the party officials have worked themselves back into the party apparatus, others have died, and some have been appointed to quasi-diplomatic ministerial positions. None have fully recovered their former party eminence, while additional party and government officials have been shifted to diplomatic careers.

The Channels of Soviet Diplomacy. It is general practice for Soviet envoys to report to the ministry through routine bureaucratic channels—that is, through the appropriate geographical divisions in the ministry—but ambassadors in important posts frequently report directly to the foreign minister. Reports of an exceptionally important character are also sent directly to the

---

[54] See Potemkin, *Istoriya Diplomatii,* 3: 778–80. The date of the decree is mistakenly given as June 14, 1943, in this work.

foreign minister or his first deputies, rather than through normal channels. The close supervision of the diplomatic service by the party center cannot be overemphasized; and diplomatic channels remain deliberately flexible.

Not all Soviet representatives abroad report to the Foreign Ministry. Envoys to other communist states, particularly those holding high party rank, probably report to the Central Committee or the Presidium, except for reports of essentially protocol or legalistic significance, which are funneled through normal channels. The jurisdiction of the Foreign Ministry over envoys to communist countries appears marginal at best.

Although the ambassador, as the chief legal representative of the Soviet Union in foreign countries, is charged with general supervision over the activities of Soviet representatives and missions abroad to ensure that they are in accord with the general policy of the government, this responsibility is often of little more than formal or legal significance. According to defectors like Igor Gouzenko and Vladimir Petrov, Soviet missions abroad are organized into five separate divisions, each with separate and independent channels of communication: (1) the ambassador and his staff, reporting directly to the Ministry of Foreign Affairs; (2) the commercial counsellor, reporting to the Ministry of Foreign Trade; (3) the secret police representative, disguised as a minor diplomat, reporting directly to the foreign section of the Security Ministry (now Security Committee); (4) the attachés, reporting directly to the director of military intelligence in Moscow; (5) the party representative, also disguised as a minor diplomatic functionary, communicating directly with the foreign section of the Central Committee of the party.

All of these representatives, with the exception of the ambassador and the embassy staff proper, may be actively engaged in the overt or clandestine collection of intelligence information. In order to comply with the letter of their agreements with foreign countries, the ambassador is scrupulously insulated from all knowledge of illegal espionage activities organized by the other sections, and although the Foreign Ministry statute gives him the power to determine whether their activities are in accordance with government policy, in practice the ambassador rarely sees the reports dispatched by the other sections through their respective channels.

In addition to espionage and intelligence activities, the secret police and party sections maintain general surveillance over the other members of the mission and over each other. If the accounts of high-ranking defectors from the diplomatic and police service are accurate, Soviet missions abroad are often centers of intrigue, personal vendettas, and institutional rivalries and jealousies.

Information coming through various channels is screened, coordinated, and evaluated by a special agency of the Central Committee, which then submits its reports to the Presidium to be used as a factor in the formulation of foreign policy and in the making of decisions.

As instruments, rather than makers of policy, Soviet professional diplomats play a minor role in the formulation of foreign policy. Their work is essentially technical and legalistic; their reports are concerned primarily, if not exclusively, with observations and suggestions for more effective implementation of existing policy. Their area of initiative is carefully circumscribed, and often they are ignorant of the exact intentions of their superiors in the Kremlin. Their reports constitute but a minute fraction of the information on which the Presidium acts, and final disposition of all information from routine diplomatic channels and intelligence sources is made by the Presidium as it sees fit. As Merle Fainsod points out, accurate evaluation of information in the Soviet Union is often subjected to special hazards:

The mountains of material have to be reduced to manageable proportions before they are brought to the attention of the leadership. What the rulers read reflects the selection and emphasis of an editorial staff which may be guided by its own preconditioning as well as its sensitivity to the anticipated reactions of its readers. The tendency to embrace data that confirm established predilections while rejecting the unpalatable facts that offend one's preconceptions is a weakness . . . [to] which . . . totalitarian societies appear to be particularly susceptible. . . . Every dictatorship has a tendency to breed sycophancy and discourage independence in its bureaucratic hierarchy. When the pronouncements of the dictator are sacred and unchallengeable, the words which subordinates must throw back at him tend to flatter his whims rather than challenge his analyses. . . . The ideological screen through which facts are received, filtered, and appraised constitutes an additional possibility of misrepresentation. . . . Not even the most pragmatically oriented member of the ruling group can wholly liberate himself from the frame of responses that represent the residue of a lifetime in Communist thought patterns.[55]

Khrushchev's explanation of why Stalin ignored repeated warnings, from Churchill and from his own efficient espionage networks, that the Nazis were planning to attack the Soviet Union appears to confirm Fainsod's perceptive appraisal when he revealed that "information of this sort

concerning the threat of German armed invasion of Soviet territory was coming in also from our own military and diplomatic sources . . . [but] because the leadership was conditioned against such information, such data were dispatched with fear and assessed with reservation."

SELECTED BIBLIOGRAPHY

ASPATURIAN, VERNON V. *Process and Power in Soviet Foreign Policy*. Boston: Little, Brown and Co., 1971.

————. *The Union Republics in Soviet Diplomacy*. Paris: Libraire Droz, 1960.

BARGHOORN, F. C. *The Soviet Cultural Offensive*. Princeton: Princeton University Press, 1960.

————. *The Soviet Image of the United States*. New York: Harcourt, Brace & World, 1950.

————. *Soviet Russian Nationalism*. New York: Oxford University Press, 1956.

BELOFF, MAX. *The Foreign Policy of Soviet Russia, 1929–1941*. New York: Royal Institute of International Affairs, 1947.

————. *Soviet Policy in the Far East, 1944–1951*. London: Royal Institute of International Affairs, 1953.

CARR, E. H. *The Bolshevik Revolution, 1917–1923*. Vol. 3. London: Macmillan & Co., 1953.

————. *German-Soviet Relations between the Two World Wars*. Baltimore: Johns Hopkins Press, 1951.

DALLIN, ALEXANDER, ed. *Soviet Conduct in World Affairs*. New York: Columbia University Press, 1960.

DALLIN, D. J. *Soviet Espionage*. New Haven: Yale University Press, 1955.

————. *Soviet Foreign Policy After Stalin*. New York: J. B. Lippincott Co., 1961.

DEGRAS, JANE, ed. *Soviet Documents on Foreign Policy*. 3 vols. New York: Oxford University Press, 1951–1953.

DEUTSCHER, I. *Stalin*. New York: Oxford University Press, 1949.

DINERSTEIN, HERBERT. *War and the Soviet Union*. 2d ed. New York: Praeger, 1963.

[55] Fainsod, *How Russia Is Ruled*, p. 283.

FAINSOD, M. *How Russia Is Ruled.* 2d ed. Cambridge: Harvard University Press, 1963.

FISCHER, LOUIS. *Russia's Road From Peace to War.* New York: Harper & Row, 1969.

———. *The Soviets in World Affairs.* 2 vols. Princeton: Princeton University Press, 1951.

HILGER, G., and MEYER, A. G. *The Incompatible Allies.* New York: Macmillan Co., 1953.

HORELICK, ARNOLD, and RUSH, MYRON. *Strategic Power and Soviet Foreign Policy.* Chicago: Chicago University Press, 1966.

KEEP, JOHN, ed. *Contemporary History in the Soviet Mirror.* New York: Praeger, 1965.

KENNAN, GEORGE. *Soviet Foreign Policy Under Lenin and Stalin.* Boston: Little, Brown and Co., 1961.

KULSKI, W. W. *Peaceful Co-existence.* Chicago: Henry Regnery Co., 1959.

LAQUEUR, WALTER. *Russia and Germany.* Boston: Little, Brown and Co., 1965.

LEITES, NATHAN. *A Study of Bolshevism.* New York: Free Press, 1953.

MACKINTOSH, J. M. *Strategy and Tactics of Soviet Foreign Policy.* New York: Oxford University Press, 1962.

MARX, KARL, and ENGELS, FRIEDRICH. *The Russian Menace to Europe.* New York: Free Press, 1952.

MOORE, BARRINGTON. *Soviet Politics: The Dilemma of Power.* Cambridge: Harvard University Press, 1950.

MOSELY, PHILIP E. *The Kremlin and World Politics.* New York: Alfred A. Knopf, Vintage Books, 1960.

———, ed. *The Soviet Union, 1922–1962: A Foreign Affairs Reader.* New York: Praeger, 1963.

Nazi-Soviet Relations, 1937–1941. Washington, D.C.: Government Printing Office, 1948. Selected documents from the German archives.

RESHETAR, J. S., JR. *Problems of Analyzing and Predicting Soviet Behavior.* Garden City, N.Y.: Doubleday & Co., 1955.

ROBERTS, H. L. *Russia and America.* New York: Harper & Row, 1956.

ROSSER, RICHARD. *An Introduction to Soviet Foreign Policy.* Englewood Cliffs, N.J.: Prentice-Hall, 1970.

ROSSI, A. *The Russo-German Alliance, 1939–1941.* Boston: Beacon Press, 1951.

RUBINSTEIN, ALVIN Z. *The Foreign Policy of the Soviet Union.* New York: Random House, 1960.

SHULMAN, MARSHALL. *Stalin's Foreign Policy Reappraised.* Cambridge: Harvard University Press, 1963.

SOKOLOVSKII, V. M., ed. *Soviet Military Strategy.* Translated by H. S. Dinerstein, L. Goure, and T. Wolfe. Englewood Cliffs, N.J.: Prentice-Hall, 1963.

SOVIET INFORMATION BUREAU. *Falsifiers of History.* Moscow, 1948. Official explanation of the diplomacy of the Nazi-Soviet Pact and its aftermath.

STALIN, J. V. *Economic Problems of Socialism.* New York: International Publishers Company, 1952.

———. *The Great Patriotic War of the Soviet Union.* New York: International Publishers Co., 1945.

———. *Problems of Leninism.* Moscow: Universal Distributors, 1947.

TARACOUZIO, T. A. *The Soviet Union and International Law.* New York: Macmillan Co., 1936.

———. *War and Peace in Soviet Diplomacy.* New York: Macmillan Co., 1940.

TOWSTER, JULIAN. *Political Power in the U.S.S.R.* New York: Oxford University Press, 1948.

TRISKA, JAN F., and FINLEY, DAVID D. *Soviet Foreign Policy.* New York: Macmillan Co., 1969.

TRISKA, JAN, and SLUSSER, ROBERT. *The Theory, Law and Policy of Soviet Treaties.* Stanford, Calif.: Stanford University Press, 1962.

ULAM, ADAM B. *Expansion and Coexistence.* New York: Praeger, 1968.

———. *Titoism and the Cominform.* Cambridge: Harvard University Press, 1952.

WOLFE, B. D. *Khrushchev and Stalin's Ghost.* New York: Praeger, 1957. Khrushchev's secret report in full text, with commentary.

WOLFE, THOMAS W. *Soviet Power and Europe, 1945–1970.* Baltimore: Johns Hopkins Press, 1970.

———. *Soviet Strategy at the Crossroads.*

Cambridge: Harvard University Press, 1964.

ZIMMERMAN, WILLIAM. *Soviet Perspectives on International Relations.* Princeton: Princeton University Press, 1960.

Chapter Six

THE SOVIET UNION AND INTERNATIONAL COMMUNISM

VERNON V. ASPATURIAN

THE SOVIET UNION AND WORLD COMMUNISM UNDER LENIN AND STALIN

As rulers of the first country in which a Marxist revolutionary party had been elevated to power, the Bolsheviks early had to define their relationship with kindred Marxist parties engaged in revolutionary activity in other countries. Although the international communist movement has been institutionalized only in two organizations, the Comintern and the Cominform, Moscow's relations with foreign Communist parties before 1957 fall into three distinct, but closely interrelated, periods: (1) the Leninist period (1919–1928), (2) the Stalinist period (1928–1953), and (3) the residual Stalinist period (1953–1956). These distinctions are purely arbitrary, based neither on the programmatic nor the institutional metamorphosis of the world communist movement, but exclusively on the degree to which foreign Communist parties participated in the formulation of decisions concerning revolutionary strategy or Soviet foreign policy.

The Leninist Phase: Partners in World Revolution

The Comintern, founded by Lenin in 1919, was invested with two basic and interdependent functions: (1) to coordinate the strategy and direction of the world revolutionary movement, and (2) to defend the Soviet state against counterrevolution and foreign intervention. These two purposes, in turn, rested upon two fundamental assumptions concerning the world revolutionary movement: (1) the Russian Revolution was merely the first phase of a general revolution, and had neither a justification nor a purpose independent of it; (2) the revolution in Western Europe, particularly in Germany, was imminent.

The entire history of the relationship between Moscow and foreign Communist parties has been determined by the two essentially contradictory purposes—world revolution, and the defense of the Soviet Union. The proper defense of the Soviet Union, in turn, has rested on the shifting assumptions concerning the fortune and direction of the revolutionary movement outside Russia.

When Lenin convened the first Congress of the Comintern, in 1919, neither the concept of a world communist movement nor that of foreign Communist parties existed. Under Bolshevik sponsorship, radical or left-wing factions of the social-democratic parties splintered off to form separate Communist parties which affiliated with the new Third International. At the Second Congress, in 1920, statutes were drawn up defining the Communist International as "a universal Communist party of which the parties operating in each country [including Russia] form individual sections," whose aim was "the establishment of . . . the international Soviet Republic."[1] Although the Russian party was the only Communist party in power—except for the Hungarian during a brief period—and although a Russian, Grigori Zinoviev, was installed as president, the party was not invested with a privileged and dominant status in the organization, but, like all the others, was subordinate to the deci-

sions of the World Congress and its executive committee. However, since the Soviet Union was the only Soviet state in the world, and since the headquarters of the Comintern could be established only in Moscow, it was inevitable that, as the prospects of the worldwide revolution faded, the position of the Soviet party would be correspondingly enhanced.

Disagreements between Bolshevik leaders and foreign Communist parties, particularly the German, were frequent. Revolutionary doctrine and strategy and the role of Soviet diplomacy were discussed in the World Congress and in the meetings of its executive committee. The participation of foreign Communist parties was by no means a mere formality, and the Soviet state, which was conceived primarily as an instrument of the world revolution, frequently had to adjust its foreign policy to the views of these other parties, over which it did not exercise full control. The failure of revolution to take hold in Hungary and Germany, plus the ability of the Bolshevik regime to survive, forced a corresponding modification of the assumptions upon which the Comintern rested.

The struggle for power unleashed by Lenin's death in 1924 also found its reflection in the Comintern and within Communist parties abroad. A reexamination of the previous estimates of the revolution in Germany, and the victory of Stalin's policy of "socialism in one country," in opposition to Trotsky's idea of "permanent revolution," forced leaders in the Comintern and in foreign Communist parties to choose sides. As Stalin squeezed out his rivals at home, his supporters in the Comintern and in foreign Communist parties carried ou corresponding purges in their organizations. By 1930, Stalin had established his mastery over the party apparatus at

[1] W. H. Chamberlin, ed., *Blueprint for World Conquest* (Chicago: Human Events, 1946), p. 36.

home, and this was immediately followed by a corresponding subjugation of the Comintern.

The Stalinist Phase: The Primacy of Soviet Interests

The Soviet state soon assumed an identity and existence of its own, separate from, yet related to, that of the Comintern. The entire history of Soviet relationships, first with foreign Communist parties, then with other communist states, and then with rivals for leadership (i.e., China), has been determined by the Soviet Union's two essentially contradictory purposes—to serve the interests of foreign constituencies (world revolution, other communist states, China), and to reflect its internal interests (survival as a state, national interests, Soviet elites). This contradiction was resolved by adjusting the interests and behavior of the Comintern and foreign Communist parties to those of the Soviet Union. From 1928 to 1953, foreign Communist parties, even after they assumed power in their own countries, played little part in the formulation of Soviet foreign policy and were, on the contrary, completely subservient to it as pliable and expendable instruments.

The world communist movement during the Stalinist period rested upon assumptions radically divergent from those upon which the Comintern was originally founded. These were (1) the Soviet Union is the center and bulwark (not simply the advanced guard) of the world revolution; (2) revolution independent of Moscow's support is impossible; and (3) the preservation of the Soviet Union as the indispensable base of the world revolution is the most important objective of all Communists, who must demonstrate undeviating loyalty to the USSR as the "proletarian fatherland." These new assumptions were incorporated into the 1928 "Program of the Comintern," and the extension of world revolution became identified with the expansion of Soviet power:

The U.S.S.R. inevitably becomes the base of the world revolutionary movement. . . . In the U.S.S.R., the world proletariat for the first time acquires a country that is really its own. . . . In the event of the imperialist declaring war upon and attacking the U.S.S.R., the international proletariat must retaliate by organizing bold and determined mass action and struggle for the overthrow of the imperialist governments.[2]

The basic philosophy justifying this submission to Moscow's control was euphemistically defined by Stalin himself as "proletarian internationalism":

A *revolutionary* is he who without evasions, unconditionally openly and honestly . . . is ready to uphold and defend the U.S.S.R. . . . . An *internationalist* is he who unconditionally, without hesitation and without provisos, is ready to defend the U.S.S.R. because the U.S.S.R. is the base of the world revolutionary movement, and to defend and advance this movement is impossible without defending the U.S.S.R.[3]

Communist parties abroad were subordinated as expendable instruments manipulated in the interests of the Soviet state. Orders transmitted through the Comintern were followed with unquestioning obedience, even if their implementation invited self-destruction (as in China and Germany) or conflicted with the fundamental interests of their own people (as in France). As Moscow changed its policies, foreign Communists followed suit, even if the new policies were diametrically opposed to the current line. The Kremlin functioned as a GHQ of the world communist

2 Ibid., pp. 220–23.
3 J. V. Stalin, *Sochineniya* (Moscow, 1949), 10:61.

movement, sacrificing a division or corps here and there in the interest of the movement as a whole.

The dissolution of the Comintern in 1943 did not materially alter the relationship between Moscow and foreign parties, except that, as noted by Andrei Zhdanov at the founding of the Cominform in 1947, "some comrades understood the dissolution of the Comintern to imply the elimination of all ties, of all contact, between the fraternal Communist Parties, [which] . . . is wrong, harmful and . . . unnatural."[4]

After World War II, when Communist parties were installed in power in the countries of Eastern Europe and the Soviet Union was deprived of its unique position as the only communist state in the world, the theory of "proletarian internationalism" was transformed from a system justifying Moscow's control of parties into a system justifying her control of entire countries and subordinating their interests to those of the Soviet Union. Some satellite communist leaders considered the Soviet theory of "proletarian internationalism" applicable only to parties in capitalist countries, otherwise it became a philosophical jusification for Soviet colonialism.

As satellite leaders betrayed signs of uneasiness and independence in their new role as government leaders with the interests of their own countries and peoples to consider, Stalin organized the Cominform, ostensibly as an organ of mutual consultation based on the equality and independence of its members, but in reality to solidify his control over the satellites and to root out all tendencies toward independence. Unlike the Comintern, the new organization was carefully restricted to only the seven

communist states of Eastern Europe (Albania was denied membership) and to the two largest parties in the West, the Italian and the French. The refusal of Tito and other satellite leaders to place the interests of the Soviet Union above those of their own communist countries and to act as Moscow's subservient agents of plunder and exploitation of their own people led to the expulsion of Yugoslavia from the Cominform and the wholesale slaughter of satellite leaders who showed signs of independence. "Loyalty to the Soviet Union," ran the Moscow line, "is the touchstone and criterion of proletarian internationalism."[5] This was echoed by satellite communists and by communist leaders in capitalist countries, who agreed with Dimitrov that "proletarian internationalism . . . means complete coordination of the activities of Communist Parties and of the leading role of the Bolshevik [i.e., Soviet] Party."[6]

In rebuttal, Yugoslav leaders complained:

The leaders of the U.S.S.R. consider that Yugoslavia as a state should be subordinated . . . and its entire development in a general way should be made dependent upon the U.S.S.R. At the same time, they have forced other socialist states to act in a similar manner. . . . The political relations . . . are also based upon . . . the need to maintain in the various socialist countries the kind of regimes that will always be prepared to agree . . . to accept such unequal status and exploitation of their country. Thus—subservient and vassal governments and vassal states are actually being formed.[7]

[4] Strategy and Tactics of World Communism (Washington, D.C.: Government Printing Office, 1948), p. 229.

[5] For a Lasting Peace, For a People's Democracy, June 30, 1950.

[6] G. Dimitrov, Report to the Fifth Congress of the Bulgarian Communist Party (Sofia, 1948), p. 55.

[7] Milovan Djilas, Lenin on Relations between Socialist States (New York, 1949), pp. 16, 31.

Stalin's insistence that the Communist parties in Eastern Europe and in the Far East continue their subservience to Soviet interests introduced serious strains in the communist orbit, of which Tito's defection was merely the most obvious manifestation. Moscow continued to interfere crudely in the internal development of the satellite states, while disclaiming interference; it plundered their economies and called it disinterested aid; and it rigidly dictated their progress toward socialism, while paying lip service to national peculiarities. On all these matters, satellite leaders were not consulted before decisions were taken in the Kremlin, but were simply commanded to carry them out as efficiently as possible.

Whereas the small communist states of Eastern Europe were at the mercy of Soviet power, the attempt to dictate to Peking provoked considerable resistance. Satellite leaders elsewhere were slaughtered by the score, but no Stalinist purges took place in the Chinese party. One measure of Stalin's patent contempt for Chinese interests or national sensitivities was his refusal to relinquish the Soviet stranglehold on Manchuria, dissolve joint-stock companies, or surrender the special extraterritorial interests in Port Arthur and Dairen, although this refusal was clearly resented by the Chinese. According to Walter Ulbricht, Stalin's brazen attempts to treat China like an ordinary satellite almost forced Mao to desert the Soviet camp.

The Residual Stalinist Phase: The Primacy of Soviet Interests Defied

When Stalin died in March, 1953, the dominance of the Soviet Union in the communist system appeared fixed and permanent, and the primacy of its interests established and as-sured. His death, however, unleashed rivalries among his successors, and this created opportunities for other communist states to stir and come back to life. Since Stalinist sycophants were installed in all the satellite countries, and their constituency was in Moscow rather than at home, they had no vested interest in loosening the Soviet grip. With their patron dead, however, they faced an uncertain future. As they anxiously sought to identify their new patron in Moscow, "collective leadership" was proclaimed. Malenkov was invested only with the formal trappings of state authority, and he clearly was forced to share power with Beria and Molotov. Factional groupings assumed shape in the satellite capitals, corresponding to those in the Kremlin, and Beria's arrest, in June, sent a ripple of fear throughout Eastern Europe. Soon, collective leadership became the new orthodoxy, as party and state posts in Eastern Europe were separated and redistributed.

Stalin's successors were thus almost immediately confronted with the vexing problem of trying to perpetuate his system of vassalage, or of modifying it. This reexamination unleashed a "great debate" within the Kremlin, one which divided the leadership into one faction which insisted that the old system be retained with minor adjustments and another which advocated a liberalization that bordered on revolutionizing the entire relationship between Moscow and her allies. While Malenkov was premier, no radical departures from Stalin's policies toward Eastern Europe could be detected, but it now appears that the faction headed by Khrushchev and Bulganin was pressing for a complete rupture with the past. Its program included (1) elimination of the developing schism with Marshal Tito, (2) rapprochement with

Marshal Tito, (3) halting the economic exploitation of the satellites, and (4) permitting the gradual evolution of partial political autonomy. These proposals presupposed not only a break with the past, but also an actual repudiation of Stalin's policies, and consequently they were strongly resisted by Molotov and others, as dangerous to the unity of the communist movement.

As the internal controversy became more acute, uncertain, and incapable of resolution on the basis of the internal political balance, the factions in the Kremlin reached out into their empire for incremental support. Communist leaders were once again about to become power constituencies, starting with the most powerful and the most independent, China and Yugoslavia. China had been humiliated by Stalin, who had tried to make her subservient, and this was clearly resented by the Chinese, not only as unconsonant with its national pride and dignity, but as contrary to proper relations between communist states.

Obviously, Chinese resentment promised possible political support to some in the Kremlin. We can date the beginnings of the Soviet Union's loss of primacy in the communist world from Khrushchev's opportunistic use of China and Yugoslavia against his rivals. Presumably, both Mao Tse-tung and Tito would reciprocate by supporting Khrushchev. And for the next three years, both China and Yugoslavia played significant roles in shoring up Khrushchev's position at home and vis-à-vis the Eastern European communist countries.

The defeat of the Malenkov-Molotov policy was clearly apparent by July, 1954. Neither Premier Malenkov nor Foreign Minister Molotov accompanied the Khrushchev-Bulga-

nin mission to Peking, in the autumn of 1954, where it was their purpose to assuage Peking's resentments and inaugurate a new era in the relations between the two countries. The Soviet grip on Manchuria was relinquished, the joint-stock companies liquidated, and full Chinese sovereignty restored over Dairen and Port Arthur.

The Chinese apparently submitted an additional list of grievances and demands. Mao apparently interpreted the Soviet action as a sign of fear and weakness, and demanded further adjustments: the return of Mongolia; a rectification of Sino-Soviet frontiers in China's favor; and perhaps a demand that the Soviet Union cancel Chinese debts incurred as a result of the Korean War, which, after all, was fought in the interests of the socialist camp as a whole. All these were presumably rejected. The Mongolian issue and the general territorial question became matters of public record only in August, 1964, when Mao raised them in an interview with a visiting delegation of Japanese socialists:

In keeping with the Yalta Agreement the Soviet Union, under the pretext of insuring Mongolia's independence, actually placed this country under its domination. . . . In 1954 when Khrushchev and Bulganin were in China we took up this question but they refused to talk to us. . . . Some people have declared that the Sinkiang area and the territories north of the Amur must be included in the Soviet Union.[8]

The Soviet version of the 1954 events placed them in a broader context, as revealed in a rebuttal by *Pravda*:

Maps showing various parts of the Soviet Union . . . as Chinese territory continued to be published in the CPR. Chinese representatives recently began mentioning with increasing frequency

8 *Pravda*, September 2, 1964.

hundreds of thousands of square kilometers of Soviet territory which allegedly belong "by right" to China. . . . In his talk, Mao Tse-tung bemoaned the fate of Mongolia which, as he said, was put by the Soviet Union "under its rule. . . . " The existence of an independent Mongolian state, which maintains friendly relations with the U.S.S.R. . . . does not suit the Chinese leaders. They would like to deprive Mongolia of its independence and make it a Chinese province. The CPR leaders offered "to reach agreement" on this with N. S. Khrushchev and other Soviet comrades during their visit to Peking in 1954. N. S. Khrushchev naturally refused to discuss this question.[9]

Thus, by 1954, China felt assertive enough to demand territorial restitution in the name of Chinese national interests. Mao was also apparently informed of the impending resignation of Malenkov, an unprecedented gesture on the part of Soviet leaders, in that it was an implicit request for clearance from a foreign communist leader.

The decision to seek a reconciliation with Tito proceeded more cautiously, but it, too, was a Khrushchev-Bulganin gesture in search of new external constituencies. And since the effort to return Yugoslavia to the communist fraternity was bound to have repercussions in Eastern Europe, Khrushchev saw a need to ameliorate conditions in other communist states as well. Comecon (Council of Mutual Economic Assistance) was converted from a vehicle of exploitation into an institutionalized conference, and regular meetings were devoted to mutual economic problems. In November, 1954, a conference in Moscow laid the foundations for the Warsaw Pact, which was signed on May 14, 1955, binding all the European communist states in a military alliance. While the Pact did little more than legalize the presence of Soviet troops on the territories of the Eastern European states, it was significant psychologically. Unilateralism was replaced with formal multilateralism, and Stalin's devisive, bilateral arrangements were disowned.

The rapprochement with the Yugoslavs was preceded by a bitter controversy in the Kremlin, and Molotov, who was strenuously opposed to the whole idea, was overruled. At Tito's insistence, the following measures were taken: (1) Stalin's satellite policies were openly condemned and repudiated; (2) Stalin's victims in Eastern Europe, like Rajk in Hungary and Kostov in Bulgaria, were posthumously rehabilitated, their trials pronounced a fraud, and Tito absolved of all implications of subversion and deviation; (3) "national deviationists" or "Titoists" still alive, like Gomulka in Poland and Kadar in Hungary, were released from prison and restored to high rank in the party; (4) "Stalinists" in Eastern Europe were dethroned and replaced with personalities more acceptable to Tito; (5) the Cominform was liquidated; (6) Molotov was ousted as foreign minister because he was *persona non grata* to Tito; and (7) Moscow accepted the Yugoslav theory "that the roads and conditions of socialist development are different in different countries. . . . that any tendency of imposing one's views in determining the roads and forms of socialist development is alien."[10] Never before had a foreign communist leader—and a former outcast, at that—demanded and received such an influential role in the policies of the Kremlin.

9 Ibid.

10 *New York Times,* June 21, 1956.

THE SOVIET UNION AND INTERNATIONAL COMMUNISM: THE EROSION OF SOVIET PRIMACY

The Soviet Union's Twentieth Party Congress (1956) represented a new level in the evolution of Soviet relations with the rest of the communist world. Locally responsive Communists, like Gomulka and Nagy, were catapulted into power in Poland and Hungary by powerful internal pressures which were set into motion by the revelations of the Twentieth Party Congress. The demolition of Stalinism at home could only have resulted in the progressive disintegration of Stalinist structures in Eastern Europe. The repercussions in China, Yugoslavia, and Albania were smallest, since they were governed largely by indigenous Stalinist regimes, particularly China and Albania.

The Polish and Hungarian "Octobers" were the immediate and most serious consequences of de-Stalinization, and the demands these two events placed upon the communist system, as then organized, threatened to reduce it to ruins. Nationalism of the Soviet variety could no longer be obscured, and nationalism of the smaller states could no longer be denied. The year 1956 thus inaugurated the gradual dissolution of proletarian internationalism into its constituent proletarian or communist nationalisms. This process unfolded gradually and pragmatically in response to situations and events.

Before Stalin's death, the flow of demands in the communist system had been in one direction only, from the center to the periphery. After Stalin's death, and especially after 1956, the flow was substantially and progressively altered. First Peking in 1954, then Yugoslavia in 1955, then Poland in 1956 made demands upon the Soviet Union which were met and which have since been repeated by other communist states. By 1958, the Soviet Union was bombarded with demands, trivial and serious, from all directions. Moscow's demands on other communist states became more limited and less coercive. During the years 1957–1961, demands flowing in from the periphery gradually exceeded those flowing outward from the center.

The Council of Mutual Economic Aid (Comecon), for example, which was originally operated to the economic advantage of the Soviet Union, was reorganized to control and arrest Soviet exploitation. No sooner had this happened then it was converted into a vehicle for channeling economic aid from the Soviet Union to the other communist states, as demands came in for restitution, reparations, economic assistance, and commercial autonomy. The joint-stock companies were dissolved, and deliveries of raw materials and finished goods were made in accordance with world market prices. Eastern European states asserted the right to receive economic assistance from, and engage in profitable commercial transactions with, capitalist countries.

Economic demands upon the Soviet Union spilled over into the political and ideological realms, as individual states demanded and received greater autonomy. Institutions modeled after those in the Soviet Union were, in many cases, dissolved or modified, while Soviet-type ideological controls over the arts, sciences, professions, education, and media of information were renounced in accordance with the local demands of each state. No overt attempt was made to organize joint or concerted action on Moscow until 1961, however, when China and Albania forged an anti-Soviet factional alliance.

The role of the Soviet Union underwent modification with each successive stage in the continuing evolution of the system and movement. Four distinct phases and the beginning of a fifth are discernible in the Soviet Union's relationship to the communist universe of states and parties during the period from 1956 to 1967.

The first phase was a short one, covering the period from the Twentieth Party Congress to the World Conference of Communist Parties in November, 1957. During this period, the Soviet Union was clearly a crippled leader, mauled and bruised as a consequence of its de-Stalinization program. Divided at home, its prestige tarnished and its power tattered and ragged, using both Belgrade and Peking as crutches, it hobbled its way from one capital to another seeking to preserve its authority.

The world conference of November, 1957, marks the end of the first phase and the beginning of the second, which lasted until the Twenty-second Party Congress of the Communist Party of the Soviet Union (CPSU), in October, 1961. Unable to assert its former primacy, the Soviet Union was soon challenged by China, which attempted to introduce Chinese interests as a prime factor in proletarian internationalism, by making successive demands on the Soviet Union, on the system, and then on the movement itself. Khrushchev's excommunication of China's echo, Albania, at the Twenty-second Party Congress, signaled a successful Soviet quashing of the Chinese bid for primacy and an attempt to reassert positive Soviet leadership in Eastern Europe and over Western Communist parties.

The third phase, which covers the period from the Twenty-second Party Congress to the Limited Nuclear Test Ban Treaty of July, 1963, was marked by the progressive transformation of a polycentric communist universe into a movement grouped around two opposite poles, Moscow and Peking. This meant that not only was Marxism-Leninism incapable of guaranteeing an ideological consensus, but that the international communist movement was no longer even capable of containing the conflict.

The fourth phase, beginning with the test ban treaty, was marked by open mutual denunciation and abuse, the potential transformation of a polarized communist universe into two hostile camps, and the dissolution of the communist world as a military bloc. Peking accused Moscow of conspiring with the United States against her, while Moscow charged Peking with seeking to maneuver the Soviet Union into a thermonuclear war of mutual annihilation with the United States so that China might pick up the pieces and dominate the ruins. The ouster of Khrushchev in October, 1964, postponed the climax of this phase, but China's refusal to send a delegation to the Twenty-third Party Congress of the CPSU in April, 1966, may have contributed to the development of a new phase in the evolution of the world communist movement, the phase of two hostile communist camps and movements, with the re-emergence of a more compact Soviet bloc within the communist movement.

The occupation of Czechoslovakia by the military forces of the Soviet Union and four of its Warsaw Pact allies and the enunciation of the "Brezhnev doctrine" inaugurated a fifth phase in the evolution of the world communist movement. The most conspicuous characteristic of this phase was the Soviet reversion to the employment of military coercion, under the cover of "socialist commonwealth" multilateralism, to enforce its will upon recalcitrant members of the communist community of states. The first concrete result of this development was the reemergence of a Soviet bloc, but on a smaller scale (largely Eastern Europe), based upon the narrower foundations of national self-interest and the threat of Soviet intervention, and less reliance upon ideological communion and charismatic Soviet leadership. The new, smaller Soviet bloc emerges more distinctively as the hegemonic instrument of the Soviet state as an imperial rather than revolutionary power, and is a politico-military coalition that may be mobilized against both the West and Communist China.

The other main characteristics of this phase are (1) further fragmentation of the world communist movement as a *movement*, (2) continued polarization within the communist world around either Moscow and Peking, (3) progressive alienation of a large number of parties from both communist giants, (4) massive military confrontation on the Sino-Soviet border and the continuing danger of military conflict on a scale greater than the border clashes of 1969, and (5) possible conversion of the Warsaw Treaty Organization into an anti-Chinese alliance.

Crippled Leader: The Primacy of Soviet Interests Subdued

Theoretically, of course, proletarian internationalism demands that national interests be subordinated to an international interest. In the case of the Soviet Union, the subordination of its interests to proletarian internationalism could only mean to reverse roles and allow the national interests of other communist states to prevail over its own. This, Moscow was not prepared to do. From 1956 to 1958, therefore, an attempt was made to

find a way to coordinate several national interests. The effort proved futile, however, as it became apparent that the Chinese were demanding a disproportionately large role for their national interests in the calculation of proletarian internationalism. Soviet recognition of the primacy of proletarian internationalism, under these conditions, would have been tantamount to the subordination of its national interests to those of the Chinese.

The cracking of the monolith in Eastern Europe approached its climax in October, 1956, with an independent-minded Gomulka in Warsaw and a secessionist-minded Nagy in Budapest. Moscow fluctuated between adventurism and paralysis. The Poznan uprising and its aftermath elicited a Soviet threat to intervene militarily but, according to Chinese accounts, Chinese pressures exerted a moderating influence and Poland was saved from Soviet military occupation. The Hungarian national uprising, which threatened to sweep communism out entirely, was met with hesitation and vacillation in Moscow; according to the Chinese version, it was only the wisdom and firmness of Mao Tse-tung which induced Khrushchev to save Hungary for the socialist camp.

Soviet intervention in Hungary also evoked divergent reactions in various capitals. Peking pressured for military intervention, the other satellites applauded it, Warsaw deplored it, and Belgrade condemned it. This brought Tito into direct conflict with Peking. Tito openly condemned the Soviet explanation of the revolution and deplored the use of troops. The situation over Hungary was so serious that Moscow asked Peking for support. A statement was issued condoning the Hungarian repression and repudiating the Yugoslav criticisms. Belgrade temporarily lost influence, but Peking and Belgrade were to emerge as the two poles of the communist axis.

On October 30, 1956, the Soviet leaders, in consultation with Peking, issued a statement entitled "The Foundations of the Development and Further Consolidation of Friendship and Cooperation between the Soviet Union and other Socialist States," in which Moscow conceded grave errors in its relationships with other communist states, promised amends (and eventually reparations), and called for the transformation of the communist system into a commonwealth of socialist nations:

In the process of constructing a new system and effecting profound revolutionary changes in social relationships, there have arisen many difficulties, unsolved problems and outright errors. The latter have included infringements of the mutual relationships between socialist countries and mistakes which have weakened the principle of the equality of rights in the mutual association of the socialist countries.[11]

Moscow also pledged that "the Soviet Government is ready to discuss, together with the governments of other socialist states, measures . . . to remove the possibilities of violating the principle of national sovereignty and . . . equality."

The dissolution of the Cominform —the only multilateral party organization in the entire movement—made it a matter of urgency to devise new processes and institutions of mutual consultation as quickly as possible. Since the Cominform was viewed as a discredited symbol of Soviet primacy and Stalinist domination, Moscow's stated preference for a new, permanent, multilateral organization was rejected by Peking, Warsaw, and Belgrade as too suggestive of the Cominform and Comintern. It was also op-

posed by the Italian Communist party. In all cases, the opponents of a revival of institutionalized multilateral forms betrayed a fear that this might relegitimize Soviet primacy, in view of Moscow's command of the loyalty of a majority of both communist states and parties. Moscow, accordingly, resigned itself to a position of flexibility.[12]

With Tito discredited, Peking boldly moved in and unilaterally assumed the role of an honest broker between Moscow and its rebellious Eastern European client states. On December 29, 1956, the Chinese issued a long statement in which they condemned the extremes of both Stalinism and Titoism and, at the same time, attempted to suggest a new orthodoxy for the entire system. The legitimacy of national interests in determining common action was explicitly recognized:

Marxism-Leninism has always strongly advocated that proletarian internationalism be combined with patriotism. . . . The Communist Parties of all countries must . . . become the spokesmen of the legitimate national interests and sentiments of their people [and] . . . effectively educate the masses in the spirit of internationalism and harmonize the national sentiments and interests of these countries.[13]

Chou En-lai was dispatched by Peking on a fence-mending tour designed to find a new common ground between Moscow and its recalcitrant satellites in Eastern Europe. The Chinese action was welcomed by Gomulka, who saw in Peking's intervention a useful counterpoise to Soviet pressure. Chou carefully steered a course which simultaneously renounced "great-power chauvinism"

[11] *Pravda,* October 31, 1956.

[12] See Mikoyan's speech to the Eighth Congress of the Chinese Communist Party, *Pravda,* September 18, 1956.
[13] *Pravda,* December 31, 1956.

and preserved the "leading role" of the Soviet Union. Peking's intervention apparently also helped to improve Khrushchev's position in the Soviet hierarchy.

The forging of a new international interest or communist consensus was, during most of 1957, restricted mainly to bilateral discussions between Communist parties and leaders and consultations at various party congresses, but this soon proved inadequate and ineffective. Warsaw continued its refusal to accept even the formalities of Soviet primacy, while Peking became an increasingly assertive spokesman for the camp as a whole. During the "antiparty group" crisis in June, 1957, Khrushchev again apparently sought and received support from Mao, which further contributed to the image of China as a virtual codirector of the socialist camp. In return for Chinese support, Khrushchev apparently agreed to contribute to China's nuclear development, and an agreement on nuclear technology was signed in October, 1957.

Not only did the communist countries fail to agree upon new forms of supranational organizations of consultation, but they failed to find any operational consensus at all. In 1957, the Soviet Union was unable to convince the other communist countries of the necessity for a new multilateral communist organization similar to the Cominform in structural outlines. And by 1964, Moscow was unable even to persuade the communist states to convene a general conference of Communist parties. None has been convened since November, 1960. An alternative pattern of multilateral consultation, reportedly suggested by Moscow, was the exchange of permanent party representatives. Both suggestions were frowned upon by Peking, Warsaw, and the Italian Communist party, and Belgrade was not consulted.

The principal resistance to a new Cominform came from Yugoslavia, although both Poland and China also opposed a revival of the organization in any form, which they still feared might once again be employed by Moscow as an instrument of centralization and domination. The Yugoslav-Polish view was that consultation should be primarily a bipartisan affair.[14]

Pending the formation of definitive institutions and methods of consultation, bilateralism and ad hoc multilateralism have been the general rule. This has followed three patterns: (1) mutual exchanges of party delegations to party conferences and congresses; (2) bilateral discussions throughout the communist world, followed by the issuance of joint communiqués, which have deviated interestingly from the crude uniformity of the past; (3) multiparty conferences, in the form of periodic gatherings of delegates from all communist parties, and selective conferences restricted to parties which exercise power in their respective states. The first of these post-Cominform conferences was a rump meeting held in Budapest in January, 1957, which was attended only by delegates from Moscow, Budapest, Sofia, Prague, and Bucharest.

November, 1957, saw the first attempt to establish a multilateral process for arriving at a communist consensus. It is now known that serious controversies between Moscow and Peking developed at this conference. The expulsion of the "antiparty group" and the successful disposition of Zhukov had improved Khrushchev's position to the point where Peking's support was no longer required or desired. A number of Mao's proposals were successfully resisted, but the Chinese leader was successful in altering

14 See *New York Times*, January 1, 1957.

a Soviet draft declaration which proved unacceptable to Yugoslavia.

The Yugoslav representatives refused to accept the declaration issued by the ruling Communist parties, which embodied a common core of ideological principles and policy positions which had been hammered out after long and arduous negotiation. The purpose of the declaration was to restore unity among the various ruling parties, but it became impossible to reconcile the extreme positions of China and Yugoslavia, in spite of the wide latitude which the "November declaration" afforded for individual variation within a common program.

The concessions made by Moscow, however, did earn the public support of Peking for the ideological innovations introduced at the Twentieth Party Congress, as well as the denunciation of at least some aspects of Stalinism, but the Chinese could not accept positions which would be acceptable to Belgrade. Now that China supported the Russian position, Warsaw had no alternative but to alter its heretical position and support the declaration.

The net result was the elimination of Yugoslavia as a factor in making decisions for the communist orbit, and the elevation of Peking to a position of rivalry with Moscow for power and influence in the communist world. The November, 1957, meeting signaled China's political and ideological independence from Moscow and underlined the voluntary character of her recognition of Soviet primacy, with the implication that she could withdraw this recognition at will. The auspicious inauguration of the "people's communes" in China in 1958, and the bitter attacks leveled against them by Soviet leaders, betrayed a bold attempt on the part of China to claim primacy for the Chinese state as the most advanced society in the

world. Outwardly, however, the 1957 conference seemed to reflect harmony and concord, and its declaration outlined new procedures for determining the content and direction of proletarian internationalism:

Following their exchange of views, the participants in the discussion have come to the conclusion that in the present circumstances it would be expedient, in addition to the meetings of leading officials and in addition to an exchange of information on a bilateral basis, to arrange more far-reaching conferences of the communist and workers' parties in order to discuss topical international problems, to exchange experiences, to get to know one another's views and attitudes and to coordinate the common struggle for common aims, for peace, democracy, and socialism.[15]

Challenged Leader: The Chinese Bid for Primacy

The full implications of the resurgence of nationalism were not immediately apparent in 1956–1957. The enthronement of the nation-state as the definitive form of the communist state meant that the idea of a world communist state had been jettisoned in favor of a communist interstate system for the indefinite future. Party conflicts would inevitably be transformed into state conflicts, and state conflicts would inexorably reflect national conflicts, as the nation-state once again preempted the highest loyalty of its citizens. Highest loyalty to the proletariat, yes, but to the *national* proletariat and its nation-state.

The Chinese were caught in a peculiar dilemma. They insisted that the movement required a center or leader, But more than any other communist state, they demanded autonomy. What Peking wanted, of course, was to as-

[15] *Pravda*, November 22, 1957.

sume direction herself, but since there was little immediate prospect of displacing Moscow directly, the Chinese sought to use Moscow as an unsuspecting instrument in their drive for power and influence.

Under Khrushchev's direction, however, Soviet policies were gradually oriented toward the avoidance of thermonuclear war and a relaxation of international tensions, based on a limited accommodation with the United States. By achieving an agreement with the United States when Soviet prestige was high, the diplomatic consequences might be correspondingly advantageous. This strategy, however, conflicted with Chinese aspirations. Mao made dramatically clear, at the 1957 Moscow meeting, that he calculated the Soviet Union to be militarily superior to the United States and that instead of settling for an accommodation, his superior wisdom dictated that the Soviet Union should use its military superiority to oust American power from marginal areas, particularly in the Far East.

These divergent national interests were bound to collide, although Peking apparently thought that its leverage was still sufficient to force Moscow's acceptance of its demands. The Chinese decided to press the issue and confront Khrushchev with an agonizing choice between supporting a major ally or seeking an accommodation with the major enemy and thus risking a rupture with Peking. The Chinese leaders apparently thought that Khrushchev would hardly dare to alienate Peking in return for an uncertain and fragile accommodation with the United States. Mao probably calculated—on the basis of past experience—that Khrushchev would not dare oppose him for fear that his rivals might use his opposition as a pretext to successfully discredit his leadership.

From Peking's standpoint, China possessed all the necessary credentials for primacy in the communist world except two: (1) nuclear weapons, and (2) a sufficiently advanced stage of economic development. Sometime in late 1957 or early 1958, the Chinese leaders decided to overcome these two deficiencies. Apparently, Mao perceived an opportunity, in the summer of 1958, to force the issue of nuclear weapons with the Soviet Union and, at the same time, to disrupt Khrushchev's attempts to to bring about a new summit meeting in order to establish some sort of accommodation with the United States.

Peking's fears and suspicious were apparently reinforced by Moscow's mild response to the landing of U.S. Marines in Lebanon and by Khrushchev's assent to Eisenhower's suggestion that a summit conference be held, within the framework of the United Nations Security Council, to discuss the Middle Eastern crisis. Such a conference would not only exclude Peking, but possibly include India and even Chiang Kai-shek, since Nationalist China continued to occupy China's seat on the Security Council.

Peking's reaction was sufficiently violent to impel Khrushchev not only to withdraw his acceptance, but also to make a hurried and unannounced trip to Peking to offer explanations. On August 4, Khrushchev withdrew his assent to a summit meeting altogether.

The Chinese had apparently prevailed again. It appears, however, that they may have used the opportunity to make an additional demand—that Moscow supply China with sample atom bombs—and that Moscow refused. The Chinese may also have demanded that Khrushchev be prepared to issue a public statement of nuclear support for a forthcoming Chinese initiative in the Taiwan Strait to test

American determination and, perhaps, also to force Moscow to choose between communist unity and an agreement with the United States. The unsatisfactory nature of the Soviet response during the Taiwan Strait crisis of 1958 was confirmed in 1963, when the entire episode was raked over in acrimonious public debate after the test ban treaty was signed.

It seems clear that the Soviet Union began to resist Chinese demands after Khrushchev's return from Peking in 1958, when he decided, instead, to pursue his policy of seeking an agreement with the United States. This was confirmed by the Chinese in September, 1963:

> The leaders of the C.P.S.U., eager to curry favor with U.S. imperialism, engaged in unbridled activities against China. . . . They thought they had solved their internal problems and had "stabilized" their own position and could therefore step up their policy of "being friendly to enemies and tough with friends."[16]

The Chinese later complained bitterly that the Soviet refusal to supply them with nuclear assistance and bombs was a betrayal of "proletarian internationalism."

The Chinese demands, in 1958, for a nuclear arsenal of some sort were paralleled by a series of bold moves designed to secure an ideological foundation for a future Chinese claim to primacy. According to a subsequent account, Moscow interpreted Chinese behavior at that time as follows:

> In the spring of 1958 the Chinese leadership began to change its line sharply. Instead of the approximately 15 years that had been envisioned for setting up the base for socialism in China, in 1958 a period of only three years was proclaimed to be adequate even for the transition to communism. The so-called "great leap" was announced—a political-economic adventure unprecedented in both design and scale. This was a policy . . . built on the desire to solve grandiose tasks faster and to "teach" others the newly invented methods of building socialism and communism. It was then that the slogan was proclaimed of the "people's communes," which formed the basis of the attempt to leap over natural stages of socialist construction in the . . . effort to get "ahead of progress" here.[17]

Khrushchev, a resourceful politician, quickly perceived the challenge, and while he did not overtly condemn the communes or criticize the Chinese "Great Leap Forward" at the time, he ignored it publicly and ridiculed it privately. The Soviet press was conspicuously silent about the entire affair, but the Yugoslavs openly denounced the communes, and other Eastern European leaders privately expressed disgust and apprehension over Mao's abrupt leftward turn. In April, 1964, Khrushchev revealed what he had obviously discerned, six years earlier, to be the motivation behind China's behavior:

> But in that same year, 1958, the Chinese leaders unexpectedly proclaimed the so-called course of the "great leap" and the "people's communes." The idea behind this course consisted in skipping over the stages of socialist development into the phase of communist construction. At the time, Chinese propaganda asserted that China would show everyone an example of entry into communism ahead of schedule.[18]

Who was ahead of whom was no idle question, since both Moscow and Peking were aware that spearheading the dialectic of history was a necessary

16 *Peking Review,* September 13, 1963, no. 37, pp. 6–23.

17 L. Llyichev, "Revolutionary Science and the Present Day," *Kommunist,* July, 1964, no. 11, pp. 12–35.
18 *Pravda,* April 16, 1964.

ideological prerequisite for a serious and legitimate claim to primacy, although it could not by itself be sufficient. Nuclear power was also necessary. Consequently, Khrushchev took immediate and effective steps to deny both nuclear weapons and economic success to the Chinese. Moscow curtailed its economic and technical assistance to China on the pretext that the Great Leap Forward was disrupting and distorting Chinese economic development, and hence, that Soviet aid constituted a waste of Soviet resources. Although Peking later confessed that the Great Leap Forward had failed, the episode remained a sobering experience for the Soviet Union's leaders.

Since Soviet interests required a rapprochement with the United States, and Chinese interests dictated an aggravation of Soviet-American relations, the interests of the two countries were to drift further and further apart. On this point, compromise was impossible. Each was convinced that its vital interest—the avoidance of thermonuclear war, from the Soviet point of view, and the expulsion of the Americans from the Far East, from the Chinese—dictated the proper course to pursue. If Moscow, China's chief ally, were to become reconciled to the United States, her major enemy, then of what value was the Sino-Soviet alliance to the Chinese? On the other hand, if solidarity with China required that the Soviet Union risk nuclear annihilation in a confrontation with the United States, her alliance with China was tantamount to a suicide pact. These divergent interests made it imperative that each chart its own policy toward the United States in accordance with its individual goals.

Khrushchev, in a series of ripostes to the Chinese bid for primacy, continued to apply various forms of political, military, and economic pressure. On August 3, 1959, two months after the nuclear agreement with China was nullified by Moscow, it was announced in Moscow that Khrushchev would meet with Eisenhower in the United States. Almost simultaneously, Marshal Peng Teh-huai was dismissed by Peking. The Chinese military leader, who had been Peking's observer to the Warsaw Treaty Organization, apparently shared Khrushchev's misgivings about Mao and, furthermore, was professionally concerned over the imminent suspension and withdrawal of Soviet military support. The Chinese have hinted that Khrushchev tried to bring about the ouster of Mao by intriguing with his rivals.

On August 7, while the Chinese Central Committee plenum which dismissed Marshal Peng was still in session, the Sino-Indian border conflict flared up, leading to an invasion of Indian territory by the Chinese which continued into September. The Sino-Indian dispute, which Moscow interpreted as a device to frustrate the Eisenhower-Khrushchev meeting, unleashed acrimonious discussion between the two communist giants, culminating in a Soviet statement deploring the conflict and virtually disassociating Moscow from Chinese actions.

Peking charged that Khrushchev further sacrificed Chinese interests by informing Eisenhower that the Soviet Union would not give nuclear weapons to China and that Moscow would accept a "two Chinas" solution to the Taiwan problem. After the Camp David talks, which Khrushchev considered a signal success, the Soviet leader's stature and prestige visibly increased. In his next confrontation with Mao in Peking, almost immediately afterward, his self-assertion did not go unnoticed:

Back from the Camp David talks, he went so far as to try to sell China the U.S. plot of "two Chinas" and, at the state banquet celebrating the 10th anniversary of the founding of the C.P.R. he read China a lecture against "testing by force the stability of the capitalist system."[19]

Serious conflicts of national purpose and interests were only obliquely revealed in the Sino-Soviet dialogue but, as the conflict continued and intensified, they gradually broke through the ideological shells in which they were encrusted. Although ideology and national interests are so intimately intertwined in communist politics that they cannot be distilled out completely, yet they were separating out as visible quantities in the equation of conflict. Soviet interests veered more and more in the direction of an acceptance of the status quo, whereas Chinese interests demanded that the United States be expelled from the Far East.

What the Chinese failed to do, Gary Francis Powers and the flight of an American U-2 over Soviet territory succeeded in doing, on May Day, 1960. The Chinese felt themselves justified and congratulated themselves on their superior wisdom. Three years later, they were still exulting: "The 'spirit of Camp David' completely vanished. Thus, events entirely confirmed our views." Khrushchev, however, berated both Eisenhower and Mao, the former for cupidity or stupidity, and the latter for belligerent dogmatism. Relations with China deteriorated even faster than those with the United States, however. In June, Moscow suggested that the forthcoming Rumanian party congress be turned into an ad hoc meeting of ruling parties to discuss the implications

of the abortive summit meeting with the West; Peking accepted only grudgingly, because it was opposed to Moscow's purpose in calling the meeting. Moscow's interest in seeking a détente with the United States seemed to coincide with the interests of the Eastern European states, and the Chinese were unenthusiastic about placing themselves in the minority, so they had the meeting broadened into a general conference of Communist parties. Peking's relations with the Kremlin were not visibly improved by the shooting down of the U-2, but it appears that Khrushchev's rivals at home were strengthened and Soviet attitudes toward the United States hardened.

The Chinese initiated their new strategy of reaching outward from the fraternity of communist countries into the larger movement for support by engaging in factional activity against Soviet positions at a meeting held in Peking on June 5–9, 1960. This was the first instance of one communist state, other than the Soviet Union, organizing opposition against another. This factional activity was to accelerate and become the main organizational weapon against Moscow's seemingly permanent majority in the fraternity.

Anticipating China's factional strategy, Khrushchev laid an ambush for the Chinese at Bucharest:

At Bucharest, to our amazement, the leaders of the C.P.S.U. . . . unleashed a surprise assault on the Chinese Communist Party. . . . In the meeting, Khrushchev took the lead in organizing a great converging onslaught against the Chinese Communist Party as "madmen," "wanting to unleash war" . . . "being pure nationalist" on the Sino-Indian boundary question and employing "Trotskyite ways" against the C.P.S.U.[20]

[19] *Peking Review*, September 13, 1963, no. 23.

[20] Ibid.

Khrushchev's crude—but probably warranted—retaliation against the Chinese failed to halt them. Instead, the Chinese escalated the level of their demands, expecting that Moscow would back down eventually. Moscow had no alternative but to retaliate again. In the words of the Chinese:

Apparently the leaders of the C.P.S.U. imagined that once they waved their baton, gathered a group of hatchetmen to make a converging assault, and applied immense political and economic pressures, they could force the Chinese Communist Party to abandon its Marxist-Leninist and proletarian internationalist stand and submit to their revisionist and great power chauvinist behests. But the tempered and long-tested Chinese Communist Party and the Chinese people could neither be vanquished nor subdued. Those who tried to subjugate us by engineering a converging assault and applying pressures miscalculated.[21]

Nationalism continued to spill over from the communist system into the larger movement. Nonruling parties were drawn more and more into the struggle, as the twelve ruling Communist parties failed to find an area of common agreement for the movement as a whole. A separate conference of all Communist parties has not been convened since 1957, and is not likely to occur in the future, although the European group has met, as the Warsaw Treaty Organization and as Comecon, and several rump "world conferences" have also met, but without the participation of the Chinese and several other parties.

The second conference of all the Communist parties was convened in November, 1960. Both the Chinese and Soviet leaders lobbied vigorously before, during, and after the conference. The Chinese found themselves in the minority. They made virtually no headway among the European and Western parties, and their behavior completely bewildered and confused the others, most of whom did not want to be placed in the uncomfortable position of being forced to choose, although they were not averse to exploiting the dispute to their own ends. Stung by Chinese charges of greatpower chauvinism, the Soviet leaders emphasized that theirs was the majority position and correctly claimed that, of the eighty-one parties represented at the conference,

the overwhelming majority of the fraternal parties rejected the incorrect views and concepts of the C.C.P. [Chinese Communist Party] leadership. The Chinese delegation at this meeting stubbornly upheld its own particular views and signed the Statement only when the danger arose of its complete isolation. Today it has become absolutely obvious that the C.C.P. leaders were only maneuvering when they affixed their signatures to the 1960 Statement.[22]

The Chinese ruefully conceded a Soviet majority at the conference, which reaffirmed the primacy of the Soviet Union as the senior partner in an association of equal members.

Khrushchev, in a widely publicized speech on January 6, 1961, virtually renounced the dubious distinction of being the leader of a movement which was fractured beyond repair. It was also, simultaneously, a signal that Moscow could no longer be held responsible for, or be associated with, Peking's actions:

The C.P.S.U. in reality does not exercise leadership over other parties. All communist parties are equal and independent. . . . The role of the Soviet Union does not lie in the fact that it leads other socialist countries but in the

21 Ibid.

22 *Pravda*, July 14, 1963.

fact that it was the first to blaze the trail to socialism, has the greatest positive experience in the struggle for the building of socialism, and was the first to enter the period of comprehensive construction of communism. . . . It is stressed in the Statement that the universally acknowledged vanguard of the world communist movement has been and still remains the C.P.S.U. . . . At the moment, when there exists a large group of socialist countries, each of which is faced with its own tasks, when there are eighty-seven communist and workers' parties functioning, each of which, moreover, is faced with its own tasks, it is not possible for leadership over socialist countries and communist parties to be exercised from any center at all.[23]

Rump Leader: Polarization of the International Communist Movement

The course of the controversy between the Soviet Union and China since the conference in November, 1960, and the nature of the demands each has placed upon the other has resulted in the release of more information, greater employment of abuse and invective, less sophistication and discretion in argumentation, and greater visibility of underlying motives and intentions—all, more or less, variations on themes which are by now familiar.

The deterioration of the ideological quality of the conflict revealed the naked national interests which were in conflict. This did not signify that ideology has been rendered insignificant, but it did mean that it was becoming progressively national and internationalized. Furthermore, issues of national interest are more likely to mobilize popular support than are abstract ideological imperatives. The emergence of Communist China as well as of national communist states

in Eastern Europe required the dozen communist states involved to reconcile their divergent interests into a common ideology which could command universal respect. The result appears to be little more than a demand that the nonruling Communist parties subordinate their interests to those of the twelve communist states. The debilitating struggle between Moscow and Peking has further revealed the degeneration of a once universalistic ideology into a vehicle of national power.

The polarization of the communist system and movement has largely followed lines of geography, stage of economic development, and even race, rather than ideology, although each pole continues to justify its position ideologically. More and more, the Soviet Union is being forced to surrender its pretensions to universalism as it emerges as essentially the leader of a coalition of European communist nations and a group of Western Communist parties.

By the time of the Twenty-second Party Congress in October, 1961, the crystallization of national conflicts was already yielding to a new polarization. Soviet primacy had been dethroned, and the Chinese bid for leadership rebuffed. Each communist state was chartering its own road to socialism, and Soviet classifications of each country's stage of development seemed to be essentially a barometer of its relationship to Moscow. The Soviet position in the communist world was largely defined by its military power and economic strength, rather than by its ideological wisdom. Moscow adjusted to the new distribution of power in the system with grudging grace, although residual aspects of its former aspiration to centralized control continued to assert themselves. More out of habit than conviction, Soviet leaders continued to pose as the source of ideological innovation.

Khrushchev announced a grandiose plan for the construction of communism; promulgated new statutes for the party, which introduced the principle of rotation; and proclaimed a new party program, after discussion of a draft which had been widely circulated. Innovations like the "all-people's state" and the "all-people's party" were evidences more of the ideological exhaustion of the Soviet regime than its creativity. Although these enunciations were offered as guides to other states and parties, it was evident that each Communist party and country would examine the new ideological wares and carefully select and reject in accordance with its own needs.

After halfhearted attempts to oust the Albanian leader, Enver Hoxha, had failed, Khrushchev publicly excommunicated the Albanian party. As the most outspoken defender of the Chinese position, Tirana was a thorn in Khrushchev's side and had to be removed from the communist bloc.

Albania was China's first recruit in her anti-Soviet campaign within the system. She was soon joined by North Korea (which has since assumed a neutral position), and then by an ambivalent, but practical, North Vietnam. The Chinese were also ultimately able to entice the numerically powerful Indonesian party (which has since been all but destroyed) to their side, but they succeeded in generating factionalism and splinter groups in other countries more often than they won over their parties. Some communist states and Communist parties, in Europe and elsewhere, offered and tried to mediate, since most of the parties had a vested interest in preventing an open and formal break, although few were really interested in healing the split. As long as the two most powerful communist states were locked in controversy, it allowed the widest latitude of autonomy for the others. The advantages for the non-ruling parties, however, were not as clear.

As early as December, 1961, the Italian communist leader, Luigi Longo, openly admitted the pattern of polarization which was assuming shape in the communist world:

The quarrel between the Soviet and the Chinese Communist Parties refers to a much more important question than that of peaceful coexistence, possibilities of avoiding atomic war or the dispute over the cult of Stalin's personality. The real issue is a difference between their views on the true way to socialism and communism. The Chinese believe that the development of communism in the various countries of the socialist bloc should be indivisible. The countries that are more advanced economically should therefore take more interest in the troubles and sufferings of the more backward socialist countries and place all their material resources at their disposal. Those who hold this view cannot accept the competition between the Soviet Union and the United States and the capitalist countries. Nor can they accept peaceful coexistence or Soviet aid to underdeveloped countries. This help should be given to the economically backward countries in the socialist camp. The Chinese comrades do not hide their misgivings but we Italian communists believe that the Soviet policy of competition with the United States is more useful for the development of world communism than a concern for the equal economic development of all the countries in the socialist camp. The effect of Soviet policy is to accelerate the development of conflicts within the capitalist camp and to draw the colonial peoples in the socialist camp.[24]

The Cuban missile crisis, resulting at least in part from a Soviet attempt to demonstrate its ability to protect

[24] *L'Unita,* December 23, 1961.

all socialist countries, accelerated the fragmentation and polarization, and brought into question the credibility of what Moscow was seeking to demonstrate. Accusing Khrushchev of engaging in both "adventurism" and "capitulationism," and of risking thermonuclear war without prior consultation of other communist states (by dispatching missiles and then withdrawing them over Cuban objections), the Chinese sought to cast doubt on Moscow's willingness to defend other communist states against American imperialism. The Chinese gesture backfired, as the European parties rallied to the support of the Soviet Union, although Castro was obviously humiliated and peeved by the quick Soviet retreat.

The episode served to isolate China even more. Moscow organized its counterstroke against the Chinese, as Peking was subjected to an unprecedented crossfire of invective and abuse at a series of European party congresses held between November, 1962, and January, 1963 (Bulgarian, Hugarian, Italian, Czechoslovak, and East German). Moscow concentrated its fire on Albania, while the European parties converged upon the Chinese directly. Some parties, including the Cuban, attempted to preserve a posture of neutrality, but as the conflict escalated, polarization accelerated. Peking struck back in a series of unusually long documented and systematically organized attacks on Western parties, still adhering to the phrase "certain comrades" when referring to the Soviet leaders, but naming Italian and French leaders in their indictments. The conflict flared into the open in March, 1963, when Khrushchev's position seemed precarious at home. But the test ban treaty was soon signed, and the first phase of the long-sought-after détente with the United States was a reality.

Compromised Leader: The Soviet-American Détente and World Communism

After conclusion of the test ban treaty in 1963, the Soviet Union's relations with both the United States and Yugoslavia improved rapidly, and Moscow's image of American intentions underwent a radical change. From the Chinese point of view, something resembling a *reversement des alliances* had taken place, and they saw the Soviet Union and the United States as conspiring to deny China nuclear weapons and plotting to jointly dominate the world:

The leaders of the C.P.S.U. have completely reversed enemies and comrades. . . . The leaders of the C.P.S.U. are bent on seeking Soviet-United States cooperation for the domination of the world. They regard United States imperialism, the most ferocious enemy of the people in the world, as their most reliable friend and they treat the fraternal parties and countries adhering to Marxism-Leninism as their enemy. They collude with United States imperialism, the reactionaries of various countries, the renegade Tito clique and the right-wing Social Democrats in a partnership against the socialist fraternal countries. When they snatch at a straw from Eisenhower or Kennedy or others like them, or think that things are going smoothly for them, the leaders of the C.P.S.U. are beside themselves with joy, hit out wildly at the fraternal parties and countries adhering to Marxism-Leninism, and endeavor to sacrifice fraternal parties and countries on the altar of their political dealings with United States imperialism.[25]

The Chinese, having failed in their bid for primacy, and Moscow, having failed equally to bring the Chinese to heel, have tried to fasten responsibility for an organizational split upon

[25] *New York Times,* February 7, 1964.

each other. Recognizing that few Eastern European or Western Communist parties can identify their interests with those of the Chinese, Peking has virtually abandoned the Eastern Europe states and Western parties as possible instruments with which to organize a new revolutionary movement which would embrace both communists and noncommunist revolutionaries. Since Moscow has succeeded in virtually isolating Peking from the European communist states, the Chinese have retaliated by trying to freeze the Soviet Union out of Asia, Africa, and Latin America. Resorting to bonds of race and underdevelopment, Peking appears to be seeking to mobilize the nonwhite underdeveloped world against the white developed world, whether communist or noncommunist. Chinese representatives vigorously propagate the view that racial bonds are stronger than class bonds in Soviet calculations, and that Moscow will inevitably associate itself with whites against nonwhites. According to a Soviet indictment, the Chinese reason that, since nonwhites outnumber whites, the most effective road to Chinese hegemony is to organize the former under Chinese direction, in preparation for the day when they will displace the white race as the dominant element on the globe. This, according to Moscow, is the real meaning of the Chinese slogan, "The East Wind prevails over the West Wind":

The Chinese leaders represent matters as though the interests of the peoples of Asia, Africa, and Latin America were especially close and understandable to them, as though they were concerned most of all for the further development of the national liberation struggle in order to turn them into a tool for the realization of the hegemonic plans. . . . The Chinese . . . suggested to the representatives of the African and Asian countries that inasmuch as the Russians, Czechs, and Poles are white, "you can't rely on them," that they will allegedly "always be in collusion with the Americans—with whites," that the peoples of Asia and Africa have their special interests. . . . The Chinese leaders are trying to fan these feelings, in the hopes of setting the peoples of the former colonies against the socialist countries, against the working people of the developed capitalist countries. . . . China, they reason, is the largest country of the East and embodies its interests; here are born the "winds of history" that are to prevail over the "winds of the West." Thus this slogan is nothing but an ideological and political expression of the hegemonic aspirations of the Chinese leadership.[26]

The Chinese strategy emerged as follows: (1) to undermine the traditional Soviet claims to a special position in the communist world, by charging its leaders with "modern revisionism" and "the restoration of capitalism"; (2) to undermine the credibility of Soviet promises to defend and look after the military security of its smaller allies; (3) to isolate the Soviet Union from the underdeveloped countries and from the revolutionary movement in Latin America, Africa, and Asia. They were, in effect, energetically preparing the groundwork for a separate and rival revolutionary movement in these continents.

One of the consequences of the Sino-Soviet split was that it left the Soviet Union as a badly wounded leader of a rump, essentially Western, communist movement. And within this orbit, it has been defied even by its formerly most servile minions, the leaders of the Rumanian Communist party.

The sudden and unexpected ouster of Khrushchev from his posts of authority in October, 1964, diminished

[26] *Pravda*, April 3, 1964.

Soviet prestige further. The humiliating manner of Khrushchev's removal conveyed the impression that Chinese pressure and demands on the Soviet Union had somehow prevailed again. And the sense of outrage expressed by Eastern European leaders and by Western parties, most of whom had associated their interests with Khrushchev's policies, indicated that they were using the removal of their champion as an occasion to assert their increasing independence and autonomy. Some parties, like the Polish, Hungarian, Yugoslav, Italian, and French, were critical of Khrushchev mainly because he did not pursue the ultimate logic of de-Stalinization with sufficient vigor. Disturbed in particular by the nature of Khrushchev's ouster, they demanded and received an explanation. Togliatti's testament, issued in September, 1964, explicitly called for a greater public disclosure of factional and policy differences among Soviet leaders:

> It is not correct to refer to the socialist countries (including the Soviet Union) as if everything were always going well in them. . . . Some situations appear hard to understand. In many cases one has the impression there are differences of opinion among the leading groups, but one does not understand if this is really so and what the differences are. Perhaps it could be useful in some cases for the socialist countries also to conduct open debates on current problems, the leaders also taking part. Certainly, this would contribute to a growth in the authority and prestige of the socialist regime itself.[27]

This represented a further development in the reverse flow of demands from the periphery to the center in the communist world. Up to now, only Moscow exercised the right to inter-

fere and intervene in the factional squabbles in other communist states, while changes in Moscow were immune from outside scrutiny and intervention. The chorus of demands and criticisms which descended on Khrushchev's detractors and successors resulted, first, in arresting any further design to downgrade and degrade Khrushchev and, second, in accepting the demands for a detailed explanation of the sudden change in Soviet leadership. Further, the concern expressed by Eastern European and Western party leaders is a reflection of their determination to complete the transition from pawns to actors in the world communist system and movement. Either they participate in decisions pertaining to communism as a whole, and their interests are taken into account in arriving at these decisions, or they will assert their right to chart their own course.

Although the escalation of the Vietnam war in 1965, and the systematic bombing of North Vietnam by the United States, has caused a deterioration in Soviet-American relations and has arrested the détente, it has poisoned Sino-Soviet relations even more. In March, 1966, just prior to the opening of the Soviet Union's Twenty-third Communist Party Congress, which the Chinese refused to attend, Moscow and Peking once again exchanged denunciations. These summarized their complaints against one another, revealed new information about their past relations, and disclosed additional sources of continuing conflict and rivalry. In a secret letter circulated to Communist parties, Moscow leveled a series of changes against the Chinese leaders which seemed almost deliberately designed to provoke the Chinese into absenting themselves from the congress. In this letter, the Soviet leaders made the following charges: (1) China has inter-

27 *New York Times,* September 5, 1964.

fered with Soviet attempts to send material and military assistance to North Vietnam; (2) Chinese leaders have rebuffed all Soviet overtures for a meeting in order to settle their differences; (3) the Chinese have organized anti-Soviet demonstrations and have tried to incite the Soviet population against its leadership; (4) "the C.P.R. [Chinese People's Republic] leadership propagates ever more obstinately the thesis of potential military clashes between China and the Soviet Union"; (5) the Chinese have been "provoking border conflicts . . . [which] have increased again in recent months, . . . [and] allegations are being spread to the effect that the Soviet Union unlawfully holds Chinese territory in the Far East"; (6) and, finally;

there is every reason to assert that it is one of the goals of the policy of the Chinese leadership in the Vietnam question to cause a military conflict between the U.S.S.R. and the United States. They want a clash of the U.S.S.R. with the United States so that they may, as they say themselves, "sit on the mountain and watch the fight of the tigers."[28]

In conclusion, the Soviet letter reiterated the charge that Peking was manipulating the international communist movement and the national liberation movement for its own hegemonic purposes.

The Chinese leaders retorted, in a public statement, that the circulation of "an anti-Chinese letter to other parties, instigating them to join you in opposing China," was eloquent proof of insincerity in inviting the Chinese to attend the Twenty-third Congress of the CPSU. Peking accused Moscow of spreading false rumors that China was obstructing Soviet assistance to Vietnam, and "encroach-

ing on Soviet territory," The Soviet leaders were charged with stating that China was no longer to be viewed as a socialist country and of viewing the Chinese Communist party as an "enemy." The Chinese statement made a brief but spirited defense of Stalin, and accused Khrushchev's successors of intensifying his "revisionism" and "splittism," but the major thrust of its attack was that Moscow, far from wanting to aid North Vietnam, was encouraging the North Vietnamese to negotiate with the United States in order to clear the way for the Soviet Union and the United States to accelerate their joint conspiracy against China:

Despite the tricks you have been playing to deceive people, you are pursuing United States-Soviet collaboration for the domination of the world with your whole heart. . . . You have all along been acting in coordination with the United States in its plot for peace talks, vainly attempting to sell out the struggle of the Vietnamese people against United States aggression and . . . to drag the Vietnam question into the orbit of Soviet-United States collaboration. You have worked hand in glove with the United States in a whole series of dirty deals inside and outside the United Nations. In close coordination with the counterrevolutionary "global strategy" of United States imperialism, you are now trying to build a ring of encirclement around socialist China. . . . You have even aligned yourselves with United States imperialism . . . and established a holy alliance against China, against the movement and against the Marxist-Leninists.[29]

Thus, beginning in late 1958 and continuing into the sixties, was the gradual emergence of Peking and Moscow as the two poles of ideology and power in the communist camp. A new Soviet policy was to seek to

28 *New York Times*, March 24, 1966.   29 Ibid.

solidify Soviet control and influence over the Eastern European communist states, as a separate and distinct process from maintaining the unity of the communist world as a whole. This led to the creation of a European communist bloc, led by the Soviet Union. Only Albania, whose special fear is Yugoslavia—the main focus of attack by Peking—remains outside the Soviet bloc, playing a strange game of pitting Peking against Moscow. China has not yet organized a comparable regional communist bloc; indications are that Peking would like to organize such a regional grouping, made up of the four Asian communist states—China, North Korea, Mongolia, and North Vietnam—but her geographical position vis-à-vis the smaller Asian countries is not as decisive as the Soviet position with respect to Eastern Europe, since three of the four Asian communist countries border on the USSR itself. Mongolia, which fears Chinese power, has solidly associated itself with Moscow, while North Korea has issued a plague on both houses, and North Vietnam straddles the fence, using the Soviet Union as a counterpoise against Chinese domination, and relying upon Chinese threats to deter the United States from carrying the war to the north.

The eruption of the "Great Proletarian Cultural Revolution" in China, however, temporarily arrested the polarization of the world communist movement into two rival camps, as domestic turmoil, economic dislocation, and political disorientation served to diminish the Chinese role and prestige in the international community and among communist states and Communist parties. Between 1965 and 1968, Mao was locked in a titanic power struggle with Liu Shao-chi, the chief of state, and Teng Hsiao-ping, the general secretary of the Chinese Communist party, and with other prominent Chinese political and military leaders. Supported by Marshal Lin Piao and the People's Liberation Army—the "Red Guards"—and subsequently by Premier Chou En-lai, Mao succeeded in dislodging his opponents, whom he accused of Soviet-type "revisionism," but at the same time forfeited at least temporarily the opportunity to organize a rival bloc of communist states and Communist parties from among those disenchanted with the apparent Soviet loss of revolutionary zeal and those who would wish to use Peking as a counterpoise to Moscow in order to achieve greater autonomy from Soviet direction. As a result of the domestic turbulence in China, many Communist parties sympathetic to the Chinese position or at least "neutral" in the Sino-Soviet conflict were disaffected by the excesses and seeming irrationalities of the Cultural Revolution.

THE REEMERGENCE OF A SOVIET BLOC

Taking advantage of Moscow's agonies and indecisiveness, and relying upon both Peking and Washington to deter drastic action, Communist parties and states continued to widen their latitude of action in charting their own courses and policies. Although China was temporarily crippled as a rival center by the Cultural Revolution, the Soviet leaders were initially unable to arrest the disintegrative forces unleashed by the Sino-Soviet conflict, the Soviet-American détente, and the ouster of Khrushchev, and their power and influence in the world communist movement continued to slip. The loss of primacy in the movement at large now fed back to erode Soviet primacy in Eastern Europe itself. But Eastern Europe, for the Soviet Union, is not simply an ideological sphere but, more importantly, a regional sphere of political and security interest that constitutes the foundation of the Soviet claim as a regional, hegemonic, and global power, in contradistinction to her role as the center of a world revolutionary movement. And this slippage in Eastern Europe was taking place just at the time when, as a result of a series of Soviet diplomatic debacles culminating in the Arab defeat in June, 1967, Soviet prestige and power had reached a low ebb.

Challenged in the East by China and in the West by the United States and a West Germany flexing its diplomatic muscles with a new flexible and threatening *Ostpolitik*, the Soviet leaders were now unexpectedly confronted with insurgent Eastern European states moving progressively from recalcitrance to defiance, and even threatening renunciation of Soviet control over their destinies. This movement actually started before Khrushchev's ouster, when in April, 1964, Rumania announced what amounted to a virtual declaration of economic independence, with her leaders refusing to subordinate their economic development to the central coordination and planning to the bloc's Council of Mutual Economic Assistance (Comecon) by supinely accepting its dictate that Rumania concentrate on agricultural development and spurn industrialization.[30] Other Eastern European states continued selectively and cautiously to assert the priority of their own national interests in one area after another, as the defiance or recalcitrance of one state encouraged or emboldened other states to follow suit.

[30] See D. Floyd, *Rumania, Russia's Dissident Ally* (New York: Praeger, 1965), and Ghita Ionescu, *The Break-up of the Soviet Empire in Eastern Europe* (Baltimore: Penguin Books, 1965).

The Erosion of Soviet Control in Eastern Europe[31]

Khrushchev's ouster in October, 1964, accelerated the erosion of Soviet influence in Eastern Europe, as the expansion of the Eastern European states' autonomy in domestic affairs spilled out into the realm of foreign policy, when Rumania in 1965 refused to accept a Soviet demand that all the Warsaw Pact countries adopt uniform rules on military conscription and instead reduced the military obligation of her conscriptees to below the suggested level. In 1966, Rumania issued her first independent call for the dissolution of all military blocs and in the same year demanded that Moscow not employ nuclear weapons without consulting the other members of the Warsaw Treaty Organization. At the same time, Rumania questioned the right of Moscow to select the commander of the Warsaw Treaty forces and suggested that it be rotated among the other members.[32] The same year saw Rumania concluding a number of important commercial arrangements with Western countries, which reduced her trade with the Soviet Union to about 30 percent of the total by 1968, thus further reducing Moscow's capability to take punitive action.

Beginning in 1964 and continuing to the present, Rumanian leaders have refused to condemn Red China and side with Moscow in the Sino-Soviet split, and have adopted a policy

[31] Some of the material in the following pages is adapted from the following articles previously published by the author: "The Aftermath of the Czech Invasion," *Current History*, November, 1968; "Soviet Aims in East Europe," *Current History*, October, 1970; and "Soviet Foreign Policy at the Crossroads," *International Organization*, Autumn, 1969.

[32] See excerpts from Ceausescu's speech in *New York Times*, March 14, 1966.

of pursuing friendly relations with *all* countries, including the United States. In apparent pursuance of this policy, Rumania has served as a diplomatic conduit between the United States and North Vietnam, has established normal diplomatic relations with West Germany, has refused to condemn Israel as the aggressor in the June, 1967, Arab-Israeli war, and has continued to maintain diplomatic relations with Israel while also voting independently of the Soviet bloc on a number of issues in the United Nations.

During the first half of 1968, Rumania's defiance of the Soviet Union accelerated and was no doubt encouraged by developments in Czechoslovakia that alarmed the Soviet leaders and prompted Brezhnev to personally intervene in Prague in an unsuccessful attempt to forestall the ouster of Antonin Novotny, the reliable pro-Soviet conservative leader. Novotny was forced to resign as party secretary in favor of liberal reformer Alexander Dubcek, while General Ludvik Svoboda replaced him as president in January, 1968. Events accelerated as Novotny was suspended from the party and the Czech secret police was discredited and pilloried by sensational revelations, while the Czech press, in an unprecedented outburst of freedom, sharply criticized and even condemned Soviet policies and Soviet-modeled institutions in Czechoslovakia.

Although the situation in Eastern Europe was also deteriorating from Moscow's standpoint, the Soviet leaders were still convinced that they could restore their centrality if not primacy in the world communist movement by tolerating diversity in Eastern Europe in order to gather support for the excommunication of China. By initially indulging dissidence in Eastern Europe, China might be excluded from the movement, and once China was eliminated as a factor in communist affairs, then Moscow could reimpose controls in Eastern Europe. In this way—as Soviet leaders may have reasoned—the Soviet Union could reimpose "unity" on the world communist movement and preserve its regional ideological-security base on its western flank. Unfortunately for the Soviet leaders, too many Eastern European leaders saw through this strategy and refused to play the game.

By 1967, the turmoil in China had become incomprehensible and frightening to many European communist leaders. Hoping to capitalize on their anxieties and incredulity, the Soviet leaders, after being rudely rebuffed by Peking when they extended an olive branch, resurrected Khrushchev's earlier effort to have China declared anathema and excommunicated from the world communist movement.[33] Beginning in 1967, the traumatized Soviet leaders futilely sought to reestablish their authority, if not primacy, in the world communist movement by convening another world conference of Communist parties that could be prevailed upon to demand either that Peking conform with the Moscow line or be thrown out of the movement. The Soviet leaders moved cautiously and prudently, and attempted to accommodate the uncomfortable diversity that was threatening to metamorphose into disintegration. They begged and pleaded, cajoled and importuned, solicited counsel and advice, conducted rounds of consultation, and at times reverted to bribery and threats. Moving cautiously, they sought first to convene a purely European "Consultative Conference," hoping in this way to incrementally reestablish their authority by firmly reinforcing their primacy

[33] See *Pravda*, January 20, 1967.

in Europe. The first concrete result was a European conference held at Karlovy Vary, Czechoslovakia, on April 24–26, 1967, where they incautiously attempted to mobilize support against Peking, although it was called ostensibly to discuss European problems.[34]

The conference was far from successful; six of the thirty-one parties invited refused to attend, including the key Rumanian, Yugoslav, and Albanian parties, whose dissidence the conference was convened to eliminate. But the wary European communist leaders refused to lend themselves as Moscow's pawns against Peking, and were generally reluctant to excommunicate China from the world communist movement when it was her heretical presence and menacing rivalry to Moscow that impelled the Soviet leaders to be so reasonable and solicitous of Eastern European diversity. Eager to curry favor with the leaders of the European Communist parties, the Soviet leaders exhibited remarkable self-restraint, if not diplomatic dexterity, in an effort to convey an image of maturity and reasonableness in contrast to the infantilism and irrationality of the Chinese. Instead, they succeeded only in creating an impression of weakness, indecision, vacillation, drift, and paralysis of will. This was further reinforced by the Arab defeat a few months later, which cast a pall over the golden jubilee celebration of the Bolshevik Revolution, which was further tarnished by the conspicuous refusal of China and Albania to dispatch delegates to the commemoration ceremonies in November.

Although the golden jubilee conclave constituted the largest gathering of high-ranking communist officials ever convened in one place, the disarray in the communist movement was made more than manifest when Brezhnev's appeal for unity and his condemnation of Mao were less than enthusiastically received. Moscow, however, infelicitously used the occasion to gather support for yet another "consultative meeting" of all Communist parties to be held in Budapest.[35] Of the eighty-one parties invited, only sixty-seven attended, with the powerful and influential Chinese, Cuban, Albanian, North Korean, and North Vietnamese parties absent. Yugoslavia was not invited to the conference, which was convened in February, 1968, and the Rumanians only agreed to attend reluctantly after concessions and importunings by Moscow, only to bolt the conference after opposing Moscow's attempts to reimpose conformity and mobilize the conference against China.

Moscow's attempt to mobilize Eastern Europe against China proved to be counterproductive. Rumania and Czechoslovakia not only openly opposed any excommunication procedure that might serve as a precedent for future action against them, but were also encouraged to press forward with their own independent courses because Moscow's desperation was perceived as a sign of growing impotence and loss of control over events in Eastern Europe itself. The situation in Czechoslovakia, for example, deteriorated (from the Soviet standpoint) even more rapidly after the conference than before.

As the Czechs expanded their area of freedom in domestic affairs, Rumania expanded hers in foreign policy, and the two processes appeared to feed upon one another. One week after Rumania walked out on the

[34] For details, see *New York Times*, April 23 and 24, 1967.

[35] See *Pravda* and *Izvestia*, November 23, 1967.

Budapest conference (February 29, 1968), she refused to sign a "unanimous" declaration of the Warsaw Pact powers at Sofia endorsing the draft treaty against the spread of nuclear weapons sponsored by the Soviet Union and the United States.[36]

This was followed by Rumania's refusal to participate in the Dresden conference of Warsaw Pact powers and their crude threat to intervene in Czechoslovakia (March 23–24, 1968). She similarly refused to participate in the Warsaw meeting of the alliance (Czechoslovakia also refused to attend) on July 14–15, 1968, which issued an even more threatening ultimatum to Dubcek's Czech regime. During this period, Rumanian leaders publicly encouraged the Czech reformers, and at the height of the crisis, Rumanian President Nicolae Ceausescu offered to lend his personal presence in Prague in a joint gesture of defiance. Czech party leader Alexander Dubcek prudently declined the offer, although Ceausescu later followed Yugoslav President Tito to Prague in a display of solidarity. To the Soviet Union, it might have seemed that the pre-1939 Little Entente was being resurrected as a hostile grouping of communist states in its erstwhile placid garden of client and vassal states. After the Soviet intervention in Czechoslovakia, Rumania continued her gestures of defiance: she condemned the invasion; demanded that all communist states be masters of their own affairs; vowed never to allow Warsaw Pact forces on Rumanian territory; and placed the entire country on the alert, threatening to resist actively any possible Soviet encroachment on her sovereignty.

As events in Czechoslovakia took an ominous turn in the Soviet view, factional cleavages developed within

the Soviet leadership, as it grappled with the relative costs and risks of intervention or nonintervention in dealing with both the fracturing movement and the Soviet Union's deteriorating position in Eastern Europe. Diplomatic and military restraint after the Egyptian defeat, reasonableness in dealing with China, and maturity in handling diversity in Eastern Europe, while admirable qualities in the abstract, were nevertheless projecting an image of Soviet impotence and paralysis. In what may have been a final effort on the part of a divided Soviet leadership to assess the situation more accurately, an extraordinary series of meetings were held in Bratislava and Cierna, Czechoslovakia, early in August, between virtually the entire Soviet leadership and that of Czechoslovakia. Although the meeting was acrimonious enough, it appeared that the Soviet leadership was given sufficient assurance by the Czechs that the situation would not take a turn dangerous to Soviet interests and, hence, that intervention would be unnecessary.

On August 21, 1968, after an apparent and sudden shift in Soviet sentiment, the Red Army, leading a massive force of 650,000 Warsaw Pact troops, intervened to arrest developments in Czechoslovakia, allegedly in response to the pleas of "loyal" (i.e., pro-Soviet) Czech leaders, who invited them to expel the "Western imperialists," subdue the "counter-revolutionaries," and crush the treacherous "Dubcek clique."[37] Unable to pressure

---

[36] See New York Times, March 1, 1968.

[37] The "invitation" was necessary to provide the bare minimum basis of legality for the intervention, since the Warsaw Treaty does not give the member states the blanket authority, collectively or individually, unilaterally to declare the existence of "counter-revolutionaries" and/or external "imperialist forces" and intervene on their own initiative. The so-called invitation, published by Pravda

an aged but unyielding President Svoboda to legalize Soviet intervention and unable to persuade even a handful of Czechoslovakian Communists to betray their country by signing the prefabricated Soviet document of invitation and to form a Quisling government, the Soviet Union was forced to deal with the very government which its military forces had arrested. Svoboda was whisked off to Moscow and given a shameless red carpet welcome, while Dubcek, Premier Oldrich Cernik, and National Assembly President Josef Smirkovsky were transported to the Soviet capital in chains to "negotiate" a compromise settlement.

Erosion Arrested: The Occupation of Czechoslovakia

The Soviet occupation of Czechoslovakia in August, 1968, the thirtieth anniversary of the Munich Pact and the twentieth anniversary of the internal Communist party coup of 1948, thus signaled an ominous turn in Soviet relationships with Eastern Europe, whose full implications for internal Soviet developments, Sino-Soviet relations, the world communist movement, East-West relations, and particularly for Soviet-American relations are as yet not fully predictable. Clearly, however, it signifies a phase in which the naked security and national

interests of the Soviet Union have been unambiguously given a higher priority in Soviet calculations than ideological considerations. Whatever the rationalizations that were used by the USSR to justify its intervention in Czech affairs, they were only cursorily invoked and failed to persuade most of the Communist parties of the world. The Soviet action provoked condemnation by China, Rumania, Yugoslavia, and Albania among communist countries and elicited denunciation by the leadership of the French and Italian Communist parties. The flimsiness of Moscow's ideological pretext was further exposed by the frank Polish admission that Warsaw cooperated in the venture on grounds of "reasons of state." By resorting to the military occupation of Czechoslovakia, the Soviet leaders signified their determination to maintain a sphere of influence in the traditional great-power sense and have thereby implied that the Eastern European countries, for all practical purposes, can no longer serve as a springboard for the further communization of Europe. This signifies the full flowering of the Soviet state as a traditional imperialist state, whose influence and role in the world are determined less by the attractiveness of its ideology and more by the enormity of its power and its determination to employ it in its own interests.

When the Soviet Union established its sphere of influence in Eastern Europe after World War II, Soviet state interests and ideological interests were conveniently and logically in tandem. The establishment of a Soviet bloc simultaneously satisfied the historic and strategic necessity of a security belt and the convenience of a springboard for the further communization of Europe in accordance with the self-imposed mission assumed by Moscow.

---

and *Izvestia* on August 21, 1968, justified the intervention on both internal and external grounds: "Tass is authorized to state that party and state leaders of the Czechoslovak Socialist Republic have requested the Soviet Union and other allied states to give the fraternal Czechoslovak people immediate assistance, including assistance with armed forces. The reason for this appeal is the threat posed to the socialist system existing in Czechoslovakia and to the constitutionally established state system by counterrevolutionary forces that have entered into collusion with external forces hostile to socialism."

Increasingly, however, these two purposes of the Soviet presence in Eastern Europe have been rendered incompatible, as the Soviet role and position in the world communist movement have been challenged from within and eroded by obstacles and hazards from without. As a consequence, the Soviet leaders were forced to reexamine the basic premises of their presence in Eastern Europe and to face more realistically the uneven consequences of the further deterioration of their control.

The Soviet interest in Eastern Europe continues to reflect the dual character of the Soviet Union: as a great power with tendencies toward regional hegemony and as the guardian of an ideological movement with universalist purposes.[38] And while this dichotomy persists, its character has undergone a subtle transformation. During the first decade following World War II, Soviet leaders managed to coordinate their purposes in Eastern Europe with minimum conflict. Soviet ideological purposes were at first dominant, but as the needs of security began to conflict with the demands of ideology, Soviet actions and decisions favored Soviet security and national interest over ideology and world communism. The Soviet Union was faced with just such a dilemma during the Czech crisis of 1968, and resolved it by giving higher priority to its interests as a regional hegemonic power than to its position as guardian of an ideological movement. Although the Soviet leaders justified their action largely in ideological terms, the Soviet occupation of Czechoslovakia clearly reflected the dominance of the interests of the Soviet Union as a regional and global power.

The conspicuous role of the Soviet

military presence as the chief vehicle of Soviet control in Eastern Europe is revealed by the often forgotten fact that no less than four of the eight Eastern European communist states— Czechoslovakia, East Germany, Hungary and Poland—are under some form of military occupation. Yugoslavia and Albania are lost to the Soviet bloc, while Rumania persists in limiting her military responsibilities and obligations to Moscow at the Soviet leaders desperately search for some pretext to station Soviet troops on Rumanian soil. Of the six remaining members of the Soviet bloc, the USSR can safely rely only on Bulgaria to follow the Soviet lead without the presence or threat of Soviet troops.

Clearly, the Soviet leadership has failed to transform Stalin's rigid neocolonial system into a socialist commonwealth of states. The common characteristic of the communist countries—i.e., of the "socialist system"— was insufficient to generate a common interest. When a number of Eastern European states began to chart their separate roads—not necessarily in the direction of "communism"—the incompatibility rather than the compatibility of interest within the bloc became clear. The basic divergencies of interest materialized not only in the domestic realm—threatening to undermine the common features of the sociopolitical order—but in foreign policy as well, posing a threat not only to the "socialist order" but also to Soviet security. By reverting to naked military power to reestablish its slipping grip on its crumbling Eastern European empire, Moscow has ushered in a new phase in Soviet-Eastern European relations that will once again redefine its role in the world communist movement.

The developments culminating in the Soviet occupation of Czechoslovakia and the reconstitution of a So-

---

[38] For a fuller treatment of this theme, see chap. 5.

viet bloc were the consequences of two distinct, but closely interrelated, processes set into motion by the policies of the Khrushchev era: "de-Stalinization" and "desatellitization." Although both concepts are defined in terms of a reaction against the starting point of each process and hence by now have assumed a more positive character in each case, it might still be useful to employ these terms in spite of their etymological obsolescence and inappropriateness. *De-Stalinization* refers primarily to the dismantling of Stalinist institutions and practices in domestic life, and in Eastern Europe it originally closely followed the de-Stalinization taking place in the Soviet Union itself. *Desatellitization* refers to the process whereby the individual countries of Eastern Europe gradually reasserted their autonomy and independence from Soviet control, a process that is still continuing. Both processes have contributed to the process of substantively transforming the principle of "proletarian internationalism" from a doctrine justifying unilateral Soviet penetration into the sociopolitical systems of other communist states into one justifying multilateral and reciprocal intervention, or interpenetration.

Desatellitization has been a universal phenomenon, but de-Stalinization has not involved all communist countries. At a certain stage of development the two processes came into conflict, since some countries asserted their independence in order to retain certain Stalinist institutions and norms or to resist their complete dismantling. In Albania, for example, desatellitization has resulted in the intensification of Stalinist norms rather than greater internal liberalization. De-Stalinization was also resisted in varying degrees in Rumania, Bulgaria, and Czechoslovakia, although it had recently been almost completely repu-

diated in Czechoslovakia. De-Stalinization is, in effect, a process of internal liberalization, a process that has progressed at varying tempos in Eastern Europe, sometimes faster and sometimes slower than in the Soviet Union itself. The two most independent countries of Eastern Europe reflect opposing tendencies with reference to Stalinism, with Yugoslavia the most distant in its departure from Stalinist doctrines and Albania the least.

The terms *de-Stalinization* and *desatellitization* are thus no longer entirely accurate in describing the manifold transformations taking place in Eastern Europe. Both processes, it is now clear in retrospect, were but transitional episodes in the drive for greater autonomy internally and greater independence in foreign policy. In the case of de-Stalinization, the process had moved into the phase of de-Sovietization in some countries and could eventuate even in decommunization, whereas desatellitization might logically result not only in withdrawal from the Soviet alliance and neutralization, but eventually culminate in a reversal of alliances. Either development would affect the balance of power between East and West, and both taken together could alter the balance irreversibly. All of these fears and hazards, which were repeatedly and candidly expressed by Moscow, Warsaw, and East Germany, congealed to trigger the Soviet occupation of Czechoslovakia.

It is not always easy to determine which of the two processes—internal autonomy or independence in foreign policy—is perceived by the Soviet leadership as posing the greater danger to its interests. Undoubtedly the Soviet leaders are sharply divided on this point, as they are on many others, and the relative danger of the threat of each process varies over time and from one country to another. The Soviet leadership might thus tolerate varying degrees of autonomy and independence, which would in turn depend upon their perception of the strategic importance of the country concerned or the reliability and prudence of its leadership, which further involves an intuitive calculation of the historical images of the USSR prevailing in each country. The two processes pose distinct, unrelated sets of dangers and risks for Moscow, which seem to coincide not only with the two main purposes of the Soviet presence in Eastern Europe but also with the two major factional cleavages in the Soviet leadership. Thus growing internal autonomy challenges directly the ideological values and norms of the Soviet system and indirectly the security of the Soviet state, while independence in foreign policy erodes directly Soviet power in world affairs and constitutes indirectly a challenge to Soviet ideological goals and values. Concomitantly, some Soviet leaders, especially those that are ideologically conservative, are more likely to be disturbed by deviations and departures from the Soviet system, while others might be agitated more by the degree of independence asserted in foreign policy, and still others might find both processes equally unpalatable and any combination of the two downright intolerable. Aside from factors such as inertia, factional paralysis, and the impact of cumulative developments, these conflicting perceptions of the "main" danger may account for the extraordinary self-restraint exercised by Moscow toward Rumania's growing independence in foreign policy and her intolerance of developments in Czechoslovakia.

While the Soviet leaders have accommodated and adjusted to the impulse of the Eastern European states to manage their own affairs, as long as they remain "socialist," the absence of any common or universal criteria of what constitutes "socialism" since Khrushchev's denunciation of Stalin in 1956 creates a wide area of ambiguity which causes anxiety in Moscow and inspires boldness and innovation in Eastern European capitals. What started out as "de-Stalinization" in Czechoslovakia was soon legitimized in the doctrine of "separate roads to socialism," but it quickly became evident that the "separate roads" doctrine created both logical possibilities and practical opportunities for subverting and displacing the social orders inspired and established by the Soviet Union. Thus was born the Soviet equivalent of the "falling dominoes" theory. De-Stalinization leads to "separate roads," which proliferate into various "national deviations," which may in turn inspire "modern revisionism," which is but a prelude to "social democracy" that quickly degenerates into "bourgeois democracy" and the "restoration of capitalism," which Russia cannot tolerate in Czechoslovakia or anywhere else.

At what point in this process are Soviet leaders apt to intervene? Has Soviet armed intervention provided clearcut criteria for judging what might be called the Soviet "threshold of intolerance"? On the surface, it might appear that the threshold of intolerance in the case of Czechoslovakia was reached at a point somewhere between "modern revisionism" and "social democracy," and that a precedent for future interventions has thus been established. In concrete terms, the intervention in Czechoslovakia suggests that the Soviet Union may intervene under the following conditions:

1. when censorship, restraints, and sanctions on freedom of expression in the press, arts, and sciences are removed

and freedom of expression and assembly are generally restored;[39]

2. when pressures develop for the restoration of a multiparty system that would jeopardize the political monopoly and control of the Communist party;[40]

3. when economic innovations are planned that would seriously dilute the "socialist" character of the economic order, returning some sectors of the economy to private hands and allowing a greater latitude for further expansion of the private sector; and

4. when parliamentary government—whose power, responsibility and accountability would be to the electorate rather than to the Communist party—is restored.

In Czechoslovakia, such internal policy changes were not sufficient in themselves to provoke Soviet intervention, given the grave risks and costs that such intervention would entail. If changes could have been *contained* and *restricted* to Czechoslovakia, then intervention might have been averted. It appears that it was precisely this assurance that Dubcek and his reformist colleagues gave and which the Soviet leaders initially accepted. Upon further reflection, however, it was judged that Dubcek was either unwilling or unable to control the situation

at home and was certainly unable to prevent the contagion of liberalization from spreading across Czech frontiers.[41]

Another major risk in allowing internal autonomy is that it might create pressures for far greater independence in foreign policy. Some movements in the direction of an independent Czechoslovakian foreign policy raised apprehensions in Moscow, frightened Polish Premier Wladyslaw Gomulka, and appeared downright ominous to East German party leader Walter Ulbricht. These included not only a possible political and diplomatic rapprochement with West Germany (encouraged by Bonn's repudiation of the Munich agreement of 1938) originating within the Dubcek regime, but also the prospect of a large hard-currency loan from West Germany that might set the stage for a radical reorientation of Czechoslovakia's trade from the Soviet Union and Eastern Europe to Western countries.[42] The fact that such a rearrangement of trade relations coincided with Czech economic interests and was indispensable for economic recovery served to reinforce the Soviet fear that a change in trade relations would soon be followed by significant alterations in Czechoslovakia's political and ideological alignments.

Furthermore, when Brezhnev's mission to save Czech Premier Novotny failed in December, 1967, and particularly after Novotny's suspension from the party and the discrediting of the secret police by the Dubcek regime,

[39] For the ventilation of Soviet fears concerning freedom of expression in Czechoslovakia, see Yuri Zhukov, "Strange Undertaking of *Obrana Lidu,*" *Pravda,* July 27, 1968, and "Double Game," *Pravda,* July 28, 1968. For Soviet atttacks on Czech "revisions" of recent history, see A. Nedorov, "Contrary to the Facts," *Izvestia,* June 29, 1968, and "What Does 'The Student' Teach?—The Prague Weekly 'for Young Intelligentsia' and Its Concept of Democracy," *Komsomolskaya Pravda,* June 21, 1968.

[40] This was reflected in the vicious Soviet attacks upon the political manifesto, "2000 Words," which called upon the Dubcek regime to purge the party of Novotny followers, and contained a savage criticism of the party as the source of Prague's ills for the past twenty years.

[41] This was the crux of the warnings in the Dresden and Warsaw statements and a major reason given for the necessity of intervention in *Pravda,* August 22, 1968.

[42] Moscow feared that not only Prague but also other Eastern European states might be attracted by the blandishments of West Germany's "new Eastern policy," which became a focus of Soviet attack.

Czech opinion on foreign policy became bolder and—from the Soviet point of view—outrageous. A prominent Czech general[43] challenged Soviet domination of the Warsaw Pact command structure; others called for a reexamination of Czechoslovakia's role in the Warsaw Treaty Organization; while still others demanded that future Czech foreign policy be based on Czech national interests and not on the interests of the Soviet Union, other communist states, or the world communist movement. Some even called for a frankly "neutralist" policy.

The decisive factor in a sharply divided Soviet leadership may well have been the real fear that Ulbricht would not be able to resist the pressures for liberalization in East Germany that would inevitably be generated if Dubcek were successful in resisting Soviet pressures. Greater internal autonomy in East Germany would inevitably result in further popular pressures for an independent reexamination of East Germany's role as a separate state bound in permanent vassalage to the USSR. Under these conditions, the Soviet Union would be confronted with a crisis of incalculable magnitude. The situation might spin out of control and result in a reunited Germany that would fundamentally alter the entire balance of power in Europe and conjure up the nightmare of another German march to the east. At best, an autonomous East Germany would sap Soviet energies and constitute a permanent drain on Soviet power, resources, and nerves.

Soviet Options Before the Invasion of Czechoslovakia: Lost Opportunities

It is apparent in retrospect that the Czechoslovakian crisis confronted the

[43] Lieuteuant General Vaclav Prchlik, head of the Military Department of the Central Committee of the Czech Communist party.

Soviet leaders with their moment of truth in Eastern Europe: to intervene or not to intervene? Either course would have produced unpalatable and distasteful consequences. Clearly the Soviet Union had reached an important crossroads in its relationship with Eastern Europe. Before the intervention in Czechoslovakia, the Soviet position in Eastern Europe had been clearly slipping in response partly to the apparent erosion of NATO and the diminution of the U.S. threat to the communist system. Either the Soviet empire was on the verge of dissolution, as Rumania virtually seceded from the Warsaw alliance and Czechoslovakian liberalization appeared to be irresistible and threatening to infect all of Eastern Europe, or it was on the brink of a fundamental transformation. The transformation of relationships could have assumed one of three forms:

1. The Warsaw Treaty Organization and Comecon could be *converted* into an authentic socialist "commonwealth of nations," in which the individual members would be allowed a wide latitude of internal deviation from the Soviet norms of socialism, exercise greater freedom, and engage in trade and cultural relations with the West, while remaining tightly bound to the Soviet Union in a purely defensive alliance. Such a transformation would presuppose a continuation and expansion of the détente, a tacit disavowal of ideological aggressiveness in foreign policy, and give greater form and shape to the new commonwealth as a purely regional association, in which the interests of the smaller members would no longer be sacrificed to those of the Soviet Union in the name of the bogus principle of "proletarian internationalism" or subordinated to purely Soviet "great-power diplomacy" in its dealings with

the United States or Communist China. The chief objections to such a transformation before August, 1968, were that it threatened to isolate East Germany, render Poland even more dependent upon the Soviet Union vis-à-vis West Germany, and deprive the Soviet Union of some useful levers and pressures in dealing with the German problem, the United States, and Communist China.

2. The spontaneous *devolution* of the Warsaw Treaty Organization, Comecon, and other multilateral organizations might occur; they could be replaced with a series of bilateral and trilateral agreements. The Soviet Union could make periodic ad hoc adjustments to the situation, allowing the natural interests of each state to more or less shape its internal development and its individual relationship with the Soviet Union and with the every Eastern European state to take a policy stand on each and every facet of Moscow's global foreign policy or to allow the Soviet leaders to determine ideological orthodoxy on internal matters. In matters remote to the interests of the smaller states (for example, American-Soviet competition in such countries as those of Africa and Latin America), they would be permitted to remain uninvolved. Global policy would be properly the province of the global powers and not of their client or allied states. The United States, for example, has learned to live with some of its allied and client states which are reluctant or even opposed to becoming involved in America's global enterprises. Czechoslovakia's internal innovations and Rumania's semi-independent foreign policy were clearly the prototypes of the kinds of behavior the Soviet leaders would have to live with in this kind of arrangement. Moscow would rely upon a common ideology, intersecting interests, the prudence and good sense of the smaller countries, and the reservoir of goodwill toward Moscow that would flow from such a policy to become the foundations of a new relationship. Under these conditions, the relationship of the individual member states with the Soviet Union could vary considerably, as would their relations with one another. The artificiality of imposed "fraternal" relations would be replaced by something more uncertain but perhaps more durable and natural.

The Soviet leaders found this second alternative to be clearly unacceptable, and the invasion of Czechoslovakia was the immediate consequence. A choice of this alternative would involve all of the hazards of the first alternative and, furthermore, undermine the foundations of the existing sociopolitical structure at home through Moscow's implicit legitimization of all changes taking place in Czechoslovakia and those that might take place elsewhere. The possible feedback effects into the Soviet Union were apparently too much to contemplate.

3. The Soviet empire could be *reconstituted* as a "sphere of influence" or domination. Wherever and whenever necessary, naked force and fear would replace reliance on the shibboleths of ideology, pliable local leaders, and a common social system, in order to preserve Soviet control. This would clearly require a partial restoration of Stalinist hegemonic controls in Eastern Europe, which, however, would inevitably entail the risk of their recrudescence at home. Just as the liberalization of communism in Czechoslovakia threatened to infect the Soviet Union itself, the reappearance of Stalinist practices in Eastern Europe would probably encourage residual Stalinists in Soviet society to agitate for similar measures at home.

The Soviet leaders apparently opted for this third alternative as a stopgap —more as a *threat* to impose Soviet military controls in all Eastern Europe rather than as a full-fledged policy. But in the process of selecting this option, even on a temporary basis, they may have effectively foreclosed the other two. It would seem that the Soviet Union, by its action in Czechoslovakia, has not only expended whatever remained of the reservoir of goodwill associated with the historical, cultural, and ideological considerations of the past, but has reduced its options to preserving its position by force, threat, and periodic intervention, or allowing its control of Eastern Europe to completely disintegrate. For the moment, the Soviet Union has enhanced the credibility of its determination to use its immense power to control its immediate environment, but simultaneously it has restored its reputation for diplomatic perfidy, impetuous brutality, and psychological insecurity. Not only the communist world, but the communist states of Eastern Europe seem irrevocably split.

Before the Soviet invasion and occupation of Czechoslovakia, the countries of Eastern Europe could be grouped into four distinct categories in reference to their relationship to the Soviet Union: (1) Yugoslavia, an independent, virtually "neutralist" and "nonaligned" communist state that exercised complete sovereignty in its domestic and foreign policy; (2) Albania, an independent, anti-Soviet (antirevisionist) communist state, ideologically allied to but not under the control of China or any other communist state; (3) the Warsaw Pact countries of Poland, Czechoslovakia, Bulgaria, East Germany, and Hungary, which are residual satellite states, or, more properly, client states of Moscow; (4) Rumania, a dissident and uncooperative member of the Warsaw Treaty Organization and Comecon, a "neutral" in the Sino-Soviet conflict, and quasi-independent in its foreign policy. After the invasion of Czechoslovakia, both Yugoslavia and Rumania were further alienated from Moscow and the bloc, Albania formally withdrew from the Warsaw Treaty Organization, and Czechoslovakia was returned to vassalage, while Poland was forced into greater dependence on the Soviet Union and, like East Germany, was threatened with de facto diplomatic isolation. The alignments in Eastern Europe now coincided more closely with the national self-interests of individual communist states rather than with ideological affinities. Thus, the three communist states that were openly opposed to and hostile to the occupation of Czechoslovakia represent three *doctrinally* different regimes. Albania is a neo-Stalinist communist state and Yugoslavia is a "liberal" communist state, while Rumania is doctrinally very close to Soviet orthodoxy. In terms of foreign policy, Yugoslavia is "neutralist" and "nonaligned" and Rumania is a Warsaw alliance member, while Albania is allied to Moscow's rival, Peking. Yet all three are engaged in informal and indirect consultations regarding their opposition to any attempt by the Soviet leaders to apply the "Brezhnev doctrine" to their countries.

The liberalization in Czechoslovakia has been arrested and is being reversed. Soviet leaders have not only announced their intention to keep Soviet troops on the Czechoslovak-West German frontier indefinitely, but are also imposing their dictates on purely internal Czechoslovakian affairs, and have refused to allow Prague to expand its trade relations outside the Soviet bloc. Like Hungary, Czechoslovakia has been demoted from clientage to vassalage. While the initial reaction in the other countries of Eastern Europe was fear and apprehension combined with outrage and shame, they have been given notice that Moscow will not hesitate to reduce its fraternal allies to vassalage if the Soviet Union disapproves of their internal and external policies.

Legitimizing Soviet Intervention: The "Brezhnev Doctrine"

Before the Soviet invasion of Czechoslovakia in August, 1968, all Soviet interference in the internal affairs of Eastern European countries had been defined in terms of intraparty relationships. When intervention was necessary, the Soviet party dictated or directed changes in the leadership structure and ideological orientation of the particular satellite's Communist party, which in turn altered the structure and composition of the government to introduce new policies and directions. Theoretically, there was no Soviet state interference in the domestic affairs of another state. While Soviet intervention in Eastern European states was frequently blatant and ruthless, particularly from 1947 to 1953, the USSR was nevertheless scrupulous in disclaiming any right to intervention, and perennially reaffirmed its devotion to the norms of nonintervention and noninterference and to the concept of the absolute sovereignty of states under international law. The Soviet leaders were thus careful to avoid any precedent that might justify intervention on the part of other powers.

For the first time in its history, the Soviet Union has fashioned a theory that justifies in advance the right of the Soviet Union, as a state and not by means of the party, to intervene in the affairs of another communist state. On the grounds that the subversion or displacement of the socialist system in one country endangers its existence in others, each individual communist state is precluded from the right to replace its socialist system with another. Theoretically, any communist state enjoys the same right, but at this time only the Soviet Union possesses the power to exercise it. In some respects, the "Brezhnev doctrine" resembles very closely the Monroe and Wilson doctrines, which have been multilateralized and institutionalized in the Organization of American States. In each instance, a collective or multilateral right to intervene in the affairs of member states is largely a juridical figleaf concealing the unilateral right of a regional Great Power to intervene.

The Brezhnev doctrine, which was incrementally developed via a series of Soviet statements, speeches, declarations, and resolutions, is theoretically applicable to the entire "socialist commonwealth of nations," including China, Yugoslavia, and Albania, although its immediate concrete effect is to transform the Warsaw Pact countries into a quasi-legal Soviet sphere of influence. The doctrine simultaneously legalizes and legitimizes the occupation of Czechoslovakia and provides the ideological and legal rationale for future Soviet interventions in the affairs of other communist countries. Hence, it has been condemned by China, Yugoslavia, Albania, Rumania, and many other ruling and nonruling parties.

Thus, Foreign Minister Andrei Gromyko, in order to give the doctrine a quasi-juridical status under international law, in a speech before the U.N. General Assembly on October 3, 1968, in effect declared that the "socialist commonwealth" constituted a legal-ideological entity whose total sovereignty was superior to that of its individual members:

The countries of the socialist commonwealth have their own vital interests, their own obligations, including those of safeguarding their mutual security and their own socialist principles of mutual relations based on fraternal assistance, solidarity and internationalism. This commonwealth constitutes an inseparable entity cemented by unbreakable ties such as history has never known. . . . The Soviet Union and other socialist countries have on many occasions warned those who are tempted to try to roll back the socialist commonwealth, to snatch at least one link from it, that we will neither tolerate nor allow that to happen. . . . The Soviet Union deems it necessary to proclaim from this rostrum, too, that the socialist States cannot and will not allow a situation where the vital interests of socialism are infringed upon and encroachments are made on the inviolability of the boundaries of the socialist commonwealth and, therefore, on the foundations of international peace. It goes without saying that such an action as military aid to a fraternal country to cut short the threat to the socialist order is an extraordinary step, it can be sparked off only by direct actions of the enemies of socialism inside the country and beyond its boundaries, actions creating a threat to the common interests of the camp of socialism.

Brezhnev, whose name graces the doctrine, in his definitive statement merged ideological sovereignty and state sovereignty into what might essentially be called a doctrine of "limited sovereignty":

The socialist states stand for strict respect for the sovereignty of all countries. We emphatically oppose interference into the affairs of any states, violations of their sovereignty. At the same time the establishment and defense of the sovereignty of states, which have embarked upon the road of building socialism, is of particular significance for us, Communists. . . . The C.P.S.U. has always advocated that each socialist country

determine the specific forms of its development along the road of socialism with consideration for its specific national conditions. However, it is known, comrades, that there also are common laws governing socialist construction, a deviation from which might lead to a deviation from socialism as such. And when the internal and external forces hostile to socialism seek to revert the development of any socialist country toward the restoration of the capitalist order, when a threat to the cause of socialism in that country, a threat to the security of the socialist community, as a whole, emerges, this is no longer only a problem of the people of that country but also a common problem, concern for all socialist states.[44]

And an authoritative article in *Pravda* had earlier explicitly emphasized that "the sovereignty of individual Socialist countries cannot be counterposed to the interest of world Socialism and the world revolutionary movement."[45]

The enunciation of the "Brezhnev doctrine" of limited sovereignty thus creates new horizons of possible Soviet abuse in relations with other communist countries. The doctrine attempts, first of all, to unilaterally legalize the presence of Soviet troops in Czechoslovakia; secondly, to justify the selective reimposition of Soviet military and political controls over the Warsaw Pact states; and finally, to provide in advance a legitimate rationale for Soviet military intervention in any communist state, including China, Yugoslavia, and Albania. The intent to the doctrine was quickly appreciated in all communist capitals, particularly Peking:

[44] *Pravda*, November 13, 1968.
[45] *Pravda*, September 26, 1968. See also Vernon V. Aspaturian, "East European Relations with the U.S.S.R.," in *The Changing Face of Communism in Eastern Europe*, ed. Peter Toma (Tuscon: Arizona University Press, 1970).

"Limited sovereignty" in essence means that Soviet revisionism can encroach upon the sovereignty of other countries and interfere in their domestic affairs at will, and even send its aggressor troops into the territory of these countries to suppress the people there, while the people invaded have no right to resist aggression and safeguard their own sovereignty and independence. This is an out-and-out fascist "theory." . . . The fascist theories of the Soviet revisionist renegade clique are of the same kind as the tsars' imperialist ones created to invade other countries.[46]

The New Soviet-Czech Treaty: Legal Model for the Brezhnev Doctrine. The first concrete juridical application of the Brezhnev doctrine was the Soviet-Czechoslovak Treaty of Mutual Assistance signed on May 6, 1970.[47] Its provisions constitute a fundamental departure from previous bilateral treaties between Moscow and other communist states, and the treaty clearly constitutes the model that Soviet leaders would like to impose on other communist countries, although Rumania successfully thwarted such an imposition when the Soviet-Rumanian treaty was renewed two months after the Czech treaty. In line with the provisions of the Brezhnev doctrine, and affirming the frankly juridico-ideological nature of the treaty, Czech party leader Husak made the extraordinary statement that the treaty was based on the recognition that

Czechoslovakia's western borders are also the borders of the Socialist camp, and . . . our state can develop only in close alliance and friendship with the Soviet Union and other friendly Socialist states.[48]

Essentially, the new Soviet-Czech treaty of alliance departs from previ-

ous Soviet bilateral treaties in that: (*a*) it declares that the defense and consolidation of "socialist gains are a common internationalist responsibility" and therefore a multilateral obligation (preamble and article 5); (*b*) it omits geographical limitations on the application of the alliance (article 10); (*c*) it places no ideological limitations on its application—i.e., it is not directed against particular types of "aggression," e.g., fascist aggression (article 10); (*d*) it attempts to extrapolate its provisions into the Warsaw Pact (article 9), although the latter is specifically limited in its geographical application to an "attack in Europe," is aimed at Germany or those supporting Germany, and is scrupulously non-ideological in its formal provisions. The implications of the new treaty are as follows: (1) it goes into effect when either party is attacked anywhere by anybody, presumably including China; (2) by making defense of "socialist gains" a duty of the entire "socialist commonwealth," it implies that the Warsaw Pact powers are obligated to come to the defense of either party if they are subject to attack from any quarter; and (3) it converts Czechoslovakia into a de facto protectorate of the Soviet Union, and provides the legal basis for extending this status to other Warsaw Pact countries.

The new Soviet-Czech treaty, if we are to highlight its distinctiveness, should be compared with other Soviet bilateral treaties renewed during the past decade. It most closely resembles the Soviet-Mongolian treaty, renewed in 1966, which dropped Japan as its ostensible target, in favor of any aggressor. Since China is the only state bordering on both Mongolia and the USSR, the treaty appears clearly aimed at China. The Soviet treaties with East Germany (1964) and with Poland (renewed in 1965) are more

[46] *Jenmin Jihpao,* March 17, 1969.
[47] See *Pravda,* May 7, 1970, for full text.
[48] Ibid.

closely linked with the Warsaw Pact, although the East German treaty includes ideological provisions excluded from the Polish treaty. In other words, at least three Soviet treaties—those with East Germany, with Mongolia, and with Czechoslovakia—are explicitly based upon the ideological principles of "socialist internationalism," the most recent authoritative interpretation of which is the "Brezhnev doctrine."[49]

Two months after the Soviet-Czech treaty, the Soviet Union and Rumania renewed their treaty of alliance, after two years of negotiation. Although Rumania has, since the Soviet invasion of Czechoslovakia, proceeded more cautiously and prudently in defying the Soviet leaders, Moscow was unable to impose a Czech-type treaty upon Bucharest. The Soviet-Rumanian treaty, unlike the Czech treaty, is essentially a state document, and was signed only by the two premiers, whereas party leaders Brezhnev and Husak had also signed the Soviet-Czech treaty. None of the provisions of the Brezhnev doctrine has been incorporated into the Rumanian treaty, and whereas the treaty does not specifically limit its application to Europe, neither does it stipulate that the casus foederis be an armed attack against either party by "any state or group of states," as stated in the Czech treaty. Furthermore, the Rumanian treaty specifically mentions NATO in connection with the Warsaw Pact, and thus its restricted geographical application can be inferred. And finally, while the Soviet-Czech treaty clearly states that in foreign policy the two parties will proceed "from their common position agreed upon in the interests of both states," the Rumanian treaty merely states that the partners will consult "with a view toward coordinating their positions."[50]

It should be reemphasized that the occupation of Czechoslovakia, the Brezhnev doctrine, and the new treaties with Mongolia and Czechoslovakia are designed to transform Eastern Europe into a constellation of military-ideological protectorates not only to be used as a possible within-system grouping against China, but also to render Eastern Europe less vulnerable to the blandishments of West Germany's *Ostpolitik* and to the U.S. policy of "bridge-building" set into motion under the Johnson administration. The Soviet leaders perceive three major external sources of possible intrusion in their Eastern European sphere: the United States, China, and West Germany. For more than a decade, they have been denouncing an alleged Bonn-Washington axis within NATO, and in more recent years they have publicly conjured up nightmares of a Sino-American combine in the East constituting one side of a giant nutcracker working in concert with a German-American axis in the West. Since the United States plays a prominent role in both hallucinations because of its overarching global position, it might not take too much uncontrolled imagination to conjure up the image of an artful United States skilfully orchestrating a squeeze play, employing Bonn as its instrument in the West and Peking as its unwitting foil in the East. The force of this nightmare, however, has been substantially mitigated because of the domestic disturbances and eroding social consensus within the United States and the quagmire of war in Vietnam, both of which have served

---

49 For details, see Vernon V. Aspaturian, "Soviet Aims in East Europe," *Current History*, October, 1970.

50 For text of the Rumanian treaty, signed on July 7, 1970, see *New York Times*, July 8, 1970.

to blunt United States will and purpose to function as a militant global power.

It has been the grand strategy of Khrushchev's successors to deal with each of their main rivals within the context of an overall design embracing policies on three separate levels, each corresponding to one of the three threats. With regard to the United States, the Soviet leaders operate at the global level, in terms of strategic balances, nuclear stockpiles, missile development and overall rivalry in all parts of the globe. The arena within which the Soviet Union contests China is somewhat smaller and is restricted largely to the world communist movement and the "Third World." Eastern Europe is relevant to the Sino-Soviet confrontation only because it is part of the ideological arena.

Within this context, West Germany operates in the smallest arena of all, at the regional level, but Bonn's choice of battlefields is precisely Moscow's Eastern European garden. Consequently, Eastern Europe has become the primary focus of West Germany's challenge. But since the Soviet sphere of influence in Eastern Europe is the irreducible desideratum underpinning the Soviet Union's existence as a hegemonic power, West Germany's *Ostpolitik* threatened the foundations of the Soviet role as a global power and an ideological center.

As a consequence of the Brezhnev doctrine, the old *Ostpolitik* is dead, as are the old United States policies of "bridge-building." In their place, as a result of the victory of the Social Democrats in the elections of 1969, a new controversial *Ostpolitik* fashioned by Chancellor Willy Brandt has emerged, which, while acceptable to Moscow, is largely unacceptable to the Christian Democrats. The new *Ostpolitik* does not parallel any new

United States policy in the area, aside from the tacit acceptance by the United States of Soviet hegemony there.

The occupation of Czechoslovakia effectively nullified the initial successes of the old *Ostpolitik*, and the Brezhnev doctrine insured that it could not be resumed in its existing form. As a temporary measure, the Brezhnev doctrine must therefore be judged a success in terms of Moscow's position as a global and as a regional power. It has compelled the United States to abandon whatever residual elements of the old "rollback" and "liberation" policies remained and virtually to jettison its new policies of "bridge-building." For all practical purposes, the United States now accepts the Eastern European status quo and tacitly recognizes that the Eastern European region is immune from outside interference.

The Brezhnev doctrine has also complicated Peking's options in utilizing Eastern Europe as a lever against Moscow, or rather it has made it virtually impossible for the Eastern European countries to exploit the Sino-Soviet conflict to their advantage. Peking is being squeezed out of the world communist movement, and the Warsaw Treaty Organization may become an anti-Chinese alliance.

The Brezhnev doctrine thus constitutes a hermetic seal rendering the countries of Eastern Europe immune to political, ideological, and military penetration, while allowing limited cultural and economic contacts. The course of liberalization has been arrested in Eastern Europe, but the forces that impelled it remain intact and may later be revived. Similarly, any immediate hope that the other countries of Eastern Europe could imitate Rumania's developing autonomy in foreign affairs is being frustrated.

THE IDEOLOGICAL PLURALIZATION OF THE COMMUNIST WORLD

The Soviet occupation of Czechoslovakia thus foreshadows new realignments in the world communist movement and, most importantly, new cleavages and alignments in Eastern Europe. Whereas in the past, conflicts of interest among communist states were articulated as doctrinal conflicts, it is likely now that conflicts of interest and ideological differences may be expressed independently of one another as well as be intertwined. Even in the absence of basic ideological conflicts, differences among communist states over territorial frontiers, treatment of minorities, economic and trade matters, administrative and institutional implementation of ideological principles, and external relations and attitudes toward individual communist and noncommunist states will probably become more manifest. Moscow can be expected to counter these tendencies, and individual instances may succeed, but it appears that basic trends have been set into motion that will continue to express themselves in greater diversity internally and more variation in foreign policy.

Thus the communist world today, after more than two decades of communist rule, represents an interesting kaleidoscope of ideological deviations and sociopolitical development within a broad common philosophical and institutional framework. This diversity, however, remains diversity with a given ideological, social, and historical context. All communist states remain "Marxist-Leninist" states; all share a common ideological point of departure; all bear the same birthmarks, which remain ineradicably "Stalinist," "Soviet," and "Russian," although each has attempted to surmount and compensate for its stigmata in different ways.

The diversity that has characterized the communist world since 1956 is usually referred to as "polycentrism" to distinguish it from the "monocentrism" of the Stalinist era. While the term has gained general currency, it is somewhat awkward, since the notion of many centers of communism is not only an inaccurate description but a logical absurdity. While China and the Soviet Union might conceivably consider themselves as rival communist "centers," most of the communist states are not centers of anything. A more descriptive term might be "pluralistic" communism. Because of this common ideological framework, which has resulted in the establishment of a common sociopolitical system with its peculiar pattern of institutional and political interpenetration, domestic politics in individual communist states has been, and continues to be to some degree, intimately connected with communist interstate relations. Institutionally, this pattern of political interpenetration has been expressed through the Cominform (1947–1956), multilateral and bilateral conferences of Communist party representatives, the Warsaw Treaty Organization (since 1955), and Comecon (since 1949). Although these institutions were initially established to legitimize and facilitate unilateral Soviet penetration and control of smaller communist states in the guise of multilateral interpenetration, in later years the pattern assumed a more authentic interpenetrative character, with other communist states and leaders demanding a voice in the determination of Soviet internal politics and foreign policy. As noted earlier, this reverse pattern of penetration was set into motion by Khrushchev when he sought the assistance of Mao and Tito against his internal factional rivals.

This pattern of interpenetrative politics in the communist world is ideologically legitimized by the principle of "proletarian internationalism," whose most recent operational manifestation is the "Brezhnev doctrine," which, as noted earlier, declares that certain internal state matters are not shielded by the doctrine of state sovereignty but are the legitimate concern of the entire "socialist commonwealth." Despite its outrageous implications, the Brezhnev doctrine, like the "multilateral" invasion of Czechoslovakia, represents a sort of progress over previous Soviet policy. The Brezhnev doctrine legitimizes the right of the collective "socialist community" to intervene in the affairs of any individual socialist state, including the Soviet Union. This is surely an advance over the previous practice of "proletarian internationalism," which gave to Moscow a sort of monopolistic guardianship over the communist movement, entitling it to unilaterally intervene, with or without consultation.

Thus, although the Brezhnev doctrine was enunciated by Moscow primarily to provide Soviet intervention in Czechoslovakia with an ideological figleaf in the form of multilateralism, "multilateral" intervention in the affairs of small communist states may logically lead to multilateral *demands* for intervention in Soviet affairs. Although Peking has condemned the Brezhnev doctrine, the Chinese leaders have been insisting since about 1957 that they have a right under the doctrine of "proletarian internationalism" to call attention to Soviet doctrinal errors and even to rectify matters if necessary in the interests of world socialism. While the Soviet leaders have rejected this particular Chinese impertinence and have sought protection behind the shield of "state sovereignty," it should be noted that

the Brezhnev doctrine would not only assert a right to collective intervention in Chinese affairs, but also provide a basis for *legitimating a demand* that the Soviet Union accept collective intervention, although in practice the likelihood of such an intervention remains remote.

The Soviet military occupation of Czechoslovakia ushers Soviet relations with Eastern Europe into a new transitional phase—a phase of Soviet military control. This new phase is "Stalinesque," but it should not be confused with the earlier Stalinist period. During the Stalin era, Moscow relied not only upon the Soviet military presence, but upon a common ideology, upon the reliability and servility of the local Communist party, and, most importantly, upon the prestige of Soviet power and Stalin's charisma. This is no longer even residually the case in Rumania, Yugoslavia, Albania, or Czechoslovakia (in spite of the occupation). Communist parties in Eastern European countries will continue to pay greater and greater attention to national needs than to Soviet dictates and interests, although the danger of a desperate Soviet intervention has increased. But interventionism itself is a wasting asset and cannot be sustained indefinitely; thus the Soviet military occupation of Czechoslovakia, while it signifies a Soviet determination to reintensify its control, at the same time risks contracting its range of control.

Thus, for the immediate future, we can expect the Soviet leaders to limit the necessity for intervention by both warnings and inducements. The fragmentation of national interests in the Soviet bloc demonstrated by the Warsaw Pact countries' invasion of Czechoslovakia makes it imperative for the Soviet leaders to formulate separate policies toward each country tailored to the peculiarities of each set of relationships. And increasingly these policies will be shaped by factors such as ideological loyalty, mutual interests, demands and claims, the range of levers and pressures available, and the degree of importance each Eastern European country has to Soviet interests. Soviet leaders may thus further deideologize their dealings with Eastern European countries, recognizing that bloc unity can no longer function as a credible operative norm of behavior, and this is bound to result in the cynical manipulation of differences among Eastern European countries by Soviet policy.

Among other functions, the communist subsystem of states ("socialist commonwealth") also served as a conflict-resolving and conflict-containing mechanism, and as long as the entire communist bloc was confronted by an overriding common threat and motivated by a common higher purpose, these local conflicts could be subordinated to a higher mission in the name of bloc unity. But, just as the weakening of NATO in the face of a receding Soviet threat has resulted in the revival of temporarily submerged local conflicts (the Greek-Turkish dispute over Cyprus, for example), the erosion of the Soviet bloc in Eastern Europe threatens to unleash the latent conflicts in Eastern Europe that antedate the advent of communism. Many Eastern European states have serious territorial claims against one another and against the Soviet Union. Some of these are purely historical in character, while others represent the failure to correlate political frontiers with ethnographic boundaries, while still others are reflections of incompleted processes of national unification or arrested demands for national self-determination. With respect to Poland and Rumania, sensitive territorial issues may become an increasingly

overt factor in their relations with Moscow. Soviet leaders may have to pay more or risk more, as the case may be in individual instances. This also probably means that Moscow may pay greater attention to latent conflicts between individual countries (the Rumanian-Hungarian dispute over Transylvania, for example) in the calculation of its policies, as it searches for new levers and pressures to exert its will in Eastern Europe.

The Soviet leaders are still confronted with the awesome alternatives of dissolution or transformation, but their range of options as far as transformation goes is now severely limited. The audacious attempt to transform a collection of vassal states into an ideological commonwealth of socialist states bound together by a common ideology and common sociopolitical system has failed. The primary reason for the failure was the inability of the Soviet system to transform itself and to adapt itself to the transformations taking place in Eastern Europe. It is now clearer than ever that the fate of the Soviet system is irrevocably tied more closely to the nature of the Soviet relationship to Eastern Europe than to its relationship to the world communist movement.

THE SOVIET FUTURE: GLOBAL POWER OR LEADER OF THE WORLD COMMUNIST MOVEMENT

Although the Soviet occupation of Czechoslovakia and the omnipresent menace of the Brezhnev doctrine has served to domesticate the Warsaw Pact powers in Eastern Europe—decelerating, if not completely arresting, internal liberalization trends, and certainly acting as a brake on Rumania's developing autonomy in foreign affairs—the Soviet position in the world communist movement has not improved appreciably. Even her position in Eastern Europe rests more upon force and the threat of force than ideological leadership. Nevertheless, after the Czech occupation, the Soviet leaders proceeded with the plans to convene a "unity conference" of world Communist parties as if nothing had transpired to complicate the decision taken before the Czech crisis. In accordance with the decision laboriously squeezed out by Moscow at the Budapest consultative conference, a series of acrimonious and bitter preliminary meetings were convened in order to implement the convocation of a new conference.[51] Not only the Czech occupation but the bloody border encounter on the Amur between Soviet and Chinese troops in February, 1969, intervened to widen the deep fissures that continued to trigger the ideological and political earthquakes that periodically manifested themselves in the movement.

Eventually, a conference was convened in Moscow in June, 1969. Envisaged as a "unity conference" by the Soviet leaders, it was essentially a forum where the dirty linen of the communist movement was once again exposed to public view.[52] The conference was boycotted by no less than five of the fourteen ruling parties (Yugoslavia, Albania, China, North Vietnam, and North Korea), while Cuba dispatched "observers" rather than delegates. Thus, of the four ruling Asian parties, only Mongolia participated, while eleven other Asian parties refused to attend, which served to emphasize the Europocentric character of the meeting.[53]

Only sixty-one of the seventy-five delegations in attendance could be persuaded to sign the main document of the conference without reservations. Five, including the Cuban "observer" group, refused to sign outright; three signed in part; while six, including Rumania, signed with reservations. Although seventy-five parties attended the conference, at first glance numerically impressive, it was nevertheless misleading, since the sixteen parties not in attendance represented nearly half of the total 45,200,000 Communist party members in the world. Furthermore, the geographical-racial imbalance at the conference was reflected in the fact that the only parties from Asia (excluding the Near East) represented were the Indian, Mongolian, and East Pakistani. The fragmentation of the movement in 1970 was further reflected in the fact that of the nearly ninety parties (including splinters and fractions), only thirty-nine could be adjudged as Moscow-oriented, five took their cue from Peking, thirty were badly split, while fourteen were independent or neutral.[54]

As an instrument of Soviet foreign policy, the world communist movement is now of considerably diminished utility, and in some respects may even be a handicap to Moscow's posture as a global power. While the range of Soviet authority shrinks and the intensity of its controls attenuates, the individual Communist parties and states within the movement have become more assertive, and exert their demands upon the Soviet Union with greater militancy, and thus become even more influential in the shaping of Soviet foreign policy. This assertion of influence ranges all the way from Chinese attempts to intrude in Soviet factional affairs and demands for ter-

[51] See *Pravda*, March 28, 1969.
[52] See Michel Tatu, "The Moscow Conference," *Interplay*, August–September, 1969.
[53] See *Pravda*, June 6, 1969.

[54] See *World Communism, 1967–1969: Soviet Efforts to Establish Control* (Washington, D.C.: Government Printing Office, 1970), pp. 154 ff.

ritory to the demands of smaller parties that Soviet policy devote more attention to their problems, in return for their support against China.

In a real sense, the world communist movement is being increasingly transformed from an instrument of Soviet foreign policy into, first, an arena of conflict, controversy, and debate among Communist parties (chiefly between the Soviet Union and other parties) and, second, into one of the international environments in which it must act and react. It functions increasingly like a microcosmic counterinternational system, not in accordance with the placid and idyllic visions of "socialist internationalism," but more like a replica of the international order it seeks to supplant. Organized on the basis of nation-states or Communist parties that are potential communist nation-states,[55] divided along developmental, racial, and geographical lines, structured vertically and hierarchically with the Soviet Union at the apex, polarized by great-power rivalries, spheres of influence, and constellations of client and vassal states and parties, and regulated by an internal balance-of-power mechanism, its principal mark of distinction from the existing order its seeks to displace is its ideological and sociopolitical content.

As the Soviet Union comes increasingly to occupy essentially identical roles in both international systems, imperatives and responsibilities generated by each are brought into collision, forcing the Soviet Union to establish priorities not only within each system but across systems. These contradictory imperatives stem from the fact that in the communist interna-

tional system, the Soviet Union's challenging power is China, whereas in the general interstate system, Moscow's principal rival is the United States. In other words, Soviet responsibilities in the communist system have been colliding with its responsibilities and interests as a global power in the general interstate system, with Moscow frequently assigning higher priority to the latter. This followed from the Soviet realization that its security and well-being depended more upon its relationship to the United States than upon its role and position in the communist system. Since the United States has the capability independently to annihilate the Soviet Union, regardless of the latter's degree of solidarity with its allies in the communist world, Soviet security interests demand some sort of accommodation with the United States. No amount of solidarity between Peking and Moscow can deprive the United States of this objective and independent capability. Thus, if the price of solidarity with China is a more militant or aggressive policy toward the United States, Soviet security interests must come into conflict with system interests: the Soviet Union has a vital area of common interest with the United States, and the intensification or expansion of this interest in view of the current Chinese position almost automatically insures the shrinkage of its area of common interest with China. The security interests of the Eastern European states also seem to dictate an accommodation with the West. Their interests being thus in harmony with those of the Soviet Union, they are deaf to Peking's charges that the Soviet leaders have lost their revolutionary zeal.

Moscow's dilemma was both politically and ideologically enervating. Revolutionary ideological imperatives dictated solidarity with China, while Soviet defensive instincts demanded a

---

[55] Parties representing large countries or the Great Powers—e.g., the Italian, French, and Japanese—increasingly behave as potential ruling parties of large states rather than as supplicants and outsiders.

détente with the United States. Since these two impulses conflicted, Khrushchev sought an alternative that proved nonexistent: he hoped to transform a détente into a disarmed world which would deprive the United States of its capability to "export counter-revolution" when revolutions spontaneously erupted around the world. Peking considered this an incredible expectation, and viewed Soviet justifications as puerile at best and perfidious at worst.

In the general interstate system, the Soviet Union, as the second most powerful economic and military state in the world, functions as a global power with self-proclaimed rights and responsibilities in all parts of the world. At many points its role in the communist system intersects harmoniously with its role in the general interstate system, particularly in supporting revolutionary movements and regimes in the underdeveloped areas; but they also often collide, as noted above. This dual role imposed upon the USSR calls for both conflict and cooperation with the United States—conflict as the leader of the communist camp, and cooperation as a partner-rival in the general international scene. This cooperative imperative has been intensified by Soviet awareness that its very physical existence depends upon the exercise of mutual nuclear self-restraint on the part of Washington and Moscow. It means assigning a premium to the relaxation of international tensions, since this not only tends to maximize Soviet physical security but enhances the possibility of more intensified internal development. On the other hand, such a course involves the sacrifice of the interests of some of its allies and the postponement or abandonment of certain of its diplomatic and ideological objectives in foreign policy.

To minimize these conflicts, Soviet leaders have endeavored to find surrogates for the obligations they have deferred or renounced in the communist subsystem. They are providing greater material assistance to communist states; and in underdeveloped countries they are supporting local nationalist revolutionary regimes and movements rather than focusing exclusively on communist revolutionary movements. Soviet flirtation with such leaders as Nasser, Ben Bella, Nkrumah, Sukarno, and Nehru was designed to move their countries gradually into the Soviet diplomatic orbit and then, as in the case of Cuba, to orient their "ethnic" socialisms in a Soviet direction.

This pattern of Soviet behavior virtually abandons local communist movements to their own devices, and tends to frustrate the development of Communist parties where they are weak or nonexistent. This has created a gap that the Chinese have begun to exploit. Communist parties in underdeveloped countries tend to have a greater interest in becoming constituencies of China than of the Soviet Union, since China shows a preference for working through them, while Moscow upholds regimes which it may temporarily support but which it ultimately seeks to subvert and replace. Thus, Soviet policy increasingly resembles the behavior of a Great Power seeking client states, rather than the leader of a revolutionary movement cultivating spiritual adherents. And this abandonment of local Communist parties is reflected in the fragmented character of the world communist movement, as outlined above, with thirty divided parties, five oriented toward Peking, and fourteen pursuing an independent or neutral course.

The erosion of the Soviet commitment to violence and world revolution represents the growing maturity and responsibility of the Soviet Union in world affairs. The control and manipulation of a world revolutionary movement is no longer either indispensable or desirable as an instrument of Soviet policy and purpose. In some ways, it has actually become counterproductive and dysfunctional. In retrospect, one might say that the Soviet Union used its control of a world revolutionary movement as a de facto (not necessarily an intentional) surrogate for other attributes to great-power status and behavior. As the Soviet Union developed economic and military power, the world revolutionary movement correspondingly lost its former utility: it was no longer necessary, for the Soviets had the acquired conventional instruments of great-power status.

On the other hand, China finds herself in a condition of impotence comparable to that of the Soviet Union before World War II. China is an aspiring world power, and she still perceives a world revolutionary movement and support of Communist parties as significant and useful power-substitutes during the current transition period. As in the case of the Soviet Union, China's success in organizing and manipulating a world revolutionary movement will depend upon her ability to find foreign constituencies who believe they can best serve their interests by becoming instruments of China's great-power aspirations.

As a global power in the general interstate system, the Soviet Union demands and is accorded all of the legal rights and privileges of such status: permanent membership on the U.N. Security Council and the right to be heard on all major problems of international relations. It also asserts its informal prerogatives as a global power by unilaterally intervening in any dispute or problem in any part of the world to the degree that its power permits. It organizes alliances and coalitions, seeks client states, and buys the support of smaller powers. The Soviet Union has interjected its presence in Latin America, Africa, and Southeast Asia, and it maintains an extensive program of military and economic assistance. As a global power, the world, not merely the communist system, is its sphere of activity.

The emergence of the Soviet Union as a thermonuclear power with global interests and responsibilities, the resurgence of nationalism within the communist system, the emergence of China as a rival to the Soviet Union, and the unmitigated fear of thermonuclear annihilation—all these have all combined to give the Soviet Union a greater interest in maintaining the status quo than in attempting, through high-risk policies, to alter it in its favor. Moreover, the increasing cleavage between the interests of developed and underdeveloped nations, the fading prospects for revolution in the former, and the growing prospects for revolution in the latter might serve to enhance Chinese, not Soviet, power. The proliferation of communist regimes under these conditions would alter the balance between developed and underdeveloped, European and non-European communist states—a situation which Moscow increasingly perceives as both dysfunctional and counterproductive to its interests.

As a consequence, the Soviet Union has been impelled to restructure the order of priorities among its obligations and interests in the Communist party-state subsystem and the general interstate system. This means, as the Chinese have charged, that the Soviet Union will protect its interests in the general interstate system, even if doing so adversely affects the interests of its communist allies in the subsystem.

The Soviet Union and China continue to be significantly divided on questions of ideology and policy sufficient to prevent the development of a common outlook and the forging of a common policy toward the noncommunist world. These divisions reflect a basic conflict of national interests between a maturing social and industrial order—the Soviet Union and the Eastern European satellites—which has a greater stake in avoiding nuclear war, and a preindustrial revolutionary society which feels that its political and economic goals can be achieved only by destroying the vestiges of the old social and economic order.

Irrespective of the detailed nature, causes, and motivations of Sino-Soviet controversies—and these range from traditional, historical, and territorial questions to fundamental differences between the basically European character and culture of Moscow and the orientalism of China, and transcend ideological matters—the significant point is that the world communist movement has been divested of its single directing center and threatens to fragment into several centers. Regardless of what institutional forms of cooperation are adopted, the Kremlin has abdicated its monopoly on making decisions for the entire communist world and to some extent must coordinate its foreign policy with that of its allies, rather than the other way around.

Although the Soviet Union appears more interested in preserving its role as a global power than reclaiming its position as the center of world revolution so long as the two roles continue to collide, the Soviet leaders still retain the residual hope of reconciling these two imperatives. Unfortunately, however, this will depend more and more upon events in the external environment beyond Soviet control, and, in particular, upon the increasing triangulation of power among Moscow, Peking, and Washington. As Chinese power grows, its influence spills outside the communist system and into the general interstate system; China thus threatens to become a dual rival of the Soviet Union, unlike the United States, which relates to Moscow only in one international environment. Thus, Moscow's role within both the communist movement and the general interstate system will be increasingly influenced by Chinese power and policies.

It should be noted that surprises are always possible in the communist world. And while Moscow's current favorite hallucination is a Sino-American rapprochement that would enable both China and the United States to contend more effectively in the respective international environments in which they confront the Soviet Union, it is also possible that a fortuitous death in China might create the basis for a Sino-Soviet rapprochement—or that Peking's favorite nightmare, Soviet-American collusion against China, may become an active reality rather than a passive game.

SELECTED BIBLIOGRAPHY

ASPATURIAN, VERNON V. *The Soviet Union in the International Communist System.* Stanford, Calif.: Hoover Institution Studies, 1966.

BORKENAU, F. *The Communist International.* London: Faber & Faber, 1938.

———. *European Communism.* New York: Harper & Row, 1953.

BRZEZINSKI, ZBIGNIEW K. *The Soviet Bloc.* 2d ed. Cambridge: Harvard University Press, 1967.

CHAMBERLIN, W. H., ed. *Blueprint for World Conquest.* Chicago: Human Events, 1946.

DALLIN, ALEXANDER, et al., eds. *Diversity in International Communism.* New York: Columbia University Press, 1963.

FLOYD, DAVID. *Mao Against Khrushchev.* New York: Praeger, 1963.

GITTINGS, JOHN. *Survey of the Sino-Soviet Dispute.* New York: Oxford University Press, 1968.

GOODMAN, ELLIOT R. *The Soviet Design for a World State.* New York: Columbia University Press, 1960.

GRIFFITH, WILLIAM E. *Albania and the Sino-Soviet Rift.* Cambridge: M.I.T. Press, 1963.

———. *The Sino-Soviet Rift.* Cambridge: M.I.T. Press, 1964.

GRZYBOWSKI, KAZMIERZ. *The Socialist Commonwealth of Nations.* New Haven: Yale University Press, 1964.

HINTON, HAROLD. *China's Turbulent Quest.* New York: Macmillan Co., 1970.

IONESCU, GHITA. *The Politics of the European Communist States.* New York: Praeger, 1967.

LAQUEUR, WALTER, and LABEDZ, LEOPOLD, eds. *Polycentrism.* New York: Praeger, 1962.

LOWENTHAL, RICHARD. *World Communism.* New York: Oxford University Press, 1964.

MCKENZIE, KERMIT. *Comintern and World Revolution.* New York: Columbia University Press, 1962.

ROYAL INSTITUTE OF INTERNATIONAL AFFAIRS. *The Soviet-Yugoslav Dispute.* London, 1948.

RUSSIAN INSTITUTE OF COLUMBIA UNIVERSITY. *The Anti-Stalin Campaign and International Communism.* New York: Columbia University Press, 1956. A selection of documents.

SCALAPINO, ROBERT, ed. *The Communist Revolution in Asia.* Englewood Cliffs, N.J.: Prentice-Hall, 1965.

SCHWARTZ, HARRY. *Tsars, Mandarins and Commissars.* New York: J. B. Lippincott Co., 1964.

TOMA, PETER, ed. *The Changing Face of Communism in Eastern Europe.* Tucson: Arizona University Press, 1970.

TRISKA, JAN F., ed. *Communist Party States.* Indianapolis: Bobbs-Merrill, 1969.

WHELAN, JOSEPH G., ed. *World Communism, 1967–1969: Soviet Efforts to Reestablish Control.* Washington, D.C.: Government Printing Office, 1970.

ZAGORIA, DONALD. *The Sino-Soviet Conflict, 1956–1961.* Princeton: Princeton University Press, 1962.

ZINNER, P. E., ed. *National Communism and Popular Revolt in Eastern Europe.* New York: Columbia University Press, 1947. A selection of documents.

Chapter Seven

FOREIGN POLICY OF COMMUNIST CHINA

ALLEN S. WHITING

CONCEPTUAL FRAMEWORK

Despite the fact that, in taking China as our subject, we are dealing with the world's oldest continuous civilization, our analysis of Chinese foreign policy must be largely inferential. Very little primary research in Chinese archival materials has been completed to provide us with an evidential base for understanding the perceptual framework, the organizational interaction, and the political determinants which combine to make foreign policy. Too few detailed case studies exist of specific interactive situations involving the People's Republic of China (PRC) to lay a foundation for systematic generalization about behavior. Even the conventional historical record provides relatively little help. Although its political systems date back more than 2,000 years, China is a relative newcomer to contemporary foreign relations. For centuries, its relations with the outside world remained tributary in nature. No concept of sovereignty or equality interfered with domination by the Middle Kingdom over dependencies such as Tibet and Mongolia, or vassal states such as Korea and Annam.

The collapse of the Manchu empire and the birth, in 1912, of the Republic of China failed to produce a united nation entering the world community on equal terms. Foreign governments continued to post their own troops and police in enclaves of extraterritoriality, enjoying foreign law and privilege on Chinese soil. Civil war rent China apart during the decade 1918–1928, as a northern government at

Peking, dominated by shifting military factions, vied for power with a southern government at Canton, headed by Sun Yat-sen and his Kuomintang cohorts. Officially, Peking enjoyed recognition as the legal voice of China until its final defeat by the Nationalist (Kuomintang) army in 1928. Its actual power, however, extended through only a small section of the country. During the turbulent twenties, most of South China, Tibet, Sinkiang, Mongolia, and the northeast (Manchuria) lay beyond control of the capital. No sooner was the new government of Chiang Kai-shek established at Nanking in 1928, however, than Soviet troops fought to protect Soviet interests in Manchuria against the local warlord. In 1931 Japan overran this rich industrial area to create the puppet state of Manchukuo. Then, at the opposite end of China, Soviet authorities gave military and economic assistance to the local governor of Sinkiang, concluding formal agreements without reference to Nanking and informally extending influence over its policy and army. Warlord autonomy, Japanese invasion, and growing Chinese communist dissidence combined to deprive Chiang of control over more than a dozen provinces throughout most of the period 1931–1945. Meanwhile, each of these uncontrolled areas enjoyed varying degrees of independence in its relations with foreign powers.

In fact, not until 1949 and establishment of the People's Republic of China did the world's most populous nation achieve sufficient sovereignty and unity throughout its vast domain to enjoy a monopoly of full control over foreign relations in the central government. This provides a natural starting point for our analysis. Unlike its immediate predecessor, however, the People's Republic was not formally admitted to "the family of nations" for many years, lacking diplomatic recognition from most countries outside the Soviet bloc, and denied participation in the United Nations until the 1970s. Thus, on the one hand, we have historical evidence of foreign policy conducted by a somewhat fictitious central government, ruling largely in name only from 1911 to 1928, followed by a highly fragmented regime from 1928 to 1949. This approximates forty years of seemingly "normal" international relations for a weak and divided China, formally allied with the victorious powers in two world wars and a member of the League of Nations. On the other hand, our principle object of interest, the PRC, spans more than two decades of semi-isolation from much of the international system, including the United Nations and such traditional Great Powers as the United States, Britain, and Japan.

These historical anomalies obviate the standard approach of focusing on the nation-state as actor. Despite appearances, foreign governments were not dealing with a highly stable and continuous regime prior to 1949. To be sure, the entity "China" was an obvious empirical referent for whatever group assumed authority at whatever point in the society. Treaties were negotiated, commerce carried out (albeit through foreign-controlled customs until the 1930s), and wars fought in the name of China. However, our inquiry will concern itself primarily with the perceptions and behavior of Chinese elites, particularly the communist, which have tried to manage China's foreign relations over the past half-century. It is their values and views, rather than the inheritance of tradition or the bureaucratic inertia of continuing organizational entities within government, which have shaped the ends, means, and style of Chinese foreign policy.

Our general conceptual framework begins with the physical environment, both real and perceived, into which these elites moved as international actors. In addition to actual size and geography, policy is shaped by perceptions of spatial relationships. Borders may be seen as secure or threatened, as inviolate or flexible, as indisputable or contentious and negotiable. Space may be conceived as providing isolation or inviting attack. Size may be held an asset of strength or a liability for defense. Perceptions, in turn, are in part a function of received experience, of history as it is transmitted within a culture or political system. Received experience provides "lessons" from the past whose "truth" may be reinforced through the "real experience" of the present. Just as there are objective inputs of wars and diplomacy, as in the physical attributes of geography, to shape perception and behavior, so too there is the subjective element of anticipation, which may create a "self-fulfilling prophecy" effect whereby expected hostility from an outside power is prepared for in such a way as to cause or increase hostility. Alternatively, "selective perception" focuses only on evidence of behavior which conforms with expectation and dismisses that which does not fit anticipation. These inputs of geography, history, and psychology combine to constitute what we shall call the *Chinese components* of foreign policy.

In addition, we must consider ideology or the *communist component* of policy. Ideology is not unique to elites and cultures which articulate it in the highly formalized and conscious manner of communist systems, but its explicitness and omnipresence in their political communications makes it even more of a determinant than in less ideologically structured systems. From Marx to Mao, a corpus of litera-ture provides definitions of goals and prescriptions of means that shape the view of the world from Peking.

These basic factors in the Chinese and communist components do not explain everything. They will be differentially affected by specific organizational roles and responsibilities such as defense, trade, diplomacy, and revolutionary activity abroad. Moreover, they will have an idiosyncratic impact upon policy as filtered through the different "operational codes" of such individuals as Mao Tse-tung, Liu Shao-ch'i, Lin Piao, and Chou En-lai. The sum of these internal interactions constitutes the decision-making process, but this in turn must interact externally for the dynamic of international relations to be complete. Foreign policy does not operate in a vacuum, nor is it the exclusive initiative of one country, least of all China over the past half-century. Unfortunately, however, in the absence of any concrete data on the effect of organization and personality in Chinese foreign policy, we must remain content with a larger, looser inferential framework that deals primarily with the factors we have subsumed under the Chinese and communist components. Moreover, in the space at our disposal we cannot hope to do justice to interaction analysis except for selective illustrative purposes. Within these limits, nevertheless, we can appreciate the goals of recent Chinese foreign policy and assess the means available and likely to be adopted by present and future elites in pursuit of these goals.

Physical Factors—Real and Perceived

One cannot look at any map of the world, regardless of its projection, and not be awed by the proportion encompassed by China. So extensive is its reach from north to south and from east to west as to conjure up images of supracontinental domination "over-shadowing" Southeast Asia and India, while "menacing" the Soviet Far East and Japan. Coupled with emphasis on China's population of roughly 800 million, "expansionism" seems the inevitable threat confronting China's neighbors.

These images receive reinforcement from Chinese official statements. Although the days of the Chinese empire are long past, contemporary Chinese leaders continue to pay obeisance to the memory of vanished glory in their delineation of China's territorial goals. Chiang Kai-shek, borrowing Adolf Hitler's concept of *Lebensraum* ("living space"), laid claim to past holdings on the basis of population pressure as well as of historical possession:

In regard to the living space essential for the nation's existence, the territory of the Chinese state is determined by the requirements for national survival and by the limits of Chinese cultural bonds. Thus, in the territory of China a hundred years ago [i.e., c. 1840], comprising more than ten million square kilometers, there was not a single district that was not essential to the survival of the Chinese nation, and none that was not permeated by our culture. The breaking up of this territory meant the undermining of the nation's security as well as the decline of the nation's culture. Thus, the people as a whole must regard this as a national humiliation, and not until all lost territories have been recovered can we relax our efforts to wipe out this humiliation and save ourselves from destruction.[1]

Although Chiang did not specify his "lost territories," a Chinese textbook published shortly after his statement contains a table listing them (see table 7.1).

[1] Chiang Kai-shek, *China's Destiny* (New York: Roy Publishers, 1947), p. 34.

Nor do communist leaders remain indifferent to China's past holdings, although they temper their immediate claims according to time and place. Thus, Mao Tse-tung staked out his future realm in an interview more than thirty years ago:

It is the immediate task of China to regain all our lost territories. . . . We do not, however, include Korea, formerly a Chinese colony, but when we have reestablished the independence of the lost territories of China, and if the Koreans wish to break away from the chains of Japanese imperialism, we will extend them our enthusiastic help in their struggle for independence. The same thing applies for Formosa. . . . The Outer Mongolian republic will automatically become a part of the Chinese federation, at their own will. The Mohammedan and Tibetan peoples, likewise, will form autonomous republics attached to the Chinese federation.[2]

True to his word, at least in part, Mao, despite Indian protests, drove his Red Armies to the Tibetan heights one year after the establishment of the People's Republic of China in 1949. His implicit definition of Korea as within China's sphere of interest received implementation when Chinese armies hurled back United Nations troops from the Yalu River to the 38th parallel during 1950–51. Sinkiang, which is presumably the region referred to above as "the Mohammedan people" (because of its predominantly Moslem population), became an autonomous region in 1955 after considerable pacification by the Chinese Red Army. Only Taiwan ("Formosa"), held by Chiang Kai-shek, and Outer Mongolia, recognized as independent by the Treaty of Friendship and Alliance concluded between the Nationalist government and Mos-

[2] Quoted in Edgar Snow, *Red Star over China* (New York: Random House, 1944), p. 96. Interviews with Mao Tse-tung in 1936.

TABLE 7.1

China's "Lost Territories"

Date	Area, in Square Kilometers	Location	New Ownership
1689	240,000	North side Khingan Mountains	Russia
1727	100,000	Lower Selenga Valley	Russia
1842	83	Hong Kong	United Kingdom
1858	480,000	North of Heilungkiang	Russia
1858	8	Kowloon	United Kingdom
1860	344,000	East of Ussuri River	Russia
1864	900,000	North of Lake Balkhash	Russia
1879	2,386	Liuchiu Islands	Japan
1882–1883	21,000	Lower Ili Valley	Russia
1883	20,000	Irtysh Valley east of Lake Zaysan	Russia
1884	9,000	Upper Koksol Valley	Russia
1885–1889	738,000	Annam and all Indochina	France
1886	574,000	Burma	United Kingdom
1890	7,550	Sikkim	United Kingdom
1894	122,400	West of the upper Salween	United Kingdom
1894	91,300	West of the upper Yangtze	United Kingdom
1894	100,000	Upper Burma, Savage Mountains	United Kingdom
1895	220,334	Korea	Japan
1895	35,845	Taiwan	Japan
1895	127	Pescadores	Japan
1897	760	The edge of Burma	United Kingdom
1897	2,300	The edge of Burma	United Kingdom
Total	4,009,093		

Source: Hou Ming-chiu, Chen Erh-shiu, and Lu Chen, *General Geography of China* (in Chinese), 1946, as reproduced in G.B. Cressey, *Land of the 500 Million* (New York: McGraw-Hill Book Co., 1955), p. 39.

cow in 1945 and adhered to in this particular by Peking, have remained beyond Mao's control.

Similarly, both Nationalist and communist maps place China's borders far down in the South China Sea, off the shores of Borneo. Mao would subscribe to the statements of the official Nationalist handbook:

Both the southernmost and westernmost borders remain to be defined. The Pamirs in the west constitute a contested area among China, the U.S.S.R., and Afghanistan. The sovereignty of the Tuansha Islands [Coral Islands] in the south is sought by China, the Republic of the Philippines, and Indo-China.[3]

[3] *China Handbook, 1955–56* (Taipei, Taiwan, 1955), p. 15.

At least some of these are more than mere verbal aspirations. In the past decade Chinese Communist troops have twice fought over disputed border areas. The movement of Peking's forces into Indian-claimed checkpoints along the Himalayas following the Tibetan revolt of 1959 triggered small clashes with Indian border guards that year. Subsequent Indian efforts in 1962 to recoup claimed land, long unoccupied until the advent of Chinese road building and patrols in 1958–61, ignited a smoldering confrontation which finally exploded that fall in a massive Chinese offensive at both ends of the 1,500-mile frontier. While larger strategic considerations than the border itself underlay the

Chinese attack, the tenacity with which Peking bargained—and finally fought—with New Delhi over marginal land of little economic or strategic value illustrates the persistence of "lost territories" in shaping perceptions and goals of foreign policy.

An even more dramatic example of this phenomenon came in March, 1969, when Chinese border troops fought Soviet armored units over unoccupied islands in the Ussuri River along China's northeast frontier. These incidents, while far smaller in scope and briefer than the 1962 war with India, had far more threatening implications for China's security, since they involved the much more powerful Soviet military capabilities, potentially including nuclear weapons. Again, as with India, more was perceived to be at stake than the islands themselves. Nonetheless, the role the border played throughout 1969, both here and in Sinkiang, reminded the world that Chinese sensibilities and sensitivities can hearken back to times past to a degree unique among the major powers on the world scene today.

Does this necessarily mean that irredentism—the drive to recover "lost territiories"—literally impels Chinese leaders to restore control over thousands of square miles ruled by Russia and the Soviet Union for a century or more? In the tense summer of 1969, the official English-language journal *Peking Review* suddenly introduced a heretofore neglected quotation from Mao, "We the Chinese nation have the spirit to fight the enemy to the last drop of our blood, the determination to recover our lost territory by our own efforts, and the ability to stand on our own feet in the family of nations." Although various sources, especially Soviet, imputed a grandiose irredentist design to Peking, support-

ing this charge with alleged statements made privately by Mao, their analysis was contradicted by the consistent caution with which Peking deployed force beyond its borders since its initial intervention in the Korean War in October, 1950. Certainly, the strategic imbalance between China and the USSR is so great, now and in the foreseeable future, as to make incredible a major move against Moscow's central Asian, Siberian, or Far Eastern holdings that were once ruled from Peking. And indeed, when Sino-Soviet border negotiations began in the fall of 1969, the People's Republic issued the following declaration:

> On May 24, 1969, the Chinese Government issued a statement [which] . . . pointed out that although the treaties relating to the present Sino-Soviet boundary were unequal treaties imposed on China by tsarist Russian imperialism in the latter half of the 19th century and the beginning of the 20th century, . . . the Chinese Government was still prepared to take these treaties as the basis for an overall settlement of the Sino-Soviet boundary question and proposed that, pending a settlement, the status quo of the border should be maintained and armed conflicts averted. . . . The Chinese Government has never demanded the return of the territory tsarist Russia had annexed by means of the unequal treaties.[4]

As in the Indian case, the border problem is both less and more than the question of "lost territory" per se. It is less so in terms of the amount of land actually at issue as compared with that carried on maps and tables as the maximal extent of past Chinese rule. The problem involves more than the land, however, insofar as it involves the principles of politics, both

[4] Statement of October 7, 1969, in *Peking Review*, October 10, 1969.

domestic and foreign, which impinge on the posture adopted by Chinese leaders vis-à-vis questions of "unequal treaties" and "lost territory." One such principle is the traditional Chinese definition of a government possessing the "Mandate of Heaven" as capable of defending the frontiers against barbarian incursions while maintaining the peace against domestic insurrection. Thus, so remote and undesirable an area as Outer Mongolia became the subject of political controversy in 1912, when young Nationalists agitated against Peking's concessions to Mongolian demands for autonomy under Russian protection, using the issue as a political weapon against the regime of Yuan Shih-k'ai. In 1950 Chinese Nationalist propagandists sought to embarrass the new communist regime in Peking in a similar manner. They charged it with "selling out" Chinese soil to the Soviet Union by accepting Outer Mongolian independence despite alleged Soviet violations of the 1945 agreements. In these agreements, Chiang Kai-shek had promised to abide by a "plebiscite" in Outer Mongolia, knowing it would confirm the area's self-proclaimed independence under Soviet domination but hoping thereby to woo Stalin away from supporting the Chinese Communists. Seen in this perspective, Outer Mongolia is primarily a political issue to be exploited in domestic or foreign politics according to expediency, not a compulsive constraint on Chinese policy.

Individual leaders may not believe in the importance of a particular border section or the literal necessity of recovering "lost territory," but the manipulative use of such an issue in internal politics may constrain their position, thereby posing foreign policy goals which exacerbate relations abroad. Three instances illustrate the complexity of this problem. Outer

Mongolia would seem strategically irretrievable without Soviet acquiescence, and politically undesirable, given fifty years of Mongol escape from Chinese hegemony. Yet authoritative Japanese and Soviet sources attribute statements to Mao which seem to reflect a lingering aspiration to replace Soviet influence there, including an official Soviet claim that Mao raised the issue with Nikita Khrushchev as early as 1954. Are these statements merely an effort to press Soviet influence back, or are they also to advance Chinese influence? Is it Mao's personal *idée fixe*, or is it a shared objective within the elite? While Peking's propaganda publicly lamented Moscow's alleged transformation of the Mongolian People's Republic into a "colony" in 1969–70, Soviet radio broadcasts accused Peking of harboring "chauvinist" ambitions over this vast land of desert and steppe, inhabited by a million or so nomads and herdsmen. Logic may strengthen one or another explanation, but evidence is lacking to provide any definitive answer.

As a second instance, the Sino-Soviet border clashes of 1969 appear to have been initiated by the Chinese. Certainly, Peking's internal propaganda immediately escalated their importance to a matter of highest national prestige and priority, as illustrated by the earlier quotation from *Peking Review*. At the same time, preparations were being completed for the Ninth Congress of the Chinese Communist party, the first in more than ten years and the initial restructuring of the political system since the convulsions and internal upheaval of the so-called Great Proletarian Cultural Revolution of 1966–68. According to Edgar Snow on the basis of his later conversations with Mao Tse-tung, Mao decided to launch the Cultural Revolution because his presumed successor, Liu Shao-ch'i, had advocated patching up the Sino-Soviet quarrel to present a united front in the Indochina war.[5] Was Mao also exploiting sensitivity over borders and "lost territory" to prevail over internal opponents? Or was this a wider design to refashion national unity against an external enemy after the divisive developments of the previous three years? Or was there a genuine coincidence of events, the border clashes being genuinely related to basic Chinese anxieties aroused by the Soviet military buildup in central Asia and the Far East and Moscow's military move into Czechoslovakia in August, 1968? Again, our effort is not to provide a single explanation in the absence of proof, but to illustrate the various ways in which China's borders and territorial problems interact with domestic and foreign policy.

A final instance concerns Taiwan. Since the founding of the PRC in 1949, its leadership has ritualistically and repeatedly sworn to "recover China's province, Taiwan." Yet since imposition of the U.S. Seventh Fleet in the Taiwan Strait in 1950 and the Mutual Assistance Treaty concluded between Taipei and Washington in 1954, no serious effort from the mainland has sought to recover Taiwan by force or subversion. Is this an issue of genuine irredentism which inevitably must result in reunion with the mainland by one means or another? Is it a political matter linked to the continuing presence on Taiwan of a defeated civil-war enemy, the Chinese Nationalists, who still lay claim to representation of and rule over all China? Is it a whipping-boy for attacking "U.S. imperialism," and if so, are the impli-

cations primarily domestic—for mobilizing unity—or foreign—to isolate the United States from Asian affairs? Or is there a changing mixture of motivations, varying according to the changing perceptions and priorities of the leadership in Peking?

Suggesting these various instrumental uses of the question is not to deny objective factors which, from the perspective of those responsible for Chinese security, make China's size a defensive liability and China's borders a vulnerable point of contention. First, vague territorial claims, Chinese or otherwise, based on concepts of suzerainty and tributary relations or on disputed treaties, are an inadequate basis for determining international boundaries. Chinese Communists and Nationalists alike agree that the use of force against Tibetan leaders, whether in 1950 or 1959, is an internal affair, and does not constitute legal "aggression." Even New Delhi acquiesced, albeit reluctantly, in the earlier instance. But where runs the legal boundary resultant from a line drawn on an inadequate map by a British official before World War I and never surveyed, much less formally ratified by the government in Peking?

Second, even where such boundaries are fixed with rough approximation, precise definition is impeded by the absence of natural lines of demarcation. Except for the coast and the Amur-Yalu river complex in the northeast, none of China's frontiers can be readily identified topographically. Instead, they twist tortuously through jungle, mountain, and desert, according to the temporary dictates of local need and the relative power available to interested parties. The absence of natural demarcation is paralleled by an absence of natural barriers against migration or invasion, complicating the responsibilities fac-

[5] Edgar Snow, "Aftermath of the Cultural Revolution: Mao Tse-tung and the Cost of Living," *The New Republic*, April 10, 1971, p. 19.

ing the central government responsible for its citizens' welfare and defense.

Thus, the ability in 1959 of 80,000 Tibetan refugees to flee through Himalayan passes, in some cases claimed and ostensibly guarded by Indian patrols, raised the possibility of these refugees returning with foreign arms and training to carry on subversion and sabotage, if not actual guerrilla war. Indeed, precisely such clandestine activities followed the exodus, described by foreign participants and correspondents from bases in the sub-Himalayan area. Again, in 1962, the flight of up to 100,000 Uighur, Kazakh, and Kirghiz refugees across the Sinkiang border to ethnically related areas in adjacent Soviet central Asia raised Chinese fears of their eventual return as instruments of Soviet subversion in a province long known for anti-Chinese revolts among its predominantly Turki-speaking Moslem peoples. Small wonder that under these circumstances the Indian and Soviet borders appear so sensitive to decision makers in Peking.

Few lines of communication traverse the great distances from China's traditional power centers to its remote border provinces, whereas these provinces lie relatively close to rival centers of power. Not until well after establishment of the PRC did a railroad link Outer Mongolia with northern China, although it was circled on the north by the Trans-Siberian Railroad. Only rough roads linked Tibet with China proper until the late 1950s, while Lhasa lay within striking distance of determined troops, traders, and travelers approaching from the Indian subcontinent, as evidenced by British expeditions at the turn of the century. Nor did Peking push a railroad into Sinkiang until the mid-1950s, despite its strategic and economic importance proximate to the highly developed transportation network across the Soviet border. Even today, land communications to most points along China's southern and western boundaries are scarce and subject to the hazards of interruption by recurring natural phenomena as well as to interdiction by potential dissidents. This combination of arduous terrain and traditionally hostile non-Chinese local populaces mocks the image of size and strength projected by simple unidimensional maps of China.

China's traditional attraction for invaders was food and wealth, luring from the interior nomadic groups against whom the Great Wall was originally designed. Modern invaders came after markets (Great Britain), raw materials (Japan), or imperial prestige (Germany). Regardless of the size and distance of the predatory power, during the nineteenth and twentieth centuries China grappled with problems of defense against external pressure to a degree unique among the countries under survey in this volume. Virtually no point along the 12,600 miles of its perimeter has been safe from one or another of these pressures during the last three hundred years. At the turn of the century, many wondered whether China would become the "sick man of Asia," to be carved up by other countries as was the "sick man of Europe," the Ottoman empire.

These physical factors have combined with the behavior of other powers to make defense a major preoccupation of Chinese foreign policy elites, be they Manchu, Nationalist, or communist. We have dwelt at length on the border problem because it looms large in the foreign policy perspective of Peking—not because of communist "expansionism" or "paranoia," but rather as an outgrowth of China's remembered past. Thus, thousands of troops from the People's Liberation Army (PLA) occupied two northern provinces of Laos adjacent to China from 1962 into the 1970s. This was done, not to aid the Pathet Lao war against the Royal Laotian government, but to secure a buffer against possible penetration of China by American CIA-trained Meo hillsmen or by former Chinese Nationalist soldiers living in exile in nearby Thailand. Nor can we understand recurring tensions in the Taiwan Strait around the offshore islands of Quemoy and Matsu in 1954–55, 1958, and 1962 without an appreciation of the recurring raids against the mainland launched from these islands by Chinese Nationalist teams trained and backed by the United States. Indeed, China's only major military actions— in Korea (1950) and on its borders with India (1962) and the USSR (1969)—in the first two decades of the PRC came about in large part because of anxiety over the potential penetration by hostile powers over vulnerable borders, at times when internal tensions, economic and political, heightened fears of invasion and subversion.

Historical Factors

China's defensive attitudes intermittently explode into xenophobia. Their subjective evaluation of events during the past century convinces Chinese Nationalist and Communist alike that many, if not all, of China's ills stem from contact with the "foreign devil," now castigated as "Western imperialism." Two hundred years ago, Li Shih-yao, viceroy of Kwangtung and Kwangsi, memorialized the throne on regulations for the control of foreigners, warning:

It is my most humble opinion that when uncultured barbarians, who live far beyond the borders of China, come to our country to trade, they should estab-

lish no contact with the population, except for business purposes.[6]

Events since Li Shih-yao's day show little break in continuity, so far as interpretation of foreign relations is concerned. Chiang Kai-shek blamed the chaotic years of interregnum following the collapse of the Manchu dynasty on "secret activities of the Imperialists, . . . the chief cause of civil wars among the warlords."[7] Indeed, he attributed the empire's disintegration to the so-called unequal treaties which "completely destroyed our nationhood, and our sense of honor and shame was lost. . . . The traditional structure of the family, the village, and the community was disrupted. The virtue of mutual help was replaced by competition and jealousy. Public planning was neglected and no one took an interest in public affairs."[8]

This simplistic explanation errs in attributing cause and effect where coincidence is the phenomenon. Western pressures hastened the collapse of the empire and its Confucian traditions, but they came after the process of disintegration had begun. The ability of Japanese society to respond to the combined impact of feudal decline and Western influence by adapting the old content to new forms demonstrates the distortion of history in Chiang's analysis.

However, it is not the facts of history that condition political behavior, but the way in which men view those facts. Hence, the similarity of the following communist analysis to those preceding it is highly suggestive of xenophobia as a component of Chinese policy:

[6] Quoted in Hu Sheng, *Imperialism and Chinese Politics* (Peking, 1955), p. 9.
[7] Chiang Kai-shek, *China's Destiny*, p. 78.
[8] Ibid., pp. 79, 88.

[The imperialists] will not only send their running-dogs to bore inside China to carry out disruptive work and to cause trouble. They will not only use the Chiang Kai-shek bandit remnants to blockade our coastal ports, but they will send their totally hopeless adventurist elements and troops to raid and to cause trouble along our borders. They seek by every means and at all times to restore their position in China. They use every means to plot the destruction of China's independence, freedom, and territorial integrity and to restore their private interests in China. We must exercise the highest vigilance. . . . They cannot possibly be true friends of the Chinese people. They are the deadly enemies of the Chinese people's liberation movement.[9]

Thus, the Chinese communist devil-theory of imperialism coincides with the popular mythology that evil is inherent in foreign contacts, and produces suspicion and hostility at various levels. The popular mythology derives from experiencing the rape and pillage by Western troops during the nineteenth century. Western insistence on extraterritorial privileges so that their nationals could be tried by foreign law for crimes committed on Chinese territory rubbed salt in the wound. Insult was added to injury. While the Chinese viewed white behavior as barbaric, the whites viewed Chinese punishment as brutal. The inevitable cultural gap, widened by racial prejudice, reinforced the hostility on both sides.

Injustice was also encountered at higher levels of diplomatic relations. Chinese experience in the international arena gave good reason for bitter resentment at being cast in the role of "a melon to be carved up by the powers." Throughout the nineteenth

[9] K'o Pai-nien, "Hsin min chu chu yi te wai chiao tse" [The foreign policy of the new people's democracy] Hsüeh Hsi [Study] 1, no. 2 (October, 1949):13–15.

century, gunboat diplomacy forced China to abdicate her customary rights of sovereignty without reciprocal privileges. Extraterritorial law, economic concessions, and the stationing of foreign troops in Chinese cities were sanctified by treaty but won by force. Punitive expeditions, in 1860 and 1900, delivered the supreme insult of foreign military occupation of the venerated capital of Peking.

The twentieth century brought little relief. Japan fought Russia on Chinese soil for control of the rich provinces of Manchuria. China's own allies in World War I swept aside her protests at Versailles, and awarded to Japan concessions in China held by defeated Germany. During World War II, the Yalta Conference of 1945 rewarded the Soviet Union with important military, economic, and political privileges in China, all without consultation with Chiang Kai-shek. Although President Roosevelt reminded Premier Stalin that those inducements for Soviet entry into the war against Japan would have to be affirmed by Chiang, Allied pressure left China no alternative but capitulation.

In sum, China was the object of international relations but seldom the agent. Acted on by others, she was unable to act in her own right. Long the primary power in Asia, she has been cut deeply, during the past century, by an induced feeling of inferiority. Her fear of Japan followed a defeat caused by material inferiority. Her resentment against the West followed a capitulation caused by military inferiority and a humiliation caused by sensed cultural and ideological inferiority. Small wonder that, today, Peking's militant insistence upon being heard in regional and world councils strikes a responsive chord among wide sectors of the populace. At long last, a determined elite is working to restore China's place in the sun.

To be sure, irredentist claims to lost territories, denunciation of unequal treaties, and the playing off of power against power—"use barbarians against barbarians"—are all traditional techniques of foreign policy. The difference in their use by the Chinese lies in the psychological convictions behind these techniques. Among Western states, the exploitation of grievances is an accepted stratagem among assumed equals who are struggling for limited gains and for the coveted position of *primus inter pares*. Between China and the rest of the world, however, the bitter remembrance of things past heightens the defensive and offensive aspects of foreign policy.

The Communists' emphasis on imperialist aggression fits well into the objective and subjective factors, conditioning Chinese views of world politics. The resulting xenophobia, manifested in exaggerated attitudes of belligerence, has ultimately worked even to the Soviet Union's disadvantage. Whereas originally it was exploited by Soviet leaders against the West, eventually it exploded again over such real and sensed grievances as Soviet looting in Manchuria after World War II, the resentment against dependence on Soviet economic assistance, and the suspected Soviet subversion in Sinkiang. In the decade 1949–1959, official affirmations of the "monolithic unity of Sino-Soviet friendship" sought to repress the hostility with which many Chinese viewed the Sino-Soviet alliance. When Mao challenged Khrushchev for primacy in the communist world, however, such protestations of friendship disappeared in a wave of anti-Soviet invective which found ready acceptance among large sectors of the populace, always ready to believe the worst of any foreigner in his dealings with China.

THE PROCESS OF POLICY: THE COMMUNIST COMPONENT

Ideological Content: Marxism-Leninism

Besides those aspects of continuity in policy which we ascribe to the Chinese component, there are differences in degree or substance which stem from the dedication of the present Chinese leaders to communism. As Mao Tse-tung declared in 1945, "From the very beginning, our Party has based itself on the theories of Marxism, because Marxism is the crystallization of the world proletariat's most impeccable revolutionary scientific thought."[10]

General protestations of fidelity to Christianity, international law, and justice appear throughout statements of Western political figures. Rarely do these protestations enable us to determine the ends and means of these leaders, especially in foreign policy. Marxism-Leninism, however, carries with it a construct of goals and ways of seeking those goals that imparts form to ideology and institutions to a degree unknown in the noncommunist world.

Foremost in this ideology is its determination to advance communism throughout the world. Almost three decades ago, the fugitive Chinese Communist party, beleaguered by Nationalist armies in Kiangsi, proclaimed, "The Provisional Government of the Soviet Republic of China declares that it will, under no condition, remain content with the overthrow of imperialism in China, but, on the contrary, will aim as its ultimate objective in

[10] *The Fight for a New China*. A report of April 24, 1945, to the Seventh National Congress of the Chinese Communist party as quoted in O. Edmund Clubb, "Chinese Communist Strategy in Foreign Relations," *The Annals* 277 (September, 1951):156.

waging a war against world imperialism until the latter is all blown up."[11]

In terms of "progress" and "revolutionary scientific thought," this goal is
justified as a desirable one, the "good
society" being found in utopian drives
common to world philosophies. An
additional element, however, distinguishes this compulsion toward ideological expansion from counterparts
in Islam, Christianity, Wilsonian
democracy, and Nazism. For the Marxist, destruction of the imperialist is
not only desirable but necessary. The
maximum goal of world conquest is
the only guarantee for achieving the
minimum goal of communist survival.

Basic to this argument is the assumption of conflict as omnipresent in
human relations. The "contradictions
of the dialectical process" exist in various forms; conflict need not be military in manifestation. Marx posited
all historical development as a process
of struggle, whether between classes
within a nation or between nations
themselves. The highest and final conflict is to come between classes on the
international plane, in the world revolution springing from the basic contradiction between international communism and international capitalism.

This struggle is not one that is
created by the Communists. According to their credo, it is the imperialists who are to blame, engaging in a
death struggle to stave off the inevitable victory of the communist ideal.
As expressed by Peking's official voice,
Jen Min Jih Pao (People's daily),
"Although we have consistently held
and still hold that the socialist and
capitalist countries should co-exist in
peace and carry out peaceful competition, the imperialists are bent on destroying us. We must therefore never
forget the stern struggle with the

enemy, i.e., the class struggle on a
world scale."[12]

Thus, the minimum goal of survival
requires policies employing means
which simultaneously serve the maximum goal of world communist domination. One such means is that of
applying the classic Chinese dictum of
"using barbarian against barbarian"
so as to take advantage of the conflict
that assumedly exists among capitalists. Mao Tse-tung wrote, in 1940,
"Our tactical principle remains one of
exploiting the contradictions among
. . . [the imperialists] in order to win
over the majority, oppose the minority, and crush the enemies separately."[13]

These assumptions of conflict are
reinforced by the attitudes and actions
of the noncommunist world. In part,
this results from Chinese Communist
behavior and illustrates the phenomenon of the self-fulfilling prophecy.
When Mao Tse-tung proclaimed the
establishment of the People's Republic of China in October, 1949, Great
Britain extended recognition. Twist-
ing the lion's tail, Peking rejected the
recognition with protests against the
phraseology of the British note, as well
as against British consular relations
with the Nationalist authorities on
Taiwan. The maltreatment of British
business concerns in China undermined the economic arguments advanced in England for wooing Peking.
The subsequent British refusal to vote
for Peking's admission to the United
Nations, and British support for the

11 *Central China Post* (Hankow), November 25, 1931, as quoted in Clubb, "Chinese
Communist Strategy," 157.

12 "More on Historical Experience of Proletarian Dictatorship," *Jen Min Jih Pao*
(Peking), December 29, 1956. An article prepared by the editorial department of *Jen
Min Jih Pao* on the basis of a discussion at
an enlarged meeting of the Political Bureau
of the Central Committee of the Communist
party of China.
13 "On Policy" (December 25, 1940), as
translated in *Selected Works of Mao Tse-
tung* (Bombay, 1954), vol. 3, 218.

United States' action in Korea, aroused a violent reaction in China against the "Anglo-American imperialist bloc." In one sense, that bloc came about, in spite of the contradictions within it, largely because of the Chinese predisposition to hostility.

To a lesser extent, America's relations with the new regime were also a product of its own actions. As early as 1948, American consular officials were put under house arrest in communist-held Mukden, jailed, tried, and eventually expelled from China. The seizure of Economic Cooperation Administration stocks in 1949, the inflaming of public opinion against American personnel, both official and unofficial, and the confiscation of American consular property held through treaty agreement, in January, 1950, all served to obstruct a rapprochement between Washington and Peking. Chinese intervention in the Korean War, and the attendant defeat of American troops at the Yalu in November, 1950, wiped out whatever possibility remained of normal relations between the two countries, at least for many years to come. Yet, prior to this war, the record shows a number of instances where normal adherence by Peking to international custom might have strengthened the hand of groups within the United States which were seeking to establish ties with the new regime.

It would be misleading to attribute all Chinese Communist fears and resentments against the United States to this self-fulfilling prophecy. America's support of Chiang Kai-shek in the civil war, its obstruction of Chinese representation in the United Nations, and its promulgation of an economic embargo against Peking exacerbated relations between the two countries during the 1950s. The combination of expectation and realization reinforced the ideological content of Chinese

Communist policy, which posits conflict, overt or covert, with the noncommunist world.

The most famous formulation of this principle came in Mao Tse-tung's "lean to one side" declaration on July 1, 1949:

> "You lean to one side." Precisely so. . . . Chinese people either lean to the side of imperialism or to the side of socialism. To sit on the fence is impossible; a third road does not exist. . . . Internationally we belong to the anti-imperialist front headed by the U.S.S.R. and we can look for genuine friendly aid only from that front, and not from the imperialist front.[14]

The implementation of this principle came quickly, with the signing of the Treaty of Friendship, Alliance, and Mutual Aid of February 14, 1950, between the Chinese People's Republic and the Union of Soviet Socialist Republics. Mao and Stalin agreed that "in the event of one of the Contracting Parties being attacked by Japan or any state allied with her and thus being involved in a state of war, the other Contracting Party shall immediately render military and other assistance by all means at its disposal." A proliferation of subsequent agreements regulated Soviet economic assistance to China (loans and technical assistance), as well as military aid, cultural exchange, and routine international arrangements about telecommunications and postal regulations.

The "lean to one side" policy, precluding assistance from, much less alliance with, noncommunist countries, was antithetical to traditional Chinese politics of playing off one country against another. It can only be ex-

14 "On People's Democratic Dictatorship," July 1, 1949, as translated in *A Documentary History of Chinese Communism*, ed. C. Brandt, B. Schwartz, and J. K. Fairbank (Cambridge: Harvard University Press, 1952), pp. 449 ff.

plained in terms of the communist component of Chinese foreign policy.

Ideology: Maoism

So far, we have been discussing aspects of policy that stem from the communist component as developed in Marxism-Leninism. Assumptions of conflict, antagonism against capitalism, and promoting the world revolution are all compatible with the ideological concepts dominant in the Soviet Union, at least until the death of Stalin in 1953. Within this framework, however, divergent strategies emerged with the rise of the Chinese Communist party (CCP). As early as 1946, Liu Shao-ch'i told an American correspondent, "Mao Tse-tung has created a Chinese or Asiatic form of Marxism. His great accomplishment has been to change Marxism from its European to its Asiatic form. He is the first who has succeeded in doing so."[15] At that time, the principal Chinese innovation appeared to be Mao's building a Communist party on a peasant guerrilla army based in the countryside, as opposed to the classical Marxist method of a worker's movement which seizes power in the cities. Beneath this question of strategy, of course, lay the deeper question of historical "stages" whereby Marx posited socialism as "naturally" emerging out of advanced capitalism, in contrast with Mao's effort to move directly from China's "semifeudal" state into socialism.

Subsequent to winning power, however, new ideological differences pitted Mao's vision of the "good society" against that manifest in the Soviet Union. We cannot recapitulate the entire Sino-Soviet dispute, nor do we wish to place exclusive emphasis on ideological as contrasted with national interest conflicts. Mao recognized that both factors cause "contradictions between socialist countries and [between] Communist Parties" when he asserted these were "not the result of a fundamental clash of interests between classes but of *conflicts between right and wrong opinions* or of a partial contradiction of interests"[16] (italics added). Mao's reference to "right and wrong opinions" reflects his philosophy of "cure the illness, save the patient," in that "wrong opinions" are to be "struggled against" instead of either being passively ignored or suppressed by physical force. The "struggle" is necessitated by the importance of "thought" as a guide to "action" and it includes public confrontation between the erring individual and his peers in a "study group." In similar fashion, Mao initiated a theoretical debate with Nikita Khrushchev, conducted in public as well as private channels, beginning with the Soviet leader's sudden denunciation of Stalin at the Twentieth Congress of the Communist Party of the Soviet Union in March, 1956. Again in 1960, Mao moved from indirect, closed debate to direct, open polemics in order to persuade Khrushchev's colleagues at home and abroad of the difference between "right and wrong opinions."

This philosophy and its accompanying tactics were wholly alien to the repressive and secretive style of Stalin, much of which continued to characterize Soviet politics down to the 1970s. But more than style separated Mao from his Soviet counterpart. At issue was nothing less than the fundamental ideological goals of revolution, not merely as manifested in the century-old slogans of Marx and Engels,

[15] Quoted in Anna Louise Strong, *Dawn Out of China* (Bombay: People's Publishing House, 1948), p. 29.

[16] "More on the Historical Experience of Proletarian Dictatorship," *Jen Min Jih Pao*, December, 1956; later officially attributed to Mao.

but in the present practices and future values of the new society. Mao's primary aim in carrying out a revolution in China was to transform the society's ethos from a hierarchical, elitist, authoritarian culture to an equalitarian, mass-oriented, and eventually mass-directed culture. For him, this domestic revolution took priority over such other goals as modernization of the economy, building up national military power, and emulating foreign societies in their definition of national goals and values.

This appreciation of Mao's goals did not emerge fully until his Cultural Revolution of 1966–68. In retrospect, however, it provides a clue to the intensity with which Mao waged his attack against "revisionism" as early as 1958, initially masked as "Yugoslav" revisionism and later revealed explicitly as "Soviet" when the polemic became public in the 1960s. The important linkage between internal Soviet policy and Chinese foreign policy lay in Mao's recognition that national boundaries and governmental relations provide an inadequate frame of reference for understanding important levels of transnational interaction. Just as the missionaries and businessman of the nineteenth century provided alternative models for emulation in China and transmitted values antithetical to the Confucian ethic, so the Soviet Union threatened to shape the new Chinese society in its own image. Such Soviet "leadership" was a compulsive dictate of Stalin's era whereby emulation of all things Russian seemed mandatory for "membership in the socialist camp," meaning Soviet military and economic support. Even after death removed Stalin's personal tyranny, Soviet methods and motivational values dominated allied regimes through the continuing ascendance of the Soviet model, transmitted by translated texts and articles, technical assistance teams, training in Soviet institutes and research centers, and varying degrees of integration and standardization of technical systems, especially military.

The Sino-Soviet alliance promised to keep China permanently dependent —psychologically if not in fact—on the Soviet Union, since Peking could hardly hope ever to "catch up" with Moscow's technical and material superiority, especially given China's tremendous imbalance between an enormous, largely untrained population and scarce resources of capital, foodstuffs, and raw materials. Ideologically, the alliance confronted Mao with a model that stressed economic modernization, material incentives, and unequal rewards of power and status for political authority and acquired skill. These values, national interest conflicts apart, threatened his twin goals of developing a China "standing on its own feet" and eliminating the traditional Confucian culture.

Thus, in addition to specific foreign policy conflicts which sharply exacerbated Sino-Soviet tensions in 1958–59, the ideological conflict eroded the alliance because Mao was willing to risk the loss of Soviet military and economic support in order to shield China from Soviet "revisionism." Another ideological dimension, dominant in the polemic at the time, concerned the strategy and tactics best suited for advancing world revolution. Each side tended to caricature the other in this debate, the Chinese accusing the Soviets of "abandoning" the revolution to "peaceful coexistence with imperialism" while sacrificing local Communists through insistence on the "parliamentary path to power," which could only end in frustration or suppression. The Soviets responded by claiming Mao to be a "nuclear madman" who would risk World War III to advance Chinese "chauvinistic, expansionistic" interests while he sacrificed local Communists to bloody "people's wars" which might escalate to global proportions.

Accordingly, China's foreign policy has carried a far more militant, strident tone of support for "people's wars" since 1958 than has that of the Soviet Union. Mao believes that "power grows out of the barrel of a gun" and that "armed struggle in the countryside" is the most reliable path to power. Moreover, his confrontation with Moscow has compelled Peking to champion communist causes throughout the world to "prove" that China is revolutionary while the USSR is revisionist. These two factors illustrate the dialectic of choice and necessity which intertwines Maoist ideology with foreign policy. More important, however, is the root involvement of Mao's domestic ideological concerns which fueled his "struggle" with Khrushchev's "wrong opinions," thereby splitting the "socialist camp" and ultimately the "world revolutionary movement."

A reliable journalist subsequently explained Mao's decisions to launch the Cultural Revolution in the light of two problems. First, his presumed successor and then chief of state, Liu Shao-ch'i, was "taking the capitalist road" and refusing to "repudiate the reactionary bourgeois academic 'authorities' and the ideology of the bourgeoisie and all other exploiting classes." Second, Liu advocated reuniting with the Soviet Union in the face of American military escalation in Vietnam.[17] Liu was villified as "China's Khrushchev," thereby emphasizing Mao's first concern, domestic affairs. Mao refused to mute his dispute with Moscow after Khrushchev's fall in 1964, despite U.S.

bombing of North Vietnam and massive U.S. troop involvement in South Vietnam during 1965, deciding instead both to "go it alone" and to purge China's political system of "revisionists." This demonstrates the extent to which he saw his domestic ideological goals threatened by any affiliation with the Soviet Union.

Mao's suspicions were not without foundation. For instance, the transformation of China's military establishment from a backward army developed in guerrilla warfare against the Japanese into a modern, multiservice force moving toward a nuclear capability resulted wholly from Soviet assistance, both material and human. In Mao's eyes, however, the army is not merely for passive defense, exclusively military in function, but as in the guerrilla years of World War II, it should be intimately associated with civilian political and economic activities, serving both as an model of selfless behavior and as a direct participant in mass campaigns of flood control, reforestation, and agriculture. For him it was no coincidence that opposition to his "Great Leap Forward" experiment of 1958–59 with its mass communes and "backyard furnaces" was spearheaded by top PLA officials whose position paralleled that of Moscow. While Soviet criticism of the communes was accompanied by an apparent scaling down of promised assistance in developing China's atomic weapons, PLA leaders attacked Mao's experiment as endangering the economy. To be sure, their argument was shared by civilian officials. But to the extent it appeared to reflect Soviet priorities of technical efficiency and technological leadership, as well as self-defined (rather than Mao-defined) roles and relationships between the military and civilian systems, the interplay between Khrushchev's "revisionism" and domestic Chinese develop-

17 Snow, "Aftermath of the Cultural Revolution."

ments fueled Mao's determination to push the Sino-Soviet dispute.

Again in 1965, the connection between foreign and domestic politics appeared in the confrontation between top Chinese officials, some of whom seem to have argued for a strategy based on modern professional, military perspectives as against Mao's advocacy of a massive people's militia and a return to defensive strategies of the prenuclear era. Those who argued against Mao, implicitly or explicitly, advocated closer cooperation with the Soviet Union in support of North Vietnam in order to improve China's military capability and to deter further U.S. escalation. The potential fusion of organizational values across national lines threatened Mao's determination to fashion an indigenous, truly revolutionary society in China. In this regard, it is interesting to note that in May, 1965, only a few months after he rejected Soviet Premier Kosygin's proposals in Peking, Mao eliminated all signs of rank in the People's Liberation Army. That fall, he ousted his chief of staff and reactivated his long dormant mass militia program.

What of the external ideological goals of world revolution? How do they weigh in the scales of priority for Peking? Despite their salience in the Sino-Soviet dispute, the goals of revolution appear seriously constrained and of lower priority than other ends of foreign policy, such as national security and international prestige. Of course, "national liberation wars" may strengthen China's security if they weaken "U.S. imperialist bases" in Southeast Asia, and they can promote Peking's prestige, when they succeed, by paralleling Mao's path to power. But Mao seems to have excluded serious support for such foreign ventures, neither affording them success nor saving them from failure by significant contributions of Chinese assistance. In

part, this is ideologically determined by the theory that "revolution is not for export," but must be indigenous to a country's problems and won by that country's revolutionary leadership. Quite likely, however, this is not the only constraint which limits Chinese material help to Communist parties abroad. An amalgam of prudence and Sinocentrism reduces Peking's contribution to considerably less than might be inferred from its polemic with Moscow or from its propagandistic pledges of "support" to various insurgencies, whether in adjacent Burma, more distant Malaysia, or far-off Brazil.

In light of the above, the role of ideology in positing goals which require verbal, if not full, commitment should not be overlooked in understanding the constraints which condition choice in Peking. However tempting might seem the gains of disavowing world revolution in general or disowning a Mao-oriented group in a particular country, for purposes of improving diplomatic, economic, or military relations the leadership can move only so far in this direction without betraying its own sense of obligation as ritualistically reiterated virtually every day of its existence. By placing this goal, as well as specific means of achieving it, through "armed struggle" as well as through the "parliamentary road," at issue in the Sino-Soviet debate as far back as 1957, Peking limited its options, at least in public relations, in the competition for international influence with both Moscow and Washington. In some cases, this proved no liability regardless of whether armed struggle with Chinese support was at issue. In Indonesia, for instance, the largest Communist party in Asia (other than the Chinese) steadily expanded its influence by peaceful means from 1955 to 1965, while both it and the government under Sukarno moved ever closer to Peking and further away from Moscow and Washington. In India, however, the local communist movement was splintered over the choice between violence versus peaceful competition, with Moscow clearly winning over Peking at both the governmental and the communist levels of influence. While the Sino-Indian border conflict finally tipped the balance decisively against China at both levels, the prospects for Peking were already dim before the Himalayan clashes of October and November, 1962.

The prospects are uncertain for Mao's ideological influence on future Chinese foreign policy, as contrasted with the more general tenets of Marxism-Leninism, which are certain to complement Chinese components of policy so long as the Chinese Communist party remains in power. It is this very uncertainty which prompted Mao to implement the extreme measures of the Cultural Revolution. If, through bureaucracy, organization, and decision-making processes, routinization and institutionalization invariably dilute revolutionary ideology over time, it is no surprise that twenty years after winning power the policy establishment in Peking was not to Mao's liking. How deep has been the impact of his Cultural Revolution and how successful his successors will be in carrying on Mao's heritage remains to be seen. In subsequent conversations with Edgar Snow, Mao insisted that while state differences could be resolved with Moscow, ideological differences would remain.[18] Presumably these include not only the external differences over how to confront "U.S. imperialism" and support "national liberation struggles," but also the domestic systems of values in the two societies. If so, much will

[18] Snow, "A Conversation With Mao," *Life,* April 30, 1971.

depend on Mao's successors maintaining his revolutionary priorities even if they cut against bureaucratic and "national" interests of "modernization" and economic growth, not to mention individual preferences for promotion and material rewards. Mao's confidence that ideological differences will remain may be somewhat misplaced, but the conflicts of interest on other levels would appear to have cut so deeply into the consciousness of all Chinese involved with Sino-Soviet affairs over the last fifteen years as to preclude any return to the intimacy of the early fifties in the foreseeable future. Insofar as the ideological infusion of the Soviet ethos was a function of that intimacy, then, Mao may have no need for anxiety over his successors' handling of Soviet relations, although China may nonetheless evolve in directions contrary to his own ethos.

Institutional Structure of Decision-Making

So far, we have focused primarily on such vast aggregate concepts as "China" and "the Chinese," or on individual personalities such as Mao Tse-tung and Liu Shao-ch'i. Moving from these two extreme opposite levels of analysis to the intermediary ground of governmental decision making is essential if we are to project a model of behavior compatible with our appreciation of such processes in other large bureaucracies. Rarely, if ever, does foreign policy result from an abstract concept of a monolithic "national interest." Neither is it usually the dictate of a single official acting wholly on his own initiative. Instead, specific interests and responsibilities shape the perceptions, information intake and output, and policy preferences of organized groups whose interaction defines policy in specific situations. That interaction will change over time as different groups' relative power changes within the political system, in addition to changing in response to "feedback" from the international system. These two dynamic processes, internal and external, virtually preclude simplistic assertions of individual roles and rigid projection of future policy.

Even more than in our previous analysis we must now work by inference, since we have virtually no solid data on group interactions in the foreign policy process of China since 1949. Mountains of material reflecting public participation in the form of mass rallies, demonstrations, and petitions are superficial evidence of nongovernmental groups organized along economic, educational, and communal lines. This tells us much about the implementation and utilization of foreign policy in domestic politics, but virtually nothing about the masses' prior participation in decision making. In contrast, a few illuminating glimpses into bureaucratic relationships were provided in the turmoil of the Cultural Revolution; otherwise, logical deduction rather than hard evidence must be the primary basis for speculation concerning interactions within the government. Finally, personality analysis, the mainstay of "Kremlinology," comes hard in the wake of the Cultural Revolution, during which no individual was designated as foreign minister for three years and no constitution or state organs relevant to policy making appeared in Peking.

One additional obstacle compels us to be even more tentative about our image of the present policy-making process in Peking as compared with the pre-Cultural Revolution period of 1949–66: Mao's effort to refashion institutions and replace individual officials progressed slowly in the aftermath of the two-year upheaval. While

we can surmise the earlier difference between form and substance by juxtaposing the role of party and that of the official administrative and constitutional organs, it becomes increasingly difficult to determine who exercises what authority after 1968. On the one hand, "revolutionary committees" at various levels received public attention for combining "reformed cadres," members of the PLA, and "revolutionary mass" representatives in collective leadership. On the other hand, the omnipresence of military personnel in offices and factories suggested to observers supervisory ascendancy for the PLA. As a further complication, the Chinese Communist party enjoyed a slow, painful restoration during the years after its Ninth Congress in April, 1969, leaving uncertain its final position in the constellation of political power.

With these reservations in mind, we can sketch the outlines of interacting elements as they probably existed down to 1966, and speculate on how this "mix" might affect future policy. We should be wary of the pure authoritarian models of the individual (Mao) or the institution (party) that are suggested by China's mass media, because it does not seem logical or feasible that so large and complex a problem as Chinese foreign policy can be so simply determined. As we have seen, foreign relations, especially in the Chinese perspective, involve first of all security against attack. This requires estimates of friend and foe and the allocation of scarce resources according to felt needs and sensed future threats. Thus, one large organization necessarily concerned with foreign policy planning, implicit or explicit, is the military. It must play a role in determining the degree of risk to be accepted on behalf of beseiged friendly states, such as North Korea or North Vietnam, or in response to threats posed by the Soviet Union, India, or the United States. Its interests were intimately involved in the Sino-Soviet alliance and in the jeopardy to that alliance posed by the dispute. Its modernization and nuclear development are affected by foreign trade and the use to which China's scarce purchasing and export power is put. Intelligence requirements must be met by a clandestine foreign service and Chinese missions abroad, as well as by costly, technologically advanced systems such as satellites and long-range radar. Commitments to foreign recipients of military aid, whether governmental or subversive, involve the PLA at least peripherally. In the cases of Pakistan or the Indochina war, the involvement may become major and prolonged. These matters, while they do not exhaust the interests of the military in foreign policy, demonstrate the unlikelihood of such policy being determined solely within the walls of the Ministry of Foreign Affairs or among party leaders acting exclusively in that capacity.

More obviously, of course, the Ministry of Foreign Affairs acquires its own organizational identity and interests as formal recognition of the PRC increases its size and responsibilities. The advancement of China's prestige through diplomacy—as manifested in the signing of treaties, the establishment of embassies, exchanges of state visits, and Chinese participation in international conferences—is an important substitute for the projection of influence and power through global military and economic aid—as is possible for the Soviet Union and the United States—or through international trade—as is possible for Japan. Yet, at the same time that the People's Republic aspires to diplomatic preeminence, especially in the "Third World" of Asia, Africa, and Latin America, it professes to be the main

base supporting world revolution. These two goals can easily conflict at particular points in time and place, as evidenced by African regimes which have denied recognition to Peking or, after granting recognition, have ousted its diplomats because of Chinese subversive activity. Thus, a presumably sizeable organization within the overall bureaucracy argues for more resources and policy support to promote revolution, even if this conflicts with the dictates of diplomacy advanced by the foreign ministry. Still another point of contention comes with the need to present a public posture in accordance with one or another of these conflicting interests through domestic media and their global counterparts, such as Radio Peking, *Peking Review*, and the tons of pamphlets distributed in a dozen languages, including Esperanto.

So far, we have identified agencies within the government whose responsibilities are primarily, if not exclusively, externally directed. However, no agency concerned with internal development can be wholly disinterested in foreign relations if its activity is in any way dependent on foreign trade, either as a means of acquiring technology to facilitate development or as a demand on domestic production of exports to fund imports. Despite the insistence of both Chiang Kai-shek and Mao Tse-tung that China be "self-reliant," foreign trade, while small relative to the country's size, can play an important role in the domestic economy. At the crudest level, maintenance of the delicate food-population balance throughout the 1960s depended on annual imports of wheat from Canada, Australia, Argentina, and France. Improving that balance required major purchases abroad of chemical fertilizers and entire factories for their manufacture. At the minimum, this trade called for avoidance of unnecessary risks which might involve China in hostilities disruptive to seaborne commerce. In addition, the purchasing power for such imports could not be generated in bilateral trade, because China's products had insufficient demand. Consequently, the unique role of Hong Kong, which provided China with $500 million or more in annual trade surplus, made Sino-British relations critical for domestic development. Despite this remnant of imperialism on China's doorstep, occasioning Soviet ridicule of Mao's revolutionary pretensions, the preponderance of nonrevolutionary interests in Peking safeguarded Hong Kong against internal or external takeover.

These linkages virtually preclude the possibility that foreign affairs are the prerogative of a few men, although detailed management undoubtedly falls within narrow sectors of particular competence, with highest-level guidance from the apex of the policy pyramid. Before focusing on that apex, however, we must add one more dimension to our model: time. Over time, developments occur, internally and externally, which affect the weight of each component in the policy process. Capabilities change, threats shift, and projections are borne out or fail to prove correct. Successes and failures affect the credibility of policies and of those who advocate or oppose them. Individuals rise or fall in the process, with changing degrees of influence. While avoiding an exclusive concern with personalities, we cannot ignore the significance of the political game, with its unwritten rules for assuring personal survival and its invisible struggles to win out over one's rival, either within an organization or in opposite areas of interest. The temptation is strong to see all policy decisions as rationally arrived at within a wholly logical and consistent model, thereby explaining why past events occurred and providing hopeful predictability for future events. However, in reality accident and mismanagement are far more frequent than could ever be believed by the outside observer. Tidiness is not the hallmark of large bureaucracies in foreign or domestic affairs. Therefore, not only may the whole be larger than the sum of its parts, but also its shape is subject to change as its parts change in the course of time.

Let us look schematically, then, at the apex of decision making as it existed down to the Cultural Revolution, and as it may reemerge in modified form. The arena of action is the Chinese Communist party's top organ, the political bureau (Politburo)—or, more accurately, the party's Standing Committee. A top-ranking party official, Teng Hsiao-p'ing analyzed the relationship between party and state in his report to the Eighth National Congress of the CCP, in September, 1956, as follows:

The Party is the highest form of class organization. It is particularly important to point this out today when our Party has assumed the leading role in state affairs. . . . [This] means first, that Party members in state organs and particularly the leading Party members' groups formed by those in responsible positions in such departments should follow the unified leadership of the Party. Secondly, the Party must regularly discuss and decide on questions with regard to the guiding principles, politics, and important organizational matters in state affairs, and the leading Party members' groups in the state organs must see to it that these decisions are put into effect with the harmonious cooperation of non-Party personalities. Thirdly, the Party must . . . exercise constant supervision over the work of state organs.[19]

[19] "Report on Revision of Party Constitution," delivered to the CCP Eighth National Congress on September 16, 1956, as quoted by NCNA, Peking, September 18, 1956.

This frank analysis lent substance to an analysis of party control of state organs based upon interlocking direction by high-ranking party members. The State Council, corresponding to the Council of Ministers in the Soviet Union or to the Western cabinet, allocated controlling positions to party members—the premiership, all ten vice-premierships, and positions in such key ministries as foreign affairs, defense, public security, finance, state planning agencies, machine industries, electric power, railways, and foreign trade. Noncommunists held ministries concerned primarily with public consumption, such as food, textiles, and aquatic products, or posts concerned with cultural affairs and health.

Similarly, the Standing Committee of the National People's Congress was studded both with Politburo members (its chairman and secretary general) and with party members (six of its fifteen vice-chairmen). Although this group was vested, by the constitution of 1954, with powers akin to those of legislative bodies in the West, its membership seem to have been politically impotent in view of the extreme range of decree power held by the State Council. The inclusion of such dignitaries as Madame Sun Yat-sen (Soong Ch'ing-ling); China's outstanding literary polemicist, Kuo Mo-jo; and Tibet's Panchen Lama among its vice-chairmen suggests that this body was an honorific gathering to provide public sanction for decisions arrived at elsewhere.

The party's constitution made clear the absolute duty of all members to carry out policies and practices decreed by the Central Committee or, in its absence, by the Politburo:

Article 19. (6) The decisions of the Party must be carried out unconditionally. Individual Party members must yield to Party organizations, the minority to the majority, the lower organizations to the higher organizations, and all the organizations throughout the country must yield centrally to the National Congress and the Central Committee.[20]

That such decisions were seldom those of the Central Committee was evidenced by the infrequency of its sessions, the size of its membership, and the relatively short intervals during which lengthy reports were read and accepted. The Eighth Central Committee, elected in 1956, had more than 190 regular and alternate members. Although it met approximately twice yearly, as stipulated by the party constitution, its plenums seldom lasted more than five days. Moreover, in crisis-ridden 1960, no Central Committee plenum was reported, despite nationwide famines, reorganization of the communes, and the growing differences with Soviet Russia.

Judging by appearances, albeit with little first-hand evidence, key decisions come from a small, self-perpetuating CCP elite whose composition remained fairly constant from 1945 to 1966. The active members of the Politboro's Standing Committee—Mao, Liu, Chou, and Teng Hsiao-p'ing—dated their association back to the 1920s. Despite the wealth of reported accusations and other documentation of the Cultural Revolution, we are still unable to pinpoint at what time and over what issues Mao and Liu began to drift apart. In the absence of such information, it may be safe to assume that consensus emerged under the leadership of Mao more readily in foreign than in domestic affairs until

[20] The Constitution of the Communist Party of China adopted by the Eighth National Congress of the CCP on September 26, 1956, as translated in *Current Background* (Hong Kong: United States Consulate General), no. 417 (October 10, 1956).

the two became inextricably inter-twined in the Sino-Soviet dispute. This surmise is supported by the ease with which the PRC resumed estab-lished lines of foreign policy in 1968–71, made familiar from its earlier period when Liu was chief of state, and by the continuity of Chou En-lai's service as China's most prominent spokesman in world affairs despite the Cultural Revolution.

While we have cautioned against an exclusive personality focus, it is worth recalling that both Mao and Chou have long shown flexibility and adaptability in foreign relations, in contrast with the more rigid posture adopted by Peking's propaganda at home and abroad concerning world revolution and the struggle against imperialism. This permitted emergent organizational and interest groups to adopt an equally diverse set of ap-proaches to the outside world, as the CCP moved from a beleaguered guer-rilla army in the hills and plains of northern China to command of the People's Republic. As early as Decem-ber, 1944, Mao and Chou requested a secret meeting with President Roose-velt in Washington, and the follow-ing spring Mao talked at length with an American official concerning his hope for U.S. investments and indus-trial assistance after the civil war had been won.[21] Significantly, Mao did not announce his celebrated "lean to one side" formula until 1949, well after CCP experience with U.S. support for

Chiang Kai-shek had confirmed expec-tations of "imperialist" opposition as compared with "socialist" support. In 1946, Chou En-lai had warned Ambas-sador George C. Marshall, President Truman's special emissary in an abor-tive attempt to mediate between the Nationalist and Communists, "Of course we will lean to one side, but how far depends upon you."[22] Thus the leadership roles of Mao and Chou permit an overall framework of flexi-bility for the discussions of foreign policy, within which specific interests represented through members of the Politboro contend for different poli-cies. In addition, a ready rationale for different strategies, tactics, and specific policies is provided by the Marxist philosophy of the dialectical progres-sion of history and by Mao's emphasis on understanding "contradictions"—both "antagonistic" and "nonantago-nistic"—among foreign powers as well as between a foreign power and China. How these "contradictions" are to be handled, wherein lies "the main threat," and how to "translate theory into practice" become the stuff of policy debate as applied to each situa-tion.

This does not mean that policy dis-putes never split the leadership or that they never leave an aftermath of bitter acrimony. Clearly, Sino-Soviet relations played an important part in the confrontation between Mao and his Politboro associate Marshal P'eng Teh-huai in 1959. P'eng's role and responsibilities as minister of defense took priority over his collegial role in the party, prompting his challenge to Mao's "Great Leap Forward" and his Soviet policy. P'eng's chief of staff fell with him at this time, as did other military figures and a former ambas-

---

21 For details on these and related devel-opments, see the telegram of Ambassador Hurley to Secretary of State Hull, February 7, 1945, paraphrasing message from Mao and Chou sent "eyes only via General Wedemey-er," January 9, 1945, and Mao's conversa-tion with John S. Service of March 13, 1945, *Foreign Relations of the United States: Diplomatic Papers, 1945*, vol. 7, *The Far East: China* (Washington, D.C., 1969), pp. 209 ff.

22 Personal reminiscence of John F. Melby, foreign service officer on Marshall's staff, as to the author.

sador to Moscow.[23] Mao's subsequently named successor, Marshal Lin Piao, became minister of defense, and Lo Jui-ch'ing moved from head of internal security to chief of staff. However, six years afterward, Lo's socialization shifted his identification so close to the viewpoint of professionals in the PLA as to prompt him to challenge Mao's policy vis-à-vis Moscow in the context of U.S. escalation in Vietnam, and once again, purge settled policy differences. These developments suggest the relative weight of individual predilection as compared with organizational roles and responsibilities.

Of course, no organization is purely monolithic. Differences exist within them on the basis of sectional and subsectional interests and perspectives on issue areas. Dramatic evidence of factionalism in the Ministry of Foreign Affairs came in May, 1967, when Red Guards ransacked the ministry, seized its files, and attacked its leading officials. Led by an official formerly in the Chinese embassy in Jakarta, the militants won control by mid-summer. By August, they had succeeded in pushing China's relations with several countries, most particularly Burma and Great Britain, to the brink of rupture through violent demonstrations against foreign missions and their personnel in Peking as well as through turbulent public demonstrations by Chinese embassy staffs abroad.[24] In Burma, these demonstrations triggered an anti-Chinese reaction in which two Chinese diplomatic personnel and many local Chinese residents were killed. In response, Peking adopted a harsh position, throwing its full propaganda support against the regime of Ne Win and behind the Burmese White Flag (Communist party) insurgents. Meanwhile, in the Chinese capital, massive demonstrations against the missions of the Soviet Union, India, and Britain climaxed with the sacking of the British chancery on August 22 and the manhandling of its occupants. Beginning in May, coincident with the assault on the foreign ministry, the Cultural Revolution spillover in Hong Kong threw the colony into a summer-long crisis complete with riots, bombings, and border incidents.

These tumultuous events coincided with intense struggles at every level of the political system and throughout the country, threatening civil war as military units and services became divided in their support for contending factions. With this last prospect imminent and with foreign relations in shambles, enough temporary unity emerged at the top to quiet the worst violence. More particularly, control of the Ministry of Foreign Affairs was wrested from the militants, and nominal control was reassumed by the besieged foreign minister, Ch'en Yi, with substantive direction returning to the strong hand of Chou En-lai. In September, Cambodian Prince Norodom Sihanouk's vigorous protest of the undiplomatic behavior of Chinese embassy personnel in Phnom Penh evoked a prompt personal apology from Chou. More quiet and discreet amends were communicated to the British in Peking, while negotiations at the Hong Kong border restored the previous status quo by mutual agreement.

Although the circumstances surrounding the 1967 eruption are unique in the history of the People's Republic, the issues at stake may not

[23] David Charles, "The Dismissal of Marshal P'eng Teh-huai," *The China Quarterly*, no. 18 (October–December 1961):63–77.

[24] A detailed examination of this period, based on Chinese sources of the time, is provided by Melvin Gurtov, "The Foreign Ministry and Foreign Affairs in China's 'Cultural Revolution,'" RAND Corporation Report RM-5934-PR (March, 1969).

have been. The confrontation between radical, revolutionary interests and those of professional diplomacy is inherent in China's dual mission, derived from its national heritage and its Marxist-Maoist ideology. Equally illuminating is the light this period throws on the linkage between domestic and foreign politics. This linkage is obvious in the case of those noncommunist societies where public opinion or political parties can affect foreign policy issues. It is, nonetheless, even present in the closed authoritarian system when perceptual and interest differences at various levels are permitted to coalesce in concert with struggles within the leadership. Neither does this mean that China's 800 million inhabitants remain ignorant of or uninvolved in foreign affairs. Special mass organizations, such as the Communist Youth League and the All-China Democratic Women's Federation, link entire sectors of society in a closely coordinated network of communications media directed from the Department of Propaganda of the CCP. Governmental gatherings, such as the National Committee of the Chinese People's Political Consultative Conference, bring together representatives of "democratic parties and mass organizations" to receive reports from leaders and to endorse contemporary policies. Additional ad hoc meetings at provincial, municipal, and county levels provide ritualized support for policy as a prelude to mass rallies and parades, as do small group discussions at places of employment and in neighborhood and commune gatherings.

Thus, both parties and interest-group organizations exist in the PRC, but their function is basically within the context of one-way communication from the top downward, as distinguished from their dual role of influencing and explaining policy in

the West. In this sense, public opinion exists to be mobilized by the party but not to direct the party. It may fail to respond to party propaganda, thereby compelling some revision of policy. It may articulate grievances by indirection, thereby stimulating examination of policy at the top. When it comes to placing external pressure on the government, however, public opinion in China is not an articulate force, at least in the realm of foreign policy.

It is important, in formulating foreign policy, that parties, interest groups, and public opinion act to unify the populace. Mass campaigns are carried out for months at a time over all the media of communication, and with thousands of study groups. These means are useful in three different types of situations, discussed below.

Mass campaigns may serve a contingency purpose, preparing the populace for possible action without committing the government to such action. In 1954–55, all China signed petitions in blood, applauded speeches, and endorsed resolutions calling for the "immediate liberation of Taiwan." No invasion of Taiwan followed, nor were any decisive preparations for invasion evident. Similarly, in 1956, a shorter, less intensive campaign pledged "volunteers for Egypt" during the Anglo-French attack upon that country. Again, no action followed. Such instances serve to confuse the outside world as to the intent of Chinese policy, in addition to whatever domestic stimuli they may provide for increasing production, renewing bonds of allegiance, or promulgating symbols of national unity.

Such campaigns may also serve the function of whipping up public support for an action already decided on. In 1950, an attack on Tibet was preceded by public rallies, exhortatory articles, and ringing declarations by prominent leaders. Undoubtedly, the most extensive use of this technique came in the celebrated "Resist-American-Aid-Korea" movement which accompanied Chinese intervention in the Korean War. During the three years of that action, a steady barrage of propaganda carried the movement to every corner of China.

Finally, these campaigns serve the purpose of "feedback," much as polls of public opinion are supposed to do in the noncommunist world. Study group meetings are active discussions. They seek to bring out all questions of doubt and opposition, for the purpose of achieving final unity under the skilled leadership of prepared party personnel, activists, and cadres. Following Soviet intervention in the abortive Hungarian revolt of 1956, meetings at Chinese universities, factories, and farms discussed Peking's support for the Soviet action and attempted to quell what was reported by the communist press as "shock and confusion."

The limits on public participation in policy are extreme and explicit, however. An authoritative Chinese analysis warned against "practicing democracy merely for the sake of democracy." Specifically, it advised the youth:

Before the liberation the forms used by the people in demanding democracy from the Kuomintang consisted mainly of strikes (of workers and students), demonstrations, and parades, bringing loss to the Kuomintang and applying pressure on the enemy so that they had to accept our demands. Today, in dealing with the Anglo-French imperialists who carry out aggression against Egypt, we still adopt the form of demonstration and parade. However, in dealing with divergences of views within the internal ranks of the people, the defects and mistakes of the people, we must resort principally to argument . . . and not the

form of applying pressure. . . . The country today belongs to us, and we ourselves will bear the losses, political and economic, arising out of such forms as strikes of workers, strikes of students, and demonstrations and parades for the solution of questions.[25]

Thus, in the area of "people-to-people diplomacy" a basic asymmetry exists between China and its opposite numbers in the noncommunist world. The public applause for American table-tennis players in Peking and Shanghai provided no constraint on leadership options in handling Sino-American relations, whereas mass media publicity for this event in the United States immediately changed the context of decision making on China policy in Washington. It would be an exaggeration to say that American public opinion in the aggregate forces a particular choice on presidential policy, except when a national election coincides with the existence of an extremely sensitive foreign policy issue such as the Korean War in 1952 and the Vietnam war in 1968. Nonetheless, the degree of support for or opposition to specific foreign policies in the United States, particularly as manifested through congressional responses to perceived public opinion, is wholly without counterpart in the People's Republic, where policy is exclusively the prerogative of elite interactions within the bureaucratic and party hierarchy.

THE SUBSTANCE OF POLICY

Ends

The foreign policy of the People's Republic of China embraces a range of goals. Maintenance of internal

[25] Chiang Ming, "Democracy Is the Means, Not the End," *Chung Kuo Ching Nien* [China youth], no. 23 (December 1, 1956).

security is a minimum goal not peculiar to Peking. Intermediate goals, however, projecting what might be called "friendly influence" on Asian political and economic developments, stem from Chinese as well as communist components of policy—they are not, for instance, so evident in Burma or Thailand. Finally, the maximum goal of Peking, ascendancy in Asia through communist regimes that are political and economic satellites of China, is a more ambitious aim than is evident in any other ruling group in the area.

These different goals may be furthered by similar means. Wooing the uncommitted or neutral groups of Southeast Asia, following the Korean armistice in 1953, served the minimum goal of security by offsetting United States negotiations for the Southeast Asia Treaty Organization. It also smoothed the way for the increase of Peking's prestige, an intermediate goal in the move to influence governments in the area.

Yet it is important to recognize that this priority of goals is dictated by the necessity of circumstance. In its first decade, the People's Republic of China grappled, through its foreign policy, with the problems of uniting traditionally Chinese territory on the Asian mainland and at the same time reducing the external threats to the new states' existence. Chou En-lai's skillful diplomacy at Geneva and Bandung provided a peaceful counterpart to military intervention in Korea, but both were aimed basically at the minimum goal of security.

The intermediate goal is capable of realization only with economic development and a more flexible political atmosphere within China following the turmoil of the Cultural Revolution. These domestic developments, accompanied by an armistice in Indochina, are a prerequisite for fully realizing Peking's leadership in Asian affairs. Not until this process is completed can the maximum goal, a Chinese bloc of communist regimes in Asia, be realistically contemplated by Peking.

Thus, although both China and the Soviet Union may hold the identical maximum goal, that of extending communism throughout the world, they are not in the same stage of development toward attaining this goal. Moscow has long since disposed of its concern over internal security, and has advanced well along the path of attaining the intermediate goal, that of influencing governments along its periphery in Europe and the Middle East. Its economic and military means are far ahead of those available to China.

This difference in development may account for specific conflicts of policy between the two communist capitals. The prolongation of the Korean War during 1952–53 may have served the Soviet ends of increasing the strains on the North Atlantic Treaty Organization and weakening its available force in Europe. This would facilitate Soviet influence over its Eastern European satellites, and extend its influence, at least negatively, into Western Europe. China's need for security, however, called for throwing back the United Nations troops from the Ya Lu, but not necessarily beyond the 38th parallel. The continuation of the war drained the Chinese economy, shaky at the start, and increased the danger or retaliation upon China proper by United States airpower. Not until the death of Stalin, in March, 1953, did Peking's negotiators at Panmunjom agree to armistice terms essentially similar to those they had rejected months previously. Although not conclusive, the timing of this move lends credibility to our analysis.

This example suggests a spatial difference in goals, in addition to one derived from temporal differences of development. Europe is the Soviet Union's primary sphere of interest and concern, offensively and defensively. The Asian periphery, extending from Tokyo to Kabul, demands China's prior attention. Both countries share interests as well as concern with Japan, but basically they are oriented in opposite directions. This increases the possibility of continued conflict between Peking and Moscow, at least with respect to specific points of policy. It also suggests differences in the degree and area of conflict they will have with the United States.

Means

Any construct of probable means to be adopted must take into consideration the availability of the means, as well as the likelihood of their being adopted. The latter consideration assumes rational decision making, insofar as a decision is logically consistent with ideology. For reasons stated earlier, we cannot assume such rationality to be uniformly present in Chinese foreign policy. Compulsive belligerency—for instance, during the first years of the People's Republic of China—was "irrational" in terms of an objective appraisal of her assets and liabilities. However, such behavior seems less evident with the elite's maturing responsibility and its growing experience with international affairs. Therefore, the likelihood of rash or essentially irrational action lessens with time, although it by no means disappears entirely.

The means least likely to be employed by Peking, in pursuit of goals in Asia, are those of open military force. In the northeast, only South Korea and Japan might be targets of Chinese aggression. South Korea is definitely under United States protec-

tion; Japan is far less vulnerable, given the relative air and sea weakness of Chinese military forces. In southern Asia, transportation is sparse and primitive. The only rail lines venture from China into North Vietnam. Airbases are scattered and isolated. Terrain along the frontier is predominantly thick jungle or rugged mountains. Although this favors small-scale border incursions, it argues against mass invasions of the distant capitals of New Delhi, Rangoon, Bangkok, or Phnom Penh.

In addition, the base strength of China, presently located along the coast and the northeastern sectors, is moving gradually toward the north and northwest, more secure from United States bases of attack. This leaves China's southern and southwestern areas extremely deficient in the manpower and economic strength necessary for supporting large-scale military action. Finally, open use of force would risk the loss of influence and prestige that might be won through less costly means, and might drive uncommitted countries to the side of the United States.

More likely is limited Chinese military assistance to local insurrections or civil wars that advance Peking's interests. Strengthening North Vietnam, bolstering insurgent Pathet Lao forces, and aiding guerilla groups in Malaya served China well during 1950–54. Increased emphasis on the so-called spirit of Bandung, however, brought abandonment of this strategy for several years. The resumption of a bellicose posture from 1958 to 1960 endangered the positive influence won by Peking in circles sensitive to armed insurrection. Peking's doctrine of armed struggle and advocacy of wars of national liberation raised increasing doubt in the minds of its former friends, particularly in Africa, as newly independent regimes lost their revolutionary ardor and came to prefer the Soviet Union's emphasis on peaceful coexistence as a means for taking aid from all sides without being dominated by any one.

The least expensive and the least dangerous means of advancing intermediate goals would appear to be economic and political. Dramatic announcements of economic assistance, as in the Tanzanian railroad subject, or token teams of technical experts accompanied by loans or grants, as in Nepal, reap rewards far out of proportion to their expense. Chinese experience is closer than that of Western countries to the experience of underdeveloped countries. The cultural gap is easier to bridge, and the accomplishments of Chinese Communists provide a striking contrast with pre-1949 conditions in their country.

The political channels available for exporting influence are several. Much of Asia is opposed to private capital and to foreign investment. The communist credo supports this prejudice. Key groups in India, Burma, Indonesia, and Japan support varying degrees of Marxist or socialist ideology, and are responsive to Peking's planned economy, while communist strictures against corruption, nepotism, and sloth provide a positive appeal throughout Asia.

Local agents for communicating Chinese messages may be found in various cultural groups organized to promote, say, Sino-Nepali or Sino-Burmese friendship. They may be assisted by local Communist parties of some strength, as they were in Indonesia. In these personal contacts at the popular level, Peking enjoys a political advantage generally denied Western capitals.

Furthermore, personal contact plays a major role in Chinese diplomacy, which exploits shared attitudes of anticolonialism and bonds of so-called Afro-Asian unity. Exploiting these associations to the fullest, Chinese leaders have sought to conclude pacts of nonaggression and friendship with weaker neighbors and exchange support for their grievances receiving support, in turn, for Chinese claims to Taiwan and representation in the United Nations. In addition, growing technical assistance programs place a proliferation of efficient Chinese Communist experts throughout Africa and Asia. Their exemplary behavior and their contributions to local needs mitigate the negative impact of Peking's brutal suppression of the Tibetan revolt, or its bellicose posture on various international problems.

Finally, Chou En-lai, suave and sophisticated, has played a signal role, assuring his audiences of China's need for peace, of its exclusive concern with domestic problems, and of its interest in assisting fellow Asians. This approach pays dividends in countries where individuals play an important role in policy, unimpeded by opposition parties or by rival leaders in the bureaucracy.

These various tactics serve the familiar united-front strategy intermittently employed by Communists throughout the world since the days of Lenin. They may act from above, joining forces at the elite level, or they may act from below, infiltrating mass organizations in order to undermine present leadership. Either strategy is a temporary one designed to facilitate ultimate overthrow of the government by local Communist parties.

In view of China's power compared with that confronting it, both from local sources and from the United States, this strategy maximizes Peking's assets while minimizing its liabilities. So long as societies in southern and Southeast Asia continue to suffer from political and economic instability, we may expect increased economic and political action from the People's Republic of China, although not overt military aggression.

This past decade witnessed a new growth, both geographic and strategic, in China's foreign policies. Chinese activity in Africa increased dramatically, as Peking strengthened, by diplomatic contacts and economic assistance, its access to newly independent regimes. Its challenge to Moscow spread its influence among nascent Communist parties and splinter groups in Latin American countries where it had no official presence. And as Peking's nuclear weapons strength increases, its prestige is certain to expand among the weaker, less developed countries, especially in Asia. Whether this is accompanied by more militant behavior depends on many unknown factors, including the composition of the regime after Mao Tsetung passes from the scene, the alternative means of advancing its goals, and the posture adopted by noncommunist countries. As final determinants of Chinese policy, of course, the actions of Moscow and Washington are of prime importance. In this sense, no analysis can predict the future course of China by focusing solely on the decision makers in Peking. Only a continuous correlation of their views with the changing environment within which they must operate can enable us to outline the alternatives which lie before the People's Republic of China, the largest country of Asia.

SELECTED BIBLIOGRAPHY

Books

BARNETT, A. DOAK. *Communist China and Asia*. New York: Harper & Row, 1960.

CHEN, KING C. *Vietnam and China, 1938–1954*. Princeton: Princeton University Press, 1969.

CHIANG KAI-SHEK. *China's Destiny*. New York: Roy Publishers, 1947.

DUTT, V. P. *China and the World*. New York: Praeger, 1966.

ECKSTEIN, ALEXANDER, ed. *China Trade Prospects and U.S. Policy*. New York: Praeger, 1971.

ECKSTEIN, ALEXANDER. *Communist China's Economic Growth and Foreign Trade*. New York: McGraw-Hill Book Co., 1966.

FAIRBANK, JOHN K. *The United States and China*. Cambridge: Harvard University Press, Belknap Press, 1967.

GITTINGS, JOHN. *Survey of the Sino-Soviet Dispute*. London: Oxford University Press, 1968.

HINTON, HAROLD C. *China's Turbulent Quest*. New York: Macmillan Co., 1970.

———. *Communist China in World Politics*. New York: Houghton Mifflin, 1966.

HSIEH, ALICE L. *Communist China's Strategy in the Nuclear Era*. Englewood Cliffs, N.J.: Prentice-Hall, Spectrum Books, 1962.

HUCK, ARTHUR. *The Security of China*. New York: Columbia University Press, 1970.

LALL, ARTHUR. *How Communist China Negotiates*. New York: Columbia University Press 1968.

MAO TSE-TUNG. *Selected Works*. Vols. 1–4. Peking, 1961–65.

PASSIM, HERBERT. *China's Cultural Diplomacy*. New York: Praeger, 1962.

SCHRAM, STUART. *Mao Tse-Tung*. New York: Simon and Schuster, 1966.

SIMON, SHELDON W. *The Broken Triangle: Peking, Djakarta, and the PKI*. Baltimore: Johns Hopkins Press, 1968.

VAN NESS, PETER. *Revolution and Chinese Foreign Policy*. Berkeley: University of California Press, 1970.

WHITING, ALLEN S. *China Crosses the Yalu*. Stanford, Calif.: Stanford University Press, 1968.

YOUNG, KENNETH T. *Negotiating with the Chinese Communists*. New York: McGraw-Hill Book Co., 1968.

ZAGORIA, DONALD S. *The Sino-Soviet Conflict, 1956–1961*. Princeton: Princeton University Press, 1962.

Periodicals

Asian Survey (Berkeley).
China Quarterly (London).

Current Scene (Hong Kong).
Far Eastern Economic Review (Hong Kong).
Journal of Asian Studies (Ann Arbor), with annual bibliography.
Survey of the China Mainland Press (American Consulate General, Hong Kong).

Chapter Eight

THE FOREIGN POLICY OF
MODERN JAPAN

ROBERT A. SCALAPINO

THE BACKGROUND OF JAPANESE
FOREIGN POLICY

In geopolitical terms, there are some obvious reasons for
making a rough comparison between Japan and Great
Britain. Both are island societies lying within the Tem-
perate Zone and close to a great continental mass. From
earliest times, cultural interaction with the continent has
been vital in shaping the character of each society; each has
definitely been a part of the larger cultural orbit centering
upon the continent. The sea, however, has been both a lane
and a barrier. It has prevented recent invasions, enabling
the development of a relatively homogeneous people who,
despite many foreign adaptations, have retained a strong
quality of uniqueness. Thus the encircling sea has been
important to culture as well as to livelihood and defense.
It has also been central to the historic dilemma over isolation versus continental involvement. This has been the basic
foreign policy issue of both societies throughout their existence. And in recent eras, the interaction between internal
and external pressures has been such as to present essentially
the same answer to this question in both Japan and Great
Britain. The growth of foreign pressures and the needs flowing from modernization—the scarcity of certain domestic
resources combined with the rise of unused power—these
and other factors led to regional and then global commitment. When the costs of that commitment proved too great,
and the power of these societies relative to others declined,

a substantial withdrawal took place. Now, in the case of Japan at least, some renewed commitments are being considered, reflective of the extraordinary advances made by that nation during the last two decades. To appreciate the new trend, let us turn first to the background against which it emerges.

The Tokugawa Era

The diplomatic history of modern Japan opened in the mid-nineteenth century on a decidedly reluctant and confused note. Prior to Perry's arrival in 1853, the Japanese government had pursued a rigorous policy of isolation from the outside world for over two hundred years. It abandoned that policy only under strong pressure and with many misgivings. Isolation had first been imposed as a means of maintaining internal stability. When the Tokugawa family first came to power in Japan in 1606, the West had already been represented in the country for fifty years. Missionaries and traders had come in a steady stream, first from Portugal and Spain, then from the Netherlands and England. In the first years of the Tokugawa era, however, abuses were regularly reported to the government. Christian converts among the provincial nobility sought Western arms or alliances to fortify their position against the central regime. Western trade also became a means of augmenting local power, especially in the Kyushu area. Between 1616 and 1641, therefore, the Tokugawa government applied a series of anti-Christian and antitrade edicts, leading up to a policy of almost total exclusion of the West. As is well known, only the Dutch were allowed to trade, very restrictedly, at Nagasaki. This, together with some limited relations with China and Korea, constituted Japanese foreign relations until the middle of the nineteenth century.

To draw up a balance sheet for the policy of isolation is not easy. It can be argued that, had Western intercourse been allowed to continue, Japan might well have been plunged into chaos and warfare, subsequently suffering the colonial fate of Southeast Asia. On the other hand, isolation clearly exacted its price. This is true not merely in terms of institutions and material developments, but also in the realm of emotions and attitudes. Isolation always breeds some of the symptoms of the garrison state—exclusivism, ethnocentrism, and mounting fear of the unknown, outside world. Most of these factors have been present in the Japanese scene, helping to shape the foreign policies and attitudes of that nation.

But in its time, isolation seemed to present only one major problem to Japan: How to maintain it? The expansion of the West in Asia was building up an intense pressure on Japan by the beginning of the nineteenth century. From the north, the Russians were moving forward on a broad front; Saghalien, the Kuriles, and even Hokkaido seemed threatened. Overtures for trade and coaling stations were rejected, but, at the same time, English intrusions began to take place in the southwest. These events were climaxed by news of the Opium War and repeated warnings from the Dutch. A debate began to shape up in Japan over fundamental policies.

This debate enabled Japanese nationalism to come forward, borne aloft by intellectuals from the agrarian-military class, and rooted in the primitive mythology of Shintoism. It was a movement with many facets: in part, dedicated to a restitution of imperial prerogatives and their defense against usurpation by Tokugawa; in part, an attack on the long-standing intellectual subservience to China and a simultaneous insistence on the unique character of Japan; and finally, partly a fierce assault on Western encroachment born out of an admixture of condescension and fear. All these factors were implied in the chief slogan of the era, *sonno-joi* ("revere the emperor; oust the barbarians").

In the precise form just described, this movement did not enjoy complete success, but within it was carried the destiny of modern Japan. Its evolution followed, in some measure, the broad stages characteristic of the whole panorama of Asian-Western relations during this period, whether stated in political or intellectual terms: an initial stage, dominated by the total rejection of Westernism as barbarian, inferior, and completely incompatible with the Asian way of life; a second stage, in which Western science and technology—distilled into the unforgettable spectacle of Western power—were accorded a begrudging but nonetheless deeply felt respect, from which followed, after much soul-searching and confusion, a conscious majority decision to attain these sources of power while holding firmly to traditional values; and thence, inevitably, there developed that stage in which such a rigid and unrealistic dichotomy as that between technology and values had to be abandoned in favor of a more broadly based and integral synthesis, the exact ingredients and balance of which have depended on the background and convictions of each individual or group. It is within this general trend—its various exceptions, time lags, and all-important local distinctions not to be ignored—that the major elements of foreign policy in modern Asia have taken shape. Japan has been no exception.

Even before the arrival of Perry, a small group of Japanese intellectuals had begun to question the policy of rigid isolation. Out of "Dutch learning" had come exciting ideas; and there grew, in some minds, the desirability of leading the commercial revolution rather than fighting it, and of using foreign trade to develop power. How else could the intriguing slogan, "a rich country; a powerful soldiery," be made a reality? How else could Japan defend herself against Western imperialism? But this group was a small minority in the early period. Even the Tokugawa government supported the opening of the country only as a temporary expedient until force could be garnered to throw out the West. In accepting Perry's demands, it decided to accede rather than risk war, but it gave as little ground as possible. With the initial step taken, however, it was impossible to retreat. The first U.S. envoy, Townsend Harris, secured major liberalization of the Perry treaty in 1858, and similar rights were soon granted to other Western powers. From this date, Japan was truly opened up to Western commerce, and shortly the Tokugawa regime was even to seek assistance in developing arsenals and shipyards. "Support the government" and "open the country" seemed to be slogans indissolubly linked.

Yet basically, Tokugawa policy remained more a product of pressure than of purpose, and this fact worked against the effectiveness of the policy. Beset by many problems, the regime grew steadily weaker; its capacity to act vigorously in any direction diminished. It satisfied neither the West, which complained of its inability to control unruly elements, nor the provincial samurai, who regarded the central government as arch-appeasers. As so often happens in history, the regime in power found, by tortuous means, the only feasible policy for national survival—in this case, the policy of opening the country—but in the course of reaching that policy it was itself fatally weakened, so that the actual execution and fulfillment of the policy had to pass to other hands.

Meiji Foreign Policy

In 1867, the Tokugawa regime was finally overthrown and the young Emperor Meiji was "restored" to the position of ruler, a position which the nationalists claimed the Tokugawa family had stolen. But real power in Meiji Japan gravitated into the hands of a small group of court officials and young leaders of the former military class. Their first major objective in foreign policy became that of removing the blemish of the unequal treaties, thereby attaining "complete independence" and equity with the Western powers. This task proved more difficult than they had expected; to accomplish it took nearly three decades. The Western powers, and particularly Great Britain, saw no reason to revise the treaties until Japanese standards came close to Western norms. The Japanese discovered that treaty revision was closely connected with basic reform in such fields as law and commerce. Thus the Iwakura mission, which left for the West so hopefully, in 1871, to persuade the powers to abandon the fixed tariffs and extraterritoriality, came home realizing that many internal developments had first to be undertaken.

Through the years, "modernization" progressed by means of German, French, British, and American models. Japanese economic and military power showed remarkable gains. Law and order prevailed despite occasional domestic crises. Finally, in 1894, after repeated failures, the first great objective of Japanese foreign policy was obtained: agreements on basic treaty revisions were concluded with the West, all of which went into effect by 1899. As the nineteenth century ended, Japan had become the first nation of Asia to attain nearly complete parity with the West in legal terms. She had done so, in part, by satisfying the West that she was prepared to abide by the general rules of Western conduct, in part by the obvious facts of her internal progress and stability, and in part by her persistence and by certain clear signs that inequity toward Japan had reached a point of diminishing returns.

In the long struggle for treaty revision, latent elements of antiforeignism occasionally came to the surface in various forms. Officials deemed obsequious to foreign powers, too pro-Western in their personal habits, or disrespectful of Japanese tradition ran grave risks. The history of these years is filled with records of assassination plots, some successful, against more moderate leaders. This was one price to be paid for cultivating a nationalist movement so assiduously, while scarcely daring to admit its excesses. But quite apart from its extremists, Japanese society as a whole tended to react in pendulumlike fashion to the West. In many respects, this was most natural. Periods of intensive borrowing and adaptation at both individual and group levels would be followed by noticeable retreats, with the primary targets being those excesses and absurdities most easily discernible, but with secondary attacks ranging over as broad a front as conditions would permit. On the one hand, Japan wanted to catch up with the West, be accepted as a "progressive" and "civilized" nation, and match the West in the areas of its own talents; in addition, a very genuine fondness for things Western was entertained by many Japanese, great and small. But on the other hand, in this period of intensive nationalist indoctrination, and when the old antiforeign traditions were not yet completely dead, the periodic cry of "excessive Europeanization!" or "un-Japanese practices!" could have telling effect. Moreover, if selected aspects of Westernism appealed to almost everyone, there was no widespread desire to abandon the mainstream of Japanese culture or customs. These factors are not completely absent from contemporary Japan.

During the early Meiji era, there were strong overtones of defensiveness in Japanese policy and psychology. But the climate was also ripe for the rise of expansionism. Northeast Asia was largely a vacuum of power, tended haphazardly by the "sick man of Asia," China, on the one hand, and the somewhat stronger but essentially unstable and overcommitted tsarist forces, on the other. The Japanese mission seemed even clearer when it could be posed against the prospects of continuous Korean turmoil and the increasing threat of Western imperialism in this entire area. The theme of "Asia for the Asians" was first applied here, and ofttimes by sincere men who had a vision of liberating other Asians from backwardness and Western domination, sharing with them the fruits of the new era in Japan. Private societies like the *Genyosha* (Black Current Society) and the *Kokuryukai* (Amur River Society) emerged, to exercise a great influence on Japanese foreign policy as influential pressure groups on behalf of a forceful continental policy with some such objectives in mind.

The ideology of expansionism was complex, and it knew no single form of expression. Groups like the *Kokuryukai* represented the past: they held firm to Japanese Confucianism, exalted the primitive mythology that surrounded the emperor-centered state, and were composed of ultranationalists of a peculiarly medieval type. Yet, from another point of view, these same men were radicals associated with the new era. Wherever Asian nationalism took root, they were willing to give it nourishment, even when its ideological bases were greatly different from their own. To movements as widely disparate as those of Aguinaldo and Sun Yat-sen their assistance was given freely, and in this they often went beyond what the Japanese government was willing or prepared to do. Moreover, there was an element of radicalism in their approach to internal affairs as well, even though its source might be largely traditional. Decrying the corruption, materialism, and excessive wealth of the new order, they demanded stringent internal reforms, some of which could be considered socialist in character. Thus were connected the themes of internal reform and external expansion as twins that were to have recurrent echoes throughout modern Japanese history.

The expansionists made their first major advance in the extraordinary decade between 1895 and 1905. Prior to that time, Japan had already added the Ryukyu Islands and the Bonins to her domain, and made more secure her northern outpost, Hokkaido, by extensive colonization, but these were not spectacular ventures. By 1894, however, Japanese leadership was ready to challenge China, the weakest of her rivals, for influence on the Korean peninsula. For Japan, the war was unexpectedly short and easy, the first of a series of wars that "paid." The Western-style training and the nationalist indoctrination of her conscript military forces stood the initial test with flying colors. For China, defeat at the hands of a foe long regarded with some contempt, and treated at best as a pupil, was a profound shock. Demands for fundamental reform were now renewed, especially by younger intellectuals, and China was pushed toward accelerated change and revolution despite Manchu resistance.

In Japan, the implications of victory were fourfold. The beginnings of the Japanese empire were laid, and the first tentative steps as a modern continental power were taken; China ceded Formosa, the Pescadores, and, for a time, the Liaotung Peninsula, until the intervention of Russia, France, and Germany forced its return. And China was eliminated as a serious competitor in the Korean contest. Second, the war served as a further stimulus to industrial growth and general economic development. In an atmosphere of patriotic fervor, industrial investment and expansion were undertaken, with an emphasis upon heavy industry. The war boom brought prosperity; and afterward, Japan received both indemnities and new China markets. Third, Japan enjoyed a sharp rise in prestige; most of the West looked on approvingly as their most apt pupil demonstrated her progress and valor, and it was in the aftermath of this victory that Japan began to be received in Western circles with some semblance of equality. Finally, these factors naturally accrued to the credit of the nationalist movement and to the prestige of the military class. The professional soldier, his samurai traditions now supplemented by Western science and by a new sense of mission not present in the Tokugawa era, promised to play a vital role in determining the future of his society.

In the aftermath of the Sino-Japanese War, a crucial decision had to be made. Japan was dedicated to increasing her ties with other Asian societies and providing leadership for them when possible. But to obtain these objectives and to have any basic security for herself, she needed a major alliance with a non-Asian power. This was still the world of the nineteenth century, when Europe collectively exercised a global influence, and when the unfolding of European power politics had a direct and immediate effect upon the non-European world. With the United States, Japan needed only to achieve some general agreement that would serve to neutralize potential conflict; indeed, she could expect no more, since American commitments toward the Pacific were still very limited, even after the annexation of the Philippines. The major powers in Asia were Great Britain and Russia, and the choice had to be made between these two.

Initially, top political circles in Japan were divided. Men like Ito and Inoue hoped for an agreement with Russia that would establish long-term peace in northeastern Asia on the basis of satisfying mutual interests. Had such an agreement been reached, Japanese expansion might have been directed southward at a much earlier point. An alliance with Great Britain, on the other hand, was recognized as a step toward stabilization in the south and fluidity in the northeast. Not merely in this respect, however, but in every respect, Japanese foreign policy was affected for nearly two decades by the Anglo-Japanese Alliance of 1902. This pact was widely heralded as insuring the peace of Asia. Within certain limits, perhaps it did contribute to that end. England, now finished with isolation, needed global alliances to protect her global interests. In the Western Hemisphere, she cultivated the United States; in Asia, she directed her attentions to Japan. Once established, the alliance not only supported the status quo in southern and Southeast Asia; it also provided, within the limitations of British policy, some protection for China. In exchange, Japanese "special interests" in northeastern Asia were given recognition by the leading power of the world. Under such conditions, Japan could scarcely afford not to advance those interests.

Thus, the first fruit of the Anglo-Japanese Alliance was not peace, but war. The question of Japanese or Russian hegemony over northeastern Asia, having its antecedents back as far as the seventeenth century, was now given over to military decision. As is well known, Japanese victory against a weary and distracted foe was swift. From the Portsmouth Treaty, Japan emerged in control of much of northeastern Asia, and became the first Asian world power. The fruits of defeat and victory were similar to those of the Sino-Japanese War: for the defeated, soul-searching, unrest, and revolution; for the victor, a new gain of territory and fame. Clear title was obtained to the Kuriles, and southern Saghalien was added to the empire; control over Korea could no longer be challenged, although outright annexation did not come until 1910; the Manchurian-Mongolian area also fell under the shadow of expanding Japanese power, a situation placing new pressure upon China. Again, Japanese industry had enjoyed great expansion as a part of the war effort, with some support from British and American loans. And once more Japanese nationalism had risen to the test. Only a handful of intellectual pacifists and radicals denounced the war; the great majority of the people had been deeply loyal to the cause of a greater Japan.

Some of the costs of victory could also be tabulated. One lay on the surface. Nationalist propaganda had been carried so far during the war that many patriots assumed that the peace would be dictated in Moscow, not realizing that a long war of attrition might be dangerous for a smaller country. Consequently, ugly riots broke out over the Portsmouth settlement, and the government had difficulty in restoring order. There were also deeper costs to be tallied. At home, militarism had grown stronger; the nonconformist had little protection, either in law or by the customs of his society. Abroad, Japan was moving into a new orbit of power and influence; but as a result, she was now the object of new suspicions and fears, some of them coming from such traditional supporters as the United States and Great Britain. Already it seemed likely that the critical test might be China.

In partial recompense, immediately ahead lay an era of unprecedented influence for Japan throughout Asia. It was an influence, moreover, derived from much more than mere military prowess. There is no doubt that most of the Asian world experienced a thrill at the Japanese victory over Russia, because it gave hope that the West could be beaten at its own game. But in the broader sense, Japan had become the symbol of the new Asia, a society that had successfully made the transition toward modernization by a process of synthesizing new ideas with its indigenous culture. Western science and progress had come alive within the Japanese context, and from this experience the rest of Asia had much to learn. The success of Japanese nationalism was also a tremendous stimulus, even though its precise ideological forms might not be acceptable elsewhere. Thus, as this era unfolded, Japan embarked upon an extensive career as model, tutor, and leader to eager Asians everywhere. Thousands of students flocked to Tokyo and other Japanese centers of learning and industry. The majority came from China, but every section of Asia was represented in some degree. Likewise, Asian nationalist movements found in Japan a haven and source of support.

Their leaders in exile wrote polemics, collected funds, and sometimes obtained official encouragement. Tokyo became a revolutionary center for the Far East. Japan was riding the crest tide of the developing "Asia for the Asians" movement.

Already, however, the central problem of Japanese foreign policy was becoming that of distinguishing the thin line between acceptable leadership in Asia and unwelcome domination. This problem could be put in various forms. Would Japanese national interests, in the long run, be made compatible with the Asian march toward independence? Would Japanese technological, economic, and political assistance to Asia rest on mutual benefit and truly cooperative bases, or were the methods and intentions such as to be readily labeled the underpinnings of Japanese imperialism? Did the Japanese have, or would they acquire, a fitting psychology for world leadership, or would their actions and attitudes be marked by ethnocentrism, insecurity, and brutality, thereby producing the hatred of those whom they wished to persuade? From these, the universal questions of twentieth-century relations between advanced and lagging societies, Japanese foreign policy was by no means immune. The events of World War I accentuated the issues.

The Rise of Japan as a World Power

World War I was the third conflict within a generation to pay handsome and immediate dividends to the cause of Japanese prestige. It is not difficult to understand why later glorification of war by Japanese militarists produced such weak rebuttals from the society as a whole. Against the true desires of her ally, Japan entered the war "to fulfill her obligations under the Anglo-Japanese Alliance." She

proceeded to capture, without difficulty, the German holdings on the Chinese Shantung peninsula and in certain other parts of the Pacific. With this mission accomplished, she directed her energies to supplying the Asian markets cut off from their normal European contacts, and to providing her Western allies with the materials of war. These tasks required enormous industrial expansion. Indeed, it was at the close of this period that industrial productivity overtook agrarian productivity in yen value, and Japan could thereby claim to have moved into the ranks of industrial societies.

These trends, and complemental factors elsewhere, stimulated the drive for a more intensive policy toward China. The Manchu dynasty had fallen in the revolution of 1911, but that revolution had failed in its major objectives. The Chinese scene was now marked by deep political cleavages, with rival factions striving desperately for both internal and external support. With Europe fully engaged in a bloody "civil war" and the United States prepared to go no further than a policy of moral suasion, Japan was soon heavily involved in Chinese politics. In 1915, the Japanese government demanded an extensive list of concessions from the Yuan Shih-k'ai regime, known as the "Twenty-one Demands." These were bitterly resisted by China, with some success. Japanese influence moved steadily forward by means of loans, advisers, and technical assistance, yet Japan soon acquired a new image in China—that of the chief threat to Chinese nationalism. This era was climaxed by the historic May Fourth Movement, now widely heralded by the Chinese Communists as their point of origin, a fervent demonstration against Versailles and against Japanese imperialism, spearheaded by Peking students and spreading throughout China in May, 1919.

At the close of the World War I, however, there could be no question that Japan had become a world power. She was the one major nation besides the United States to emerge from that war in a stronger position. Her preeminence in eastern Asia could not be doubted, despite the uncertain new force of Bolshevism. What were the ingredients of this power as the third decade of the twentieth century began?

One source of Japan's new power clearly was her evolving economic capacities. Perhaps the full secret of the Japanese industrial revolution still escapes us. However, in its essence, it seems to have involved the capacity of Japanese society to utilize selected elements of Western technique and experience, adapting these to its own culture and timing, without duplicating either the historical context of Western development or the precise set of Western drives, impulses, and incentives. Toward this process were contributed both the conscious purposes of state and the remarkable talents of a people who could display creativeness through integration and discipline. By 1920, Japan was already becoming the workshop of Asia. Her large factories, equipped in many cases with the most modern machinery, contributed such basic products as textiles in great volume; at the same time, an infinite variety of cheap manufactured items flowed out of the thousands of small and medium-sized plants that formed the base of the pyramidal Japanese industrial structure. Sharing with management the credit for such productivity was the new Japanese labor force, abundant in numbers, cheap in cost, malleable (within limits) to its new task, moving out of the paddy fields into the factories, and acquiring sufficient know-how to give Japan an industrial character of which their fathers could not have dreamed.

But if manpower was a strength, it was also a problem—and one that now began to have an overt influence upon policy. Shortly after World War I the Japanese population reached 60 million, more than double the figure at the beginning of the Meiji era. In many respects, the facilities existing within Japan to accommodate this great mass already seemed seriously strained, yet no leveling off was in sight. Increasing talk of *lebesraum* was inevitable. And if the population explosion had produced an abundance of cheap labor, by the same token it had placed certain limits on their consumption of goods, by throwing increased emphasis on foreign trade.

Other factors underlined Japanese dependence on foreign lands. The four main islands of Japan were not richly blessed with those natural resources vital to the industrial development of this period. Coal was present in sufficient quantities (except for high-grade coking coal), but the supply of iron ore was very limited, that of petroleum was negligible, and most essential metals were either absent or available only in modest quantity. Moreover, because of her limited land space and her location, Japan had to import many of the agricultural resources needed for industry; raw cotton and rubber were two prominent examples. The Japanese empire of this period was helpful; from Formosa, Saghalien, and particularly from Korea came important raw materials and foodstuffs. However, the more important supplies lay outside these areas, and the Manchuria-Mongolian region could be depicted in impressive economic terms.

To revert to our discussion of the sources of Japanese power, the military and political ingredients certainly cannot be overlooked. The Japanese navy had become the third largest in the world. Her army, in size, equipment, and training, dwarfed other forces readily available in this part of the world. There was no foreign force that seemed prepared to challenge a Japanese force that was fully committed in its own territories or in any part of eastern Asia. The size and equipment of the Japanese military was a testament to the lavish yearly budgetary contributions of the people; the morale of that force was a tribute to intensive indoctrination, sustained by the realities of great political power and prestige within the society.

Politics, in its broader reaches, was also a wellspring of power. For a society without totalitarian restraints (albeit one strongly paternal and authoritarian in character), Japan presented a picture of remarkable stability up to this point. Besides a handful of intellectual radicals, there were few who would dare (or think) to question *Kokutai*—"the national polity" or, more vaguely, "the Japanese way of life." Thus, decisions of state, especially in the realm of foreign policy, could be taken on the assumption that they would be accepted with a maximum of conformity. The oracles of national interest could speak without fear of discordant responses, at least so long as they spoke within a consistently nationalist framework. What leadership group has not found some advantage in this?

Yet, as the postwar era began, there were indications that Japanese politics might be drastically affected by the democratic tide. The influence of Western liberalism, crowned by the global idealism of Woodrow Wilson, was strongly felt in Japanese intellectual and urban circles. Party government had assumed new importance, the office of premier was held for the

first time by a commoner, and the movement for universal suffrage was receiving widespread support. Japan's liberal era was opening, bringing with it some serious efforts to establish parliamentary and civilian supremacy in Japanese politics. Temporarily, at least, the long-entrenched bureaucrats and even the military had to move to the defensive. For the latter, the Siberian expedition was the first clearly unrewarding venture abroad. And however strong the attempt to shift the blame to political timidity and lack of resolution at home, the army could not prevent some questions from arising in the public mind.

Hence, moderation in foreign policy was possible during this period. At the Washington Armament Conference of 1921, Japan accepted the famous 5:5:3 naval ratio with the United States and Great Britain, despite the bitter protests of her naval authorities. She agreed to the return of the Shantung concessions. Withdrawal from Siberia was slowly and cautiously undertaken. One cabinet even had the audacity to cut the military budget sharply, and there were some discussions (although no action) on a permanent reduction in the institutional power of the military in Japanese government. During this era, no figure symbolized moderation in foreign policy more than Kijuro Shidehara, foreign minister under the Minseito cabinets. Shidehara was a conservative, a nationalist, and a loyal servant of the emperor. He believed that Japan had special interests in northeastern Asia and a special responsibility toward China. But he wanted to avoid a "get-tough" policy which would only provoke boycotts, anti-Japanese hostility, and possibly war. Rather, he hoped Japanese influence could be exerted through trade, financial agreements, and political negotiation.

Militarism and Defeat

The liberal era was short-lived. With its collapse went much of the hope for moderation, either at home or abroad. This is not the place to spell out the story of democratic failure in prewar Japan, but its more immediate causes are familiar: economic crisis and depression; political confusion and corruption; and the consequent rise of opponents from left and right. The repercussions were felt almost immediately in Japanese foreign policy. In 1928, under the Tanaka cabinet, there was a sharp turn toward a more militant nationalism in both the economic and political fields. State support to home industry was combined with a more "positive" program of support for Japanese interests abroad, especially in China. Overtures from Chiang Kaishek—who had just broken with the Communists—were rejected, partly because of fear that his successful northern expedition would jeopardize the future Japanese position in Manchuria and northern China. Ironically, while the Tanaka China policy was provoking sharp Chinese reaction because of its strengths, it was under simultaneous attack by Japanese military extremists because of its weaknesses. Some of these elements, working through the Kwantung army in Manchuria, engineered the murder of Chang Tso-lin in June, 1928, hoping to force a decisive Japanese move in this area. The Japanese government was posed with the first of a series of direct military challenges to civilian control, challenges which went unmet.

Japanese foreign policy, in the fifteen years between 1930 and 1945, represented the natural culmination of these new trends. To be sure, not all the old themes were reversed, particularly those that could be read with different inflections. Stress continued to be placed upon Sino-Japanese cooperation, and on the need for a stable, friendly China, purged of communist and anti-Japanese elements. But action continually interfered with words. As the Japanese militarists gained control of the strategic heights of policy, especially in the field, any cooperation had to be strained through the tightening net of aggression, fanatical patriotism, and individual, sometimes mass, acts of brutality. Through these field actions, and as a result of a contrived incident, war came to Manchuria in September, 1931. The weaker Chinese forces were quickly defeated, but Manchukuo remained, to the great body of the Chinese, an acceptable symbol of Japanese aggression.

With the Manchurian region at last under complete Japanese control, the militarists could not avoid spreading outward toward Mongolia and northern China. Thus the Second China Incident erupted, in 1937, and led eventually to total war and defeat. Throughout this entire period, Japan could always find some Chinese allies, whether as a result of the acrid internal rivalries for power in China, sheer opportunism, or some genuine hopes that this route might lead to a new and better Asia, freed from Western control. Indeed, the allies garnered from all of these sources were not inconsiderable either in number or in influence. In Wang Ch'ing-wei, Japan finally found an able if embittered leader. But, as against these facts, Japanese policy achieved what had always been feared most: a union of the dominant wing of the Kuomintang with the Communists and many independents into a nationalist popular front that was bitterly anti-Japanese. Although it had as one of its supreme goals the salvation of Asia from communism, Japanese policy, in the end, contributed more than any other single factor to communist success.

To concentrate solely on China, however, would be to examine only the weakest link of a general Asian policy which, for all its militant, aggressive qualities, had elements of real power and appeal. Building from the old "Asia for the Asians" theme, Japanese policy moved, in the 1930s, toward the concept of a Greater East Asia Co-Prosperity Sphere. The economic background for this policy lay in the rapid strides made by Japanese trade throughout Asia. By means of general deflation, changes in currency valuation, industrial rationalization, and extensive state support, Japanese trade came to enjoy highly favorable competitive conditions in eastern Asia by the mid-thirties. Western Europe complained vigorously about the practice of "social dumping" onto the colonial markets. Japan retorted with charges of economic discrimination and attempted monopoly. The fact remained, however, that Japanese penetration of the Asian market, during this period, was substantial. The basis was thus provided for later proposals of greater economic integration of an Asian region led by Japan and divorced from Western control.

The center of the Japanese appeal to greater Asia, however, remained in the sphere of politcal nationalism. As Japan drifted toward the fascist bloc, Western imperialism in Asia could be attacked with less inhibition than in the past. These attacks were particularly effective in areas where nationalism was still treated as subversive by Western governors, and where Japanese policies could not yet be tested. Once again, an attempt was made to develop an expanded program of cultural relations and technical assistance. Students flocked to Japan from all parts of Asia; cultural missions were exchanged on an increasing scale; Japanese technicians went forth; and, as the Pacific war approached, the Japanese government provided underground assistance to various Asian nationalist movements in the form of funds, political advice, and even the training and equipping of military forces.

Most of the presently independent governments of southern and Southeast Asia owe an enormous debt to Japanese propaganda, military successes, and political concessions—even when the latter were self-serving, empty, or last-minute gestures. There can be no doubt that Japan, both in victory and in defeat, contributed mightily to the end of the old era and the emergence of a more independent, dynamic Asia. Yet her record was tarnished, and today she must combat a legacy of suspicion and even hatred in some of these countries. In part, this can be attributed to such factors as the misconduct of her troops, but, more importantly, it is the product of the great cultural barriers that separated her from the regions she occupied and of her inability—through lack of experience, insecurity, and because of her own traditions—to develop the type of flexibility and broad tolerance necessary in leadership. In considerable degree, Japanese hopes for cooperation and friendship were strangled by the nationalism that pushed them forward.

As a corollary to her new Asian policy, Japan naturally developed a new policy with respect to the West. Nearly a decade earlier, at the time of the Washington conference of 1921, Japan had reluctantly given up the Anglo-Japanese alliance, her shield and support for twenty years. In its place were substituted the more general agreements among the major powers. This concept of collective agreement (not, it should be emphasized, collective security) was especially attuned to the American position. The United States wanted an end to exclusive alliances, but it was prepared to undertake only the most limited of commitments, and it still wished to rely essentially upon moral suasion for policy enforcement. The great symbol of this hope and this era was the famous Kellogg-Briand Pact, outlawing war.

Thus, the decline of Japanese liberalism at home was complemented by the absence of effective external checks or controls. The old system of alliances, and the type of checks they imposed upon unilateral action, had been declared obsolete in the Pacific, but no effective international order had replaced them. Consequently, in the name of her national interests, Japan could successfully defy the Nine-Power Agreement and the League of Nations, with no single nation or group making an effective stand against her. Inevitably, as she challenged the status quo powers, Japan gravitated toward Germany and Italy, the dissidents of Europe. The Anti-Comintern Pact sealed an alliance of mutual interest, though not one of great intimacy.

But the real decision that confronted Japan as the Pacific war approached had a familiar ring: Was she to seek a stabilization of her northern or her southern flanks? Who was to be engaged, the Soviet Union or the Western allies? The decision was not an easy one. In the late 1930s, Japan had participated in large-scale clashes with Soviet forces in the Mongolian region, and her historic rivalry was augmented by her hatred of communism. In the final analysis, however, she decided to count on a German victory on the steppes of Russia, and she turned to the south, whose resources had to be unlocked and whose Western masters had to be over-

thrown if the Japanese vision of the future were to be attained. Possibilities for agreement with the West to avoid this fateful step were explored, as all the moderates desired, but hopes were broken on the rock of China. Too much had been invested in blood and treasure to concede to Chiang Kai-shek, and so, infinitely more was to be invested—and all in vain.

THE FORMULATION OF FOREIGN POLICY IN PREWAR JAPAN

In the Tokyo trials of major war criminals that followed the Japanese surrender, the Allied prosecutors repeatedly sought the answer to one central question: Who bears the responsibility for leading Japan toward aggression and war? If they did not obtain a completely satisfactory answer, no blame should be assigned. Few questions involve greater difficulties. The problem has taken on universal dimensions as the modern state has grown in complexity and as foreign policy has developed into the composite, uncertain product of a myriad of technicians, men rigidly compartmentalized, skilled and jealous of these skills, but almost always frustrated by the limits of their power; an indeterminate number of free-roaming generalists, yet not so free, being bound by the limits of the single mind, the niceties of group decision, and the pressures—subtle or direct—of subalterns; and, finally, the larger, vaguer public, varying in size but never comprising the whole of its society nor the sum of its parts—alternately indifferent and excited, overwhelmed by the complexities and focusing on some vital issue, ignored and watched with anxiety, molded and breaking out of molds.

Japan was a modern state. In the

narrow sense, Japan appeared as a society of great personal absolutism. In both the family and the nation, the head was invested with absolute powers. Inferiors owed complete and unswerving obedience. There seemed no measure of egalitarianism or individualism to alleviate the rigidities of a hierarchical system which, through primogeniture and an emperor-centered mythology, found its apex in a single source. But in fact, the essence of power in Japanese society has not been that of personal absolutism. The vital center of decision making has uniformly lain in its collective or group character, and in its extensive reliance on consensus as the primary technique. It is critical to understand that, despite all superficial signs to the contrary, the basic nature of Japanese society can only be approached by a thorough appreciation of the intricate refinements of small group interaction, the great importance of induced voluntarism, and the generally eclectic quality of final agreements.

In all likelihood, it is only because these things were true that the outward signs of rigid hierarchy and absolutism were so well maintained into the modern era. Elaborate methods had already been developed to integrate theory and appearance with the needs of a dynamic society. Just as the system of adopted sons had long preserved the necessary flexibility in the Japanese family, so the institutions of senior councillor, adviser, and go-between had each, in its own way, facilitated the making of group decisions. That process, giving extraordinary attention to form and status, was often wearisome and prolonged, but every care had to be taken to make concessions and consensus possible, with a minimum of violence to the position and prestige of those involved. Necessarily, equals were wary of confronting each other in person until the formula for consensus seemed assured; and inferiors developed, to a fine art, all forms of subtle pressures and persuasive devices, so that successful superiors paid silent homage to these in the course of final action.

Not all these conditions sound strange to Western ears, although the aggregate process might seem foreign or extreme. In any case, how were such basic factors in Japanese social relations translated into politics and the making of foreign policy? In theory, the Meiji Constitution of 1889 paid its highest tribute to imperial absolutism but, for successful practice, it demanded a unity or consensus of its disparate working parts. The weakest of these, the two-house Diet, its lower house elected, had at least the power to withhold its consent from basic policies. The administrative bureaucracy, culminating in such executives as the prime minister, and the members of the cabinet and the Privy Council, had a vast range of powers and had legal responsibility only to the emperor, but it could not be effective alone. The military also drew their power from the emperor and had direct access to him; in practice, moreover, this branch acquired a potent weapon in that the ministers of war and navy had to come from its ranks, which served to limit sharply the independent power of the Japanese cabinet. The military, however, could operate effectively only in conjunction with the other major branches.

There was never any serious thought of having these forces coordinated by the emperor personally, despite the awsome nature of his stipulated powers. Instead, that task was handled, for some thirty years, by a small oligarchy of Meiji restoration leaders who acted in the name of the emperor as his "chief advisers." Ultimately, this group came to be known as the *genro* or "senior councillors," an institution without a vestige of legal recognition or responsibility, but central to the process of Japanese politics. Every basic policy decision was placed before the *genro*, and their approval was a prerequisite to action. Even the daily affairs of state frequently engaged their attention. With protégés in every branch of government, and with their own vast accumulation of experience, these men were at once the source of integration, the court of final appeal, and the summit of power. To be sure, agreement among them was not always easy; there were deep personal and political cleavages in this, as in other Japanese groups. Timed withdrawals and temporary concessions, however, enabled a consensus to operate with a minimum of crises. Until the close of the World War I, with rare exceptions, the fountainhead of Japanese foreign policy was this group.

With the postwar era, however, basic changes in government began to emerge, paralleling those in society. The members of the *genro* became old, and their ranks were not refilled. No group came forth to undertake the integrative role. Instead, Japanese politics was marked by an increasing struggle for supremacy and control among the parties, the bureaucracy, and the military. It is interesting to note that, at the outset of this era, an attempt was made to establish a liaison council under the aegis for the prime minister for the development of a unified foreign policy. It was intended to include major party, official, and military representation, but it was never accepted by the major opposition party, and it ultimately faded away.

Without a supreme coordinator such as the *genro*, Japanese consti-

tutionalism, in both its written and unwritten aspects, revealed serious flaws. In the hectic party era, foreign policy decisions taken in cabinet or government party circles were subject not only to legitimate attacks in the Diet, but also to extensive sabotage by the ranks of the subordinate bureaucracy, and to angry challenges by the military groups. The parties never attained more than a quasi supremacy and, as they faded, the military moved from verbal challenge to open defiance. Japanese society, in the period after 1928, was a classic example of a government divided against itself. Important segments of the military operated, both in the field and at home, in such a manner as to scorn the government. They received substantial support from within the bureaucracy, and from certain party figures as well. Every branch of government was riddled with dissension. Within the Ministry of Foreign Affairs, various cliques maneuvered for position—the militarist clique, the Anglo-American clique, and numerous others. For a time, consensus was impossible, and conditions close to anarchy prevailed.

Gradually, however, greater stability was achieved. Making full use of traditional procedures, top court officials surrounding the emperor involved themselves in unending conferences with representatives of all major groups; innumerable go-betweens explored the possible bases of compromise; certain voluntary withdrawals, strategic retreats, and silent acquiescences were effected. Slowly, a new basis for interaction developed, one which gave due recognition to military superiority but still was broad enough to include essential elements of the civil bureaucracy, court officials, and important pressure groups. Once again, the basic decisions were reached by consensus, but with somewhat greater cognizance of the realities of power. In this period, a new group of senior councillors, the *jushin*, was organized. Although lacking the influence of the *genro*, it was fashioned after that model, indicating the continuing search for an integrative center. That search was destined never to be completely successful. Another experiment was conducted in a liaison council, the purpose being to pool military and civilian policy with particular reference to the foreign scene. Ultimately, the imperial conference, with the emperor himself presiding over a small group of top military and administrative officials, became the final decision-making body. Indeed, it was this group that determined the Japanese surrender, the emperor personally settling this great issue. Perhaps this was the only basis left for the organic unity envisaged by the Meiji constitution.

The foregoing trends are not completely meaningful without some brief reference to other important social groups. First, however, it should be noted that the type of consensus being developed during the militarist era was abetted by an increasing control over all media of communication. One of the most literate societies in the world, Japan had national newspapers and magazines with massive circulation. After the early thirties, prominent dissent from ultranationalism became increasingly dangerous and, after the Second China Incident, all the public organs were echoing the official line.

Meanwhile, a process of accommodation had been taking place between conservative militarists and the industrial and commercial world of Japan. In the initial stages of the military revolt against liberalism and a weak-kneed foreign policy, the strong notes of a radical, anticapitalist theme were heard; the historic cry of "internal reform, external expansion" once again sounded forth. However, after the February 26th Incident, in 1936, when army units in Tokyo under radical command rebelled, this type of revolutionary activity was suppressed. Although some liberal business elements were regarded with suspicion, and certain onerous controls were sharply protested by entrepreneurs, still the necessary compromises were made, and all of Japanese industry rose to the war effort.

Japanese labor reacted in the same way. Its radical and liberal elements had long since been silenced, and the great masses worked with patriotic fervor. It was from the rural areas, however, that the bedrock of Japanese conservatism derived. The alliance between peasant and soldier now held more meaning than at any time since the Meiji restoration. As is so frequently the case, rural provincialism bred its own type of ultranationalism. The Japanese common man played a role in the formulation of foreign policy in his own way: he posed no obstacles to expansionism, his complete loyalty was assured, and no sacrifice would be too great if it contributed to the nationalist cause.

JAPAN SINCE 1945: OCCUPATION AND ITS AFTERMATH

When Japan surrendered in August, 1945, both her leaders and her people were forced to reconcile themselves to being a vanquished nation. By the terms of the Yalta and Potsdam agreements, the Japanese empire was to be dissipated and Japan reduced in size to the approximate boundaries of the restoration era. The homeland was to be occupied for an indefinite period by foreign forces. For the first time in recorded history, Japanese sovereignty was to be superseded by foreign rule. Some of the broad objectives of this rule had already been stipulated: action was to be taken to insure that Japan never again would become a world menace, or a world power. Total disarmament was to be carried out, and those responsible for past aggression were to be punished; even the fate of the emperor was unclear, although Japanese leaders sought desperately to gain assurances on this point during the surrender negotiations. Along with these essentially negative tasks, the occupation was also to encourage Japanese democratic forces and movements, so that Japan could eventually take her place in a peaceful world. Thus was inaugurated, in September, 1945, a radically new era for Japan, one that might well be labeled "the era of the American Revolution."

If the contemporary processes and substance of Japanese foreign policy are to be discussed meaningfully, certain pertinent aspects of this period must be set forth. In the first place, the American occupation and its aftermath can easily be divided into three broad phases: (a) the early revolutionary era, when the emphasis was upon punishment and reform; (b) the era of reconstruction, when the stress was shifted to stabilization and economic recovery; and (c) the era of proffered alliance, which is continuing at present. Each of these eras, in its own way, has contributed to the current nature and problems of Japanese society.

The Revolutionary Era

The American Revolution in Japan was that of 1932, not that of 1776, although some of the spirit of the latter, as it applied to basic democratic values, was certainly present. The New Deal had new opportunities along the bombed-out Ginza and in the rice fields. But first, the old order had to be eradicated. Japanese milita-ry forces were totally disbanded in a remarkably short time; before the end of 1947, some 6 million Japanese troops and civilians had been returned from overseas, demobilized, and poured into the homeland. The military forces within Japan proper had also been completely dissolved. The ministries of war and navy were abolished. And, in an effort to seal these actions with the stamp of permanency, the now-famous Article 9 was written into the new Japanese Constitution:

Aspiring sincerely to an international peace based on justice and order, the Japanese people forever renounce war as a sovereign right of the nation and the threat or use of force as means of settling international disputes.

In order to accomplish the aim of the preceding paragraph, land, sea, and air forces, as well as other war potential, will never be maintained. The right of belligerency of the state will not be recognized.

The American vision for Japan during this period became widely associated with the phrase, "the Switzerland of the Far East," although, in this case, pacifism was added to neutralization. It was a vision that had a powerful appeal to many Japanese who lived amidst rubble, without adequate food or warmth, and with vivid memories of lost ones, fire raids, and the final holocaust of the atom bomb. There could be no question as to whether this war had paid. Moreover, the extraordinary vulnerability of the great Japanese cities had been fully demonstrated during the war's last, terrible months. For most thoughtful Japanese, the early postwar era was a period of deep reflection. Its dominant theme was trenchant criticism of past leaders and institutions. Once more, there was a Japanese surge toward new ideas and ways; MacArthur, no less than Perry, symbolized the end of an old order, and a war-weary people turned hopefully to *demokurashi*, without being precisely sure of its contents. These sentiments, widespread as they were, aided the revolution that was getting under way.

Among the various SCAP[1] actions, none had more long-range implications than those which affected the nature and position of Japanese pressure groups. As we have noted, for more than a decade the most powerful group in Japanese society had been the military. Suddenly it was entirely liquidated, and it has not yet reappeared as a significant political force. Liquidation was not merely demobilization, but also the purge that barred all professional military officers from future political activity, and the war crimes trials, after which the top military men of the nation were executed or sentenced to prison. Although many of these actions were subsequently modified or rescinded, their total effect, combined with other circumstances, has thus far been sufficient to render postwar militarism in Japan weak, recent Chinese charges notwithstanding.

Through the purge and other measures, SCAP ate still further into prewar conservative ranks. For the old guard it seemed like the reign of terror, although without violence or brutality. Most professional politicians of the old conservative parties had to step aside because they had belonged to some ultranationalist group or had been endorsed by the Tojo government in the elections of 1942. Conservative leadership was hastily thrust into the hands of the one

group that could be cleared: the so-called Anglo-American group, from within the Foreign Ministry. Kijuro Shidehara, Shigeru Yoshida, and Hisashi Ashida, all from this group, became the top conservative leaders of Japan for nearly a decade. Even the commercial and industrial world felt the shock of reform. Beset by purges, a program to break down the *zaibatsu* ("big combines"), and the general toll of wartime ravage and postwar inflation, most business elements sought merely to survive, as if seeking shelter during a gale.

Meanwhile, with American encouragement, the labor union movement attained a massive size; within a brief period it numbered some 6 million workers, whereas, in the prewar period, bona fide union membership had never exceeded one-half million. These postwar figures masked many divisions and weaknesses, but there could be no doubt that Japanese organized labor was a new force with which to reckon on the economic and political scene. And in the rural areas, the "American Revolution" was operating in the most forceful fashion. Under a far-reaching program of land reform, absentee landlordism was almost completely abolished, tenancy was reduced to less than 10 percent of total agrarian families, and land holdings were equalized beyond the wildest imagination of prewar advocates of land reform. Basically, this program was dedicated to the creation of a huge independent yeomanry. The political repercussions in the rural areas, especially among younger age groups, have only recently become measurable.

Certain reforms cut across class lines and into the broadest categories of society. Legal attempts were made to abandon primogeniture and to emancipate women. Women were given full equality before the law, including equal rights of inheritance, divorce, and suffrage. Sweeping reforms in education were inaugurated, with the purpose of developing freer, more independent students, unshackled from the old chauvinism and submissiveness. Even that very special category of men, the subordinate government officials, were given lectures on democracy, in the hope that some of the old attitude of *kanson mimpi* ("officials honored, people despised") could be removed.

To recite these various efforts in such bald fashion may lead to the supposition that a total social revolution took place in Japan during the first years after 1945. Any such impression would be false. Conservatism, both in the form of certain dominant classes and in the form of certain traditions that operated in every class, was a sturdy force. Moreover, as might be surmised, not all SCAP experiments were successful and, by the end of 1947, in any case, the era emphasizing reform was drawing to a close. In its ripest forms, it had lasted only about two years. The conservatives definitely survived.

It would be equally misleading, however, to underestimate the changes that took place during this era, whether because of SCAP reforms or as a result of the total complex of postwar circumstances. Some of these changes should be regarded as part of the continuum inherited from prewar days. Others were largely the product of foreign intervention or the new conditions prevailing as a result of military defeat. In any case, the changes which developed during this period had a direct influence on the processes and substance of Japanese foreign policy. Most important have been the altered composition of Japanese pressure groups and the accelerated movement toward a mass society.

The nature of Japanese conservatism has been strongly affected by the demise of the military, the leveling of agriculture, and the combined impact of defeat and technology. The Japanese "left" has been equally affected by the rise of organized labor and the freedom accorded the intellectuals and students. The political path that will be taken in the coming decade remains unclear. One thing, however, seems apparent: the trend has been toward a closer balance of competing pressure groups within that society than there was in the prewar era. As a result of this and other factors, the Japanese common man has become the object of increasing political solicitation and concern. As we shall note, public opinion has become an important factor in the shaping of Japanese foreign policy.

Stabilization

Before we turn to the current status of foreign policy, some brief consideration should be given to the second and third phases of the occupation and the gradual emergence, once again, of an independent Japan. The shift of emphasis in occupation policy, from punishment and reform to economic stabilization and recovery, began as early as 1947. The change was motivated by many problems. Certain earlier American premises about the postwar world now seemed unjustified. The prospects for a China that would be friendly and democratic by American definition were dim; the honeymoon with the Soviet Union was clearly over and the Cold War was beginning; the threat of communism throughout Europe and Asia, as a result of postwar chaos and economic misery, was a matter of profound concern. In Japan itself, the close relation between economic recovery and the prospects for democratic success could no longer be slighted or ignored. In addition, the expenses of occupation and relief constituted a heavy burden for the American taxpayer; at its peak, the cost ran close to a half-billion dollars a year.

The new emphasis brought many changes. Increasingly, the supreme test to which any policy could be put was: Does it advance productivity and economic stabilization? An assessment was made of the primary obstacles—war damage, inflation, the lack of raw materials, and low industrial morale. SCAP began to interest itself in Japanese productive efficiency, and moved from merely keeping Japan alive to furnishing her with raw materials and acquainting her entrepreneurs with the most advanced machinery and techniques. The complex problem of inflation was finally faced. Under the Dodge Nine-Point Stabilization Program, stringent reforms were put into effect. These were unpopular in many quarters, but the inflationary tide was at last turned.

Meanwhile, other disruptions to production were dealt with. The deconcentration program was relaxed and gradually abandoned, after successful initial attempts to reduce certain large zaibatsu families and cartels. The United States also progressively receded from its early severity on the issue of reparations. By the end of this era, the American government had indicated its acceptance of the thesis that the Japanese ability to repay war damages was strictly limited, that large reparations would indirectly become a responsibility to the United States, and that the heavy industry on which the Japanese future was so dependent could not be used for these purposes. Finally, SCAP took a sterner attitude toward the labor movement, amending its earlier generous legislation on unionism to give the employer, and especially the government, a stronger position.

The net effect of these actions, accompanied by certain broader trends at home and abroad, was to stimulate rapid economic recovery. Japanese society could build on an industrial revolution already well advanced, and on a legacy of technical know-how. Deflation and internal readjustments were followed by new opportunities for industrial expansion. The Korean War and the great prosperity of the free world were of major assistance. Beginning in 1950, therefore, Japan entered a period of amazing economic development. For the next twenty years, the average annual rise in gross national product was approximately 10 percent, one of the most spectacular rates of growth in the world.

This second phase of the occupation, which triggered the economic surge, was not without internal political reverberations. In the revolutionary era, American actions had been an anathema to the conservatives; now, the conservatives became the new allies. The liberal left, which had cheered in the early days, was filled with dismay and resentment at many actions of which it did not approve but from which it had no recourse. Japanese democracy was still under the tutelage of American military rule, and criticism and opposition were strictly limited by that fact. Inevitably, however, the United States and its policies became the central issue in Japanese politics, paving the way for the sharp divergencies that came into the open later. For every political group, moreover, this second era was one of reflection and reconsideration of Western values. There was an unmistakable tendency, at all levels, to emphasize synthesis and adjustment rather than uncritical acceptance of foreign concepts. The pendulum had begun to swing back.

As can be seen, the beginnings of postwar Japanese foreign policy were established in this era, albeit under American direction. These beginnings followed a course that Japanese leadership itself might well have taken and even labeled "in the national interest," had it been an independent agent. Indeed, on issues like reparations and trade, the United States was widely accused of being excessively pro-Japanese. One policy which was emphasized was that of rehabilitating Japanese heavy industry and encouraging its orientation toward the needs and markets of the late-developing societies, particularly those of non-communist Asia. Again, the concept of Japan as the workshop of Asia was advanced, but without certain former connotations. As a concomitant to this policy, the United States also tried to adjust Japanese political and economic relations with erstwhile enemies. Like a benevolent warden convinced of the successful rehabilitation of his charge, the United States pressed for Japanese reentry into the world community.

But with the second phase of the occupation, there also began an intimate and largely new relationship between Japan and the United States, a relationship founded on a rising tempo of economic interaction. Japanese products began to flow into the United States in exchange for American raw materials, foodstuffs, and machinery. Technical assistance from the United States smoothed the way for investments and patent sharing. The economic interaction was thus very broadly based. It was supported, moreover, by an expanding cultural exchange of customs, ideas, and patterns of life.

The Era of Alliance

Within these trends lay the seeds of the third era, that of alliance proffered by the United States to Japan.

By 1949, American authorities realized, on the one hand, that the occupation was reaching a point of diminishing returns, and, on the other, that continuing economic and political ties between the two countries were a mutual necessity. The explorations which led to the San Francisco Peace Treaty of 1951 involved a series of decisions that added to the new Japanese foreign policy and provoked heated political debate.

The critical issue pertained to the question of Japanese defense. Two broad alternatives seemed to exist. One was Japanese pacifism, which involved seeking universal agreements guaranteeing the sanctity of Japanese territory and backing these with pledges of protection by the United Nations, and possibly by the United States, separately. The alternative was to acknowledge the Japanese need for, and right to, military defense, and to underwrite Japanese rearmament with American power. Obviously, the choice between these two broad courses would affect and shape most other aspects of Japanese foreign policy.

The Yoshida government did not hesitate to support the second alternative, that of political, military, and economic alliance with the United States, as the only course compatible with world conditions and Japanese needs. To adopt a policy of neutralism, the conservatives argued, would make Japan dependent on the mercurial policies of the communist world. It would provide neither security nor prosperity. They insisted that both the economic and the political interests of Japan were best served by alignment with the free world, particularly the United States.

These arguments prevailed. While making known its desire for an overall peace treaty, the Japanese government agreed to sign a treaty with the noncommunist allies alone, if necessary. The Cold War had become hot in Korea while preliminary treaty negotiations were getting under way. Because of this, and because of the wide divergence between Soviet and American views on Japan, no serious attempt was made to obtain communist approval for the treaty draft, as the Japanese socialists had wished. In exchange for their willingness to sign a separate treaty, the conservatives were given a treaty considered generous by all, and soft by some. Reparations, and certain territorial issues (the Kurile and Ryukyu Islands), were left open, providing Japan with some bargaining power. The treaty contained no stipulations concerning SCAP reforms. Japan was left free to make any changes desired in her internal institutions. This included the right to rearm.

Official independence for Japan finally came on April 28, 1952, the day on which the San Francisco treaty came into effect. Accompanying the main treaty was a bilateral Mutual Security Treaty with the United States providing for the continuance of American military bases in Japan until adequate defenses were prepared by the Japanese government. At least as early as 1949, the creation of a Japanese defense force was being urged in some American and Japanese circles, and Japanese rearmament was first started in the summer of 1950, shortly after the outbreak of the Korean War. The National Police Reserve was activated in August of that year with an authorized component of 75,000 men. With the coming of Japanese independence, this number was increased to 110,000, and a small Maritime Safety Force was established, in May, 1952. In August, these were brought together under the National Safety Agency. Two years later, on July 1, 1954, the name was

changed to the Defense Agency, and the armed forces were brought directly under the office of the prime minister, who was authorized to add a small Air Self-Defense Force. The slow build-up of Japanese defense forces continued. By the end of 1955, there were about 200,000 men in the total defense force. Seventeen years later, in 1972, the force numbered some 236,000 men in all branches. While this represented a small force in comparison with the military establishment of the People's Republic of China or even that of the divided Koreas and Vietnams, it was ultramodern and capable of being rapidly expanded. Indeed, as we shall soon note, military-strategic issues seem likely to loom large in American-Japanese relations during the 1970s.

Meanwhile, economic relations between the United States and Japan have grown to gigantic proportions. By the end of 1970, total Japanese trade was approaching $35 billion, and roughly 30 percent of that trade was still with the United States. Since the trade has grown at the staggering rate of over 16 percent per annum during the last decade, two critical facts immediately become clear: first, Japanese-American economic relations provide the foundation for the alliance, being of vital importance to both nations; second, those relations now present some extremely serious problems which must be confronted in the period just ahead.

THE FORMULATION OF FOREIGN POLICY IN POSTWAR JAPAN

Before exploring the basic issues and alternatives currently involved in Japanese foreign policy, let us look briefly at the way in which decision-making and administrative processes in this field operate. The post-1945 state inherited a troubled, complex record. In the critical Meiji era (between 1867 and 1910), as we have indicated, the apex of the decision-making process lay with a small group of elder statesmen, the *genro*. The political genius of Japan has always lain in oligarchy and a consensus process involving intricate negotiations and compromises. After World War I, however, centripetal forces multiplied, with the *genro* institution fading away. For more than two decades thereafter, the problems of coordination mounted, with various parts of the political-economic-military elite increasingly in conflict.

In this period, the role of the bureaucracy was naturally of critical importance. In theory, this bureaucracy was an instrument of the emperor, not the Diet. Institutional limitations combined with socioeconomic realities to reduce the independent role of the political parties. The parties were significant only as they were linked with one or another faction of the bureaucracy and its senior officialdom. Public opinion was of very limited significance. Divisions within the bureaucracy, however, were serious, and tended to grow deeper with the passage of time. It has been customary to see these divisions largely as reflecting a cleavage between civilian and military. In fact, however, they were much more complex, with many competitive, conflicting civilian-military alliances. As our knowledge of decision making in the foreign policy field for the 1920–1945 era grows, the problems of coordination, the depth of policy conflicts, and the instances of open or subtle insubordination on the part of junior officials in various branches of the government have come into sharp focus. The series of crises preceding Pearl Harbor were built out of deep fissures within the conservative-radical nationalist elites that in some measure shared power during those tumultuous years.

Has the decision-making process been more coordinated in the postwar era? The new Japanese constitution of 1947 did much to clarify the ultimate responsibility for policy, domestic and foreign. Patterned almost wholly after Anglo-American institutions, it drastically altered the old system. Under its provisions, the emperor's functions became ceremonial and symbolic. Sovereignty was assigned to the people, to be exercised by their elected representatives. A parliamentary system modeled after that of Great Britain was established, with certain modifications of a distinctly American flavor.

The Diet, instead of being peripheral to the political process, is now its center, and both houses are elective. The upper house, the House of Councillors, is constructed in a complicated fashion, with both nationwide and prefectural constituencies; the lower house, the House of Representatives, is based on medium-sized election districts (three to five members chosen from each district, depending upon its size. Executive responsibility to the Diet is clearly stipulated. The prime minister must be approved by the Diet or, if the houses disagree, by the lower house. In case of a vote of no confidence, the government must either dissolve the lower house and call for new elections, or resign.

A new law pertaining to the Diet was enacted to accompany the constitution of 1947. Among other things, it provided for a system of standing committees—in contrast to the prewar, British-style, ad hoc committees. Thus, each house of the Diet now has a Foreign Affairs Committee. After agreement among the parties on the allocation of committee seats, members are selected by each party on the basis of training, experience, and political connections. The standing committees exist to hold hearings on government legislation or any policy matters within their general jurisdiction. Special ad hoc committees, however, are still used extensively in the Japanese Diet, sometimes on issues involving foreign policy.

Despite these institutional changes, the Japanese Diet committee system, as it currently operates, does not give either to the Diet as a whole or to individual Diet members the degree of power possessed in the United States Congress. Party or, more accurately, factional discipline interacts with the traditions of Japanese parliamentarism to make this true. Initiative and power in foreign policy continue to lie overwhelmingly with the executive branch of government—in concrete terms, currently with the key leaders of the Liberal Democratic party. In certain respects, of course, party supremacy has been strengthened by the new institutional structure. Under a Western-style parliamentary system, major party leaders constitute the apex of authority. The emperor no longer serves as an independent and legally omnipotent channel of power. The military branch of government is no longer a separate and competitive source of influence. And even the civil bureaucracy is now clearly subordinated in law to a political administration that must be consonant with a majority of the popularly elected members of the House of Representatives.

How do the bureaucracy and the parties cooperate in foreign policy formulation today? The evidence suggests that the dominant leaders of the conservative Liberal Democratic party play the major role in determining the broad framework within which foreign policies shall be developed; then such Ministries as those of Foreign Affairs, Finance, and International Trade and Industry draft specific policies within this framework. The draft is then subject to scrutiny and approval by the party leaders, after which the designated officials proceed to execute policy in its final forms. To understand how this actually works out, however, one must have a general appreciation of the present Japanese party system and bureaucracy.

Perhaps four general trends within the party system are significant for foreign policy. First, the conservatives have continued to hold a commanding position in Japanese politics. They currently hold a wide margin in both houses of the Diet, as has been the case almost continuously during the post-1945 era. Perhaps the major reasons for regular conservative victories have been their prewar ties and strength at local levels, especially in rural areas; their prominent, well-known candidates; the funds at their disposal; the extraordinary prosperity of Japan since 1950; the divided and weak nature of the opposition; and last, but by no means least, the capacity of the conservatives to adjust to changing conditions. Will this LDP dominance continue throughout the 1970s? The signals are mixed.

The conservatives do have some reasons for concern. Their percentage of the total vote in House of Representatives elections has dropped below 50 percent in recent years. It is clear, moreover, that the conservatives are in trouble in the metropolitan areas, where urban issues are becoming of critical importance. In Tokyo, Osaka, and Kyoto, for example, they do badly, especially in local elections. The rural vote upon which the conservatives traditionally counted, meanwhile, continues to decline in percentage terms. These and other factors have led some observers to predict

that Japan is enroute to coalition government at some point in the 1970s.
It is by no means clear, however, when
or even whether such a political shift
will take place. The opposition parties
continue to be badly split, and with
no obvious candidate for central leadership. The *Komeito*, Japan's newest
and most novel party, has parlayed
religion (Buddhism of the Soka Gak-
kai sect), Asia-centered nationalism,
domestic reform, and antiestablish-
ment imagery into a considerable
measure of success. At the moment,
however, the *Komeito* appears to have
run into problems, both internal and
vis-à-vis the Japanese public, making
its further advances problematic. The
Japan Socialist party has long been
deeply divided and politically stag-
nant, dominated by a preoccupation
with ideology and seemingly afraid of
actually coming to power. At some
point, it is possible that the labor
movement will reshape this party—or
some successor—in a more moderate,
realistic fashion. Until that time, the
JSP's impotence will probably continue—unless a major economic crisis
were to emerge. The Democratic Socialist party, meanwhile, is a moderate
party—closely akin to the British
Labour party in some respects. Its
base of support, however, has remained small, and there are few signs
that this will change. There remains
the Communist party of Japan—a
party that has finally established an
"autonomous" or "independent" position vis-à-vis both Peking and Moscow. The Communists, despite some
gains in recent years, remain much
weaker than their counterparts in
France and Italy.

United-front politics thus far has
been most easily established and most
successful at metropolitan and local-
regional levels. In general, however,
the conservatives (with almost all of
the independents affiliated with them)
dominate local and prefectural politics even more thoroughly than at the
Diet level. Only in the key cities have
they slipped badly. Barring some
major crisis such as war or depression,
therefore, it is difficult to foresee any
early demise of the conservatives. In
a functional sense, Japan can be said
to have a "one and one-half" party
system: one dominant party that
knows only how to govern, and half-
parties that know only how to oppose.
If this should change in the near
future, the most likely cause would be
the deepening fissures within the LDP
and the development of new party
alignments.

This suggests that there is still
another way in which the Japanese
party system can be defined and explained: as a system of rival federa-
tions within which operate the real
parties—namely, the smaller factions
that are based upon intimate personal ties and mutual interests. Each
of the major parties is composed
of such factions. Thus, the Liberal
Democratic party currently has eight
to ten principal factions. The shifting
alliances among these factions determine leadership of the "federation,"
or party. Factional loyalty generally
takes precedence over loyalty to the
federation; hence, in many respects,
the real party is the faction.

Considering the circumstances noted
above, it is not surprising that bipartisanship on foreign policy issues does
not exist in Japan. Indeed, such issues
are often used as weapons in the struggle for power among rival factions
within a major party. Within the Liberal Democratic party, for example,
such issues as policies toward the
Republic of Korea, adjustments in the
Mutual Security Treaty with the
United States, and —above all—China
policy have been made heated intraparty issues. Sometimes, issue divergence stems from genuine differences

of opinion. More frequently, it becomes a means of soliciting public or elitist support.

In sum, Japanese foreign policy is largely determined today by the dominant party, the Liberal Democratic party, and within that party by the so-called "mainstream" factions—namely, those factions closely aligned with the prime minister. Changes of whatever character in Japanese foreign policy are at least as likely to come via the evolution of the Liberal Democratic party itself as via some new party, a coalition government or the emergence of an opposition group into power. It is appropriate, however, to note at this point that the advent of *any* opposition party to power (with the partial exception of the Democratic Socialists) would result in major foreign policy changes, assuming that current views were retained. The *Komeito* takes a position favoring a gradual phasing out of the Mutual Security Treaty, to be replaced by a policy of "complete neutrality"—that is, of nonparticipation in any military alliance, the maintenance of an "equal distance" from other nations, and the retention of an "absolute minimum force of national guards." The Japanese Socialist party has advocated "unarmed neutrality" (a totally pacifist position in principle, but one linked up with strong anti-American positions) and—on the part of one major faction—a high level of sympathy for the People's Republic of China. The Communists, curiously, have opted for a more nationalistic "armed neutrality" position, and nonalignment with either Peking or Moscow, reflective of the new nationalist currents within many Asian communist movements. Needless to say, however, the JCP is bitterly opposed to the American-Japanese alliance, and to all U.S. policies in Asia.

Thus, when we refer to Japanese foreign policy or government attitudes, the sharp divisions between contending political forces must be constantly kept in mind. One final point, moreover, deserves emphasis. The party system as a whole is still on trial with the Japanese people, although the Japanese political system, in comparison with those in other democratic societies, looks remarkably stable at present. Popular commitments to parties and to the party concept may be growing, but they are still weak. There is always the danger that parties and the Diet may be circumvented, with the left protesting via the streets and the ultraright via the knife. That danger, however, does not seem greater at the moment in Japan than in certain other "advanced" nations, including the United States.

Although the LDP leaders play the critical role in setting the basic positions for Japanese foreign policy, the Japanese bureaucracy nevertheless merits special attention. In relative terms, it is probably correct to assert that the prestige of the Japanese official has been declining. The popular homage he receives, his emoluments, and his own attitude toward his status seem to point in this direction. But the changes taking place in these respects are relative to the Japanese past. In comparison with other democratic societies, the Japanese official still enjoys considerable prestige and power. And many young Japanese aspire to careers as officials. Indeed, competition for the available civil-service positions is as intense as for top positions in industry or the leading professions.

In some respects, the bureaucracy has changed less than most other facets of postwar Japan. It remains strongly hierarchical, and its modes of operation have been altered only slowly. Yet, in its socioeconomic composition, the Japanese bureaucracy is undergoing significant evolution. Young men from the upper and upper-middle classes still have sizeable advantages—the educational opportunities and the proper social connections—but others have been pushing their way into the civil service in increasing numbers. Tokyo University, moreover, does not have the monopoly on training it possessed before 1945; a larger proportion of successful candidates come from other institutions. Above all, Japanese civil servants are now receiving a much broader college education, on the one hand, and much more advanced technical training, where it is desired, on the other hand. The premium on specialized skills has grown steadily. Some observers believe that the Japanese civil service not only attracts top talent in such fields as economics, but gives it more opportunity than does the academic world.

Another vital fact cannot be ignored. As in the prewar period, an increasing bureaucratic infiltration of the conservative group has been taking place. The percentage of conservative Diet members who have been officials in the national civil service has steadily risen since 1946. Approximately one-fourth of the Liberal Democratic Diet members are in this category, and the percentage of party leaders and cabinet members who are former officials is much higher. This fact explains the close interaction between party leadership and government bureaucracy at the topmost levels in contemporary Japan.

The Ministry of Foreign Affairs (or Foreign Office), it should be noted, is less prestigious than the Ministry of Finance, generally regarded as the most powerful branch of the Japanese bureaucracy. Moreover, the Foreign Office does not handle all matters involving foreign affairs, particularly those dealing with trade, aid, and similar matters. Both the Ministry of Finance and the Ministry of International Trade and Industry (MITI) are of major importance in the foreign policy arena. And like all advanced nations, Japan has major problems of bureaucratic coordination. The Ministry of Foreign Affairs is itself relatively small and simply organized. It has approximately 2,000 men of civil-service rank. Its major subdivisions are bureaus of two types—those covering geographic areas and those representing specialized functions. The latter include treaties, economic affairs, information and culture, and international cooperation. Within the ministry, there is also a Secretariat which serves as a central coordinating and administrative unit. It includes a policy planning staff charged with overall evaluation and planning of basic policy positions. Official liaison with the Diet is maintained through a parliamentary vice-minister, normally appointed from the Diet membership.

In comparison with the prewar period, the formulation of Japanese foreign policy is clearly more coordinated and efficient. Prior to 1945, as we have noted, the struggle to control foreign policy was a complex one waged by diverse forces. The ultimate cost to Japan was enormous. In the immediate postsurrender period, neither party leaders nor bureaucratic leaders could play a major role. Both foreign and domestic policies were laid down by occupation authorities. The Japanese function was, essentially, to discern what the policy was and then to exercise—with uncertain results—the right of suggestion. Diplomacy had to be directed almost wholly toward the United States. As the occupation drew to a close, Japanese initiative was gradually reasserted. Initially, diplomacy, which was in the hands of Prime Minister Yoshida, himself a former Foreign Office man, was highly personalized. His opponents charged him with "one-man diplomacy." Party participation in foreign policy was very limited, and the Foreign Office still struggled to overcome its earlier weak and ineffectual position.

Down to the present, Japanese prime ministers have continued to keep a firm hand on their nation's foreign policy, and for most, indeed, some major personal accomplishment in this field has tended to mark the climax of each leader's political career. Gradually, however, the base for the conduct of foreign policy has broadened, with elements of the Liberal Democratic party and the various Ministries centrally involved. By the time of the Kishi era (Kishi became prime minister in February, 1957), bureau chiefs in the Ministry of Foreign Affairs had begun to maintain close contacts with party leaders. Many of these contacts were with the pertinent commitees of the Liberal Democratic party: the Research Committee on Foreign Relations, the Policy Research Committee, and the General Affairs Board. These committees, particularly the General Affairs Board, officially determine the foreign policy of the party. At least equally important were the contacts maintained with "mainstream faction" leaders.

Relations between career officials and the Liberal Democratic party relating to foreign policy issues have not always been smooth or uncomplicated. As we have noted, the factional character of Japanese parties can be a major problem, especially if a faction is encouraged by external pressure groups. Thus, at the time of negotiations between Japan and the Soviet Union for a treaty of peace, some leaders within the Liberal Democratic party, supported by certain fishery and commercial groups, built up pressure for a rapid settlement. This was resisted by top Foreign Office officials but, for a time, Japan suffered once again from dual diplomacy. The Foreign Office has also faced jurisdictional and policy quarrels with other ministries on occasion. As yet, however, Japan has not had the massive problem of reconciling and integrating a Pentagon-State Department-White House staff triumvirate in the foreign policy field. On the whole, the coordination of Japanese foreign policy has been more satisfactory in recent years than at any other time in the history of modern Japan.

Yet, there is another side to the coin. Japanese pressure groups and public opinion, when combined with the opposition parties, have added many new complexities to the scene. As we noted earlier, pressure groups of all types now exist. Their number, diversity, and influence on Japanese foreign policy have increased greatly. On several recent occasions, for example, and notably with respect to textile trade regulations, the evidence suggests that the prime minister himself was not able to prevail over a powerful internal interest group. It is not appropriate here to attempt any detailed discussion of this development; only a few salient points can be presented. As in the prewar era, the commercial and industrial groups have the greatest single influence on the Liberal Democratic party, especially in the field of foreign policy. These speak through the Japan Employers Association and many similar organizations. It would be a mistake, however, to assume that the Japanese business and industrial world speaks with a single voice. On such an issue as China policy, for example, it is far from unanimous. Still, the broad outlines of Japanese foreign policy at present are deeply influenced by the interests and views of leading industrial and commercial pressure groups. They remain the chief financial support for the Liberal Democratic party, they include the most intimate confidants of conservative politicians, and, hence, they are the most powerful unofficial influence on public policy, domestic and foreign.

The pressures emanating from rural Japan have decreased substantially in recent years, particularly in the area of foreign policy. While the farmer continues to vote conservative in substantial measure, he has progressively become a smaller fraction of the Japanese electorate, and very frequently, in occupational terms, he now represents a mixed element, with some of his income derived from labor or small to medium-sized business.

The more serious of the factors that complicate the formulations of Japanese foreign policy are not the traditional Japanese pressure groups, but certain new ones, in addition to the force of public opinion as it is revealed in countless polls. Among the opposition pressure groups, the most important is organized labor. *Sohyo*, the General Council of Trade Unions of Japan, has been especially vocal on foreign policy. It has hewed closely to, and helped to shape, the socialist positions on neutralism, on relations with the communist world, on "American imperialism," and on many other issues. In addition, it has supported these positions with demonstrations, work stoppages, and quantities of political literature.

Sohyo, with 4.2 million members, is probably the most formidable of the opposition pressure groups (although it should not thereby be implied that it can commit all its members on any issue). There are, however, a number of others. Most of them represent intellectual, student, and labor elements in Japanese society. As in the case of "conservative" interest groups, these diverse forces by no means speak with a single voice. At the same time, such groups cannot totally be ignored by the governing elite, particularly since they maintain a substantial forum by means of newspapers, magazines, TV, and radio. Their various messages now reach the Japanese public—especially the urban public—regularly. Hence, in the last twenty years, foreign policy has become a central part of the political battlefield in Japan, sometimes the most vital part. The conservatives have been forced to recognize a far more significant opposition than any experienced in the prewar era, despite the weaknesses in that opposition noted earlier. Suppression or indifference is no longer feasible. Consequently, the conservatives are also resorting to the media and other forms of public appeal.

It is very difficult to assess the present influence of Japanese public opinion on foreign policy. In recent years, polling has become popular in Japan. It is carried out by a number of organizations, the most widely regarded polls being those which resemble the leading American polls. The major Japanese newspapers, in particular, poll the public at regular intervals on a wide variety of subjects, including many issues of foreign policy. Opinions on rearmament, the Mutual Security Treaty, Okinawa, constitutional revision, and relations with China have been frequently requested. And, in a number of cases, the polls have indicated that either a large minority or an actual majority of those polled differed with government policy. They also revealed a considerable amount of public apathy and ignorance.

There is little doubt that public opinion, now being presented in these concrete, measured forms, has had a rising impact on decision making in

Japan. Increasingly, it is a factor which Japanese leaders take seriously. Sometimes, to be sure, public opinion is used to justify a decision based mainly on other grounds. But more frequently, when the polls indicate substantial public opposition to a given policy, conservative leaders respond with modifications, a shift in timing, or a more intensive public relations campaign. However, the reluctance of recent conservative administrations to rearm rapidly or to seek the repeal of Article 9 of the Constitution, the long and fairly firm Japanese bargaining in connection with the revised Mutual Security Treaty, and the cautious, ambivalent position toward China are all indications of the new political power of the Japanese common man.

At the same time, the Japanese conservatives are well aware of the fact that elections in Japan are not won primarily on the basis of issues of foreign policy. To the extent that elections hinge on issues in Japan, domestic concerns have been of overwhelming importance. Throughout their long tenure in office, the conservatives have consequently played upon such themes as prosperity and progress; and they count heavily upon their superior organization, their greater funds, and their local leadership. And where they have lost elections, as noted earlier, domestic issues have been paramount.

Thus, the Liberal Democratic leaders can afford to take some chances in the area of foreign policy, even when they know or suspect that there is strong public opposition to specific policies. When confronted with evidence of hostile public opinion, the government tactic is to camouflage or alter a policy slightly, so as to disarm some of the opposition, but rarely if ever to make basic changes. With respect to the socialists (and other ele-

ments of the "left") also, a caveat must be entered regarding the influence of public opinion: the record would indicate that such parties have often ignored public opinion when it conflicted with their ideological stance.

In sum, the process of formulating, executing, and defending Japanese foreign policy today is in the hands of a conservative elite. The formal and informal institutional processes have been greatly refined in the postwar era, and now operate at a fairly high level of efficiency. Collaboration between the Liberal Democratic party and the Ministry of Foreign Affairs (or other appropriate branches of government) is close and continuous. The prime minister continues to play the dominant role, together with the factions supporting him, and, in the final analysis, the political rather than the bureaucratic element now tends to predominate on most basic issues of foreign policy (although many top conservative leaders have been ex-officials). The military has been very subordinate thus far, but it is likely that its influence will increase somewhat in the decade ahead—how much depending upon both internal and external developments. Meanwhile, the newer generations of Ministry officials are more broadly recruited and trained than they were before World War II, and they possess a higher level of technical proficiency.

The conservative elite that directs Japanese foreign policy is sustained and influenced mainly by the industrial, commercial, and agrarian segments of Japanese society. Contradictory pressures, however, sometimes flow from these elements. In any case, no simple economic analysis does justice to the realities of the situation. Japan is becoming, among other things, a mass society in which the conservative elite is forced to pay increasing attention to public opinion. While not of commanding importance, public opinion now serves to effect modifications both of substance and of timing in certain policies, and causes the Japanese leaders to give more attention to the public image of their policies.

CONTEMPORARY ISSUES IN JAPANESE FOREIGN POLICY

At present, three dominant considerations underlie the debates and decisions pertaining to foreign policy in Japan. First, there is the high priority that must be accorded economic considerations in foreign policy—the extreme importance attached to maintaining Japanese economic growth, and the need to face the problems which that phenomenal growth has already bequeathed. Second, there is the major issue of security, an issue involving Japanese relations with the United States, the communist nations, and the world—particularly the Pacific-Asian world. Finally, there is the broader, vaguer question of what role Japan should play in the world, and what mix of economic, political, and military commitments is desirable, both from the standpoint of her national interest and from the standpoint of the changing psychological needs of the Japanese people.

The Economic Basis of Japanese Foreign Policy

Today, Japan is an economic giant, with an annual productivity exceeded only by the United States and the Soviet Union. In 1970, her GNP (gross national product) was $200 billion, her foreign trade was approaching $35 billion, her overseas investments totaled $3 billion, and her average annual per capita income was approximately $1,500—making her people the most prosperous in eastern Asia by a wide margin. As is well known, this series of achievements did not occur suddenly. In the decade after 1960, the Japanese GNP averaged a gain of approximately 12 percent per annum, with exports growing at an average annual rate of 16.5 percent, imports at 15 percent.

This accomplishment is all the more remarkable when one considers certain basic socioeconomic facts with which Japan must live. In 1970, the population of the relatively small four islands comprising this nation had reached 104 million. Present trends indicate that that population will increase at the rate of approximately 1 million per year for the next decade, with Japan being the first society in Asia to practice population planning on a massive (and effective) scale. This means, of course, that the Japanese labor force will gradually become older, and the problem of labor scarcity will become more serious. Meanwhile, only 14 percent of the land is currently under agricultural cultivation, with about 25 percent of the population (27.9 million) engaged in agricultural pursuits. Only 20 percent of Japan's farm households depend exclusively on farm incomes, and agriculture, forestry, and fisheries account for only 9 percent of the net domestic product. Thus, the Japanese economy is heavily geared to manufacturing (31 percent of the net domestic product) and services (44 percent). Yet, most of the mineral resources and many other raw materials crucial to the industrial sector must be imported from overseas. Japan is almost totally dependent for her crude oil and iron ore supplies from abroad, as well as the great bulk of such essential commodities as cotton, copper, coking coal, and many other items.

The slogan, "Export or die," stems from these elemental facts. Yet they neither explain the essential ingredients of Japanese success in the recent decades, nor do they signal all of the problems that lie ahead. Japanese political leaders see the phenomenal growth of the postwar era as the product of combining correct policies of centralized economic planning with a vigorous private enterprise system. On the one hand, the state has continued—as in the past—to provide extensive direction, "rewarding" those sectors of the economy regarded as most suitable to the national needs via subsidies, tax benefits, and protection. Indeed, this has led to the charge of "Japan Inc.," a collusion of government and business to the detriment of foreign competitors. On the other hand, the extraordinary vitality and capacities of the private sector manifested themselves in a variety of ways. Japanese society had long been acculturated to modernity, with organizational talents, high levels of discipline, and a truly remarkable work ethic having permeated the entire community. In specific terms, the primary causes of the recent Japanese "economic miracle" would appear to be these: a very high savings ratio (currently over 20 percent of disposable income); very high ratios of governmental and private capital investment; rapidly rising labor productivity, as a result of advanced levels of education and discipline on the part of the working force—all contributing to a very strong competitive position in the international market.

What are the prospects for the future, and how do these prospects affect Japanese foreign policy? Until recently, very rapid growth rates of 8–10 percent were being projected officially for the 1970's. By 1975, it was predicted, Japan would have a $400 billion economy, double that of 1970, with major increases in trade and overseas investment. With the uncertainties surrounding American and West European trade and fiscal policies, future Japanese growth rates may now be in question. Real growth in 1971, a year of considerable crisis in American-Japanese economic relations, was reported unofficially at 5.5 percent. This is certainly not a negligible growth rate, especially for a highly developed nation, but it represented a substantial drop from previous years.

At this point, there is little reason to believe that Japan is entering an era of economic crisis, although earlier growth projections may have been overly optimistic. Unquestionably, however, a number of problems must be faced. Internally, Japan is confronted with competitive demands for her available state capital. The ratio of governmental expenditures for social services up to date has been low, amounting to less than 8 percent. Now, environmental problems together with other social welfare needs can be ignored by the ruling party only at its political peril. Defense expenditures, extraordinarily low in the past, have also begun to rise—with only the amount of increase in doubt. Meanwhile, the high savings propensity may decline, as the Japanese public becomes consumption-oriented, and certain demands—for example, for automobiles and better housing—rapidly mount. Moreover, as we have noted, the labor market is going to become increasingly tighter, given present demographic trends. Inflation is also a problem; consumer prices have been rising on an average of 5 percent per annum since 1960.

The more complex problems in connection with Japan's economic goals, however, are likely to be in the international arena. Let us look first at the question of trade expansion.

Where does Japan hope to score major advances in the years immediately ahead? Current official projections envisage gains spread over the entire globe. Hopes are not to be pinned to a single nation or region. However, only modest gains are expected with respect to the markets of communist states. It is assumed that the China market will gradually develop, and might develop more quickly if long-term credits were granted. Forecasts concerning this market, nevertheless, are considerably less optimistic than was the case a decade ago—partly because of a greater appreciation of China's longer range economic problems and partly because of the obstacles presented by her chosen economic-political policies. Some hope is attached to the future of Japanese-Soviet economic relations. Potentially, a considerable expansion in these relations could take place, with Siberia being its focal point. The extent of this development, however, is highly dependent upon the political as well as the economic decisions of Soviet leadership.

In any case, primary hopes are pinned on the noncommunist world—both the so-called advanced states and the less developed countries. Despite recent troubles, Japan continues to gamble heavily upon being able not merely to hold, but to increase, her share in the U.S. import market. By 1975, for example, she hopes to occupy nearly 20 percent of that market, having had approximately 14 percent of it in 1970. Meanwhile, however, the extensive increases in Japanese imports into the United States over the past decade have already created a major domestic issue in the latter country. Such American industries as textiles, steel, automobiles, television and radio, and the entire electronics field have felt seriously threatened, and have demanded remedial action.

Initially, "voluntary quotas" served to reduce pressure in the United States for more stringent protectionist measures, but in recent years the charges of Japanese "dumping" and the serious inroads made by Japanese products in a wide range of fields traditionally controlled by American producers have heightened the demand for firmer controls.

Another complication must be added. It is an uncomfortable fact that the American economy has long been ailing. Coupled with a rising inflation has been a relative decline in labor productivity. Thus, on the international front, a serious deficit of payments problem had emerged by mid–1971, forcing the Nixon administration to take dramatic steps, including the floating of the dollar and the imposition of a ten percent surcharge on all foreign imports. The United States asserted that these measures were to be temporary, and primarily for the purpose of forcing basic changes in the fiscal, trade, and investment policies of Japan and West Europe. Intensive negotiations got underway in the fall of 1971, looking toward a new international monetary policy. Meanwhile, an agreement on Japanese textile exports to the US was reached. Yen revaluation appeared likely. But many basic problems in the economic sphere remain unsettled.

Clearly, economic issues have become a vital and potentially dangerous point of division in American-Japanese relations. Japan must bear a substantial responsibility for the crisis. She acted much too slowly in accepting import liberalization, with the major strides in this field having come only in the last few years. Resistance to liberalization of capital transactions continues. Meanwhile, extraordinary inroads into the American market were made, sometimes via questionable techniques. At the same time, the issue of whether the United States is, or can become truly competitive in the international arena increasingly beclouds the picture, and signals the element of American responsibility.

Are there alternatives to economic nationalism? Trade-offs in quotas will provide some temporary relief. The yen should, and probably will be, revalued. Moreover, Japan has promised an accelerated liberalization program directed toward the continued removal of import duties. On the American side, the adjustments necessary are more complex, involving as they do economic policies to slow inflation, raise productivity, and increase American competitiveness.

As has been indicated, the current economic difficulties plaguing American-Japanese relations cannot be solved bilaterally. Nontariff barriers imposed by the European Economic Community (EEC) clearly discriminate at present against the Japanese, and as one result, the Japanese share of European imports has been less than 2 percent. A reduction or removal of such discrimination—together with the movement of Japan toward total import liberalization—might increase Japanese economic interaction with the EEC, and thereby reduce the pressures involved in such a heavy concentration upon the American market. The involvement of GATT (General Agreement on Tariffs and Trade) in a basic multilateral set of rules on fair trade may represent the only alternative to a serious deterioration of economic relations among advanced states in the coming years. Barring significant global advances, can a Pacific regionalism offer any hope? The EEC illustrates the advantages and limitations of economic regionalism. While the Pacific community is a very different type of community, and much more complex, it remains true that trade and economic relations between four Pacific-Asian states—the United States, Japan, Canada, and Australia—are critical to each of the countries involved, and form the vital heart of their international economic relations. Thus, a case can be made out for multilateralism via a "Pacific Economic Community." It is easier to define the problems in this area, however, than to solve them.

Meanwhile, Japan also faces problems in expanding her economic interaction with the less developed countries. Here again, the hope is to develop broad new markets in such areas as Latin America and Africa, while extending trade and investment in those areas where the Japanese presence is already substantial. The plans call for Japan to hold over 40 percent of the Southeast Asian import market by 1975 (presently, she controls 30 percent of that market), and to push the Japanese import quotient from 9 to 15 percent in the Oceania-southern Asia area. If these plans are realized, Japan will clearly be the dominant economic power throughout eastern Asia; indeed, that is already the case in major degree. Naturally, this creates both political and economic problems. Resentment against Japanese control has recently been growing in these regions, and there is particularly grave concern over the unbalanced nature of the trade. In 1970, Japan sold commodities valued at some $5 billion to Southeast Asia while importing from that area only $3 billion worth of commodities.

What policies are available to Japan to offset the risks involved in current economic expansion plans as these relate to the less developed countries? By 1975, Japan is pledged to increase her economic and technical aid to developing countries to 1 percent of her GNP (in 1971, such aid had almost reached that figure). Most of this aid goes to the South and Southeast Asian regions. Present policies also dictate the development of Japanese enterprises overseas—many of them in the Asian area—not merely to take advantage of lower production costs, but also to alleviate current economic imbalances. In the nonmanufacturing areas, at least, consortium arrangements in this connection, as well as an acceptance of indigenous participation, could reduce charges of Japanese domination of the domestic economy.

Nevertheless, as the single most powerful nation in Asia economically, Japan is destined to face complex difficulties as well as significant opportunities in the years ahead. Her rising economic involvement in eastern Asia will give her a chance to participate in developmental experimentation crucial not merely to Asia, but to the entire world. And clearly, as Japanese trade and investment increase in this region, she will have an ever-greater stake in its peace and economic growth. Whether her major economic presence can continue to grow without adverse political repercussions is, of course, a central question. Much will depend upon Japanese conduct—governmental, corporate, and individual—and here, substantial improvements are in order. The image of the Japanese as mere "economic animals" is even more deeply implanted in the non-Western world today than the earlier image of the Japanese as "militarists." Of critical importance also is the question of whether Japan's economic role in Asia will bring her into greater cooperation or deeper competition with the communist states of that region. If China grows militarily but continues to enjoy only modest

economic advances, and Japan continues her rapid economic growth but remains at relatively modest levels militarily, will tensions between the two states mount?

The Security Issues in Japanese Foreign Policy

Already, in our discussion of economic factors in the preceding section, we have moved to issues within the realm of the political—more specifically, issues relating to the security of this unique nation. If Japan is an economic giant, she is currently a political pygmy. Nor is her military strength impressive at present, all of the charges of an incipient Japanese militarism notwithstanding. It is true, as noted earlier, that the Japanese military establishment is a highly modern one, geared to the use of the latest defensive techniques on land, in the air, and at sea. The total personnel involved, however, number less than one-quarter of a million individuals, with 158,000 of these in the Ground Self-Defense Forces. In 1970, the Japanese navy consisted of 210 ships totaling some 125,000 tons, and the air force was made up of 960 planes, including 15 jet fighter squadrons. In comparison with the major powers of the world, this is a very modest military structure, and certainly not one capable of playing the American role in Asia, as certain observers earlier suggested might soon come to pass. It is legitimate, however, to raise the question of whether the future will be more than a mere continuance of the past with respect to Japanese security policies.

At the outset, let us note the two basic factors that have governed Japanese security policies in the post-1945 era. The single most critical determinant of those policies has been the military alliance with the United States via the Mutual Security Treaty. In essence, Japan has had her security underwritten by the American nuclear umbrella, and by the sizeable American conventional force present in eastern Asia, some of it utilizing bases in Japan and Okinawa. With such a formidable shield available, it was considered neither necessary nor desirable to develop a large independent military capacity. Consequently, to date, Japan has spent less than 1 percent of its annual GNP on defense. In 1968, for example, when Japan was allocating 0.8 percent of its GNP to such expenditures, the German Federal Republic was spending 3.9 percent, Great Britain 5.3 percent, the Chinese People's Republic 9 percent, the United States 9.2 percent, and the Soviet Union 9.3 percent.

It is true, of course, that because her GNP was rising very rapidly, Japan in actuality was spending substantially increased amounts on defense. Indeed, those expenditures have doubled approximately every six years since 1952, and by 1969 they had reached a level of $1.3 billion. In 1970, moreover, a 17.7 percent increase in defense expenditures was authorized, making gross expenditure for that year some $1.6 billion. Nevertheless, in the crucial years between 1950 and 1970, capital investment could be concentrated in industries vitally important to the total Japanese economy in unprecedented degree because defense spending was very low in comparison with those nations against whom Japan found herself in primary competition.

A second factor of equal significance relates to the political-psychological environment in which Japanese defense policy has evolved. The postwar era began with the shattering impact of the war breeding in most Japanese varying commitments to pacifism, withdrawal, and minimal risk. These sentiments were particularly strong among the immediate postwar generations. As we shall shortly suggest, there are now signs that the psychological trends of yesteryear are changing. To date, however, the Japanese public has not had a deep sense of external threat to its security. Public opinion polls are revealing in this respect. On the one hand, the Japanese public *does* dislike the two communist giants more than it dislikes any other nation (although antipathy to Korea is also high). Moreover, antagonism to the People's Republic of China grew markedly in the aftermath of the first Chinese nuclear tests and the Cultural Revolution. In comparative terms, the United States does well in these popularity contests, although the general trend in recent years has been that of increasing independence, with a refusal to identify any country as "most liked." But in some conflict with the above data, when questioned about the purpose of American military bases in Japan, most Japanese see these as primarily intended for the defense of the United States and other Asian nations, *not* for the defense of Japan. Moreover, many Japanese perceive the threat of becoming involved in war via the American alliance as equally great as, or greater than, the threats emanating from the Soviet Union or the People's Republic of China. There is a disposition to rate the dangers of an attack by these or other states upon Japan as very low.

Naturally, these views—shared by a certain portion of the Japanese political elite—have influenced policy in various ways. Even the most security-conscious leaders are not disposed to seek a repeal of the so-called antiwar clause (Article 9 of the Japanese Constitution), because under present conditions there would be no public support for such a move. The public apparently supports limited rearmament—for defense purposes only—at approximately the levels currently established. But all recent public opinion polls register strong opposition to extensive rearmament, the use of Japanese military forces abroad, or the acquisition of nuclear weapons. It is not surprising, therefore, that Japanese leaders speak cautiously when discussing security policy alternatives —and even among the conservative elite, there are presently substantial differences of opinion on security issues and the basic direction to be pursued in the future.

Before exploring these differences, and the policy alternatives which they imply, it might be wise to note that, under certain conditions, public opinion is subject to radical changes. Within a few years, the Chinese People's Republic will have operational ICBMs quite capable of being directed at Japan. The military power of the Soviet Union in the Pacific-Asian area has sharply increased in recent years. Meanwhile, the Japanese economic-political stake in eastern Asia steadily grows. If one or both of the major communist powers were to undertake political-military blackmail against Japan, or view Japanese economic expansion as contrary to their national interests, present Japanese public opinion could presumably change as dramatically as Japanese policies. There is also the complex phenomenon of a new Japanese nationalism, to which we shall refer shortly—a phenomenon having uncertain bearings upon attitudes toward power and security.

Thus, Japanese security policies in the 1970s will evolve in the context of a swiftly changing international scene, and one marked by many uncertainties. Not the least of these, of course, are trends in the East Asian policies of the United States. Today, the "Nixon doctrine" sets the basic outlines of American policy. In security terms, the central theme of the Nixon doctrine is that, while the United States will maintain its treaty commitments, each of its allies will be expected to provide for its own ground defense, and that the American contribution will be primarily that of a deterrent to major-power involvement —by virtue of its nuclear weapons, and by supplying aerial-naval aid if necessary. For many Japanese, however—and for many other Asians as well—the issue is not the merits of the Nixon doctrine, but whether that doctrine can withstand the heavy tides of isolationism that are now sweeping over the American scene.

Any precipitous American withdrawal from Asia would almost certainly produce an increased polarization within Japan over the basic direction to be taken in foreign policy. Three quite different possibilities suggest themselves. One would be an accelerated nationalism of a Gaullist character, manifesting itself initially in some combination of an independent political-military program (including the development of nuclear weapons) and a new/old type of pan-Asianism. It is some variant of this policy that has been most widely discussed and predicted, from communist and noncommunist sources alike.

An entirely opposite set of policies might flow from the same set of circumstances: the fears and antagonisms caused by an abrupt American withdrawal might further strengthen the political position of the Japanese left, with a coalition government emerging which would in turn opt for "non-alignment," with the premium upon friendly relations with the communist bloc and a very low military profile. This would require a dramatic reorientation, and one probably involving economic as well as political and psychological dimensions.

There is yet a third response that might develop as a response to American isolationism—one which seems more probable than the second course outlined above, and at least as possible as the first course suggested: American withdrawal and the psychological pangs accompanying it might well result in locking Japan into a position of uncertainty—and hence, inaction—for the next few crucial years. During this time, such signs of greater political initiative and of concern over the security of northeastern Asia as have appeared would fade away. A moderate leadership, remaining in power, would revert to an exceedingly cautious economics-only policy, one involving the minimum possible risks and commitments. The effect would be to freeze Japanese foreign policy in the mold of the recent past, with Japan unable or unwilling to accept any new role in the absence of confidence in American policy or in the American will.

In all probability, such a "freeze" could not be sustained beyond a few years. Pressures would surely rise, both at home and abroad, pushing Japan in the direction of one or the other of the first two policies set forth above. Indeed, the pressures would probably accelerate on behalf of both policies simultaneously, with differences over Japanese foreign policy becoming a growing source of political instability. In any case, however, the element of timing under the circumstances just outlined could be crucial. If uncertain Japanese leaders felt themselves forced to follow a minimal, weak foreign policy, while

at the same time widespread American withdrawal became an accomplished fact, the Asian-Pacific area would be cast into a state of political-military disequilibrium. If the international peacekeeping mechanisms remained as inadequate as they are at present, and the military capacities of some states as formidable, the temptations to engage in "wars of liberation" might increase, casting a long shadow over the peace of the region. Is the recent India-Pakistan conflict an ominous harbinger of Asia's future?

Let us assume, however, that the Nixon doctrine in its basic outline prevails. Even under those conditions, a considerable reduction of the American presence in eastern Asia will take place, particularly in military terms. Questions concerning American credibility will mount, and debate will revolve around the basic alternatives set forth above.

In the near future, Japan will continue to allocate about 1 percent of her GNP to defense expenditures. If projected growth rates are realized, this means that by 1975 Japan will be spending about $2.5 billion annually in the military field. Such expenditures, moreover, will be oriented most heavily toward modern military aircraft, missiles, and naval expansion. In the course of this period, Japan will assume defense responsibilities for Okinawa, as well as for the air and sea approaches to Japan proper. The presence of American military personnel in the Japan-Okinawa military base complex will continue to be phased out, with naval facilities being the primary bases in Japan proper at the close of this period.

If such a projection is correct, Japan will be a "middle power" militarily by 1975, spending approximately one-half the amount being spent in the military field by each of the major European states or by the People's Republic of China. The Mutual Security Treaty will continue to be the linchpin in Japan's defense program, providing as it does America's nuclear guarantee, and the Japanese government will continue to be deeply concerned about the credibility of the American defense pledge. There will be no move to develop nuclear weapons; but, in the broadest sense, the nuclear option will be kept open, with the ultimate decision dependent upon developments throughout the world, and particularly in northeastern Asia.

Under such circumstances, Japan will not be capable of engaging in any military confrontation with China or the Soviet Union, nor will she be prepared—militarily or psychologically—to play any power role in southern Asia. Her first security concern after that involving her own territory will be with the Republic of Korea, as Prime Minister Sato has made clear. Given the complex political relations that have existed historically between these two societies, however, as well as the reluctance of the Japanese people to accept any overseas military obligations, the Japanese commitment is not likely to go beyond certain forms of military aid, together with permission for the United States to use Japanese bases in the event of strife on the Korean peninsula.

Developments in foreign policy during the later 1970s are more difficult to project. Certainly, there are no financial inhibitions upon a more extensive military buildup, should that course become necessary or desirable in the eyes of Japanese leaders. Given the present and probable future rate of growth, Japan could raise her military expenditures to 2 percent of her GNP or more without major financial strain. Nor are there serious technical restraints. Japan will soon be manufacturing F-4 fighter planes, and such missiles as the Nike-Hercules and Hawk missiles are already being constructed there. Japan could also construct nuclear weapons in a very brief period of time, if she chose to do so.

The arguments for developing nuclear weapons generally put forth in private discussions include the following: the American defense commitment cannot be trusted, especially in the light of recent domestic U.S. trends and the growing nuclear threat likely to be presented by the CPR; only nuclear powers have major political status; and without nuclear weapons, Japan will be subject to blackmail by either China or the Soviet Union. Additional reasons are presented for substantially augmenting Japan's conventional defenses: the protection of her vital sea lanes to the Middle East and throughout eastern and southern Asia; the critical importance of South Korea and Taiwan to Japan's own defenses; and the likelihood that the conventional forces of both China and the Soviet Union will grow, enabling them to bargain—or threaten—from a position of power.

The arguments against nuclear weapons are equally potent: nuclear power has conferred upon neither France nor Great Britain a significantly enhanced political position, while representing a massive drain on their economies; as a state containing a huge population concentrated in a very small area, Japan is at a unique disadvantage in contemplating any nuclear conflict, even one involving only tactical nuclear weapons; and a large-scale military arsenal has not proven particularly useful in protecting overseas markets and investments.

Whatever the logic of these various arguments, many outside observers believe that as her economic strength steadily grows and her global position becomes both massive and critical to her future, Japan will not be able to tolerate military-political dependence upon others and the status of a mere medium-sized power. Thus, it is argued that by carefully measured but steadily accelerating stages, Japan will once again be a major military power by the end of the 1970s, probably with nuclear weapons—unless vastly more effective steps toward worldwide nuclear disarmament have been taken in the interim. Under any circumstances, it is assumed that the Japanese military establishment would place primary emphasis upon air and sea power, as befits an island nation heavily dependent upon her overseas markets. Will this prediction prove correct? At this point, no one can be certain. The new Japanese nationalism may abet such a tendency. But the truly decisive influence is likely to be the nature of the perceived threat (specifically, the policies and attitudes of China and the Soviet Union); the perception of the American commitment and the American will; and the degree of progress attained in such fields as those of disarmament and "peaceful coexistence," especially as these relate to eastern Asia.

Meanwhile, certain special problems will exist with respect to the Japanese bases—especially those on Okinawa, which reverted to Japanese administrative control in 1972, with the United States retaining base rights there on the same terms that apply to the bases in Japan proper. The next few years are likely to be difficult ones concerning this change. Japanese and Okinawans now have to become reacquainted, and on the most intimate social, political, and economic grounds. The autonomy of Okinawa is being dismantled as it becomes just one more prefecture in the Japanese system, albeit one with a very special recent history. The psychological tensions involved in this transitional period, together with some very concrete economic and political problems, are likely to be substantial. In such a setting, the United States can, under certain circumstances, become a very useful scapegoat. It will take extraordinary skill—and luck—to prevent "the Okinawa issue" from periodically emerging as a disruption in American-Japanese relations.

The Quest for the Japanese Role in World Affairs

Thus far, we have been discussing the two vital sets of problems with which contemporary Japan must concern itself in constructing her foreign policy—those in the economic field and those in the military-security arena. Beyond such specific issues, however, there lies a broader question: What is the Japanese role to be in the late-twentieth-century world? Here, we are involved in probing the political culture of this remarkable society, and the deeper psychological as well as economic-political trends now governing the Japanese people. As was suggested earlier, Japanese political culture has been traditionally based upon strictly hierarchical relations; consequently, the concept of equality in foreign as well as domestic relations has been extremely difficult to accept or to practice. Thus, the American occupation of Japan in 1945 began with a little appreciated advantage—a people conditioned to accept tutelage if they could not exercise dominance. On the other hand, the United States was fully prepared to assume leadership—not necessarily in terms of her specialized knowledge of the area, but in terms of her moral and political self-confidence. Total victory in a global war, unprecedented prosperity at home, and the accelerating, upward thrust of the "American Revolution" in Japan combined to abet those psychological qualities that had always underwritten American internationalism in its most expansive forms: great self-confidence in one's abilities; a pervasive optimism concerning the future; a strong belief in the efficiency that stems from total commitment (and thus produces policies wedded to an impressive use of resources and a brief time-span of operations); and finally, a genuine humanistic attitude, sometimes resting uneasily with deeply rooted feelings of political and racial superiority.

The post-1945 American-Japanese relationship was successful in part because it was consonant with both the underlying psychological traits of the two societies *and* their prevailing political moods. Americans undertook the costly, dangerous tasks of rehabilitation and security, not merely for Japan but for various other parts of Asia as well. The Japanese, for their part, accepted a dependent status, one with minimal external responsibilities, as they set about the reconstruction of a devastated society. What division of labor could have accorded better with the psychological proclivities of these two diverse societies at that time?

The times have changed. Once again, after an enormous expenditure of resources, material and human, the United States is tired, querulous, and in a "withdrawal" mood. Meanwhile, complex and somewhat contradictory psychological trends are manifesting themselves in Japan. Any individual living outside the Japanese cultural orbit seeks to define these trends with trepidation. Japanese observers are

themselves by no means agreed upon their import. However, we appear to be witnessing a shift away from the mood that dominated the generation of Japanese deeply scarred by World War II. Many in that generation harbored intense feelings of inferiority and guilt, and showed a proclivity for dependency and withdrawal. This proclivity was naturally abetted by the harsh economic conditions that prevailed.

How substantial has the change in Japanese psychology been? To equate the newest generation of adult Japanese with their counterparts of the 1920s and 1930s, or to draw close parallels between Japanese nationalism in that era and today, is to commit a major error. Political institutions and values on the one hand, and socioeconomic developments on the other, have undergone radical changes. Moreover, the regional environment is entirely different. A new mood, however, is emerging in Japan. Recent Japanese generations seem more self-confident, more optimistic concerning their personal future and that of their nation, less inhibited in personal and group relations, and more willing to stand comparison with others—Asian and Western. Naturally, such qualities vary with the individual and also with the socioeconomic group, but it is impossible to overlook their increasing importance. In the aggregate, these and related trends can be said to constitute the new Japanese nationalism.

It would be surprising, indeed, if this new nationalism did not contain some xenophobic—and, more specifically, anti-American—elements. Dependency upon the United States, after all, has been the most enduring symbol of the post-1945 era. As yet, however, this is not the predominant characteristic of the new atmosphere. The current thrust appears more in the direction of a willingness and a desire to assert Japanese "self-interest"—especially in the economic sphere, and more strongly in bargaining relations at the official level and in other forms of interchange at the private level. Will this mood ultimately project a demand in Japan for recognition in all fields, the political and military as well as the economic? Will the new nationalism combine with unprecedented economic power to make Japan a major actor on the political stage by the 1980s?

Thus far, the Japanese government has contented itself with the pledge to attain an "independent diplomacy," and with pursuing a foreign policy in keeping with the nation's "national interests, economic and security"— words that are suitably flexible and vague. Full cognizance, moreover, should be given the fact that the enormous success of Japan's minimal-risk–maximal-gain foreign policy operates against any rapid or massive changes. Why should one abandon a policy that has been extraordinarily successful, unless altered circumstances force such an abandonment? Nor can the Japanese ignore the fact that dramatic changes in military technology in recent decades have tended to enhance the relative power of continental-mass societies. It is difficult to conceive of a restoration of the nineteenth-century principles of military and political power that favored Japan's geography.

These facts are not lost upon the leaders of Japan. When they talk of playing a greater role in the international community, they are currently thinking of an enhanced role in the United Nations and in other international bodies, particularly those involved in social and economic activities; an enlarged political role for Japan in Asia, via ASPAC and similar regional groups; a middleman

position between Asia and the West, and possibly, if circumstances permit it, a peacekeeping role as well. The most immediate problem, therefore, should American withdrawal from Asia be substantial, is more likely to be Japan's minimal performance, not her maximal performance; in the longer run, however, the picture still remains cloudy.

In the meantime, despite the strains to which it is currently subject, the American-Japanese alliance is likely to remain the cornerstone of Japanese foreign policy throughout the coming decade. For both countries, this alliance is of vital importance. Indeed, modern Japan has never had a relationship so significant, not merely in economic and military terms, but in political and cultural terms as well. It can also be assumed that Japan will seek a normalization of her relations with both the People's Republic of China and the Soviet Union, as noted earlier. Such a normalization, however, even if it occurs, is more likely to be a supplement to, rather than a substitute for, close Japanese-American ties. The prospects for truly close relations between Japan and the communist giants are dim. The great differences in stages of development, ideological-political systems, current cultural trends, and economic structures preclude a Japanese-Chinese or Japanese-Soviet alliance in the foreseeable future. At best, Japan can achieve a form of peaceful coexistence with these countries that permits improved economic and political interaction.

Thus, the prospects are for modifications of past foreign policies, but no sharp break with the traditions of the last twenty-five years. Japan will add to her economic role certain political and military increments in the years that lie immediately ahead, but she will not seek to play the role of a superpower—in Asia or elsewhere. Her dilemma, however, lies in the fact that whether she wills it or not, she is becoming an economic superpower, with enormous influence upon the policies of many nations and the lives of their peoples. How to mesh this fact, and its implications, with her relatively limited military capacity and her still low political profile constitutes the central problem for Japanese policy makers in the 1970s, and the approach taken to this problem will powerfully affect every nation in the Pacific-Asian region.

SELECTED BIBLIOGRAPHY

There is a wealth of primary and secondary source materials on Japanese foreign policy for the reader who can use the Japanese language. Memoirs of prominent statesmen are abundant; a number of documentary collections and good secondary works exist; and many of the Japanese Foreign Office Archives, having been microfilmed during the American occupation, are obtainable through the Library of Congress. To list even the most essential Japanese materials would be a lengthy task, and one not appropriate here. Fortunately, the reader of Japanese can refer to a number of sources for bibliographic assistance. We shall merely suggest some English-language materials, with emphasis upon more recent books.

Although English-language materials are still far too limited, the last fifteen years have seen an increasing number of worthy articles, monographs, and general studies, many of which deal in some fashion with Japanese foreign policy.

To start with the historical background of Japanese international relations, one might mention the older work of R. H. Akagi, *Japan's Foreign Relations, 1542–1936* (Argus, 1936); but the historical

writings of Sir George Sansom provide an excellent introduction to this subject as well as to other facets of traditional Japan: *Japan—A Short Cultural History* (New York: Appleton-Century-Crofts, 1943), *A History of Japan to 1334* (Stanford, Calif.: Stanford University Press 1958), *A History of Japan, 1334–1615* (Stanford, Calif.: Stanford University Press, 1960), and *The Western World and Japan* (New York: Alfred A. Knopf, 1950). See also Herschel Webb, *The Japanese Imperial Institution in the Tokugawa Period* (New York: Columbia University Press, 1968).

To these should be added C. R. Boxer's *Christian Century in Japan* (Berkeley: University of California Press, 1951) for a careful exposition of initial Western contacts.

For the modern period, a few general works include materials on foreign policy. One might select Hugh Borton's *Japan's Modern Century* (New York: Ronald Press Co., 1955) and Chitoshi Yanaga's *Japanese People and Politics* (New York: Wiley, 1956) as recent works of this type.

For those particularly interested in early Meiji period, we are fortunate in having the work of W. C. Beasley. His *Great Britain and the Opening of Japan, 1934–1858* (Luzac, 1951) was followed by *Select Documents on Japanese Foreign Policy, 1853–1868* (London: Oxford University Press, 1955). These serve as an admirable introduction to the problems of the early Meiji era, which began in 1867. The memoirs and accounts of Western diplomats and other residents are also of interest: E. M. Satow, *A Diplomat in Japan* (Philadelphia: J. B. Lippincott Co., 1921); Sir Rutherford Alcock, *The Capital of the Tycoon*, 2 vols. (London, 1963); J. H. Gubbins, *The Progress of Japan, 1853–1871* (London: Oxford University Press, 1911).

There are also a few monographs of special interest, mainly pertaining to the later Meiji period. Two of these are Marius B. Jansen, *The Japanese and the Chinese Revolutionary Movements, 1895–1915*, and Shumpei Okamoto, *The*

Japanese Oligarchy and the Russo-Japanese War (New York: Columbia University Press, 1970).

The Taisho period (1912–1926) is rather sparsely covered as yet. Masamichi Royama has written one work in English, *The Foreign Policy of Japan, 1914–1939* (Tokyo, 1941); the older work by T. Takeuchi, *War and Diplomacy in the Japanese Empire* (Garden City, N.Y.: Doubleday & Co., 1935), may still have some utility.

The books by A. M. Young, especially his *Japan in Recent Times, 1912–1926* (New York: William Morrow & Co., 1928), are of interest as contemporary accounts and the Young newspaper, the *Kobe* (later *Japan*) *Chronicle*, is a most important source for many events of the entire period between the mid-Meiji and prewar Showa eras.

For most readers, the Showa period is likely to be of greatest interest. For the militarist era of the 1930s, the most important materials are contained in two memoirs: the so-called *Harada-Saionji Memoirs* and the *Kido Diary;* neither of these has been published in English, but both are available at certain leading libraries in the United States in mimeographed form, in whole or in part.

Perhaps no single English source is as valuable as the voluminous *War Crimes Trial Documents,* running into thousands of pages, which were translated for the famous Tokyo trials. These also can be obtained; a complete set exists, for instance, at the University of California, Berkeley library.

Among existing Western memoirs, special mention should be made of J. C. Grew, *Ten Years in Japan* (New York: Simon & Schuster, 1944), and Sir R. Craigie, *Behind the Japanese Mask* (London: Hutchinson & Co., 1946). From the Japanese side, see Mamoru Shigemitsu, *Japan and Her Destiny* (New York: E. P. Dutton & Co., 1958).

We have a general account of this wartime period in F. C. Jones, *Japan's New Order in East Asia: Its Rise and Fall, 1937–1945* (London: Oxford University Press, 1954).

A growing number of monographs dealing with this general period are available. Yale Maxon explores the problems involved in formulating Japanese foreign policy in his *Control of Japanese Foreign Policy: A Study of Civil-Military Rivalry, 1930–1945* (Berkeley: University of California Press, 1957).

For other worthy studies, see Harry J. Benda, *The Crescent and the Rising Sun* (Institute of Pacific Relations, 1958); Robert Butow, *Japan's Decision to Surrender* (Stanford, Calif.: Stanford University Press, 1955), and *Tojo and the Coming of the War* (Stanford, Calif.: Stanford University Press, 1961); Willard H. Elsbree, *Japan's Role in Southeast Asian Nationalist Movements, 1940–1945* (Cambridge: Harvard University Press, 1953); James B. Crowley, *Japan's Quest for Autonomy* (Princeton: Princeton University Press, 1966); Ernst Preusseisen, *Germany and Japan: A Study in Totalitarian Diplomacy, 1933–1941* (The Hague, 1958); Sadako N. Ogata, *Defiance in Manchuria—The Making of Japanese Foreign Policy, 1931–1932* (Berkeley: University of California Press, 1954); and Paul Schroeder, *The Axis Alliance and Japanese-American Relations, 1941* (Ithaca, N.Y.: Cornell University Press, 1958).

Japanese accounts of the war are available in Saburo Hayashi, in collaboration with Alvin D. Cox, *Kogun: The Japanese Army in the Pacific War* (Marine Corps Association, 1959) and Nobutaka Ike (trans. and ed.), *Japan's Decision for War* (Stanford, Calif.: Stanford University Press, 1967); T. Kase, *Journey to the Missouri* (New Haven: Yale University Press, 1950); M. Kato, *The Lost War* (New York: Alfred A. Knopf, 1946); and Mamoru Shigemitsu, *Japan and Her Destiny* (New York: E. P. Dutton, 1958).

Various aspects of the postwar period are covered in certain general books: Ardath Burks, *Government in Japan* (New York: Praeger, 1961); Allan B. Cole, *Japanese Society and Politics* (Boston, 1956); Esler Dening, *Japan* (New York: Praeger, 1961); Nobutaka Ike, "Japan," in *Major Governments of Asia,* ed. George

Kahin (Ithaca, N.Y.: Cornell University Press, 1958); Kazuo Kawai, *Japan's American Interlude* (Chicago: University of Chicago Press, 1960); Ivan Morris, *Nationalism and the Right Wing in Japan* (London: Oxford University Press, 1960); and Harold Quigley and John Turner, *The New Japan: Government and Politics* (Minneapolis: University of Minnesota Press, 1956). See also *Parties and Politics in Contemporary Japan* by Robert A. Scalapino and Junnosuke Masumi (Berkeley: University of California Press, 1962).

In his book *The Japanese People and Foreign Policy* (Berkeley: University of California Press, 1962), Douglas Mendel, Jr., present an important collection of public opinion polls pertaining to foreign policy issues.

Naturally, the American reader will tend to have a special interest in American-Japanese relations. A substantial number of books have been written on this subject. Among the older works, those of Payson J. Treat are well known: *Japan and the United States*, rev. ed. (Stanford, Calif.: Stanford University Press, 1928), and *Diplomatic Relations between the United States and Japan*, 3 vols. (Stanford, Calif.: Stanford University Press, 1932, 1938). See also Foster Rhea Dulles, *Forty Years of American-Japanese Relations* (New York: Appleton-Century-Crofts, 1937).

A broad cultural account is to be found in T. Dennett, *Americans in Eastern Asia* (New York: Macmillan Co., 1922). More recently, such an approach has been effectively used by Robert Schwantes in his *Japanese and Americans: A Century of Cultural Relations* (New York: Harper & Row, 1955).

For current political relations, the reader can refer to E. O. Reischauer, *The United States and Japan*, rev. ed. (Cambridge: Harvard University Press, 1957); Robert A. Scalapino, "The United States and Japan," in *The United States and the Far East*, ed. Willard L. Thorp, rev. ed. (Englewood Cliffs, N.J.: Prentice-Hall, Spectrum Books, American Assembly Series, 1962), and *United States Foreign Policy: Asia,* a study prepared for the United States Senate Committee on Foreign Relations (Washington, D.C.: Government Printing Office, 1959); Herbert Passin (ed.), *The United States and Japan* (Englewood Cliffs, N.J.: Prentice-Hall, Spectrum Books, American Assembly Series, 1966), Donald C. Hellman, *Japanese Domestic Politics and Foreign Policy* (Berkeley: University of California Press, 1969); Gerald L. Curtis (ed.), *Japanese-American Relations in the 1970's* (Washington, D.C.: American Assembly, 1970); Herman Kahn, *The Emerging Japanese Superstate: Challenge and Response* (Englewood Cliffs, N.J.: Prentice-Hall, 1970); Martin E. Weinstein, *Japan's Postwar Defense Policy, 1947–1968* (New York: Columbia University Press, 1970).

Official publications from the U.S. State Department, such as the series *Foreign Relations of the United States and Japan,* contain useful major documents. See also various congressional hearings, especially those of the Senate Committee on Foreign Relations, *United States Security Agreements and Commitments Abroad—Japan and Okinawa,* 91st Congress, 2d sess., on January 26–29, 1970, pt. 5.

In addition, there are a number of more specialized accounts, limited in scope or time. Only three will be mentioned here: H. L. Stimson, *The Far Eastern Crisis* (New York: Harper & Row, 1936); Herbert Feis, *The Road to Pearl Harber* (Princeton: Princeton University Press, 1950); and Ray W. Curry, *Woodrow Wilson and Far Eastern Policy* (Twayne, 1957).

No serious study of Japanese foreign policy should be undertaken, of course, without reference to the periodical literature. Among the English-language journals, those carrying articles of significance at rather regular intervals include *Contemporary Japan, Japan Quarterly* (formerly *Far Eastern Quarterly*), *Foreign Affairs, Pacific Affairs,* and *Asian Survey* (formerly *Far Eastern Survey*).

Some reference should also be made to the increasing number of English-language materials being published by the

Japanese government, including valuable items, pertaining to foreign policy problems and policies, from the Ministry of Finance, the Ministry of Trade and Commerce, and the Foreign Office. In reference to contemporary issues, it will be helpful to consult the translations of the vernacular press and of selected articles from Japanese vernacular magazines which are put out by the American embassy, if one can obtain access to these.

Such newspapers as the *Japan Times* (formerly *Nippon Times*), the *Osaka Mainichi* (English-language edition), and the *Asahi Evening News* should also be examined. Naturally, many of the above materials will contain further leads and much fuller biographies.

Chapter Nine

INDIA'S FOREIGN POLICY

RICHARD L. PARK

India's policy of nonalignment, and the conciliatory diplomacy advocated by the late Prime Minister Jawaharlal Nehru, have combined to elevate the Republic of India to a major role in the conduct of world affairs, despite its relatively low rank on the ladder of major powers. This remarkable achievement of international eminence, reduced in stature only in part by recent conflicts with China (1962) and Pakistan (1965 and 1971), involved skillful strategy and a shrewd reading of current events. History also helped to shape the circumstances.

The emergence of India as an independent state in 1947, and the coming to power of the Chinese Communists two years later, represent the consequences of two major forces in the social and political revolutions that have been waged in Asia throughout the present century. The results of the competition between a liberal, democratic Republic of India and a communist People's Republic of China are recognized as being of critical importance to the ultimate success or failure in the spread of the communist movement throughout the world. More than half the people on earth are encompassed in the great arc of nations from Japan and Korea in eastern Asia westward to Pakistan and the Middle East. What happens in India and in China, and between them, will affect the whole of Asia. For the noncommunist as well as the communist worlds, what comes of the Indian experiment with democratic government will not be of immediate significance only; it may well have repercussions in every other part of the globe. From this point of view, the stability of India's domestic politics, her effectiveness in developing her economy, and her ability to solve her social problems would seem to outweigh, by far, India's external influence on contemporary world affairs.

The leaders of India view their role in international politics from a different perspective. They place special emphasis on the fact that the whole of Asia, and increasingly the Middle East and Africa as well, at last are escaping from the dominance and imposed tutelage of Western imperial power. With freedom attained, the next objective is to raise living standards appreciably and to revitalize old civilizations with the best of modern technology and the most far-reaching of social reforms. The communist issue, according to leaders in the highest political circles in India, cannot be allowed to obscure the fact that internal national development must take priority over external involvement, and for reasons of domestic rather than ideological or international concern. World communism and Asian nationalism have grown up together and have come to critical junctures calling for commitment and decision at about the same time, but for India, at least, foreign policy must be exercised in the immediate interests of India, and not in accordance with the wishes and interests of other world powers. India believes that her own national interests are best served by creating conditions of peace, encouraging cultural and economic cooperation on an unrestricted international scale, and fostering conditions favorable to political coexistence between competing forms of government. Under these circumstances, it is felt India might enjoy an atmosphere conducive to the development of her own material and human resources. In this view, domestic and foreign policies necessarily interlink; foreign policy is a safeguard for the national interest.

The failure of India's effort to reach an understanding with China, and the continuation of heated and sometimes violent relations with Pakistan over Kashmir and related boundary issues, have compelled India to modify her foreign policy and her defense arrangements. The commitment to nonalignment nevertheless remains the backbone of India's posture in international politics.

To understand the dynamics of India's foreign policy, it is advisable to look with some care at the historical factors that have influenced her outlook on the world community, and to examine India's pattern of domestic problems and her plans for their solution, out of which stem policies for external affairs.

THE NATIONAL BACKGROUND

Political History

Any full-scale inquiry into Indian foreign policy would lead one to range widely through history to identify the infinite variety of influences which flowed between India and her neighbors and which characterized the early relations among the peoples of Asia. The relative isolation of segments of the region during the past few centuries was, in large part, the result of the parceling out of spheres of influence between the several Western imperial powers. But cultural memories are lasting. Although India is a young nation, its civilization is ancient. Contemporary leaders are mindful of past greatness at home and abroad, and are unwilling to build toward anything less than a new image of greatness that will efface the memories of subordination during centuries of Western dominance.

The cultural vehicles of the Hindu and Buddhist ways of life carried Indian philosophy, art, and literature throughout Asia. No major part of that continent was untouched by Buddhism, which arose in India but flourished on its borders and beyond. Pilgrims from the Buddhist world were drawn back to India, the birthplace of Gautama Buddha, bringing with them new ideas and taking back to their own countries diaries of their observations in the holy land. Through this interchange of culture and faith, ties were made that centuries of neglect could not entirely break.

From the north and west came the Islamic invasions which culminated in the Mogul empire, spendidly exemplified by the rule of the Emperor Akbar. Akbar, like the Hindu-Buddhist Asoka long before him, is an Indian hero, remembered for combining compassion with strength, and honor with efficiency—terms now reserved for modern leaders such as Mahatma Gandhi and Jawaharlal Nehru. Akbar represents Islam and the tie of India to the cultural traditions of the Middle East.

Much later, particularly after the seventeenth century, when European powers battled for trading rights in the Indian subcontinent, Western and Indian ideas and institutions met, clashed, and in part coalesced in the creation of a pattern of political and social doctrine and forms of social organization that have persisted to a remarkable extent, and are clearly represented in the constitution of the Republic of India.

Our concern must be directed toward more recent history, to the direct line of development of independent India's foreign policy. In concentrating on these latter years, however, it would be well to remember that India's leaders keep at least one eye reserved for 5,000 years of history, and not a few of their contemporary decisions are made with due regard for this background of experience.

By the middle of the nineteenth century, India had become an administrative and political unity. Between 1600, when Elizabeth I chartered the British East India Company for trading rights in the East, and about 1858, most of the lands of the Indian subcontinent were brought under British administration and control. The rapid decline of the Mogul empire in the eighteenth century, plus the skill of the British in administration and in warfare, had led to the gradual absorption and political control of local Indian rulers' lands. This process involved, first, revenue collecting and imposition of law and order to assure trading rights, and, then, possession itself, for the ultimate assurance of commercial security that such political control allows.

India had never before had an opportunity to draw together the many cultural strands that formed the basis of its unique community. In the Sanskritic tradition and in Indian philosophy, there were ties that for millennia had given a sense of unity to the many Hindu peoples who inhabited the larger part of the subcontinent. But diversity of expression —in language, art, literature, religious belief, and intensity of loyalty—was the rule rather than the exception before the nineteenth century and the age of British dominance. The institutions of caste and the joint family, cemented by local symbols of loyalty and social custom, contributed to the patchwork quilt of cultures on the subcontinent—a condition, incidentally, which continues to divide the Indian people into competing regional groups.

British administration, to be effective and efficient, had to be tightly organized and centralized. Thus the country was divided and subdivided, not always rationally or in accordance with an integrated plan, but in any event in line with considerations that would bolster imperial British control. The objective was to organize an administrative state: one where revenues could be collected regularly and sufficiently; where a few top British political officers, and a small corps of Indian civil-service members, could funnel orders from the top of the hierarchy to the grass roots, and conversely, where local sentiments could be channeled upward; where law and order—and proximate justice—could be enforced; and where British ideas about the ultimate destiny of the Indian people could be carried forward by the Indians by means of education, imitation of colonial behavior, and experience in the use of Western social and political institutions.

The year 1858 was a turning point in Indian history. The year before, a mutiny, now often called the First War of Indian Independence, had broken out in several parts of northern India. The ostensible objective of the mutiny was to restore the Mogul emperor to his throne in Delhi. Underneath, however, were a number of grievances against the East India Company's rule, grievances based on its failure to give adequate attention to the social and economic needs of the people. Agreements with local rulers had been set aside, often without consultation, and, in general, the social well-being of the population was subordinated to the personal and economic interests of the rulers themselves. Often ignorant of local customs, and sometimes oblivious to the social consequences of enforced rule and regulations, the East India Company was suddenly confronted with crises on many fronts that led to outright revolt against the company's

power. London's response to the situation was to give control of India to the British crown, and for Parliament to assume the supervisory responsibilities for the conduct of state affairs.

Nationalism

From 1858 to 1947, authoritarian British rule in India conceded gradually to the liberal British view that a people should be trained to govern themselves, at least in local affairs. Indian nationalist opinion developed with the view that a people *must* be allowed to govern themselves. It was perhaps inevitable that the growth of Indian nationalism would be encouraged by the liberal British tradition that dominated the Indian educational system from the middle of the nineteenth century.

Indian nationalism commenced more as a movement for social and religious reform than as a political and economic movement. Faced with the facts of an earlier Muslim domination of a basically Hindu society, and then with the rapid takeover of Mogul reins by the British, nineteenth-century Indian leaders were led to question the inherent strength of Hindu social institutions. Men such as Raja Rammohan Roy, often called the "father of Indian nationalism," vigorously fought, in the early nineteenth century, for a liberalization of Hindu social institutions, and for English education so that the new ideas of Europe might be brought to bear on the reform of Indian life. Rammohan Roy founded the *Brahmo Samaj*, in 1828, as an institutionalized means for giving opportunities to liberal Indians to make over Hindu society along more enlightened lines. Other reformers, such as Dayananda Saraswati, founder of the *Arya Samaj*, urged a return to the purer—less historically and socially overladen—philosophy of the ancient Vedic age, unhindered by caste divisions, as his more indigenous response to the impact of the West. Late-nineteenth-century developments along the same general lines included the work of Annie Besant of the Theosophical Society and Swami Vivekananda of the Ramakrishna Mission.

But poverty, illiteracy, and disease, deep-rooted and widespread, were the facts of Indian life that served as the mainsprings for a vigorous nationalism and, later, for the insistent demand for freedom from British rule. Centralized imperial administration provided the means for improving transportation and communication, broadening markets for industry and agriculture, and encouraging modern finance and commerce. In the process, British capital, more than Indian, reaped the profits, and it was British industry and commerce that benefited more by the construction of a colonial economy in which India provided the raw materials for a profitable European industry. And in the Indian backwaters, the relatively self-sufficient village economy broke down as middle-scale industrialization came to India. No longer could village craftsmen hope to compete with the factories of the towns and cities. The tightly woven fabric of Indian village society, with its ancient system of interrelated economic functions and social services, was struck a heavy blow. The economy and the related aspects of the society grew in a lopsided manner. The tiny fraction that was urban India grew further apart from the four-fifths that was village India. Education, better health, and the benefits of modern technology hardly touched the countryside; indeed, even in the towns and cities the cleavages between the well-off and the down-and-out were all too evident.

Indian National Congress

It was under these conditions of dominance by British power, of internal division between the several layers of Indian society, of separatist tendencies between Hindu and Muslim and between linguistic regions, plus a pervasive stagnation in the culture and in the general economy, that the Indian National Congress was founded in 1885. The Congress, destined to be the vehicle of the Indian nationalist movement and the organization in which the main lines of independent India's foreign policy would be tested and formed, was a moderate body with modest objectives in the years preceding World War I. Congress leaders of those days, such as Pherozeshah Mehta, Surendranath Banerjea, and G. K. Gokhale, were mainly concerned with increasing Indian membership in the Indian Civil Service, extending the benefits of higher education, and arguing a persuasive case to the Parliament and people of Great Britain for a greater measure of Indian participation in running the affairs of India. In this effort, the Congress was encouraged by liberal British leaders in both Great Britain and India. It was the belief of those concerned with this early phase of nationalist expression that, with experience and time, the good sense of the British would recognize the obvious need for a loosening of British control over Indian affairs. Such optimism proved unwarranted, and a vigorous but uniquely nonviolent nationalist movement, led by Mohandas K. Gandhi from 1919 onward, was the result. The National Congress-backed nationalist movement expanded its program of action to the masses of the Indian people, pressing harder and harder for the concessions from their rulers that ultimately led to an independent India in 1947.

As freedom came near, however, the bitter feeling between the Hindu and Muslim communities grew more intense. The common nationalist cause against an alien ruler broke down and, after 1940, a large proportion of the Muslims demanded a separate state, Pakistan, in which to develop a nation based on Islamic brotherhood. Pakistan was founded in 1947, after widespread rioting, terrible bloodshed, and the fearful migration of millions of people had forced the issue. Needless to say, the circumstances of partition contributed much to the mutual fear and enmity that has colored relations between Pakistan and India ever since.

This brief survey of the Indian nationalist movement and of the general conditions of nineteenth- and twentieth-century India is intended to convey one important lesson in the better understanding of India's view of world affairs: Indians have been concerned—one might almost say obsessed—during the past half-century with the imperial or colonial question. Almost everything else in world history has been read in terms of the colonial theme, including the communal rivalry between Muslims and Hindus, which is felt to be the product of a British policy of "divide and rule." It is understandable that leaders like Nehru, who fought for independence for over a quarter-century, would not easily forget their experiences in earlier years. As a colony, India considered herself isolated from active participation in world affairs, and yet subject to the forces of world politics because she was bound to the decisions of Great Britain. In particular, India resented its involuntary, if legal, involvement in two world wars. This involuntary alignment with Great Britain and its allies in times of war and peace undoubtedly contributed to India's decision to develop its

foreign policy along lines of nonalignment with blocs of power, especially with the Western, or free-world, alignment with which she had been all too familiar.

Economic Geography

However internationally isolated, in a formal sense, the Indian National Congress may have been in the years before independence, Indian leaders certainly were alert to the geographical, economic, and political facts of Indian life which formed the conditions of any Indian foreign policy, even as interpreted by Great Britain.

First, India was recognized as being strategically located in the west of Asia: her peninsula stretches across the main lines of sea and air communications from west to east, and her northern, mountainous boundaries touch important centers of the Middle East, central Asia, and the Far East. India's near neighbors include several of the most powerful nations in the world—particularly the Soviet Union and China—but also Burma, Indonesia, and the other countries of Southeast Asia with which India feels she has much in common. India has been relatively isolated, historically, by mountains to the north and seas on her peninsular sides; nevertheless, it has been recognized that India's geographic location, in the age of air travel, involves a natural intercourse with the many economic, political, and cultural forces that cross or abut on its territory. Not only is protection from invasion the crucial question; also of importance is the skill with which India may take advantage of interrelations with the many who come her way.

Economically, India has been and remains a country poor in the level of its exploited natural resources, in the rate of its industrial and agricultural development, and in the prospect for rapid rises in its standards of living. These facts were early recognized by the Indian National Congress. One of the great urges of the nationalist movement was the hope that, with greater freedom to plan and legislate, adequate steps might be taken to improve the economic lot of the Indian people. Nationalist thinking on foreign affairs was never far removed from the economic implications of whatever steps might be taken abroad. And the first major step toward sound economic development was the attainment of the political freedom which would permit national economic planning.

Competing Ideologies

The geographic and economic facts affecting India's international position discussed above, however, are of relatively minor significance to National Congress leaders when these facts are compared with the influence of political ideas. The first major ideological influence was that of liberalism; the second, closely following on the first in historical sequence, was socialism.

The farthest-reaching legacy of the period of British rule in India was the infusion of a liberal philosophy of government in the mental frame of India's educated hierarchy of leadership. The process by which this intermixture of ideas and institutions took place over the past 150 years is, in large part, the total social history of India of the period. Education in English from the mid-nineteenth century on, both at the secondary and higher educational levels, brought to Indian students the story of western European political achievement which assumed that law, politics, and civil and military administration would be subject to the responsible control of

the people. The connection between a vital liberal democracy and rapid economic and social development was not lost on those Indians who examined European experience. Moreover, significant numbers of Indian students took their higher degrees in London, or at Oxford or Cambridge, and a few on the continent, thus pouring back into Indian society leaders fully on a par, intellectually, with their European classmates.

As the British administrators of India faced novel problems for which no ready indigenous solution seemed present, it was only natural that they look to British experience for ideas and institutions applicable in India. Indian judges and lawyers, accountants and teachers, agricultural economists and engineers, editors and reporters, and, of course, politicians as well, grew up in an institutionalized atmosphere that was reflective of the British liberal view of society's proper organization. Although this process of macrocosmic acculturation was largely an urban phenomenon and affected only a small segment of India's society, the influence was nevertheless great, for it touched the lives of the greater part of India's educated ruling classes. By the 1920s, when the Indian National Congress under Gandhi opened its mass campaign for political freedom, liberalism was well established as the common core of political agreement concerning the kind of government and the kind of society that India's leaders wished to develop under their own guidance. In fact, one of the most powerful weapons that leaders of the National Congress used against the British was the assertion that Great Britain was denying to the Indian people the goals of liberal democracy extolled so vociferously in London.

The second major ideological influence in twentieth-century India has been socialism. For many, socialism was seen as a combination of utopian propositions and Fabian interpretations of social democracy. These ideas equated rather easily with the main tenets of liberalism as they had been developed in India. For others, Marxism and Marxian socialism were more influential, although organized political parties favoring Marxian socialism did not gain prominence until the 1930s. Most Indian intellectuals, and many politicians, were convinced that India's economic and social conditions required active, regularized legislative and administrative direction if needed social and economic changes were to come about. The Russian Revolution was closely followed by Indian leaders, since it was felt that here was an experiment in a social and economic situation not unlike that of India. The fact that the Soviet Union and spokesmen for the Comintern endorsed India's aspirations for independence and condemned British imperial power, at a time when others were silent, has not been forgotten. At least a portion of the sympathetic hearing now given to Soviet views on world affairs may be traced to the Communists' early support of Indian nationalism.

Ideologically, then, India's leaders had grown accustomed, by the mid-1920s, to the liberal democracy of western Europe, combined with an infusion of socialist solutions to economic problems, and they were fully committed to the perpetuation of such a mixed form of government in an independent India. This was true even though it was well understood by these leaders that some of the principles of liberal democracy, when applied in India, would conflict with the localized groups of village India, which relied more on caste or class, and less on the individual, for the exercise of political responsibilities.

Foreign Policy in the Making

The Indian National Congress did not, of course, have a foreign policy, in any formal sense, until it became the body conducting the government of the Republic of India. But as a strategy in the nationalist movement, the Congress adopted a policy of expressing itself by resolutions on foreign affairs at its annual sessions, or through statements by its officers at other times. The same policy was adopted for matters of domestic concern. This process was called "parallel government": the Congress, in this case, speaking for the Indian people who were unable to speak effectively through British-Indian organs of government.

By the mid-1920s, the National Congress turned its attention more regularly to international politics. The new emphasis arose partially as a consequence of India's failure to secure a greater measure of freedom following the end of World War I, but perhaps more so because of the insistence of a young Congressman from the United Provinces, son of a then-prominent Congress leader, Motilal Nehru.

Jawaharlal Nehru, a London-trained lawyer educated at Harrow and Cambridge, began to make his influence felt in circles of the National Congress by the mid-1920s. Although he was primarily interested in domestic politics, his special contribution to the nationalist movement was the education of several generations of Indians in the facts of international life. Nehru believed that India was inevitably to play an important role in international affairs, and that the Indian National Congress had the responsibility of preparing the people for the years ahead. An examination of the resolutions of the Congress from

1926 to 1947 reveals an acute awareness of the dangers in the growth of fascism, a sympathetic approach to the aspirations of the Soviet Union, a consistent criticism of the continuation or expansion of Western imperial power anywhere in the world, and a sensitive exposure of all forms of racial, social, and economic discrimination. Such an examination of the record reveals the growth of the view that international disputes require peaceful means of solution, and that peaceful means for resolving disputes would be encouraged by a world organized to enforce the exclusive use of such means. The influence of Gandhi in the growth of this policy of nonviolent methods in international affairs is obvious. Jawaharlal Nehru, as general secretary of the Indian National Congress, reestablished, in 1936, a Foreign Department (originally formed in 1925) to study world affairs and to disseminate literature on the subject throughout India. Although it is unfair to credit Prime Minister Nehru for the whole construction of India's foreign policy, it can be said that he was the architect and the guide who prepared the way, from 1926, for policies that, by 1947, were acceptable to and taken for granted by the vast majority of the citizens of India.

THE POLICY-MAKING PROCESS

For the personal and historical reasons outlined above, Jawaharlal Nehru was able to impress his personal stamp on the foreign policy of India. One measure of Mr. Nehru's lasting influence on foreign policy has been the pledge made by his successors, the late Lal Bahadur Shastri and Mrs. Indira Gandhi, to continue the policies he shaped. As a politically powerful, highly intelligent nationalist leader with a deep concern for world affairs, Mr. Nehru articulated a policy based on his view of the present and future, bearing in mind the strengths and weaknesses of his country and people, and that policy was affirmed by all but rather small sectors of Indian political opinion. After the Sino-Indian dispute over the Himalayan border in 1962, there was a sharp increase in public criticism of foreign policy, criticism which brought into focus the bureaucratic and legislative apparatus that supports the voice of the prime minister on matters of foreign policy.

Governmental Agencies

The executive authority. India's constitution places formal executive responsibility with the president of the republic. But, like Great Britain's queen, the president acts on the advice of his Council of Ministers. The cabinet, which does not necessarily include all ministers, is composed of senior ministers nominated by the prime minister and appointed by the president, who then act with collective responsibility to Parliament.

From 1947 to 1964, India had one prime minister, Jawaharlal Nehru, who continuously held the portfolio for external affairs as well. Since Nehru's Congress party enjoyed a substantial majority in every session of Parliament over that period, continuity in foreign policy was sustained to the degree that Nehru wished to sustain it. Although, as minister of external affairs, Mr. Nehru could and did take counsel with his colleagues in the cabinet, as prime minister he held such broad responsibility for the domestic and external well-being of his country that explanations, rather than questions, appear to have been his normal presentations to the cabinet on foreign matters. The holding of the two portfolios by a man of such experience—one, moreover, who was held in near-reverence by the bulk of his people—combined with the Congress party's control of a substantial majority in Parliament, gave Mr. Nehru what amounted to a free hand in constructing and executing India's foreign policy. Following Mr. Nehru's death in 1964, the new prime minister, Lal Bahadur Shastri, selected Sardar Swaran Singh to head the Ministry of External Affairs. M. C. Chagla and then Dinesh Singh led the ministry during Mrs. Indira Gandhi's first term starting in 1966, but Sardar Swaran Singh was returned to the post after Mrs. Gandhi's sweeping victory in 1971.

The Ministry of External Affairs is a large and professionally staffed organization. A minister of state assists the minister of external affairs both in the ministry and in Parliament. A secretary general presides over much of the general administration, and a bank of senior secretaries and their many assistants compose the working staff of the ministry. It is from the "country desks," from the research branches, and from the technical staffs that analytical materials flow to the minister, giving him the raw materials and statements of alternative policies on which foreign policy is based.

The secretary general supervises the administration of the ministry, aided by a Commonwealth secretary for British Commonwealth matters; a special secretary for managing the finances, personnel, communications, supplies, and records; and a foreign secretary to cover the world other than the Commonwealth, as well as protocol, historical research, and related subjects.

The Foreign Service. Over 7,000 staff members man the Ministry of External Affairs and its offices abroad. Personnel recruited into the foreign service—now scattered throughout the world in the high commissions and commissions within the Commonwealth of Nations; in the embassies, legations, consulates-general, and consulates; and in the United Nations and international missions elsewhere—are carefully selected by competitive examination and thoroughly trained for their positions. At the highest levels—ambassadors and high commissioners—what might be called "political appointments" sometimes occur. But the tradition is to use the professional service to the maximum.

The foreign service, somewhat similar to its counterpart in Great Britain, is an elite service, admission to which is much sought after by India's most able university graduates. The pressure to expand India's external representation rapidly was very great after 1947, but trained personnel were in short supply. Now the service is nearly stabilized, and its standards have increased year by year. Protected from personal criticism by the restraints of responsible ministers, the foreign service has been able to give an even greater maturity to India's assessment of the facts of international affairs. More adequate linguistic skills, an improvement in the analysis of intelligence, and much greater information on world situations provide the Ministry of External Affairs with substantial resources to use in pursuing the global implications of India's foreign policy.

Parliament. Parliament is not concerned with the day-to-day making or execution of foreign policy. But debates in the *Lok Sabha* (House of the People) or the *Rajya Sabha* (Council of State)—initiated by the prime minister or the minister of external affairs, or by questions raised during the question period, or following the president's addresses opening Parliament or concerning the budget—give several opportunities for members to influence policy. Since the prime minister necessarily is concerned daily with foreign affairs, reports tend to be made to Parliament regularly, often, and in detail. Seldom is Parliament in doubt about the government's views. But Parliament does not have a standing committee on foreign affairs. This prerogative remains with another organ of Parliament, the cabinet, and, of course, with the minister of external affairs and the prime minister.

It should not be assumed, however, that members of Parliament are not an integral part of the process of making foreign policy. To the contrary, articulate members of the Opposition, including several members of the Communist party of India, as well as Congress party members who disagree with accepted policy, often are heard, their words recorded, and the debate disseminated widely throughout the country in official records and in the press. Spokesmen in Parliament help to identify the controversial issues for the public. Public opinion, in turn, acts as a restraint upon the Congress party's parliamentary majority. Members of Parliament have become far more vocal in their criticism of government policy since India's confrontation with China in 1962.

Nongovernmental Agencies

Political Parties. The Congress party, through its annual sessions (usually held in December), through its policy-suggesting organ—the Working Committee—and through the party's administrative secretariat—the All-India Congress Committee—regularly discusses foreign policy and proposes policy changes to the parliamentary Congress party. The prime minister, as a prominent leader of the party, remains in close communication with party headquarters and party leaders, on foreign as well as on domestic matters. The considered opinion of the Congress party today is likely to be official policy tomorrow.

As we have already mentioned, certain respected leaders from other parties, or from among the independents, can be influential, in Parliament or from the public platform, on matters relating to foreign affairs—but only to the extent that their personal standing is high in the country. For example, the various socialist parties have not been effective critics of foreign policy. But a socialist leader of proven ability can personally have significant impact, as can a former socialist like Jayaprakash Narayan, who holds no political office at all. The Communists, too, are not backward in voicing opposition to given policies. The pro-Peking and pro-Moscow Communist parties both express opinions on foreign affairs, both in and out of Parliament.

But since the Congress party rules India more or less as if India were, in fact, a one-party state, debate *within* the Congress party is the most critical locus of political controversy on domestic and world affairs. The Congress party is not inclined, substantively and for good political reasons, to deny the prime minister's conclusions if a positive stand is taken and support is requested. The exceptional cases tend to be issues involving China or Pakistan, where debate is less disciplined.

Interest Groups. For the most part, interest groups do not have much influence in shaping India's foreign policy. Tradition excludes them from indirect involvement as informal advisers, and the law bars them from direct pressures. Such groups do, of course, have spokesmen in Parliament; they publish their views; they influence individuals. But groups such as the trade unions, professional societies, commercial, financial, and industrial organizations, and caste lobbies have a most limited scope of influence. To the extent that these groups find a congenial home in a political party, their interest can be more effectively passed on through recognized political channels.

The Indian Council of World Affairs, at its Sapru House headquarters in New Delhi and in its many branches throughout the country, as well as in its publications, can be influential. However, the council has tended to be tender in its criticism of established policy in foreign affairs.

Media of Mass Communications and Public Opinion. World news is given extended and generally fair treatment in the English-language newspapers, in the best of the Indian-language newspapers, and in the thousands of weeklies, fortnightlies, and monthlies published in all parts of the country. Indian newspapers are inclined to carry very long articles and informative editorials, which may run two full columns, about crucial foreign affairs questions. These publications also make suggestions intended to influence foreign policy in their editorials. Newspapers of the quality of the *Hindu* (Madras), the *Times of India* (Bombay and New Delhi), the *Hindustan Times* (New Delhi), and the *Statesman* (Calcutta and New Delhi) are read meticulously by officers in the Ministry of External Affairs. Party organs such as *Vigil* and the *Organiser*, or papers of opinion like *Thought* (Delhi), *Economic and Political Weekly* (Bombay), *Seminar* (Delhi), and *Quest* (Bombay), to name a few of the special publications, help to shape opinion indirectly. Television is not yet an important means of communication in India, and the All-India Radio is nationalized and without significant editorial influence on foreign policy.

These stimuli of public opinion, plus books and pamphlets, appear to have made an impact on the urban intelligentsia. But India is 70 percent illiterate, and much of the country is out of the range of radios that function. Thus, public opinion, even at best, is expressed only by relatively few people, and these largely in urban centers.

On the whole, the Indian press supports the government's conclusions on foreign affairs, and such criticism as does appear is usually minor. The exceptions have involved the Sino-Indian disputes and the old Kashmir question. In these two cases, India's territorial integrity is at stake, and critics, including many journalists and editors, have been outspoken—and perhaps, thereby, somewhat influential.

India is not a country of opinion pollsters. However, the Indian Institute of Public Opinion (New Delhi) has produced two serial publications, one on public issues and one on economic matters (using George Gallup's methods), which supply useful material on public attitudes.

THE SUBSTANCE OF FOREIGN POLICY

The remarkable consistency in public expressions of India's foreign policy can, as we have already noted, be traced to the continuity of leadership held by Jawaharlal Nehru and the Congress party from 1947 to 1964.

The trying circumstances of India's political and economic life have induced wide public support for the government of India's stand on world affairs, particularly since this stand has resulted in the growth of India's prestige. Although the cases of Kashmir, Korea, Suez, Hungary, China, and East Pakistan (1971) have produced bends and kinks in the main lines of foreign policy, India's principal international objectives and her diplomatic strategy have not been changed fundamentally since independence.

On September 26, 1946, Mr. Nehru, as the leader of the Interim Government, issued the following statement on foreign policy—a statement that would be applicable today:

In the sphere of foreign affairs India will follow an independent policy, keeping away from the power politics of groups aligned one against another. She will uphold the principles of freedom for dependent peoples and will oppose racial discrimination wherever it may occur. She will work with other peace-loving nations for international cooperation and goodwill without exploitation of one nation by another.

It is necessary that, with the attainment of her full international status, India should establish contact with all the great nations of the world and that her relations with neighboring countries in Asia should become still closer. . . .

Towards the United Nations Organization India's attitude is that of wholehearted cooperation and unreserved adherence, in both spirit and letter, to the Charter governing it. To that end, India will participate fully in its varied activities and endeavor to play that role in its Councils to which her geographical position, population and contribution toward peaceful progress entitle her. In particular, the Indian delegate will make it clear that India stands for the independence of all colonial and dependent people and their full right to self-determination.[1]

[1] Statement issued at a press conference in New Delhi on September 26, 1946, and published in *Indian Information* (New Delhi: Government of India Information Bureau), October 15, 1946.

One finds in this statement a number of principles that highlight the main strands of India's foreign policy:

1. the independence in outlook of a people who had been dominated for too long;
2. the fear that involvement in the affairs of others would restrict India's ability to construct a new and better social and economic order for itself;
3. the determination to assist others in attaining the political freedom for which India fought for so many years;
4. the hatred of second- and third-class citizenship, and particularly of an inferior status awarded because of race;
5. the confidence in cooperation and mutual goodwill, exemplified by the United Nations; and
6. the urge for international contacts throughout the world, but with special attention given to neighboring countries in Asia.

Theory in Practice

In practice, the principles enumerated above have made it relatively easy to anticipate the government of India's response to issues as they have arisen in world politics.

Nonalignment. The policy of nonalignment (or of "neutralism," as some prefer to call it) assured that India would not participate in the Southeast Asia Treaty Organization (SEATO) or the Baghdad Pact (later CENTO). What was (and is) less well known is that India, in order to help create "conditions of peace," would exercise its influence to lessen the effectiveness and the range of membership in such mutual defense arrangements, particularly those which, like SEATO and CENTO, impinge on the region of southern Asia. To the extent possible, it appears that India has advised its diplomats to endorse nonmilitary, peaceful solutions, and to bring into question military solutions. The exceptions, perhaps, are those military agreements (e.g., the North Atlantic Treaty or the Warsaw Pact) that do not relate directly to Asian concerns and are geographically distant from India.

During the period of negotiations leading to the signing of the Mutual Defense Assistance Agreement between the United States and Pakistan on May 19, 1954, India pushed its nonalignment policy one step further, in this case arguing that a military agreement entered into by Pakistan—a country whose eastern and western sectors enclose India like bookends—inevitably involved India in dangerous military consequences not of India's choosing and without mutual consent. In Parliament, Mr. Nehru explained why he felt it necessary to object to Pakistan's decision to sign such an agreement, even though Pakistan, a sovereign state, claimed that the matter was none of India's business:

Of course, they are a free country; I cannot prevent them. But if something affects Asia, India especially, and if something, in our opinion, is a reversal of history after hundreds of years, are we to remain silent? We have thought in terms of freeing our countries, and one of the symbols of freedom has been the withdrawal of foreign armed forces. I say the return of any armed forces from any European or American country is a reversal of the history of the countries of Asia, whatever the motive. . . .

I am not prepared to express my opinion except in the most philosophic manner about the distant problems of Europe. India has not the slightest desire to impose its views or wishes on any other country. But because in Asia we have passed through similar processes of history in the last two hundred years or so, and thus can understand each other a little better, it is likely that I am in tune with some of my neighbor countries when I speak. If the great powers think that the problems of Asia can be solved minus

Asia or minus the views of Asian countries, then it does seem to be rather odd.[2]

Pakistan did sign the agreement, of course, and India's earlier differences with Pakistan, especially those over Kashmir, were hardened. Whether the defense agreement was wise, or not, depends on one's point of view. But from the perspective of India's foreign policy and India's sense of the situation in Asia, an American offer of a similar defense arrangement with India to parallel the Pakistan arrangement, intended to offset the charge of upsetting the balance of power in southern Asia, was both ill-advised and impertinent. Leaders in India could read the United States' offer only as a total misunderstanding or, worse, an indifference to India's policy of nonalignment and to the diplomatic strategy which India felt helped to create conditions of peace. India's foreign policy gave a clear indication of its probable response to a proposal for a defense agreement with the United States, but the United States ignored the signs. This case provides a useful lesson in the dilemmas of international politics. Assuming a mutual understanding of the issues involved in a dispute, a resolution need not necessarily follow. Indeed, a sharp identification of the issues may well make an agreement less likely, particularly if the probable ramifications of alternative solutions are rendered explicit.

Needless to say, conditions changed radically after 1954. Pakistan, originally closely tied to American strategy in Asia, later sought an accommodation with China—and at the very time that Pakistan's enemy, India, became

2 Speech of February 22, 1954, given in full in *Jawaharlal Nehru's Speeches,* vol. 3, March, 1953–August, 1957 (New Delhi: Ministry of Information and Broadcasting, 1958), pp. 344–46.

embroiled in border conflicts with China. As India had anticipated, American arms in Pakistan, intended to contain China, were used by Pakistan against India in 1965.

The independence movement of 1971 in East Pakistan again embroiled India and Pakistan in a controversy over styles of nonalignment. The government of Pakistan in Islamabad accused India of interference in Pakistan's internal affairs because of India's sympathy for the "freedom fighters" and criticism of the Pakistan army's effort to quell revolt in East Pakistan. Prime Minister Gandhi replied that India cannot remain still when military force is used against an unarmed public. The East Pakistan case again shows the tendency for India's foreign policy to be more narrowly self-interested the closer the case in dispute rests to home.

Nationalist Movements. India's foreign policy has led, in the past, to consistent support of groups aspiring to national independence from Western imperial control. On the subcontinent itself, French Indian territory was claimed by India and eventually was handed over without a struggle. The dispute with Portugal over Goa and the rest of Portuguese India was ended when India occupied these territories by force of arms in 1961. In the neighboring country of Nepal, whenever influence could be exercised, it has been intended to maintain Nepal's independence and to encourage internal changes that would transfer political power from authoritarian leaders to responsible political hands. In recent years, Nepal (with Bhutan and the protectorate Sikkim) has been subjected to firmer influence from India because of the critical importance of these regions to India's policy of defense of the territory which borders China. But Nepal, in particu-

lar, has resisted Indian influence, and Bhutan has successfully sought membership in the United Nations to assert its independence. Thus, India has not been very successful in courting friendships with its immediate neighbors.

Nationalists further afield—in Algeria, Kenya, Malaysia, the Congo, Angola, Egypt, and many other areas—have enjoyed India's open support. In the more recent cases, especially after the tempering years of experience in the United Nations, India has been somewhat more cautious about supporting nationalist movements in Africa. But her support of the principles of self-determination and the national right to independence remains firm.

India has been unwilling, however, to apply this principle to the communist world, except in the case of Yugoslavia—where a solution other than national revolt was found. The uprisings in Poland and the notorious cases of Hungary and Czechoslovakia tested India's intentions. India was not, in these cases, willing to stretch her policy to help to sustain national strivings behind the communist shield. The contrast between India's reluctant and basically neutral reaction to the Soviet Union's behavior in Hungary and Czechoslovakia and her immediately hostile reaction to British, French, and Israeli behavior in Suez in 1956 underscores an inconsistency that would appear to be difficult to explain except in ideological or opportunistic terms. India's official reaction to revolts in Tibet and to the escape of the Dalai Lama from the Chinese also was cautious and noncommittal, at first. After 1959, when the Sino-Indian border dispute, involving Tibet, involved the national interests of India, she altered her previous strategy of fostering peace by recognizing the monolithic character of the communist world system. Under the pressure of the struggle with China over the Sino-Indian boundaries in the Himalayas, India recognized more clearly the nature and substance of Tibetan resistance to Chinese cultural and political absorption. The Indian government's implication that a communist form of imperialism exists—especially in Asia, from China —has been made more explicit in public and private forums over the past years. But the legend that imperialism is uniquely the final stage of capitalism, grounded on Lenin's analysis and known to every schoolboy in India, dies hard.

Racial Discrimination. For many years preceding independence, Indian leaders objected to discrimination based upon race or creed. Mahatma Gandhi established his world reputation, before World War I, by organizing effective nonviolent resistance to such discrimination in South Africa. The continuation in South Africa of racial policies, and the enactment of permanent and legal discrimination in the form of apartheid, have led India to boycott South Africa and sever diplomatic relations. The withdrawal of South Africa from the British Commonwealth of Nations is in no small part due to the adamant stand against apartheid taken by India, Pakistan, Ghana, and other African and Asian Commonwealth members, powerfully supported by Canada. India has followed a similarly strong stand against the racist policies of the all-white government of Southern Rhodesia.

The South Africa case is only the most dramatic instance of India's involvement in international anti-discriminatory policies. Australia's "white" policy, the plight of the Negro in the United States, and the Sinhalese-Buddhist attacks on the

rights of the minority of Tamil-speaking Hindus in Ceylon are three among the many other instances in which India speaks, but more cautiously, in behalf of equality.

The United Nations and the Afro-Asian Bloc. India's record in the United Nations is far too extensive to review here. The record reveals the great importance she places on the United Nations as an international forum for the resolution of conflicts, the prevention of possible conflicts, and the spreading of mutual understanding and cooperation, especially through the work of the specialized agencies. The Kashmir case, first brought to the attention of the United Nations by India in late December of 1947, resulted in some disillusionment for India, since the Security Council's actions did not coincide with India's wishes. The handling of the Kashmir dispute by the United Nations was a lesson in the political operations of the Security Council. It is not likely that India will again bring a case of that sort to the United Nations, except after the most careful consideration.

The Afro-Asian consultative conference within the United Nations has become, since its formation in 1950, a significant force in the General Assembly, especially as the number of Afro-Asian member nations increases yearly. India and Egypt have played leading roles in this group. Although several shades of political outlook are encompassed in the bloc, it is dominantly neutralist. Partially by means of this informal organization of states, India has been able to advance its formula for the conditions of peace, by limiting military defense arrangements in Africa and Asia and by gaining United Nations membership for potential members of the bloc. The growing power of this group has been shown in the steady rise in the proportion of states willing to vote for the admission of China to the United Nations, even though India now advocates this less actively than before.

Circles of Interest

Pakistan. India's most important foreign policy problem is neighboring Pakistan. Partition was the consequence of bloodshed, arson, rape, abduction, tremendous losses of property, the transfer of 12 million people, plus a general ill will of a virulent and lasting variety. India's conciliatory and generous approach to more distant problems has not been applied to Pakistan.

More than two decades have passed since partition, and functional ties between the two countries—in transportation, communications, exchange of persons, commerce, and culture—have not been restored. Piecemeal, a few of the thorny differences over trade, boundaries, and the like have been settled. And with the help of the International Bank, a spectacular technological solution of the Indus valley (canal waters) dispute, one which benefited both countries, was achieved. On the other hand, Indians and Pakistanis seldom meet each other on the subcontinent. Customs rules make it difficult for Indians to read about Pakistan, and vice versa. What could be a natural avenue for the exchange of goods on the subcontinent now is almost devoid of Indo-Pakistani traffic.

The fight for Bangla Desh (Bengali nation) in the area of East Pakistan was the most recent—and most serious—confrontation between India and Pakistan since 1965. The Pakistani elections of December of 1970 resulted in the spectacular political rise of East Pakistan's Awami League and of the party's leader, Sheikh Mujibur Rahman, who won so handsomely that he was declared prime minister-designate. The Sheikh's demand for radical autonomy for East Bengal, however, led from March 25 to a deadly purge of intellectuals and followers of Rahman by the Pakistani Army, the arrest of the Sheikh, and a sweeping military suppression of the independence movement for Bangla Desh—a movement spearheaded by the guerrillas, the Mukti Bahini (freedom fighters). In the turmoil and fear thus created, ultimately more than nine million East Bengalis, mostly Hindus, fled to India, presenting to India an intolerable refugee problem in border regions. India assisted the guerrilla movement with military training and armaments, and provided artillery cover for guerrillas seeking safety in Indian territory after completing operations in East Bengal. When no political solution was offered by Pakistan by the winter of 1971, the Indian Army moved early in December in direct support of the Mukti Bahini and forced the surrender of the Pakistani Army in the East after two weeks of fighting. A western front had opened in the meantime, but it too closed with a ceasefire at the time of surrender. India had occupied 1400 square miles of Pakistani territory in the western sector, and Pakistan had occupied about 60 square miles of India.

The 1971 war was local, but Peking and Washington supported the Pakistan case, whereas Moscow encouraged the Indian case and an independent Bangla Desh—a solution that now appears to be a settled fact. As the result of the war, Indo-American relations have hit a new low, and the Soviet Union's reputation in India could not be higher.

Kashmir currently remains the most vivid symbol of past differences and deep antagonisms between the two countries. The issue is too complex to detail here. In sum, each country proceeds from different premises. Pakistan argues that possession of the territory should be settled by a plebiscite, as recommended by the United Nations; India argues that the state of Jammu and Kashmir is an integral part of India by reason of the accession agreement of 1947, and that referral to the people already has taken place during elections conducted legally in the state.

The case has not advanced a step toward solution over the years, except that time has tended to stabilize India's possession of the larger part of the area. This, in turn, has resulted in an authoritarian rule in Jammu and Kashmir, in order to squash opinion favoring secession to Pakistan or Kashmiri independence from both India and Pakistan. Azad ("Free") Kashmir, on Pakistan's side, is equally disturbed, and also ruled with a hard hand.

In 1965, a major armed conflict broke out between India and Pakistan over Kashmir, threatening to engulf the subcontinent in a war going far beyond the Kashmir controversy. Pressure from the United Nations, the United States, and the Soviet Union led to a ceasefire. The Soviet Union, in 1966, invited the president of Pakistan and the prime minister of India to meet in Tashkent to work out an amicable solution. The Tashkent declaration, drawn up at the conclusion of the meetings, resulted in a gradual reduction of militant feelings in both countries, and the two armies have moved back to the boundaries existing before the conflict opened in the late summer of 1965, except for the military movements opened by the Bangla Desh war of 1971.

There are several feasible solutions to the Kashmir problems: (a) the territory could be ceded, in whole, to one party or the other; (b) they could agree on the status quo; (c) they could agree on a repartitioning; (d) they could agree on a partition, plus a plebiscite in the Vale of Kashmir; (e) Kashmir could be granted condominium status, supported by India and Pakistan; or (f) Kashmir could be granted independence. And there are variations on these themes, of course. But solutions have been barred, thus far, because India sees in Kashmir not only an important link in its geographic line of security and in its economy, but also a largely Muslim area, possession of which tends to justify India's secular political philosophy. Pakistan, in turn, sees Kashmir as advantageous to her military security; as a largely Muslim area of some economic value; and as a land contiguous to Pakistan, one that should, under the principles of partition, have come to Islamic Pakistan. Military, political, and economic issues are here intertwined with questions of religion and prestige, a deadly combination. Only India can resolve the deadlock, since India controls the richest, largest, and most populous part of the territory. Such initiative has not been forthcoming, and her reluctance to move has undoubtedly reduced her effectiveness in world affairs. In fairness, it should be said that India's reluctance to take initiative stems, in part, from the inability or unwillingness of many world powers to try to comprehend the position of India and to understand the enormous complexites of the case. The basically communal argument of Pakistan has convinced the majority of impatient ears, since that side of the matter is much easier to present. Only one willing to dig deeply will ever understand the Indian case and, even when one understands, it is possible to disagree with India's solutions.

China. India was one of the first to recognize the People's Republic of China in 1949, has worked for its recognition elsewhere, and has argued for China's membership in the United Nations from the start. Under the ambassadorship of K. M. Panikkar, India developed a policy of friendship toward China based on a large nation's shrewd respect for a more powerful neighbor. India's was a strategy of functional and cultural involvement. Rather than allow China to become isolated, and thus ever more closely tied to the Soviet Union, India hoped for a China that would be at least as Asian as it was communist—and the more Asian, the better.

In the process of building these relationships, India withstood many a Chinese affront: first over Tibet, then over trading rights, and finally over territory. In retrospect, it must be conceded that India's policy toward China was misconceived. India failed adequately to weigh China's traditional territorial claims along India's northern borders, and she understimated the militancy of the Chinese Communists in confrontations with Asian bourgeois nationalist regimes.

Since at least 1957, China has laid positive claim to over 50,000 square miles of land in Ladakh, in the North East Frontier Agency, and elsewhere along the Himalayan frontier, and has actually entered and occupied some of this territory, including large segments in the Ladakhi sector of Kashmir. In 1959, when these Chinese military maneuvers were announced in Parliament, an uproar arose in India. The fact that Parliament was kept in the dark for so long on a matter of national concern also led to an unusually heated and extended debate, the end of which is not yet in sight. The armed conflict with China, in October of 1962, resulted in a military defeat for India that approached a debacle. China quietly occupied most of the key areas it claimed and then drew back its armies unilaterally.

Others. India is interested in safeguarding Nepal, Sikkim, and Bhutan as integral parts of the subcontinental security line. Afghanistan, to the northwest, is given special attention because of its proximity to the Soviet Union. Relations with Ceylon, to the south, and with Burma, Malaysia, Singapore, and Indonesia, to the southeast, are mutually supportive of nonalignment and neutralism. Members of SEATO are less cordially viewed, and Taiwan is officially ignored. Japan is increasingly of special interest to India, as more detailed knowledge of Japan is accumulated, but their foreign policies clash. The Philippines remains a curiosity, largely a mystery, even to well-informed Indians.

India's relations with the Soviet Union and with the United States have been alternately cordial and testy, in both cases in response to Cold War pressures that have tended to make India suspicious of proposals coming from either side. When, more recently, economic aid and technical assistance began to predominate over ideological wooing, and continued aid from the United States showed its goodwill to be genuine, some shift toward the United States occurred. However, India has nevertheless given higher priority to her relations with the Soviet Union, especially to offset pressure from China. Soviet military assistance to India has been substantial, and the enhancement of political accord has accompanied military cooperation.

The British Commonwealth of Nations is another of India's links around the world. Membership in the Commonwealth provides an easy means for maintaining close relations with Great Britain, and is also a comfortable and noncommittal way for India to keep informed on the affairs of old Commonwealth friends and new members from Asia and Africa. At first, the most valuable assets of Commonwealth membership were the sterling balances held in London to India's credit and the consultative facilities in London. Now, India, rapidly taking on the status of an old constituent, is in a position to lead in discussions and to use the Commonwealth as a forum to promote the Indian outlook on world affairs. But one should not overemphasize the Commonwealth tie. For India, the Commonwealth is *a* connection, not *the* connection above all others. The Commonwealth, nevertheless, does provide exclusive and clublike contacts with Canada, New Zealand, Australia, and with the many members in Africa and Asia.

Relations with Western Europe—especially France, West Germany, Italy, and the Scandinavian countries —tend to be commercial and cultural, except as colonial issues arise. Latin America, to all but a few in India, is a distant mystery of no great significance, except when votes are counted in the United Nations.

Panch Shila

Panch Shila ("the five principles") of India's diplomacy were first incorporated in the communiqué on the Trade and Intercourse Agreement between India and China issued in Peking on April 29, 1954.[3] This communique put forward the principles as follows:

[3] The full text can be found in *Foreign Policy of India: Texts of Documents, 1947–1958* (New Delhi: Lok Sabha Secretariat, 1958), pp. 87–93.

Both parties agreed to negotiate on the basis of the principles of [1] mutual respect for each other's territorial integrity and sovereignty, [2] mutual non-aggression, [3] mutual non-interference in each other's internal affairs, [4] equality and mutual benefit, and [5] peaceful co-existence.

Since the signing of the 1954 agreement, India has signed similar agreements with a good many countries in Asia. The hope was that promises to respect one another's territory and national aspirations would, in time, strengthen the likelihood of peace. The outbreak of conflicts between *Panch Shila* nations, especially after the seven-point adaptation was affirmed at the 1955 Bandung Conference, was disappointing to India. China's demand, in 1957, for substantial segments of territory occupied and claimed by India, and the conflict with China in 1962, seem to have dealt a devastating blow to the *Panch Shila* ideal. One hears little of it today.

International Trade and Economic Aid

India's chief economic problem is to raise living standards as quickly as possible, with limited material and excessive human resources. Customs, tariff, taxation, and import-export rules are closely calculated to promote industrialization, to discourage or prohibit imports, to extend the exploitation of India's natural resources and to decrease their import, and to increase exports of all kinds. A favorable balance of trade is the object. But the fact is that India can go only so far in developing her economy. Savings are relatively modest and, in any event, inadequate to the necessary investment; goods and services must be imported from hard-currency countries, especially the United States;

and food still must be bought outside the country.

India's international economic policy is therefore directed not so much at the regulation of trade as at the gaining of economic aid from abroad in massive amounts. The United States has been the largest subscriber of help since 1947. Loans and grants from the United States have been more than four times as extensive as those from the Soviet Union. The United States is expected to guarantee more in the future, as is the Soviet Union. In addition, Great Britain, Canada, West Germany, and Japan, to name a few, have contributed a good deal as well.[4]

SUMMARY

The foreign policy of India has three, interrelated, main themes:

1. the policy of nonalignment, to obviate involvement in military or political commitments, thus permitting each issue to be decided on its intrinsic merits as it arises;
2. the policy of positive neutralism, as a technique for unrestricted cultural and personal interrelationships on a global basis, thus opening opportunities for extending the area of peace by all legitimate means; and
3. the policy of national self-interest, to assure the military security of the country and the social and economic well-being of its citizens.

The last point has gained in importance since 1962. Defense policies are now more adequately geared to meet immediate threats to India's territorial interests than they were before the conflict with China.

Nonalignment provides the independent status that, in turn, makes neutralism possible; these two policies seem best calculated, in an interdependent world, to satisfy the national goals of the third and crucial policy, security and progress.

The political aspirations of India rest firmly on the democratic base of parliamentary and party government, on adult suffrage, on the rule of law, on responsible administrative and military services, and on the positive search for individual liberty and national freedom. India's foreign policy, as its leaders see it, is devised to serve these ideals of national life.

SELECTED BIBLIOGRAPHY

AIYAR, S. P. *The Commonwealth in South Asia.* Bombay: Lalvani Publishing House, 1969.

BERKES, ROSS N., and BEDI, MOHINDER S. *The Diplomacy of India.* Stanford, Calif.: Stanford University Press, 1958.

BOWLES, CHESTER. *Ambassador's Report.* New York: Harper & Row, 1954.

BRECHER, MICHAEL. *India and World Politics: Krishna Menon's View of the World.* New York: Praeger, 1968.

————, *Nehru: A Political Biography.* New York: Oxford University Press, 1959.

————, *The New States of Asia: A Political Analysis.* New York: Oxford University Press, 1963.

————, *The Struggle for Kashmir.* New York: Oxford University Press, 1953.

CHAKRAVARTI, P. C. *India's Foreign Policy.* Bloomington: Indiana University Press, 1962.

CRABB, CECIL V., Jr. *The Elephants and the Grass: A Study of Nonalignment.* New York: Praeger, 1965.

FISHER, MARGARET W., ROSE, LEO E., and HUTTENBACK, ROBERT A. *Himalayan*

---

[4] For an analytical treatment of economic aid to India and to the rest of southern Asia, see Charles Wolf, Jr., *Foreign Aid: Theory and Practice in Southern Asia* (Princeton: Princeton University Press, 1960). See also John P. Lewis, *Quiet Crisis in India* (Garden City, N.Y.: Doubleday & Company, Inc., 1963).

Battleground: Sino-Indian Rivalry in Ladakh. New York: Praeger, 1963.

GALBRAITH, JOHN KENNETH. *Ambassador's Journal.* Boston: Houghton Mifflin Co., 1969.

GUPTA, SISIR, *Kashmir: A Study of India-Pakistan Relations.* New Delhi: Indian Council of World Affairs, 1966, New York: Taplinger Publishing Co., 1966.

HIGGINS, ROSALYN, *United Nations Peacekeeping, 1946–1967: Documents and Commentary.* Vol. 2, *Asia.* London: Oxford University Press, 1970.

India Quarterly (journal). New Delhi: Indian Council of World Affairs.

KORBEL, JOSEPH, *Danger in Kashmir.* Rev. ed. Princeton: Princeton University Press, 1966.

LAMB, ALASTAIR, *The China-India Border: The Origins of the Disputed Boundaries.* New York: Oxford University Press, 1964. Issued under the auspices of the Royal Institute of International Affairs.

LEVI, WERNER, *Free India in Asia.* Minneapolis: University of Minnesota Press, 1952.

LEWIS, JOHN P. *Quiet Crisis in India.* Garden City, N. Y.: Doubleday & Co., 1963.

MAXWELL, NEVILLE, *India's China War.* Bombay: Jaico Publishing House, 1970.

MISRA, K. P., ed. *Studies in Indian Foreign Policy.* Delhi: Vikas Publications, 1969.

NEHRU, JAWAHARLAL, *Independence and After: A Collection of Speeches, 1946–1949.* New York: John Day Co., 1950.

——, *Speeches, 1949–1953.* New Delhi: Government of India, 1954.

——, *Speeches, 1954.* New Delhi: Government of India, 1955 (and annually thereafter to 1964).

NORMAN, DOROTHY, ed. *Jawaharlal Nehru The First Sixty Years.* 2 vols. New York: John Day Co., 1965.

PALMER, NORMAN D. *South Asia and United States Policy.* Boston: Houghton Mifflin Co., 1966.

POPLAI, S. L., ed. *India, 1947–1959.* Vol. 1, *Internal Affairs* (including Kashmir). Vol. 2, *External Affairs.* Bombay: Oxford University Press, 1959. Issued under the auspices of the Indian Council of World Affairs.

STEIN, ARTHUR. *India and the Soviet Union.* Chicago: University of Chicago Press, 1969.

TALBOT, PHILLIPS, and POPLAI, S. L. *India and America: A Story of Their Relations.* New York: Harper & Row, 1958. Published for the Council on Foreign Relations.

WOLF, CHARLES, Jr. *Foreign Aid: Theory and Practice in Southern Asia.* Princeton: Princeton University Press, 1960.

Chapter Ten

THE AMERICAN TRADITION IN FOREIGN POLICY

An Overview

HANS J. MORGENTHAU

Throughout its history, the United States has pursued a consistent foreign policy. Beneath the clamor of contending philosophies, the controversies of factions, the contradictions and reversals of individual moves on the international scene, the foreign policy of the United States presents a simple and coherent pattern. This pattern results from the nature of the interests which the United States has traditionally pursued on the international scene.

In the Western Hemisphere, the United States has always endeavored to preserve its unique position as the predominant, unrivaled power. The United States has recognized from the very beginning that its predominance could not be effectively threatened from within the hemisphere without support from outside it. This peculiar situation has made it imperative for the United States to isolate the Western Hemisphere from the political and military policies of non-American nations. The interference of these nations in the affairs of the Western Hemisphere, especially through the acquisition of territory, was the only way in which the predominance of the United States could have been challenged from within the hemisphere itself. The Monroe Doctrine, and the policies implementing it, express the permanent national interest of the United States in the Western Hemisphere.

Since the interests of the United States in the Western Hemisphere can be effectively threatened only from outside —historically, from Europe—the United States has always striven to prevent the development of conditions in Europe

which would be conducive to interference in the affairs of the Western
Hemisphere, or contemplation of a
direct attack upon the United States.
These conditions would be most likely to arise if a European nation having unchallenged predominance in
Europe could look across the sea for
conquest without fear of being threatened at the center of its power.

It is for this reason that the United
States has consistently pursued policies aiming at the maintenance of the
balance of power in Europe. (The
War of 1812 is the sole major exception to this tradition.) The United
States has opposed whatever European nation was likely to gain ascendancy over its European competitors and to jeopardize the hemispheric
predominance and, eventually, the
very existence of the United States as
an independent nation. Conversely, it
has supported whatever European nation appeared capable of restoring the
balance of power by offering successful resistance to the would-be con-
queror. While it is hard to imagine a
greater contrast in political philosophy than that between Alexander
Hamilton and Woodrow Wilson, they
agree in their concern for the maintenance of the balance of power in
Europe. It is with this in mind that
the United States has intervened in
both world wars on the side of the
initially weaker coalition, and has
pursued European policies largely
paralleling those of Great Britain; for
from Henry VIII to Sir Edward Grey,
on the eve of World War I, Great
Britain's single objective in Europe
was the maintenance of the balance
of power.

Asia has vitally concerned the
United States only since the turn of
this century, and the meaning of Asia
for American interests has never been
obvious or clearly defined. In consequence, American policies in Asia

have never as unequivocally expressed
the permanent national interest as
have the hemispheric and European
policies. Yet, beneath the confusions
and incongruities which have sometimes marred American policy in Asia,
one can detect a consistency that reflects, however vaguely, the permanent interest of the United States
in Asia. And this interest is again
the maintenance of the balance of
power.

The principle of the "open door" in
China expresses this interest. At the
beginning, its meaning was purely
commercial. But when other nations,
especially Japan, threatened to close
the door to China, not only com-
mercially but also militarily and politically, the United States sought to
keep open the door to China in order
to safeguard the latter's territorial integrity and political independence for
political as well as commercial reasons. However unsure the United
States may have been in the particular
moves of its Asian policy, it has always assumed that the domination of
China by another nation would create
so great an accumulation of power as
to threaten the security of the United
States.

This extraordinary position of safety, which could be threatened only
sporadically from afar, gave rise to a
peculiarly American attitude toward
foreign policy and war. All other politically active nations have been
forced, by their continuous exposure
to danger from abroad, to recognize
the truth of Karl von Clausewitz's dictum that war is the continuation of
policy by other means. The peaceful
and warlike means by which a nation
pursues its interests vis-à-vis other
nations form a continuous process in
which, although one means may replace the other, the end remains the
same. Foreign policy itself is a continuum beginning with the birth of

the nation and ending only with its death.

Yet under the impact of the extraordinary position in which the United States found itself vis-à-vis other nations from the beginning of its history to the end of World War II, Americans came to embrace a different philosophy. According to this philosophy, it was "normal" for a nation to have no foreign policy at all. If a crisis should require a temporary departure from that normalcy in the form of an active foreign policy or of intervention in a foreign war, it was taken for granted that after the crisis was settled the nation ought to return to the normalcy of detachment. On this assumption—that the nation had a choice between involvement in or detachment from world affairs, and that the latter was to be preferred—both the isolationists and internationalists of the interwar period agreed. They disagreed only in their assessment of the urgency of intervention in a particular crisis situation. Furthermore, the internationalists believed that, in order to forestall the next crisis and meet it with the greatest chance for success, the United States should participate in the development and support of international organizations seeking to maintain international order and peace.

Foreign policy was thus regarded as something like a policeman's night stick, to be used only when necessary to bring a disturber of the peace to reason; war, in turn, was assigned the function of the policeman's gun, to be used only *in extremis* to rid the world of a criminal. But here the analogy ends: the policeman always carries his gun with him, but the United States threw its gun away twice—after it had done the job in two world wars.

The United States could see that war did have a necessary connection with what it considered the criminal aggression that preceded and provoked it, but it did not realize the organic relation that exists between war and what follows it. The purpose of war appeared to be the elimination of a disturbance by eliminating the disturber; once that was done, the world would presumably settle back into normalcy and order. War, as prepared for and waged by the United States, was a mere technical operation to be performed according to the rules of the military art—a feat of military engineering like building a dam or flattening a mountain. The organic relationship between foreign and military policy was lost and, in consequence, foreign policy was without strength, and military policy lacked purpose.

THE REVOLUTION IN AMERICAN FOREIGN POLICY

The aftermath of World War II witnessed a drastic change, not in the traditional interests, but in the traditional policies and attitudes of the United States. This change was imposed by the conditions of unprecedented novelty under which the United States had to pursue its traditional interest in the preservation of the balance of power in Europe and Asia. When the United States was called on, in the two world wars, to redress the European balance of power, the German threat was being contained, however precariously, by a counterweight located in Europe itself. The Japanese threat, in turn, was contained on the Asian mainland by the power of China. The United States only needed to add its strength to these counterweights until victory was achieved, and then it expected to return to the normalcy of isolation. This is what it did after World War I, and what it was prepared to do after World War II. After some months of hesitation and confusion, the United States realized that the nations of Western Europe had become too weak to contain the Soviet threat to the European balance of power and that the United States, in order to prevent a Soviet hegemony over all of Europe, had to commit itself in virtual permanence to the defense of Western Europe. When, in 1949, China fell to communism and nothing stood in the way of its expansion except Chiang Kai-shek's forces, the United States took upon itself similar permanent obligations in Asia.

By 1947, the new pattern of American foreign policy was set. It manifested itself in four political innovations: the Truman doctrine, the policy of containment, the Marshall Plan, and the American alliance system. Foreign aid and liberation were added to these in the fifties. These policies have in common the permanent assumption, by the United States, of responsibilities beyond the limits of the Western Hemisphere.

The Truman doctrine is contained in President Truman's message to Congress of March 12, 1947. The president recommended the appropriation of $400 million for assistance to Greece and Turkey and the authorization to send civilian and military personnel as well as commodities, supplies, and equipment to these two countries. The immediate occasion for these requests was the inability of Great Britain to continue the historic function, which she had performed for almost a century and a half, of protecting the eastern shores of the Mediterranean from Russian penetration. Since the end of the Napoleonic wars, one of the basic assumptions of British foreign policy had been that Russian control of Greece and of the Dardanelles constituted a threat to

the European balance of power. Great Britain was no longer able to shoulder the overall responsibility for the maintenance of the balance of power in Europe, and she had just notified the United States that she no longer possessed the military and economic resources to defend Greece.

The interest of the United States in the maintenance of the European balance of power had been historically identical with that of Great Britain and, by the beginning of 1947, the United States had already become—by the logic of the distribution of power, if not by design—the successor to Great Britain as the main counterweight against a threat to the independence of the nations of Europe. It then became almost inevitable for the United States to take over the particular British burden for the protection of the independence of Greece and the territorial integrity of Turkey, an action justified both by traditional interest in the European balance of power and by the particular conditions prevailing in the eastern Mediterranean at the beginning of 1947.

Yet the Truman doctrine went beyond the immediate occasion by committing the United States to the defense of democratic nations everywhere in the world against "direct or indirect aggression" and against "subjugation by armed minorities or by outside pressure." At this point, the Truman doctrine merges into the policy of containment.

The policy of containment was never officially formulated. It grew as an almost instinctive reaction to the threat of Soviet imperialism. It called a halt to the territorial expansion of Soviet power beyond the line of military demarcation drawn at the end of World War II between the Soviet orbit and the Western world. It said, in effect, to the Soviet Union: "Thus far and no farther, else you will be at war with the United States." Or as the London *Economist* of December 2, 1950, put it: "The object of the endeavor in which the nations of the free world are now united is to contain Russian imperialism without having to fight another world war."

The United States recognized that the policy of containment could not succeed so long as the nations of Western Europe remained economically prostrate and politically unstable. Thus, Secretary of State George Marshall declared, in an address at Harvard on June 5, 1947, that the United States would welcome the initiative and cooperation of the European countries in the elaboration of an economic program of self-help combined with American assistance. The Western European nations quickly responded to this "Marchall Plan," forming as their vehicle of cooperation a Committee of European Economic Cooperation which laid the foundation for the establishment, the following year, of the Organization for European Economic Cooperation (OEEC). In April, 1948, Congress approved the bill creating the Economic Cooperation Administration (ECA) as the instrument for channeling billions of dollars to the nations of Europe in a four-year program.

The American tradition limited to the Western Hemisphere the continuous presence of the United States on the stage of foreign policy. The great reversal of 1947 extended the permanent military commitments of the United States immediately beyond the Rhine and, potentially, to any region, anywhere, threatened by communist aggression or subversion. It further committed the economic resources of the United States immediately to the support of the nations of Western Europe, of Greece and Turkey, and potentially of any nation anywhere which needed it to preserve its freedom. It had become the policy of the United States, in the words of the Truman doctrine, "to support free peoples who are resisting attempted subjugation by armed minorities or by outside pressures." Since peoples throughout the world, in Europe, Africa, Asia, and Latin America, are resisting such subjugation, the commitments of the United States, by virtue of the Truman doctrine, have become worldwide, unlimited geographically, and limited only by the lack of need for support or a nation's unwillingness to accept it.

Of the traditional foreign policy of the United States, this revolution in America's relations to the outside world made short shrift. Nothing is left of it but a memory and, in some, a vain desire to return to an age when the United States was committed to defend only its own territory and the Western Hemisphere—not the nations of Western Europe, Berlin, Greece, Turkey, Australia, New Zealand, Pakistan, Thailand, South Vietnam, South Korea, Japan, and Taiwan—and when the United States endeavored to transform the world by its own example rather than by intervening, assisting, and advising.

America, once its policy of containment had met successfully the Soviet military threat to Western Europe, had to achieve three difficult tasks. First of all, it had to create, out of the makeshift arrangements aimed at meeting the Soviet military threat, a viable international order which would translate common interests into a common purpose, fuse the power of individual nations, and assign to them responsibilities commensurate with their interests and power. Second, it had to create a relationship with the uncommitted new nations of Africa and Asia which would be conducive to the development of domestic and international stability. Third, it had to establish a relationship conducive both to peace and freedom with those nations who were unwilling objects of communist domination, such as the nations of Eastern Europe.

How did the United States endeavor to meet these tasks? It developed three policies to serve them: alliances; foreign aid; and liberation.

The Policy of Alliances

Since the end of World War II, the United States has concluded four collective alliances: the Inter-American Treaty of Mutual Assistance of 1947, also called the Rio Pact; the North Atlantic Treaty of 1949, under which the North Atlantic Treaty Organization (NATO) was established; the Security Treaty with Australia and New Zealand (ANZUS) of 1951; and the Southeast Asia Treaty Organization of 1954 (SEATO). To these collective agreements must be added individual alliances the United States has concluded with Japan, the Philippines, South Korea, South Vietnam, and the Republic of China. The Baghdad Pact of 1955, concluded among Turkey, Iraq, Great Britain, Pakistan, and Iran, and succeeded, after the defection of Iraq in 1958, by the CENTO Pact, has been actively supported, but was not formally joined, by the United States.

The Rio Pact, of which the United States and all Latin American nations are members, serves the common defense of the Western Hemisphere by transforming the Monroe Doctrine from a unilateral American declaration into a collective arrangement. NATO, to which the United States and all nations of Western Europe— with the exception of Austria, Ireland, Sweden, Switzerland, and Spain —as well as Greece and Turkey, belong, serves the defense of Western

Europe. The ANZUS treaty serves the defense of the Pacific. SEATO, of which the United States, Great Britain, France, Australia, New Zealand, the Philippines, Thailand, and Pakistan are members, serves the defense of southern and Southeast Asia.

The relationships within an alliance are determined by two fundamental factors—the interests and the power of its members. In this respect, the alliance between the United States and the nations of Western Europe must be distinguished from the other U.S. alliances. The interests which tie the United States to its European allies are more profound, more comprehensive, and more stable than the interests upon which alliances have traditionally been based. Far from concerning nothing more than a limited territorial advantage against a temporary enemy, these interests enclose the national identity of all the members within a common civilization, threatened by an alien and oppressive social system. Thus, this alliance was not formed through a process of bargaining among suspicious temporary associates, but rather sprang naturally and almost inevitably from a concern with a common heritage which had a chance to survive only through common support. The members of the alliance had to choose between the alliance and the loss of their national identity and cultural heritage; that is to say, they had no choice at all.

The cement that has maintained that alliance has been the paramount power of the United States. Although, in past alliances, power had been unequally distributed, with one ally predominant, rarely had there been such a concentration of power, with all other allies in a subordinate position. The United States was not only paramount in the military and economic fields, but also in the intangible sphere of the values of Western civilization, and had become, in every respect, the predominant power of the alliance.

If the institutions and operations of the alliance had been as comprehensive and intense as its underlying interests, and if the influence of the United States had been commensurate with its power, the alliance might have amounted to a confederation of states merging their most vital activities in the fields of foreign policy, defense, finance, and economics. However, during the fifties, the United States did not play its required role in the Western alliance. Three inherited patterns of thought and action prevented this: the traditional limitation of the direct exercise of American power to the Western Hemisphere; the principle of equality; and the military approach to foreign policy.

On the two previous occasions when American power went beyond the limits of the Western Hemisphere, America retreated to its traditional confines after it had failed to establish itself firmly beyond them. The liquidation of the conquests of the Spanish-American War, in view of its accidental and peripheral connection with the American tradition of foreign policy, were able to begin as soon as the conquests had been made. The failure of Wilson's attempt to "make the world safe for democracy" rendered pointless the presence of American power in Europe. The nature of the Soviet threat after World War II left the United States no rational choice but to establish its power in virtual permanence at the circumference of the Soviet empire. But should that power be established in terms of American supremacy, which would reduce America's allies to the status of satellites, or was there to be equality among all members of the alliance,

which would, ideally, result in the harmonious cooperation of like-minded nations? This dilemma had to be solved in a way that would not deny either of these essentials of American policy—military supremacy and harmonious cooperation.

American power had to operate in the territory of friendly nations whose consent provided the only title for the American presence, the purpose of which was the defense of the freedom and territorial integrity of the allies. If the United States had reduced its allies to the status of satellites, the very purpose of the European alliance would have been defeated. On the other hand, the establishment of the alliance on the basis of complete equality was feasible only on the assumption that the identity of interests among the allies was so complete that they could pursue common ends, with common measures, through free and equal cooperation. If this cooperation fell short of the ideal expectation, the purpose of the alliance, as a cooperative effort on behalf of the common interests, would be defeated.

Of these alternatives, the United States chose the latter. It refused to bring its superior power to bear on the alliance on behalf of common interests which would compete with divergent ones. When the United States left the Western Hemisphere, it carried only its military and economic power, not its creative imagination and its constructive will. Significantly, this imagination and will played its greatest role in that sphere closest to the American tradition in foreign affairs, the military sphere.

The United States emerged from World War II as the most powerful nation on earth by chance and not by design, and it assumed the leadership of the coalition of free nations by virtue of necessity and not of choice. In consequence, its will and mind were not equal to its power, responsibility, and opportunity. Since America's responsibility was not the result of conscious choice, it approached the tasks incumbent upon the paramount power of the Western alliance with unbecoming humility and unwarranted self-restraint.' The political predominance required by its power was incompatible with its anti-imperialist tradition, which is the manifestation abroad of the principle of equality. Confronted with the choice between assuming the position of leadership and treating its allies as equals, the United States chose the latter. Accustomed to expanding its rule into politically empty spaces but not to imposing it on existing political entities, it endeavored to establish a consensus within the Western alliance by the same methods of rational persuasion and economic inducements with which the American commonwealth had been created, maintained, and developed.

Yet the application of the egalitarian principle of democratic consensus to alliances resulted in disintegration and anarchy. The integrating effects of the domestic egalitarian consensus depend upon a preestablished hierarchical relationship in the form of a sovereign central government; any equality among allies drastically differing in power and responsibility must be subordinated to a hierarchical relationship between the paramount power and the rest. This relationship was lacking between the United States and its allies. As a result, the alliance was either incapable of pursuing new, positive policies in common, or else the most determined ally was able to impose its will on the United States.

NATO is the outstanding example of the former consequence. The principle of equality among its fifteen members, applied to the political operations and overall military planning of the alliance, put a virtually insurmountable obstacle in the way of new policies to be pursued in response to new opportunities or threats. The principle of equality would have been compatible with new departures in policy only on the unattainable conditions that all members of the alliance had an equal interest in such departures, were equally aware of these interests, and agreed completely on the means to be used in support of them. Short of an open threat of military conquest or revolution, such as confronted the members or NATO in the late 1940s, these conditions cannot be expected to be present at the same time. In the absence of one of them, the best an alliance can achieve is to translate the lowest common denominator of agreed interests into common action. While the objective conditions under which the fifteen allies live require a degree of unity in purpose and action far transcending that of a traditional alliance, and while NATO was designed to be the instrument of that kind of unity, NATO has become more and more undistinguishable from a traditional, loosely knit alliance.

The other consequence of the egalitarian approach to alliances has been most marked in the bilateral relations between the United States and its allies. Governments which govern only because the United States maintains them or which have no alternative to the American association have been able to play a winning game in which the United States holds all the trumps. The United States has not been disposed to play these trumps for two reasons. Its commitment to the principle of equality made it impossible to bring its superior power to bear upon a weak ally on behalf of its own interests. These interests were conceived in terms of what might be called the "collector's approach" to alliances. The United States, in the fifties, was primarily interested in the conclusion of alliances per se, regardless of the specific and concrete interests these alliances were supposed to serve. An alliance thus conceived is a standing invitation for a weak ally to make the alliance serve its specific and concrete interests. Thus, the United States has paid for the willingness of weak and even unviable nations to become its allies by underwriting the interests of these nations, regardless of whether these interests coincide with, or even run counter to, its own.

This relationship, unhealthy even by the standards of traditional foreign policy, is a far cry from the new order through which the United States was called upon to realize the common purpose of the nations of Western civilization in the atomic age. The United States was not able to free itself from the pattern of thought and action established both by its tradition and by its successful reaction to the threat of Soviet power in the aftermath of World War II—it continued to conceive of its relations to the outside world primarily in military terms. It saw itself surrounded by allies, by uncommitted nations which thus far had refused to become allies, and by satellites which Soviet power had prevented from becoming allies. From this picture of the world, three militarily oriented objectives ensued. The allies had to be kept in the American orbit, the uncommitted nations had to be drawn into it, and the satellites had to be liberated in order to enable them to join it. SEATO and the abortive Eisenhower doctrine of March, 1957, were open-ended—and largely unsuccessful—invitations to the uncommitted nations of Asia and the Middle East, respectively, to become allies of the United States, or at least to accept military assistance from it.

These policies were largely unsuccessful because the picture of the world from which they derived was at odds both with the facts of experience and the interests of the United States. What the United States had to cope with, outside Europe, was not the threat of Soviet military power but the promise of a new political and economic order. A policy of military alliances was irrelevant to the problems raised by that promise. It was also counterproductive; for by strengthening the forces of the status quo and the military establishments in the allied nations, it tended to identify the United States with those forces and with preparations for war. This, in turn, gave communism the opportunity to identify itself with the forces of progress and peace.

The Policy of Foreign Aid

The policy of foreign aid, considered the main instrument for strengthening the uncommitted nations in their uncommitted position, has similarly suffered from this predominantly military orientation. But it has also suffered from two other handicaps.

The American theory and practice of foreign aid, during the fifties, was derived largely from certain unexamined assumptions which are part of the American folklore of politics. The popular mind has established a number of simple and highly doubtful correlations between foreign aid, on the one hand, and a rising standard of living, social and political stability, democratic institutions and practices, and a peaceful foreign policy on the other. The simplicity of these correlations is so reassuring that the assumption of a simple and direct relationship between foreign aid and economic, social, and political progress is rarely questioned.

Thus, fundamental questions like the following were hardly ever asked explicitly: What are the social, political, and moral effects of foreign aid likely to be under different circumstances? Does successful foreign aid require a particular intellectual, political, and moral climate, or will the injection of capital and technological capability from the outside create this climate? To what extent, and under what conditions, is it possible for one nation to transform, through outside intervention, the economic and technological life of another nation? More specifically, in terms of the political objective of keeping the uncommitted nations uncommitted, how is one to create that positive relationship in the mind of the recipient between the aid and its beneficial results, on the one hand, and the political philosophy, system, and objectives of the giver, on the other? As long as the recipient disapproves of the politics of the giver, the political effects of the aid are lost. These effects are similarly lost as long as the recipient remains unconvinced that the aid received is but a natural manifestation of the politics of the giver. Foreign aid, then, remains politically ineffective as long as the recipient says either, "Aid is good, but the politics of the giver are bad," or, "Aid is good, but the politics of the giver have nothing to do with it."

Answers to questions such as the ones above require policies of extraordinary subtlety and intricacy. The simple correlation between foreign aid and what the United States desires in the uncommitted nations could not provide the answers. That correlation is a projection of the domestic experience of America onto the international scene. Capital formation and investment and technological innovation created the wealth and prosperity of America, and so it was assumed that the export of American capital and technology into the underdeveloped nations would bring forth similar results there. The similarity between this and the Wilsonian expectation is striking. Wilson wanted to bring the peace and order of America to the rest of the world by exporting its democratic institutions. His contemporary heirs wanted to bring the wealth and prosperity of America to the rest of the world through the export of American capital and technology. Yet, the failure of the Wilsonian experiment was quick and drastically revealed; the failure of foreign aid, simplistically conceived, has been less obvious, albeit no less drastic.

Even if the United States had developed a well-planned philosophy of foreign aid, however, its application would have come up against the same egalitarian principle which has frustrated the alliance policy of the United States. While the application of this principle to the alliance policy was not warranted by the objective situation, foreign aid has confronted the United States with a real dilemma. If we apply the egalitarian principle expressed in the slogan, "no strings attached," to foreign aid, we put ourselves at the mercy of unenlightened or corrupt governments which might misuse foreign aid through incompetence or by design. If, on the other hand, we assume responsibility for the way our aid is used, we feed the nationalistic suspicion of "imperialist" motives. By choosing the former method, the United States gave the recipient governments at least a potential leverage against itself, similar to that its allies enjoy. This leverage is increased by the competitive participation of the Soviet Union in foreign aid, which allows the recipient governments to play one superpower against the other. Yet, while the Soviet Union used foreign aid as an integral part of its political policy, seeking the expansion of its influence either directly or through communist movements, the United States was at a disadvantage in trying to serve consistently either its own purpose or the purposes of the underdeveloped nations.

The Policy of Liberation

The weakness of the foreign policies of the United States, as conducted in the fifties, came to a head in the total failure of its policies toward the satellites of the Soviet Union. The character of that failure suggests, as we shall see, the nature of the remedy. The inspiration from which the policies toward the satellites were derived is within the American tradition of seeking the expansion of the area of freedom. These policies continue the anti-imperialistic tradition of America, yet with one significant difference. The anti-imperialistic tradition has operated on two levels, the general one of revulsion against the normal practices of European power politics, and the specific one of revulsion against a particular case of oppression of one nation by another. The political consequences of the first type were the abstention and isolationism of Washington's farewell address. The second type had almost no political consequence at all, but led to the emotional commitment to what appeared to be the cause of freedom and humanitarian assistance to its suffering supporters. Thus, the American anti-imperialism of the nineteenth century favored the national movements of Europe against monarchical enemies and opposed certain colonial ventures of European nations, and the American anti-imperialism of the

early twentieth century took its stand against imperial and Nazi Germany and against tsarist and Soviet Russia, and both received the fighters in the lost causes of freedom as citizens.

The new anti-imperialism, aimed at the conquests of the Soviet Union, obviously partook of these characteristics, but possessed a quality its predecessors lacked; it became an integral and crucial part of the foreign policy of the United States. The traditional anti-imperialism of America was without a political objective, either by virtue of its very nature or else because the radius of an active American foreign policy was limited to the Western Hemisphere. The new anti-imperialism could no longer afford to condemn the suppression of liberty from afar and limit its tribute to freedom to charitable deeds. Committed to the containment of communism, to the preservation of national freedom wherever it was threatened by Soviet imperialism, the United States could reconcile itself to the loss of national freedom only if it altogether ceased being anti-imperialistic. If it wanted to remain faithful to its anti-imperialist tradition, it would have had to embark upon positive political and military policies on behalf of both the preservation and the expansion of national freedom. Yet at this point, when it came to adapting the traditional attitude of America to the opportunities and limitations of the contemporary world, American foreign policy failed.

The traditional American goal of expanding the area of freedom encountered a new opportunity and a new limitation in the foreign policy of the United States. It did not come to terms with either. Of this failure, the policy of liberation and the explicit inaction on the occasion of the Hungarian revolution of 1956 and of the Soviet occupation of Czecho-

slovakia in 1968 have been the outward manifestations.

The policy of liberation must be
seen as a logical extension of the policy of containment and as the positive
implementation of the American refusal to recognize the Soviet Union's
European conquests. Stalin and his
successors attempted to liquidate the
Cold War by concluding an agreement with the United States which
would have divided Europe into two
spheres of influence, with the European conquests of the Soviet Union
recognized as definite and legitimate.
The United States has consistently
refused to consider even the possibility of such an agreement. The
United States could let it go at that,
satisfied with containing Soviet power
within the limits reached in 1945,
and that is essentially what it did up
to the beginning of 1953. The impulse
to go beyond this negative policy of
containment and nonrecognition, and
to give that policy a positive implementation, stems from the traditional
American purpose of expanding the
area of freedom. But once America
yielded to that impulse, it was up
against the problem of what kind of
positive policy it should pursue.

In accordance with its general conception of foreign policy, the United
States conceived of liberation essentially in military terms—as the evacuation of Eastern Europe by the Red
Army. Such evacuation could be
brought about only through military
pressure which carried the risk of war.
As the London *Economist* put it on
August 30, 1952, when the policy of
liberation was first proclaimed: "Unhappily 'liberation' applied to Eastern
Europe—and Asia—means either the
risk of war or it means nothing. . . .
'Liberation' entails no risk of war only
when it means nothing." Since liberation was to be achieved without resort
to war, according to repeated official

statements, it was, as conceived by
American policy, incapable of achievement. Thus, the fear of war contained
not only the Soviet Union, but also
the United States.

What pretended to be a new
dynamic policy turned out to be no
policy at all, nothing more than a
verbal commitment incapable of implementation by action. However,
that commitment was taken as a
threat by the Soviet Union and as a
promise by the satellites. Instead of
contributing anything to the liberation of the satellites, it served as a
pretext for the Soviet Union to maintain its military rule of Eastern
Europe, and as an incentive for the
satellites to entertain illusions about
what the United States might do,
only to be disillusioned with American policy and reconciled to their fate
when no action was forthcoming. The
policy of liberation not only did not
liberate, it actually strengthened the
forces opposed and detrimental to
liberty.

The Hungarian revolution of 1956
provided the definitive test of the self-
defeating unreality of the policy of
liberation. For here the United States
was faced, not with the impossible
task of liberating without resort to
war, but with the opportunity to support a liberation already achieved. By
remaining inactive under these most
favorable circumstances, it demonstrated that there was no such thing
as a policy of liberation, but only
verbal pronouncements designed to
give the appearance that there was
one. The United States declared from
the outset, through its most authoritative spokesman, the president, that it
would abstain from active interference. While it is a moot question as
to how much the United States could
have done, it is obvious, in view of
the since-revealed dissension within
the Soviet government over the use of

force, that it could have done more than nothing.

THE REVOLUTION IN THE INTERNATIONAL ENVIRONMENT

These weaknesses, inherent in the foreign policy of the United States as it developed during the fifties, were aggravated by fundamental changes in the international environment to which American foreign policy did not adapt itself. At the end of the period, the international scene was different in four fundamental respects from what it had been at its beginning.

First of all, the balance of military power had changed radically. In the aftermath of World War II, the United States was unquestionably the most powerful nation on earth. Under the umbrella of its monopoly of atomic weapons, the United States formed the European alliance, implementing the policy of containment. The monopoly provided a virtually absolute protection for the nations which felt themselves threatened by communist aggression. This protection has disappeared. It has been replaced by a stalemate, or by what Winston Churchill called a "balance of terror." The United States is able to destroy the Soviet Union and the Soviet Union is able to destroy the United States in an all-out war.

In view of this stark and simple situation, an alliance with the United States is no longer regarded as an unmixed blessing. It still provides a certain protection, but it also implies a certain liability. Can the United States be relied upon to come to the aid of an ally at the risk of its own destruction? And would not such aid, even if provided, seal the doom of the ally, since it would probably be in the nature of nuclear war to be countered in kind by the enemy? The allies of the United States are raising questions such as these, and they answer them by seeking safety in greater independence from the United States. Either they try to develop foreign and military policies of their own, with or without are independent nuclear deterrent, or else they tend to move away from the United States into a neutral or at least a more detached position.

The second great transformation in the political world during the fifties was the restoration of the economic and, to a certain extent, the political health of most of the nations of Western Europe. At the beginning of the fifties, the alliance with the United States was, for nations such as Italy, France, and Great Britain, a matter not of choice but of life and death. Without the economic, political, and military support of the United States, those nations might not have survived as independent national entities and would have been in great danger of being subverted by communism or swallowed up by the Soviet Union. Today, this dependence on the United States has to a great extent disappeared, especially in the economic area. It has become rather ineffective in the political area, and its military ambivalence has become obvious.

Furthermore, and most importantly, the foreign policy of the Soviet Union has fundamentally changed. In the years immediately following World War II, the greatest asset of United States foreign policy was the foreign policy of Stalin. Whenever there was a slackening in the Western effort or a weakening of the alliance system, Stalin would make a drastic move which demonstrated how necessary the American connection was.

Khrushchev's foreign policy, during the fifties, was of an entirely different nature. His was not a policy of direct military aggression or of direct military threats. Even the threat against the Western presence in Berlin, uttered for the first time in November, 1958, and repeated many times since, was quite different from the threats Stalin would have made or would have followed up by action, as in the case of the Berlin blockade in 1948. Khrushchev's policies aimed not so much at the conquest of territories by diplomatic pressure or military threats as at the subversion of the whole noncommunist world through the impact of Soviet power and technological and economic accomplishments. This is a much more insidious, a much subtler, way of undermining the position of the United States and of the Western world.

To these three fundamental changes must be added a fourth: the rise of the former colonial nations in Africa and Asia. These enormous masses of land and populations no longer belong to any of the power blocs. Most of them are no longer under the control of any of the Great Powers. But they were expected to seek the support of stronger nations and fashion their political, economic, and social lives in the image of one of the great political and social systems competing for their allegiance. Hence, they became the great prize in the struggle between East and West. Whichever power could attract the loyalties of these uncommitted nations and impress them with the excellence and superiority of its form of government, of its social and economic system, was expected to have gained a great victory in the struggle for the world. And Khrushchev proclaimed that the Soviet Union, through the attractiveness and achievements of communism, would conquer the minds of the uncommitted peoples and thereby inherit the earth. As it has turned out, however, the new and emerging nations of Africa, Asia, and Latin America have by and large preferred to be miserable in their own way to being made happy in the American, Chinese, or Soviet way.

These four fundamental changes in the international environment imposed on the United States the task of rethinking and refashioning American foreign policy in five major areas: relations with its allies; its relations with the uncommitted nations; the relationship between its domestic politics and foreign policy; relations with the communist bloc; and, finally, the supranational control of nuclear power.

The several alliances of which the United States is a member owe their existence, as we have seen, to two different factors: the need of the United States' European allies, as well as its former enemies, after World War II, to have American economic, military, and political support; and the objective of the United States to contain, by military means, the Soviet Union and Communist China throughout the world. During the fifties, the foundations for the first type of alliance changed radically; the foundations for the second type were weak from the very outset.

The economic recovery of the nations of Western Europe and the former enemies made them less dependent on American support than they once had been. As a consequence, they have, at times, been able to pursue their own narrower interests regardless of the common interests of the alliance. The United States must find a new foundation for these alliances. France is the principal case in point. These alliances were primarily conceived in military terms. They must now be given an economic, political, and cultural content as well.

The transformation of the Cold

War into what is now called "competitive coexistence" has revealed the essential unsoundness of the policy of military containment as extended to Asia and the Middle East. The conflict between East and West has taken on the aspects of a struggle for the minds of men, especially in the uncommitted nations of Asia, Africa, and Latin America—a struggle to be fought with the weapons of prestige, subversion, political pressure, foreign aid, and foreign trade. Military alliances—in any contest for men's minds—are likely to be, at best, of minor importance and, at worst, a political handicap. Indochina provides a telling example.

If the United States is to wage this struggle for the minds of men with any chance of success, it must devise a new grand strategy. Two fundamental reforms are called for: the integration of all the factors involved in the struggle—military, political, economic—for the single purpose of maintaining and expanding the influence of the noncommunist world; and the adaptation of these various factors to the local conditions prevailing in different countries. The United States must develop, and act on, a coherent philosophy of foreign aid and foreign trade.

The uncommitted nations also confront the United States with a problem in political organization. Many of the new nations owe their existence to mere accidents of colonial history, and are therefore not likely to become viable political, economic, and military units within the boundaries they now occupy. They present a standing invitation for a new imperialism to establish a new order where the old colonial order has disappeared, or they are threatened with an anarchy which might well involve the rest of the world. This enormously complex problem will test the political creativity and determination of the United States.

It is obvious that the domestic policies pursued by the United States, especially in the field of race relations, are bound to have a direct influence upon its ability to wage the struggle for the minds of men. The United States needs to be fully aware of this influence in its conduct of domestic policies. Where it cannot entirely control these policies, it must at least give moral support to the positions which conform most closely to the best traditions of America. Throughout the better part of American history, the foreign policy of the United States drew strength and its attractiveness to other nations from the character of its domestic politics. The American experiment in government and social organization was intended, from the very outset, not only for America but for the world. It was meant as a model for other nations to emulate. The United States must restore that meaning.

The outcome of these new policies will depend upon the kind of relations the United States is able to establish with the communist world. If these relations should deteriorate further, the very success of the new policies might turn out to be self-defeating, bringing closer the probability of a third world war fought with nuclear weapons. Thus, the United States must accomplish the supreme task of statesmanship—it must successfully wage the competitive struggle with the communist world, without at the same time increasing the risk of war.

The first condition for minimizing that risk is the stabilization of the contested territorial frontiers, especially in Southeast Asia. The second condition is the maintenance of the Western deterrent to nuclear war. The risk of war will diminish only in the measure that the points of conflict which might ignite a war can be reduced, at the same time that deterrence to the starting of a war is maintained. The third condition is the abatement of the nuclear armaments race through arms control—that is, the stabilization of nuclear arms and delivery systems at a level sufficient to maintain the balance.

Finally, even if the United States should be successful in the pursuit of all these policies, the United States and the world will still be confronted with the mortal danger of the spread of atomic weapons to an indefinite number of nations. This danger the United States can cope with only in cooperation with the other great nations of the world. The prospect of such a spread is bound to become a reality unless the present trend is reversed. If the trend continues, it is likely to cause unprecedented anarchy which will finally get out of control. To bring the nuclear arms race and the proliferation of nuclear weapons under control is the overriding task of the age. History is likely to judge the United States by its approach to this task and its success in accomplishing it.

THE CONDUCT AND FORMATION OF AMERICAN FOREIGN POLICY

The character of a foreign policy conducted in a democracy is not determined by the requirements of sound foreign policy alone. It is also characterized by the willingness of the domestic political forces, whose approval is either required by the constitution or necessary for political reasons, to support the foreign policies favored by the executive branch of the government. To secure that support becomes a prerequisite for the conduct of for-

eign policy. While it is certainly an exaggeration to say, as an eminent observer of American foreign policy has done, that 90 percent of American foreign policy consists of domestic politics, it is no less certain that an American administration which fails to secure domestic political support for its foreign policies will find itself incapable of pursuing those policies effectively.

To secure support is bound to be a difficult task, for there exists an inevitable incompatibility between the requirements of good foreign policy and the preferences of a democratically controlled public opinion. As Tocqueville wrote, with special reference to the United States,

foreign politics demand scarcely any of those qualities which are peculiar to a democracy; they require, on the contrary, the perfect use of almost all those in which it is deficient. . . . A democracy can only with great difficulties regulate the details of an important undertaking, persevere in a fixed design, and work out its execution in spite of serious obstacles. It cannot combine its measures with secrecy or await their consequences with patience.

The history of foreign policy conducted under democratic conditions illustrates the truth of these observations. The conditions under which popular support can be obtained for a foreign policy are not necessarily identical with the conditions under which a foreign policy can be successfully pursued. Whenever these two sets of conditions diverge, those responsible for the conduct of foreign policy are confronted with a tragic choice. Either they must sacrifice what they consider good policy on the altar of public opinion, or they must, by devious means, gain popular support for policies whose true nature is concealed from the public.

Nations with a long experience in the conduct of foreign policy and a vivid awareness of its vital importance, such as Great Britain, have developed constitutional devices and political practices which tend to minimize the dangers to the vital interests of the nation inherent in the democratic conduct of foreign policy. Parliamentary democracy, especially under the conditions of the two-party system, provides in the cabinet a mechanism which insures the support, by the majority of the elected representatives of the people, of the foreign policies pursued. The collective parliamentary responsibility of the cabinet compels the government to speak in foreign affairs with one voice, so that there can be no doubt, either at home or abroad, about the government's foreign policy at a particular moment.

It is the peculiar quality of the conduct of foreign policy in the United States that it maximizes the weaknesses inherent in the formulation and execution of foreign policy under democratic conditions, and that it aggravates these inherent weaknesses by unique constitutional devices and political practices.

The method of conducting U.S. foreign policy is determined by four general characteristics of the Constitution: (a) its lack of definition in assigning functions to the different agencies of the government; (b) the separation of powers, which allows the executive and legislative branches of the government to hold office and, within certain limits, to pursue policies, without regard to the other; (c) the system of checks and balances, which, within certain limits, makes it possible for one branch of the government to prevent another branch from pursuing its policies; and (d) the requirement that, under certain conditions, measures can be taken by neither branch alone, but only through the concerted action of both.

The Constitution nowhere makes clear with whom the ultimate responsibility for the conduct of foreign policy rests. It assigns to the president alone certain specific functions, such as the reception of foreign diplomatic representative; it assigns others, such as the regulation of foreign commerce and the declaration of war, to Congress alone; it provides for still others, such as the conclusion of treaties, which the president can discharge only in cooperation with the Senate. Apart from these specific grants, the Constitution limits itself to an over-all distribution of powers between the president and Congress by vesting in the former the executive power and making him commander in chief of the armed forces, and by vesting all legislative powers and the power of appropriations in Congress.

To locate, with the guidance of these "great generalities" and specific instances, the ultimate authority for the conduct of foreign policy is a task for constitutional theory and political practice. Jefferson's dictum that "the transaction of business with foreign nations is executive altogether" has claimed that ultimate authority for the president. On the other side of the argument, there is a chorus of voices which claim for the Senate, if not for both houses of Congress, at least an equal share in the conduct of foreign policy. Constitutional theologies have covered these two positions with clusters of legalistic cobwebs, and have left the issue where the Constitution has left it—undecided. For, in view of the affirmative powers granted by the Constitution to the president and Congress, the issue cannot be decided through constitutional interpretation. By giving some powers to the president, some to the Senate, some to the entire Congress, and by remaining silent on the ultimate responsibility for the conduct of foreign policy, the Constitution, in the words of Professor Corwin, an eminent expounder of its law, "is an invitation to struggle for the privilege of directing American foreign policy." Just as the question of the location of sovereignty in the United States, an issue similarly held in abeyance by the Constitution, had to be answered by a civil war, so the issue of the ultimate responsibility for the conduct of American foreign policy is being decided individually each time it arises, in a series of running battles between the Senate or the two houses of Congress, on one side, and the executive branch, on the other. Each side uses the weapons provided by the Constitution as well as the extraconstitutional ones which have grown in its shadow.

The political relations between the president and Congress are determined by the fact that the president can hardly ever be certain of the support of a majority of both houses of Congress for his policies. This is obviously so when the president and the majority of Congress belong to different parties; but even if the president is a member of the majority party, a minority of his own party will regularly vote against the policies with which he is identified. This defection is somewhat offset by a minority of the opposition party generally voting in favor of the president's policies. Yet the traditional jealousy with which any Congress guards its prerogatives against any president tends to give the edge to the hostile minority of the president's party. The president operates under the perpetual threat that his policies will be dis-

avowed by a bipartisan majority of Congress.

To make such a threat come true, Congress has at its command legislation, appropriations, and resolutions. To the same end, the Senate alone has power to approve treaties and to approve the appointment of diplomatic representatives and the high officials of the executive branch. This power of the Senate over appointments—by virtue of article II, section 2, of the Constitution—is a potential threat in the field of foreign policy rather than an active weapon. The Senate has sometimes refused to confirm individuals nominated by the president to ambassadorial positions or to high positions in the Department of State, but it has not used that power for the purpose of making it impossible for the president to pursue a certain foreign policy.

The weapon of legislation can be used in two different ways. Whenever a foreign policy needs to be implemented by legislation, Congress can modify, emasculate, or negate the foreign policy pursued by the executive branch. Congress can also take the initiative and, as in the case of the neutrality legislation of the thirties and the successive immigration acts, limit the president's freedom of action through restrictive statutory provisions.

The weapon of appropriations can be wielded in two different ways. Congress can either withhold, in part or in whole, appropriations necessary to the execution of a certain foreign policy, and thus cripple that policy or make its execution altogether impossible. The customary congressional changes in appropriations for the Department of State, for foreign aid, and for information policies illustrate the potentialities of this weapon. The Cooper-Church amendment of December 29, 1970, prohibiting expenditures for American ground troops and advisors operating in Cambodia, is another case in point. The financial requirements of present American foreign policy make it the most potent of all the weapons at the disposal of Congress. Or Congress can attach a rider to an appropriation bill, providing expenditures for purposes not contemplated by the executive branch. In that case, the president must either reject the appropriation bill *in toto* and forego the policy for which the appropriation was to be used, or he must accept the appropriation bill *in toto* and, against his better judgment, execute a policy imposed upon him by Congress. Thus, Congress in 1948 earmarked, in the bill providing aid to Western Europe, an appropriation for aid to China, a rider which the President had to accept, since he did not want to jeopardize the European aid program.

Through resolutions, either joint or by one of the houses, Congress expresses its preference for certain policies. While such expression of preference has no legally binding effect upon the executive branch, it indicates what kind of foreign policies Congress is likely to approve when called upon to act by way of legislation or appropriation. The Vandenberg resolution of June 11, 1948, for instance, calling for the conclusion of regional compacts for the purpose of mutual defense, influenced the form in which the North Atlantic Treaty was submitted to the Senate. The Tonkin Gulf resolution of August 7, 1964, was taken into consideration by the Johnson administration for the military measures it subsequently took in Vietnam.

Public opinion has come to regard the constitutional provision which requires approval of two-thirds of the Senate for treaties negotiated by the president as the main weapon by which one-third of the Senate members, plus one, can veto the foreign policies of the executive branch which have taken the form of international treaties. In view of the relations between majority and minority party mentioned above, and given a politically controversial issue calling for a partisan stand, the chances of a treaty's being approved by two-thirds of the Senate are slim. "A treaty entering the Senate," wrote Secretary of State Hay in summing up his bitter experience, "is like a bull going into the arena. No one can say just how and when the final blow will fall. But one thing is certain—it will never leave the arena alive." The death blows which the Senate dealt, in the interwar years, to presidential policies of international cooperation are remembered, for whatever different reasons, by president and Senate. Their memory has exerted a powerful influence toward avoiding conflict situations and securing, in advance, bipartisan support for the foreign policies to be pursued by the executive branch.

The general power of Congress in the field of foreign affairs has been met by the president with the general weapon put at his disposal by his position as chief executive and commander in chief. The president has a natural eminence in the conduct of foreign affairs from which constitutional arrangements and political practices can detract, but which they cannot obliterate. His powers in this field are, in the words of the Supreme Court, "delicate, plenary, and exclusive." Short of the expenditure of money, the binding conclusion of treaties, and the declaration of war, the president can almost do as he pleases in formulating and executing foreign policies. He can, without reference to any other agency of government, make a public declaration of policy, such as the Monroe or Truman doctrines. He can recognize or refuse to recognize a foreign government, as successive presidents did with respect to the government of the Soviet Union. He can give advice, make promises, and enter into informal commitments as he sees fit. He can send the armed forces of the United States anywhere in the world and commit them to hostile acts short of war. In sum, he can narrow the freedom of choice which constitutionally lies with Congress to such an extent as to eliminate it for all practical purposes. If, for instance, the president had wanted to use armed force during the Berlin crisis of 1948, or in response to the military operations of China in the Straits of Taiwan during the late fifties, he could have done so on his own responsibility, and thus he could have committed Congress to war regardless of the latter's preferences. The course of American policy toward Germany and Japan during the initial phase of World War II was determined primarily by presidential action, and it was left to Congress to ratify or, at worst, to retard and weaken the consummation of that course.

The ascendancy of the president over Congress in the determination of American foreign policy is dramatically revealed by the extent to which the president has been able to circumvent Senate participation by substituting executive agreements, not requiring legislative approval, for formal treaties. The executive agreement has recently become the normal medium for international compacts. Most of the great political understandings of the Warld War II years, from the destroyer deal to Potsdam, were concluded by the president alone, in the

form of executive agreements. In 1939, ten treaties were concluded by the United States as opposed to twenty-six executive agreements. The corresponding figures for the following years are eloquent: 1940, 12 and 20, respectively; 1941, 15 and 39; 1942, 6 and 52; 1943, 4 and 71; 1944, 1 and 74; 1945, 6 and 54. They are even more eloquent for the decade starting in 1950; 1950, 12 and 59; 1951, 13 and 200; 1952, 20 and 356; 1953, 12 and 128; 1954, 9 and 251; 1955, 23 and 291; 1956, 10 and 241; 1957, 19 and 227; 1958, 6 and 178; 1959, 13 and 227. The trend continued in the sixties: 1963, 9 and 248; 1964, 13 and 231; 1965, 5 and 197; 1966, 10 and 242; 1967, 10 and 218; 1968, 57 and 226.

The relations between president and Congress, however, must be conceived not only in terms of actual or potential conflict, but also in terms of cooperation. For while the power of the president is preeminent in starting the course of American foreign policy, Congress's potential for obstruction remains, and the dependence of the chief executive upon congressional consent has increased with the expanding financial requirements of American foreign policy. Since the end of World War II, successive presidents and secretaries of state have developed a system of cooperation with Congress in the formulation and execution of foreign policy. Its main purpose is the avoidance of the situation, which was the undoing of Wilson, in which the minority party opposes presidential policies primarily because they are the president's and his party's policies. It has become the established practice of the executive branch to brief, and consult with, the foreign policy experts of the two parties, especially those of the Senate, in advance of major steps to be taken, to secure their consent and to take their advice into account. This practive has worked with different results in different fields of American foreign policy. At times, the executive branch has not dared to take a step for fear of congressional disapproval and, on other occasions, Congress has not dared to oppose certain policies proposed or initiated by the executive branch for fear it be accused of partisan obstruction. The overall result, however, has been the formation of a coalition, composed of the majority of the two parties, in support of the president's foreign policy.

Bipartisanship, as originally conceived at the end of World War II, carried the negative implication that a foreign policy ought not to be opposed by one party solely because the president and the secretary of state, who belonged to the other party, were carrying it out. In positive terms, bipartisanship implied that the minority party should support sound foreign policies and oppose unsound ones, regardless of the party affiliation of those carrying them out. Conceived in these terms, bipartisanship recognized the elementary fact that the consequences of foreign policy are not limited, as are those of many domestic ones, to a particular segment of the population identified with one or the other party, but affect the whole nation for generations to come. Bipartisanship drew from this fact the sound and indispensable conclusion that party strife for its own sake must stop at the point where the whole nation meets other nations in defense of its interests and its very existence.

Thus far, we have referred to the president and the executive branch in their relations with Congress and foreign powers as though the president and the executive branch were one single entity pursuing one single policy. Nothing could be farther from the truth. It is true that the president, as chief executive and commander in chief, has the constitutional power to impose his own conception of foreign affairs upon the executive and military departments. In reality, however, even so strong and astute a president as Franklin D. Roosevelt was unable to assume full control even of the State Department, the constitutional executor of his foreign policies.

The reason for this anomaly must be sought in two factors. One is the absence of a cabinet which could integrate the policies of the different executive departments in the field of foreign policy, the American cabinet being an informal advisory body. The other factor is the frequent inability of the president to definitely resolve major dissensions between executive departments or to meet head-on resistance to his policies on the part of an executive department, without risking inopportune conflicts with Congress. Congress is always ready to take advantage of open dissensions within that branch. President Roosevelt, rather than take on a reluctant State Department, entrusted the execution of his more delicate and controversial foreign policies to special representatives, operating directly from the White House, or created special agencies for the performance of special functions. Sometimes Roosevelt pursued foreign policies of his own without even the knowledge of the State Department. The classic example is Roosevelt's approval, in June, 1944, of the division of the Balkans into British and Soviet spheres of influence, while for almost three weeks afterward the State Department continued to pursue a policy of opposition to the Anglo-Soviet agreement. Sometimes, as with regard to certain phases of Middle Eastern policy, the

State Department has emerged victorious from the struggle with the president.

The problem of unity of action arises not only between the president and the executive departments, but also—especially when strong leadership from the White House is lacking —among the executive departments themselves, and even within them. Washington is the scene of continuous interoffice feuds, sometimes growing from real differences of policy, more often the result of a mere struggle for power. The Hoover Commission on Organization of the Executive Branch of the Government counted about forty-five executive agencies, aside from the State Department, which are concerned with some phase of foreign policy. While most of them deal only with minor matters, some have exerted an important influence upon the conduct of American foreign policy. Among them, the military establishment is outstanding. The main vehicle for its influence is the National Security Council, composed of the president, the vice-president, the secretaries of state and defense, and the director of the Office of Civil and Defense Mobilization, as statutory members. Its purpose is "to advise the President" in those fields of policy "relating to the national security." In a period of Cold War, the whole field of foreign policy becomes the proper object of the council's advice. The National Security Council has become the key agency through which the views of the executive departments are filtered. Through the daily reports of its executive secretary, it exerts a potent influence upon the president's mind.

The task of coordinating American foreign policy under the president's direction does not end with the settlement of disputes between executive departments. It extends to the executive departments themselves and their representation abroad. Certain ambassadors, such as Dodd in Berlin and Kennedy in London in the thirties, and Hayes in Madrid during World War II, were able for months to pursue foreign policies at variance with the policies of the State Department, if not the president. Generals Clay in Germany and MacArthur in Japan, during the period immediately following World War II, in large measure formulated and executed their own policies which the executive departments concerned could do little about except ratify.

The success of the American way of conducting foreign affairs is due to that elusive factor which gives direction and unity to the American political system on all levels—public opinion. The Constitution makes public opinion the arbiter of American policy by calling upon the American voter to pass judgment on the president and his party every four years, and on all members of the House of Representatives and one-third of the membership of the Senate every other year. The American people live perpetually in a state of preelection or election campaigns. Presidential and congressional policies are always fashioned in anticipiation of what the voter seems likely to approve. The president, as the most exalted mouthpiece of the national will and the initiator of foreign policies, will test the state of public opinion by submitting new policies in the tentative form of public addresses and messages to Congress. These new policies will then be pursued or shelved, according to the reaction of the public. Democratic control of American foreign policy will depend largely on the correctness of the president's estimate of the willingness of public opinion to support his policies, and on his ability to marshal public opinion to that support. It is here that another, perhaps fundamental, weakness of the conduct of American foreign policy becomes apparent.

The state of American public opinion is ascertained by public opinion polls and by the intuitive estimates of individuals on the basis of the mass media, opinions of members of Congress, and private communications. Yet the result is a distorted picture of the actual state of the American mind. While such indicators may point with approximate accuracy to the public's lack of information, they give only a hint of its susceptibility to strong and wise leadership, derived from its native intelligence and moral reserves. The president and State Department seem to be taking at face value the picture conveyed, by the mouthpieces of public opinon, of the moral and intellectual qualities of the American people. In particular, fear of what Congress might do to their policies has at times been a veritable obsession with many members of the executive department, a fear derived from a misjudgment of the powers of Congress as an organ of public opinion.

That this fear is not justified by the actual control of Congress over the conduct of foreign affairs has already been pointed out. That the temper of Congress, and especially of the Senate, is not necessarily representative of public opinion is evident from a consideration of the four factors which limit the representative function of Congress: the disproportionate influence of rural over urban representatives by virtue of the apportionment of congressional districts favoring the former; the disproportionate influence of the less populous states by virtue of the representation of all states, regardless of population, by two senators; the disproportionate influence, on members of Congress, of the spokesmen of special interest groups; and finally, the limited representative character of members of Congress from a number of Southern states by virtue of the limitation of the franchise.

The mistaken identification of the mass media, polls, and Congress with public opinion has had a distorting as well as a paralyzing influence on American foreign policy. It is here that the way American foreign policy is conducted has a direct bearing on the kind of foreign policy pursued by the United States. By equating what Congress will approve with what the American people might be willing to support, president and State Department underrate the intellectual and moral resources of the American people. In consequence, the foreign policies they present to public opinion for approval often stop short of what they deem necessary in the national interest.

This fear of public opinion, especially in the form of congressional opinion, together with the ever-present risk of conflict between the executive branch and Congress and within the executive branch itself, constitutes a very serious handicap for any fresh departure in foreign policy. If one wants to win the next election, if one wants to advance in the bureaucratic hierarchy, if one wants to retain and increase the powers of one's office, it is well to avoid conflict and to swim with the prevailing current. Yet any fresh departure in foreign policy means conflict—conflict with a half-informed and at times hysterical public opinion, conflict with a suspicious and reluctant Congress, conflict between and within executive departments. Thus, the foreign policy of the Cold War, with its emphasis on mili-

tary preparations and its minimiza-
tion of the traditional methods of
diplomacy, is in a sense the foreign
policy which the procedures of the
American government are best fitted
to conduct, although it is not the best
fitted to preserve peace. The overriding concern for the preservation of
peace makes imperative a change in
the methods by which—and, more important, a change in the spirit in
which—American foreign policy is
conducted.

The factors which determine the
conduct of American foreign policy
cooperate as a brake upon executive
initiative in foreign affairs. The deficiencies which Tocqueville found in
the democratic conduct of foreign
affairs are compounded by the peculiarities of the American constitutional and political system. Not only
does Congress act as a brake upon the
executive branch, as it should, but so
does public opinion, which ought to
provide the fuel to carry American
foreign policy forward. In that task
of reestablishing public opinion as
an independent positive force, the
responsibility of the president is
paramount.

The president must reassert his
historic role as both the initiator of
policy and the awakener of public
opinion. Only a strong, wise, and
shrewd president can marshal, to the
support of wise policies, the strength
and wisdom latent in that slumbering
giant, American public opinion. Yet
while it is true that great men have
rarely been elected president of the
United States, it is upon that greatness, which is the greatness of its people personified, that the United States
has had to rely in the conduct of its
foreign affairs. It is upon that greatness that Western civilization must
rely for its survival.

SELECTED BIBLIOGRAPHY

BEMIS, SAMUEL FLAGG. *American Foreign Policy and Diplomacy*. New York: Holt, Rinehart & Winston, 1959.

BLOOMFIELD, LINCOLN P. *The United Nations and U.S. Foreign Policy*. Boston: Little, Brown & Co., 1960.

BRANDON, DONALD. *American Foreign Policy: Beyond Utopianism and Realism*. New York: Appleton-Century-Crofts, 1966.

GERBERDING, WILLIAM P. *United States Foreign Policy*. New York: McGraw-Hill Book Co., 1966.

HALLE, LOUIS. *Dream and Reality: Aspects of American Foreign Policy*. New York: Harper & Row, 1959.

HOFFMANN, STANLEY. *Gulliver's Troubles, or the Setting of American Foreign Policy*. New York: McGraw-Hill Book Co., 1968.

JACOBSON, HAROLD K. *America's Foreign Policy*. New York: Random House, 1960.

KENNAN, GEORGE F. *American Diplomacy, 1900–1950*. Chicago: University of Chicago Press, 1951.

———. *Realities of American Foreign Policy*. Princeton: Princeton University Press, 1954.

KOLKO, GABRIEL. *The Politics of War*. New York: Random House, 1968.

LISKA, GEORGE. *Imperial America: The International Politics of Primacy*. Baltimore: Johns Hopkins Press, 1967.

MORGENTHAU, HANS J. *In Defense of the National Interest*. New York: Alfred A. Knopf, 1951.

———. *A New Foreign Policy for the United States*. New York: Praeger, 1969.

———. *The Purpose of American Politics*. New York: Alfred A. Knopf, 1960.

OSGOOD, ROBERT. *Alliances and American Foreign Policy*. Baltimore: Johns Hopkins Press, 1968.

————. *Ideals and Self-Interest in America's Foreign Relations.* Chicago: University of Chicago Press, 1953.

PERKINS, DEXTER. *The American Approach to Foreign Policy.* Cambridge: Harvard University Press, 1952.

————. *The Diplomacy of a New Age.* Bloomington: Indiana University Press, 1967.

————. *The Evolution of American Foreign Policy.* New York: Oxford University Press, 1948.

SPANIER, JOHN W. *American Foreign Policy Since World War II.* New York: Praeger, 1960.

TUCKER, ROBERT W. *Nation or Empire?* Baltimore: Johns Hopkins Press, 1968.

INDEX